GOOD WINE GUIDE 2000

ROBERT JOSEPH

DK PUBLISHING, INC.

A DK PUBLISHING BOOK

www.dk.com

Produced by RJ Publishing Services

www.robert-joseph.com

EDITOR Robert Joseph

DEPUTY EDITOR Kitty Johnson

EDITORIAL ASSISTANTS Susie Barrie, Simon Meads

RESEARCHERS Nick James-Martin, Terry Copeland

PHOTOGRAPHY Steve Gorton

except, E.T. Archive: Correr Museum, Venice p. 64

Mary Evans Picture Library pp. 58, 76; Scope: Jacques Guillard p. 63

Telegraph Colour Library: J. Sims p. 50

Published in the United States by DK Publishing, Inc.

95 Madison Avenue, New York, New York 10016

First American Edition, 1998

2 4 6 8 10 9 7 5 3 1

oseph, Robert

Robert Joseph's Good Wine Guide / Robert Joseph -

2nd American Ed.

p. cm.

Includes index.

ISBN 0-7894-4637-5

1. Wine and wine making. I Title

TP548. J72 1999

641.2'2–dc21 98-16437

CIP

Typeset by RJ Publishing Services

Film outputting bureau: Personality

Printed and bound in Germany by

Graphischer Grossbetrieb Pössneck

Contents

Introduction

As winemakers around the globe celebrate the dawn of the new millennium, we would like to welcome you to the 2nd edition of *The Good Wine Guide*. As in the past, the Guide is really three books in one. In the first section – *The Basics* – you will find all the grounding you need to get through a dinner party among wine experts, as well as guidance on styles, flavors, vintages, and the most compatible marriages between hundreds of wines and dishes.

The following section – *The A–Z of Wine* – is an encyclopedia of some 2,700 wines, terms, regions, and producers that will enable you to find your way as easily through the intricacies of an auctioneer's catalog as around the wine shelves of a liquor store. Unlike any other encyclopedia of its kind, the *A–Z* goes on to recommend currently available vintages and examples that show off specific wines and winemakers at their best.

The *A–Z* also uniquely tells you how to pronounce the names of all those wines. So, with the book to hand, you will never have to pause before ordering a bottle of Ngatarawa from New Zealand or Beaulieu Napa Valley Cabernet (it's ***boh-lyoo*** by the way, not ***boh-lyuh*** as a French-speaker might reasonably expect).

Having chosen your wine, you won't have to search for a decent retailer from whom to buy it. Simply turn to the third section of the book – the *US Retailers* – where you will find details of over 230 America's best stockists, ranging from multistate chains and discount stores, to specialists, wine clubs, and gourmet delis. Then, finally, in the fourth section, there are listings for auctioneers, wine vacations, places to store your wine - and to learn about it.

Taken as a whole, the *2000 Good Wine Guide* should (as a reviewer once wrote) be the "only wine book you need" when choosing, buying, or drinking wine in the first year of the 21st century.

This year's *Guide* owes much to stalwart editorial assistants Susie Barrie and Simon Meads, and to researchers Nick James-Martin and Terry Copeland. Without my brilliant and long-suffering deputy editor Kitty Johnson, however, the *Guide* simply would not exist.

I also have to thank Piers Russell-Cobb and, at Dorling Kindersley: David Lamb, Chuck Wills, Derek Coombes, and Sonia Charbonnier. Elfreda Pownall at the *Sunday Telegraph* in London and Susan Vumbach Low, Chris Orr, and Colin Bailey-Wood at *WINE* Magazine were as indulgent as ever. All of these people share any credit for this book; the criticism should fall on my shoulders alone.

THE BASICS

NEWS

VIN DE SIÈCLE

When the wine makers and distributors or the world gathered at the biannual Vinexpo trade fair in Bordeaux in June 1999, there was a strong demand for crystal balls. How, at least a few people wondered, would the wine industry handle the years when every vintage begins with a "2" or a zero?.

Genes Blues

Starting, as it were, at the factory floor, there was the question of whether 21st century grapes will have been subject to GM - genetic modification. Moët & Chandon, admitted to research on GM vines, which had been "put on hold because of public concern." For its supporters, genetic engineering merely extends the technological progress that has already been made. Winemakers throughout the world have, after all long been planting cloned grapes onto carefully selected strains of rootstock. Once the fruit has been picked, the natural yeasts on its skins will more than likely have been killed off to allow fermentation to be "managed" more efficiently with yeasts that have been specially cultured by commercial laboratories.

Grape growers have also been increasingly concerned by the resistance pests and diseases have developed to chemical treatments. GM vines might need less – or possibly even no – protection at all. Alternatively, grapes could be programmed to ripen earlier or to be susceptible to the desirable noble rot which helps to create Sauternes and Trockenbeerenauslese, but not to the undesirable gray rot which makes wines taste musty. GM yeasts already developed by the Genetic Plant Research Institute in Montpellier will, it seems, enable winemakers to produce rich, flavorsome wines with less alcohol.

Sceptics in the New and Old Worlds, are less convinced, foreseeing a future in which wine will be like beer: a standardized product that tastes the same, irrespective of region or vintage. More significantly, winemakers who grow their vines organically and use natural yeasts, are concerned that their neighbors' GM vines might jeopardize their own efforts. Paul Draper of Ridge Vineyards in California, for example believes that bees play a crucial role in storing and distributing the yeast spores that end up on the skins of his grapes. What will happen if the bees, like the butterflies that are already menaced by GM agriculture, are no longer around?

Losing Contrôlée?

Among the most vociferous opponents of GM viticulture are a group of Burgundians who want Appellation Contrôlée legislation to keep genetically modified vines out of their – and other – classic French regions. It would be ironic if the authorities ignored this call, given the restrictions they place in the path of quality-conscious producers who favour more natural forms of innovation. Appellation Contrôlée is a rusty 60-year old machine in need of a full-scale overhaul. It is still, for example, as illegal to give a thirsty French vine a drink of water as it is for a winemaker to make a delicious, sweet, late harvest Pouilly Fumé. Almost every French wine region has refined its choice of grapes over the centuries (most Sancerre used to be red, for example); by outlawing this kind of experimentation, the appellation system has effectively halted evolution in its tracks.

Eastern Promise

Another concern for winemakers lies in the style of wine the world wants to drink. After years of international Chardonnamania, the pendulum has now swung back towards red wine. In 1999, the British, for the first time in decades, drank more red than white. In Asia and the United States, where the so-called "French paradox" has been most keenly promoted, red wine of any kind is associated with health. Japan once a white wine-drinking country has also switched to red, quietly - despite its financial troubles - taking first place among the world's importers of Bordeaux and Burgundy.

Exports to Asia are especially welcome in France, given the fact that, according to recent surveys, most young Frenchmen and women would rather drink vodka or beer than wine. If and when they do turn to the fruit of the grape, they apparently disdain the dry red favored by their parents, prefering the same kind of "international" fruity white Chardonnay as their contemporaries in the USA.

Chinese wine drinkers keenly concentrating on claret

The Bigger the Better

Some of the highest profile members of the wine industry often seem to be less interested in making wine than in working together and/or taking each other over. So, at Vinexpo, while Robert Mondavi was promoting the wines he's helping to make in Italy and South America, Mouton Rothschild was launching its own Almaviva Chilean co-production; The owners of Penfolds in Australia were talking about

Taittinger: still family owned.

their Californian wines, Moët & Chandon was showing off its Argentinian reds, and the Lurton brothers of Bordeaux were offering wines they are making just about everywhere.

Wherever you look, the giants are growing more gigantic. Moët & Chandon's owners LVMH have recently bought Krug, adding it to an arsenal that already includes Veuve Clicquot, Ruinart, Mercier, Pommery, and Canard Duchêne; in California, the mammoth Canandaïgua has, in two gulps, swallowed Franciscan and Simi (two of my favorite producers) and, in Australia, Mildara Blass has bought Maglieri, regular winners of International Wine Challenge Shiraz awards. The message is clear, in the wine world today, if you want to remain independent, it's better to be an ant or an elephant. Anything in between is likely to make you a target for takeover.

Squealing Ego

Some ants of course do pretty well out of being tiny. Newly established Bordeaux "micro wines" like le Pin, Valandraud and la Mondotte have demonstrated the advantage of only making a thousand or so cases rather than the 20,000 produced every year by long-established Médoc estates such as Margaux, Lafite and Latour. Hardly surprizingly, it hasn't taken long for clever and ambitious winemakers elsewhere to discover that they too can play the "Small is Beautiful – and Pricy"card. So despite their recent arrival on the scene, Californian miniaturists like Screaming Eagle and Harlan Estate now have no problem in selling their wine for $100 or more. Which, in turn, allows other, bigger producers to stick $40 tags on wines that might have been offered at $30 a few vintages ago – and to pretend that a $20 bottle is now something of a bargain. Well, sometimes it may be – but proof of the poor value offered by a great many $10-25 Californian wines lies in the difficulty they have competing overseas with more fairly priced efforts from other countries.

Value Judgment

Unfortunately, for the moment at least there is no real incentive for any Californian or Bordeaux winery to ask a moderate price for its produce. The less change you give a buyer from a $100 bill, the greater the chance of scoring a mark in the 90s from the all-important critics. But this is a shrinking world, and one in which the chances of a somebody pointing out the transparency of the emperor's new clothes are growing every day. Or to be more precise, every time somebody opens an older bottle from the Hype Winery or Château Prix-Fou, focuses on the flavor for a second or two and discovers that the wine maybe hasn't aged as gracefully as some of the longer-established (and more modestly priced) alternatives.

Net Benefit

Until now, disgruntled or enthusiastic wine drinkers were lonely voices who could only share their opinions with their friends and – occasionally – through the letters pages of specialist magazines. But the internet is already changing all that. Movie buffs have already proved that the views they post on the net can affect the box office success of the latest Hollywood blockbuster, and reviews by book lovers can help to shift new novels at amazon.com. But you can be just as influential when it comes to wine. Just head for sites like winespectator.com, or my own goodwineguide.com and tell the world what you think.

The rarely-mentioned but surprizingly widespread incidence of moldy barrels which, for a while, spoiled the quality of such high-profile wines as Château Canon in Bordeaux, for example, will be far harder to keep under wraps in the future – as will the differences in the prices asked by rival stockists for the same wine.

And that's where the net will probably have its greatest impact. As authorities throughout the nation are discovering, it's going to be very hard to maintain the old protectionist system that prevented individuals and retailers from dealing directly with producers in the US and overseas. Sometime soon, wine drinkers almost anywhere in the country will hopefully find that wine is almost as easy to buy over the net as books and cds already are today. And that's a future to which I will certainly be very happy to raise a glass in celebration.

A PERSONAL SELECTION

An unashamedly quirky list of varied wines that, out of the thousands I have tasted this year, have caught my attention. Wines are listed by price, alphabetically, and are rounded to the nearest 50 cents. (For retailers, see page 267).

RED WINES FOR DAILY DRINKING

1996 Château Saint Benoit Minervois $6 Rich and surprisingly classy wine with the flavor of wild rosemary.

1998 Pedras do Monte $6 Modern Portuguese wine with flavors of rich dried fruit and tobacco.

1997 Balbi Mendoza Shiraz $7.50 A lovely fresh, licoricey Argentinian example of this variety. Watch out, Australia.

1997 Beaujolais la Barreille $7.50 Strawberries, squashy strawberries! Wonderful easy-drinking wine.

1997 Berberana Dragon Rioja $7.50 Just what I'm looking for in an easy-drinking, young, strawberryish Spanish red.

1997 Chasse du Pape, Côtes du Rhône, Meffre $7.50 An attractive, peppery, typical Rhône red.

1996 Domaine Força Réal Côtes du Roussillon Villages $7.50 Tasty, berryish wine from Languedoc-Roussillon. Great with stew.

1998 Domaine Jeune Vin de Pays du Gard $7.50 An inventive tobaccoey wine, made from the local Counoise grape.

1997 Four Corners Merlot $7.50 Côtes de Castillon claret. Plummy, rich, unusually good-value Bordeaux.

1997 LA Cetto Petite Sirah $7.50 Spices – and value – galore from this reliable Mexican winery.

1996 Vallone Salice Salentino $7.50 The perfect, gamey, Italian partner for almost any kind of herby dish.

1997 d'Arry's Original Shiraz Grenache $10 Maybe this Australian is too rich and flavorsome to drink every day, but it's very fairly priced and would be my choice for a cold winter night.

1997 Spiropoulos Porfyros $10 A deliciously spicy, oaky example of modern Greek winemaking, using a traditional Greek grape variety.

1995 Ch Tour de Marchesseau $12 Lovely Merlot-based Bordeaux from Lalande de Pomerol with lingering, rich, plummy, cherryish flavors.

Red Wines for Special Occasions

1998 Coldstream Hills Pinot Noir $15 Raspberryish, Aussie Pinot from wine writer and confirmed Burgundy lover James Halliday.

1995 Moulin à Vent, Ch. du Moulin à Vent Cuvée Exceptionelle $15 Serious, maturing, plummy wine that proves that good Beaujolais can be worth keeping.

1997 Pedroncelli Special Vineyard Selection Dry Creek Mother Clone Zinfandel $15 A real mouthful of a name – and a real mouthful of rich, spicy, chocolatey wine.

1996 Marqués de Griñon Domaine de Valdepusa Petit Verdot $16 Once a little-known ingredient in red Bordeaux, the violetty Petit Verdot here performs solo in Spain.

1996 Chapel Hill "The Vicar" $17.50 A glorious, berryish, Aussie blend of Cabernet and Shiraz matured in a mixture of American and French barrels. One to keep.

1997 Felton Road Pinot Noir $18 The newest name in New Zealand Pinot.World-class raspberryish stuff.

1997 Chorey-lès-Beaune $20 Affordable real Burgundy produced in a little-known village opposite Corton.

1991 Crozes Hermitage, La Guiraude, Graillot $20 Smokily intense northern Rhône Syrah that's now at its best.

1994 Chateau Pibarnon, Bandol $25 Wonderful rich, gamey, herby wine with lingering plummy, cherryish fruit.

1995 Osar, Masi $30 Intense, smoky, dark-berryish wine made in the Veneto from the little-known Osar grape.

1996 Roberto Voerzio Vignaserra $30 A brilliant blend of Nebbiolo and Cabernet Sauvignon from one of the finest winemakers in Piedmont.

1996 Domaine de Trevallon $32 Extraordinary blueberry flavors that linger on and on. Not bad for a Vin de Pays!

1997 Casa Lapostolle Clos Apalta $35 Chile's finest red? A deeply intense berryish red from very old vines – and showing the winemaking skills of Michel Rolland.

1996 Andrew Will Cabernet Sauvignon $40 Rich, deeply blackcurranty and mulberryish class in a glass from one of the best wineries in Washington State.

1994 Barolo Pira $40 Proof that traditional Barolo can match Bordeaux at its best. Long, spicy and floral.

1996 Chateau Haut-Bailly $40 Great red Graves from one of the top châteaux in the region. Lovely, lingering complex raspberry and blackberry flavors.

1995 Opus One $100 Glorious modern blackcurranty wine made by Mondavi and Mouton Rothschild and offering the complexity of great Bordeaux.

WHITE WINES FOR DAILY DRINKING

1998 Caballo de Plata Torrontes $6 Typical of the Argentinian Torrontes grape, this smells grapily and sweetly like Muscat, but tastes bone dry and of peaches and apples.

1997 Arius Reserve Chardonnay $7.50 Fairly priced Chardonnay with tropical fruit flavors and sweet, spicy oak.

1997 Ch la Raz Montravel $7.50 Good, freshly dry alternative to white Bordeaux from a little-known appellation to the east of that region.

1998 Lindemans Bin 65 Chardonnay $7.50 A regular favorite, this fresh, easy-going, melony-pineapply wine is still offers some of the best value around.

1996 Simonsig Chenin Blanc $7.50 Great value unoaked, appley wine from South Africa.

1998 Tramontane Reserve Viognier, Dom. Viennets $7.50 A great-value, limey, floral version of this very tricky grape.

1999 35 Sur Sauvignon Blanc $8 Proof that Chile can make wines from this grape that can compete on level terms with efforts from New Zealand.

1996 Bourgogne Chardonnay, Laroche $8 This tastes just like classy Chablis selling at nearly twice this price.

1998 Oxford Landing Estate Limited Release Viognier $8 Wonderful perfumed wine with apricot and spice.

1998 Cape Mentelle Ironstone Semillon Chardonnay $10 A New World (Western Australian) white to delight Chablis fans. Fresh, peachy and pineapply with a hint of mineral.

1997 Gaia Thalassitis $10 One of Oddbins' laudable range of New-Wave Greek wines, this is exciting pineappley-licoricey wine made from the indigenous Assyrtiko grape.

1997 Martin Codax Albariño $10 My favorite of the new wave of seductively floral dry white wines from Galicia.

1997 Muscadet de Sevre et Maine sur Lie Château de la Ragotière $10 Serious lemony Muscadet that seems to be breaking the rule that this wine doesn't age.

1997 Bonny Doon Malvasia $12 A wonderful grapey, peary Californian version of a classic Italian style.

1997 Graacher Himmelreich Riesling Spätlese, von Kesselstatt $12 Refreshing, delicate, floral, young Mosel with the typical appley character of the Riesling.

1996 Domaine Antonopolous £15 Win money from your friends by challenging them to blind-taste and guess the nationality of this classy modern Greek Chardonnay.

1997 Carmen Reserve Chardonnay $17 Unashamedly oaky, but with lots of really classy fruit flavors to go with all that wood.

White Wines for Special Occasions

1998 Nepenthe Lenswood Sauvignon Blanc $13.50 From one of the newest stars in Australia; impeccable, asparagussy, dry Sauvignon.

1996 Bellondrade y Lurton Rueda $15 A glorious peachy, oaky pure Verdejo made by Brigitte Lurton (of Château Climens) and her husband.

1998 Grosset Watervale Riesling $15 One of the world's great Rieslings, from Clare Valley. Wonderful, fresh, complex dry wine to drink or keep.

1997 Savennières "Clos du Papillon," Dom. du Closel. $15 Honey and apples. Textbook Loire Chenin Blanc to drink now or to leave for a decade or so.

1997 Pouilly Fumé, Ch de Tracy $16 Loire white at its best: asparagus and fresh peas and the smoke that is supposed to have given this region its name.

1996 Domaine Castera Jurançon Cuvée Privilége $18 An impeccably made, lemony, spicy example of an under-appreciated French wine region.

1994 Graacher Himmelreich Riesling Spätlese $22 Maturing Riesling that is beginning to take on the spice of age. Still fresh and limey though.

1994 Planeta Chardonnay $22 A great, tropical-fruit packed wine from Sicily – a wine region to watch.

1993 Tyrrell's Vat 1 Semillon $27 Classic Hunter Valley unoaked wine with a characteristic peachy, strawy character.

1997 Petaluma Chardonnay $30 The best Chardonnay yet from this reliable producer. Sheer Elegance.

1997 Domaine de Monteillet Condrieu $30 Ultra-typical Condrieu with the tell-tale flavor of ripe apricot. Ripely exotic.

1996 Riesling, Knoll $30 A perfect example of ultra-ripe Austrian wine with intense peachy, raspberry fruit.

1996 Pouilly-Fuissé Vieilles Vignes, Ch. de Fuissé $50 Southern Burgundy at its nutty, pineappley best. Intense but subtle, with just enough oak.

1996 Domaine Zind Humbrecht Pinot Gris Clos Windsbuhl $60 Lovely, rich, peary, and spicy wine from one of the most reliable producers in the Alsace region.

1998 Chablis les Butteaux, Raveneau $70 Classic complex Chablis from a master of this region. Rich, but with a characteristic "mineral" character.

1996 Corton Charlemagne, Bonneau de Martray $75 Serious multilayered white Burgundy which really ought to be locked away for a decade or so.

SPARKLING WINES AND ROSÉ

Jacob's Creek Sparkling Chardonnay Pinot Noir $10 A recently launched wine – and an instant success with great, fresh, raspberry Pinot Noir fruit.

1995 Seaview Pinot Noir-Chardonnay $12 Another Aussie wine that's brilliantly balanced, dangerously easy-to-drink and ludicrously fairly priced.

1997 Seppelt Show Sparkling Shiraz $14 Some hate red sparkling wine; I love its intense plum and cinnamon flavors.

1996 Domaine Chandon Green Point Sparkling Wine $16 Creamily classy wine from Moët & Chandon's Australian offshoot.

1994 Montana Deutz Blanc de Blancs $20 Classy pure Chardonnay sparkling wine from the biggest producer in New Zealand.

Roederer Estate Quartet, Anderson Valley $20 Champagne quality from California, with some lovely yeasty-biscuity richness.

Lanson Black Label Brut $25 Probably the most reliable of widely available Champagnes at the moment. Good ripe but subtle fruit.

Mis-en-Cave 1995 Charles Heidsieck Champagne $30 Non-vintage sparkling wine whose label bears the year it was blended. Vintage quality, rich, biscuity wine.

1990 Billecart-Salmon Champagne Cuvée Nicolas François $50 Stylish sparkling wine for a special occasion, with food or just to sip at.

1990 Veuve Clicquot Rosé Champagne $65 Gorgeous raspberry and dark chocolate flavors in one of the best examples of pink sparkling wine.

ROSÉ

1998 Balatonboglar Chapel Hill Pinot Noir Rosé $6.50 Emphatically easy drinking from Hungary.

1998 Big Frank's Deep Pink Rosé $6.50 Why do decent pink wines have to have silly names? Well, whatever it's called, this is good dry, cherryish, stuff.

1998 Château Val Joanis $7.50 Peppery, berryish rosé from a go-ahead estate in Luberon, close to Marseilles.

1997 Bloody Good Pink $11 A rare example of serious dry Zinfandel, made by Randall Grahm of Bonny Doon

1998 Château de Marsannay Rosé $15 Burgundy rosé is a rarity, but one that I, at least, enjoy for its fresh, raspberryish flavor.

SWEET AND FORTIFIED WINES

1996 Cranswick Estate Botrytis Semillon $15 37.5cl Australia's answer to Sauternes, with an intensely luscious marmalade flavor. Irresistibly seductive.

1996 Saussignac Dom. Léonce Cuisset $15 An exciting, toffeeish, yet fresh alternative to nearby Sauternes.

1994 Forster Ungeheur Riesling Auslese, von Buhl $25 Indulgent appley, raisiny Riesling with some lovely fresh acidity in the background.

1996 Vouvray le Marigny Moelleux, Domaine des Aubuisières $25 Honeyed, appley wine with a touch of the praline Vouvray develops with age.

1996 Kracher Chardonnay-Welschriesling Nouvelle Vague Trokenbeerenauslese No.4 $30 Extraordinary lemony wine from one of Austria's finest winemakers.

1996 Condrieu les Eguets, Vendange Tardive $30 for 50cl A rare masterpiece, combining the perfume of the Viognier with late harvest luscious, apricotty sweetness.

1997 Château Climens $80 Perfect sweet white Bordeaux. Subtle but beautifully balanced and with an apricot and mandarin flavor that lasts for ever.

FORTIFIED

Penfolds Magill Tawny $7.50 for 37.5cl Great, rich, toffeeish Aussie "port" with gorgeous fruitcake flavors.

Lustau Fino Jarana Reserva $14 An ultra-serious toasty example of light, dry sherry which simply screams for olives.

Brown Brothers Liqueur Muscat $16 Liquid Christmas pudding in a glass. Sheer indulgence.

Vya Extra Dry Vermouth $16 After proving it could compete with port, the Quady winery in California has now made the ultimate spicy vermouth.

Henriques & Henriques 10 Year Old Sercial $20 Limey, dry, classic Madeira. Due for a comeback.

1990 Warre's Bottle Matured LBV $20 "Traditional" Late Bottled Vintage port that – unlike most – needs decanting, and tastes like vintage port.

1984 Fonseca Guimaraens $50 My vote for the most reliable, best-value top-quality vintage port.

Reid Wines Very Old Amontillado $60 Sheer extravagance, but who cares? Complex old woody sherry that made me think of old wooden desks and leather chairs.

Gonzalez Byass Noe $70 Ultraconcentrated raisiny stuff that I'd trickle over very good vanilla ice cream.

WINEMAKERS' CHOICES

Great wine deserves great food. I asked four of the world's top winemakers to reveal their favorite three dishes and the wines they would most enjoy drinking with them. I have also recommended some of their own wines that I think would complement the chosen dishes.

VITTORIO & LEONARDO FRESCOBALDI

The Frescobaldi family stands at the heart in the history of Italian wine – and wine as a whole. They have been making Chianti for seven centuries and can count among their early fans such illustrious customers as King Henry VIII of England. As long ago as 1855, it was a Frescobaldi who introduced Cabernet Sauvignon, Merlot, Pinot Noir, and Chardonnay to their Nipozzano estate in Tuscany and, more recently, it was Marchese Vittorio, the current head of the firm, who helped to spearhead the general renaissance in Chianti of the fine Sangioveto clone which had been widely supplanted by more productive strains of the Sangiovese.

Apart from the Chiantis with which Frescobaldi is associated, there are superb "Super Tuscan" wines such as Mormoreto, and the Pomino Il Benefizio, one of Italy's most successful modern whites. In 1997, Vittorio and Leonardo, the company vice-president, joined forces with Robert Mondavi to produce the instantly successful Luce and Lucente.

Vittorio & Leonardo Frescobaldi's Meal and Wines

Risotto with herbs, guinea-hen, and white truffles.
The Italian classic.
Marinated wild boar cooked in its sauce, served with fresh polenta.
A great traditional dish.
Millefeuille, served with marron glacé and caramel.

1997 Hamilton Russell Chardonnay.
South Africa's top dry white?
1986 Vega Sicilia.
Spain's top red – and a wine with enough richness of flavor to match the wild boar.
1967Château d'Yquem.
A wonderfully hedonistic wine for a very hedonistic dish.

Editor's Note

The oaky 1996 Frescobaldi Pomino Benefizio would also go brilliantly with the risotto, while the red for the boar might be the 1990 Montesodi. As for the millefeuille: a raisiny 1992 Pomino Vin Santo.

RANDALL GRAHM OF BONNY DOON

I suspect that Randall Grahm rather relishes being described as the *wunderkind* and *enfant terrible* of the California wine industry – and the winemaker who has always preferred to lead (or sidestep) fashion than to follow it. Starting out as a student of philosophy (among several other subjects), he first became passionate about wine after tasting some great French examples at the Beverly Hills shop where he was employed to sweep the floors. In 1979 while studying winemaking, he surprised teachers and fellow students by focusing on the then still unfashionable Pinot Noir, which he then tried to produce at the tiny Bonny Doon winery he launched two years later in the Santa Cruz Mountains. In 1986, however, he admitted defeat and switched his allegiance to the grape varieties of the Rhône. Le Cigare Volant, the Châteauneuf-du-Pape-lookalike with a tongue in cheek label, brought fame – and the nickname of the "Rhone Ranger" which, in 1992 was given to an asteroid (rather than a star or planet, you'll notice) in Graham's honor.

By the early 1990s, Randall Grahm had become idealogically commited to what he calls the "meridional" varieties of Italy and Southern France. Plus the Zinfandel he makes into a wine called Cardinal Zin and the Riesling he calls "the noblest white cepage," an example of which , he says, brought him to the understanding that wine could also be a psychoactive substance. In 1994. he was named Wine & Spirits professional of year by the James Beard Foundation.

Randall Grahm's Meal and Wines

A panoply of smoked fish, beluga caviar, and blinis	1982 Maximin Grünhauser Riesling Spätlese *The perfect match!*
Quail in molé sauce. *A Mexican dish, made with chocolate, cinnamon, and peppers*	1949 Musigny Comte de Vogue (en magnum) *Ultimate Pinot Noir*
Dead-ripe Hawaiian mango. *As if the wine needed any more hedonism...*	1971 Scharzhofberger Auslese Gold Cap Riesling, Egon Müller.

Editor's Note

If Randall Graham wanted to drink his own wines with these dishes, he could opt for the lovely fresh 1998 Pacific Rim Riesling with the fish – or his Italian-style Malvasia. With the quail, he would almost certainly opt for his Pinot Meunier, an unusual raspberryish, truffley red made from a variety very rarely seen outside Champagne. This "felicitous" combination apparently raised a round of spontaneous applause from an entire restaurant in Indianapolis.

ROBERT & MARGRIT MONDAVI

If one man deserves the credit for creating the international reputation of California wine, it has to be Robert Mondavi. From the moment he launched the Robert Mondavi Winery in Oakville in 1966 vowing that California could produce world-beating wines, he has broken new ground with style and quality. He was a pioneer of Carneros Pinot Noir, dry Sauvignon Blanc, and top quality Reserve Chardonnay and Cabernet Sauvignon. Wine tourism was led by his winery which attracts 300,000 visitors a year, and foreign investment in Napa was encouraged by the Opus One joint venture with Mouton Rothschild.

In recent years, with his sons, Michael and Tim at the helm, the company has followed the success of Opus One with co-productions in Italy with Frescobaldi and in Chile with Errazuriz and Caliterra.

The long list of awards won by Robert Mondavi, includes *Decanter Man of the Year* and Lifetime Achievement Awards from the *Society of Bacchus* and the *European Wine Council*. Margrit Mondavi, Robert's wife since 1937, has always been involved in the winery. In the 1960s she introduced displays of artworks and the Summer Music Festival, and the sponsorship of the *Great Chefs of France* culinary instruction program. Robert Mondavi particularly credits Margrit with developing and promoting the art of marrying fine food and wine.

Robert & Margrit Mondavi's Meal and Wines

Grilled seabass with avocado slices and escarole and olive oil and lemon vinaigrette,	1997 Flora Springs, Carneros Chardonnay. *A complex Californian white to match the fish and escarole.*
Grilled rack of lamb jus naturel with morels, potato, and celery puree. Baby carrots and green peas.	1985 Chateau Mouton Rothschild *Sublime Bordeaux from a lovely ripe vintage. A wine that has always given pleasure.*
Tarte Tatin Vanilla-bean ice cream	1994 Egon Müller Scharzhfberger Ice Wine

Editor's Note

The Robert Mondavi Reserve Chardonnay would be a perfect alternative to the wine made in nearby vineyards by Flora Springs. Alternatively, a Viognier or a Riesling would be a good choice. The only dangerous element in the dish will be the lemon vinaigrette which could quarrel with an older wine. The 1985 Mouton Rothschild is at its best now and would be sublime with lamb, as would be a younger Opus One or a Robert Mondavi Reserve Cabernet Sauvignon. With the Tarte Tatin, I would be delighted to drink the Mondavi Moscato d'Oro.

CHRISTIAN & CHERISE MOUEIX

Château Pétrus in particular and Pomerol in general have become so famous and sought-after throughout the world that it is worth recalling that, without the commitment of a merchant called Jean-Pierre Moueix after World War II, this region might have remained – like the still unfashionable Fronsac – a backwater of Bordeaux.

Jean-Pierre Moueix's son Christian, who now heads the family company is internationally associated with top class wines from Pomerol, St Emilion and, more recently with his Dominus from Napa, California.

Despite his international fame, however, in a world where the highest critical acclaim often seems to go to reds that are described as "big" and "voluptuous" and offer "gobs of fruit," Christian Moueix and the wines he makes and sells stand, rather unfashionably, for finesse and elegance.

Like almost every Bordelais – if not every Frenchman – he prefers to consider wine in the context of food. His wines which do not always shine at their brightest when tasted "blind" alongside other more showy efforts, always come into their own at the dining table where some of those bigger wines can seem clumsy. The meal and wines below were chosen by Christian and his American-born wife Cherise who met through their mutual love of fine art.

Christian & Cherise Moueix's Meal and Wines

Ecrevisses Sauvages à la Nage *Crawfish cooked in white wine, onions, garlic, and parsley.*	1982 Montrachet, Ramonet *The greatest white Burgundy of all – from one of the greatest of all Burgundy estates.*
Truffes Gros Sel *Truffles encased in coarse salt and baked in the oven. A very traditional style of cooking.*	1990 Château Petrus *A brilliant vintage for Bordeaux, whose wines, though worth keeping, are already delicious.*
Perdreau Rôti *Partridge wrapped in vine leaves and bacon before roasting.*	1982 Château Cheval Blanc *Perfect maturing St Emilion with myriad layers of flavor.*

Editor's Note

Having chosen three of the world's very finest wines, Christian and Cherise Moueix have understandably opted to accompany them with fine but simple dishes. I can imagine no finer white than the Burgundy to drink with the crawfish – but might happily enjoy them with a mature white Bordeaux such as a Domaine de Chevalier Blanc, or Haut Brion. The 1995 Château Canon-Moueix which has 80% Merlot would be an affordable match for the truffles, while another Moueix wine, the Canon de Brem, with rather more Cabernet Franc, would be a humbler but delicious alternative for the Cheval Blanc.

TASTING & BUYING

SPOILED FOR CHOICE

Buying wine today has become wonderfully – and horribly – like buying a gallon of paint. Just as the manufacturer's helpful chart can become daunting with its endless shades of subtly different whites, the number of bottles and the information available on the supermarket shelves can make you want to give up and reach for the one that is most familiar, or most favorably priced.

If you're not a wine buff, why should you know the differences in flavor to be found in wines made from the same grape in Meursault in France, Mendocino in California, and Maipo in Chile? Often, the merchant has helpfully provided descriptive terms to help you to imagine the flavor of the stuff in the bottle. But, these too can just add to the confusion. Do you want the one that "tastes of strawberries or raspberries," the "refreshingly dry," or the "crisp, lemony white?"

Over the next few pages, I can't promise to clear a six-lane highway through this jungle but, with luck, I shall give you a path to follow with rather more confidence when you are choosing a wine, and one from which you can stray to explore for yourself.

Arm yourself with a good corkscrew (see page 66) and let's get tasting

THE LABEL

Wine labels should reveal the country or region where the wine was produced (see page 30), and possibly the grape variety (see page 50) from which it was made. Both region and grape, however, offer only partial guidance as to what you are likely to find when you pull the cork.

Bear in mind the following:

1) Official terms such as Appellation Contrôlée, Grand or Premier Cru, Qualitätswein, and Reserva are often as trustworthy as official pronouncements by politicians.
2) Unofficial terms such as Reserve Personnel are, likewise, as trustworthy as unofficial pronouncements by the producer of any other commodity.
3) Knowing where a wine comes from is often like knowing where a person was born; it provides no guarantee of how good the wine will be. Nor, how it will have been made (though there are often local rules). There will be nothing to tell you, for instance, whether a Chablis is oaky nor, quite possibly, whether an Alsace or Vouvray is sweet.
4) "Big name" regions don't always make better wine than supposedly lesser ones. Inexpensive Bordeaux is far worse than similarly priced wine from Bulgaria.
5) Don't expect all wines from the same grape variety to taste the same: a South African Chardonnay may taste far drier than one from California and less fruity than one from Australia. The flavor and style will depend on the climate soil and producer.
6) Just because a producer makes a good wine in one place, don't trust him to make others either there or elsewhere. The team at Lafite Rothschild produce dull Los Vascos wines in Chile; Robert Mondavi's inexpensive Woodbridge wines bear no relation to the quality of his Reserve wines.
7) The fact that there is a château on a wine label has no bearing on the quality of the contents.
8) Nor does the boast that the wine is bottled at said château.
9) Nineteenth-century medals look pretty on a label; they say nothing about the quality of the 20th-century stuff in the bottle.
10) Price provides some guidance to a wine's quality: a very expensive bottle may be appalling, but it's unlikely that a very cheap one will be better than basic.

A Way with Words

Before going any further, I'm afraid that there's no alternative to returning to the thorny question of the language you are going to use to describe your impressions.

When Washington Irving visited Bordeaux 170 years ago, he noted that Château Margaux was, "a wine of fine flavor – but not of equal body." Lafite, on the other hand, had "less flavor than the former but more body – an equality of flavor and body." As for Latour, well, that had "more body than flavor." He may have been a great writer, but he was evidently not the ideal person from whom to learn about the individual flavors of the great Bordeaux – and how they actually tasted.

Michelangelo was more poetic, writing that the white wine of San Gimignano "kisses, licks, bites, thrusts and stings...". Modern pundits refer to wines as having "gobs of fruit" and tasting of "kumquats and suede." Each country and each generation simply comes up with its own vocabulary. Some descriptions, such as the likening to gooseberry and asparagus of wines made from the Sauvignon Blanc, can be justified by scientific analysis, which confirms that the same aromatic chemical compound is found in the fruit, vegetable, and wine.

Then there are straightforward descriptions that could apply to almost anything we eat or drink. Wines can be fresh or stale, clean or dirty. If they are acidic, or overfull of tannin, they will be "hard"; a "soft" wine, by contrast might be easier to drink, but boring.

There are other less evocative terms. While a downright watery wine is "dilute" or "thin," subtle ones are called "elegant." A red or white whose flavor is hard to discern is described as "dumb." Whatever the style of a wine, it should have "balance." A sweet white, for example, needs enough acidity to keep it from cloying. No one will ever enjoy a wine that is too fruity, too dry, too oaky, or too *anything*.

The flavor that lingers in your mouth long after you have swallowed or spat it out is known as the "finish." Wines whose flavor – pleasant or unpleasant – hangs around, are described as "long;" those whose flavor disappears quickly are "short."

Finally, there is "complex," the word that is used to justify why one wine costs ten times more than another. A complex wine is like a well-scored symphony, while a simpler one could be compared to a melody picked out on a single instrument.

TASTING

Wine tasting is surrounded by mystery and mystique. And it shouldn't be – because all it really consists of is paying attention to the stuff in the glass, whether you're in the formal environment of a wine tasting, or drinking the house white in your local bar. The key questions are: do you like the wine? And is it a good example of what it claims to be. Champagne costs a lot more than basic Spanish Cava, so it should taste recognizably different. Some do, some don't.

See

The look of a wine can tell you a lot. Assuming that it isn't cloudy (in which case send it straight back), it will reveal its age and may give some hint of the grape and origin. Some grapes, like Burgundy's Pinot Noir, make naturally paler wines than, say, Bordeaux's Cabernet Sauvignon; wines from warmer regions tend to have deeper colors. Tilt the glass away from you over a piece of white paper and look at the rim of the liquid. The more watery and brown it is, the older the wine (Beaujolais Nouveau will be violet through and through).

Swirl

Vigorously swirl the wine around the glass for a moment or so to release any reluctant smells.

Sniff

You sniff a wine before tasting it for the same reason that you sniff a carton of milk before pouring its contents into coffee. The smell can tell you more about a wine than anything else. If you don't believe me, try tasting anything while holding your nose, or while you've got a cold. When sniffing, concentrate on whether the wine seems fresh and clean, and on any smells that indicate how it is likely to taste.

What are your first impressions? Is the wine fruity, and, if so, which fruit does it remind you of? Does it have the vanilla smell of a wine that has been fermented and/or matured in new oak barrels? Is it spicy? Or herbacious? Sweet or dry? Rich or lean?

A brief look then swirl the wine round in the glass to release the aromas

Sip

Take a small mouthful and – this takes practice – suck air between your teeth and through the liquid. Look in a mirror while you're doing this: if your mouth looks like a cat's bottom and sounds like a child trying to suck the last few drops of soda through a straw, then you're doing it right. Hold the wine in your mouth for a little longer to release as much of its flavor as possible.

Focus on the flavor. Ask yourself the same questions about whether it tastes sweet, dry, fruity, spicy, herbacious. Is there just one flavor, or do several contribute to a "complex" overall effect?

Now concentrate on the texture of the wine. Some like – Chardonnay – are mouth-coatingly buttery, while others – e.g., Gewürztraminer – are almost oily. Muscadet is a good example of a wine with a texture that is closer to that of water.

Reds, too, vary in texture, some seeming tough and tannic enough to make the inside of one cheek want to kiss the inside of the other. Traditionalists were tolerant of that tannin, believing it necessary to a

Does the wine smell fresh and inviting? Simple or complex? Let it wash around your palate, and focus on the range of flavors it has to offer.

wine's longevity. More modern winemakers, including the men and women responsible for the best estates in Bordeaux and Burgundy, take a different view. For them, there is a difference between the harsh tannin and the "fine" (non-aggressive) tannin to be found in wine carefully made from ripe grapes. A modern Bordeaux often has as much tannin as old-fashioned examples – but is far easier to taste and drink.

Spit

The only reason for spitting a wine out – unless it is actively repellent – is quite simply remain upright at the end of a lengthy tasting. I still have the notes I took during a long banquet in Burgundy at which there were dozens of great wines and not even the remotest chance to do anything but swallow. The descriptions of the first few are perfectly legible; the thirtieth apparently tasted "very xgblorefjy." If all you are interested in is the taste, not spitting is an indulgence; you should to have gotten 90 percent of the flavor while the wine was in your mouth.

Pause for a moment or two after spitting the wine out. Is the flavor stili there? How does what you are experiencing now compare with the taste you had in your mouth? Some wines have a surprisingly unpleasant aftertaste; others have flavors that linger deliciously in the mouth.

SHOULD I SEND IT BACK?

Wines are subject to all sorts of faults, though far less than they were even as recently as a decade ago.

Acid

All wines, like all fruit and vegetables, contain a certain amount of acidity. Without it they would go very stale very quickly. Wines made from unripe grapes will, however, taste unpalatably "green" and like unripe apples or plums – or like chewing stalky leaves or grass.

Bitter

Bitterness is quite different. On occasion, especially in Italy, a touch of bitterness may not only be forgivable, it may even be an integral part of a wine's character, as in the case of Amarone. Of course, the Italians like Campari too. Even so, a little bitterness goes a very long way.

Cloudy

Wine should be transparent. The only excuse for cloudiness is in a wine like an old Burgundy whose deposit has been shaken up.

Corked

Ignore any cork crumbs you may find floating on the surface of a wine. Genuinely corked wines have a musty smell and flavor that comes from moldy corks. Some corks are moldier, and wines mustier, than others, but all corked wines become nastier with exposure to air. Between 4-6 percent of wines – irrespective of their price – are corked.

Crystals

Not a fault, but included because people often think there is something wrong with a white wine if there is a layer of fine white crystals in the bottom of the bottle. These are just tartrates that fall naturally.

Maderized/Oxidized

Madeira is fine fortified wine that has been intentionally exposed to the air and heated in a special oven. Maderized wine is stale, unfortified stuff which has been accidentally subjected to warmth and air.

Oxidized is a broader term, referring to wine that has been exposed to the air – or made from grapes that have cooked in the sun. The taste is reminiscent of poor sherry or vinegar – or both.

Sulfur (SO_2/H_2S)

Sulfur dioxide is almost universally used as a protection against the bacteria that would oxidize (qv) a wine. In excess, sulfur dioxide, may make you cough or sneeze. Even worse, though, is hydrogen sulfide and *mercaptans,* its associated sulfur compounds, which are created when sulfur dioxide combines with the wine. Wines with hydrogen sulfide smell of rotten eggs, while mercaptans reek of all sorts of nastiness, ranging from rancid garlic to burning rubber. If you think you have found these characteristics, pop a copper coin into your glass. It may clear up the problem completely.

Vinegary/Volatile

Volatile acidity is present in all wines, but only in small proportions. In excess – usually the result of careless winemaking – what can be a pleasant component tastes downright vinegary.

READING THE LABEL

INTRODUCTION

Labels – in all their different forms – are so much part of the business of wine that it may come as a surprise that, even a century ago, they barely existed. Wine was sold by the barrel and served by the jug or decanter. Indeed, the original "labels" were silver tags that hung on a chain around the neck of a decanter and were engraved with the word "claret," "hock," "port," or whatever.

Today, however, printed wine labels include legally required information such as the amount of liquid in the bottle, its strength, the place where it was made and the name of the producer, brand-owner, or importer. Confusingly, though, the rules governing what may be said on a label can vary between countries and between regions. Labels may also reveal a wine's style – the grape variety, oakiness, or sweetness, for example. And lastly, they are part of the packaging that helps to persuade you to buy one wine rather than another. The following examples should help you through the maze.

CHAMPAGNE

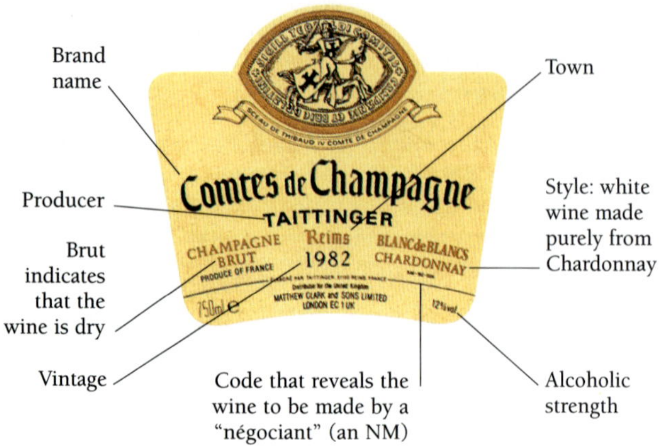

Whites

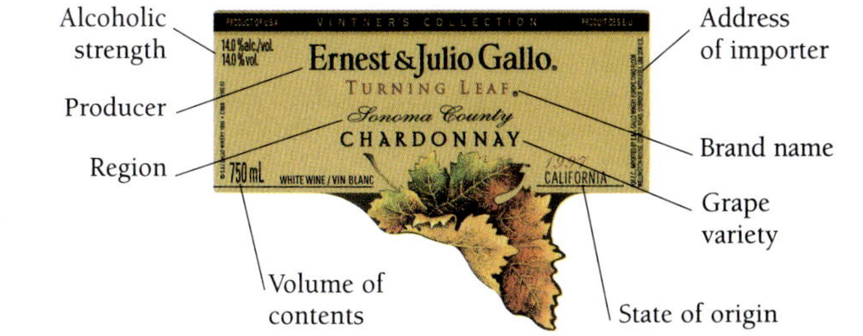
Alcoholic strength
Producer
Region
Volume of contents
Address of importer
Brand name
Grape variety
State of origin
VINTNER'S COLLECTION
14.0 %alc./vol.
14.0 % vol.
Ernest & Julio Gallo.
TURNING LEAF
Sonoma County
CHARDONNAY
750 mL
WHITE WINE / VIN BLANC
CALIFORNIA

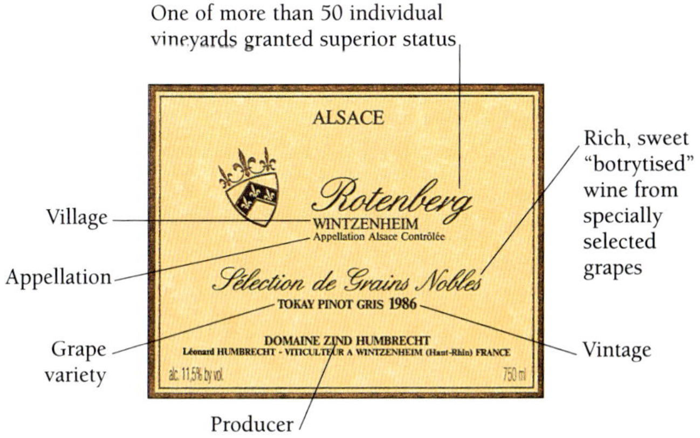
One of more than 50 individual vineyards granted superior status
Village
Appellation
Grape variety
Producer
Rich, sweet "botrytised" wine from specially selected grapes
Vintage
ALSACE
Rotenberg
WINTZENHEIM
Appellation Alsace Contrôlée
Sélection de Grains Nobles
TOKAY PINOT GRIS 1986
DOMAINE ZIND HUMBRECHT
Léonard HUMBRECHT - VITICULTEUR A WINTZENHEIM (Haut-Rhin) FRANCE
alc. 11,5% by vol.
750 ml

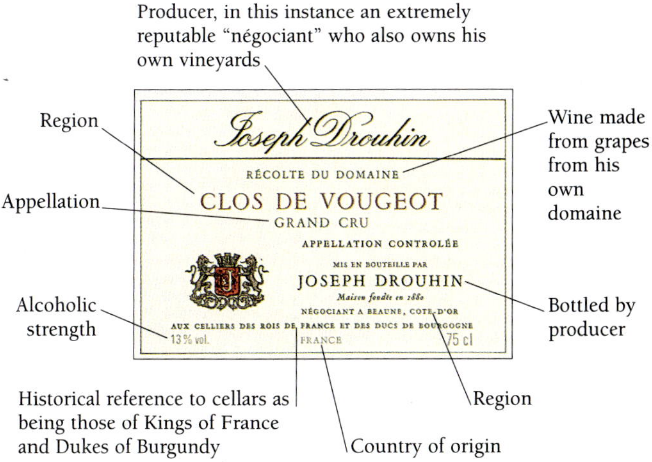
Producer, in this instance an extremely reputable "négociant" who also owns his own vineyards
Region
Appellation
Alcoholic strength
Wine made from grapes from his own domaine
Bottled by producer
Historical reference to cellars as being those of Kings of France and Dukes of Burgundy
Region
Country of origin
Joseph Drouhin
RÉCOLTE DU DOMAINE
CLOS DE VOUGEOT
GRAND CRU
APPELLATION CONTROLÉE
MIS EN BOUTEILLE PAR
JOSEPH DROUHIN
Maison fondée en 1880
NÉGOCIANT A BEAUNE, COTE-D'OR
AUX CELLIERS DES ROIS DE FRANCE ET DES DUCS DE BOURGOGNE
13% vol.
FRANCE
75 cl

REDS

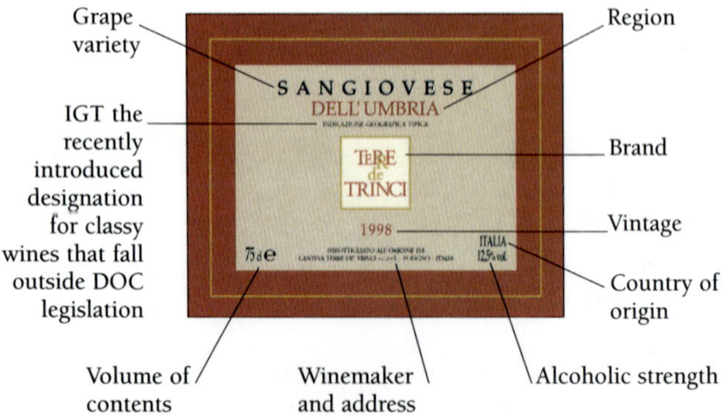
SANGIOVESE
DELL'UMBRIA
TERRE de TRINCI
1998
75 cl e
ITALIA
12.5% vol
Grape variety
Region
IGT the recently introduced designation for classy wines that fall outside DOC legislation
Brand
Vintage
Country of origin
Volume of contents
Winemaker and address
Alcoholic strength

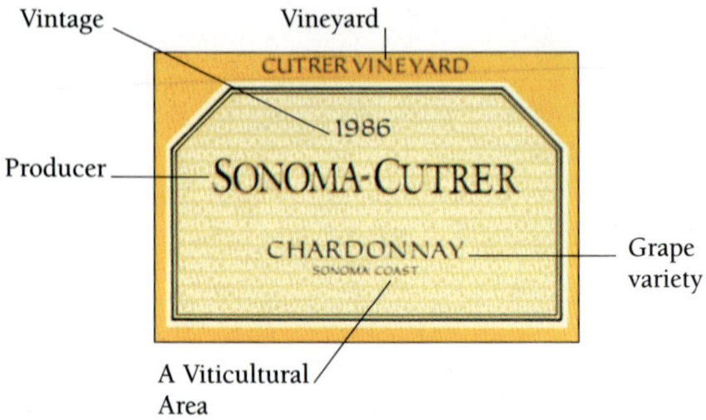
CUTRER VINEYARD
1986
SONOMA-CUTRER
CHARDONNAY
SONOMA COAST
Vintage
Vineyard
Producer
Grape variety
A Viticultural Area

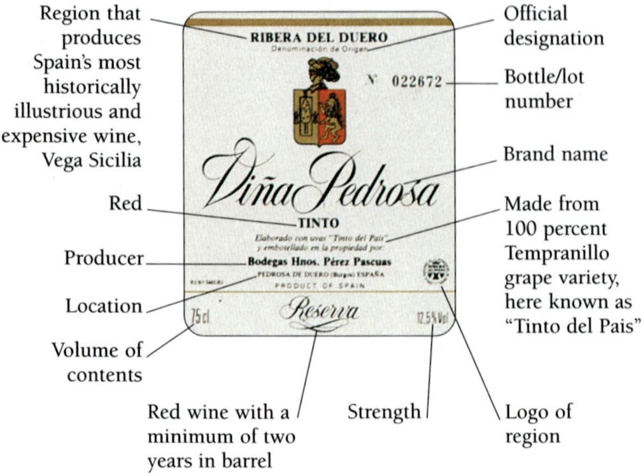
RIBERA DEL DUERO
Denominación de Origen
Nº 022672
Viña Pedrosa
TINTO
Bodegas Hnos. Pérez Pascuas
PRODUCT OF SPAIN
Reserva
75cl
12.5% Vol
Region that produces Spain's most historically illustrious and expensive wine, Vega Sicilia
Official designation
Bottle/lot number
Brand name
Red
Made from 100 percent Tempranillo grape variety, here known as "Tinto del Pais"
Producer
Location
Volume of contents
Red wine with a minimum of two years in barrel
Strength
Logo of region

DESSERTS/FORTIFIEDS

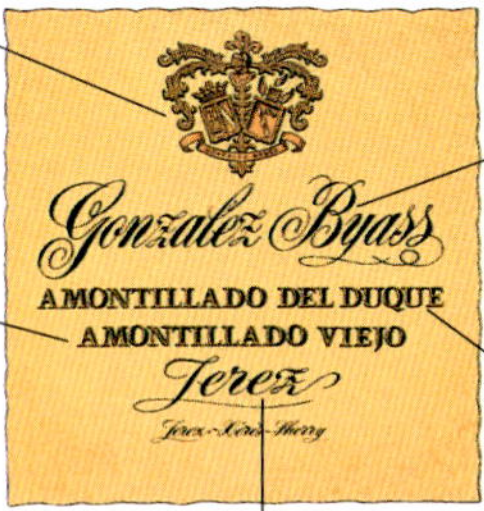

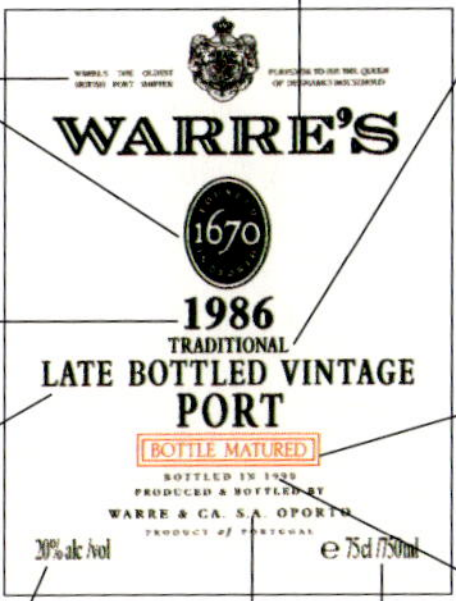

COUNTRIES

WHERE IN THE WORLD?

Despite the plethora of bottles whose labels bear the name of the same grape variety, the country, and the region in which a wine is made – with its climate, traditions, and local taste – still largely dictate the style of the stuff that ends up in your glass. In the next few pages, we'll take a whirlwind tour of the wine world, which should give you a clearer idea of what to expect from all of the most significant winemaking nations. (For more information on grapes, terms and regions, see the A–Z, which starts on page 97.)

AUSTRALIA

Reading the label: Late harvest/noble harvest – *sweet.* Show Reserve – *top-of-the-range wine, usually with more oak.* Tokay – *Australian name for the Muscadelle grape, used for rich liqueur wines.* Verdelho – *Madeira grape used for limey dry wines.* Mataro – *Mourvèdre.* Shiraz – *Syrah.* Tarrango – *local success story, fresh, fruity, and Beaujolais-like.*

Twenty or so years ago, Australian wines were the butt of a Monty Python sketch. Today, these rich and often intensely fruity wines are the reliable vinous equivalent of Japanese stereo gear and cameras. It is hard to explain quite how this switch happened, but I would attribute much of the credit to the taste the Australians themselves have developed for wine. Having a populace that treats wine almost as casually as beer, milk, or coffee has helped to provide the impetus for two of the best wine schools in the world – and for a circuit of fiercely fought competitions in which even the humblest wines battle to win medals.

Another strength has been the spirit of exploration which led to the establishment of regions like the Barossa and Hunter Valleys, and which is now fueling the enthusiastic planting of vines in previously unknown places, such as Orange, Robe, Mount Benson, Young, and Pemberton.

Remember these names; they are already appearing on a new generation of subtler Australian reds and whites that will make some of today's stars look like amateurs. And look out too for unconventional blends of grape varieties, as well as delicious new

flavors none of us has ever tasted. Australia is the only region or country to have drawn up a master plan to dominate the world's premium wines within 25 years. Judging by what's been achieved so far, I think the Australians may well be on track to achieving their ambitions.

AUSTRIA

Reading the label: Ausbruch – ***late harvested, between Beerenauslese and Trockenbeerenauslese***. Erzeugerabfüllung – ***estate-bottled.*** Morillon – ***Chardonnay.*** Schilfwein – ***made from grapes dried on mats.***

Austrian winemakers are riding high, with brilliant, late harvest wines, dry whites and increasingly impressive reds. Names to look out for include Alois Lang, Kracher, and Willi Opitz.

CANADA

Reading the label: VQA (Vintners Quality Alliance) – ***local designation seeking to guarantee quality and local provenance.***

The Icewines, made from grapes picked when frozen on the vine, are the stars here, though the Chardonnays are fast improving and progress is also being made with reds made from the Pinot Noir and Merlot.

EASTERN EUROPE

Some parts of Eastern Europe are coming to terms with life under capitalism a lot more successfully than others, but throughout the region, winemaking is improving by fitfully.

BULGARIA

The pioneer of good Iron Curtain reds, Bulgaria remains a reliable source of inexpensive, ripe Cabernet Sauvignon and Merlot, as well as creditable examples of the earthy local Mavrud. Whites are getting better too, thanks largely to the efforts of visiting Australian winemakers.

HUNGARY

Still probably best known for its red Bull's Blood, Hungary's strongest card today lies in the rich Tokajis, the best of which are being made by foreign investors. Reds are improving, as are affordable Australian-style Sauvignons and Chardonnays.

ROMANIA, MOLDOVA, AND FORMER YUGOSLAVIA

It is too early to see whether the new Yugoslav republics can export as many bottles of wine as used to go out under the Laski Rizling label, but Romania produces decent if atypical Pinot Noir, while Moldova's strength lies in whites.

ENGLAND AND WALES

Despite an unhelpful climate and government, the vineyards of England and Wales are steadily developing a potential for using recently developed German grape varieties to make Loire-style whites, high-quality, late harvest wines, and good sparkling wines. There are reds, too, but these are only really of curiosity value and are likely to remain so until global warming takes effect.

FRANCE

Reading the label: Appellation Contrôlée (or AOC) – *designation referring to the region and style of what are supposedly France's better wines.* Blanc de Blancs – *white wine made from white grapes.* Blanc de Noirs – *white wine made from black grapes.* Cave – *cellar.* Cave des Vignerons de – *usually a cooperative.* Cépage – *grape variety.* Château – *wine estate.* Chêne – *oak barrels, as in Fûts de Chêne.* Clos – *(historically) walled vineyard.* Côte(s)/Coteaux – *hillside.* Crémant – *sparkling.* Cuvée – *a specific blend.* Demi-sec – *medium sweet.* Domaine – *wine estate.* Doux – *sweet.* Grand Cru – *higher quality, or specific vineyards.* Gris – *pale rosé, as in Vin Gris.* Jeunes Vignes – *young vines (often ineligible to produce Appellation Contrôlée wine).* Méthode Classique – *used to* *indicate the Champagne method of making sparkling wine.* Millésime – *year or vintage.* Mis en Bouteille au Château/Domaine – *bottled at the estate.* Moelleux – *sweet.* Monopole – *a vineyard owned by a single producer.* Mousseux – *sparkling.* Négoçiant (Eleveur) – *a merchant who buys, matures, bottles, and sells wine.* Pétillant – *lightly sparkling.* Premier Cru – *"first growth," a quality designation that varies from area to area.* Propriétaire (Récoltant) – vineyard owner/manager. Reserve (Personelle) – *legally meaningless phrase.* Sur Lie – *aged on the lees (dead yeast).* VDQS (Vin Délimité de Qualité Supérieur) – *perpetually "soon-to-be-abolished" official designation for wines which are better than Vin de Pays but not good enough for Appellation Contrôlée.* Vieilles Vignes – *old vines (could be any age from 20–80 years), should indicate higher quality.* Villages – *supposedly best part of a larger region, as in Beaujolais or Côtes du Rhône Villages.* Vin de Pays – *wine with regional character.* Vin de Table – *basic table wine. Stupid rules mean that these wines are banned from mentioning their provenance, grape varieties, or vintage on their labels.*

Still the benchmark, or set of benchmarks, against which winemakers in other countries test themselves. This is the place to find

the Chardonnay in its finest oaked (white Burgundy) and unoaked (traditional Chablis) styles; the Sauvignon (from Sancerre and Pouilly Fumé in the Loire, and in blends with the Sémillon, Bordeaux); the Cabernet Sauvignon and Merlot (claret); the Pinot Noir (red Burgundy and Champagne); the Riesling, Gewurztraminer, and Pinots Blanc and Gris (Alsace). The Chenin Blanc still fares better in the Loire than anywhere else and, despite their successes in Australia, the Syrah (aka Shiraz) and Grenache are still at their finest in the Rhône.

France's problem remains the unpredictability of the climate in most of its best regions, and the unreliability of far too many of its winemakers, who are often happy to coast along on the reputation of the region in which they happen to work.

ALSACE

Reading the label: Sélection de Grains Nobles – *lusciously sweet wine made from grapes affected by Noble Rot.* Vendange Tardive – *late harvested.* Edelzwicker – *blend of white grapes, usually Pinot Blanc and Sylvaner.*

Often underrated, and confused with German wines from the other side of the Rhine, Alsace deserves to be more popular. Its odd assortment of grapes make wonderfully rich, spicy wine, both in their customary dry and more unusual, late harvest styles. This is my bet to follow the success of its spicy red counterparts in the Rhône.

BORDEAUX

Reading the label: Chai – *cellar.* Cru Bourgeois – *level beneath Cru Classé but possibly of similar quality.* Cru Classé – *"Classed Growth," a wine featured in the 1855 classification of the Médoc and Graves, provides no guarantee of current quality.* Grand Cru/Grand Cru Classé – *confusing terms, especially in St. Emilion, where the former is allocated annually on the basis of a sometimes less-than-arduous tasting, while the latter is reassessed every decade.*

For all but the keenest wine buff, Bordeaux is one big region (producing almost as much wine as Australia) with a few dozen châteaux that have become internationally famous for their wine.

Visit the region, or take a look at the map, however, and you will find that this is essentially a collection of often quite diverse subregions, many of which are separated from each other by farmland, forest or water.

Heading north from the city of Bordeaux, the Médoc is the region which includes the great communes of St. Estèphe, Pauillac, St. Julien, and Margaux where some of the finest reds are made. Largely gravel soil suiting the Cabernet Sauvignon, though

lesser Médoc wines, of which there are more than enough, tend to have a higher proportion of the Merlot. For the best examples of wines made principally from this variety, though, you have to head eastward to St. Emilion and Pomerol where the Merlot is usually blended with the Cabernet Franc.

To the south of Bordeaux lie Pessac-Léognan and the Graves which produce some of Bordeaux's lighter, more delicate reds. This is also dry white country, where the Sémillon and Sauvignon Blanc hold sway. A little farther to the southeast, the often misty climate provides the conditions required to make the great sweet whites of Sauternes and Barsac.

Each of these regions produces its own individual style of wine In some years, the climate suits one region and/or grape variety more than others. So, beware of vintage charts that seek to define the quality of an entire vintage across the whole of Bordeaux.

BURGUNDY

Reading the label: Hospices de Beaune – ***wines made and sold at auction by the charitable Hospices de Beaune.*** Passetoutgrains – ***a blend of Gamay and Pinot Noir.*** Tasteviné – ***a special label for wines that have passed a tasting by the Confrérie des Chevaliers de Tastevin.***

The heartland of the Pinot Noir and the Chardonnay, this is the region that produces such wines as Chablis, Nuits-St-Georges, Gevrey-Chambertin, Beaune, Meursault, Puligny-Montrachet, Mâcon Villages, Pouilly-Fuissé, and Beaujolais. According to the official quality pyramid, the best wines come from the Grands Crus vineyards; next are the Premiers Crus, followed by plain village wines and, last of all, basic Bourgogne Rouge or Blanc.

Despite the simplicity of the system, however, it can be tough to find a good bottle. The region's many individual producers make their wines with varying measures of luck and expertise, generally selling in bulk to merchants who are just as variable in their skills and honesty. So, one producer's supposedly humble wine can be finer than another's pricier Premier or Grand Cru.

CHAMPAGNE

Reading the label: Blanc de Blancs – ***white wine from white grapes, ie pure Chardonnay***. Blancs de Noirs – ***white wine made from black grapes***. Brut Sauvage/Zéro – ***bone dry***. Extra-Dry – ***(surprisingly) sweeter than Brut***. Grand Cru – ***from a top-quality vineyard***. Négoçiant-manipulant (NM) – ***buyer and blender of wines***. Non-Vintage – ***a blend of wines usually based on wine of a single vintage***. Récoltant manipulant (RM) – ***individual estate***.

Top-class Champagne has a unique blend of toasty richness and subtle fruit. Beware of cheap examples, however, and poor wine from big-name Champagne houses who should know better.

LOIRE

Reading the label: Moelleux – ***sweet***. Sur Lie – ***on its lees (dead yeast), usually only applied to Muscadet***. Côt – ***local name for the Malbec***.

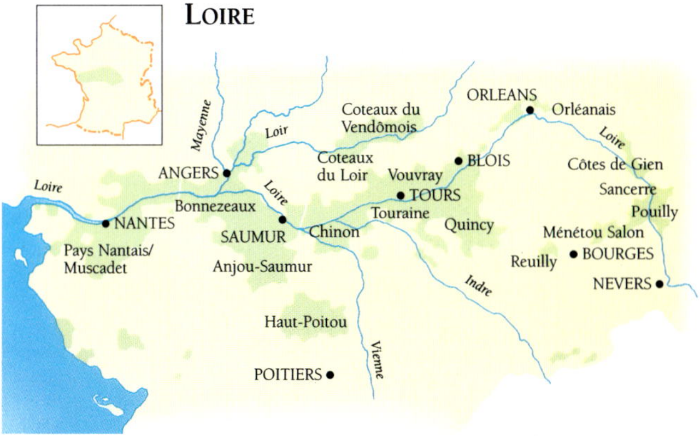

This is the heartland of fresh, dry Sauvignons as well as honeyed sweet wines from Vouvray, Quarts de Chaume, and Bonnezeaux, fresh sparkling wine in Saumur and Vouvray, and juicy blackcurranty reds in Chinon and Bourgeuil. Buy with care. Shoddy winemaking and sulfur dioxide abuse can give wines – particularly late harvest, sweet ones – an unpleasantly "woolly" character.

RHÔNE

Reading the label: Vin Doux Naturel – ***fortified wine, such as Muscat de Beaumes de Venise***. Côtes du Rhône Villages – ***wine from one of a number of better sited villages in the overall Côtes du Rhône appellation, and thus, supposedly finer wine than plain Côtes du Rhône***.

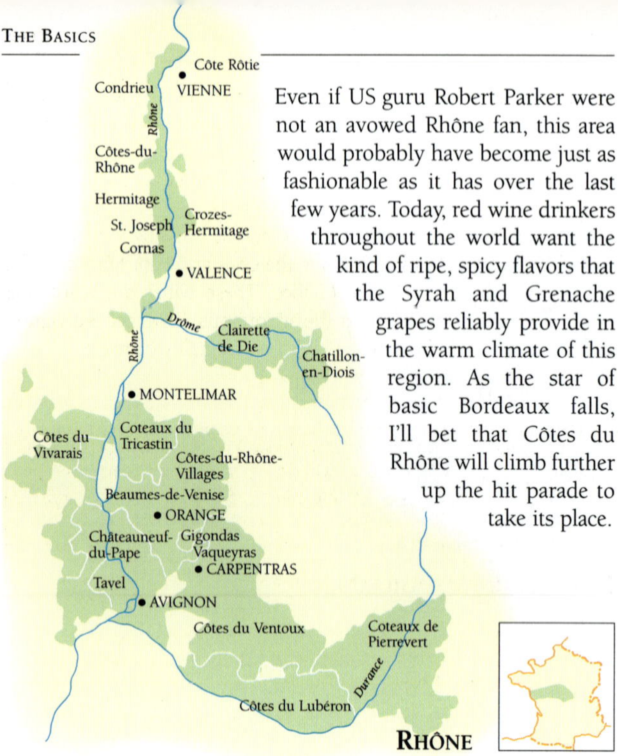

Even if US guru Robert Parker were not an avowed Rhône fan, this area would probably have become just as fashionable as it has over the last few years. Today, red wine drinkers throughout the world want the kind of ripe, spicy flavors that the Syrah and Grenache grapes reliably provide in the warm climate of this region. As the star of basic Bordeaux falls, I'll bet that Côtes du Rhône will climb further up the hit parade to take its place.

THE SOUTHWEST

Reading the label: Perlé or Perlant – *gently sparkling, used in one of the styles of Gaillac.*

The conservative corner of France, heading inland from Bordeaux. This is the place to find wines like Jurançon, in its sweet and dry form, Gaillac, Cahors, and Madiran. Once upon a time these wines, though famous among French wine buffs, were often quite old-fashioned in the worst sense of the term.

Today, a new wave of winemakers is learning how to extract unsuspected fruit flavors from grapes like the Gros and Petit Manseng, the Tannat, the Mauzac, and the Malbec. These wines are worth the detour for anyone bored with the ubiquitous Cabernet Sauvignon and Chardonnay and dissatisfied with poor-quality claret.

THE SOUTH

Reading the label: Vin de Pays d'Oc – *country wine from the Languedoc region. Often some of the best stuff in the region.* Rancio – *woody, slightly volatile character in Banyuls and other fortified wines that have been aged in the barrel.*

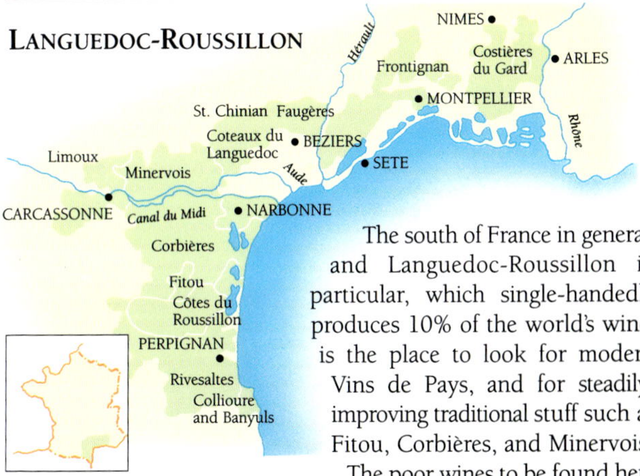

The south of France in general, and Languedoc-Roussillon in particular, which single-handedly produces 10% of the world's wine, is the place to look for modern Vins de Pays, and for steadily-improving traditional stuff such as Fitou, Corbières, and Minervois.

The poor wines to be found here can be blamed on the conservatism of the producers. Even so, the combination of an ideal climate and increasingly dynamic winemaking (and substantial foreign investment) is raising the quality here, as well as in Provence to the east, where classics such as Cassis and Bandol now attract as much attention as the ubiquitous rosé.

EASTERN FRANCE

Reading the label: Vin de Paille – *sweet, golden wine from grapes dried on straw mats.* Vin Jaune – *sherry-like, slightly oxidized wine.*

Savoie's zingy wines are often only thought of as skiing fare but, like Arbois' nutty, sherry-style whites, they are characterfully different, and made from grape varieties that are grown nowhere else.

GERMANY

Reading the label: Amtliche Prüfungsnummer (AP number) – *official identification number.* Auslese – *sweet wine from selected grapes above a certain ripeness level.* Beerenauslese – *luscious, sweet wines from selected, ripe grapes (Beeren), hopefully affected by botrytis.* Erzeugerabfüllung – *bottled by the grower/estate.* Halbtrocken – *off-dry.* Hock – *English name for Rhine wines.* Kabinett – *first step in German quality ladder, for wines which fulfil a certain natural sweetness.* Kellerei/Kellerabfüllung – *cellar/producer/estate-bottled.* Landwein – *a relatively recent quality designation – the equivalent of a French Vin de Pays.* QbA (Qualitätswein bestimmter Anbaugebiete) – *basic quality German wine, meeting certain standards.* QmP (Qualitätswein mit Prädikat) – *QbA wine with "special qualities" subject to (not very) rigorous testing. The QmP blanket designation is broken into five sweetness rungs, from Kabinett to Trockenbeerenauslese plus Eiswein.* Schloss – *literally "castle," the equivalent of Château, designating a vineyard or estate.* Sekt – *very basic, sparkling wine.* Spätlese – *second step in the QmP scale, late harvested grapes, a notch drier than Auslese.* Staatsweingut – *state-owned wine estate.* Tafelwein – *table wine, only the prefix "Deutscher" guarantees German origin.* Trocken – *dry.* Trockenbeerenauslese – *wine from selected dried grapes which are usually botrytis-affected.* Weingut – *estate.* Weinkellerei – *cellar or winery.*

Ignore the oceans of sugar-water cynically exported by Germany under such labels as Liebfraumilch, Piesporter Michelsberg, and Niersteiner Domtal. Ignore too, some of the big-name estates that still seem to get away with producing substandard fare. For real quality, look for Mosel Rieslings from producers like Dr. Loosen and Richter, and new wave Rhine wines now being made by winemakers such as Künstler, Müller Catoir, and Kurt Darting, not to mention the occasional successful red from Karl Lingenfelder. But, however convincing an explanation anyone might offer you for them, avoid dry "Trocken" Kabinett wines from northern Germany unless you want the tartar and enamel removed from your teeth.

ITALY

Reading the label: Abboccato – *semi-dry*. Amabile – *semi-sweet*. Amaro – *bitter*. Asciutto – *bone dry*. Azienda – *estate*. Classico – *the best vineyards at the heart of a DOC*. Colle/ colli – *hills*. DOC(G) Denominazione di Origine Controllata (e Garantita) – *designation, based on grape variety and/or origin*.

Dolce – *sweet*. Frizzante – *semisparkling*. IGT, Indicazione Geografica Tipica – *questionable new designation for quality Vino da Tavola*. Imbottigliato nel'origine – *estate-bottled*. Liquoroso – *rich, sweet*. Passito – *raisiny wine made from sun-dried grapes*. Recioto – *strong, sweet (unless designated Amarone)*. Vino da Tavola – *table wine that does not fit into the DOC system. Includes basic stuff as well as some of Italy's top wines. To be replaced for the latter by* IGT.

Three facts about Italy. **1)** It is more a set of regions than a single country. **2)** There is a tradition of interpreting laws fairly liberally. **3)** Style is often valued as highly as content. So when it comes to wine, this can be a pretty confusing place. Producers do their own frequently delicious thing, using indigenous and imported grape varieties and designer bottles and labels in ways that leave legislators – and humble wine drinkers – exhilarated and exasperated in equal measure.

NEW ZEALAND

This New World country has one of the most unpredictable climates, but produces some of the most intensely flavored wines. There are gooseberryish Sauvignon Blancs, Chardonnays, and innovative Rieslings and Gewürztraminers, as well as some improving reds.

Hawke's Bay seems to be the most consistent region for these, while Gisborne, Marlborough, Auckland, and Martinborough share the honors for white wine (though the last has had some success with the Pinot Noir).

NORTH AFRICA

Islamic fundamentalism has done little to encourage winemaking of any description in North Africa. Even so, Algeria, Morocco, and Tunisia can all offer full-flavored, old-fashioned reds that will probably delight people who liked Burgundy when it routinely included a slug of Algerian blackstrap.

PORTUGAL

Reading the label: Adega – ***winery***. Branco – ***white***. Colheita – ***vintage***. Engarrafado na origem – ***estate-bottled***. Garrafeira – ***a vintage-dated wine with a little more alcohol and minimum ageing requirements***. Quinta – ***vineyard or estate***. Reserva – ***wine from a top-quality vintage, made from riper grapes than the standard requirement***. Velho – ***old***. Vinho de Mesa – ***table wine***.

Like Italy, Portugal has grapes grown nowhere else in the world. Unlike Italy, however, until recently the Portuguese had done little to persuade foreigners of the quality of these varieties.

But now, thanks to two Australian winemakers, Peter Bright and David Baverstock, and the efforts of dynamic, innovative Portuguese producers like Luis Pato in Bairrada, we are beginning to see what the native grapes can produce.

Try any of Pato's Bairradas, Bright's New-Wave Douro reds and Baverstock's tasty Quinta do Crasto red wines from the Douro.

PORTUGAL

SOUTH AFRICA

Reading the label: Cap Classique – ***South African term for Champagne method sparklers***. Cultivar – ***grape variety***. Edel laat-oes – ***noble late harvest***. Edelkeur – ***"noble rot," a fungus affecting grapes and producing sweet wine***. Gekweek, gemaak en gebottel op – ***estate-bottled***. Landgoedwyn – ***estate wine***. Laat-oes – ***late harvest***. Oesjaar – ***vintage***. Steen – ***local name for Chenin Blanc***.

At long last, South Africa's winemakers are beginning to live up to the promise that has always been claimed for their wines. Until recently, as visitors from Bordeaux, Britain, and Australia have noticed, too many wines have had the "green" flavor of over-cropped and under-ripe grapes. Wineries like Thelema, Saxenburg, Plaisir de Merle, Vergelegen, and Fairview show what can be done, while Grangehurst, Kanonkop, and Vriesenhof support the cause for South Africa's own spicy red grape, the Pinotage.

South Africa's late harvest and sparkling wines can also be of world class.

THE CAPE

SOUTH AMERICA

ARGENTINA

Reading the label: Malbec – *spicy red grape*. Torrontes – ***unusual grapey white***.

As it chases Chile, this is a country to watch. The wines to look for now are the spicy reds made from the Malbec, a variety once widely grown in Bordeaux and still used in the Loire. Cabernets can be good, too, as can the grapey but dry white Torrontes.

CHILE

Reading the label: Envasado en Origen – ***estate-bottled.*** Carmenaire/Grand Vidure – ***grape variety once used in Bordeaux but no longer found there.***

One of the most exciting wine-producing countries in the world, thanks to ideal conditions, skilled local winemaking, and plentiful investment. The most successful grape at present is the Merlot, but the Cabernet, Chardonnay, Pinot Noir, and Sauvignon can all display ripe fruit and subtlety often absent in the New World.

SOUTHEASTERN EUROPE

GREECE

Finally casting off its image as purveyor of Europe's worst wines, Greece is beginning to show what can be done with "international" grapes and highly characterful indigenous varieties. Prices are high (so is demand in smart Athens restaurants), but as the New-Wave wines trickle out into the outside world, producers like Château Lazaridi, Gentilini, and Hatzimichali are set for international success.

CYPRUS

Still associated with cheap sherry-substitute and dull wine, but things are changing. Look out for the traditional rich Commandaria.

TURKEY

Lurching out of the vinous dark ages, Turkey has yet to offer the world red or white wines that non-Turks are likely to relish.

LEBANON

Château Musar has survived all the tribulations of the last few years, keeping Lebanon on the map as a wine-producing country.

ISRAEL

Once a source of truly appalling wine, Israel can now boast world-class Cabernet and Muscat, from the Yarden winery in the Golan Heights. The big Carmel winery now produces adequate fare too.

SPAIN

Reading the label: Abocado – *semi-dry.* Año – *year.* Bodega – *winery or wine cellar.* Cava – *Champagne method sparkling wine.* Criado y Embotellado (por) – *grown and bottled (by).* Crianza – *aged in wood.* DO(Ca) (Denominacion de Origen (Califacada)) – *Spain's quality designation, based on regional style, with a newly-introduced higher level* (Califacada) *to indicate superior quality.* Elaborado y Anejado Por – *made and aged for.* Gran Reserva – *a quality wine aged for a designated number of years in wood; more than for an ordinary Reserva.* Joven – *young wine, specially made for early consumption.* Reserva – *official designation for wine that has been aged for a specific period.* Sin Crianza – *not aged in wood.* Vendemia – *harvest or vintage.* Vino de Mesa – *table wine.* Vino de la Tierra – *new designation similar to the French "Vin de Pays."*

Spain used to be relied on for a certain style of highly predictable wine: soft, oaky reds with flavors of strawberry and vanilla, and whites that were either light, dry, and unmemorable (Marqués de Cáceres Rioja Blanco), oaky and old-fashioned (traditional Marqués

de Murrieta Rioja), or sweet and grapey (Moscatel de Valencia). Suddenly, however, like a car whose driver has just found an extra gear, Spanish wines have begun to leap ahead – into often largely uncharted territory. The first region to hail the revolution was Penedés, where winemaker Miguel Torres made a specialty of using both traditional and imported grape varieties.

Others have overtaken Torres, in regions like Somontano, Rueda, and Navarra. In Rioja itself experiments are quietly going on to see whether the Cabernet Sauvignon can improve the flavor of this traditional wine. There are traditionalists who would prefer all this pioneering business to stop, but the wine genie is out of the Spanish bottle and there seems little chance of anyone forcing it back inside again.

SWITZERLAND

Reading the label: Gutedel, Perlan, Fendant – *local names for the Chasselas*. Grand Cru – *top designation which varies from one canton to the next*. Süssdruck – *off-dry, red wine.*

Ferociously expensive for non-Swiss wine drinkers, but recommendable wines on their own terms. This is one of the only places the Chasselas produces anything even remotely memorable. (Incidentally, Switzerland is also the only country I know that has largely switched from corks to screw-caps, so you're unlikely to get a nasty, musty bottle.)

USA

Reading the label: Blush – *rosé*. Champagne – *any sparkling wine*. Fumé – *oak-aged white wine, especially Sauvignon (Blanc Fumé)*. Meritage – *popular, if pretentious, name for a Bordeaux blend (white or red)*. Vinted – *made by (a vintner, or winemaker)*. White Grenache/Zinfandel, etc) – *refers to the unfashionable rosé, slightly pink wines, sometimes also referred to as "blush."*

CALIFORNIA

These are busy days for the best-known winemaking state of the Union. After 20 years of almost single-minded devotion to the Chardonnay and Cabernet Sauvignon and to the Napa Valley, the focus has broadened to take in a wider range of grapes (particularly Italian and Rhône varieties) and regions (Sonoma, Santa Barbara, especially for the Pinot Noir, plus San Luis Obispo, Santa Cruz, Mendocino, and Monterey).

Within the Napa Valley too, where vineyards are being replanted in the wake of the damage caused by the phylloxera louse, there is growing acknowledgement that some subregions produce better wines than others. Carneros is already famous for its Pinot Noir, Oakville for its Chardonnay, while Rutherford and Stag's Leap are known for their Cabernet. But do try other worthwhile areas, such as Mount Veeder and Howell Mountain.

THE PACIFIC NORTHWEST

Outside California, head north to Oregon for some of the best Pinot Noirs in the US (at a hefty price) and improving, but rarely earth-shattering Chardonnays, Rieslings and Pinot Gris. Washington State has some Pinot too, on the cooler, rainy west side of the Cascade Mountains. On the east, the irrigated vineyards produce great Sauvignon and Riesling, as well as top-flight Chardonnay, Cabernet, Syrah, and a very good Merlot.

NEW YORK AND OTHER STATES

Once the source of dire "Chablis" and "Champagne," New York State is now producing worthwhile wines, particularly in the microclimate of Long Island, where the Merlot is thriving. The Finger Lakes are patchier but worth visiting, especially for the Rieslings and cool-climate Chardonnays. Elsewhere Virginia, Missouri, Texas, Maryland, and even Arizona are all producing wines to compete with California and indeed some of the best that Europe can offer.

NORTH EASTERN STATES

THE GRAPES

BLENDS OR SINGLE VARIETIES?

Some wines are made from single grape varieties – e.g., red or white Burgundy, Sancerre, German Riesling, and Barolo – while others, such as red or white Bordeaux, California "Meritage" wines, port, and Châteauneuf-du-Pape, are blends of two or more types of grape. Champagne can fall into either camp, as can New World so- called "varietal" wines which, though labeled as "Chardonnay," "Cabernet Sauvignon," etc., can contain up to 25 percent of other grape varieties, depending on local rules. Blends are not, per se, superior to single varietals – or vice versa.

Freshly picked black grapes ready for crushing

WHITE WINE GRAPES

CHARDONNAY

Ubiquitous but hard to define because of the influences of climate, the soil and the particular clone that has been planted. In Burgundy and the best California examples, (Kistler, Peter Michael, Sonoma Cutrer) it tastes of butter and hazelnuts; lesser New World efforts are sweet and simple and often very melony (a flavor which comes from the clone). Australians range from subtle buttery pineapple to oaky tropical fruit juice. Petaluma, Coldstream Hills and Leeuwin show how it can be done. New Zealand's efforts are tropical too, but lighter and fresher (Te Mata, Cloudy Bay). Elsewhere, Chile is beginning to hit the mark, as is South Africa, though some examples still taste unripe. In Europe, look around southern France, Italy, Spain, and Eastern Europe, but beware of watery cheaper versions.

CHENIN BLANC

Loire variety producing fresh fizzy wine, dry, and luscious honeyed wines; also raw stuff like unripe apples and, when over-sulfured, old socks. Most California Chenins are semisweet and ordinary. South Africans call it the Steen, use it for sweet wines. There are few good Australians (but try Moondah Brook) or New Zealanders (Millton).

GEWÜRZTRAMINER

Outrageous stuff that smells of parma violets and tastes of lychee nuts. At its best in Alsace, dry and sweet, as a Vendange Tardive or Sélection de Grains Nobles (Zind Humbrecht, Schlumberger, Faller). Try examples from Germany, New Zealand, and Italy too.

Chenin Blanc

Gewürztraminer

MARSANNE

A classic, flowery, lemony variety used in the Rhône in wines like Hermitage (from producers like Guigal), and in Australia – especially in Goulburn in Victoria (Chateau Tahbilk and Mitchelton); in southern France (in Vin de Pays d'Oc blends such as La Pérousse and from Mas de Daumas Gassac) and in innovative wines from California. At its best young or after five or six years.

MUSCAT

The only variety whose wines actually taste as though they are made of grapes, rather than some other kind of fruit or vegetable. In Alsace, southern France, and Northeast Italy it is used to make dry wines. Generally, though, it performs best as sparkling wine (Moscatos, and Asti Spumantes from Italy and Clairette de Die Tradition from France) and as sweet fortified wine. Look out for Beaumes de Venise and Rivesaltes in southern France, Moscatel de Setúbal in Portugal, Moscatel de Valencia in Spain, and Christmas-puddingy Liqueur Muscat in Australia (Morris, Chambers, Yalumba).

PINOT BLANC/PINOT BIANCO

As rich as Chardonnay, but with less fruit. At its worst – when overcropped in Alsace and Italy, it makes neutral wine. At its best,however,(also in Alsace) it can develop a lovely cashew nut flavor. When well handled it can also do well in Italy, where it is known as Pinot Bianco (Jermann), and in Germany, where it is called Weissburgunder. Most California Pinot Blancs are really made from the duller Melon de Bourgogne of Muscadet fame.

PINOT GRIS

An up-and-coming Alsace variety also known as Tokay but unrelated to any of the world's other Tokays. Its wines can be spicy, and appear in both sweet and dry versions. In Italy where it is often used to make dilute wine, it is called Pinot Grigio, and in Germany it is known as Grauerburgunder. Look for New World examples from Oregon (Eyrie), California, and New Zealand.

RIESLING

For purists this, not the Chardonnay, is the king of white varieties. Misunderstood – and often mispronounced as Rice-ling rather than Rees-ling – it carries the can for torrents of cheap German wine made from quite different grapes. At its best, it makes dry and sweet, grapey, appley, limey wines that develop a spicy, gasoline character with age. Quality and character depend on soil – ideally slate – more than climate and while the best examples come from Germany, in the Mosel, (Dr Loosen) and Rhine and Alsace (Zind-Humbrecht, Faller),this variety can perform equally well in such different environments as Washington State (Kiona), and Australia (Grossett, Tim Adams) and New Zealand (Matua Valley). Don't confuse the Riesling with such unrelated varieties as Laski, Lutomer, Welsch, Emerald, or White Riesling.

Riesling

Sauvignon Blanc

SAUVIGNON/FUMÉ BLANC

The grape of Loire wines, such as Sancerre and Pouilly Fumé, and white Bordeaux, where it is often blended with the Sémillon. This gooseberryish variety now performs brilliantly in Marlborough in New Zealand (where the flavors can include asparagus and pea-pods), in South Africa (Thelema), and Australia (Shaw & Smith, Cullens). Chile has some good examples (from Casablanca) – and poor ones, made from a different variety called the Sauvignonasse. Washington State can get it right, but in California it is often horribly sweet or overburdened by the flavor of oak. (Oaked versions here and elsewhere are usually labeled Fumé Blanc.) Only the best ones improve after the first couple of years.

SÉMILLON

A distinctive peachy variety with only two successful homes. In Bordeaux, usually in blends with the Sauvignon Blanc, it produces sublime dry Graves and sweet Sauternes – and over-sulfured stuff that tastes like old dishcloths. In Australia there are brilliant, long-lived dry wines which are made purely from the Semillon in the Hunter Valley (often unoaked) and Barossa Valley (usually oaked). Good "noble" late-harvest examples have also been produced (by de Bortoli) in Riverina. Elsewhere in Australia the grape is sometimes blended with the Chardonnay, a cocktail which has proved popular in California (in Geyser Peak's Semchard). Progress is being made in Washington State but most examples from California, New Zealand, and Chile are disappointing.

SYLVANER

A characterful grape rarely found outside Alsace and Franken in Germany, the Sylvaner has a recognizably "earthy" character at odds with most modern wines. Crossing the Sylvaner with the Riesling, incidentally, produced the the Scheurebe and the Müller-Thurgau.

Sémillon

Viognier

VIOGNIER

Now a cult grape, the Viognier was once more or less confined to the small appellations of Condrieu and Château Grillet in the Rhône, where good examples showed off its extraordinary perfumed, peach blossomy character, albeit at a high price. Today, however, it has been widely introduced to the Ardèche and Languedoc-Roussillon, California – where it is made with loving care (and over-generous exposure to oak barrels) – Eastern Europe, Argentina, and Australia (Heggies Vineyard). While affordable examples are welcome, many are disappointing.. Buy with care.

RED WINE GRAPES

BARBERA

An Italian variety at its best in Piedmont. The keynote is a wild berryish flavor. Increasingly successful in blends with the Nebbiolo and Cabernet. Making inroads into California and Australia.

CABERNET SAUVIGNON

A remarkable success story, historically associated with the great red wines of the Médoc and Graves (where it is blended with the Merlot) and, more recently, with some of the best reds from the New World, especially California, Chile, and Australia. Eastern Europe has good value examples (Bulgaria), as does southern France (Vin de Pays). Spain is rapidly climbing aboard (in the Penedès, Navarra, and – though this is kept quiet – Rioja). The hallmark to look for is blackcurrant, though unripe versions taste like a blend of weeds and bell peppers. There are some great Cabernets in Italy, though the "Italian wine" flavor somehow always dominates the grape. Good New World Cabernets can smell and taste of fresh mint, but with time, like the best Bordeaux, they develop a rich, leathery "cigar box" character.

Cabernet Sauvignon

Grenache/Garnacha

GRENACHE/GARNACHA

Pepper – freshly ground black pepper – is the distinguishing flavor here, sometimes with the fruity tang of penny candy. At home in Côtes du Rhône and Châteauneuf-du-Pape, it is also used in Spain (as the Garnacha) in blends with the Tempranillo. Seek out "Old Vine" or "Bush" examples from Australia.

Merlot *Nebbiolo/Spanna*

MERLOT

The most widely planted variety in Bordeaux and the subject of eager planting in California. In Bordeaux it is at its best in Pomerol, where wines can taste of ripe plums and spice, and in St. Emilion, where the least successful wines show the Merlot's less lovable dull and earthy character. Wherever it is made, the Merlot should produce softer wines than the Cabernet Sauvignon, though some California examples have been tough. Elsewhere, Washington State and Chile are places to look, along with Italy and Eastern Europe.

NEBBIOLO/SPANNA

The red wine grape of Barolo and Barbaresco in Piedmont now, thanks to modern winemaking, increasingly reveals a lovely cherry and rose-petal character, often with the sweet vanilla of new oak casks.

PINOT NOIR

The wild raspberryish, plummy, and licoricey grape of all red Burgundy, is also a major component of white and pink Champagne. It is used to make red and pink Sancerre, as well as light reds in Alsace and Germany (where it is called Spätburgunder). Italy makes a few good examples, but for the best, modern efforts, look to California – espcially Carneros (Saintsbury) and Santa Barbara (Au Bon Climat) – Oregon (Domaine Drouhin), Australia (Coldstream Hills), New Zealand (Martinborough), Chile (Cono Sur, Valdivieso), and South Africa.

PINOTAGE

Almost restricted to South Africa, this cross between the Pinot Noir and the Cinsaut can make berryish young wines that may develop rich gamy-spicy flavors. Try Kanonkop and Vriesenhof.

SANGIOVESE

The grape of Chianti, Brunello di Montalcino, and of a host of popular Vino da Tavola wines in Italy, not to mention "new wave" Italian-style wines in California. The recognizable flavor is of sweet tobacco, wild herbs, and berries.

SYRAH/SHIRAZ

The extraordinary spicy, brambly grape of the Northern Rhône (Hermitage, Cornas, etc.) and the best reds of Australia (Henschke Hill of Grace and Penfolds Grange), where it is also blended with the Cabernet Sauvignon (just as it once was in Bordeaux). Elsewhere in Europe, the Marqués de Griñon has a great Spanish example, and Isole e Olena has made an unofficial one in Tuscany. Increasingly successful in California and Washington State.

Syrah/Shiraz *Zinfandel*

TEMPRANILLO

Known under all sorts of names around Spain, including Cencibel (in Navarra) and Tinto Fino (in Ribeira del Duero), the grape gives Spanish reds their recognizable strawberry character. Often blended with the Garnacha, it works well with the Cabernet Sauvignon.

ZINFANDEL

California's "own", related to the Italian Primitivo. In California, it makes spicy, blueberryish reds (see Ridge Vineyards) and "ports" and, when blended with sweet Muscat, sweet pink "White Zinfandel". Outside California, Cape Mentelle makes a good example in Western Australia and Delheim a floral one in South Africa.

OTHER GRAPES

WHITE

Albariño/Alvarinho Floral. Grown in Spain and Portugal.
Aligoté Lean Burgundy grape.
Arneis Perfumed variety in Piedmont.
Colombard Appley, basic; grown in S.W. France, US, and Australia.
Furmint Limey variety, traditionally used for Tokaji.
Grüner Veltliner Limey. Restricted to Austria and Eastern Europe.
Kerner Dull German grape. Can taste leafy.
Müller-Thurgau/Rivaner Dull variety, grown in Germany and England. Can have a similar "cat's pee" character to Sauvignon.
Roussanne Fascinating Rhône variety that deserves more attention.
Scheurebe Grapefruity grape grown in Germany.
Torrontes Grapey, Muscatlike variety of Argentina.
Ugni Blanc/Trebbiano Basic grape of S.W. France and Italy.
Verdejo Interesting Spanish variety of Rueda.
Verdelho Limey grape found in Madeira and Australian table wine.
Viura Widely planted, so-so Spanish variety.
Welschriesling Basic. Best in late harvest Austrians.

RED

Cabernet Franc Kid brother of Cabernet Sauvignon, grown alongside it in Bordeaux and by itself in the Loire and Italy.
Carmenère/Grand Vidure Exciting, spicy, smoky variety once grown in Bordeaux; now limited to Chile.
Charbono Fun, spicy berryish, grape only grown in California.
Cinsaut Spicy Rhône variety; best in blends.
Carignan Toffeeish nonaromatic variety widely used in S. France.
Concord US grape better used for grape juice or jelly.
Dolcetto Cherryish Piedmont grape.
Dornfelder Successful, juicy variety grown in Germany.
Gamay The Beaujolais grape; less successful in the Loire and Gaillac.
Gamay Beaujolais/Valdiguié Mulberryish cousin of the Pinot Noir, grown in California. Confusingly unrelated to the Gamay.
Lemberger/Limberger/Blaufränkisch Berryish; successful in Washington State.
Malbec/Côt Once in Bordeaux blends; now Cahors, Loire, Argentina.
Mourvèdre (Mataro) Spicy Rhône grape; good in California and Australia, but can be hard and "metallic".
Petit Verdot Spicy ingredient of Bordeaux. Now being used straight.
Petite-Sirah Spicy; thrives in California and Mexico, and as Durif in Australia.
Ruby Cabernet Basic Carignan-Cabernet Sauvignon cross.
Tannat Tough variety of Madiran and Uruguay.

STYLES

1880 A formal dinner party, by Georges du Maurier

STYLE COUNSEL

In simple terms, wine can be separated into a few easily recognizable styles: red, white and pink; still and sparkling; sweet and dry; light and fortified. To say that the contents of a bottle are red and dry does little, however, to convey the way a wine tastes. It could be a fruity Beaujolais, a mature Rioja, a blueberryish California Zinfandel, or a tough young Bordeaux.

Knowing the grape and origin of a wine can of course give a clearer idea of what it is like, but it won't tell you everything. The human touch is as important in wine as it is in the kitchen. Some chefs like to assemble often eclectic flavors while others prefer more conservative ingredients. The wine world is similarly divided between producers who focus on obvious fruit flavors, and winemakers, in France for example, who talk about the *goût de terroir* – the taste of the earth or soil.

In a world that is increasingly given to instant sensations, it is perhaps unsurprising that it is the fruit-lovers rather than the friends of the earthy flavor who are currently in the ascendant.

NEW WORLD/OLD WORLD

Until recently, these two winemaking philosophies could be broadly defined as belonging to the New and Old World. Places like California and Australia made wine that was approachably delicious when compared with the more serious wine being produced in Europe, which demanded time and food.

Life is never quite that cut-and-dried, however. Today, there are Bordeaux châteaux that are taking a decidedly New World approach and South Africans who take a pride in making wine as resolutely tough and old-fashioned as a Bordeaux of a hundred years ago.

Flying Winemakers

One phenomenon that has contributed to these changes in philosophy has been the "flying winemakers" – mostly Antipodeans who, like hired guns, are contracted to produce wine all over the world. Today, you can choose between a white Loire made by a Frenchman – or one bearing the fruity fingerprint of Australian-rules winemaking.

Fruit of Knowledge

European old timers like to claim that the Australians use alchemy to obtain those fruity flavors. In fact, their secret lies in the winemaking process. Picking the grapes when they are ripe (rather than too early); preventing them from cooking beneath the midday sun (as often happens in Europe while work stops for lunch); pumping the juice through pipes that have been cleaned daily rather than at each end of the harvest; fermenting at a cool temperature (overheated vats can cost a wine its freshness); and storing and bottling it carefully, will all help a wine made from even the dullest grape variety to taste fruitier.

COME HITHER

If the New Worlders want their wines to taste of fruit, they are – apart from some reactionary South Africans and Californians – just as keen to make wine that can be drunk young. They take care not to squeeze the red grapes too hard, so as not to extract bitter, hard tannins, and they try to avoid their white wines being too acidic.

Traditionalists claim that wines made this way do not age well.. It is too early to say whether this is true in the long term, but there is no question that the newer wave red Bordeaux of, say 1985, have consistently given more people more pleasure since they were first released, than the supposedly greater 1970 vintage, whose wines remained dauntingly hard throughout their lifetime. A wine does not have to be undrinkable in its youth to be good to drink later on; indeed wines that start out tasting unbalanced go on tasting that way.

SPOTTING THE WOOD FROM THE TREES

Another thing that sets many new wave wines apart has nothing to do with grapes. Wines have been matured in oak barrels since Roman times, and traditionally new barrels were only bought to replace old ones that had begun to fall apart. Old casks have little flavor but, for the first two years or so of their lives, the way the staves are bent over flames gives new ones a recognizable vanilla-caramel character. Winemakers once used to rinse out their new casks with dilute ammonia to remove this flavor. Today, however, they often take the choice of forest, cooper, and charring (light, medium, or heavy "toast") as seriously as the quality of their grapes.

Oak-mania began when Bordeaux châteaux began to spend the income from the great vintages of the 1940s on replacements for their old barrels – and when New World pioneers like Mondavi noticed the contribution the oak was making to these wines. Ever since, top producers and would-be top producers internationally have introduced new barrels, while even the makers of cheaper wine have found that dunking giant "teabags" filled with small oak chips into wine vats could add some of that vanilla flavor too.

If you like oak, you'll find it in top flight Bordeaux and Burgundy (red and white), Spanish Crianza, Reserva or Gran Reserva, and Italians whose labels use the French term "Barrique." The words "*Elevé en fût de Chêne*" on a French wine could confusingly refer to new or old casks. Australian "Show Reserve" will be oaky, as will Fumé Blanc and New World Reserve and "Barrel Select"wines.

RED WINES – FRUITS, SPICE AND . . . COLD TEA

If you enjoy your red wines soft and juicily fruity, the styles to look for are Burgundy and other wines made from the Pinot Noir, Rioja, and reds from Spain, inexpensive Australians, Pomerol, good St. Emilion from Bordeaux, and Merlots from almost anywhere. Look too for Nouveau, Novello, and Joven (young wines).

The Kitchen Cupboard

Italy's Sangiovese is not so much fruity as herby, while the Syrah/Shiraz of the Rhône and Australia, the peppery Grenache and – sometimes – the Zinfandel and Pinotage can be surprisingly spicy.

Some Like it Tough

Most basic Bordeaux and all but a few wines from St. Estèphe and Listrac in Bordeaux are more tannic, as are most older-style wines from Piedmont, California, and most South Africans. The Cabernet Sauvignon will make tougher wines than the Merlot or Pinot Noir.

WHITE WINES – HONEY AND LEMON

If dry wines with unashamedly fruity flavors are what you want, try the Muscat, the Torrontes in Argentina, basic Riesling and Chardonnay, and New World and Southern French Sauvignon Blanc.

Non-Fruit

For more neutral styles, go for Soave or Frascati from Italy, Muscadet, Grenache Blanc, and most traditional wines from Spain and Southern France.

Riches Galore

The combination of richness and fruit is to be found in white Burgundy, better dry white Bordeaux and in Chardonnays, Semillons, and oaked Sauvignon (Fumé) wines from the New World.

Aromatherapy

Some perfumed, spicy grapes, like the Gewürztraminer, are frankly aromatic. The Tokay-Pinot Gris, the Gewürztraminer's neighbor in Alsace, fits the bill, as do the Viognier in France, the Arneis in Italy, the Albariño in Spain and the Grüner Veltliner in Austria.

Middle of the Road

Today, people want wine that is – or says it is – either dry or positively sweet. The Loire can get honeyed semisweet wine right. Otherwise, head for Germany and Kabinett and Spätlese wines.

Pure Hedonism

Sweet wine is making a comeback as people rebel against the health fascism that sought to outlaw such pleasures. The first places to look are Bordeaux, the Loire (Moelleux), Alsace (Vendange Tardive or Sélection des Grains Nobles); Germany (Auslese, Beerenauslese Trockenbeerenauslese); Austria (Ausbruch); the New World (late harvest and noble late harvest); and Hungary (Tokaji 6 Puttonyos).

All of these wines should not only taste sweet, but have enough fresh acidity to prevent them from being in the least cloying. Also, they should have the additional, characteristic dried-apricot flavor that comes from grapes that have been allowed to be affected by a benevolent fungus known as "botrytis" or "noble rot."

Other sweet wines such as Muscat de Beaumes de Venise are fortified with brandy to raise their strength to 15 percent or so. These wines can be luscious, but they never have the flavor of "noble rot."

PINK

Tread carefully. Provence and the Rhône should offer peppery-dry rosé just as the Loire and Bordeaux should have wines that taste deliciously of blackcurrant. Sadly, many taste dull and stale. Still, they are a better bet than California's dire sweet "white" or "blush" rosé. Look for the most recent vintage and the most vibrant color.

SPARKLING

If you find Champagne too dry, but don't want a frankly sweet grapey fizz like Asti Spumante, try a fruity New World sparkler like the Cuvée Napa from California or Seaview from Australia. If you don't like that fruitiness, try traditional Cava from Spain, Prosecco from Italy, and Blanquette de Limoux from France.

STORING

Keep track of your bottles

STARTING A CELLAR

THE RESTING PLACE

Not so long ago, when winemaking was less sophisticated and there were fewer ways to counter tricky vintages, there were two kinds of wines: the basic stuff to drink immediately, and the cream of the crop that was left in the barrel and/or bottle to age. So, a good wine was an old wine. And vice versa. Young wine and old wine had as much in common as hamburgers and *haute cuisine*.

Today, just as fast food now includes delicious sushi, there are brilliant wines that never improve beyond the first few years after the harvest, and are none the worse for that. On the other hand, some wines – German Riesling, fine claret, and top Australian Shiraz, for example – by their very nature, still repay a few years' patience in the cellar.

While many of us – myself included – live in homes that are ill-suited for storing wine, one can often find an unused grate or a space beneath the stairs that offers wine what it wants: a constant temperature of around 44–60°F (never lower than 40°F nor more than 68°F), reasonable humidity (install a cheap humidifier or leave a sponge in a bowl of water), sufficient ventilation to avoid a musty atmosphere and, ideally, an absence of vibration (wines stored beneath train tracks – or beds – age faster). Alternatively, invest in a fridgelike Eurocave that guarantees perfect conditions.– or even adapt an old freezer.

RACKS AND CELLAR BOOKS

Purpose-built racks can be bought "by the hole", and cut to fit awkwardly shaped bits of wall. Square chimney pots can be used too. If you have plenty of space, simply allocate particular racks to specific styles of wine. Unfortunately, even the best laid-out cellar plans tend to fall apart when a generous gift of two cases of Australian Shiraz has to be squeezed into a part of the cellar with space enough for just one.

If the size of the cellar warrants it, give each hole in the rack a cross-referenced identity, from A1 at the top left to, say, Z100 at the bottom right. As bottles arrive, they can then be put in any available hole, and their address noted in a cellar book in which youn can record when and where you obtained it, what it cost and how each bottle tasted (is it improving or drying out?). Some people, like me, prefer to use a computer (Filemaker Pro or Microsoft Excel).

TO DRINK OR KEEP?

A guide to which corks to pop soon and which bottles to treasure for a few years in the rack:

Drink as Soon as Possible

Most wine at under $8, particularly Muscadet, Vins de Pays, white Bordeaux; Nouveau/Novello/Joven reds; Bardolino, Valpolicella; light Italian whites; most Sauvignon Blanc; almost all rosé.

Less than 5 Years

Most Petit-Château Bordeaux and Cru Bourgeois, and lesser Cru Classés clarets from poorer vintages; basic Alsace, Burgundy and better Beaujolais; Chianti, Barbera, basic Spanish reds; good mid-quality Germans; English wines; cheaper New World Chardonnays; all but the finest New and Old World Sauvignons; basic South African, Chilean, and Australian reds.

5-10 Years

Most Cru Bourgeois Bordeaux from good years; better châteaux from lesser vintages; all but the best red and white Burgundy and Pinot and Chardonnay from elsewhere; middle-quality Rhônes; southern-French higher flyers; good German, Alsace, dry Loire and white Bordeaux; Portuguese reds; California and Washington State; South African, Chilean, and New Zealand Merlots.

Over 10 Years

Top-class Bordeaux, Rhône, Burgundy, and sweet Loire from ripe years; topflight German late harvest, Italian Vino da Tavola and Barolo; best Australian Shiraz, Cabernet, Rieslings and Semillon, and California Cabernet.

SERVING

From the Correr Museum in Venice. Graeco-Venetian School, 16th Century: 'The Marriage Feast at Cana'

THE RULES OF THE GAME

"The art in using wine is to produce the greatest possible quantity of present gladness, without any future depression."
The Gentleman's Table Guide, 1873

The Romans used to add salt to their wine to preseve it, while the Greeks favored pine resin (which helps to explain the pine-flavored Retsina that is still so popular today). Burgundians who like to refer to Napoleon's taste for Chambertin, rarely mention that the great man used to dilute his red wine with water. A century ago, the English used to add ice to claret and – in winter, in Europe today, skiiers– drink hot "mulled" wine, adding sugar, fruit, and spices. Today, Chinese wine drinkers apparently prefer their Mouton Cadet with a dash of Sprite. And why not? Millions of American wine drinkers got their first taste of wine in the form of a "cooler," which after all is only a blend of wine, sugar, and flavored soda. I'm sure the addition of soda pop would do many a skinny Bordeaux a world of good – it's just rather a pity when it's added to a classier glass of Médoc or St. Emilion. As with food and sex, it's well worth questioning accepted rules – especially when they vary between cultures. Have no fear, the advice that follows is all based on common sense and experience – and offered only to help you to decide how you enjoy serving and drinking wine.

SOME LIKE IT HOT

Particular styles of wine, like types of food, taste better at particular temperatures. Warm Champagne is as appetizing as warm strawberries. At many restaurants, though, white and sparkling wine are more often served too cold than too hot. Paradoxically, it is the reds that suffer most from being drunk too warm. Few of the people who serve wines at "room temperature" recall that, when that term was coined, there wasn't a lot of central heating. Be ready to chill a fruity red by putting the bottle in a bucket of ice and water for five to ten minutes before serving.

Don't cook your reds – or freeze your whites...

Red Wine

When choosing the temperature for a red, focus on the flavor of the wine. Tough wines are best slightly warmer. The following temperatures provide a rule-of-thumb guide:

1) Beaujolais and other fruity reds: 50–57°F (an hour in the fridge).
2) Younger red Burgundy and Rhônes and older Bordeaux, Chianti, younger Rioja, New World Grenache, and Pinotage: 58–62°F.
3) Older Burgundy, tannic young Bordeaux, and Rhônes, Zinfandel, bigger Cabernet Sauvignon, Merlot, and Shiraz, Barolo, and other bigger Italian and Spanish reds: 62–67°F.

Rosé

Rosé should be chilled at 54–57°F, or for five to ten minutes in a bucket of ice and water.

White Wine

The cooler the wine, the less it will smell or taste. Subtler, richer wines deserve to be drunk a little warmer.

1) Lighter sweeter wines and everyday sparklers: 39–46°F (two or three hours in the icebox or 10–15 minutes in ice and water).
2) Fuller-bodied, aromatic, drier, semidry, lusciously sweet whites; Champagne, simpler Sauvignons, and Chardonnays: 46–53°F.
3) Richer dry wines: Burgundy, California Chardonnay: 54–57°F.

THE PERFECT OUTCOME

The patented Screwpull is still the most reliable way to get a cork out of bottle. The "waiter's friend" is the next best thing; otherwise choose a corkscrew that comes in the form of a wire spiral rather than that looks like a large screw.

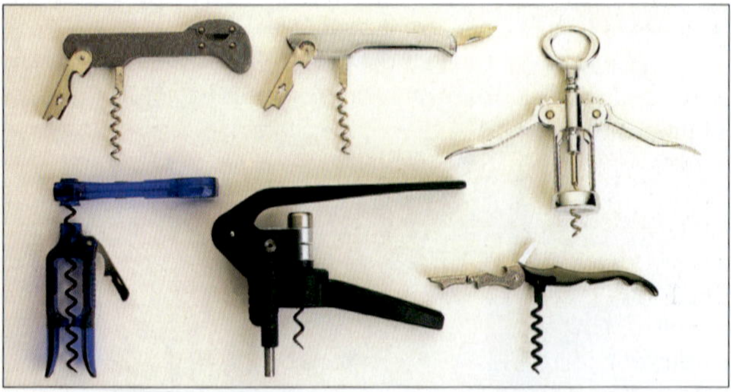

Good corkscrews all have spirals rather than screws.

WHICH GLASSES?

On occasions when no other glass was available I have enjoyed great wine from a toothbrushing mug. I suspect I'd have gotten more out of the experience if something a bit more stylish had come to hand. Glasses should be narrower across the rim than the bowl. Red ones should be bigger than white because they are best kept chilled in the bottle rather than warming in the glass. If you like bubbles in your sparkling wine, serve it in a flute rather than a saucer from which they will swiftly escape. Dartington Crystal, Schott, and Riedel are among a number of companies that now produce attractive glasses that are specially designed to bring out the best in particular styles of wine.

Wines definitely benefit from purpose-designed glasses like these

TO BREATHE OR NOT TO BREATHE?

Some reds have an unwelcome mudlike deposit; some reds and whites may benefit from the aeration of being poured into a decanter or another bottle. But don't decant every red wine you encounter. A tannic young Cabernet or Italian may soften to reveal unexpected flavors, but old Burgundy or Rioja will have very little deposit and may be too light-bodied to gain from decanting.

Stand the bottle for up to a day before decanting it. Pour it very slowly, in front of a flashlight or candle, watching for the first signs of the deposit. Coffee filters suit those with less steady hands.

Airing a wine by simply opening it a few hours in advance of serving achieves little (the contact with oxygen offered by the neck of the bottle is far too limited to have much effect). So, to be aired properly a wine normally needs to be poured out of the bottle. A small device exists however, that bubbles air into wine to mimic the effect of decanting.

Although this is not often appreciated, white wine can also sometimes benefit from the aeration that comes from being poured into a decanter. Try it for any wine that seems to smell of throat-tickling sulfur dioxide or one that seems to smell and taste more restrained than you might have anticipated.

Decant red – or white – wine to bring out the flavor

ORDER OF SERVICE

The rules say that white wines and youth respectively precede red wines and age; dry goes before sweet (most of us prefer our main course before the dessert); the lighter the wine, the earlier. These rules are of course often impossible to follow. What are you to do, for example, if the red Loire is lighter-bodied than the white Burgundy? Can the claret follow the Sauternes that you are offering with the foie gras? Ignore the absolutes but bear in mind the common sense that lies behind them. Work gently up the scale of fullness, "flavorsomeness," and quality, rather than swinging wildly between styles.

INVESTING

LIQUID ASSETS

The value of wine – like that of a great many other commodities – often has little to do with the quality of the contents of the bottle. The 1997 vintage in Bordeaux, though undeniably inferior to the 1995 and 1996, sold for higher prices, *as futures,* – in the barrel – as the producers took advantage of the wine boom in Asia. When the 1998 vintage arrived in early 1999, however, the Asian economies were looking feeble and merchants' cellars were awash with unsold 1997s. So, the price went down by around 25 percent. As Asia pulled itself back together, the Bordelais were feeling confident about the prospects for the 1999 vintage while it was still on the vine. There was, they said, almost sure to be a huge demand for the 1999 and 2000 vintages by Westerners who will be eager to get these fin-de-siècle wines into their cellars, almost irrespective of their quality.

Given the uncertainties that still surround the US and UK stock markets and the speed of the Asian recovery, I'd tread carefully when investing in any wine, but buying the right wine from the right vintage at the right price is undoubtedly a good long-term investment.

SUPPLY AND DEMAND

There are reportedly over 100,000 new dollar millionaires produced every year – people who are naturally attracted by the traditional trappings of wealth – like classic wine. And with just 240,000 bottles made annually by an average Médoc château, let alone the 12,000 or so on offer from a small Pomerol estate, it's hardly surprising that wines like these with established reputations, and critically approved new offerings, are easy to sell. It remains to be seen whether the "micro-wines" now being made in Pomerol, St. Emilion, and California, which are produced in hundreds rather than thousands of cases, will sustain ludicrously high prices that are unquestionably based on rarity rather than on quality.

THE RULES

1) The popularity and value of any wine can vary from one country to another. **2)** Wines are not like works of art; they don't last forever, so be ready to see their value fall. **3)** Tread carefully among wines like le Pin and Valandraud from Bordeaux and Screaming Eagle from California which have yet to prove their *long-term* potential. The prices of the new Bordeaux superstars began to fall during the first few months of 1998 and I wouldn't be surprised to see them fall further over the next year or so. **4)** When buying *as futures*, deal with financially solid merchants. **5)** At auction, favor wines that are known to have been carefully cellared. **6)** Store your wines carefully and securely – in your own cellar or elsewhere. **7)** Follow your wine's progress; read critics' comments, and watch auction prices. **8)** Beware of falling reputations: the 1975 Bordeaux came after a series of poor vintages and sold at high prices; within a decade they had been eclipsed by the 1970 and 1982 vintages, and today are on few people's shopping lists. The 1974 Californian Cabernets, once heavily hyped, are now similarly questioned. The following wines are worth investing in:

FRANCE

Bordeaux

Châteaux l'Angélus, Ausone, Cheval Blanc, Cos d'Estournel, Ducru-Beaucaillou, Eglise-Clinet, Figeac, Grand-Puy-Lacoste, Gruaud-Larose, Haut-Brion, Lafite, Lafleur, Latour, Léoville Barton, Léoville Las Cases, Lynch Bages, Margaux, la Mission-Haut-Brion, la Mondotte, Montrose, Mouton-Rothschild, Palmer, Pétrus, Pichon Lalande, Pichon Longueville, le Pin, Rauzan Segla (recent vintages) Rol Valentin, Valandraud. Vintages: 1982, 1983 (for Margaux), 1985, 1986, 1988, 1989, 1990, 1995, 1996.

Burgundy

Drouhin Marquis de Laguiche, Gros Frères, Hospices de Beaune (from *négociants* such as Drouhin, or Jadot), Méo-Camuzet, Romanée-Conti (la Tâche, Romanée-Conti), Lafon, Leroy, de Vogüé.

Rhône

Chapoutier, Chave, Guigal (top wines), Jaboulet Aîné "La Chapelle."

PORTUGAL (PORT)

Cockburn's, Dow's, Fonseca, Graham's, Noval, Taylor's, Warre's.

CALIFORNIA

Beaulieu Private Reserve, Diamond Creek, Dominus, Duckhorn, Dunn Howell Mountain, Grace Family, Heitz Martha's Vineyard, (varied in the late 1980s and early 1990s), Matanzas Creek, Robert Mondavi Reserve, Opus One, Ridge, Spottswoode, Stag's Leap.

AUSTRALIA

Jim Barry "The Armagh," Henschke Hill of Grace and Mount Edelstone, Leeuwin Chardonnay, Penfolds Grange and Bin 707, Petaluma Cabernet, Wynns "John Riddoch," Virgin Hills, Yarra Yering.

Vintages

Time Will Tell

Twenty-five years ago, a vintage chart was as necessary for the enjoyment of wine as a corkscrew and a glass. But that was in the days when wine of quality was produced only in a limited number of places, and in years when the climate was just right. Man had yet to develop ways – physical, chemical, and organic – of combatting pests and diseases that used to spoil wine with dreadful regularity.

Really disastrous vintages are a rarity now. Though frost can cut production, every year the most skilled and the luckiest producers in almost every region manage to make drinkable wines. Some places, however, are naturally more prone to tricky vintages than others. Northern Europe, for example, suffers more from unreliable sun and untimely rain than more southerly regions, let alone the warm, irrigated vineyards of Australia and the Americas.

A dependable climate does not necessarily make for better wine, however. Just as plants often bloom best in tough conditions, grapes develop more interesting flavors in what is known as a "marginal" climate – which is why New World producers are busily seeking out cooler, higher-altitude sites in which to plant their vines.

It's an Ill Wind

Some producers can buck the trend of a climatically poor year – by luckily picking before the rainstorms, carefully discarding rotten grapes, or even using new techniques to concentrate the flavor of a rain-diluted crop. In years like these, well-situated areas within larger regions can, in any case, make better wines than their neighbors. So, *Grand* and *Premier Cru* vineyards in France, for example, owe their prestige partly to the way their grapes ripen. The difference in quality between regions can, however, also be attributed to the types of grapes that are grown. Bordeaux had a fair-to-good vintage for red wine in 1997, but a great one for Sauternes. Similarly, there are vintages where, for example, the St Emilion and Pomerol châteaux have already picked their Merlot grapes in perfect conditions before rainstorms arrive to ruin the prospects of their counterparts' later-ripening Cabernet Sauvignon in the Médoc, only a few miles away.

The following pages suggest regions and wines for the most significant vintages of this century.

THE LAST FIVE YEARS

1999 (SOUTHERN HEMISPHERE)

A patchy year in Australia, with finest wines coming from Coonawarra and Victoria. New Zealand made better whites than in 1998. Also look out for successes from Chile and Argentina.

1998

Untimely Rain made for a very mixed vintage almost everywhere in the northern hemisphere. There were some great red Bordeaux (St. Emilion, Pomerol, and top châteaux in the Médoc and Graves), lovely Sauternes, and a few fine Burgundies and Californians.

1997

Bordeaux produced light, attractive reds and some brilliant sweet whites, and there were good white Burgundies. Elsewhere in Europe, though, the vintage was variable. Alsace, Italy, Germany, and Austria, however, made terrific wines, as did the port houses of the Douro and producers in California, Washington, Australia, and New Zealand. South African reds will be slow to mature.

1996

A classic vintage for the Médoc, Graves, and Sauternes (though less so in Pomerol and St. Emilion) and for white Burgundy and the Loire. There were vintage-quality Champagnes, but Alsace and the Rhône were patchy. Germany made good but austere Kabinett and Spätlese wines, while Italy, Spain, and Portugal had a fair vintage. California, New Zealand, and Australia produced top-class red and white wines.

1995

There were attractive, approachable red Bordeaux and white Burgundy. Italian and Loire reds, Rhône, Alsace, German, Rioja, and Ribera del Duero are all worth buying, as are wines from Australia, New Zealand, South Africa, North and South America.

1994

Bordeaux made a few really good reds that are now ready to drink. Alsace was only average in quality, as was the Loire. There were fine northern Rhône reds and red Burgundy for drinking now. Vintage port and Portuguese table wines were excellent. Italy's reds were average-to-good – and less impressive than the best from Austria and Germany. California had a great vintage, while the wines in Australia were good to very good – unlike the disappointing fare from South Africa and New Zealand.

1993

Bordeaux made light reds for early drinking. Elsewhere the quality was very patchy. There is excellent Tokaji, Alsace, and Loires (red and white), good – if tough – red Burgundy and top-class whites, but only reasonable Rhônes. Wines were good in South Africa and New Zealand, but variable in Australia.

1992

A generally average year, and mostly poor in Bordeaux, but Champagne and white Burgundy were good. Red Burgundy is for early drinking. Taylor's and Fonseca produced great vintage port. Californian Cabernets are fine – and longer-lived than efforts from Australia.

1991

Bordeaux are ready to drink, but reds from the Northern Rhône are as good. Best year for vintage port since 1985. Spain, South Africa, California, New Zealand, and Australia all had a good vintage.

1990

A great year for red and white Bordeaux, Champagne, German Rieslings, and Alsace. Also Loire whites, red Rhônes, Burgundies, Australians, and Californians. Spain too had a good year for reds, especially from the Duero, and Italy had a great year for Barolo.

1985-1989

1989 Top-class, juicy ripe red and good white Bordeaux and Champagne. Stunning German wines (from Kabinett to TBA) and excellent Alsace. Outstanding Loires (especially red), good red and superb white Rhône, good red Burgundy. **1988** Slow-evolving claret, exquisite Sauternes, fine Champagne, long-lasting Italian reds, Tokaji, German, Alsace, Loire reds and sweet whites, good red and white Rhône, and excellent red Burgundy. **1987** Fading Bordeaux and Burgundy. **1986** Powerful, long-lasting claret, good dry white and Sauternes, Australian reds, white Burgundy. **1985** California reds, claret, vintage port, Champagne, Spanish and Italian reds, Alsace, sweet Loire, red Rhône, Burgundy.

1980-1985

1984 South African reds, Australian reds, and Rieslings. **1983** claret, red Rhône, Portuguese reds, Sauternes, Madeira, vintage port, Tokaji, sweet Austrians, Alsace. **1982** Claret, Champagne, Australian reds, Portuguese reds, Spanish reds, Italian reds, red and white Burgundy, and Rhône. **1981** Champagne, Alsace. **1980** California and Australian Cabernets, Madeira, vintage port, Portuguese reds.

1970-1979

1979 Champagne, Sassicaia, sweet Austrians. **1978** Red and white Rhône, Portuguese reds, Bordeaux and Burgundy, Barolo, Tuscan and Loire reds. **1977** Port, sweet Austrians. **1976** Champagne, Loire reds and sweet whites, sweet Germans, Alsace, Sauternes. **1975** Top claret and port, Rioja, Eiswein, Sauternes, Penfolds Grange. **1974** California and Portuguese reds. **1973** Napa Cabernet, sweet Austrians. **1972** Tokaji. **1971** Bordeaux and Burgundy, Champagne, Portuguese reds, Barolo and Tuscan reds, sweet Austrians, Germans, red Rhône, Penfolds Grange. **1970** Port, Napa Cabernet, red Bordeaux, Champagne, Rioja, Chateau Musar.

1960-1969

1969 Sweet Austrians, red Rhône, Burgundy. **1968** Madeira, Rioja, Tokaji. **1967** Sauternes, Tuscan reds, Châteauneuf-du-Pape, German TBA. **1966** Port, red and white Burgundy, Champagne, Portuguese reds, claret, Australian Shiraz, **1965** Barca Velha. **1964** Claret, Tokaji, Champagne, Barca Velha, Vega Sicilia, Rioja, sweet Loire, red Rhône. **1963** Vintage port, Tokaji. **1962** Champagne, top Bordeaux and Burgundy, Rioja, Australian Cabernet and Shiraz. **1961** Claret, Sauternes, Champagne, Brunello, Barolo, sweet Austrians, Alsace, red Rhône. **1960** Port, top claret.

1950-1959

1959 Claret, Sauternes, Champagne, Tokaji, sweet Austrians, Germans, Loire and Alsace, red Rhône, and Burgundy. **1958** Barolo. **1957** Madeira, Vega Sicilia, Chianti, Tokaji. **1956** Château Yquem. **1955** Claret, Sauternes, port, Champagne, Brunello, Penfolds Grange. **1954** Madeira. **1953** Claret, Tokaji, Champagne, Vega Sicilia, sweet Germans, Côte Rôtie, Burgundy. **1952** Claret, Madeira, Champagne, Barolo, Tokaji, red Rhône, red and white Burgundy. **1950** Madeira.

1940-1949

1949 Red and white Bordeaux, Champagne, Tokaji, sweet Germans; red Rhône, and Burgundy. **1948** Port, Vega Sicilia. **1947** Bordeaux and Burgundy, port, Champagne, Tokaji, sweet Loire. **1946** Armagnac. **1945** Brunello, port, Bordeaux, Champagne, Chianti, sweet Germans, Alsace, red Rhônes and Burgundy. **1944** Madeira, port. **1943** Champagne, red Burgundy. **1942** Port, Rioja, Vega Sicilia. **1941** Madeira, Sauternes. **1940** Madeira.

ANNIVERSARY WINES

1930 Madeira. **1920** port, claret, Sauternes. **1910** Madeira. **1900** Madeira, claret. The Antique Wine Co. of Great Britain specialises in supplying wines for specific birth years. 01144 1827 830 539

WINE & HEALTH

WINE AND HEALTH

"Drink a glass of wine after your soup.
And you steal a rouble from your doctor."

Russian proverb

RED OR DEAD ?

In May 1999, the British Medical Journal carried a report from the Wolfson Institute of Preventative Medicine in London attempting to debunk the "French paradox" link between red wine and health by proposing that differences in Anglo-Saxon and Gallic rates of heart disease could be explained by the fact that the French traditionally eat less animal fats. Most observers were more convinced by the increasingly cumulative international research into the subject described below. Similarly, a report suggesting that wines bottled with synthetic corks might carry health risks, was treated with suspicion, after suggestions that it was paid for and disseminated by the manufacturers of natural corks.

WINE AND HEART DISEASE

Tests carried out by the Université de Bourgogne suggest that wine combats heart disease in two ways. People who daily drink up to half a liter of red wine have higher levels of HDL (high density lipoproteins) – "good" cholesterol which escorts "bad" cholesterol away from the artery walls and to the liver where it is destroyed. Also Resveratrol, an antifungal compound found in high concentration in grape skins, especially in the Pinot Noir grape, has been shown to improve the lipid profile of volunteers, drinking three glasses of red wine a day for two weeks. Resveratrol appears to be 20 times more powerful in its antioxidant affect than Vitamin E.

WINE AND DIGESTION

Wine of both colors also helps to counter both constipation and diarrhea, while white wine in particular stimulates the urinary functions. Wine has also been shown to kill cholera bacteria and to combat typhoid and trichinella, the poisonous compound in "bad" pork. Surprisingly, leading researcher Dr. Heinrich Kliewe actually recommends that moderate amounts of wine can counteract some of the side effects of antibiotics.

Wine and Aging

Antioxidants found in red wine protect us against the degenerative effects of oxidation on the body, such as graying and the clogging of arteries leading to strokes. Wine is also believed to give some protection against Alzheimer's Disease.

Wine and Viruses

According to Dr. Jack Konowalchuk and Joan Speirs of Canada's Bureau of Microbial Hazards, the polyphenols in tannic red wine, derived mainly from the skins, are effective against such viruses as cold sores, and possibly – though this remains hypothetical – even against the supposedly incurable genital Herpes 2.

Wine and Pregnancy

Despite the fears it arouses, Fetal Alcohol Syndrome is rare outside the poorest inner cities of the US. In 1997, the UK Royal College of Obstetricians and Gynecologists reported that up to 15 units of alcohol per week should do no harm to a fetus.

Wine and Calories

There is no difference in calories between a Muscadet or a claret. (around 110 per glass). Sweeter, but less alcoholic Liebfraumilch has about 79. A Stanford University survey suggests the action of the wine on the metabolism somehow makes its calories less fattening.

Hangovers

All alcohol – especially vintage port – is hangover-fare. The only way to avoid this fate is to drink plenty of water before going to bed.

Wine and Cancer

Alcohol has been linked to rare occurrences of mouth and throat cancer – but only among smokers. Red wine is rich in gallic acid, an acknowledged anticarcinogenic, and wine's role in reducing stress has been associated with a lower incidence of certain forms of cancer.

Wine and Migraine

Red wine, like chocolate, can inhibit an enzyme called phenosulfotransferase-P, or PST-P, which naturally detoxifies all sorts of bacteria in the gut. An absence of PST-P is linked to migraine. In some people, red wine is also associated with episodic skin allergies.

Wine and Asthma

Wines that are heavily dosed with sulfur dioxide (used to combat bacteria in most dried, bottled, and canned foods) can trigger asthma attacks. New World and organic wines have lower sulfur levels.

FOOD & WINE

Suspicions of a previously uncorked bottle, Paris, 1890's

MATCHMAKING FOR BEGINNERS

One of the most daunting aspects of wine has always been the traditional obsession with serving precisely the right wine with any particular dish – of only ever drinking red with meat and white with fish or shellfish.

It may be reassuring to learn that some of these time-honored rules are just plain wrong. In Portugal, for example, fishermen love to wash down their sardines and salt cod with a glass or two of harsh red wine. In Burgundy they even poach fish in their local red.

On the other hand, the idea that a platter of cheese is somehow incomplete without a bottle of red wine can be exploded in an instant. Just take a mouthful of claret immediately after eating a little goat's cheese or Brie. The wine will taste metallic and unpleasant, because the creaminess of the cheese reacts badly with the tannin – the toughness – in the wine. A fresh, dry white would be far more successful (its acidity would cut through the fat), while the claret would be shown to its best advantage alongside a harder, stronger cheese such as a Cheddar or a Parmesan. If you don't want to offer a range of wines to go with the platter, I'd advise sticking to one or two cheeses that really will complement the stuff in the glass.

Don't take anything for granted. Rare beef and Bordeaux surprisingly fails the test of an objective tasting. The protein of the meat somehow makes all but the fruitiest wines taste tougher. If you're looking for a perfect partner for beef, uncork a Burgundy. If it's the claret that takes precedence, you'd be far better off with lamb.

The difference between an ideal and a passable food-and-wine combination can be very subtle. Most of us have after all happily quaffed claret with our steak, but just as a keen cook will tinker with a recipe until it is just right, there's a lot to be said for making the occasional effort to find a pairing of dish and wine that really works. Like people who are happier in a couple than separately, some foods and wines simply seem to bring out the best in each other.

A SENSE OF BALANCE

There is no real mystery about the business of matching food and wine. Some flavors and textures are compatible, and some are not. Strawberry mousse is not really delicious with chicken casserole, but apple sauce can do wonders for roast pork.

The key to spotting which relationships are marriages made in heaven, and which have the fickleness of Hollywood romances, lies in identifying the dominant characteristics of the contents of the plate and the glass. And learning which are likely to complement each other, either through their similarities or through their differences.

LIKELY COMBINATIONS

It is not difficult to define particular types of food and wine, and to guess how they are likely to get along. A buttery sauce is happier with something tangily acidic, like a crisp Sauvignon Blanc, rather than a rich, buttery Chardonnay. A subtly poached fish won't appreciate a fruit-packed New World white, and you won't do pheasant pie any favors by pulling the cork on a delicate red.

WHAT TO AVOID

Some foods and their characteristics, though, make life difficult for almost any drink. Sweetness, for example, in a fruity sauce served with a savory dish seems to strip some of the fruitier flavors out of a wine. This may not matter if the stuff in your glass is a blackcurranty New World Cabernet Sauvignon, but it's bad news if it is a bone-dry white or a tough red with little fruit to spare.

Cream is tricky too. Try fresh strawberries with Champagne – delicious; now add a little whipped cream to the equation and you'll spoil the flavor. Creamy sauces can have the same effect on a wine.

Spices are problematical – due to the physical sensation of eating them rather than any particular flavor. A wine won't seem nasty after a mouthful of chili sauce; it will simply lose its fruity flavor and taste of nothing at all. Curiously, too, the way a tannic red dries out the mouth will also have the side effect of apparently accentuating the heat of the spice. The ideal wine for most Westerners to drink with any spicy dish would be a light, possibly slightly sweet, white.

Chinese palates often react differently to these combinations. They like the burning effect of the chili and see no point in trying to put out the fire with white wine.

ALWAYS WORTH A TRY

Some condiments actually bring out the best in wines. A little freshly ground pepper on your meat or pasta can accentuate the flavor of a wine, just as it can with a sauce. Squeezing fresh lemon onto your fish will reduce the apparent acidity of a white wine – a useful tip if you have inadvertently bought a case of tooth-strippingly dry Muscadet. And, just as lemon can help to liven up a dull sauce, it will also help to make a dull white wine, such as a basic Burgundy or a Soave, taste more interesting – by neutralizing the acidity in the wine, and allowing its other flavors to make themselves apparent. Mustard performs a similar miracle when it is eaten with beef, somehow nullifying the effect of the meat protein on the wine.

MARRIAGE GUIDANCE

In the following pages, I have suggested wines to go with a wide range of dishes and ingredients, taking the dominant flavor as the keypoint. Don't treat any of this advice as gospel – use it instead as a launchpad for your own food and wine experiments.

And, if no wine seems to taste just right, don't be too surprised. Heretical as it may seem, some dishes are actually more enjoyable with other drinks. The vinegar which is a fundamental part of a good pickle, for example, will do no wine a favor. Even keen wine lovers might well find beer a far more pleasurable accompaniment.

COOKING WITH WINE

Finally, a word or two about how to make best use of wine in the kitchen (apart from its role as refreshment following a vigorous session of egg-beating, and as a tranquilizer for the moments when sauces curdle and soufflées refuse to rise). The first – and most often forgotten – rule to remember is that wine that's not good enough to drink is probably not good enough to pour into the frying pan or casserole. At least, not unless you take a perverse pleasure in using and eating substandard ingredients. On the other hand, despite the advice of classic French recipes, your "coq au vin" won't be spoiled by your unwillingness to make it with a pricy bottle of Grand Cru Burgundy. A decent, humbler red will do perfectly well, though it is worth trying to use a similar style to the one suggested.

Second – and just as important – remember that, with the exception of a few dishes such as sherry trifle or zabaglione, in which wine is enjoyed in its natural state, wine, used as an ingredient needs to be cooked in order to remove the alcohol. So, add it early enough for the necessary evaporation to take place.

A

Trout with Almonds Bianco di Custoza, Pinot Blanc.

Anchovies

Salted Anchovies Rioja red or white, Manzanilla or Fino sherry.

Fresh Anchovy (Boquerones) Albariño, Vinho Verde, Aligoté.

Salade Niçoise Muscadet, Vinho Verde, or Beaujolais.

Tapenade Dry sherry or Madeira.

Aniseed Dry white.

Apple

Apple Pie or Strudel Austrian off-dry white.

Blackberry and Apple Pie Late harvest Riesling, Vouvray demi-sec.

Roast Pork with Apple Sauce Off-dry Vouvray or Riesling.

Waldorf Salad Dry Madeira.

Apricot Late harvest Sémillon or Riesling, Jurançon Moelleux.

Artichoke White Rhône.

Artichoke Frittata Dry Loire whites, Pinot Gris.

Artichoke Soup Dry Loire whites, Pinot Gris.

Arroz con Pollo Côtes du Rhône, young Zinfandel, Navarra or Rioja "Joven."

Arugula Pinot Grigio, young Viognier.

Asparagus

Asparagus Crêpes au Gratin Muscadet, Vinho Verde, Cider.

Asparagus Soup Fresh dry whites, Sauvignon Blanc.

Avocado

Avocado Mayonnaise Unoaked Chardonnay, Chablis.

Avocado Stuffed with Crab Champagne, Riesling Kabinett, Sauvignon Blanc, Pinot Gris, Australian Chardonnay.

Guacamole Fumé Blanc or unoaked Sauvignon Blanc.

B

Bacon Rich Pinot Gris or Alsace Riesling.

Bacon with Marinated Scallops Fino sherry or mature Riesling, Shiraz-based Australians, Zinfandel from the States, or a heavy Cape red.

Warm Bacon Salad New World Sauvignon Blanc, California Fumé Blanc, or a good Pouilly Fumé.

Warm Bacon Salad

Banana

Flambéed Banana with Rum Jurançon, Tokaji, Pedro Ximénez sherry, rum.

Barbecue Sauce Inexpensive off-dry white or a simple, fruity Cabernet.

Spare Ribs with Barbecue Sauce Fruity Australian Shiraz, Grenache or Zinfandel, spicy Côtes du Rhône from a ripe vintage, or an off-dry white.

Basil Slightly sweet Chardonnay (i.e. California, commercial Australian).

Pasta in Pesto Sauce New Zealand Sauvignon Blanc, Valpolicella.

Beans

Boston Baked Beans Light Zinfandel, Beaujolais, dry rosé, or beer.

Bean Salad Spanish reds such as Rioja Reserva and Rueda, or New Zealand Sauvignon Blanc.

Cassoulet Serious white Rhône, Marsanne or Roussanne, or reds including Grenache and Syrah from the Rhône, crunchy Italian reds, or Zinfandel.

Mexican Beans Côtes du Rhône, Beaujolais, dry Grenache rosé.

White Bean Stew (Estouffat) Young Corbières, light Merlot.

Beef

Beef with Green Peppers in Black Bean Sauce Off-dry German Riesling or characterful dry white, like white Rhône or Marsanne.

Beef with Scallions and Ginger Off-dry German Riesling or one of the more serious Beaujolais Crus.

Beef Stew Pomerol or St. Emilion, good Northern Rhône like Crozes-Hermitage, Shiraz, or Pinot Noir from the New World.

Beef Stroganoff Tough, beefy reds like Amarone, Brunello di Montalcino, Barolo, Côte Rôtie, or really ripe Zinfandel.

Beef Stroganoff

Beef Wellington Top Burgundy, Châteauneuf-du-Pape.

Boeuf Bourguignon Australian Bordeaux-style, Barolo, or other robust reds with sweet fruit.

Boiled Beef and Carrots Bordeaux Rouge, Valpolicella Classico, Australian Shiraz.

Bresaola (Air Dried Beef) Beaujolais, Barbera, and tasty reds from the Languedoc.

Carpaccio of Beef Chardonnay, Champagne, Cabernet Franc, and other Loire reds, Pomerol.

Chilli Con Carne Robust fruity reds, Beaujolais Crus, Barbera or Valpolicella, spicy reds like Zinfandel or Pinotage.

Corned Beef Hash Characterful spicy reds from the Rhône or Southern France.

Creole-Style Beef Cheap Southern Rhône reds or Côtes du Rhône, Zinfandel.

Hamburger Zinfandel or country reds, from Italy or France e.g. Corbières.

Hungarian Goulash East European reds, Bulgarian Cabernet, or Mavrud and Hungarian Kadarka, or Australian Shiraz.

Meatballs Spicy rich reds from the Rhône, Zinfandel, Pinotage and Portuguese reds.

Panang Neuk (Beef in Peanut Curry) New World Chardonnay, New Zealand Sauvignon Blanc, or a spicy, aromatic white Rhône.

Pastrami Zinfandel, good Bardolino, light Côtes du Rhône.
Rare Chargrilled Beef Something sweetly ripe and flavorsome, but not too tannic. Try Chilean Merlot.
Roast Beef Côte Rôtie, good Burgundy.
Steak Pinot Noir and Merlot from the New World, Australian Shiraz, Châteauneuf-du-Pape, good, ripe Burgundy.
Steak with Dijon Mustard Bordeaux, Cabernet Sauvignon from the New World, or Australian Shiraz.
Steak and Kidney Pie/Pudding Bordeaux, Australian Cabernet Sauvignon, Southern Rhône reds, or Rioja.
Steak au Poivre Cabernet Sauvignon, Chianti, Rhône reds, Shiraz, or Rioja.
Steak Tartare Bourgogne Blanc, fruity reds, light on tannin; Beaujolais, Bardolino, etc. or traditionally vodka.
Thai Beef Salad New Zealand or South African Sauvignon Blanc, Gewürztraminer, Pinot Blanc.

Beer (in a sauce)
Carbonnade à la Flamande Cheap Southern Rhône or Valpolicella.

Beets
Borscht Rich, dry Alsace Pinot Gris, Pinot Blanc, or Italian Pinot Grigio.

Black Bean Sauce
Beef with Green Peppers in Black Bean Sauce Off-dry German Riesling or characterful, dry white like white Rhône or Marsanne.

Blackberry
Blackberry and Apple Pie Late harvest Riesling, Vouvray demi-sec.

Black Cherry
Black Forest Cake Fortified Muscat, Schnapps, or Kirsch.

Blackcurrant
Blackcurrant Cheesecake Sweet, grapey dessert wines.
Blackcurrant Mousse Sweet sparkling wines.

Blinis Vodka or good Champagne.

Blood Pudding Chablis, New Zealand Chardonnay, Zinfandel, or Barolo.

Blueberries
Blueberry Pie Tokaji (6 Puttonyos), late harvest Semillon or Sauvignon Blanc.

Brandy
Christmas Pudding Australian Liqueur Muscat, tawny port, rich (sweet) Champagne, Tokaji.
Crêpe Suzette Asti Spumante, Orange Muscat, Champagne cocktails.

Brie Sancerre or New Zealand Sauvignon.

Broccoli
Broccoli and Cheese Soup Slightly sweet sherry – Amontillado or Oloroso.

Butter
Béarnaise Sauce Good dry Riesling.
Beurre Blanc Champagne Blanc de Blancs, dry Vinho Verde.

Butternut Squash
Butternut Soup Aromatic Alsace Gewurztraminer.

C

Cabbage
Stuffed Cabbage East European Cabernet.

Cajun Spices Beaujolais Crus.
Gumbo Zinfandel or maybe beer.

Camembert Dry Sauvignon Blanc or unoaked Chablis.

Capers Sauvignon Blanc.
Skate with Black Butter Crisply acidic whites like Muscadet or Chablis.
Tartare Sauce Crisply fresh whites like Sauvignon.

Chicken Vol-au-Vents White Bordeaux.
Cock-a-Leekie Dry New World white, simple red Rhône.
Coq au Vin Shiraz-based New World reds, red Burgundy.
Cream of Chicken Soup Big dry unoaked white (Chablis, Pinot Blanc).
Curry Chicken Gewürztraminer, dry white Loire, fresh Chinon.
Deviled Chicken Australian Shiraz.
Fricassée Unoaked Chardonnay.
Lemon Chicken Muscadet, Chablis, or basic Bourgogne Blanc.
Poached Chicken Beaujolais, Valpolicella.
Roast/Grilled Chicken Reds or whites, though nothing too heavy – Burgundy is good, as is Barbera, though Soave will do just as well.
Roast/Grilled Chicken with Bread Sauce Côtes du Rhône or herby Provençal reds.
Roast/Grilled Chicken with Sage and Onion Stuffing Italian reds, especially Chianti, soft, plummy Merlots, and sweetly fruity Rioja.
Roast/Grilled Chicken with Tarragon Dry Chenin (Vouvray or perhaps a good South African).
Saltimbocca (Cutlet with Mozzarella and Ham) Flavorsome, dry Italian whites, Lugana, Bianco di Custoza, Orvieto.
Smoked Chicken Oaky Chardonnay, Australian Marsanne, or Fumé Blanc.
Southern Fried Chicken White Bordeaux, Muscadet, Barbera, light Zinfandel.
Tandoori Chicken White Bordeaux, New Zealand Sauvignon Blanc.

Chicken Liver (Sauté) Softly fruity, fairly light reds including Beaujolais, Italian Cabernet or Merlot, or perhaps an Oregon Pinot Noir.
Chicken Liver Paté Most of the above reds plus Vouvray Moelleux, Monbazillac, or Amontillado sherry.

Chili Cheap wine or cold lager.
Chili Chipped Beef Robust fruity reds, Beaujolais Crus, Barbera or Valpolicella, spicy reds like Zinfandel or Pinotage.
Hot and Sour Soup Crisply aromatic English white, Baden Dry.
Szechuan-Style Dry, aromatic whites, Alsace Pinot Gris or Riesling.

Chilli con Carne

Thai Beef Salad New Zealand or South African Sauvignon Blanc.

Chinese (general) Aromatic white (Gewürztraminer, Pinot Gris, English).

Chives Sauvignon Blanc.

Chocolate Orange Muscat, Moscatel de Valencia.
Black Forest (Chocolate and Cherry) Gâteau Fortified Muscat or Kirsch.
Chocolate Cake Beaumes de Venise, Bual or Malmsey Madeira, Orange Muscat, sweet German, or fine Champagne.
Chocolate Profiteroles with Cream Muscat de Rivesaltes.
Chocolate Roulade Canadian icewine or German or Austrian Eiswein.
Dark Chocolate Mousse Sweet Black Muscat or other Muscat-based wines.
Milk Chocolate Mousse Moscato d'Asti.

Chorizo (spicy pork sausage) Red or white Rioja, Navarra, Manzanilla sherry, Beaujolais, or Zinfandel.

Cinnamon Riesling Spätlese, Muscat.
Clams Chablis or Sauvignon Blanc.
Clam Chowder Dry white such as Côtes de Gascogne, Amontillado sherry, or Madeira.
Spaghetti Vongole Pinot Bianco or Lugana.
Cockles Muscadet, Gros Plant, Aligoté, dry Vinho Verde.
Coconut (milk) California Chardonnay.
Green Curry Big-flavored New World whites or Pinot Blanc from Alsace.
Cod Unoaked Chardonnay, good, white Burgundy, dry Loire Chenin.
Cod and French Fries Any light, crisp, dry white, such as a Sauvignon from Bordeaux or Touraine. Alternatively, try dry rosé or Champagne. Remember, though, that English-style heavy-handedness with the vinegar will do no favors for the wine. For vinegary fries, stick to beer.
Lisbon-Style Cod Vinho Verde. Muscadet, light, dry Riesling.
Salt Cod (Bacalhão de Gomes) Classically Portuguese red or white – Vinho Verde or Bairrada reds.
Smoked Cod Vinho Verde.
Cod Roe (smoked) Well-oaked New World Chardonnay.
Coffee
Coffeecake Asti Spumante.
Coffee Mousse Asti Spumante, Liqueur Muscat.
Tiramisu Sweet fortified Muscat, Vin Santo, Torcolato.
Coriander
Carrot and Coriander Soup Aromatic, dry Muscat.
Coriander Leaf Dry or off-dry English white.
Coriander Seed Dry,, herby Northern Italian whites.
Corn Rich and ripe whites – California Chardonnay.
Corn on the Cob Light, fruity whites – German Riesling.
Corn Soup with Chicken Chilean Sauvignon, Southern French whites, Soave, Chilean Merlot.
Corn Soup with Crab Sancerre, other Sauvignon Blanc.
Couscous Spicy Shiraz, North African reds, or earthy Southern French Minervois.
Crab Chablis, Sauvignon Blanc, New World Chardonnay.
Crab Cakes (Maryland-style) Rias Baixas Albariño.
Crab Cioppino Sauvignon Blanc, Pinot Grigio.
Crab Mousse Crisp dry whites – Baden Dry or Soave.
Deviled Crab (spicy) New World Sauvignon, Albariño.
Cranberry
Roast Turkey with Cranberry and Orange Stuffing Richly fruity reds like Shiraz from Australia, Zinfandel, or modern Rioja.
Crayfish
Freshwater Crayfish South African Sauvignon, Meursault.
Salad of Crayfish Tails with Dill Rich South African Chenin blends or crisp Sauvignon, white Rhône.
Cream When dominant, not good with wine, particularly tannic reds.
Curry
Beef in Peanut Curry New World Chardonnay, spicy, aromatic white Rhône.
Coronation Chicken Gewürztraminer, dry, aromatic English wine, or a fresh Chinon.
Curried Turkey New World Chardonnay.
Curried Beef Beefy, spicy reds; Barolo, Châteauneuf-du-Pape and Shiraz/Cabernet or off-dry aromatic whites – Gewürztraminer, Pinot Gris. Or try some Indian sparkling wine or cold Indian lager.
Tandoori Chicken White Bordeaux, New Zealand Sauvignon Blanc.
Thai Green Chicken Curry Big New World whites or dry, tasty Pinot Blanc from Alsace.

D

Dill Sauvignon Blanc.
 Gravlax Ice cold vodka, Pinot Gris, or Akvavit.
Dover Sole Sancerre, good Chablis, unoaked Chardonnay.
Dried Fruit Sweet sherry, tawny port.
 Bread and Butter Pudding Barsac or Sauternes, Monbazillac, Jurançon. Muscat de Beaumes de Venise, or Australian Orange Muscat.
 Mince Pie Rich, late harvest wine or botrytis-affected Sémillon.
Duck Pinot Noir from Burgundy, California or Oregon, or perhaps an off-dry German Riesling.
 Cassoulet Serious white Rhônes, Marsanne or Roussanne, or try reds including Grenache and Syrah from the Rhône, berryish Italian reds, or Zinfandel.
 Confit de Canard Alsace Pinot Gris or a crisp red like Barbera.
 Duck Paté Chianti or other juicy herby red, Amontillado sherry.
 Duck Paté with Orange Riesling or Rioja.
 Peking Duck Rice wine, Alsace Riesling, Pinot Gris.
 Roast Duck with Orange Sauce Loire red or, surprisingly, a sweet white like Vouvray demi-sec.
 Smoked Duck California Chardonnay or Fumé Blanc.
Duck Liver
 Foie Gras de Canard Champagne, late harvest Gewürztraminer or Riesling, Sauternes.

E

Eel
 Jellied Eels A pint of stout.
 Smoked Eel Pale, dry sherry, simple, fresh white Burgundy.
Egg
 Baked Eggs Bordeaux Blanc, Côtes de Gascogne or other simple white, young, fruity red
 Crème Brulée Jurançon Moelleux, Tokaji.
 Omelettes Cheap Beaujolais, Bardolino.

F

Fennel Sauvignon Blanc.
Fig Liqueur Muscat.
Frankfurter Côtes du Rhône or lager.
Fish (general – see individual entries)
 Bouillabaisse Red or white Côtes du Rhône, dry rosé or peppery dry white from Provence, California Fumé Blanc, Voignier, Marsanne, or Verdicchio.
 Cumberland Fish Pie California Chardonnay, Alsace Pinot Gris, Sauvignon Blanc.
 Fish and Chips Most fairly simple, crisply acidic dry whites (white Bordeaux, Sauvignon Blanc) or maybe a good dry rosé or Champagne. (See Cod).In any case go easy on the vinegar.

Fish Cakes White Bordeaux, Chilean Chardonnay or dry rosé from Provence.

Fish Soup Manzanilla, Chablis, Muscadet.

Kedgeree Aligoté, crisp Sauvignon.

Mediterranean Fish Soup Provençal reds and rosés, Tavel, Côtes du Rhône, Vin de Pays d'Oc.

Seafood Salad Soave, Pinot Grigio, Muscadet, or a lightly oaked Chardonnay.

Sushi Saké.

Foie Gras (see Duck and Goose Liver)

Fruit (general – see individual entries)

Fresh Fruit Salad Moscato d'Asti, Riesling Beerenauslese, or Vouvray Moelleux.

Fruit Flan Vouvray Moelleux, Alsace Riesling or Tokay Pinot Gris Vendange Tardive.

Summer Pudding Late harvest Riesling, German or Alsace, Asti Spumante or Moscato d'Asti.

G

Game (general – see individual entries)

Cold Game Fruity Northern Italian reds – Barbera or Dolcetto – good Beaujolais or light Burgundy.

Roast Game Big reds, such as Brunello di Montalcino, old Barolo, good Burgundy.

Well-hung Game Old Barolo or Barbaresco, mature Hermitage, Côte Rôtie or Châteauneuf-du-Pape, fine Burgundy.

Game Pie Beefy reds, Southern French, Rhône, or Australian Shiraz.

Garlic

Aïoli A wide range of wines go well including white Rioja, Provence rosé, California Pinot Noir.

Garlic Sausage Red Rioja, Bandol, Côtes du Rhône.

Gazpacho Fino sherry, white Rioja.

Roast/Grilled Chicken with Garlic Oaky Chardonnay or red Rioja.

Roast Lamb with Garlic and Rosemary Earthy soft reds like California Petite Sirah, Rioja, or Zinfandel.

Snails with Garlic Butter Aligoté and light white Burgundy or perhaps a red Gamay de Touraine.

Ginger Gewürztraminer or Riesling.

Beef with Onions and Ginger Off-dry German Riesling or Beaujolais Crus.

Chicken with Ginger White Rhône, Gewürztraminer.

Ginger Ice Cream Asti Spumante or late harvest Sémillon.

Goat Cheese Sancerre, New World Sauvignon, Pinot Blanc.

Grilled Goat Cheese Loire reds.

Goose A good Rhône red like Hermitage, Côte Rôtie, or a crisp Barbera, Pinot Noir from Burgundy, California or Oregon, or perhaps an off-dry German Riesling.

Confit d'Oie Best Sauternes, Monbazillac.

Goose Liver

Foie Gras Best Sauternes, Monbazillac.

Gooseberry

Gooseberry Fool Quarts de Chaume.

Gooseberry Pie Sweet Madeira, Austrian Trockenbeerenauslese.

Grapefruit Sweet Madeira or sherry.

Grouse

Roast Grouse Hermitage, Côte Rôtie, robust Burgund, or mature Claret.

Guinea Fowl Old Burgundy, Cornas, Gamay de Touraine, St. Emilion.

H

Haddock White Bordeaux, Chardonnay, Pinot Blanc.
Mousse of Smoked Haddock Top white Burgundy.
Smoked Haddock Fino sherry or oaky Chardonnay.
Hake Soave, Sauvignon Blanc.
Halibut White Bordeaux, Muscadet.
Smoked Halibut Oaky Spanish white/Australian Chardonnay, white Bordeaux.
Ham
Boiled/Roasted/Grilled/Fried Ham Beaujolais-Villages, Gamay de Touraine, slightly sweet German white, Tuscan red, lightish Cabernet (eg Chilean), Alsace Pinot Gris, or Muscat.
Braised Ham with Lentils Light, fruity Beaujolais, other Gamay, Côtes du Rhône.
Honey-Roast Ham Riesling.
Oak-Smoked Ham Oaky Spanish reds.
Pea and Ham Soup Beaujolais.
Prosciutto Try a dry Lambrusco, Tempranillo Joven, or Gamay de Touraine.
Hare
Hare Casserole Good Beaujolais Crus or, for a stronger flavor, try an Australian red.
Jugged Hare Argentinian reds, tough Italians like Amarone, Barolo and Barbaresco, inky reds from Bandol or the Rhône.
Hazelnut Vin Santo, Liqueur Muscat.
Warm Bacon, Hazelnut, and Sorrel Salad New World Sauvignon Blanc, California Fumé Blanc, or a good Pouilly Fumé.
Herbs (see individual entries)
Herring
Fresh Herrings Sauvignon Blanc, Muscadet, Frascati, or cider.
Roll-Mop Herring Savoie, Vinho Verde, Akvavit, cold lager.
Salt Herring White Portuguese.
Sprats Muscadet, Vinho Verde.
Honey Tokaji.
Baklava Moscatel de Setúbal.
Horseradish
Roast Beef with Horseradish California Pinot Noir or mature Burgundy.
Houmous French dry whites, Retsina, Vinho Verde.

I

Ice Cream Try Marsala or Pedro Ximénez sherry.
Indian (general) Gewürztraminer (spicy dishes); New World Chardonnay (creamy/yogurt dishes); New Zealand Sauvignon Blanc (Tandoori).

J

Japanese Barbecue Sauce
Teriyaki Spicy reds like Zinfandel or Portuguese reds.
John Dory Good, white Burgundy or Australian Chardonnay.

K

Kedgeree New World Sauvignon Blanc or Sauvignon.

Kidney

Lambs' Kidneys Rich, spicy reds; Barolo, Cabernet Sauvignon, Rioja.

Steak and Kidney Pie/Pudding Bordeaux, Australian Cabernet Sauvignon, Southern Rhône reds or Rioja.

Kippered Herrings New World Chardonnay or a good fino sherry. Or, if you are having it for breakfast, Champagne, a cup of tea, or Dutch gin.

L

Lamb

Cassoulet Serious white Rhône, Marsanne or Roussanne, or reds including Grenache and Syrah from the Rhône, berryish Italian reds or, Zinfandel.

Casserole Rich and warm Cabernet-based reds from France or California Zinfandel.

Cutlets or Chops Cru Bourgeois Bordeaux, Chilean Cabernet.

Haggis Beaujolais, Côtes du Rhône, Côtes du Roussillon, Spanish reds, malt whiskey.

Irish Stew A good simple South American or Eastern European Cabernet works best.

Kebabs Modern (fruity) Greek reds or sweetly ripe Australian Cabernet/Shiraz.

Kleftiko (Lamb Shanks Baked with Thyme) Greek red from Nemea, Beaujolais, light Cabernet Sauvignon.

Lancashire Hotpot Robust country red – Cahors, Fitou.

Moussaka Brambly Northern Italian reds (Barbera, Dolcetto, etc), Beaujolais, Pinotage, Zinfandel, or try some good Greek wine from a modern producer.

Roast Lamb Bordeaux (especially Médoc and Graves), New Zealand Cabernet Sauvignon or Merlot,South African Cabernet, Cahors, Rioja crianza or reserva, Merlot or Cabernet from Chile and Malbec from Argentina. Alternatively try a new wave Greek red (especially made from the St. George).

Roast Lamb with Thyme Try a New Zealand or South African Merlot or Cabernet Sauvignon, Bourgeuil or Chinon.

Shepherd's Pie Barbera, Cabernet Sauvignon, Minervois, Zinfandel, Beaujolais, Southern French red.

Langoustine Muscadet, Soave, South African Sauvignon.

Leek

Cock-a-Leekie Dry New World white, simple red Rhône.

Leek and Potato Soup Dry whites, Côtes de Gascogne.

Leek in Cheese Sauce Dry white Bordeaux, Sancerre or fruity Australian Semillon.

Vichysoisse Dry whites, Chablis, Bordeaux Blanc.

Lemon

Lemon Cheesecake Moscato d'Asti.

Lemon Meringue Pie Malmsey Madeira.

Lemon Sorbet Late harvest Sémillon or sweet Tokaji.

Lemon Tart Sweet Austrian and German wines.

Lemon Zest Sweet fortified Muscats.

Lemon Grass New Zealand Sauvignon, Sancerre, Viognier.

Lemon Sole Chardonnay.
Lentils Earthy country wines, Côtes du Rhône.
Chicken Dhansak Sémillon or New Zealand Sauvignon.
Dhal Soup Try Soave or Pinot Bianco.
Lime Australian Verdelho, Grüner Veltliner, Furmint.
Kaffir Lime Leaves (in Thai Green Curry, etc.) Big-flavored New World whites or Pinot Blanc from Alsace.
Thai Beef Salad New Zealand or South African Sauvignon Blanc, Gewürztraminer, Pinot Blanc.
Liver
Calves' Liver Good Italian Cabernet, St Emilion, New World Merlot or mature Chianti.
Fegato alla Veneziana Nebbiolo, Zinfandel,, or Petite Sirah.
Lambs' Liver Chianti, Australian Shiraz, or Merlot.
Liver and Bacon Côtes du Rhône, Zinfandel, Pinotage.
Lobster Good white Burgundy.
Lobster Bisque Grenache rosé, fresh German white, Chassagne-Montrachet, dry Amontillado sherry.
Lobster in a Rich Sauce Champagne, Chablis, fine white Burgundy, good white Bordeaux.
Lobster Salad Champagne, Chablis, German or Alsace Riesling.
Lobster Thermidor Rich beefy Côtes du Rhône, oaky Chardonnay, or a good deep-colored rosé from Southern France.

M

Mackerel Best with Vinho Verde, Albariño, Sancerre, and New Zealand Sauvignon.
Smoked Mackerel Bourgogne Aligoté, Alsace Pinot Gris.
Smoked Mackerel Paté Sparkling Vouvray, Muscadet.

Mackerel

Mallard Côte Rôtie, Ribera del Duero, or Zinfandel.
Mango Best eaten in the bath with a friend and a bottle of Champagne. Otherwise, go for Asti Spumante or Moscato.
Marjoram Provençal reds.
Marsala
Chops in Marsala Sauce Australian Marsanne or Verdelho.
Mascarpone
Tiramisu Sweet fortified Muscat, Vin Santo, Torcolato.
Meat (general – see individual entries)
Cold Meats Juicy, fruity reds, low in tannin ie Beaujolais, Côtes du Rhône, etc.

Consommé Medium/Amontillado sherry.
Meat Paté Beaujolais, Fumé Blanc, lesser white Burgundy.
Mixed Grill Versatile uncomplicated red – Australian Shiraz, Rioja, Bulgarian Cabernet.

Melon Despite its apparently innocent, juicy sweetness, melon can be very unfriendly to most wines. Try tawny port, sweet Madeira, or sherry, Quarts de Chaume, late harvest Riesling.

Mincemeat
Mince Pie Complemented by rich, sweet, late-harvest wine or botrytis-affected Sémillon.

Mint Beaujolais, young Pinot Noir, or try a New Zealand or Australian Riesling.
Thai Beef Salad New Zealand or South African Sauvignon Blanc, Gewürztraminer, Pinot Blanc.

Monkfish A light, fruity red such as Bardolino, Valpolicella, La Mancha Joven, or most Chardonnays.

Mushroom Merlot-based reds, good Northern Rhône, top Piedmontese reds.
Mushroom Soup Bordeaux Blanc, Côtes de Gasgogne.

Mushroom Soup

Mushrooms à la Greque Sauvignon Blanc or fresh, modern Greek white.
Risotto with Fungi Porcini Top-notch Piedmontese reds – mature Barbera, Barbaresco, or earthy Southern French reds.
Stuffed Mushrooms Chenin Blanc, Sylvaner.
Wild Mushrooms Nebbiolo, red Bordeaux.

Mussels Sauvignon Blanc, light Chardonnay, Muscadet Sur Lie.
Moules Marinières Bordeaux Blanc or Muscadet Sur Lie.
New Zealand Green-Lipped Mussels New Zealand Sauvignon Blanc.

Mustard Surprisingly, can help red Bordeaux and other tannic reds to go with beef which might otherwise accentuate their tough, tannic character.
Dijon Mustard Beaujolais.
English Wholegrain Mustard Beaujolais, Valpolicella.
French Mustard White Bordeaux.
Steak with Dijon Mustard Cabernet Sauvignon from the New World or Australian Shiraz.

N

Nectarine Sweet German Riesling.

Nutmeg Rioja, Australian Shiraz or, for sweet dishes, Australian late harvest Semillon.

Nuts Amontillado sherry, Vin Santo, and Tokaji.

O

Octopus Rueda white or a fresh, modern Greek white.
Olives Dry sherry, Muscadet, Retsina.
  Salade Niçoise Muscadet, Vinho Verde or Beaujolais.
  Tapenade Dry sherry or Madeira.
Onion
  Caramelized Onions Shiraz-based Australians, Zinfandel from the States, or a good Pinotage.
  French Onion Soup Sancerre or dry, unoaked Sauvignon Blanc, Aligoté, white Bordeaux.
  Onion/Leek Tart Alsace Gewürztraminer, New World Riesling or a good unoaked Chablis.
Orange
  Caramelized Oranges Asti Spumante, Sauternes or Muscat de Beaumes de Venise.
  Crêpe Suzette Sweet Champagne, Moscato d'Asti.
  Orange Sorbet Moscato or sweet Tokaji.
  Orange Zest Dry Muscat, Amontillado sherry.
Oregano Provençal reds, red Lambrusco, more serious Chianti or lightish Zinfandel.
Oxtail Australian Cabernet, good Bordeaux.
Oyster Sauce
  Beef and Snow Peas in Oyster Sauce Crisp, dry whites like Muscadet or a Northern Italian Lugana or Pinot Bianco, white Rhône, Gewürztraminer.
Oysters Champagne, Chablis, or other crisp, dry white.

P

Paprika
  Goulash Eastern European red like Bulgarian Cabernet or Mavrud, Hungarian Kadarka, or Australian Shiraz.
Parmesan Salice Salentino, Valpolicella.
  Baked Chicken Parmesan with Basil Chenin Blanc, Riesling.
Parsley Dry, Italian whites – Bianco di Custoza, Nebbiolo, or Barbera.
  Parsley Sauce Pinot Grigio, Hungarian Furmint, lightly oaked Chardonnay.
Partridge
  Roast Partridge Australian Shiraz, Gevrey-Chambertin, Pomerol, or St. Emilion.
Pasta
  Lasagne Valpolicella, Barbera, Teroldego, Australian Verdelho or Sauvignon.
  Pasta with Meat Sauce Chianti, Bordeaux Rouge.
  Pasta with Pesto Sauce New Zealand Sauvignon Blanc, Valpolicella.
  Pasta with Seafood Sauce Soave, Sancerre.
  Ravioli with Spinach and Ricotta Pinot Bianco/Grigio, Cabernet d'Anjou.
  Spaghetti with Tomato Sauce California Cabernet, Zinfandel, Chianti.
  Spaghetti Vongole Pinot Bianco, Lugano.
  Tagliatelle Carbonara Pinot Grigio or a fresh, red Bardolino or Beaujolais.
Peach Sweet, German Riesling.
  Peaches in Wine Riesling Auslese, Riesling Gewürztraminer Vendange Tardive, sweet Vouvray.
Peanuts
  Beef in Peanut Curry New World Chardonnay, an aromatic, white Rhône.
  Satay Gewürztraminer.

Pepper (corns)
Steak au Poivre Cabernet Sauvignon, Chianti, Barbera, Rhône reds, Shiraz, or Rioja.
Peppers (fresh green, red) New Zealand Cabernet, Loire reds, crisp Sauvignon Blanc, Beaujolais, Tuscan red.
Peppers (yellow) Fruity, Italian reds, Valpolicella, etc.
Stuffed Peppers Hungarian red – Bull's Blood, Zinfandel, Chianti, or spicy, Rhône reds.
Pheasant Top-class, red Burgundy, good American Pinot Noir, mature Hermitage.
Pheasant Casserole Top class, red Burgundy, mature Hermitage.
Pheasant Paté Côtes du Rhône, Alsace Pinot Blanc.
Pike Eastern European white.
Pine Nuts
Pesto Sauce New Zealand Sauvignon Blanc, Valpolicella.
Pizza
Fiorentina Pinot Bianco, Pinot Grigio, Vinho Verde, Sauvignon Blanc.
Napoletana Verdicchio, Vernaccia de San Gimignano, white Rhône.
Quattro Formagi Pinot Grigio, Frascati, Bianco di Custoza, Lugana or serious single-vineyard Soave.
Quattro Stagioni Valpolicella, Bardolino, light Chianti, good single-vineyard Soave.
Plaice White Burgundy, South American Chardonnay, Sauvignon Blanc.
Plum
Plum Pie Trockenbeerenauslese, Côteaux du Layon.
Pork
Cassoulet Serious white Rhône, Marsanne or Roussanne, or reds including Grenache and Syrah from the Rhône, berryish, Italian reds, or Zinfandel.
Pork Casserole Mid-weight, earthy reds like Minervois, Navarra, or Montepulciano d'Abruzzo.
Pork Pie Spicy reds, Shiraz, Grenache.
Pork with Prunes Cahors, mature Chinon, or other Loire red or rich, southern French wine such as Corbières, Minervois, or Faugères.
Pork Rillettes Pinot Blanc d'Alsace, Menetou-Salon Rouge.
Pork Sausages Spicy Rhône reds, Barbera.
Pork and Sage Sausages Barbera, Côtes du Rhône.
Pork Spare Ribs Zinfandel, Australian Shiraz.
Roast Pork Rioja reserva, New World Merlot or Pinot Noir,Chenin Blanc, or dry Vouvray.
Roast Pork with Apple Sauce Off-dry Vouvray, Riesling, or good South African Chenin Blanc.
Saucisson Sec Barbera, Cabernet Franc, Alsace Pinot Blanc, or Beaujolais (Villages or Crus).
Spare Ribs with Barbecue Sauce Fruity Australian Shiraz, Grenache, or Zinfandel, spicy Côtes du Rhône from a ripe vintage or a good off-dry white such as Vouvray.
Szechuan-Style Pork Dry, aromatic whites, Alsace Pinot Gris, Riesling, Grenache rosé or beer.
Prawns White Bordeaux, dry, Australian Riesling, Gavi.
Prawn Cocktail Light, fruity whites – German Riesling.
Prawns in Garlic Vinho Verde, Pinot Bianco.
Prawn Vol-au-Vents White Bordeaux, Muscadet.
Thai Prawns Gewürztraminer, dry, aromatic Riesling, or New Zealand Sauvignon Blanc.
Prunes Australian, late harvest Semillon.
Pork with Prunes and Cream Sweet, Chenin-based wines, or good Mosel Spätlese.
Prune Ice Cream Muscat de Beaumes de Venise.

Q

Quail Light, red Burgundy, full-flavored, white Spanish wines.
Quince Lugana.
Braised Venison with Quince Jelly Rich and fruity Australian or Chilean reds, good, ripe Spanish Rioja, or a Southern French red.

R

Rabbit
Rabbit Casserole New World Pinot Noir or mature Châteauneuf-du-Pape.
Rabbit in Cider Muscadet, demi-sec Vouvray, cider, or Calvados.
Rabbit with Mustard Franken wine or Czech Pilsner beer.
Rabbit in Red Wine with Prunes Good, mature Chinon or other Loire red.
Roast Rabbit Tasty, simple, young Rhône, red, white or rosé.
Raspberries New World, late harvest Riesling or Champagne, Beaujolais, demi-sec Champagne.
Raspberry Fool Vouvray Moelleux.
Raspberry Vinegar Full-bodied Pinot Noir.
Warm Bacon and Sorrel Salad New World Sauvignon Blanc, California Fumé Blanc, or a good Pouilly Fumé.
Redcurrant

Ratatouille

Cumberland Sauce Rioja, Australian Shiraz.
Red Mullet Dry rosé, California, Washington or Australian Chardonnay, Sauvignon Blanc.
Rhubarb
Rhubarb Pie Moscato d'Asti, Alsace, German or Austrian late harvest Riesling.
Rice
Rice Pudding Monbazillac, sweet Muscat, Asti Spumante, or California Orange Muscat.
Roquefort The classic match is Sauternes or Barsac, but almost any full-flavored, botrytized sweet wine will be a good partner for strong, creamy blue cheese.
Rosemary Light red Burgundy or Pinot Noir.
Roast Lamb with Garlic and Rosemary Earthy soft reds like California Petite Sirah, Rioja, or Zinfandel.
Rum
Flambéed Banana with Rum Jurançon, Tokaji, Pedro Ximénez sherry, and, naturally, rum.

S

Saffron Dry whites especially Chardonnay.

Bass in Saffron Sauce Riesling (German, Australian, or Austrian), Viognier.

Paella with Seafood White Penedés, unoaked Rioja, Navarra, Provence rosé.

Sage Chianti, or country reds from the Languedoc. Otherwise Sauvignon Blancs are great, especially Chilean.

Roast Chicken, Goose, or Turkey with Sage and Onion Stuffing Italian reds, especially Chianti, soft, plummy Merlots, sweetly fruity Rioja, and brambly Zinfandel.

Salami Good, beefy Mediterranean rosé, Sardinian red, Rhône red, Zinfandel, dry aromatic Hungarian white.

Salmon

Carpaccio of Salmon Cabernet Franc, Chardonnay, Australian reds, red Loire, Portuguese reds, Puligny-Montrachet.

Grilled Salmon White Rhône (especially Viognier).

Poached Salmon Chablis, good, white Burgundy, other Chardonnay, Alsace Muscat, white Bordeaux.

Poached Salmon with Hollandaise Muscat, Riesling, good Chardonnay.

Salmon Paté Best white Burgundy.

Salmon Trout Light Pinot Noir from the Loire, New Zealand, good, dry, unoaked Chardonnay, Chablis, etc.

Sardines Fresh Muscadet, Vinho Verde, very light and fruity reds such as Loire, Gamay.

Scallops Chablis and other unoaked Chardonnay.

Coquilles St. Jacques White Burgundy.

Marinated Scallops with Bacon Fino sherry or mature Riesling.

Scallops Mornay White Burgundy, Riesling Spätlese.

Sea Bass Good white Burgundy.

Bass in Saffron Sauce Riesling (German, Austrian or Australian), Viognier.

Seafood (general – see individual entries)

Paella with Seafood White Penedés, unoaked Rioja, Navarra, Provence rosé.

Platter of Seafood Sancerre, Muscadet.

Seafood Salad Soave, Pinot Grigio, Muscadet, lightly oaked Chardonnay.

Sesame Seeds Oaked Chardonnay.

Shrimps Albariño, Sancerre, New World Sauvignon, Arneis.

Potted Shrimps New World Chardonnay, Marsanne.

Skate Bordeaux white, Côtes de Gascogne, Pinot Bianco.

Smoked Salmon Chablis, Alsace Pinot Gris, white Bordeaux.

Avocado and Smoked Salmon Lightly oaked Chardonnay, Fumé Blanc or Australian Semillon.

Sole

Smoked Salmon Paté English oaked Fumé Blanc, New Zealand Chardonnay.
Smoked Trout
Smoked Trout Paté Good, white Burgundy.
Snapper Australian or South African, dry white.
Sorbet Like ice cream, these can be too cold/sweet for most wines. Try Australian fortified Muscats or see under individual entries (orange, lemon, etc).
Sorrel Dry Loire Chenin or Sauvignon Blanc.
Soy Sauce Zinfandel or Australian Verdelho.
Spinach Pinot Grigio, Lugana.
Eggs Florentine Chablis or unoaked Chardonnay, Pinot Blanc, Aligoté, Sémillon.
Spinach/Pasta Bakes Soft, Italian reds (Bardolino, Valpolicella) rich whites.
Spring Rolls Pinot Gris, Gewürztraminer, or other aromatic whites.
Squab Good, red Burgundy, rich Southern Rhône. Chianti also goes well.
Warm Squab Breasts on Salad Merlot-based Bordeaux or Cabernet Rosé.
Squid Gamay de Touraine, Greek or Spanish white.
Squid in Batter Crisp and neutral dry white – Muscadet.
Squid in Ink Nebbiolo or Barbera.
Stilton Tawny port.
Strawberries – No Cream Surprisingly, red Rioja, Burgundy (or other young Pinot Noir), especially if the berries are marinated.
More conventionally, sweet Muscats or fizzy Moscato.
Strawberries and Cream Vouvray Moelleux, Monbazillac
Strawberry Mousse Sweet or fortified Muscat.
Sweet and Sour Dishes (general) Gewürztraminer, fruity young Sauvignon Blanc (unoaked), or beer.
Sweetbreads Lightly oaked Chardonnay, Chablis, Pouilly-Fuissé, or light, red Bordeaux.
Sweetbreads in Mushroom, Butter and Cream sauce Southern French whites, Vin de Pays Chardonnay.

T

Taramasalata Oaked Chardonnay or Fumé Blanc.
Tarragon White Menetou-Salon or South African Sauvignon Blanc.
Roast/Grilled Chicken with Tarragon Dry Chenin Blanc or Vouvray
Thyme Ripe and fruity Provençal reds, Rioja, Northern Italian whites.
Roast Lamb with Thyme New Zealand Cabernet Sauvignon, Bourgeuil.
Toffee Moscatel de Setúbal, Eiswein.
Banoffee Pie Sweet Tokaji.
Tomato
Gazpacho Fino sherry, white Rioja.
Pasta in a Tomato Sauce California Cabernet, Zinfandel, Chianti.
Tomato Soup Sauvignon Blanc.
Tripe Earthy, French country red, Minervois, Cahors, Fitou.
Trout Pinot Blanc, Chablis.
Smoked Trout Bourgogne Aligoté, Gewürztraminer, Pinot Gris.
Trout with Almonds Bianco di Custoza, Pinot Blanc.
Truffles Red Burgundy,, old Rioja, Barolo or Hermitage.
Tuna
Carpaccio of Tuna Australian Chardonnay, red Loire, Beaujolais.
Fresh Tuna Alsace Pinot Gris, Australian Chardonnay, Beaujolais.
Turbot Best white Burgundy, top California or Australian Chardonnay.
Turkey
Roast Turkey with Chestnut Stuffing Rhône, Merlot or mature Burgundy.

V

Vanilla Liqueur Muscat.
- **Crème Brulée** Jurançon Moelleux, Tokaji.
- **Custard** Monbazillac, sweet Vouvray.

Veal
- **Blanquette de Veau** Aromatic, spicy whites from Alsace or from the Northern Rhône.
- **Roast Veal** Light, Italian whites or fairly light reds – Spanish or Loire, or St Emilion.
- **Wienerschnitzel** Austrian Grüner Veltliner or Hungarian Pinot Blanc.

Vegetables
- **Roasted and Grilled** Light, juicy reds, Beaujolais, Sancerre and Sauvignon Blanc. Unoaked or lightly oaked Chardonnay.
- **Vegetable Soup** Pinot Blanc or rustic reds such as Corbières or Southern Italian reds.
- **Vegetable Terrine** Good New World Chardonnay.

Venison Pinotage, rich red Rhône, mature red Burgundy, earthy, Italian reds.
- **Venison Casserole** Australian Shiraz and Cabernet-Shiraz, Zinfandel, South African red.

Vinegar
- **Choucroute Garnie** White dry Alsace (especially Riesling), Italian Pinot Grigio or Beaujolais.
- **Sauerkraut** Pilsner beer.

W

Walnut Tawny port, sweet Madeira.

Watercress
- **Watercress Soup** Aromatic dry Riesling (Alsace or Australia).

Whitebait Fino sherry, Spanish red/white (Garnacha, Tempranillo) or single-vineyard Soave.

Y

Yams Depends on the sauce. When subtly prepared, try Alsace Pinot Blanc.

Yogurt Needs full-flavored wines, such as Australian Semillon or New World Chardonnay.

Z

Zabaglione Marsala, Australian Liqueur Muscat or a French Muscat such as Muscat de Beaumes de Venise.

A-Z *of* Wine

How to read the entries

Names of wines are accompanied by a glass symbol (🍷); grape varieties by a bunch of grapes (🍇). Wine regions appear in a orange band.

Words that have their own entry elsewhere in the A–Z appear in italics. Recommended wines may also be cross-referenced.

Poor vintages are not listed. Particularly good years that are ready to drink now are featured in bold; vintages that will improve with keeping are in orange

🍷 **Ch. l'Angélus** [lon jay-loos] (*St. Emilion Grand Cru Classé, Bordeaux,* France) Flying high since the late 1980s, this is a lovely, plummy *St. Emilion* to watch. The *second label* Carillon d'Angélus is also well worth seeking out. **79 82 83 85 86** 87 88 89 90 **92 93** 94 95 96 97 98 ☆☆☆☆☆ **1990 $$$$**; ☆☆☆ **1991 $$$**

Throughout this section, examples are given of recommended vintages, producers or wines which represent good examples of the region, style or maker.

Recommended wines are accompanied by stars.
☆☆☆☆☆ = outstanding in their style.
☆☆☆☆ = excellent in their style.
☆☆☆ = good in their style.

Prices are indicated, using the following symbols:

$	*Under $5*
$$	*$5–10*
$$$	*$10–20*
$$$$	*Over $20*

Pronunciation Guide

All but the most common words are followed by square [ ] brackets enclosing pronunciation guides. These use the "sounding-out" phonetic method, with the accented syllable (if there is one) indicated by capital letters. For example, **Spätlese** is pronounced as *SHPAYT-Lay-Zuh.*

The basic sounds employed in this book's pronunciations are as follows:

a as in **can**	**ah** as in **father**	**ay** as in **day**	**ur** as in **turn**
ch as in **church**	**kh** as in **loch**	**y** as in **yes**	**zh** as in **vision**
ee as in **see**	**eh** as in **get**	**g** as in **game**	**i** as in **pie**
ih as in **if**	**j** as in **gin**	**k** as in **cat**	**o** as in **hot**
oh as in **soap**	**oo** as in **food**	**ow** as in **cow**	**uh** as in **up**

Foreign sounds: eu is like a cross between oo and a; an italicized n or m is silent and the preceding vowel sounds nasal; an ñ is like an n, followed by a y (as in Bourgogne); an italicized r sounds like a cross between r and w; rr sounds like a rolled r.

A

Abboccato [ah-boh-kah-toh] (Italy) Semi-dry.
Abfüller/Abfüllung [ab-few-ler/ ab-few-lerng] (Germany) Bottler/bottled by.
Abocado [ah-boh-KAH-doh] (Spain) Semi-dry.

Abruzzi/zzo [ah-broot-zee/zoh] (Italy) Region on the east coast, with often dull *Trebbiano* whites and fast-improving *Montepulciano* reds. **Barone Cornacchia; Farnese, Castello di Salle; *Cantina Tollo*; Edoardo Valentini.**

AC (France) See *Appellation Contrôlée.*

🍷 **Acacia** [a-kay-shah] (*Carneros*, California) Fine producer of *Chardonnay* and *Pinot Noir*. Under the same ownership as the similarly excellent *Chalone, Edna Valley* and *Carmenet*. ☆☆☆☆☆ **1995 Pinot Noir Beckstoffer Vineyard $$$$;** ☆☆☆☆☆ **1995 Chardonnay Carneros Reserve $$$**

🍷 **Accordini** [a-kor-DEE-nee] (*Veneto*, Italy) New *Valpolicella* star with fine vineyards. ☆☆☆☆ **1993 Amarone Il Fornetto $$$**

Acetic acid [ah-see-tihk] This volatile acid (CH3COOH) features in small proportions in all wines. Careless winemaking can result in wine being turned into acetic acid, a substance most people know as vinegar.

Acidity Naturally occuring (*tartaric* and malic) acids in the grapes are vital to contributing freshness, and also help to preserve the wine while it ages. In reds and many cool region whites, the malic is often converted to lactic by a natural process known as *malolactic fermentation*, which gives the wines a buttery texture and flavor. In hotter countries (and sometimes cooler ones) the acid level may (not always legally) be adjusted by adding *tartaric* and citric acid.

Aconcagua Valley [ah-kon-kar-gwah] (*Central Valley*, Chile) Region noted for blackcurranty *Cabernet Sauvignon*. The subregion is *Casablanca*. Grapes from both are used by many Chilean producers. ***Concha y Toro, Errazuriz.***

Tim Adams (*Clare Valley*, Australia) Highly successful producer of *Riesling*, rich peachy *Semillon* and deep-flavored Aberfeldy *Shiraz* and intense peppery Fergus *Grenache*. ☆☆☆☆☆ **1996 The Aberfeldy $$$**; ☆☆☆☆ **1997 Semillon $$**

Adanti [ah-dan-ti] (*Umbria*, Italy) Star producer of spicy reds and herby Grechetto whites. ☆☆☆☆ **1994 Rosso di Montefalco $$$**

Adega [ah-day-gah] (Portugal) Winery – equivalent to Spanish *bodega*.

Adelaide Hills [ah-dur-layd] (*South Australia*) High-altitude region, long known for classy lean *Riesling* and *Semillon*; now famous for *Sauvignon Blanc* and *Chardonnay* from *Ashton Hills*, *Petaluma* and *Nepenthe and Shaw & Smith, Croser sparkling wine* and the occasional Pinot Noir. See also the new sub-region of *Lenswood*. ***Heggies; Henschke; Mountadam; Penfolds.***

Weingut Graf Adelmann [graf-eh-del-man] (*Wurttemberg*, Germany) One of the region's best estates, making good reds from grapes such as the *Trollinger*, Lemberger and Urban. Look for Brüssele'r Spitze wines.

Adelsheim [a-del-sime] (*Oregon, USA*) Classy, long-lived but non-showy Pinot Noir from a producer with the look of an Old Testament prophet. ☆☆☆☆☆ **1995 Reserve Pinot Noir $$$**

Age [ah-khay] (*Rioja*, Spain) Big, modern, highly commercial winery.

Aglianico [ah-lee-AH-nee-koh] (Italy) Thick-skinned grape grown by the Ancient Greeks. Now used to make hefty *Taurasi* and *Aglianico del Vulture*.

Aglianico del Vulture [ah-lee-AH-nee-koh del vool-TOO-reh] (*Basilicata*, Italy) Tannic liquoricey-chocolatey blockbusters made in Southern Italy on the hills of an extinct volcano. **D'Angelo; Basilium; Casele; Paternoster; Sasso.** ☆☆☆☆ **1997 I Portali Aglianico del Vulture, Basilium $$**

Agricola vitivinicola (Italy) Wine estate.

Ahr [ahr] (Germany) Northernmost *anbaugebiet*, making light-bodied reds.

Ajaccio [ah-JAK-see-yoh] (*Corsica*, France) Very mixed fare, but *Comte Peraldi* makes intense reds and whites. See also: **Gie Les Rameaux.**

Airén [i-REHN] (Spain) The world's most planted variety. Dull and fortunately more or less restricted to the region of *La Mancha*.

Albana di Romagna [ahl-BAH-nah dee roh-MAN-yah] (*Emilia-Romagna*, Italy) First white *DOCG*. Improving but traditionally dull white. Passita, sweeter whites are best. ☆☆☆☆ 1996 Passita Scacco Matto, Zerbina **$$**

Albariño [ahl-BAH-ree-nyoh] (*Galicia*, Spain) The Spanish name for the Portuguese *Alvarinho* and the peachy-spicy wine made from it in *Rias Baixas*, **Lagar de Cervera; Martin Codex; Pazo de Barrantes; Salnesu; Valdamor.**

Alcohol This simple compound, technically known as ethanol, is formed by the action of yeast on sugar during fermentation.

Aleatico [ah-lay-AH-tee-koh] (Italy) Red grape producing sweet, ***Muscat***-style, often fortified wines. Produces *DOCs* A. di Puglia and A. di Gradoli.

Alella [ah-LEH-yah] (*Catalonia*, Spain) *DO* district producing better whites (from grapes including the ***Xarel-lo***) than reds. ☆☆☆☆ **1997 Marqués de Alella Clasico $$$**

Alenquer [ah-lehn-KEHR] (*Oeste*, Portugal) Coolish region producing good ***Periquita*** reds and ***Muscat***-style ***Fernão Pires*** whites. Also increasingly successful efforts from French varietals. ☆☆☆☆ **1996, Quinta da Abrigada $$**

Alentejo [ah-lehn-TAY-joh] (Portugal) Up-and-coming province north of the Algarve, where ***JM da Fonseca*** makes Morgado de Reguengo, *JP Vinhos* produces Tinta da Anfora and ***Ch. Lafite*** has its Quinta do Carmo. Herdade do Esporão is the best producer, though. **Borba; Cartuxa; Esporâo; Redondo.**

Alexander Valley (*Sonoma*, California) ***Appellation*** in which ***Simi***, ***Jordan***, ***Murphy Good***, and ***Geyser Peak*** are based. Red: 86 89 **90** 91 92 **94** 95 96 97 White: **92** 94 95 **96** 97 **Ch. St Jean; Clos du Bois; Marcassin**

Caves Aliança [ah-lee-an-sah] (Portugal) Modern ***Bairrada***, ***Douro*** and better-than-average *Dão*. ☆☆☆ **1997 Dão Reserva $$**

Alicante (*Valencia*, Spain) Hot region producing generally dull stuff apart from the sweetly honeyed ***Moscatels*** that appreciate the heat.

Alicante-Bouschet [al-ee-KONT- boo-SHAY] Unusual dark-skinned and fleshed grapes traditionally used (usually illegally) for dyeing pallid reds made from nobler fare. ***Rockford*** in Australia uses it to make a good rosé.

Aligoté [Al-lee-GOH-tay] (***Burgundy***, France) Lesser white grape, making dry wine that is traditionally mixed with ***cassis*** for ***Kir***. With care and a touch of oak it can imitate basic ***Bourgogne*** Blanc, especially in the village of ***Bouzeron***. **La Digoine; *Domaine Dujac;* G & J-H Goisot; Aubert de Vilaine.**

Alion [ah-lee-yon] (***Ribera del Duero***, Spain) New venture by the owners of ***Vega Sicilia***, with fruitier, more modern wines. ☆☆☆☆☆ **1994 Reserva $$$**

All Saints (***Rutherglen***, Australia) Good producer of ***Liqueur Muscat***, ***Tokay*** and ***late harvest*** wines.

Allegrini [ah-leh-GREE-nee] (***Veneto***, Italy) Top-class producer of single-vineyard ***Valpolicella*** and ***Soave***. ☆☆☆☆ **1990 Amarone della Valpolicella $$$**

Thierry Allemand [al-mon] (***Rhône***, France) Producer of classic, concentrated, single-vineyard ***Cornas*** from a small 6-acre (2.5-hectare) estate. ☆☆☆☆☆ **1996 Cornas Chaillot $$$**

Allier [a-lee-yay] (France) Spicy oak favored by makers of white wine.

Almaviva [al-mah-vee-vah] (***Maipo***, Chile) New, overpriced red co-production between Mouton Rothschild and Concha y Toro. ☆☆☆☆ **1996 $$$**

Almacenista [al-mah-theh-nee-stah] (***Jerez***, Spain) Fine old unblended ***sherry*** from a single ***solera*** – the ***sherry*** equivalent of a single malt whiskey. ***Lustau.***

Aloxe-Corton [a-loss kawr-ton] (***Burgundy***, France) ***Côte de Beaune commune*** with tough, slow-maturing, sometimes uninspiring reds (including the ***Grand Cru Corton***) and potentially sublime whites (including ***Corton-Charlemagne***). ***Louis Latour's*** pricey whites can be fine. White: **85 86 88** 89 **90 92** 95 96 97 Red: **78 85** 86 87 **88 89 90** 95 96 97 **Arnoux; *Bonneau du Martray;* Denis Bousse; Capitan-Gagnerot; *Drouhin;* Antonin Guyon; *Jadot; Leflaive;* Prince de Mérode; *Tollot-Beaut; Michel Voarick.***

Alsace [al-sas] (France) Northerly region whose warm microclimate enables producers to make riper-tasting wines than their counterparts across the Rhine. Wines are named after the grapes – *Pinot Noir, Gewurztraminer, Riesling, Tokay/Pinot Gris, Pinot Blanc* (known as Pinot d'Alsace), *Sylvaner* and (rarely) *Muscat*. In the right hands, the 50 or so *Grand Cru* vineyards should yield better wines. *Late harvest* sweet wines are labeled *Vendange Tardive* and *Sélection des Grains Nobles*. White: 85 86 88 89 90 93 94 95 96 97 ***Paul Blanck;*** **Bott-Geyl; Albert Boxler;** ***Ernest J & F Burn;*** **Joseph Cattin; Marcel Deiss; Jean-Pierre Dirler;** ***Dopff au Moulin;*** **Faller;** ***Hugel; Josmeyer; André Kientzler; Kreydenweiss; Albert Mann; Meyer-Fonné, Mittnacht-Klack; René Muré; Ostertag; Rolly Gassmann; Schlumberger;*** **Schoffit;** ***Bruno Sorg; Trimbach; Weinbach; Zind Humbrecht.***

Elio Altare [Ehl-lee-yoh al-TAh-ray] (*Piedmont*, Italy) The genial Svengali-like leader of the *Barolo* revolution and inspirer of *Clerico* and *Roberto Voerzio*. ☆☆☆☆☆ **1995 Langhe Larigi; $$$** ☆☆☆☆☆ **1993 Barolo $$$**

Altesino [al-TEH-see-noh] (*Tuscany*, Italy) First class producers of *Brunello di Montalcino, Cabernet* ("Palazzo") and *Sangiovese* ("Altesi"). ☆☆☆☆☆ **1993 Brunello di Montalcino Montosoli $$$**

Alto-Adige [ahl-toh ah-dee-jay] (Italy) Aka Italian Tyrol and Sudtirol. *DOC* for a range of whites often from Germanic grape varieties; also light and fruity reds from the *Lagrein* and Vernatsch. **Appiano; Gaierhof;** ***Alois Lageder;*** **Maddalena; Pojer & Sandri;** ***Tiefenbrunner;*** **Viticoltori Alto Adige.**

Alvarinho [ahl-vah-reen-yoh] (Portugal) White grape aka *Albariño*; at its lemony best in *Vinho Verde* and in the *DO* Alvarinho de Monção.

Amabile [am-MAH-bee-lay] (Italy) Semi-sweet.

Castello di Ama [ah-mah] (*Tuscany*, Italy) Brilliant small *Chianti* estate. Great single vineyard Vigna l'Apparita wines. ☆☆☆☆☆ **1993 Vigna l'Apparita $$$**

Amador County [am-uh-dor] (*California*) Intensely-flavored, old-fashioned *Zinfandel*. Look for Amador Foothills Winery's old-vine *Zinfandels* and top-of-the-range stuff from *Sutter Home* and *Montevina*. Red: 86 87 **88** 89 **90 91** 92 94 95 96 97 White: **94** 95 96 97 ***Quady.***

Amarone [ah-mah-ROH-neh] (*Veneto*, Italy) Literally "bitter"; used particularly to describe *Recioto*. Best known as *Amarone della Valpolicella*. ***Allegrini; Boscaini; Masi; Quintarelli; Tedeschi; Zenato.***

Bodegas Amézola de la Mora [ah-meh-THOH-lah deh lah MAW-rah] (*Rioja*, Spain) Eight-year-old estate producing unusually classy red *Rioja*. ☆☆☆☆ **1991 Crianza $$**

Amity [am-mi-tee] (*Oregon*, US) Maker of very high quality berryish *Pinot Noir*, good dry *Gewürztraminer* and *late-harvest* whites. ☆☆☆☆ **1995 Pinot Noir $$$**

Amontillado [am-mon-tee-yah-doh] (*Jerez*, Spain) Literally "like Montilla." Often pretty basic medium-sweet *sherry*, but ideally fascinating dry, nutty wine. ***Gonzalez Byass; Lustau;*** **Sanchez Romate.**

Amtliche Prüfungsnummer [am-tlish-eh proof-oong-znoomer] (Germany) Identification number on all *QbA/QmP* labels.

Anbaugebiet [ahn-bow-geh-beet] (Germany) Term for 11 large regions (e.g. *Rheingau*). *QbA* and *QmP* wines must include the name of their *anbaugebiet* on their labels.

Anderson Valley (*Mendocino*, California) Small, cool area, good for white and sparkling wines including the excellent *Roederer.* Do not confuse with the less impressive Anderson Valley, *New Mexico*. Red: **88** 89 **90 91 94**95 96 97 White: 91 92 **94**95 **96**97 **Roederer; Steele; Williams Selyem.**

Andrew Will (*Washington State*, US) Stunning producer of *Cabernet Sauvignon* and *Merlot*. ☆☆☆☆☆ **1996 Merlot $$$**

Ch. l'Angélus [lon jay-loos] (*St. Emilion Grand Cru Classé, Bordeaux*, France) Flying high since the late 1980s, this is a lovely plummy, oaky *St. Emilion*. The *second label* Carillon d'Angélus is also well worth seeking out. 79 81 **82 83 85 86 87 88**89 90 **93 94**95 96 97 98 ☆☆☆☆☆ **1990 $$$$**

Marquis d'Angerville [don-jehr-veel] (*Burgundy*, France) Long-established *Volnay* estate with rich, long-lived traditional wines from here and from *Pommard*. ☆☆☆☆ **1995 Volnay Champans $$$$**

Anghelu Ruju [an-jeh-loo roo-yoo] (*Sardinia*, Italy) Intensely nutty-raisiny, port'n-lemony wine made by *Sella & Mosca* from dried *Cannonau* grapes. ☆☆☆☆ **1987 $$**

Ch. d' Angludet [don gloo-day] (*Cru Bourgeois, Margaux, Bordeaux*, France) Made by the late *Peter Sichel,* classy cassis-flavored, if slightly earthy, wine that can generally be drunk young but is worth waiting for. 78 79 **82 83** 85 **86**88 89 90 **91** 93 94 95 96 97

Angoves [an-gohvs] (*Padthaway*, Australia) *Murray River* producer with improving, inexpensive *Chardonnay* and *Cabernet,* and great brandy.

Weingut Paul Anheuser [an-hoy-zur] (*Nahe*, Germany) One of the most credible supporters of the *Trocken* movement, and a strong proponent of the *Riesling*, this excellent estate is also unusually successful with its *Ruländer* and *Pinot Noir*. ☆☆☆☆ **1993 Kreuznacher Monchberg $$**

Anjou [on-joo] (*Loire*, France) Dry and *Demi-Sec* whites, mostly from *Chenin Blanc*, with up to 20 percent *Chardonnay* or *Sauvignon Blanc*. The rosé is almost always awful but there are good, light reds. Look for Anjou-Villages, in which *Gamay* is not permitted. Within Anjou, there are smaller, more specific ACs, most importantly *Savennières* and *Coteaux du Layon*. Red: **88** 89 90 95 96 97 White: 88 89 **90 94**95 96 97 98 Sweet White: **76 83 85 88 89 90 94** 95 96 97 **Arnault et Fils, *Ch. du Breuil*; Dom. du Closel; Ch de Fesles; Gaudard; Genaiserie Lebreton; Richou; Ch. la Varière.**

Annata [ahn-NAH-tah] (Italy) *Vintage*.

Roberto Anselmi [an-sehl-mee] (*Veneto*, Italy) Source of classy dry *Soave Classico* wines as well as some extremely serious sweet examples. ☆☆☆☆ **1995 I Capitelli Recioto di Soave $$$**

Antinori [an-tee-NOR-ree] (*Tuscany*, Italy) Pioneer merchant-producer who has improved the quality of *Chianti*, with his Villa Antinori and Pèppoli, while spearheading the *Super-Tuscan* revolution with *Tignanello, Sassicaia*, and *Solaia*. ☆☆☆☆☆ **1994 Castello della Sala Cervaro $$; ☆☆☆☆☆ 1995 Solaia $$$$;** ☆☆☆☆ **1985 Chianti Classico Riserva $$**

AOC (France) See *Appellation Contrôlée*.

AP (Germany) See *Amtliche Prüfungsnummer*.

Appellation Contrôlée (AC/AOC) [AH-pehl-lah-see-o*n* ko*n* TROH- lay] (France) Designation guaranteeing origin, grape varieties and method of production and – in theory – quality, though tradition and vested interest combine to allow pretty appalling wines to receive the rubber stamp.

Aprémont [ah-pray-mo*n*] (Eastern France) Floral, slightly *petillant* white from skiing region. **Ch. de la Violette.**

Apulia [ah-pool-ee-yah] (Italy) See *Puglia*.

Aquileia [ah-kwee-LAY-ah] (*Friuli-Venezia Giulia*, Italy) *DOC* for easy-going, single-variety wines. The *Refosco* can be plummily refreshing. **Ca'Bolani and Corvignano Cooperatives; Franco-Clementin; Zonin.**

Arbois [ahr-bwah] (Eastern France) *AC* region with light *Trousseau* and *Pinot Noir* reds and dry *Sauvignon* and *Chardonnay* whites. Also the *sherry*-like *Vin Jaune* and sparkling wine. **Aviet; Fruitière Viticole; Puffeney; Rolet; Tissot.**

Ch. d' Arche [dahrsh] (*Sauternes 2ème Cru Classé, Bordeaux*, France) Greatly improved, but still slightly patchy. 83 **86 88 89** 90 93 94 95 97

Viña Ardanza [veen-yah ahr-dan-thah] (*Rioja*, Spain) Highly reliable, fairly full-bodied red wines made with a high proportion (40 percent) of *Grenache*; good, *oaky* white, too. ☆☆☆☆ **1990 Tinto Reserva $$**

d'Arenberg [dar-ren-burg] (*McLaren Vale*, Australia) Excellent up-and-coming producer with memorably named, impressive sweet and dry table wines and unusually dazzling fortifieds. ☆☆☆☆☆ **1997 d'Arry's Original Shiraz $$$; 1997** ☆☆☆☆☆ **The Ironstone Pressings $$$**

Argentina Fast up-and-coming nation with fine *Malbec. Cabernet*, and *Merlot* have a touch more backbone than many efforts from Chile and there are interesting wines made from Italian red varieties. *Chardonnays* and grapey whites from the *Muscat*-like *Torrontes* are worthwhile too. **la Agricola; Leoncio Arizu; Balbi; Luigi Bosca; Canale; *Catena*; M Chandon (Paul Galard); *Etchart; Lurton; Morande*; Navarro Correas; *Norton; la Rural; San Telmo; Santa Ana;* Torino; *Trapiche; Weinert.***

Tenuta di Argiano [teh-noo-tah dee ahr-zhee-ahn-noh] (*Tuscany*, Italy) Instant success story, with top-class vineyards, and lovely juicy reds. ☆☆☆☆☆ **1996 Solengo $$$$**

Argyle (*Oregon*, US) Classy sparkling wine and still wines from *Brian Croser* (of *Petaluma*). ☆☆☆☆ **1995 Brut $$$;** ☆☆☆☆ **1995 Chardonnay $$$**

Ch. d'Arlay [dahr-lay] (*Jura*, France) Reliable producer of nutty *Vin Jaune* and light, earthy-raspberry *Pinot Noir*. ☆☆☆☆ **1994 Côtes du Jura $$$**

Leoncio Arizu [Ah-ree-zoo] (*Mendoza*, Argentina) Variable, old-established producer. Also owns *Luigi Bosca*

Dom. de l'Arlot [dur-lahr-loh] (*Burgundy*, France) Brilliant, award-winning *Nuits-St.-Georges* estate under the same – insurance company – ownership as *Ch. Pichon-Longueville*. Delicate modern reds (including an increasingly impressive *Vosne-Romanée*) and a rare example of white *Nuits-St.-Georges*. ☆☆☆☆☆ **1995 Nuits-St.-Georges Clos de l'Arlot $$$**

Ch. d'Armailhac [darh-MI-yak] (*Pauillac 5ème Cru Classé, Bordeaux*, France). Same stable as *Mouton-Rothschild*, and showing similar rich flavors. 82 83 85 **86 88 89**90 92 93 **94**95 96 **97**98 ☆☆☆☆ **1990 $$$$**

Dom. du Comte Armand [komt-arh-mon] (*Burgundy*, France) Only one wine – the exceptional *Pommard* Clos des Epeneaux. ☆☆☆☆ **1995 $$$**

Arneis [ahr-nay-ees] (*Piedmont*, Italy) Spicy white; makes good, young, unoaked wine. ***Bava*; Ceretto; Bruno Giacosa; Malvira; Serafino; *Voerzio*.**

Ch. l' Arrosée, [lah-roh-say] (*St. Emilion Grand Cru Classé, Bordeaux*, France) Small, well-sited property with fruity intense wines. 79 81 **82** 83 **85 86** 88 89 90 92 **93** 94 95 96 **97** 98 ☆☆☆☆ **1990 $$$$**

Arrowood (*Sonoma Valley*, California) Fine *Chardonnay, Merlot, Pinot Blanc, Viognier* and *Cabernet* from former *Ch. St. Jean* winemaker. ☆☆☆☆ **1994 Sonoma Merlot $$$$;** ☆☆☆☆ **1997 Saralee's Vineyard Viognier $$$**

Ismael Arroyo [uh-ROY-oh] (*Ribera del Duero*, Spain) A name to watch for flavorsome reds. ☆☆☆☆ **1996 Val Sotillo $$**

Artadi [ahr-tah-dee] (*Rioja*, Spain) Up-and-coming producer with particularly good *Crianza* wines. ☆☆☆☆ **1995 Viñas de Gain Crianza $$$**

Arvine [ah-veen] (*Switzerland*) Spicy white indigenous grape which has reminded some visiting Italians of their *Arneis*.

Giacomo Ascheri [ash-SHEH-ree] (*Piedmont*, Italy) New-wave producer. Impressive single-vineyard, tobacco 'n' berry wines, also *Nebbiolo, Syrah and Viognier* and Freisa del Langhe. ☆☆☆☆☆ **1998 Podere di Montalupa Viognier $$$**

Asciutto [ah-shoo-toh] (Italy) Dry.

Asenovgrad [ass-seh-nov-grad] (Bulgaria) Demarcated northern wine region with rich plummy *Cabernet Sauvignon, Merlot*, and *Mavrud*.

Ashton Hills (*Adelaide Hills*, Australia) Small up-and-coming winery producing good Pinot Noir as well as subtle, increasingly creditable *Chardonnay* and *Riesling*. ☆☆☆☆ **1998 Pinot Noir $$$**

Assemblage [ah-sehm-blahj] (France) The art of blending wine from different grape varieties. Associated with *Bordeaux* and *Champagne*.

Assmanhausen [ass-mahn-how-zehn] (*Rheingau*, Germany) If you like sweet *Pinot Noir*, this is the place to come looking for it.

Asti (*Piedmont*, Italy) Town famous for sparkling *Spumante*, lighter *Moscato d'Asti*, and red *Barbera d'Asti*. Red: 82 **85 88**89 90 **93 94**95 96 97 White: 98 **Bera; Bersano; *Fontanafredda; Gancia; Martini*.**

Astringent Mouth-puckering. Associated with young red wine. See *tannin*.

Aszu [ah-soo] (*Hungary*) The sweet syrup made from dried and (about 10–15 percent) "nobly rotten" grapes (see *botrytis*) used to sweeten *Tokaji*.

Ata Rangi [ah-tah ran-gee] (*Martinborough*, New Zealand) Small estate with high-quality *Pinot Noir* and *Shiraz*. ☆☆☆☆ **1996 Pinot Noir $$$**

Atlas Peak (*Napa*, California) Antinori's US venture is proving more successful with Cabernet than with Sangiovese. ☆☆☆☆ **1992 Cabernet $$$**

Au Bon Climat [oh bon klee-Mat] (*Santa Barbara*, California) Top-quality producer of characterful and flavorsome *Pinot Noir* and classy *Chardonnay*. ☆☆☆☆ **1996 Talley Reserve Chardonnay $$$**

Dom. des Aubuisières [day Soh-bwee-see-yehr] (*Loire*, France) Bernard Fouquet produces impeccable wines ranging from richly dry to lusciously sweet. ☆☆☆☆ **1995 Vouvray Moelleux le Marigny $$$**

Auckland (New Zealand) An all-embracing designation which once comprized over a quarter of the country's vineyards. Often derided, despite the fact that some vintages favor this region over starrier areas such as Marlborough. ***Collards; Goldwater Estate; Kumeu River; Matua Valley; Sacred Hill.***

Aude [ohd] (South-West France) Prolific *département* traditional source of ordinary wine. Now *Corbières* and *Fitou* are improving as are the *Vins de Pays*, thanks to new grapes (such as the *Viognier*) and the efforts of firms like *Skalli Fortant de France, Val d'Orbieu, and Domaine Virginie.*

Ausbruch [ows-brook] (Austria) Term for rich *botrytis* wine which is sweeter than *Beerenauslese* but less sweet than *Trockenbeerenauslese*.

Auslese [ows-lay-zuh] (Germany) Mostly sweet wine from selected ripe grapes, usually affected by *botrytis*. Third rung on the *QmP* ladder.

Ch. Ausone [oh-zohn] (*St. Emilion Premier Grand Cru Classé, Bordeaux*, France) Pretender to the crown of top *St. Emilion*, this old estate, which owes its name to the Roman occupation, can produce fine complex *claret*. Until the winemaking was taken over by *Michel Rolland* in 1995, however, the wine lacked the intensity demanded by modern critics. The 1998 is a delicious mouthful, but less delicately perfumed than in the past. 79 81 **82 83 85 86** 88 89 90 92 93 94 95 96 97 98 ☆☆☆☆☆ **1990 $$$$**

Austria Home of all sorts of whites, ranging from dry *Sauvignon Blancs*, greengagey *Grüner Veltliners* and ripe *Rieslings* to especially luscious *late harvest* wines. Reds are increasingly successful too – particularly the *Pinot-Noir*-like *St Laurents*. **Brundlmayer; *Freie Weingartner;* Juris; Knoll; *Alois Kracher; Alois Lang; Nicolaihof; Willi Opitz; Pichler;* Johan Tschida*; Prager; Umathum.***

Auxerrois [oh-sehr-wah] (France) Named after the town in northern *Burgundy*, this is the Alsatians' term for a fairly dull local variety that may be related to the *Sylvaner, Melon de Bourgogne* or *Chardonnay*. South Africa's winemakers learned about it when cuttings were smuggled into the *Cape* and planted there under the misapprehension that they were *Chardonnay*. In *Luxembourg* it is called the *Luxembourg Pinot Gris*.

Auxey-Duresses [oh-say doo-ress] (*Burgundy*, France) *Côtes de Beaune* village best known for its buttery whites, but producing greater quantities of raspberryish, rustic, reds. A slow developer. ***Robert Ampeau;* Dom. d'Auvenay; Coche-Dury; Jean-Pierre Diconne; Louis Jadot; *Olivier Leflaive; Michel Prunier*; Vincent Prunier; *Guy Roulot.***

AVA (US) Acronym for American Viticultural Areas, a recent attempt to develop an American *appellation* system. It makes sense in smaller, climatically coherent *appellations* like *Mount Veeder and Carneros;* much less so in larger, more heterogenous ones like *Napa*.

Quinta da Aveleda (*Vinho Verde*, Portugal) Famous estate producing disappointing dry *Vinho Verde*.

Avelsbach [ahr-vel-sarkh] (*Mosel*, Germany) *Ruwer* village producing delicate, light-bodied wines. Qba/Kab/Spät: 85 87 **88** 89 90 **91** 92 **93 94** 95 96 97 Aus/Beeren/Tba: **83** 85 **88 89 90** 91 92 **93 94** 95 97

Avignonesi [ahr-veen-yon-nay-see] (*Tuscany*, Italy) Ultra-classy producer of *Vino Nobile di Montepulciano, Super-Tuscans* such as Grifi, a pure *Merlot* described by an American critic as Italy's *Pétrus*. There are also serious *Chardonnay* and *Sauvignon* whites – plus an unusually good *Vin Santo*. ☆☆☆☆☆ **1997 Il Marzocco $$$;** ☆☆☆☆☆ **1995 Grifi $$$**

Ayala [ay-yah-lah] (*Champagne*, France) Underrated producer which takes its name from the village of Ay. ☆☆☆ **Non Vintage $$$**

Ayl [ihl] (*Mosel*, Germany) Distinguished *Saar* village producing steely wines. Qba/Kab/Spät: 86 88 **89** 90 **91** 92 **93 94** 95 96 97 Aus/Beeren/Tba: **83** 85 88 89 90 91 92 **93 94** 95 97

Azienda [a-see-en-dah] (Italy) Estate.

B

Babich [ba-bitch] (*Henderson*, New Zealand) The rich "Irongate" *Chardonnay* is the prize here, but the *Sauvignon Blanc* is good too. The reds improve with every vintage. ☆☆☆☆ **1998 The Patriarch Chardonnay $$**

Quinta da Bacalhõa [dah ba-keh-yow] (*Setúbal*, Portugal) The innovative *Cabernet-Merlot* made by *Peter Bright* at *JP Vinhos*. ☆☆☆☆ **1995 $$**

Bacchus [ba-kuhs] White grape. A *Müller-Thurgau-Riesling* cross, making light, flowery wine. ***Denbies; Tenterden.***

Dom. Denis Bachelet [dur-nee bash-lay] (*Burgundy*, France) Classy, small *Gevrey-Chambertin* estate with cherryish wines that are great young – and with five or six years of age. ☆☆☆☆☆ **1995 Vieilles Vignes Gevrey-Chambertin $$$**

Backsberg Estate [bax-burg] (*Paarl*, South Africa) *Chardonnay* pioneer, with good, quite Burgundian versions. ☆☆☆ **1998 Chardonnay $$**

Bad Dürkheim [baht duhr-kime] (*Pfalz*, Germany) Chief *Pfalz* town, producing some of the region's finest whites, plus some reds. Qba/Kab/Spät: **85 86 88 89** 90 91 92 **93 94 95** 96 97 Aus/Beeren/Tba: **83** 85 **88 89** 90 91 92 **93 94 95** 96 97 ***Kurt Darting;* Fitz-Ritter.**

Bad Kreuznach [baht kroyts-nahkh] (*Nahe*, Germany) The chief and finest wine town of the region, giving its name to the entire lower *Nahe*. **75 76 83 85** 86 88 **89 90** 91 92 **93** 94 95 96 97 ***Paul Anheuser*; von Plettenberg.**

Baden [bah-duhn] (Germany) Warm southern region of Germany, with ripe grapes to make dry (*Trocken*) wines. Some of these, such as "Baden Dry" – are good, as are some of the *Pinot Noirs*. The huge *Winzerkeller* cooperative makes good wines, as do: ***Dr Heger; Karl Heinz Johner.***

Baden Winzerkeller (ZBW) [bah-den vin-zehr-keh-luhr-rih] (*Baden*, Germany) Huge co-op whose reliability has set *Baden* apart from the rest of Germany.

Badia a Coltibuono [bah-dee-yah ah kohl-tee-bwoh-noh] (*Tuscany*, Italy) One of Italy's most reliable producers of *Chianti*, fairly priced pure *Sangiovese*, and *Chardonnay*. Great mature releases. ☆☆☆☆ **1997 Cetamura Chianti $$;** ☆☆☆☆ **1996 Chardonnay Toscana Sella del Boscone $$**

Baga [bah-gah] (*Bairrada*, Portugal) The spicily fruity red variety of *Bairrada*.

Ch. Bahans-Haut-Brion [bah-on oh-bree-on] (*Graves, Bordeaux*, France) The *second label* of *Ch. Haut Brion*. Red: 82 83 85 **86** 87 88 **89** 90 92 93 94 95 96 97 98 ☆☆☆☆ **1990 $$$$**

Bailey's (*Victoria*, Australia) Traditional, good *Liqueur Muscat* and hefty, old-fashioned *Shiraz*. Current wines are a little more subtle but still pack a punch. ☆☆☆☆ **1996, 1920's Block Shiraz $$$**

Bairrada [bi-rah-dah] (Portugal) *DO* region south of Oporto, traditionally making dull whites and tough reds. Revolutionary producers like *Sogrape, Luis Pato*, and *Alianca* are proving what can be done. Look for spicy blackberryish reds and creamy whites. **Red: 85 86 87 88 90 91 92 94** 95 96 97

Baja California [bah-hah] (*Mexico*) The part of *Mexico* abutting the Californian border, best known for exporting illegal aliens and importing adventurous Californians and hippies. A successful but little known wine region; home to the Santo Tomas, Casa de Piedra, and *LA Cetto* wineries.

Caramel

Caramelized Oranges Asti Spumante, Sauternes.

Crème Caramel Aromatic, sweet white – Muscat or Gewürztraminer Vendange Tardive.

Crème Caramel

Carp Franken Sylvaner, dry Jurançon, Hungarian Furmint.

Carrot

Carrot and Orange Soup Madeira or perhaps an Amontillado sherry.

Carrot and Coriander Soup Aromatic, dry Muscat, Argentinian Torrontes.

Cashew Nuts Pinot Blanc.

Chicken with Cashew Nuts Rich aromatic white, Pinot Gris, or Muscat.

Cauliflower

Cauliflower Cheese Fresh crisp Côtes de Gascogne white, Pinot Grigio, softly plummy Chilean Merlot or young, unoaked Rioja.

Caviar Champagne or chilled vodka.

Celery

Celery Soup Off-dry Riesling

Cheddar (mature) Good Bordeaux, South African Cabernet, port.

Cheese (general – see individual entries)

Cheeseburger Sweetly fruity oaky reds – Australian Shiraz, Rioja.

Cheese Fondue Swiss white or Vin de Savoie.

Cheese Platter Match wines to cheeses, taking care not to put too tannic a red with too creamy a cheese, and possibly even to offer white wines – which go well with all but the hardest cheese. Strong creamy cheeses demand fine Burgundy, blue cheese is made for late harvest wines, goat cheese is ideal with Sancerre, Pouilly Fumé, or other dry, unoaked Sauvignons. Munster is best paired with Alsace Gewürztraminer.

Cheese Sauce (Mornay) Oaky Chardonnay.

Cream Cheese, Crème Fraîche, Mozzarella, Mascarpone Fresh light dry whites – Frascati, Pinot Grigio.

Raclette Swiss white or Vin de Savoie.

Cheesecake Australian botrytized Semillon.

Cherry Valpolicella, Recioto della Valpolicella, Dolcetto.

Roast Duck with Cherry Sauce Barbera, Dolcetto or Barolo.

Chestnut

Roast Turkey with Chestnut Stuffing Côtes du Rhône, Merlot, or soft and mature Burgundy.

Chicken

Chicken with Bamboo Shoots and Water Chestnuts Dry German, New World Riesling.

Barbecued Chicken Rich and tasty white, Chardonnay.

Chicken Casserole Mid-weight Rhône such as Crozes-Hermitage or Lirac.

Chicken Chasseur Off-dry Riesling.

Chicken & Ham Pie Good Beaujolais.

Chicken Kiev Chablis, Aligoté, or Italian dry white.

Chicken Pie White Bordeaux, simple Chardonnay, or light Italian white.

Chicken Soup Soave, Orvieto, or Pinot Blanc.

Balance Harmony of fruitiness, *acidity, alcohol,* and *tannin.* Balance can develop with age but should be evident (if sometimes hard to discern) in youth.

Balaton [bah-la-ton] (*Hungary*) Wine region frequented by *flying winemakers*, and producing fair-quality reds and whites.

🍷 **Anton Balbach** [an-ton bahl-barkh] (*Rheinhessen*, Germany) Potentially one of the best producers in the *Erden* region – especially for *late harvest* wines. ☆☆☆☆☆ **1997 Nierstein Hipping Auslese Riesling $$$$**

🍷 **Bodegas Balbás** [bal-bash] (*Ribera del Duero*, Spain) Small producer of juicy *Tempranillo* reds, *Bordeaux*-style *Cabernet* blends and a lively rosé.

🍷 **Balbi** [bal-bee] (*Mendoza*, Argentina) Producer of good, inexpensive modern wines, including particularly appealing Malbecs and dry rosés.

🍷 **Ch. Balestard-la-Tonnelle** [bah-les-star lah ton-nell] (*St. Emilion Grand Cru Classé, Bordeaux*, France) Good, quite traditional *St. Emilion* built to last. 81 83 85 **86** 87 **88 89 90** 92 93 94 95 96 97 98

🍷 **Balgownie Estate** [bal-GOW-nee] (*Bendigo*, Australia) One of Victoria's most reliable producers of lovely, intense, blackcurranty *Cabernet* in *Bendigo*. *Chardonnays* are big and old-fashioned and *Pinot Noirs* are improving. ☆☆☆☆☆ **1996 Cabernet Sauvignon, Bendigo $$$**

🍷 **Bandol** [bon-dohl] (*Provence*, France) *Mourvèdre*-influenced plummy, herby reds, and rich whites. ***Ch. de Pibarnon; Dom. Tempier;*** **Ch. Vannières.**

🍷 **Villa Banfi** [veel-lah ban-fee] (*Tuscany*, Italy) US-owned producer with improving *Brunello* and *Vini da Tavola*. ☆☆☆☆☆ **1995 Summus Toscana $$$**

🍷 **Bannockburn** (*Geelong*, Australia) Gary Farr uses his experience of making wines at *Dom. Dujac* in *Burgundy* to produce concentrated, *Pinot Noir* and Shiraz at home. The *Chardonnay* is also pretty good, if slightly big for its boots, and the *Bordeaux* blends are impressive too. ☆☆☆☆ **1997 Shiraz $$**

🍷 **Banyuls** [bon-yools] (*Provence*, France) France's answer to *tawny port*. Fortified, *Grenache*-based, *Vin Doux Naturel*, ranging from off-dry to lusciously sweet. The *Rancio* style is rather more like *Madeira*. **L'Etoile; Dom. du Mas Blanc; *Clos de Paulilles*; Dom. de la Rectorie; Dom. la Tour Vieille; Vial Magnères.**

🍷 **Antonio Barbadillo** [bahr-bah-deel-yoh] (*Jerez*, Spain) Great producer of *Fino* and *Manzanilla*. ☆☆☆☆ **Reliquia $$**

🍷 **Barbaresco** [bahr-bah-ress-koh] (*Piedmont*, Italy) *DOCG Nebbiolo* red, with spicy fruit, depth, and complexity. Approachable earlier (three to five years) than neighboring *Barolo* but, in the right hands – and in the best vineyards – potentially of almost as high a quality. 82 **85 88** 89 90 **93 94** 95 96 97 . ***Ceretto; Gaja; di Gresy;*** **Castello di Neive; Paitin; *Alfredo Prunotto*.**

🍇 **Barbera** [Bar-Beh-Rah] (*Piedmont*, Italy) Grape making fruity, spicy, characterful wine (e.g. B. d'Alba and B. d'Asti), with a flavor reminiscent of cheesecake with raisins. Now in *California*, *Mexico* and (at *Brown Bros.*) Australia.

🍷 **René Barbier** [Ren-nay Bah-Bee-Yay] (*Penedès*, Spain) Dynamic producer of commercial wines and an impressive *Priorato*. ☆☆☆☆ **1994 Priorato Clos Mogador $$**

🍷 **Barca Velha** [bahr-kah vayl-yah] (*Douro*, Portugal) Portugal's most famous red, made from port varieties by *Ferreira*. It's tough stuff, but plummy enough to be worth keeping – and paying for. Also look out for Reserva Especial released in more difficult years. ☆☆☆☆☆ **1983 Ferreirinha $$$$**

🍷 **Bardolino** [bar-doh-lee-noh] (*Veneto*, Italy) Cherryish red. Can be dull – or fruity alternatives to *Beaujolais*. Also comes as Chiaretto Rosé. Best young unless from an exceptional producer. ***Boscaini; Fabiano Masi;*** **Portalupi.**

Gilles Barge [bahzh] (*Rhône*, France) Son of Pierre who won an international reputation for his fine, classic *Côte Rôtie*. Gilles, who now runs the estate, has also shown his skill with *St. Joseph*.

Guy de Barjac [gee dur bar-jak] (*Rhône*, France) A master of the *Syrah* grape, producing some of the best – and most stylish – *Cornas* around.

Barolo [bah-ROH-loh] (*Piedmont*, Italy) Noble *Nebbiolo* reds with extraordinary berryish, floral and spicy flavours. Old-fashioned versions are dry and tannic when young but, from a good producer and year, can develop extraordinary complexity. Modern versions are oakier and more accessible.82 **85 88** 89 90 **93** 95 96 97 ***Elio Altare; Batasiolo; Borgogno; Chiarlo; Clerico; Aldo Conterno; Giacomo Conterno; Conterno Fantino; Fontanafredda; Gaja; Bartolo Mascarello; Giuseppe Mascarello; Pio Cesare; Pira; Prunotto; Ratti; Sandrone; Scavino; Vietti;*** **Roberto Voerzio.**

Baron de Ley [Bah-Rohn Duh Lay] (*Rioja*, Spain) Small *Rioja* estate whose wines, partly aged in French oak, can be worth waiting for. ☆☆☆☆ **1995 Rioja Reserva $$**

Barossa Valley [bah-ros suh] (Australia) Big, warm region north-east of Adelaide which is famous for traditional, old vine *Shiraz* and *Grenache, 'ports'* and *Rieslings* which age to oily richness. *Chardonnay* and *Cabernet* make subtler, classier wines along with *Riesling* in the higher altitude vineyards of the *Eden Valley* and *Adelaide Hills*. ***Barossa Valley Estate; Basedow; Bethany; E&E; Wolf Blass; Grant Burge; Hardy's; Henschke; Krondorf; Peter Lehmann; Melton; Orlando; Penfolds; Rockford; Turkey Flat; Yalumba.***

Barossa Valley Estate (*Barossa Valley*, Australia) Top end of BRL *Hardy* with good old-vine *Barossa* reds. ☆☆☆☆☆ **1996 Ebeneezer Shiraz $$$**

Daniel Barraud [Bah-roh] (*Burgundy*, France) Dynamic producer of single-*cuvée Pouilly-Fuissé*. ☆☆☆☆ **1997 Pouilly Fuissé la Verchère $$$**

Barrique [ba-reek] (France) French barrel, particularly in *Bordeaux*, holding 225 litres. Term used in Italy to denote (new) barrel aging.

Jim Barry (*Clare Valley*, Australia) Producer of the dazzling, spicy, mulberryish Armagh *Shiraz* and great, floral Watervale Riesling. ☆☆☆☆☆ **1998 Watervale Riesling $$$;** ☆☆☆☆ **1996 McCrae Wood Shiraz $$$**

Barsac [bahr-sak] (*Bordeaux*, France) *AC* neighbor of *Sauternes* with similar, though not quite so rich, *Sauvignon/Sémillon* dessert wines. **71 75** 76 **78 79 80** 81 82 83 85 86 88 89 90 95 97 98 ***Ch. Broustet; Ch. Climens; Ch. Coutet; Ch. Doisy-Dubroca; Ch. Doisy-Daëne; Ch. Nairac.***

Ghislaine Barthod-Noëllat [jee-lenn Bar-Toh Noh-Way-Lah] (*Burgundy*, France) Top class Chambolle-Musigny estate. ☆☆☆☆☆ **1996 Chambolle-Musigny Beaux Bruns $$$**

De Bartoli [day bahr-toh-lee] (*Sicily*, Italy) *Marsala* for drinking rather than cooking from a revolutionary producer who has voluntarily removed his Vecchio Samperi from the DSOC system. ☆☆☆☆ **Vecchio Samperi $$**

Barton & Guestier [bahr-ton ay geht-tee-yay] (*Bordeaux*, France) Highly commercial *Bordeaux* shipper. ☆☆☆ **1994 Ch. Magnol $$**

Barwang [bahr-wang] (*New South Wales*, Australia) *McWilliams* label for cool-climate wines produced in newly-planted vineyards near Young in eastern *New South Wales*. ☆☆☆☆ **1995 Cabernet Sauvignon $$**

Basedow [baz-zeh-dohs] (South Australia) Producer of big, concentrated *Shiraz* and *Cabernet* and ultra-rich *Semillon* and *Chardonnays*. ☆☆☆☆ **1997 Barossa Shiraz $$**

Basilicata [bah-see-lee-kah-tah] (Italy) Southern wine region chiefly known for *Aglianico del Vulture* and improving *IGT wines*. **Basilium.**

🍷 **Bass Philip** (*Victoria*, Australia) Fanatical South *Gippsland* pioneer Phillip Jones makes great *Burgundy*-like *Pinot Noir.* ☆☆☆☆ **1996 Premium Pinot Noir $$$**

🍷 **Von Bassermann-Jordan** [fon bas-suhr-man johr-dun] (*Pfalz*, Germany) A traditional producer often using the fruit of its brilliant vineyards to produce *Trocken Rieslings* with more ripeness than is often to be found in this style. ☆☆☆☆ **1997 Riesling Auslese Pfalz Ruppertsberger Reiterpfad $$$**

Bastardo [bas-tahr-doh] (Portugal) Red grape traditionally used widely in *port* and previously in *Madeira*, where there are a few wonderful old bottles still to be found. Shakespeare refers to a wine called 'Brown Bastard'.

🍷 **Ch. Bastor-Lamontagne** [bas-tohr-lam-mon-tañ] (*Sauternes*, *Bordeaux*, France) Remarkably reliable classy *Sauternes*; inexpensive alternative to the big-name properties. 85 86 88 89 90 **94** 95 96 97 98

🍷 **Ch. Batailley** [bat-tih-yay] (*Pauillac 5ème Cru Classé, Bordeaux*, France) Approachable, quite modern tobacco-cassis-cedar *claret* with more class than its price might lead one to expect. 70 78 79 **82 83 85 86** 87 **88** 89 90 94 **95** 96 **97** 98

🍷 **Bâtard-Montrachet** [bat-tahr mon-rah-shay] (*Burgundy*, France) Biscuity-rich white *Grand Cru* shared between *Chassagne-* and *Puligny-Montrachet*. Often very fine; always expensive. **Cailot; Colin-Deleger; Drouhin; *J-N Gagnard; Vincent Leflaive; Pierre Morey; Michel Niellon; Ramonet; Sauzet.***

🍷 **Batasiolo** [bay-nee dee bat-tah-see-oh-loh] (*Piedmont*, Italy) Producer of top-class *Barolo*, impressive cherryish *Dolcetto*, fresh *Moscato*, intense berry-ish *Brachetto* and a subtle *Chardonnay.* ☆☆☆☆☆ **1993 Barolo Bofani $$$**

🍷 **Dom. des Baumard** [day boh-marh] (*Loire*, France) Producer of great *Quarts de Chaume* and *Savennières.* ☆☆☆☆☆ **1995 Clos du Papillon $$$$**

🍷 **Vin de Pays des Baux-en-Provence** [koh-toh day boh on pro-vonss] (*Provence*, France) Inexpensive fruity reds, whites and rosés, plus the cult *Dom. de Trévallon.* ☆☆☆☆ **1995 Chapelle de Romanin $$**

🍷 **Bava** [bah-vah] (*Piedmont*, Italy) Innovative producer making good *Moscato Barbera,* reviving indigenous grapes such as the rarely grown raspberryish *Ruche* and even producing a rather wonderful curious herb-infused *Nebbiolo.* ☆☆☆☆ **1994 Stradivario Barbera d'Asti Superiore $$**

🍷 **Béarn** [bay-ar'n] (*South West*, France) Highly traditional and often dull region. Lapeyre is the name to look out for.

🍷 **Ch. Beau-Séjour (-Bécot)** [boh-say-zhoor bay-koh] (*St. Emilion Grand Cru Classé, Bordeaux*, France) Reinstated in 1996 after a decade of demotion. Now making fairly priced, greatly improved wine. **82** 83 85 **86** 88 89 90 92 93 94 95 96 97 98

🍷 **Ch. Beau-Site** [boh-seet] (*St. Estèphe Cru Bourgeois, Bordeaux*, France) Benchmark *St. Estèphe* in the same stable as *Ch. Batailley.* 78 **82** 83 85 **86 88** 89 90 92 93 94 95 96 97 98

Ch. de Beaucastel [boh-kas-tel] (*Rhône*, France) The top *Châteauneuf-du-Pape* estate, using organic methods to produce richly gamey (for some, *too* gamey) long-lived, spicy reds, and rare but fine creamy-spicy whites. ☆☆☆☆☆ **1995 Châteauneuf-du-Pape Homage à Jacques Perrin $$$$**

Beaujolais [boh-zhuh-lay] (*Burgundy*, France) Light fruity *Gamay* red. Good chilled and for early drinking. *Beaujolais-Villages* is better, and the 10 *Crus* better still. With age, these can taste like (fairly ordinary) *Burgundy from the Côte d'Or*. Beaujolais Blanc made from *Chardonnay* is now mostly sold as *St. Véran*. See *Crus: Morgon; Chénas; Brouilly; Côte de Brouilly; Juliénas; Fleurie; Regnié; St. Amour; Chiroubles; Moulin-à-Vent.*

Beaujolais-Villages (*Burgundy*, France) From the north of the region, fuller-flavored and more alcoholic than plain *Beaujolais*, though not necessarily from one of the named *Cru* villages. ***Duboeuf*; Pivot; Large.**

Beaulieu Vineyard [bohl-yoo] (*Napa Valley*, California) Historic winery that has suffered at the hands of its multinational owners. The Georges de Latour Private Reserve *Cabernet* are impressive and keep well, and recent vintages of *Beautour* have improved. Other wines are ordinary. ☆☆☆☆ **1994 Cabernet Sauvignon Napa Valley Georges de Latour Private Reserve $$**

Beaumes de Venise [bohm duh vuh-neez] (*Rhône*, France) *Côtes du Rhône* village producing spicy dry reds and sweet, grapey, fortified *Vin Doux Naturel* from the *Muscat*. **Dom. des Bernardins; *Chapoutier; Dom de Coyeux.***

Ch. Beaumont [boh-mon] (*Haut-Médoc Cru Bourgeois, Bordeaux*, France) Impressive estate back on form since 1998. **82** 85 **86** 88 **89 90 93** 95 96 98

Beaune [bohn] (*Burgundy*, France) Large commune that gives its name to the *Côte de Beaune* and produces soft, raspberry-and-rose-petal *Pinot Noir*. As in *Nuits-St.-Georges*, there are plenty of *Premier Crus*, but no *Grands Crus*. The walled city is the site of the famous *Hospices* charity auction. Reds are best from *Michel Prunier*, *Louis Jadot*, *Bouchard Père et Fils* (since 1996), Ch. de Chorey; Albert Morot and *Joseph Drouhin* who also make a very successful example of the ultra-rare white.

Ch. Beauregard [boh-ruh-gahr] (*Pomerol*, *Bordeaux*, France) Estate that has recently begun to follow the trend towards juicy oaky *Pomerol*. **82** 85 **86** 88 89 90 **92** 93 **94** 95 96 97 98

Ch. Beauséjour-Duffau-Lagarosse [boh-say-zhoor doo-foh lag-gahr-ros] (*St. Emilion Premier Grand Cru Classé, Bordeaux*, France) Traditional tough, *tannic* St. *Emilion*. 82 93 85 86 88 89 90 93 94 95 96 98

Beaux Frères [boh frair] (*Oregon*, US) Pinot Noir winery launched by wine guru Robert Parker and his brother-in-law (hence the name).

Graham Beck (*Robertson*, South Africa) Producer of some of South Africa's best sparkling wines. Still wines are good too. ☆☆☆☆ **1997 Shiraz $$**

Beerenauslese [behr-ren-ows-lay-zuh] (Austria/Germany) Sweet wines from selected, ripe grapes (Beeren), hopefully affected by *botrytis*.

Ch. de Bel-Air [Bel-Ehr] (*Lalande-de-Pomerol*, *Bordeaux*, France) Impressive property making wines to make some *Pomerols* blush. **82 85** 86 88 **89** 90 92 93 **94** 95 96 97 98

Ch. Bel-Orme-Tronquoy-de-Lalande [bel-orm-tron-kwah-duh-la-lond] (*Haut-Médoc Cru Bourgeois, Bordeaux*, France) Highly old-fashioned estate and wines. Under the same ownership (and philosophy) as *Rauzan Gassies*.

Ch. Belair [bel-lehr] (*St. Emilion Premier Grand Cru Classé, Bordeaux*, France) Classy, delicate, long-lived, *St. Emilion* with a very impressive 1998. Compare and contraast with more "modern" neighbor Ausone. Don't confuse with the Lalande-de-Pomerol Ch. de Bel-Air – or any of the countless lesser Belairs scattered around Bordeaux). 78 **79 82 83 85 86** 88 89 90 92 93 94 95 96 97 98

Bellavista (*Lombardy*, Italy) Commercial Franciacorta producers of classy sparkling and still wines. ☆☆☆☆ **1993 Franciacorta Brut $$$**

Albert Belle [bel] (*Rhône*, France) An estate that has recently begun to bottle its own excellent red and – oaky – white Hermitage.

Bellet [bel-lay] (*Provence*, France) Tiny *AC* behind Nice producing fairly good red, white and rosé from local grapes including the Rolle, the *Braquet* and the *Folle Noir.* Pricey and rarely seen outside France. **Ch. de Bellet.**

Bellingham (South Africa) Improving, highly commercial winery. ☆☆☆☆ **1996 Premium Pinotage $$**

Bendigo [ben-dig-goh] (*Victoria*, Australia) Warm region producing big-boned, long-lasting reds with intense berry fruit. ***Balgownie;*** **Heathcote; *Jasper Hill; Mount Ida; Passing Clouds;* Water Wheel.**

Benziger [ben-zig-ger] (*Sonoma*, California) Classy wines at the top end of the *Glen Ellen* range. ☆☆☆☆ **1996 Chardonnay Carneros Yamakawa Vineyards Reserve $$**

Berberana [behr-behr-rah nah] (*Rioja*, Spain) Increasingly dynamic producer of a range of fruitier young-drinking styles, as well as the improving Carta de Plata and Carta de Oro and Lagunilla *Riojas*, plus sparkling Marquès de Monistrol and the excellent Marquès de Griñon range. ☆☆☆☆ **1989 Rioja Reserva $$$;** ☆☆☆☆ **1997 "Dragon" Tempranillo $$**

Bercher [behr-kehr] (*Baden*, Germany) Dynamic estate, producing impressive modern Burgundy-style reds and whites.

Bereich [beh-ri-kh] (Germany) Vineyard area, subdivision of an *anbaugebiet*. On its own indicates *QbA* wine, e.g. *Niersteiner.* Finer wines are followed by the name of a (smaller) *grosslage*, better ones by that of an individual vineyard.

Bergerac [behr-jur-rak] (France) Traditionally Bordeaux's 'lesser' neighbor but possibly soon to be assimilated into that regional *appellation*. The wines, though often pretty mediocre, can still be better value than basic red or white *Bordeaux*, while the *Monbazillac* can outclass basic *Sauternes*. **Ch. Belingard; Court-les-Muts; des Eyssards; Grinou; la Jaubertie; Tour des Gendres.**

Bergkelder [berg-kel-dur] (*Cape*, South Africa) Huge firm that still matures and bottles wines for *Cape* estates like *Meerlust,* which, like their counterparts in *Bordeaux*, really ought to bottle their own. The Bergkelder's own *Stellenryck* wines are worth watching out for; the cheaper Fleur du Cap range is likeable enough and *Pongracz* sparkling wine is first class. ☆☆☆☆ **1998 Two Oceans Cabernet Merlot $$**

Beringer Vineyards [ber-rin-jer] (*Napa Valley,* California) Big Swiss-owned producer, increasingly notable for its single-vineyard *Cabernet Sauvignons* (Knights Valley, *Howell Mountain, Spring Mountain* and Private Reserve), *Cabernet Francs* and *Merlots*, Burgundy-like *Chardonnays* and *late harvest* wines. ☆☆☆☆☆ **1995 Merlot Howell Mountain Bancroft Ranch $$$**

Bernkastel [berhrn-kah-stel] (*Mosel*, Germany) Town and area on the *Mittelmosel* and source of some of the finest *Riesling* (like the famous Bernkasteler Doktor), and a lake of poor-quality stuff. QbA/Kab/Spät: **85** 86 **88 89 90** 91 **92 93 94** 95 96 97 98 Aus/Beeren/Tba: **83 85** 88 89 90 91 **92** 93 **94** 95 96 97 ***Dr Loosen; JJ Prum; Von Kesselstadt; Wegeler Deinhard.***

Bernardus (*Monterey*, California) Producer of rich, unsubtle, unashamedly New World-style *Sauvignon Blanc, Chardonnay* and *Pinot Noir.* ☆☆☆☆ **Pinot Noir Santa Maria Valley Bien Nacido Vineyard $$**

Berri Renmano [ber-ree ren-mah-noh] (*Riverland*, Australia) The controlling force behind the giant *BRL Hardy*, with quality brands like *Thomas Hardy*, *Barossa Valley Estates, Château Reynella* and *Houghton*. Under its own name, it is better known for inexpensive reds and whites.

🍷 **Dom Bertagna** [behr-tan-ya] (*Vougeot*, France) Recently improved estate notable for offering the rare, (relatively) affordable *Premier Cru Vougeot* alongside its own version of the easier-to-find *Clos de Vougeot Grand Cru*. ☆☆☆☆ **1996 Clos de Vougeot Bertagna $$$**

🍷 **Bertani** [behr-tah-nee] (*Veneto*, Italy) Producer of good *Valpolicella*. ☆☆☆☆ **1995 Recioto della Valpolicella Amarone Classico Superiore $$**

🍷 **Best's Great Western** (*Victoria*, Australia) Under-appreciated winery in *Great Western* making delicious concentrated *Shiraz* from old vines, attractive *Cabernet*, *Dolcetto*, *Pinot Noir*, *Colombard* and rich *Chardonnay* and *Riesling*. ☆☆☆☆☆ **1996 Great Western Pinot Noir $$$**

🍷 **Bethany** [beth-than-nee] (*Barossa Valley*, Australia) Impressive small producer of knockout *Shiraz*. ☆☆☆☆☆ **1998 Pressings Grenache $$$**

🍷 **Dom. Henri Beurdin** [bur-dan] (*Loire*, France) White and rosé from *Reuilly*. ☆☆☆☆ **1998 Reuilly Blanc $$**

🍷 **Ch. Beychevelle** [bay-shur-vel] (*St. Julien 4ème Cru Classé, Bordeaux*, France) A fourth growth that achieves the typical cigar-box character of *St. Julien* but fails to excite. The *second label Amiral de Beychevelle* can be a worthwhile buy. 82 83 85 **86** 88 89 90 **94** 95 96 97 98 ☆☆☆☆☆ **1990 $$$$**

🍷 **Léon Beyer** [bay-ur] (*Alsace*, France) Serious producer of lean long-lived wines. ☆☆☆☆ **1990 Gewurztraminer Comtes d'Eguisheim $$**

🍷 **Beyerskloof** [bay-yurs-kloof] (*Stellenbosch*, South Africa) Newish venture, with Beyers Truter (of *Kanonkop*) on its way to producing South Africa's top *Cabernet* and *Stellenbosch Pinotage*. ☆☆☆☆ **1996 Cabernet $$**

🍷 **Bianco di Custoza** [bee-yan-koh dee koos-toh-zah] (*Veneto*, Italy) Widely exported *DOC*. A reliable, crisp, light white from a blend of grapes. A better-value alternative to most basic *Soave*. **Gorgo; Portalupi; *Tedeschi*; le Vigne di San Pietro; *Zenato*.**

🍷 **Maison Albert Bichot** [bee-shoh] (*Burgundy*, France) Big *négoçiant* with excellent *Chablis* and *Vosne-Romanée*, plus adequate wines sold under a plethora of other labels. ☆☆☆☆ **1997 Chablis Grand Cru Vaudésir $$$**

🍷 **Biddenden** [bid-den-den] (Kent, England) Producer showing impressive mastery of the peachy *Ortega*. ☆☆☆ **1997 Ortega $**

🍷 **Bienvenue-Batard-Montrachet** [bee-yen-veh-noo bat-tahr mon ra-rhay] (*Burgundy*, France) Fine white *Burgundy* vineyard with potentially gorgeous *biscuity* wines. **Carillon; Dom Leflaive; Sauzet.**

🍷 **Weingut Josef Biffar** [bif-fah] (*Pfalz*, Germany). *Deidesheim* estate that is on a roll at the moment with its richly spicy wines. ☆☆☆☆ **1997 Riesling Spätlese Pfalz Deidesheimer Kieselberg $$**

🍷 **Billecart-Salmon** [beel-kahr sal-mon] (*Champagne*, France) Producer of the stylish winners (the 1959 and 1961 vintages) of the Champagne of the Millennium competition held in Stockholm in 1999 at which I was a taster. Possibly the best all-rounder for quality and value, and certainly the one *Champagne* house whose subtle but decidedly agable *non-vintage*, *vintage* and rosé I buy without hesitation. Superlative. Buy the 1990 or 1991 vintages if you can find them. ☆☆☆☆☆ **1991 Cuvée Elisabeth Salmon Brut $$$$**

Billiot [bil-lee-yoh] (*Champagne*, France) Impressive small producer with classy rich sparkling wine. ☆☆☆☆ **Cuvée de Reserve NV $$$**

Bingen [bing-urn] (*Rheinhessen*, Germany) Village giving its name to a *Rheinhessen bereich* that includes a number of well-known *grosslage*. QbA/Kab/Spät: **85** 86 **88 89 90** 91 **92 93** 94 95 96 97 98 Aus/Beeren/Tba: **83 85** 88 89 90 91 92 **93 94** 95 96 97

Binissalem [bin-nee-sah-lem] (*Mallorca*, Spain) The holiday island is proud of its demarcated region, though why, it's hard to say. José Ferrer's and Jaime Mesquida's wines are the best of the bunch.

Biondi-Santi [bee-yon-dee san-tee] (*Tuscany*, Italy) Big-name estate making absurdly expensive and often disappointing *Brunello di Montalcino* that can be bought – after a period of vertical storage at room temperature – at the local trattoria. ☆☆☆☆ **1993 Brunello Di Montalcino $$$$**

Biscuity Flavor of savory crackers often associated with the *Chardonnay* grape, particularly in *Champagne* and top-class mature *Burgundy*, or with the yeast that fermented the wine.

Bitouzet-Prieur [bee-too-zay pree-yur] (*Burgundy*, France) If you like classic *Meursault*, built to last rather than seduce instantly with ripe fruit and oak, try this estate's 1995 *Meursault Perrières*. The *Volnays* are good too.

Dom. Simon Bize [beez] (*Burgundy*, France) Intense, long-lived and good-value wines produced in *Savigny-lès-Beaune*. ☆☆☆☆ **1995 Savigny-lès-Beaune les Vergelesses $$$**

Blaauwklippen [blow-klip-pen] (*Stellenbosch*, South Africa) Large estate, veering between commercial and top quality. The *Cabernet* and *Zinfandel* are the strong cards. ☆☆☆ **1995 Zinfandel $$**

Blagny [blan-yee] (*Burgundy*, France) Tiny source of unsubtle red (sold as Blagny) and potentially top-class white (sold as *Meursault, Puligny-Montrachet*, Blagny, Hameau de Blagny or la Pièce sous le Bois). Red: 83 **85** 86 **88 89 90** 92 95 96 97 ***Ampeau; Chavy-Chouet; Jobard; Thierry Matrot.***

Blain-Gagnard [blan gan-yahr] (*Burgundy*, France) Excellent producer of creamy modern *Chassagne-Montrachet*. ☆☆☆☆ **1997 Criots-Batard-Montrachet $$$$**

Blanc de Blancs [blon dur blon] A white wine, made from white grapes – hardly worth mentioning except in the case of *Champagne*, where *Pinot Noir*, a black grape, usually makes up 30–70 per cent of the blend. In this case, Blanc de Blancs is pure *Chardonnay*.

Blanc de Noirs [blon dur nwahrr] A white (or frequently very slightly pink-tinged wine) made from red grapes by taking off the free-run juice, before pressing to minimize the uptake of red pigments from the skin. **Paul Bara; Duval-Leroy (Fleur de Champagne); Egly-Ouiriet.**

Paul Blanck [blank] (*Alsace*, France) Top-class *Alsace domaine*, specializing in single *Cru* wines. ☆☆☆☆ **1995 Riesling Schlossberg $$$**

Blandy's [blan-deez] (*Madeira*, Portugal) Brand owned by the Madeira Wine Company and named after the sailor who began the production of fortified wine here. Brilliant old wines. ☆☆☆☆ **5 Year Old Malmsey $$**

Blanquette de Limoux [blon ket dur lee-moo] (*Midi*, France) *Méthode Champenoise* sparkling wine, which, when good, is appley and clean. Best when made with a generous dose of *Chardonnay*, as the local *Mauzac* tends to give it an earthy flavor with age. ☆☆☆☆ **Domaine de l'Aigle $$**

Wolf Blass (*Barossa Valley*, Australia) German immigrant who prides himself on producing 'sexy' (his term) reds and whites, by blending wines from different regions of *South Australia* and allowing them plentiful contact with new oak. ☆☆☆☆ **1996 President's Selection Cabernet Sauvignon $$$**

Blauburgunder [blow-boor-goon-durh] (Austria) The name the Austrians give their light, often sharp, *Pinot Noir.*

Blauer Portugieser [blow-urh por-too-gay-suhr] (Germany) Red grape used in Germany and Austria to make light, pale wine.

Blaufrankisch [blow-fran-kish] (Austria) Berryish grape used to make wines that compete with the red wines of the Loire.

Bocksbeutel [box-boy-tuhl] (*Franken*, Germany) The famous flask-shaped bottle of *Franken*, adopted by the makers of *Mateus* Rosé.

Bodega [bod-day-gah] (Spain) Winery or wine cellar; producer.

Bodegas y Bebidas [bod-day-gas ee beh-bee-das] (Spain) One of Spain's most dynamic wine companies, and maker of *Campo Viejo*.

Body Usually used as 'full-bodied', meaning a wine with mouth-filling flavors and probably a fairly high alcohol content.

Jean-Marc Boillot [bwah-yoh] (*Burgundy*, France) Small *Pommard domaine* run by the son of the winemaker at *Olivier Leflaive* with good examples from neighboring villages. ☆☆☆☆☆ **1996 Pommard Rugiens $$$**

Jean-Claude Boisset [bwah-say] (*Burgundy*, France) Dynamic *négoçiant* which now owns a long list of Burgundy *négoçiants*, including the excellent *Jaffelin* and the improved *Bouchard Aîné*. Boisset also makes passable wines in *Languedoc-Roussillon*.

Boisson-Vadot [bwah-son va-doh] (*Burgundy*, France) Classy, small *Meursault domaine*. ☆☆☆☆☆ **1992 Meursault Genevrières $$$$**

Bolgheri [bol-geh-ree] (*Tuscany*, Italy) The region in which are produced Italian superstars such as *Antinori's* Sassicaia and Ornellaia. **le Macchiole.**

Bolla [bol-lah] (*Veneto*, Italy) Producer of plentiful, adequate *Valpolicella* and *Soave*, and of smaller quantities of impressive single vineyard wines like its Jago and Creso. ☆☆☆☆ **1990 Amarone Classico della Valpolicella $$$**

Bollinger [bol-an-jay] (*Champagne*, France) Great family-owned firm at *Ay*, whose wines need age. The luscious and rare *Vieilles Vignes* is made from pre-*phylloxera* vines, while the nutty *RD* was the first late-disgorged *Champagne* to hit the market. ☆☆☆☆ **1990 Grande Année $$$$**

Bommes [bom] (*Bordeaux*, France) *Sauternes commune* and village containing several *Premiers Crus* such as *la Tour Blanche, Lafaurie-Peyraguey, Rabaud-Promis* and *Rayne Vigneau*. 70 **71** **75** 76 83 85 86 88 89 90 95 96 97 98

Ch. le Bon-Pasteur [bon-pas-stuhr] (*Pomerol, Bordeaux*, France) The impressive private estate of *Michel Rolland*, who acts as consultant – and helps to make fruit-driven wines – for half his neighbors, as well as producers in almost every other wine-growing region in the universe. 76 **82** 83 **85** **86** 87 **88** 89 90 92 93 94 95 96 97 98

Domaine de la Bongran [bon-grah] See *Jean Thevenet*.

Henri Bonneau [bon-noh] (*Rhône*, France) *Châteauneuf-du-Pape* producer with two special *cuvées* – 'Marie Beurrier' and 'des Celestins' – and a cult following. ☆☆☆☆☆ **1988 Cuvée Marie Beurrier $$$$**

Dom. Bonneau du Martray [bon-noh doo mahr-tray] (*Burgundy*, France) Largest grower of *Corton-Charlemagne* and impressive producer thereof. Also makes a classy red *Grand Cru Corton*. ☆☆☆☆☆ **1996 Corton $$$$**

Bonnes Mares [bon-mahr] (*Burgundy*, France) Rich *Morey St. Denis Grand Cru*. **Dom d'Auvenay; Bouchard Père; Clair Daü; Drouhin; Dujac; Fougeray de Beauclair; Groffier; Jadot; Laurent; Roumier; de Vogüé.**

Ch. Bonnet [bon-nay] (*Bordeaux*, France) Top-quality *Entre-Deux-Mers* château whose wines are made by *Jacques Lurton*.

F. Bonnet [bon-nay] (*Champagne*, France) Reliable producer under whose own and customers' names Winemaker, Daniel Thibault also makes *Charles Heidsieck*. ☆☆☆☆☆ **1990 Champagne Brut $$$**

Bonnezeaux [bonn-zoh] (*Loire*, France) Within the *Coteaux du Layon*, this is one of the world's greatest sweet wine producing areas, though the wines have often tended to be spoiled by heavy-handedness with sulfur dioxide. **76** 83 **85** 86 **88 89** 90 **93**94 95 96 97 **Ch. de Fesles; Dom Godineau; René Renou; Ch. la Varière.**

Bonny Doon Vineyard (*Santa Cruz*, California) Randall Grahm, sorcerer's apprentice, and original '*Rhône* Ranger' also has an evident affection for unfashionable French and Italian varieties, which he uses for characterful red, dry and *late harvest* whites. The sheep-like Californian wine industry needs more mavericks like Grahm. ☆☆☆☆☆ **1997 Malvasia $$**

Borba [Bohr-Bah] (*Alentejo*, Portugal) See *Alentejo*.

Bordeaux [bor-doh] (France) Largest (supposedly) quality wine region in France, producing reds, rosés and deep pink *Clairets* from *Cabernet Sauvignon, Cabernet Franc, Petit Verdot* and *Merlot*, and dry and sweet whites from (principally) blends of *Sémillon* and *Sauvignon*. *Bordeaux Supérieur* denotes (relatively) riper grapes. The rare dry whites from regions like the *Médoc* and *Sauternes* are (for no good reason) sold as *Bordeaux Blanc*, so even the efforts by *Châteaux d'Yquem, Margaux*, and *Lynch-Bages* are sold under the same label as basic supermarket white. See *Graves, Médoc, Pomerol, St. Emilion* etc.

Borgogno [baw-gon-yoh] (*Piedmont*, Italy) Resolutely old-fashioned *Barolo* producer whose initially tough wines can develop a sweet tobaccoey richness with age. ☆☆☆☆ **1985 Barolo $$$$**

De Bortoli [baw-tol-lee] (*Riverina*, Australia) Fast-developing firm (following its move into the *Yarra Valley*) which startled the world by making a *botrytized*, peachy, honeyed 'Noble One' *Semillon* in the unfashionable *Riverina* which (undeservingly) beats *Ch. d'Yquem* in blind tastings. ☆☆☆☆ **1996 Yarra Valley Shiraz $$**

Bodega Luigi Bosca [bos-kah] (*Mendoza*, Argentina) Top-class producer with particularly good *Sauvignons* and *Cabernets*. ☆☆☆☆ **1996 Malbec $$**

Boscaini [bos-kah-yee-nee] (*Veneto*, Italy) Innovative producer linked to *Masi* and making better-than-average *Valpolicella* and *Soave*. ☆☆☆☆ **1993 Ca de Loi Amarone Della Valpolicella Classico $$$**

Boscarelli [bos-kah-reh-lee] (*Tuscany*, Italy) Star producer of *Vino Nobile de Montepulciano*. ☆☆☆☆☆ **1995 Vigna del Nocio Poderi $$$**

Boschendal Estate [bosh-shen-dahl] (*Cape*, South Africa) Modern winery producing some of the *Cape's* best sparkling wine and fast-improving still reds and whites. ☆☆☆☆ **1996 Shiraz $$**

Ch. le Boscq [bosk] (*St. Estèphe Cru Bourgeois, Bordeaux*, France) Improving property that excels in good vintages, but still tends to make tough wines in lesser ones.
82 83 85 86 87 88 **89** 90 92 **93** 95 96 98

Le Bosquet des Papes [bos-kay day pap] (*Rhône*, France) Serious *Châteauneuf-du-Pape* producer, making wines that last.

Botrytis [boh-tri-tiss] Botrytis cinerea, a fungal infection that attacks and shrivels grapes, evaporating their water and concentrating their sweetness. Vital to *Sauternes* and the finer German and Austrian sweet wines. See *Sauternes, Trockenbeerenauslese, Tokaji*.

Bott-Geyl [bott-gihl] (*Alsace*, France) Young producer, whose impressive *Grand Cru* wines suit those who like their *Alsace* big and rich. ☆☆☆☆ **1995 Gewurztraminer Sonnenglanz Vieilles Vignes $$**

Bottle-fermented Commonly found on the labels of US sparkling wines to indicate the *Méthode Champenoise*, and gaining wider currency. Beware, though – it can indicate inferior *'transfer method'* wines.

Bouchard Aîné [boo-shahrr day-nay] (*Burgundy*, France) For a long time unimpressive merchant, now taken over by *Boisset* and now (somewhat) improving under the winemaking control of the excellent Bernard Repolt.

Bouchard-Finlayson [boo-shard] (*Walker Bay*, South Africa) Burgundy-style joint-venture between Peter Finlayson and Paul Bouchard, formerly of *Bouchard Aîné* in France. ☆☆☆☆ **1997 Galpin Peak Pinot Noir $$**

Bouchard Père & Fils [boo-shahrr pehrr ay fees] (*Burgundy*, France) Traditional merchant with great vineyards. Bought in 1996 by the *Champagne* house of *Henriot*. The best wines are the *Beaunes*, especially the Beaune de l'Enfant Jésus, as well as the La Romanée from *Vosne-Romanée*. ☆☆☆☆ **1997 Nuits St Georges $$$**

Vin de Pays des Bouches du Rhône (*Midi*, France) dynamic region around Aix en Provence, focusing on Rhône and Bordeaux varieties.

Pascal Bouley [boo-lay] (*Burgundy*, France) Producer of good, if not always refined *Volnay*. ☆☆☆ **1996 Volnay $$$**

Bouquet Overall smell, often made up of several separate aromas. Used by Anglo-Saxon enthusiasts more often than by professionals.

Ch. Bourgneuf-Vayron [boor-nurf vay-roh] (*Pomerol, Bordeaux*, France) Fast-rising star with deliciously rich plummy *Merlot* fruit. **85 86** 88 **89** 90 92 95 96 98 ☆☆☆☆☆ **1990 $$$**

Bourgogne [boorr-goyñ] (*Burgundy*, France) French for *Burgundy*.

Bourgueil [boorr-goyy] (*Loire*, France) Red *AC* in the *Touraine*, producing crisp, grassy-blackcurranty, 100 per cent *Cabernet Franc* wines that can age well in good years like 1995. **Amirault; Boucard; *Caslot-Galbrun;* Cognard; Delaunay; *Druet*.**

Ch. Bouscassé [boo-ska-say] (*Madiran*, France) See *Ch. Montus*.

Ch. Bouscaut [boos-koh] (*Pessac-Léognan, Bordeaux*, France) Good, rather than great *Graves* property; better white than red.

J. Boutari [boo-tah-ree] (*Greece*) One of the most reliable names in Greece, producing good, traditional red wines in Nemea and Naoussa.

Bouvet-Ladubay [boo-vay lad-doo-bay] (*Loire*, France) Producer of good *Loire* sparkling wine and better *Saumur-Champigny* reds. ☆☆☆ **1995 Saumur Rubis Rouge $$$**

Bouvier [boo-vee-yay] (Austria) Characterless variety used to produce tasty but mostly simple *late harvest* wines.

Bouzeron [booz-rron] (*Burgundy*, France) *Côte Chalonnaise* village known for *Aligoté*. ☆☆☆☆☆ **1997 Aligoté Aubert de Villaine $$**

Bouzy Rouge [boo-zee roozh] (*Champagne*, France) Sideline of a black grape village: an often thin-bodied, rare and overpriced red wine which, despite what its producers may say, rarely ages. 89 90 94 ☆☆☆☆ **1990 Paul Bara $$$$**

Bowen Estate [boh-wen] (*Coonawarra*, Australia) An early *Coonawarra* pioneer proving that the region can be as good for *Shiraz* as for *Cabernet*. ☆☆☆☆ **1996 Shiraz $$$**

Domaines Boyar [boy-yahr] (*Bulgaria*) Privatized producers, especially in the *Suhindol* region, selling increasingly worthwhile 'Reserve' reds under the Lovico label. Other wines are less reliably recommendable. ☆☆☆☆ **1995 Oriachovitza Cabernet Sauvignon Reserve $$**

Ch. Boyd-Cantenac [boyd-kon-teh-nak] (*Margaux 3ème Cru Classé* , *Bordeaux*, France) A third growth generally performing at the level of a fifth – or less. 78 **82 83 85 86** 88 89 90 93 **94** 95 96 97 98

Brachetto d'Acqui [brah-KET-toh dak-wee] (*Piedmont*, Italy) Eccentric Muscatty red grape. Often *frizzante*. ***Banfi; Batasiolo;*** **Marenco.**

Ch. Branaire(-Ducru) [brah-nehr doo-kroo] (*St.-Julien 4ème Cru Classé*, *Bordeaux*, France) New owners are doing wonders for this estate. Red: **82** 83 85 86 87 88 89 90 91 92 93 **95 96 97 98** ☆☆☆☆ **1985 $$$$**

Brand's Laira [lay-rah] (*Coonawarra*, Australia) Traditional producer, much improved since its purchase by *McWilliams*. Delving into the world of *Pinot Noir* and sparkling *Grenache* rosé.

Ch. Brane-Cantenac [brahn kon teh-nak] (*Margaux 2ème Cru Classé*, *Bordeaux*, France) Perennial under-achieving *Margaux*, whose *second label*, the discouragingly named Ch. Notton, can be a worthwhile buy. 75 78 79 81 82 83 85 **86** 87 88 89 90 95 96 98 ☆☆☆ **1985 $$$$**

Braquet [brah-ket] (*Midi*, France) Grape variety used in *Bellet*.

Brauneberg [brow-nuh-behrg] (*Mosel*, Germany) Village best known in the UK for the *Juffer* vineyard. ☆☆☆☆☆ **1997 Riesling Auslese Gold Cap Brauneberger Juffer-Sonnenuhr Fritz Haag $$$$**

Brazil Large quantities of light-bodied wines are produced in a rainy region close to Puerto Allegre. The Palomas vineyard on the *Uruguayan* border has a state-of-the-art winery and a good climate but has yet to make exciting wine.

Breaky Bottom (Sussex, England) One of Britain's best, whose *Seyval Blanc* rivals dry wines made in the *Loire* from supposedly finer grapes.

Marc Bredif [bray-deef] (*Loire*, France) Big, and quite variable *Loire* producer, with still and sparkling wine, including some good *Vouvray*. ☆☆☆ **1997 Vouvray $$**

Breganze (*Veneto*, Italy) Little-known DOC for characterful reds and whites. Maculan is the star here. ☆☆☆☆ **1995 Breganze Torcolato Maculan $$$**

Ch. du Breuil [doo breuh-yee] (*Loire*, France) Source of good *Coteaux de Layon*, and relatively ordinary examples of other *appellations*. ☆☆☆☆ **1995 Coteaux de Layon, Beaulieu $$**

Weingut Georg Breuer [broy-yer] (*Rheingau*, Germany) Innovative producer with classy *Rieslings* and high-quality *Rülander*.

🍷 **Bricco Manzoni** [bree-koh man-tzoh-nee] (*Piedmont*, Italy) Non-*DOC* *oaky* red blend of *Nebbiolo* and *Barbera* grapes grown on vines which could produce *Barolo* from *Monforte* vineyards. A wine that is drinkable young. ☆☆☆☆☆ **1994 Barolo Rocche $$$**

🍷 **Bridgehampton** (*Long Island*, US) Producer of first class *Merlot* and *Chardonnay* to worry a Californian.

🍷 **Bridgewater Mill** (*Adelaide Hills*, Australia) More modest sister winery to the highly regarded *Petaluma*, using grapes from other sources as well as their own. ☆☆☆☆ **1998 Sauvignon Blanc $$**

🍷 **Peter Bright** Australian-born Peter Bright of the *JP Vinhos* winery produces top class Portuguese wines, including Tinta da Anfora and Quinta da Bacalhoa, plus a growing range in countries such as Spain, Italy and Chile, under the Bright Brothers label. ☆☆☆☆ **1998 Bright Brothers Barrel Aged Nero d'Avola $$**

🍷 **Bristol Cream** (*Jerez*, Spain) See *Harvey's*.

🍷 **Jean-Marc Brocard** [broh-kahrr] (*Burgundy*, France) Very classy *Chablis* producer with well-defined individual vineyard wines, also producing unusually good *Aligoté*. ☆☆☆☆☆ **1997 Chablis Vieilles Vignes Domaine Sainte Claire $$$**

🍷 **Brokenwood** (*Hunter Valley*, Australia) Long-established, source of great *Semillon*, *Shiraz* and even (unusually for the *Hunter Valley*) *Cabernet*. Look for the 'Cricket Pitch' bottlings. ☆☆☆☆ **1997 Rayner's Vineyard Shiraz $$**

🍷 **Brouilly** [broo-yee] (*Burgundy*, France) Largest of the ten *Beaujolais Crus* producing pure, fruity *Gamay*. **94 95 96** 97 98. ***Duboeuf***; **Cotton**; ***Sylvain Fessy***; **Laurent Martray; Michaud; Piron; Roland; Ruet; Ch. des Tours.**

🍷 **Ch. Broustet** [broo-stay] (*Barsac 2ème Cru Classé*, *Bordeaux*, France) Rich, quite old-fashioned, well-oaked *Barsac* second growth. 70 **71** 75 76 **83** 85 **86 88 89 90** 95 96 97 98

🍷 **Brown Brothers** (*Victoria*, Australia) Family-owned and *Victoria*-focused winery with a penchant for new wine regions and grapes. The wines are reliably good, though for excitement you should look to the *Shiraz* and the *Liqueur Muscat*. The *Orange Muscat* and *Flora* remains a delicious mouthful of liquid marmalade, the *Tarrango* is a good alternative to *Beaujolais* and the sparkling wine is a new success. ☆☆☆☆☆ **1996 Shiraz $$$**

🍷 **David Bruce** (*Santa Cruz*, California) Long established *Zinfandel* specialist whose wines can be tougher than they ought to be. The 1996 *Petite Sirah* is approachably attractive.

🍷 **Bruisyard Vineyard** [broos-syard] (*Suffolk*, England) High-quality vineyard. ☆☆☆ **1990 Müller-Thurgau $$**

🍷 **Le Brun de Neuville** [bruhn duh nuh-veel] (*Champagne*, France) Good little-known producer with classy *vintage* and excellent rosé, non-vintage and *Blanc de Blancs*. ☆☆☆☆ **Cuvée Selection Brut $$**

🍷 **Willi Bründlmayer** [broodl-mi-yurh] (Austria) Oaked *Chardonnay* and *Pinots* of every kind, *Grüner Veltliner* and even a fairish shot at *Cabernet*. ☆☆☆☆**1995 Gruner Veltliner Beerenauslese Kamptal Ried Loiser Berg $$$**

🍷 **Lucien & André Brunel** [broo-nel] (*Rhône*, France) The Brunels' 'Les Caillous' produces good, traditional, built-to-last *Châteauneuf-du-Pape*.

🍷 **Brunello di Montalcino** [broo-nell-oh dee mon-tahl-chee-noh] (*Tuscany*, Italy) Prestigious *DOCG* red from a *Sangiovese* clone. **78 79 81 82 85 88 90 93** 94 95 96 97 ***Altesino; Argiano; Villa Banfi; Barbi; Tenuta Caparzo***; **Costanti; Lambardi; Col d'Orcia; Poggio Antico; Talenti; Val di Suga.**

Brut [broot] Dry, particularly of *Champagne* and sparkling wines. Brut nature/sauvage/zéro are even drier, while '*Extra-Sec*' is perversely applied to (slightly) sweeter sparkling wine.

🍇 **Bual** [bwahl] (*Madeira*) Grape producing soft, nutty wine – wonderful with cheese. ***Blandy's; Cossart Gordon; Henriques & Henriques.***

🍷 **Buçaco Palace Hotel** [boo-sah-koh] (Portugal) Red and white wines made from grapes grown in *Bairrada* and *Dão*, which last forever but cannot be bought outside the Disneyesque hotel itself.

Bucelas [boo-sel-las] (Portugal) *DO* area near Lisbon, best known for its intensely coloured, aromatic, bone-dry white wines. **Caves Velhas.**

🍷 **Buena Vista** [bway-nah vihs-tah] (*Carneros*, California) One of the biggest estates in *Carneros*, this is an improving producer of California *Chardonnay*, *Pinot Noir* and *Cabernet*. Look out for Grand Reserve wines.

Bugey [boo-jay] (*Savoie*, France) *Savoie* district producing a variety of wines, including spicy white Roussette de Bugey, from the grape of that name.

🍷 **Reichsrat von Buhl** [rihk-srat fon bool] (*Pfalz*, Germany) One of the area's best estates, due partly to vineyards like the *Forster Jesuitengarten*. ☆☆☆☆ **1997 Forster Kirchenstuck Riesling Spätlese $$$**

🍷 **Buitenverwachting** [biht-turn-fur-vak-turng] (*Constantia*, South Africa) Enjoying a revival since the early 1980s, a show-piece organic *Constantia* winery making tasty organic whites. ☆☆☆☆ **1998 Sauvignon Blanc $$**

Bulgaria Developing slowly since the advent of privatization and *flying wine-makers*. Bulgaria's reputation still relies on its country wines and affordable *Cabernet Sauvignons* and *Merlots*. *Mavrud* is the traditional red variety and Lovico, *Rousse*, Iambol, *Suhindol* and Haskovo the names to look out for.

🍷 ***Bull's Blood*** (*Eger*, Hungary) The gutsy red wine, aka Egri Bikaver, which gave defenders the strength to fight off Turkish invaders, is mostly anaemic stuff now, but privatization has brought some improvement. ☆☆☆ **1996 Eger Bikaver Reserve Tibor Gal Gia. $$**

🍷 **Bernard Burgaud** [boor-goh] (*Rhône*, France) Serious producer of *Côte Rôtie*. ☆☆☆☆ **1995 Côte Rôtie $$$**

🍷 **Grant Burge** (*Barossa Valley*, Australia) Dynamic producer and – since 1993 – owner of *Basedows*. ☆☆☆☆ **1997 Old Vine Semillon $$$**

Burgenland [boor-gen-lund] (Austria) Wine region bordering *Hungary*, climatically ideal for fine sweet *Auslese* and *Beerenauslese*. ***Feiler-Artinger;* Kollwentz-Römerhof; Helmut Lang; *Kracher; Opitz; Wachter***

🍷 **Weinkellerei Burgenland** [vihn-kel-ler-rih boor-gen-lund] (*Neusiedlersee*, Austria) Cooperative with highly commercial *late harvest* wines.

🍷 **Alain Burguet** [al-lan boor-gay] (*Burgundy*, France) One-man *domaine* proving how good plain *Gevrey-Chambertin* can be without heavy doses of new oak. ☆☆☆☆ **1995 Bourgogne Les Champeaux $$$**

🍷 **Burgundy** (France) Home to *Pinot Noir* and *Chardonnay*; wines range from banal to sublime, but are never cheap. See *Chablis, Côte de Nuits, Côte de Beaune, Mâconnais, Beaujolais* and individual villages.

🍷 **Leo Buring** [byoo-ring] (*South Australia*) One of the many labels used by the Southcorp (*Penfolds etc.*) group, specializing in ageable Rieslings and mature *Shiraz*'s. ☆☆☆☆☆ **1994 Watervale Riesling $$$**

🍷 **Weingut Dr Bürklin-Wolf** [boor-klin-volf] (*Pfalz*, Germany) Impressive estate with great organic *Riesling* vineyards and fine, dry wines.

🍷 **Ernest J&F Burn** [boorn] (*Alsace*, France) Classy estate with vines in the Goldert *Grand Cru*. Great traditional *Gewurztraminer, Riesling* and *Muscat*. ☆☆☆☆ **1994 Gewurztraminer Goldert Clos St. Imer $$$**

Buttery Rich, fat smell often found in good *Chardonnay* (often as a result of *malolactic fermentation*) or in wine that has been left on its *lees*.

Buzet [boo-zay] (*South-West*, France) Eastern neighbor of Bordeaux, using the same grape varieties to make generally basic wines. **Buzet; co-operative; Ch. de Gueyze; Tissot.**

Byron Vineyard [bih-ron] (*Santa Barbara*, California) Impressive *Santa Barbara* winery with investment from *Mondavi*, and a fine line in *Pinots* and *Chardonnays*. ☆☆☆☆ **1995 Pinot Noir Santa Barbara Reserve $$$**

C

Ca' del Bosco [kah-del-bos-koh] (*Lombardy*, Italy) Classic, if pricey, *barrique*-aged *Cabernet/Merlot* blends, fine *Chardonnay Pinot Noir* and *Pinot Bianco/Pinot Noir/Chardonnay Méthode Champenoise Franciacorta*, from perfectionist producer Maurizio Zanella. ☆☆☆☆☆ **1994 Pinèro $$$$**

Luis Caballero [loo-is cab-ih-yer-roh] (*Jerez*, Spain) Quality *sherry* producer responsible for the *Burdon* range; also owns *Lustau*.

Château La Cabanne [la ca-ban] (*Pomerol*, *Bordeaux*, France) Up-and-coming *Pomerol* property. **82** 83 **85 86** 88 89 90 92 93 94 95 96 97 98

Cabardès [cab-bahr-des] (*South-West* France) Region north of Carcassonne using Southern and *Bordeaux* varieties to produce good if rustic reds.

Cabernet d'Anjou/de Saumur [cab-behr-nay don-joo / dur soh-moor] (*Loire*, France) Light, fresh, grassy, blackcurranty rosés, typical of their grape, the *Cabernet Franc*. **96 97** 98

Cabernet Franc [ka-behr-nay fron] Kid brother of *Cabernet Sauvignon*; blackcurranty but more leafy. Best in the *Loire*, Italy, and increasingly in Australia, California, and Washington, of course, as a partner of the *Cabernet Sauvignon* and particularly *Merlot* in *Bordeaux*. See *Chinon* and *Trentino*.

Cabernet Sauvignon [ka-ber-nay soh-vin-yon] The great blackcurranty, cedary, green peppery grape of *Bordeaux*, where it is blended with *Merlot*. Despite increasing competition from the Merlot, this is still by far the most successful red varietal, grown in every reasonably warm winemaking country on the planet. See *Bordeaux*, *Coonawarra*, *Chile*, *Napa*, etc.

Marqués de Cáceres [mahr-kehs day cath-thay-res] (*Rioja*, Spain) Modern French-influenced *bodega* making fresh-tasting wines. A good, if anonymous, new-style white has been joined by a promising oak-fermented version and a recommendable rosé (*rosado*), plus a grapey *Muscat*-style white. ☆☆☆☆ **1994 Rioja Tinto $$**

Ch. Cadet-Piola [ka-day pee-yoh-lah] (*St. Emilion Grand Cru Classé*, *Bordeaux*, France) Wines that are made to last, with fruit and *tannin* to spare. 79 **82 83 85** 86 88 89 **90** 92 **93** 94 95 96 97 98

Cadillac [kad-dee-yak] (*Bordeaux*, France) Sweet but rarely luscious (non-*botrytis*) *Sémillon* and *Sauvignon* whites. Ch. Fayau is the star wine. Its *d'Yquem*-style label is pretty smart too. **88 89 90** 94 95 96 97 98

Cahors [kah-orr] (*South-West*, France) Often rustic wines produced from the local *Tannat* and the *Cot* (*Malbec*). Some are *Beaujolais*-like, while others are *tannic* and full-bodied, though far lighter than in the days when people spoke of "the black wines of Cahors." **Ch. du Cèdre; Clos la Coutale; Lagrezette; Lamartine; Prieuré de Cenac; Clos Triguedina.**

Cain Cellars (*Napa*, California) Spectacular *Napa* hillside vineyards devoted to producing a classic *Bordeaux* blend of five varieties – hence the name of the wine. ☆☆☆☆ **1994 Cain Five $$$**

Cairanne [keh-ran] (*Rhône*, France) Named *Côtes du Rhône* village known for good peppery reds. **85 88** 89 **90** 92 93 **95 96** 97 98 **Dom d'Ameilhaud; Brusset; Oratoire St-Martin; Richaud; Tardieu-Laurent.**

Cakebread (*Napa*, California) Long-established producer of rich reds, *Sauvignon Blanc*, *Chardonnay*, and improving *Pinot Noir*. ☆☆☆☆ **1996 Cabernet Sauvignon Napa Valley Benchland Select $$$$**

Calabria [kah-lah-bree-ah] (Italy) The "toe" of the Italian boot, making Cirò from the local Gaglioppo reds and *Greco* whites. *Cabernet* and *Chardonnay* are promising, too, especially those made by Librandi.

Calem [kah-lin] (*Douro*, Portugal) Quality-conscious, small *port* producer. The specialty *Colheita tawnies* are among the best of their kind. ☆☆☆☆ **1987 Quinta da Foz Vintage $$$$**

Calera Wine Co. [ka-lehr-uh] (*Santa Benito*, California) Maker of some of California's best *Pinot Noir* from individual vineyards such as Jensen, Mills, Reed, and Selleck. The *Chardonnay* and *Viognier* are pretty special, too. ☆☆☆☆ **1995 Chardonnay Mount Harlan 20th Anniversary Vintage $$$**

California (US) Major wine-producing area of the US. See *Napa, Sonoma, Santa Barbara, Amador, Mendocino,* etc, plus individual wineries. Red: 84 **85** 86 87 **90 91** 92 93 95 96 97 98 White: **85 90 91** 92 95 **96** 97 98

Viña Caliterra [kal-lee-tay-rah] (*Curico*, Chile) Sister company of *Errazuriz*. Now a 50-50 partner with *Mondavi* and coproducer of *Seña*. ☆☆☆☆☆ **1996 Tribute Chardonnay $$$**

Ch. Calon-Segur [kal-lon say-goor] (*St. Estèphe 3ème Cru Classé*, *Bordeaux*, France) Traditional *St. Estèphe* that has recently – with the 1995 and 1996 vintages – begun to surpass its third growth status. 78 **82** 83 **85 86 88** 89 **90** 91 93 94 95 96 97 98 ☆☆☆☆☆ **1995 $$$$**

Cambria (*Santa Barbara*, California) Huge operation in the *Santa Maria Valley* belonging to the dynamic *Kendall Jackson* and producing fairly priced and good, if rarely complex, *Chardonnay, Pinot Noir, Syrah, Viognier,* and *Sangiovese*. ☆☆☆☆☆ **1996 Katherine's Vineyard Chardonnay $$$**

Ch. Camensac [kam-mon-sak] (*Haut-Médoc 5ème Cru Classé, Bordeaux*, France) Improving property following investment in 1994. **82** 85 **86** 88 89 90 91 92 93 **94 95** 96 97 98 ☆☆☆☆ **1995 $$$**

Campania [kahm-pan-nyah] (Italy) Region surrounding Naples, known for *Taurasi, Lacryma Christi,* and *Greco di Tufo* and wines from *Mastroberadino*.

Campbells (*Rutherglen*, Australia) Classic producer of fortified *Muscat* and rich concentrated reds under the Bobbie Burns label. ☆☆☆☆☆ **Merchant Prince Rare Rutherglen Muscat $$$**

Campillo [kam-pee-yoh] (*Rioja*, Spain) A small estate producing *Rioja* made purely from *Tempranillo*, showing what this grape can do. The white is less impressive. ☆☆☆☆ **1996 Rioja Riserva $$**

Bodegas Campo Viejo [kam-poh vyay-hoh] (*Rioja*, Spain) A go-ahead, if underrated *bodega* whose *Reserva* and *Gran Reserva* are full of rich fruit. Albor, the unoaked red (pure *Tempranillo)* and white (*Viura*) are first-class examples of modern Spanish winemaking. ☆☆☆☆**1991 Gran Reserva $$**

Canada Surprising friends and foes alike, British Columbia and, more specifically, *Ontario* are producing good *Chardonnay, Riesling*, improving *Pinot Noirs,* and intense *Icewines*, usually from the *Vidal* grape.

Canard Duchêne [kan-nah doo-shayn] (*Champagne*, France) Improving subsidiary of *Veuve Clicquot*. ☆☆☆☆ **Grande Cuvée Charles VII $$$**

Canberra District (*New South Wales*, Australia) Confounding critics, a small group of producers led by Doonkuna, Helm's, and Lark Hill are making good Rhône-style reds and Rieslings in high-altitude vineyards here.

Canépa [can-nay-pah] (Chile) Good rather than great winery, making progress with *Chardonnays* and *Rieslings* as well as reds. ☆☆☆☆ **1998 Chardonnay $$**

Cannonau [kan-non-now] (*Sardinia*, Italy) An red *clone* of the *Grenache*, producing a variety of wine styles from sweet to dry, mostly in *Sardinia*.

Cannonau di Sardegna [kan-non-now dee sahr-den-yah] (*Sardinia*, Italy) Heady, robust, dry-to-sweet, *DOC* red made from the *Cannonau* grape. ☆☆☆☆ **1994 Sella & Mosca $$**

Ch. Canon [kan-non] (*St. Emilion Premier Grand Cru Classé, Bordeaux*, France) Until its purchase in 1997, Canon was a victim of the widespread but rarely mentioned Bordeaux problem of mold-infected beams and barrels. Costly replacement of all of the wood in the winery seems to have set the wines to rights. **82** 83 **85** **86** 87 88 89 90 92 93 94 95 96 97 98

Ch. Canon de Brem [kan-non dur brem] (*Canon-Fronsac*, *Bordeaux*, France) A very good *Moueix*-run *Fronsac* property. 81 **82** 83 85 86 88 89 90 92 93 **95** 96 97 ☆☆☆☆ **1995 $$**

Canon-Fronsac [kah-non fron-sak] (*Bordeaux*, France) Small *appellation* bordering on *Pomerol*, with attractive plummy, *Merlot*-based reds from increasingly good value, if rustic, petits *châteaux*. **82** **83** **85** 86 **88** **89** 90 94 95 96 96 97 ***Ch. Canon-Moueix*; Ch. Moulin Pey-Labrie.**

Ch. Canon-la-Gaffelière [kan-non lah gaf-fel-yehr] (*St. Emilion Grand Cru Classé*, *Bordeaux*, France) High-flying estate run by an innovative, quality-conscious Austrian who, in 1996, created the instant superstar *la Mondotte*. Rich, ultraconcentrated wine that impresses modern critics. 82 83 **85** **86** 88 89 90 92 **93** 94 95 96 97 98

Ch. Canon-Moueix [kan-non mwex] (*Canon-Fronsac*, *Bordeaux*, France) A characteristically stylish addition to the *Moueix* empire in *Canon-Fronsac*. A wine to beat many a pricier St. Emilion. 82 83 85 86 87 88 **89** 90 92 93 94 95 98 ☆☆☆☆ **1998 $$**

Ch. Cantemerle [kont-mehrl] (*Haut-Médoc 5ème Cru Classé*, *Bordeaux*, France) A *Cru Classé* situated outside the main villages of the *Médoc*. Classy, perfumed wine with bags of blackcurrant fruit. **61** 78 81 82 **83** 85 88 89 90 92 93 95 96 ☆☆☆☆ **1992 $$**

Ch. Cantenac-Brown [kont-nak brown] (*Margaux 3ème Cru Classé*, *Bordeaux*, France) Now under the same ownership as Ch. Pichon Baron and – in 1997 – at long last beginning to live up to its potential. 70 81 82 83 85 **86** 87 88 89 90 93 94 95 97 98

Canterbury (New Zealand) Following its early success with *Pinot Noir* by *St. Helena*, Waipara in this region of the South Island has produced highly aromatic *Riesling*, *Pinot Blanc*, and *Chablis*-like *Chardonnay*. ***Giesen; St.* Helena; Pegasus Bay; Melness; Mark Rattray; Sherwood Estate; *Waipara Springs.***

Cantina (Sociale) [kan-tee-nuh soh-chee-yah-lay] (Italy) Winery (cooperative).

Cap Classique [kap-klas-seek] (South Africa) Now that the term "*Méthode Champenoise*" has unreasonably been outlawed, this is the phrase developed by the South Africans to describe their *Champagne*-method sparkling wine.

Ch. Cap-de-Mourlin [kap-dur-mer-lan] (*St. Emilion Grand Cru Classé*, *Bordeaux*, France) Until 1983 when they were amalgamated, there were, confusingly, two different *châteaux* with this name. Good mid-range stuff. **79** 81 **82 83** 85 86 88 89 90 93 94 95 96 98 ☆☆☆☆ **1988 $$**

Caparzo [ka-pahrt-zoh] (*Tuscany*, Italy) Classy, *Brunello di Montalcino* estate producing wines that age well. ☆☆☆☆ **1994 Ca del Pazzo $$$**

Cape (South Africa) All of the vineyard areas of South Africa are located in the Western Cape, most of them close to Capetown. See under *Stellenbosch, Paarl, Franschhoek, Walker Bay, Robertson, Tulbagh, Worcester*, etc. Red: 89 **91 92** 93 94 95 96 97 White: 92 93 94 95 96 97 97

Cape Mentelle [men-tel] (*Margaret River*, Western Australia) Brilliant French-owned winery, founded, like *Cloudy Bay*, by David Hoehnen. Impressive *Semillon-Sauvignon*, *Shiraz*, *Cabernet*, and, remarkably, a wild berryish *Zinfandel*, to shame many a Californian. ☆☆☆☆ **1996 Cabernet Sauvignon $$$** ☆☆☆☆ **1996 Ironstone Zinfandel $$$**

Capel Vale [kay-puhl vayl] (*South West Coat*, Western Australia) Just to the north of the borders of *Margaret River*. Good *Riesling*, *Gewürztraminer* and an improving Baudin blended red. ☆☆☆☆ **1997 CV Shiraz $$**

Capezzana [kap-pay-tzah-nah] (*Tuscany*, Italy) Conte Ugo Contini Bonacossi not only got *Carmignano* its *DOCG*, he also helped to promote the notion of *Cabernet* and *Sangiovese* as compatible bedfellows, helping to open the door for all those priceless – and pricey – *Super-Tuscans*. ☆☆☆☆☆ **1995 Ghiaie della Furba $$$**

Capsule The sheath covering the cork. Once lead, now plastic or tin. In the case of "flanged" bottles, it is noticeable by its transparency or absence.

Caramany [kah-ram-man-nee] (*Midi*, France) New *AC* for an old section of the *Côtes du Roussillon-Villages*, near the *Pyrénées*. ***Vignerons Catalans.***

Carbonic Maceration See *Macération Carbonique*.

Ch. Carbonnieux [kar-bon-nyeuh] (*Graves Cru Classé*, *Bordeaux*, France) Since 1991, the whites have greatly improved and the raspberryish reds are among the most reliable in the region. Red: 82 85 **86** 88 89 90 91 92 94 95 96 97 98 White: 90 **92** 93 **94** 95 96 97 98 ☆☆☆☆ **1998 Red $$$**

Carcavelos [kar-kah-veh-losh] (Portugal) *DO* region in the Lisbon suburbs producing usually disappointing fortified wines.

Carema [proh-doo-tohr-ree nay-bee-yoh-loh kah-ray-mah] (*Piedmont*, Italy) Wonderful perfumed *Nebbiolo* produced in limited quantities largley by Cantina dei Produttori Nebbiolo

Carignan [kah-ree-nyon] Prolific red grape making usually dull, coarse wine for blending, but classier fare in *Corbières*, *Minervois*, and *Fitou*. The key to good Carignan, as its Californian fan Randall Grahm of *Bonny Doon* says, lies in getting low yields from old vines. In Spain it is known as *Cariñena* and Mazuelo, while Italians call it Carignano.

🍷 **Carignano del Sulcis** [ka-reen-yah-noh dehl sool-chees] (*Sardinia*, Italy) Dynamic DOC spearheaded by the Santadi cooperative. ☆☆☆☆ **1995 Terre Brune Carignano del Sulcis, Santadi $$**

🍷 **Louis Carillon & Fils** [ka-ree-yon] (*Burgundy*, France) Great modern *Puligny* estate. ☆☆☆☆☆ **1995 Puligny-Montrachet Les Champs Canet $$$$**

🍷 **Cariñena** [kah-ree-nyeh-nah] (Spain) Important *DO* of Aragon for rustic reds, high in alcohol and, confusingly, made not from the *Cariñena* (or *Carignan*) grape, but mostly from the *Garnacha Tinta*. Also some whites. ☆☆☆☆ **1996 Bodegas San Valero Santero $$**

🍇 **Cariñena** [kah-ree-nyeh-nah] (Spain) The Spanish name for *Carignan*.

🍷 **Carmel** (Israel) Huge producer offering a wide range of pleasant but generally unremarkable wines.

🍷 **Viña Carmen** [veen-yah kahr-men] (*Maipo*, Chile) Quietly developing a reputation as one of the best red wine producers in Chile. Seek out the Grand Vidure Carmenère. ☆☆☆☆ **1998 Reserve Sierra Los Andes Chardonnay $$**

🍇 **Carmenère** [kahr-meh-nehr] (Chile) Smoky-spicily distinctive grape that although almost extinct in Bordeaux is still a permitted variety for *claret*. Widely planted in Chile where it has traditionally been sold as *Merlot*. Look for examples like the Santa Inès Carmenère, *Carmen* Grand Vidure, or *Veramonte* Merlot. ☆☆☆☆ **1998 M De Gras Carmenere Reserva $$**

🍷 **Carmenet Vineyard** [kahr-men-nay] (*Sonoma Valley*, California) Excellent and unusual winery tucked away in the hills and producing long-lived, very *Bordeaux*-like but approachable reds, fairly-priced *Chardonnay*, and also (even more unusually for California) good *Semillon-Sauvignon* and *Cabernet Franc*. ☆☆☆☆ **1996 Sangiacomo Carneros Chardonnay $$**

🍷 **Les Carmes-Haut-Brion** [lay kahrm oh bree-yon] (*Bordeaux*, France) Small property neighboring *Ch. Haut-Brion* in *Pessac-Léognan*.

🍷 **Carmignano** [kahr-mee-nyah-noh] (*Tuscany*, Italy) Exciting alternative to *Chianti*, with the addition of more *Cabernet* grapes. See *Capezzana*.

Carneros [kahr-neh-ros] (California) Small, fog-cooled, high-quality region shared between the *Napa* and *Sonoma* Valleys. Producing top-class *Chardonnay*, *Pinot Noir*, and now, *Merlot*. Some of the best grapes are from from Hudson and Hyde vineyards. Red: **85** 86 87 **90 91** 92 **93** 95 96 97 White: **90 91** 92 **95 96** 97. ***Acacia; Carneros Creek; Cuvaison; Domaine Carneros; Domaine Chandon; Kistler; Marcassin; Mondavi; Mumm Cuvée Napa; Patz & Hall; Pine Ridge; Saintsbury; Shafer; Swanson.***

🍷 **Dom. Carneros** (*Napa Valley*, California) *Taittinger*'s US sparkling wine – produced in a perfect and thus ludicrously incongruous replica of their French HQ. The wine, however, is one of the best New World efforts by the Champenois. ☆☆☆☆**1992 le Reve $$$**

🍷 **Carneros Creek** (*Carneros*, California) Producer of ambitious but disappointing *Pinot Noir* under this name and the far better (and cheaper) berryish Fleur de Carneros.

🍷 **Carpineto** [Kah-pi-neh-toh] (*Tuscany*, Italy) High-quality producer of *Chianti*, and *Chardonnay* and *Cabernet* that are sold under the Farnito label. ☆☆☆☆ **1994 Farnito $$**

🍷 **Carr Taylor** (Sussex, England) One of England's more businesslike estates. Sparkling wines are the best buys.

🍷 **Ch. Carras** [kar-ras] (*Macedonia*, Greece) Greece's best-known modern producer. Disappointing when compared with *Hatzimichalis*.

🍷 **Les Carruades de Lafite** [kah-roo-ahd-dur la-feet] (*Pauillac*, *Bordeaux*, France) The *second label* of *Ch. Lafite*. Rarely (quite) as good as *les Forts de Latour*, nor *Ch. Margaux's Pavillon Rouge*.☆☆☆☆ **1996 $$**

🍷 **Ch. Carsin** [kahr-san] (*Entre-Deux-Mers, Bordeaux*, France) Finnish-owned, Aussie-style winery proving that this *appellation* is capable of producing wines of class and complexity. Australian-born Mandy Jones makes particularly tasty whites. 93 94 95 96 97 98 ☆☆☆ **1998 Cuvée Prestige Blanc $$**

Casa [kah-sah] (Italy, Spain, Portugal) Firm or company.

Casablanca [kas-sab-lan-ka] (*Aconcagua*, Chile) New region in *Aconcagua*; a magnet for quality-conscious winemakers and producing especially impressive *Sauvignons, Chardonnays* and *Gewurztraminers*. ***Caliterra; Viña Casablanca; Concha y Toro; Errazuriz; Santa Carolina; Santa Emiliana; Santa Rita; Veramonte; Villard.***

🍷 **Viña Casablanca** [veen-yah kas-sab-lan-ka] (*Casablanca*, Chile) Go-ahead winery in the region of the same name. A showcase for the talents of winemaker *Ignacio Recabarren*. ☆☆☆☆ **1997 Casablanca White Label Merlot $$**

🍷 **Caslot-Galbrun** [kah-loh gal-bruhn] (*Loire*, France) Top-class producer of serious, long-lived red *Loires*.

🍷 **Cassegrain** [kas-grayn] (*New South Wales*, Australia) Tucked away in the Hastings Valley on the East Coast, but also drawing grapes from elsewhere. The wines can be variable, but are often impressive. ☆☆☆☆ **1994 Semillon Hastings Valley $$**

Cassis [ka-sees] (*Provence*, France) Small coastal *appellation* producing (variable) red, (often dull) white and (good) rosé. **Clos Ste. Magdeleine; la Ferme Blanche.**

🍷 **Castel del Monte** [Ka-stel del mon-tay] (*Puglia*, Italy) Interesting southern region where Rivera makes excellent Il Falcone reds and Bianca di Svevia whites. Grapes grown include the local Aglianico, Pampanuto, Bombino Bianco and Nero, and Nero di Troia.

🍷 **Castelgiocondo** [kas-tel-jee-yah-kon-doh] (*Tuscany*, Italy) High-quality *Brunello* estate owned by ***Frescobaldi***.

🍷 **Castellare** [kas-tel-lah-ray] (*Tuscany*, Italy) Innovative small *Chianti Classico* estate whose *Sangiovese-Malvasia* blend, Nera I Sodi di San Niccoló, *Vino da Tavola*, is worth seeking out.

🍷 **Castellblanch** [kas-tel-blantch] (*Catalonia*, Spain) Producer of better-than-most *Cava* – but catch it young. ☆☆☆ **Cava Brut Zero $$**

🍷 **Casteller** [kas-teh-ler] (*Trentino-Alto-Adige*, Italy) Pale red, creamy-fruity wines for early drinking, made from *Schiava*. See *Ca'Vit*.

🍷 **Castello di Ama** [kas-tel-loh-dee-ah-mah] (*Tuscany*, Italy) Producer of great single-vineyard Chianti Classico, plus the stunning Vigna l'Apparita Merlot.

🍷 **Castell'sches, Furstlich Domänenamt** [kas-tel-shs foorst-likh Doh-mehn-en-ahmt] (*Franken*, Germany) Good Auslese Scheurebe and Rieslaner and dry Sylvaner. Dornfelder reds are interesting too.

Cat's pee Describes the tangy smell frequently found in typical *Müller-Thurgau* and unripe *Sauvignon Blanc*.

Catalonia [kat-tal-loh-nee-yah] (Spain) The semi-autonomous region that includes *Penedés, Priorato, Conca de Barberá, Terra Alta,* and *Costers del Segre*.

🍷 **Catena Estate** [kat-tay-nah] (Argentina) Quality-focused part of the giant Catena-Esmeralda concern, helped by the expertise of ex-*Simi* Californian winemaker Paul Hobbs. ☆☆☆☆ **1996 Chardonnay $$**

🍷 **Cattier** [Kat-ee-yay] (*Champagne*, France) Up-and-coming producer with good non-vintage wines.

🍷 **Dom. Cauhapé** [koh-ap-pay] (*South-West* France) Extraordinary *Jurançon* producer of excellent *Vendange Tardive* and dry wines from the *Manseng* grape. ☆☆☆☆ **1996 Jurançon Sec Chant des Vignes $$**

Cava [kah-vah] (*Catalonia*, Spain) Sparkling wine produced in *Penedés* by the *Methode Champenoise*, but handicapped by innately dull local grapes and aging, which deprives it of freshness. Avoid *vintage* versions and look instead for Anna de *Codorníu* and *Raimat* Cava – both made from *Chardonnay* – or such well-made exceptions to the earthy rule as *Juvé y Camps, Conde de Caralt, Cava Chandon,* and *Segura Viudas.*

Cava (Greece) Legal term for wood- and bottle-aged wine.

Cave [kahv] (France) Cellar.

Caymus Vineyards [kay-muhs] (*Napa Valley*, California) Traditional producer of concentrated Italianate reds (including a forceful *Zinfandel*) and a characterful *Cabernet Franc*. Liberty School is the *second label*. ☆☆☆☆☆ **1994 Cabernet Sauvignon Napa Valley Special Selection $$$$**

Dom. Cazes [kahrs] (*Midi*, France) Maker of great *Muscat de Rivesaltes,* rich marmaladey stuff which makes most *Beaumes de Venise* seem dull.

Cellier le Brun [sel-yay luh-bruhn] (*Marlborough*, New Zealand) Specialist producer of *Méthode Champenoise* sparkling wine founded by Daniel Le Brun, an expatriate Frenchman. ☆☆☆ **Brut NV $$$**

Cencibel [sen-thee-bell] (*Valdepeñas*, Spain) Alternative name for *Tempranillo.*

Central Coast (California) Increasingly interesting, varied set of regions south of San Francisco, including *Santa Barbara, Monterey, Santa Cruz,* and *San Luis Obispo*.

Central Otago [oh-tah-goh] (*South Island*, New Zealand) Exciting "new" region where Pinot Noir and Riesling flourish. **Black Ridge; Chard Farm; Gibbston Valley; Rippon Vineyards.**

Central Valley (California) Huge irrigated region controlled by giants who make three-quarters of the state's wines without, so far, matching the efforts of similar regions Down Under. New vineyards and a concentration on cooler parts of the region are paying off for the *Sauvignon Blanc* but I doubt the potential of the increasingly widely planted *Merlot*. Smaller-scale winemaking would probably help (this is wine-factory country). *Quady*'s fortified and sweet wines are still by far the best wines here. Red: 95 96 97 White: 96 97 98

Central Valley (Chile) The region in which most of *Chile*'s wines are made. It includes *Maipo, Rapel, Maule,* and *Curico,* but not the new cool-climate region of *Casablanca,* which is in *Aconcagua,* further north.

Cépage [say-pahzh] (France) Grape variety.

Cepparello [chep-par-rel-loh] (*Tuscany*, Italy) Brilliant pure *Sangiovese Vino da Tavola* made by Paolo de Marchi of *Isole e Olena*. ☆☆☆☆ **1996 $$$**

Ceretto [cher-ret-toh] (*Piedmont*, Italy) Producer of good modern *Barolos* and impressive single-vineyard examples, plus excellent La Bernardina varietals ☆☆☆☆ **1995 La Bernardina Monsordo $$$$**

Ch. de Cérons [say-ron] (*Bordeaux*, France) One of the best properties in *Cérons*. White: 83 86 **88** 89 **90** ☆☆☆☆ **1990 Château de Cerons $$$**

Ch. Certan de May [sehr-ton dur may] (*Pomerol, Bordeaux*, France) Top-class *Pomerol* estate with subtly plummy wine. 70 75 78 **79 81 82 83 85 86** 87 88 89 90 94 95 96 98 ☆☆☆☆☆ **1990 $$$$**

Ch. Certan-Giraud [sehr-ton zhee-roh] (*Pomerol, Bordeaux*, France) *Pomerol* at its most overtly plummy. Good vintages last well.

César [say-zahr] (*Burgundy*, France) The forgotten plummy-raspberryish red grape of *Burgundy*, still vinified near *Chablis* by Simonnet-Fèvre.

LA Cetto [chet-toh] (*Baja California*, Mexico) With wines like LA Cetto's tasty *Cabernet* and spicy-soft *Petite Sirah,* it's hardly surprizing that *Baja California* is now beginning to compete with a more northerly region across the US frontier. ☆☆☆☆ **1997 Petite Sirah $$**

Chablais [shab-lay] (*Vaud*, Switzerland) A good place to find *Pinot Noir* rosé and young *Chasselas* (sold as *Dorin*).

Chablis [shab-lee] (*Burgundy*, France) When not overpriced, Chablis offers a steely European finesse that New World *Chardonnays* rarely capture. *Grands Crus* should show extra complexity. 85 **86** 88 89 **90** 92 94 **95** 96 97 98 ***Bichot; J-M Brocard; La Chablisienne; René Dauvissat; Joseph Drouhin; Durup; William Fèvre; Laroche; Louis Michel; Raveneau; Servin; Verget; Vocoret.***

La Chablisienne [shab-lees-yen] (*Burgundy*, France) Cooperative making wines from *Petit Chablis* to *Grands Crus* under a host of labels. Rivals the best estates in the *appellation*. ☆☆☆☆ **1997 Chablis Blanchot $$$**

Chai [shay] (France) Cellar/winery.

Chalk Hill (*Sonoma*, California) Producer of rich *Chardonnay*, stylish *Sauvignon Blanc*, lovely berryish *Cabernet* and great Sauternes-style whites. ☆☆☆☆ **1994 Semillon Botrytized Estate Vineyard Selection $$$**

Chateau. Chalon [shal-lon] (*Jura*, France) Specialty *Jura AC* for a *Vin Jaune* which should keep almost indefinitely. **Jean Macle.**

Chalone [shal-lohn] (*Monterey*, California) Under the same ownership as *Acacia, Edna Valley*, and *Carmenet*, this 25-year old winery is one of the big names for *Pinot Noir* and *Chardonnay*. Unusually *Burgundian*, long-lived. ☆☆☆☆ **1996 Chardonnay $$$**

Chalonnais/Côte Chalonnaise [shal-lohn-nay] (*Burgundy*, France) Source of lesser-known, less complex *Burgundies – Givry, Montagny, Rully* and *Mercurey*. Potentially (rather than always actually) good value.

Chambers Rosewood (*Rutherglen*, Australia) Competes with *Morris* for the crown of best *Liqueur Muscat* maker. The Rosewood is worth seeking out. ☆☆☆☆ **Old Vine Muscadelle $$**

Ch. Chambert-Marbuzet [shom-behr mahr-boo-zay] (*St. Estèphe Cru Bourgeois, Bordeaux*, France) Characterful *Cabernet*-based *St. Estèphe*.

Chambertin [shom-behr-tan] (*Burgundy*, France) Ultra-cherryish, damsony *Grand Cru* whose name was adopted by the village of Gevrey. Famous in the 14th century, and Napoleon's favorite. Chambertin Clos-de-Bèze, Charmes-Chambertin, Griottes-Chambertin, Latricières-Chambertin, Mazis-Chambertin, and Ruchottes-Chambertin are neighboring *Grands Crus*. 76 **78** 79 83 **85** 87 **88 89 90 92** 93 **94** 95 96 97 ***Pierre Amiot; Bachelet; Alain Burguet; Bruno Clair; Pierre Damoy; Drouhin; Dugat-Py; Dujac; Engel; Faiveley; Groffier; Leroy; Denis Mortet; Bernard Meaume; Roty; Armand Rousseau.***

Chambolle-Musigny [shom-bol moo-see-nyee] (*Burgundy*, France) *Côte de Nuits* village whose wines can be like perfumed examples from the *Côte de Beaune*. *Georges Roumier* is the local star, and *Drouhin, Dujac*, and *Ponsot* are all reliable, as are *Bertagna, Drouhin; Anne Gros, Ghislaine Barthod, Dominique Laurent Mugnier, de Vogüe* and *Leroy*. Red: 78 83 **85 88 89 90 92** 93 **94** 95 96 97

Champagne [sham-payn] (France) Source of potentially the greatest sparkling wines, from *Pinot Noir, Pinot Meunier*, and *Chardonnay* grapes. See individual listings. **81 82 83 85** 86 **88** 89 90 91 92

Ɪ **Didier Champalou** [dee-dee-yay shom-pah-loo] (*Loire*, France) Estate with serious sweet, dry and sparkling *Vouvray*. ☆☆☆☆ **1997 Tries de Vendange $$$**

Ɪ **Ch. Champy** [shom-pee] (*Burgundy*, France) Long-established, recently much-improved *Beaune négoçiant*. ☆☆☆☆**1996 Savigny-lès-Beaune $$$**

Ɪ **M Chandon** [shahn-dahn] (*Mendoza*, Argentina) *Moët & Chandon*'s Argentinian winery now making good Terrazas reds and whites.

Ɪ **Dom. Chandon** [doh-mayn shahn-dahn] (*Napa Valley*, California) *Moët & Chandon*'s Californian winery, until recently underperforming, has finally been allowed to compete with its counterpart at *Dom. Chandon* in Australia. Wines are sold in the UK as Shadow Creek. ☆☆☆☆ **Etoile Napa Valley Non-Vintage $$$**

Ɪ **Dom. Chandon** [doh-mihn shon-don] (*Yarra Valley*, Australia) Sold as *Green Point* in the UK. and proving to its owners, *Moët & Chandon*, that Australian grapes, grown in a variety of cool climates, compete with *Champagne*. Now joined by a creditable, *Chablis*-like, still Colonades *Chardonnay*. ☆☆☆☆ **1996 $$$**

Ɪ **Dom. Chandon de Briailles** [shon-don dur bree-iy] (*Burgundy*, France) Good *Savigny-lès-Beaune* estate whose owner is related to the *Chandon* of *Champagne*. ☆☆☆☆ **1995 Savigny-lès-Beaune $$$$**

Ɪ **Chanson** [shon-son] (*Burgundy*, France) Improving *Beaune* merchant. Go for the *domaine* wines. ☆☆☆ **1996 Beaune Clos des Fèves $$$**

Ɪ **Ch. de Chantegrive** [shont-greev] (*Graves, Bordeaux*, France) Large modern *Graves* estate with excellent modern reds and whites.
Red: 82 83 85 87 88 93 94 95 96 97 98 White: 89 90 92 93 **94 95** 96 **97**

Ɪ **Chapel Down** (Kent, England) David Cowdroy's impressive winery-only operation uses grapes sourced from vineyards throughout southern England. ☆☆☆ **1997 Ortega $$$**

Ɪ **Chapel Hill Winery** (*McLaren Vale*, Australia) Pam Dunsford's impressively rich – some say too rich – reds and whites have recently been joined by a leaner, unoaked *Chardonnay*. ☆☆☆☆☆ **1996 The Vicar Cabernet Shiraz $$$**

Ɪ **Chapoutier** [shah-poo-tyay] (*Rhône*, France) Family-owned merchant rescued from its faded laurels by a new generation who are using more or less organic methods. Not all wines live up to their early promise but credit is deserved for the initiative of printing labels in braille. Now making wine in Australia. ☆☆☆☆ **1996 Hermitage La Sizeranne $$**

Chaptalization [shap-tal-lih-zay-shuhn] The legal (in some regions) addition of sugar during fermentation to boost a wine's *alcohol* content.

Charbono [shar-boh-noh] (California) Obscure grape variety grown in California but thought to come from France. Makes interesting, very spicy, full-bodied reds at *Inglenook, Duxoup* and *Bonny Doon*.

Chardonnay [shar-don-nay] The great white grape of *Burgundy, Champagne* and now just about everywhere else. Capable of fresh simple charm in *Bulgaria* and buttery hazelnutty richness in *Meursault* in the *Côte d'Or*. Given the right chalky soil, in regions like *Chablis*, it can also make wines with an instantly recognizeable "mineral" character. In the New World, it tends to produce tropical flavors, partly thanks to warmer climates and partly thanks to the use of clones and cultured yeasts. Almost everywhere, its innate flavor is often married to that of new oak. See regions and producers.

Ɪ **Vin de Pays du Charentais** [shar-ron-tay] (*South-West*, France) Competing with its brandy-producing neighbor Gasgogne, this region now makes pleasant light reds and whites. **Blanchard.**

Charmat [shar-mat] The inventor of the *Cuve Close* method of producing cheap sparkling wines. See *Cuve Close*.

Ɪ **Ch. des Charmes** [day sharm] (*Ontario*, Canada) Good maker of *Chardonnay*, *Pinot* and *Icewine*. ☆☆☆☆ **1997 Paul Bosc Estate Riesling Icewine $$$**

Charta [kahr-tah] (*Rheingau*, Germany) Syndicate formed in the *Rheingau* using an arch as a symbol to indicate (often searingly) dry (*Trocken*) styles designed to be suitable for aging and drinking with food. Recently reborn with (thankfully) less rigorously dry aspirations, as part of the *VDP*.

Chartron & Trébuchet [shar-tron ay tray-boo-shay] (*Burgundy*, France) Good small merchant specializing in white *Burgundies*.

Chassagne-Montrachet [shah-san mon-rash-shay] (*Burgundy*, France) *Côte de Beaune commune* making grassy, *biscuity*, fresh yet rich whites, and mid-weight often rustic-tasting wild fruit reds. Pricey but sometimes less so than neighboring *Puligny* and as recommendable. White: **85 86** 87 **88** 89 **90 92 93 94** 95 96 97 98 .Red: 78 83 **85** 86 87 **88 89 90** 92 93 94 95 96 97 98 ***Carillon; Marc Colin; Colin-Déleger; Jean-Noël Gagnard; Henri Germain, Ch de Maltroye; M Morey; Michel Niellon; J. Pillot; Roux; Ramonet.***

Ch. Chasse-Spleen [shas spleen] (*Moulis Cru Bourgeois*, *Bordeaux*, France) *Cru Bourgeois château* whose wines can, in good years, rival those of many a *Cru Classé*. Went into a slightly dull patch in the 1990s but is now back on form. **70 78** 79 **81** 82 **83 85 86** 87 88 89 90 94 95 96 97 **98** ☆☆☆☆ **1990 $$$**

Chasselas [shas-slah] Widely grown, prolific white grape making light often dull wine principally in Switzerland, eastern France, and Germany. Good examples are rare. **Pierre Sparr.**

Ch. du Chasseloir [shas-slwah] (*Loire*, France) Makers of good *domaine Muscadets*. ☆☆☆☆ **1998 Muscadet de Sèvre et Maine Sur Lie $$**

Château [sha-toh] (*Bordeaux*, France) Literally means "castle." Some châteaux are extremely grand, many are merely farmhouses. A building is not required; the term applies to a vineyard or wine estate. Château names cannot be invented, but there are plenty of defunct titles that are used unashamedly by large cooperative wineries to market their members' wines.

Châteauneuf-du-Pape [shah-toh-nurf-doo-pap] (*Rhône*, France) Traditionally the best reds (rich and spicy) and whites (rich and floral) of the southern *Rhône*. Thirteen varieties can be used for the red, though purists favor *Grenache*. **78** 81 **83 85 88** 89 90 93 94 95 96 ***Ch. de Beaucastel; Chapoutier; Font de Michelle; Guigal; Rayas; Clos des Papes; Clos des Mont-Olivet; Lucien & André Brunel; Les Bosquet des Papes;*** **Dom. de Beaurenard;** ***Pierre André; Henri Bonneau; La Nerthe; Vieux Télégraphe.***

Jean-Claude Chatelain [shat-lan] (*Loire*, France) Producer of classy individual *Pouilly-Fumés* ☆☆☆☆ **1996 Pouilly-Fume Pilou $$$**

Jean-Louis Chave [sharv] (*Rhône*, France) Gérard Chave and his son Jean-Louis run the best estate in *Hermitage*. These are great wines but they demand patience and are easily overlooked by those looking for richer, more instantly accessible fare. There is a first-class *St. Joseph* too which can be drunk earlier. ☆☆☆☆☆ **1996 Hermitage $$$$**

Dom Gérard Chavy [shah-vee] (*Burgundy*, France) High-quality estate. ☆☆☆☆☆ **1997 Puligny-Montrachet les Charmes $$$$**

Chenas [shay-nass] (*Burgundy*, France) Good but least well-known of the *Beaujolais Crus*. Daniel Robin, Hubert Lapierre, Bernard Santé, and *Duboeuf* make worthy examples.

Dom. du Chêne [doo-shehn] (*Rhône*, France) Small estate producing rich ripe *Condrieu* and top-class *St. Joseph*. The best *cuvée* is "Anais."

Chêne [shehn] (France) Oak, as in *Fûts de Chêne* (oak barrels).

Chenin Blanc [shur-nah-blo'n for France, shen nin blonk elsewhere] Honeyed white grape of the *Loire*. Wines vary from bone-dry to sweet and long-lived. High acidity makes it ideal for sparkling wine, while sweet versions benefit from *noble rot*. French examples are often marred by green unripe flavors and heavy handedness with *sulfur dioxide*. Grown in South Africa (where it is known as *Steen*) and, less frequently, New Zealand (where it is lovingly – and successfully – grown by *Millton*), and Australia (where it is skillfully oaked by *Moondah Brook Steen*). It is generally disappointing in California. See *Vouvray, Quarts de Chaumes, Bonnezeaux, Saumur.*

🍷 **Ch. Cheval Blanc** [shuh-vahl blon] (*St. Emilion Premier Grand Cru Classé, Bordeaux,* France) Supreme *St. Emilion* property, unusual in using more *Cabernet Franc* than *Merlot.* **75** 76 78 79 80 **81 82 83 85 86** 87 88 89 90 92 93 94 95 96 98 ☆☆☆☆ **1995 $$$$**

🍷 **Dom. de Chevalier** [shuh-val-yay] (*Graves Cru Classé, Bordeaux,* France) Great *Pessac-Léognan* estate which proves itself in difficult years for both red and white. Slightly less impressive in the 1990s. Red: **70 78** 79 **81 83** 85 86 87 88 89 90 92 93 94 95 96 White: **83 85 87** 88 89 90 92 93 94 95 96 ☆☆☆☆☆ **1996 Blanc, Pessac-Léognan $$$$**

Chevaliers de Tastevin [shuh-val-yay duh tast-van] (*Burgundy*, France) A brotherhood – *confrérie* – based in *Clos de Vougeot*, famed for grand dinners and fancy robes. Wines approved at an annual tasting may carry a special "tasteviné" label. ☆☆☆☆ **1997 Hautes Côtes de Nuits Tasteviné, Yves Chaley $$$$**

🍷 **Cheverny** [shuh-vehr-nee] (*Loire*, France) Light floral whites from *Sauvignon* and *Chenin Blanc* and now, under the new "Cour Chevern'" *appellation,* wines made from the limey local *Romarantin* grape. 97 **Caves Bellier; François Cazin; Ch de la Gaudronnière.**

🍷 **Robert Chevillon** [roh-behr shuh-vee-yon] (*Burgundy*, France) Produces long-lived wines. ☆☆☆☆☆ **1995 Nuits-St.-Georges Les Chaignots $$$**

🍷 **Chianti** [kee-an-tee] (*Tuscany*, Italy) (*Classico/Putto/Rufina*) *Sangiovese*-dominant, now often Cabernet-influenced, *DOCG.* Generally better than pre-1984, when it was usual to add wine from farther south, and to put dull white grapes into the vat with the black ones. Wines labeled with the insignia of the *Classico, Putto,* or the *Rufina* areas are supposed to be better too, as are wines from *Colli Fiorentini* and *Colli Senesi.* Trusting good producers, however, is a far safer bet. 79 **82 85 88 90 94** 95 96 97 98 ***Castello di Ama; Antinori; Frescobaldi; Castellare; Castell'in Villa; Isole e Olena; Ruffino;*** **Rocca di Castagnoli;** ***Selvapiana; Castello dei Rampolla; Castello di Volpaia.***

🍷 **Chiaretto di Bardolino** [kee-ahr-reh-toh dee bahr-doh-lee-noh] (*Lombardy*, Italy) Berryish, light reds and rosés from around Lake Garda.

🍷 **Michele Chiarlo** [Mee-Kay-Leh Kee-Ahr-Loh] (*Piedmont*, Italy) Increasingly impressive modern producer of *Barolo, Barbaresco* and *Barbera.* ☆☆☆☆☆ **1993 Barolo Vigna Rionda $$$$**

Chile Rising source of juicy blackcurranty *Cabernet* and (potentially even better) *Merlot, Carmenère, Semillon, Chardonnay.* ***Almaviva; Santa Rita; Casablanca; Carmen; Concha y Toro; Errazuriz; Caliterra; Casa Lapostolle; Montes; Veramonte.***

🍷 **Chimney Rock** (*Stag's Leap District*, California) Producer of serious *Cabernet.* ☆☆☆☆ **1996 Reserve Stag's Leap District $$$**

🍷 **Chinon** [shee-non] (*Loire*, France) An *AC* within *Touraine* for (mostly) red wines from the *Cabernet Franc* grape. Excellent in ripe years; otherwise potentially thin and green. *Olga Raffault* makes one of the best, or try Alliet, *Joguet or Couly-Dutheil.* Red: 83 **85** 86 **88 89 90 95** 96 97 98

🍷 **Chiroubles** [shee-roo-bl] (*Burgundy*, France) Fragrant and early-maturing *Beaujolais Cru*, best expressed by the likes of Bernard Méziat. 85 87 **88 89** 90 **91** 93 94 95 97 98 **Emile Cheyson; Duboeuf.**

🍷 **Chivite** [shee-vee-tay] (*Navarra*, Spain) Innovative producer which can outclass many a big name *Rioja bodega.* ☆☆☆☆ **1998 Gran Feudo $$$**

Chorey-lès-Beaune [shaw-ray lay bohn] (*Burgundy*, France) Modest raspberry and damson reds once sold as *Côte de Beaune Villages*, and now appreciated in their own right. **85** 87 **88 89 90** 92 93 94 95 96 97 ***Arnoux; Ch. de Chorey;* Maillard; *Tollot-Beaut.***

Churchill (*Douro*, Portugal) Small, dynamic young firm founded by Johnny Graham, whose family once owned a rather bigger *port* house. Unusually good White Port. Red: 82 **85** 91 92 96 97 ☆☆☆☆☆ **1992 Vintage $$$$**

Chusclan [shoos-klon] (*Rhône*, France) Named village of *Côtes du Rhône* with maybe the best rosé of the area. ☆☆☆☆ **1998 Caves de Chusclan $$**

Cinqueterre [chin-kweh-TEH-reh] (*Liguria*, Italy) Generally unmemorably dry and sweet vacation whites.

Cinsaut/Cinsault [san-soh] Fruity-spicy red grape with high acidity, often blended with *Grenache*. One of 13 permitted varieties of *Châteauneuf-du-Pape,* and also in the blend of *Ch. Musar* in the *Lebanon*. Widely grown in South Africa and Australia.

Cirò [chih-Roh] (*Calabria*, Italy) Thanks to the efforts of pioneering producer Librandi, these southern reds (made from Gaglioppo) and whites (made from Greco) can be well worth buying. ☆☆☆ **1997 Rosso Classico, Librandi $$**

Ch. Cissac [see-sak] (*Haut-Médoc Cru Bourgeois*, *Bordeaux*, France) Traditional *Cru Bourgeois,* close to *St. Estèphe,* making tough wines that last. Those who dislike *tannin* should stick to ripe vintages. **70 75 78** 81 **82** 83 **85 86** 88 89 **90** 92 **93** 94 95 96 97 98 ☆☆☆☆ **1990 $$$**

Ch. Citran [see-tron] (*Haut-Médoc Cru Bourgeois, Bordeaux*, France) Improving – though still not dazzling – *Cru Bourgeois,* thanks to major investment by the Japanese. 82 85 86 87 88 **89 90** 91 92 93 **94 95 96**

Bruno Clair [klehr] (*Burgundy*, France) *Marsannay* estate with good *Fixin, Gevrey-Chambertin, Morey-St.-Denis* and *Savigny.* ☆☆☆☆ **1995 Marsannay Les Vaudenelles $$$**

Clairet [klehr-ray] (*Bordeaux*, France) The word from which we derived *claret* – originally a very pale-colored red from *Bordeaux*. Seldom used.

Clairette [klehr-ret] (*Midi*, France) Dull white grape of southern France.

Clairette de Die [klehr-rheht duh dee] (*Rhône*, France) The dry Crémant de Die is unexciting sparkling wine, but the "Méthode Dioise Traditionelle" (previously known as "Tradition") made with *Muscat* is invariably far better; grapey and fresh – like a top-class French *Asti Spumante*. **Cave Diose.**

Auguste Clape [klap] (*Rhône*, France) Probably the supreme master of *Cornas*. Great, intense, long-lived wines. ☆☆☆☆☆ **1995 Cornas $$$$**

La Clape [la klap] (*Languedoc-Roussillon*, France) Little-known *cru* within the *Coteaux de Languedoc* with tasty *Carignan* reds and soft creamy whites.

Clare Valley [klehr] (South Australia) Old slatey soil region enjoying a renaissance with high-quality *Rieslings* that age well, and deep-flavored *Shiraz, Cabernet* and *Malbec*. ***Tim Adams; Barry;* Leo Buring; *Grosset; Knappstein; Leasingham; Penfolds; Petaluma; Mitchells; Pike; Wendouree.***

Clarendon Hills (*Blewitt Springs*, South Australia) Self-confident estate which has scored highly with US critics who like the ripe intensity and overlook what sometimes strikes me as unwelcome *volatility.* Like some Australians, I'm impressed but not *that* impressed. ☆☆☆☆ **1996 Merlot $$$$**

Claret [klar-ret] English term for red *Bordeaux*.

Clarete [klah-reh-Tay] (Spain) Term for light red – frowned on by the EU.

Classed Growth (France) Literal translation of *Cru Classé*, commonly used when referring to the status of *Bordeaux châteaux*.

Classico [kla-sih-koh] (Italy) A defined area within a *DOC* identifying what are supposed to be the best vineyards, e.g. *Chianti* Classico, *Valpolicella* Classico.

Henri Clerc et fils [Klehr] (*Burgundy*, France) Top-class white *Burgundy* estate. ☆☆☆☆ **1995 Meursault-Blagny Sous le Dos d'Ane $$$**

Ch. Clerc-Milon [klehr mee-lon] (*Pauillac 5ème Cru Classé, Bordeaux*, France) Juicy member of the *Mouton-Rothschild* stable. **78** 81 **82** 83 85 **86** 87 88 89 90 92 93 94 95 96 98 ☆☆☆☆ **1993 $$$**

Domenico Clerico [doh-meh-nee-koh Klay-ree-koh] (*Piedmont*, Italy) Makes great *Barolo* and *Dolcetto* and Arte, a *Nebbiolo, Barbera* blend. ☆☆☆☆☆ **1993 Barolo Pajana $$$**

Climat [klee-mah] (*Burgundy*, France) An individual named vineyard.

Ch. Climens [klee-mons] (*Barsac Premier Cru Classé, Bordeaux*, France) Gorgeous, but delicate *Barsac* which easily outlasts many heftier *Sauternes*. 75 78 79 **80** 81 82 **83 85 86 88** 89 **90** 95 96 97 98 ☆☆☆☆☆ **1990 $$$$**

Ch. Clinet [klee-nay] (*Pomerol, Bordeaux*, France) Starry property with lovely, complex, intense wines. 82 83 85 **86** 87 88 89 90 91 92 93 95 96 97 98

Clone [klohn] Specific strain of a given grape variety. For example, more than 300 clones of *Pinot Noir* have been identified.

Clos [kloh] (France) Literally, a walled vineyard.

Clos de la Roche [kloh duh lah rosh] (*Burgundy*, France) One of the most richly reliable *Côte d'Or Grands Crus*. **85 86** 88 89 90 95 97 **Drouhin; Dujac; Faivelay; Lecheneault; Perrot-Minot; Ponsot; Rousseau.**

Clos de Mesnil [kloh duh may-neel] (*Champagne*, France) *Krug's* single vineyard *Champagne* made entirely from *Chardonnay* grown in the Clos de Mesnil vineyard. ☆☆☆☆☆ **1989 $$$$**

Clos de Tart [kloh duh tahr] (*Burgundy*, France) *Grand Cru* vineyard in *Morey-St.-Denis*, exclusive to Mommessin. ☆☆☆☆ **1990 $$$$**

Clos de Vougeot [kloh duh voo-joh] (*Burgundy*, France) *Grand Cru* vineyard, once a single monastic estate but now divided among more than 70 owners, some of whom are decidedly uncommitted to quality. ***Arnoux; Confuron; Joseph Drouhin; Engel; Grivot; Anne Gros; JGros; Faiveley; Jean Gros; Leroy; Méo Camuzet; Dom. Rion.***

Ch. Clos des Jacobins [kloh day zha-koh-Ban] (*St. Emilion Grand Cru Classé, Bordeaux*, France) Rich and ripe, if not always the most complex of wines. **75** 78 79 81 **82 83** 85 86 87 **88 89 90** 92 93 **95 96** 97 98

Clos des Mont-Olivet [kloh day mon-to-lee-vay] (*Rhône*, France) *Châteauneuf-du-Pape* estate with a rare mastery of white wine. The top red is called "Cuvée du Papet."

Clos des Papes [kloh day pap] (*Rhône*, France) Producer of serious *Châteauneuf-du-Pape* which – in top vintages – rewards cellaring.

🍷 **Clos du Bois** [kloh doo bwah] (*Sonoma Valley*, California) Top-flight producer whose "Calcaire" *Chardonnay* and Marlstone *Cabernet Merlot* are particularly fine. ☆☆☆☆ **1995 Briarcrest Cabernet Sauvignon $$$**

🍷 **Clos du Ciel** [kloh doo see-yel] (*Stellenbosch*, South Africa) Inspiring *Chardonnay* from South African wine critic John Platter.

🍷 **Clos du Clocher** [kloh doo klosh-shay] (*Pomerol*, *Bordeaux*, France) Reliably rich, plummy wine. 93 **94** 95 **96** 97 98 ☆☆☆☆ **1995 $$$**

🍷 **Clos du Marquis** [kloh doo mahr-kee] (*St. Julien*, *Bordeaux*, France) The *second label* of *Léoville-Las-Cases*. 93 94 95 96 97 98

🍷 **Clos du Roi** [kloh doo rwah] (*Burgundy*, France) *Beaune Premier Cru* that is also part of *Corton Grand Cru*. ☆☆☆☆ **1997 Château de Santenay $$$**

🍷 **Clos du Val** [kloh doo vahl] (*Napa Valley*, California) Bernard Portet, brother of Dominique who used to run *Taltarni* in Australia, makes stylish *Stag's Leap* reds – including *Cabernet* and *Merlot*. They develop with time. ☆☆☆☆ **1994 Cabernet Sauvignon $$$**

🍷 **Clos l'Eglise** [klos lay-gleez] (*Pomerol*, *Bordeaux*, France) Attractive spicy wines from a consistent small *Pomerol* estate. 75 81 83 85 86 88 89 **90** 92 **93** 94 95 96 97 98

🍷 **Clos Floridène** [kloh floh-ree-dehn] (*Graves*, *Bordeaux*, France) Classy, oaked, white *Graves* made by superstar *Denis Dubourdieu*. **90** 92 93 **94** 95 96 ☆☆☆☆ **1998 $$**

🍷 **Clos Fourtet** [kloh foor-tay] (*St. Emilion Premier Grand Cru*, *Bordeaux*, France) Improving but traditional *St. Emilion*. **82** 83 88 89 90 92 93 95 98

🍷 **Clos René** [kloh ruh-nay] (*Pomerol*, *Bordeaux*, France) Estate making increasingly concentrated though approachable wines. **82 83** 85 86 87 88 89 90 91 92 93 94 95 96 97 98

🍷 **Clos St.-Landelin** [kloh San lon-duhr-lan] (*Alsace*, France) Long-lived wines; the sister label to *Muré*.

🍷 **Cloudy Bay** (*Marlborough*, New Zealand) Under the same French ownership as *Cape Mentelle*, this cult winery has a waiting list for every vintage of its *Sauvignon*. The *Chardonnay* is reliably impressive, as are the rare *late harvest* wines. The *Pelorus* sparkling wine, made by an American winemaker, is – to my mind thankfully – less of a buttery mouthful than it used to be.

🍷 **Clusel-Roch** [kloo-se rosh] (*Rhône*, France) Good, traditional *Côte Rôtie* and *Condrieu* producer. ☆☆☆☆ **1996 Côte Rôtie $$$**

🍷 **JF Coche-Dury** [kosh doo-ree] (*Burgundy*, France) A superstar *Meursault* producer whose basic reds and whites outclass his neighbors' supposedly finer fare. ☆☆☆☆☆ **1996 Meursault Perrières $$$**

🍷 **Cockburn-Smithes** [koh burn] (*Douro*, Portugal) Unexceptional Special Reserve but producer of great *vintage* and superlative *tawny port*. **55** 60 **63** 67 **70** 75 83 **85** 91 94 97 ☆☆☆☆ **10 Year Old Tawny $$$**

🍷 **Codorníu** [kod-dor-nyoo] (*Catalonia*, Spain) Huge sparkling wine maker whose Anna de Codorníu is good *Chardonnay*-based *Cava*. The Raventos wines are recomendable too, as are the efforts of the *Raimat* subsidiary. The Californian offshoot Codorníu Napa's sparkling wine is *Cava*-ish and dull despite using *Champagne* varieties. The Pinot Noirs are more impressive.

Colchagua Valley [kohl-shah-gwah] (*Central Valley*, Chile) Up-and-coming sub-region. ***Bisquertt ; Casa Lapostolle; Undurraga; Los Vascos;***

🍷 **Coldstream Hills** (*Yarra Valley*, Australia) Founded by lawyer-turned winemaker and wine writer *James Halliday*, now in the same stable as *Penfolds*. Stunning *Pinot Noir, Chardonnay,* fine *Cabernets* and *Merlots*. Proof that critics can make as well as break a wine! ☆☆☆☆ **1997 Reserve Pinot Noir $$$**

Colheita [kol-yay-tah] (Portugal) Harvest or vintage – particularly used to describe *tawny port* of a specific year.

🍷 **Marc Colin** [mahrk koh-lan] (*Burgundy*, France) Family estate with a small chunk of *Le Montrachet*. ☆☆☆☆ **1996 St.-Aubin Le Charmois $$$**

🍷 **Michel Colin-Deleger** [koh-lah day-lay-jay] (*Burgundy*, France) Up-and-coming *Chassagne-Montrachet* estate. ☆☆☆☆☆ **1996 Puligny-Montrachet Les Demoiselles $$$$**

🍷 **Collards** [kol-lards] (*Auckland*, New Zealand) Small producer of lovely pineappley *Chardonnay* and appley *Chenin Blanc*.

🍷 **Collegiata** [koh-lay-jee jah-tah] (*Toro*, Spain) Rich, red wine from the *Tempranillo* produced in a little-known region.

Colle/colli [kol-lay/kol-lee] (Italy) Hill/hills.

🍷 **Colli Berici** [kol-lee bay-ree-chee] (*Veneto*, Italy) Red and white *DOC*.

🍷 **Colli Orientali del Friuli** [kol-lee oh-ree yehn-tah-lee del free-yoo-lee] (*Friuli-Venezia Giulia*, Italy) Lively, single-variety whites and reds from near the *Slovenian* border. Subtle, honeyed, and very pricey *Picolit*, too.

🍷 **Colli Piacentini** [kol-lee pee-yah-chayn-tee-nee] (*Emiglia-Romagna*, Italy) A very varied *DOC*, covering characterful, off-dry Malvasia sparkling wine and the Bonarda-*Barbera*-based Guttiunio. **Fugazza; la Tosa.**

🍷 **Vin de Pays des Collines Rhodaniennes** [kol-leen roh-dah nee-enn] (*Rhône*, France) The *Vin de Pays* region of the northern *Rhône*, using Rhône varieties, *Gamay* and *Merlot*. **St Désirat Cooperative.**

🍷 **Collio** [kol-lee-yoh] (*Friuli-Venezia Giulia*, Italy) High-altitude region with a basketful of white varieties, plus those of *Bordeaux* and red *Burgundy*. Refreshing and often restrained.

🍷 **Collioure** [kol-yoor] (*Midi*, France) Intense *Rhône*-style *Languedoc-Roussillon* red, often marked by the *Mourvèdre* in the blend. **Clos de Paulilles.**

🍇 **Colombard** [kol-om-bahrd] White grape grown in *South-West* France for making into Armagnac and good, light, modern whites by *Yves Grassa* and *Plaimont*. Also planted in Australia (*Primo Estate* and *Best's*) and the US, where it is known as French Colombard.

🍷 **Jean-Luc Colombo** [kol-lom-boh] (*Rhône*, France) Oenologist guru to an impressive number of *Rhône* estates – and producer of his own modern, oaky *Côtes du Rhône* and *Cornas*. ☆☆☆☆ **1996 Cornas Les Mejeans $$$**

🍷 **Columbia Crest** (*Washington State*, US) *Second label* of *Ch. Ste. Michelle*. ☆☆☆☆ **1995 Columbia Crest Valley Estate Merlot $$$**

🍷 **Columbia Winery** (*Washington State*, US) Producer of good *Chablis* style *Chardonnay* and *Graves* like *Semillon*, subtle single-vineyard *Cabernet*, especially good *Merlot*, *Syrah* and Burgundian *Pinot Noir*. ☆☆☆☆ **1995 Red Willow Vineyard Merlot $$$**

Commandaria [com-man-dah-ree-yah] (Cyprus) Traditional dessert wine with rich, raisiny fruit.

Commune [kom-moon] (France) Small demarcated plot of land named after its principal town or village. Equivalent to an English parish.

🍷 **Vin de Pays des Comtés Tolosan** [kom-tay toh-loh-so'n] (*South West* France) Fast-improving blends of Bordeaux and indigenous grapes.

Conca de Barberá [kon-kah deh bahr-beh-rah] (*Catalonia*, Spain) Cool region where *Torres*'s impressive *Milmanda Chardonnay* is made.

🍷 **Viña Concha y Toro** [veen-yah kon-chah ee tohr-roh] (*Maipo*, Chile) Steadily improving, thanks to winemaker *Ignacio Recabarren* and investment in *Casablanca*. Best wines are Don Melchior, Marques de Casa Concha, Trio, Casillero del Diablo, and *Almaviva*, its joint-venture with *Mouton Rothschild*.

🍷 **Conde de Caralt** [kon-day day kah-ralt] (*Catalonia*, Spain) One of the best names in *Cava*. Catch it young.

🍷 **Condrieu** [kon-dree-yuhh] (*Rhône*, France) One of the places where actor Gerard Dépardieu owns vines. Fabulous, pricy, pure *Viognier*: a cross between dry, white wine and perfume. Far better than the hyped and high-priced *Ch. Grillet* next door. 82 85 **88 89 90** 91 94 95 96 94 98 ***Patrick & Christophe Bonneford; Yves Cuilleron; Georges Vernay; Etienne Guigal; de Monteillet; Antoine Montez; Robert Niero; Alain Parent (& Gerard Dépardieu); Perret; Phillipe & Christophe Pichon; Hervé Richard; Francois Villand; Gerard Villano.*** ☆☆☆☆☆ **1996 de Monteillet $$$**

Confréries [kon-fray-ree] (France) Promotional brotherhoods linked to a particular wine or area. Many, however, are nowadays more about pomp and pageantry, kudos and backslapping, than active promotion.

🍷 **Jean-Jacques Confuron** [con-foor-ron] (*Burgundy*, France) Go-ahead producer with good *Nuits-St.-Georges*, *Vosne-Romanée* and *Clos Vougeot*. ☆☆☆☆☆ **1996 Nuits-St.-Georges Aux Boudots $$$$**

🍷 **Cono Sur** [kon-noh soor] (Chile) *Concha y Toro* subsidiary with a range of varietals including a classy *Pinot Noir* from *Casablanca*. Returning to form after the arrival of a new winemaker (in 1998). The Isla Negra wines are good too. ☆☆☆☆☆ **1997 Cabernet Sauvignon Reserve $$**

🍷 **Ch. la Conseillante** [lah kon-say-yont] (*Pomerol*, *Bordeaux*, France) Brilliant property with lovely, complex, perfumed wines. **70 75** 76 79 **81 82** 83 84 **85** 88 89 90 91 93 94 95 96 97 98

Consejo Regulador [kon-say-hoh ray-goo-lah-dohr] (Spain) Administrative body responsible for *DO* laws.

Consorzio [kon-sohr-zee-yoh] (Italy) Producers' syndicate.

Constantia [kon-stan-tee-yah] (South Africa) The first New World wine region. Until recently, the big name was *Groot Constantia*. Now *Constantia Uitsig, Klein Constantia, Buitenverwachting* and *Steenberg* explain the enduring reputation. ☆☆☆☆☆ **1998 Klein Constantia Sauvignon Blanc $$**

🍷 **Aldo Conterno** [al-doh kon-tehr-noh] (*Piedmont*, Italy) Truly top-class *Barolo* estate with similarly top-class *Barbera*. Nobody does it better. ☆☆☆☆☆ **1994 Barolo Sorì Ginestra $$$$**

🍷 **Conterno Fantino** [kon-tehr-noh fan-tee-noh] (*Piedmont*, Italy) The other worthwhile Conterno. ☆☆☆☆ **1995 Barbera d'Alba Vignota $$$**

🍷 **Viñedos del Contino** [veen-yay-dos del con-tee-no] (*Rioja*, Spain) *CVNE*-owned *Rioja* Alavesa estate whose wines can have more fruit and structure than most. ☆☆☆☆ **1989 Rioja Reserva $$**

Coonawarra [koon-nah-wah-rah] (South Australia) Internationally acknowledged top-class mini-region, stuck in the middle of nowhere, with cool(ish) climate and terra rossa soil. Great, blackcurranty-minty *Cabernet*, underrated *Shiraz*, big *Chardonnays* and full-bodied *Riesling*. ***Bowen Estate; Hardy's; Katnook; Lindemans; Mildara; Orlando; Petaluma; Parker Estate; Penfolds; Penley Estate; Ravenswood (Hollick); Rosemount; Rouge Homme; Yalumba; Wynns.***

Coopers Creek (*Auckland*, New Zealand) Individualistic whites including a *Chenin-Semillon* blend, *Chardonnay, Sauvignon* and *Riesling*.

Copertino [kop-per-tee-noh] (*Apulia*, Italy) Fascinating berryish wine made from the *Negroamaro*. ☆☆☆☆ **1996 Riserva Cantina Sociale $$**

Corbans (*Henderson*, New Zealand) Big winery (encompassing *Cooks*). Good, rich *Merlot* reds (even, occasionally, from *Marlborough*). ☆☆☆☆ **1997 Cottage Block Chardonnay $$**

Corbières [kawr-byayr] (*Languedoc-Roussillon*, France) Region where a growing number of small estates are now making tasty red wines. ***Ch. Caraguilhes; Helene; Lastours; Mont Tauch; Pech-Latt; Voulte Gasparets.***

Cordon Negro [kawr-don nay-groh] (*Catalonia*, Spain) Brand name for *Freixenet's* successful *Cava*. The recognizable matte-black bottle and generous marketing must account for sales. This is not a sparkling wine I voluntarily drink.

Coriole [koh-ree-ohl] (*McLaren Vale*, Australia) *Shiraz* specialist that has diversified into *Sangiovese*. The *Semillons* and *Rieslings* are pretty good too. ☆☆☆☆ **1995 McLaren Vale Shiraz $$**

Corison [kaw-ree-son] (*Napa*, California) Winery specialising in juicy *Cabernet*. ☆☆☆☆ **1994 Cabernet Sauvignon Napa Valley $$$**

Corked Unpleasant, musty smell and flavor, caused by (usually invisible) mold in the cork. Affects 3-6% of bottles.

Cornas [kaw-re-nas] (*Rhône*, France) Smoky, spicy *Syrah*; *tannic* when young, but worth keeping. **76 78 82 83 85 88** 89 **90** 91 95 96 97 98 ***Thierry Allemand; Juge; de Barjac; Clape; Colombo;*** **Courbis; Eric & Joël Durand; Durvieu; Jaboulet Aîné; Jacques Lemercier;** ***Robert Michel;*** **Serette; Tain Cooperative;** ***Tardieu-Laurent; Noël Verset; Alain Voge.***

Corsica (France) Mediterranean island making robust reds, whites, and rosés under a raft of *appellations* (doled out to assuage rebellious islanders). *Vins de Pays* (*de l'Ile de Beauté*) are often more interesting.

Dom. Corsin [kawr-san] (*Burgundy*, France) Reliable *Pouilly-Fuissé* and *St. Véran* estate. ☆☆☆☆ **1996 Pouilly Fuissé $$**

Cortese [kawr-tay-seh] (*Piedmont*, Italy) Herby grape used in *Piedmont* and to make *Gavi*. Drink young.

Corton [kawr-ton] (*Burgundy*, France) *Grand Cru* hill potentially making great, intense, long-lived reds, and – as *Corton-Charlemagne* – whites. The supposedly uniformly great vineyards run a suspiciously long way around the hill. Reds can be very difficult to taste young; many never develop. White: **78 85 87 88** 89 **90 92** 95 96 97 98 Red: **78** 83 **85** 86 87 **88 89 90 92** 95 96 97 98 **Bertrand Ambroise;** ***Bonneau du Martray; Chandon de Briailles; Dubreuil-Fontaine; Faiveley;*** **Laleur-Piot;** ***Louis Latour*** **(white);** ***Leroy;*** **Maillard; Nudant;** ***Jacques Prieur; Tollot-Beaut; Thomas-Moillard.***

🍷 **Corvo** [kawr-voh] (*Sicily*, Italy) Brand used by Duca di Salaparuta for its recently re-packaged pleasant reds and whites.

🍷 **Ch. Cos d'Estournel** [koss-des-tawr-nel] (*St. Estèphe 2ème Cru Classé Bordeaux*, France) Recently sold *estate* making top-class wines with *Pauillac* richness and fruit. Spice is the hallmark.
61 70 **75 76 78** 79 **82 83 85** 86 88 **89** 90 91 92 93 94 95 96 97 98

🍷 **Ch. Cos Labory** [koss la-baw-ree] (*St. Estèphe 5ème Cru Classé*, *Bordeaux*, France) Good, traditional, if tough, wines. 89 90 92 93 95 96 97 98

Cosecha [coh-seh-chah] (Spain) Harvest or *vintage*.

🍷 **Cosentino** (*Napa*, California) Producer of serious, long-lived reds.
☆☆☆☆ **1995 Napa Reserve Cabernet Sauvignon $$$$**

🍷 **Cossart Gordon** (*Madeira*, Portugal) High-quality brand used by the Madeira Wine Co. ☆☆☆☆☆ **5 year old Sercial $$$**

🍷 **Costanti** (*Tuscany*, Italy) Serious Brunello di Montalcino producer with classy, long-lived wines.

Costers del Segre [kos-tehrs del say-greh] (*Catalonia*, Spain) *DO* created for the excellent *Raimat*, whose irrigated vineyards helped to persuade Spain's wine authorities to allow other producers to give thirsty vines a drink.
☆☆☆☆☆ **1994 Raimat Cabernet Sauvignon Mas Castell $$$**

🍷 **Costières de Nîmes** [kos-tee-yehr duh neem] (*Midi*, France) An up-and-coming region which can make reds to match the northern *Rhône*. ☆☆☆☆ **1998 Domaine des Cantarelles $$**

🍷 **Costières du Gard** [kos-tee-yehr doo gahr] (*South-West*, France) Fruity reds, rarer whites and rosés.

🍇 **Cot** [koh] (France) The grape of *Cahors* and the *Loire* (aka *Malbec*).

🍷 **Cotat Frères** [koh-tah] (*Loire*, France) One of the few Loire *Sauvignon* producers to achieve superstar status in the US. The Cotats' *Sancerres* repay aging and deserve their success. ☆☆☆☆☆ **1995 La Grande Côte $$$**

Côte d'Or [koht dor] (*Burgundy*, France) Geographical designation for the finest slopes, encompassing the *Côte de Nuits* and *Côte de Beaune*.

🍷 **Côte de Beaune (Villages)** [koht duh bohn] (*Burgundy*, France) The southern half of the *Côte d'Or*. With the suffix '*Villages*', indicates red wines from one or more of the specified *communes*. Confusingly, wine labelled simply '*Côte de Beaune*' comes from a small area around *Beaune* itself and often tastes like wines of that *appellation*. White: **82 85 86** 87 **88** 89 **90 92 95 96 97** Red: **78** 83 **85 88 89 90 91 92** 95 96 97

🍷 **Côte de Brouilly** [koht duh broo-yee] (*Burgundy*, France) *Beaujolais Cru:* distinct from *Brouilly* – often finer. Floral and ripely fruity; will keep for a few years. **88 89** 90 **91** 94 95 **96** 97 98 ***Duboeuf; Pivot;* Ch. Thivin.**

🍷 **Côte de Nuits (Villages)** [koht duh nwee] (*Burgundy*, France) Northern, and principally 'red' end of the *Côte d'Or*. The suffix "*Villages*" indicates wine from one or more specified *communes*. **78 80** 82 83 **85** 86 87 **88 89 90** 92 93 94 95 96 97 98

Côtes des Blancs [koht day blon] (*Champagne*, France) Principal *Chardonnay*-growing area.

Côte Rôtie [koh troh tee] (*Rhône*, France) Smoky yet refined *Syrah* (possibly with some white *Viognier*) from the northern *Rhône appellation* divided into the "Brune" and "Blonde" hillsides. Most need at least six years. **76 78 80 82 83 85 86 88** 89 90 91 95 96 **Ch. d'Ampuis. *Barge;* Bonnefond; *Burgaud;* Champet; Cuilleron; Clusel-Roch; Gallet; *Gasse;* Gentaz-Dervieuz; Gerin; *Guigal; Jamet; Jasmin; Ogier; Rostaing;* Saugère; L. de Vallouit; *Vernay; Vidal Fleury.***

Côte(s), Coteaux [koht] (France) Hillsides.

Coteaux Champenois [koh-toh shom-puh-nwah] (*Champagne*, France) Over-priced, mostly thin, light and acidic, still wine of the area. *Laurent Perrier's* is better than most, but it's still only worth buying in the ripest vintages. **85** 86 88 **89 90** 91 92 95 ☆☆☆ **Laurent Perrier $$$**

Coteaux d'Aix-en-Provence [koh-toh dayks on prov vons] (*Provence*, France) A recent *AC* region producing light floral whites, fruity reds, and dry rosés using *Bordeaux* and *Rhône* varieties.**Château Calissanne; Ch. Revelette; Mas Ste-Berthe; Ch. Vignelaure.**

Coteaux d'Ancenis [koh-toh don-suh-nee] (*Loire*, France) So far, only *VDQS* status for this region near Nantes, producing light reds and deep pinks from the *Cabernet Franc* and *Gamay*, and also *Muscadet*-style whites.

Coteaux d'Ardèche [koh-toh dahr-desh] (*Rhône*, France) Light country wines, mainly from the *Syrah* and *Chardonnay*. A popular place with Burgundians to produce affordable alternatives to their own white wine.

Vin de Pays des Coteaux de l'Aubance [koh-toh duh loh bons] (*Loire*, France) Light wines (often semi-sweet) grown on the banks of a *Loire* tributary. Quite rare outside the region.

Coteaux du Languedoc [koh-toh doo long-dok] (*Midi*, France) A big *appellation*, and a popular source of fast-improving rich reds such as *Pic St Loup* from *Rhône* and southern grapes.

Coteaux du Layon [koh-toh doo lay-yon] (*Loire*, France) *Chenin Blanc* whites that are slow to develop and long lived. Lots of lean dry wine but the sweet *Bonnezeaux* and *Quarts de Chaume* are superior. The wines of *Moulin Touchais* and Clos Ste. Catherine are fine, as are Pierre Bise, *Ch. du Breuil* and Dom. des Sablonettes. Sweet White: **76 83 85** 86 **88 89** 90 **94** 95 96 97 98 **Dom. des Baumard; Pierre Bise;Cady; Delesvaux; Godineau; Guimoniere; Ch. du Breuil; la Varière.**

Coteaux du Loir [koh-toh doo lwahr] (*Loire*, France) Clean, vigorous whites from a *Loire* tributary. 96 97 98

Coteaux du Lyonnais [koh-toh doo lee-ohn-nay] (*Rhône*, France) Just to the south of *Beaujolais*, making some very acceptable good-value wines from the same grapes. **Descottes; *Duboeuf*; Fayolle; Sain Bel Co-operative.**

Coteaux du Tricastin [koh-toh doo tris-kass-tan] (*Rhône*, France) Southern *Rhône appellation*, emerging as a source of good-value, peppery/blackcurranty reds. **Dom de Grangeneuve; de Rozets; du Vieux Micoulier.**

Coteaux Varois [koh-toh day boh on pro-vonss] (*Provence*, France) Inexpensive, fruity reds, whites, and rosés. **Deffends.**

Côtes de/Premières Côtes de Blaye [koht duh/pruh-myerh koht duh blih] (*Bordeaux*, France) A ferry ride across the river from *St. Julien*. Poor winemaking prevents many estates from living up to their potential. Premières are usually red; Côtes, white. **88 89** 90 94 95 96 97 98 **Ch. Bertinerie; Gigault; Haut-Sociondo; les Jonqueyres; Segonzac; des Tourtes.**

Côtes de Bourg [koht duh boor] (*Bordeaux*, France) Clay-soil region just across the water from the *Médoc* and an increasingly reliable source of good-value, *Merlot*-dominated, plummy reds. Red: 85 86 **88 89** 90 94 95 96 97 98 **Brulesécaille; Falfas; Robin; Roc-de-Cambes; Tayac.**

Côtes de Castillon [koht duh kass-tee-yon] (*Bordeaux*, France) Region where the *Merlot* is often a lot more lovingly handled than in nearby *St. Emilion*. **Ch. d'Aiguilhe; de Belcier; Côte Montpezat; Lapeyronie; de Parenchère; Pitray; Poupille; Robin.**

Côtes de Duras [koht duh doo-rahs] (*Bordeaux*, France) Inexpensive *Sauvignons*, often better value than basic *Bordeaux* Blanc **Duras Cooperative.**

Côtes de Francs [koht duh fron] (*Bordeaux*, France) Up-and-coming region close to *St. Emilion* producing increasingly good reds. **Charmes-Godard; de Francs; la Claverie; la Prade; Puygeraud.**

Vin de Pays des Côtes de Gascogne [koht duh gas-koyn] (*South West* France) Armagnac-producing region where dynamic producers *Yves Grassa* and the *Plaimont cooperative* used modern winemaking techniques on grapes that would in the past have been used for brandy. *Ugni Blanc* and *Colombard* are giving way to *Sauvignon Blanc*. ***Grassa; Plaimont.***

Côtes de Provence [koht dur prov-vonss] (*Provence*, France) Improving, good-value, fruity whites and ripe, spicy reds. The famous rosés, however, are often carelessly made and stored, but vacationers rarely notice that the so-called pink wine is a deep shade of bronze and decidedly unrefreshing. A region with as much appeal to organic winemakers as to fans of Mr. Mayle's rural tales. **Dom la Bernarde; la Courtade; d'Esclans; Gavoty; Ott; Rabiega.**

🍷 **Côtes de St. Mont** [koht duh san-mon] (*South-West*, France) Large *VDQS* area encompassing the whole of the Armagnac region. ***Plaimont*** is the largest and best-known producer.

🍷 **Vin de Pays des Côtes de Tarn** [koht duh tarn] (*South-West*, France) Fresh, fruity, simple reds and whites, mostly for drinking ***in situ*** rather than outside France. **Labastide-de-Levis Cooperative.**

🍷 **Vin de Pays des Côtes de Thau** [koht duh toh] (*Languedoc-Roussillon*, France) Fresh whites to drink with seafood in the canalside restaurants of Sète. **Les Vignerons des Garrigues.**

🍷 **Vin de Pays des Côtes de Thongue** [koht duh tong] (*Languedoc-Roussillon*, France) Up-and-coming region between Béziers and Toulouse where the Domaines d'Arjolle, Condamine, l'Eveque, Teisserenc and Deshenrys are making tasty modern wines.

🍷 **Côtes du Frontonnais** [koht doo fron-ton-nay] (*South-West*, France) Up-and-coming inexpensive red (and some rosé); fruitily characterful.

🍷 **Côtes du Jura** [koht duh joo-rah] (France) *Vin Jaune* and *Vin de Paille* are the styles to look for in this area close to Arbois, as well as sparkling wine and light Poulsard and Trousseau reds and **Ch d'Arlay; Boudry; Couret; Delay.**

🍷 **Côtes du Marmandais** [koht doo mahr-mon-day] (South-West France) Uses the *Bordeaux* red grapes plus *Gamay*, *Syrah* and others to make pleasant, fruity, inexpensive wines. **Ch. de Beaulieu; Les Vignerons de Beaupuy; Cave de Cocument**

🍷 **Côtes du Rhône (Villages)** [koht doo rohn] (*Rhône*, France) Spicy reds produced mostly in the southern part of the *Rhône* Valley. The best supposedly come from a set of better *Villages* (and are sold as *CdR Villages*), though some single *domaine* 'simple' *Côtes du Rhônes* outclass many *Villages* wines. *Grenache* is the key red wine grape, though recent years have seen a growing use of the *Syrah*. Whites which can include new-wave *Viogniers* are improving. Red: 89 **90** 93 94 95 96 **97** 98 **Dom. de Beaurenard; Cabasse; les Goubert; *Grand Moulas; Guigal*; Richaud; la Soumade; Ste. Anne.**

🍷 **Côtes du Roussillon (Villages)** [koht doo roo-see-yon] (*Midi*, France) *Appellation* for red, white, and rosé of pretty variable quality.. *Côtes du Roussillon Villages* is generally better. **Brial; Força Réal; Gauby; de Jau; *Vignerons Catalans.***

🍷 **Côtes du Ventoux** [koht doo von-too] (*Rhône*, France) Improving everyday country reds that are similar to *Côtes du Rhône*. 85 88 89 **90** 94 **95 96** 97 98 ***Jaboulet Aîné; Jaboulet Ainé;*** **Pascal; Perrin; la Vieille Ferme.**

🍷 **Côtes du Vivarais** [koht doo vee-vah-ray] (*Provence*, France) Light southern *Rhône*-like reds, fruity rosé and fragrant light whites.

Cotesti [kot tesh-tee] (Romania) Easterly vineyards growing varieties such as *Pinots Noir*, *Blanc*, *Gris*, and *Merlot*.

Cotnari [kot nah-ree] (Romania) Traditional and now very rare white dessert wine. Has potential.

Bodegas el Coto [el kot-toh] (*Rioja*, Spain) Small estate producing good, medium-bodied El Coto and Coto de Imaz reds. ☆☆☆☆ **1994 Coto de Imaz Reserva $$$**

Cottin Frères [cot-tah] (*Burgundy*, France) A new name that has been adopted by the Cottin Brothers who run the dynamic *Nuits-St.-Georges* négoçiant firm of *Labouré Roi*. ☆☆☆☆ **1996 Chassagne-Montrachet $$$**

Coulée de Serrant [koo-lay duh seh-ron] (*Loire*, France) Great dry *Chenin* from a top property in *Savennières* run by *Nicolas Joly*, a leading champion of "biodynamique" winemaking. The Becherelle vineyard is great too. ☆☆☆☆ **1996 $$$$**

Paul Coulon et Fils [Koo-lon] (*Rhône*, France) Serious *Rhône* producer. ☆☆☆☆ **1995 Dom. de Beaurenard, Châteauneuf-du-Pape $$$$**

Coulure [koo-loor] Climate-related wine disorder which causes reduced yields (and possibly higher quality) as grapes shrivel and fall off the vine.

Couly-Dutheil [koo-lee doo-tay] (*Loire*, France) High-quality *Chinon* from single-vineyards just behind the *château* in which Henry II of England imprisoned his wife, Eleanor of Aquitaine. ☆☆☆☆ **1996 Clos de L'Echo $$$**

Viña Cousiño Macul [koo-sin-yoh mah-kool] (*Maipo*, Chile) The most traditional producer in Chile. Reds are more successful than whites. ☆☆☆ **1995 Finis Terrae $$**

Ch. Coutet [koo-tay] (*Barsac Premier Cru Classé*, *Bordeaux*, France) Delicate neighbor to *Ch. Climens*, often making comparable wines: Cuvée Madame is top flight. **71 75** 76 **81** 82 **83** 85 **86** 87 **88 89** 90 95 96 97 98

Ch. Couvent-des-Jacobins [koo-von day zhah-koh-ban] (*St. Emilion Grand Cru Classé*, *Bordeaux*, France) Producer of juicy plummy-spicy wines. **82** 83 85 86 88 89 90 **92 93** 94 95 96 98 ☆☆☆ **1995 $$$**

Cowra [kow-rah] (*New South Wales*, Australia) Up-and-coming region, making a name for itself with *Chardonnay*, for which it will one day eclipse its better known but less viticulturally ideal neighbor, the *Hunter Valley*.

Dom. de Coyeux [duh cwah-yuh] (*Rhône*, France) One of the best producers of *Côtes du Rhône* and *Muscat de Beaumes de Venise*.

Cranswick Estate (*Riverina*, *NSW*, Australia) Successful producer making reliable, fairly-priced wines under its own and the Barramundi label and some great *late harvest* whites. ☆☆☆☆ **1996 Autumn Gold $$**

Quinta do Crasto [kin-tah doh cras-toh] (*Douro*, Portugal) An up-and-coming small *port* producer with good red table wines too. ☆☆☆☆ **1998 Douro Red $$**

Cream Sherry (*Jerez*, Spain) Popular style (though not in Spain) produced by sweetening an *oloroso*. A visitor to *Harvey's* apparently preferred one of the company's *sherries* to the then popular "Bristol Milk." "If that's the milk," she joked, "this must be the Cream."

Crémant [kray-mon] (France) Term used in *Champagne*, denoting a slightly sparkling style due to a lower pressure of gas in the bottle. Elsewhere, a term to indicate sparkling wine, e.g. Crémant de *Bourgogne*, de *Loire* and d'*Alsace*.

Crème de Cassis [kraym duh kas-seess] (*Burgundy*, France) Fortified fruit essence perfected in *Burgundy* using blackcurrants from around Dijon. Commonly drunk mixed with sharp local *Aligoté* as *Kir*, or sparkling wine, as *Kir* Royale. Crème de Mûre (blackberries), Framboise (raspberries), Fraise (strawberries) and Pèche (peaches) are also delicious. **Vedrenne**

Crépy [kray-pee] (*Savoie*, France) Crisp floral white from *Savoie*.

Criado y Embotellado (por) [kree-yah-doh ee em-bot-tay-yah-doh] (Spain) Grown and bottled (by).

Crianza [kree-yan-thah] (Spain) Literally keeping "con Crianza" means aged in wood – often preferable to the *Reservas* and *Gran Reservas*, which are highly prized by Spaniards but can taste dull and dried-out.

Crichton Hall [krih-ton] (*Rutherford*, California) Small winery specializing in top-class *Chardonnay*. ☆☆☆☆ **1996 Chardonnay $$$**

Crisp Fresh, with good *acidity*.

Ch. le Crock [lur krok] (*St. Estèphe Cru Bourgeois*, *Bordeaux*, France) Traditional property which, like *Léoville-Poyferré*, its stablemate, has shown great recent improvement. 82 83 85 86 88 **89** 90 92 93 95 96 98

Croft (Spain/Portugal) *Port* and *sherry* producer making highly commercial but rarely memorable wines. The *vintage port* is back on form. 55 60 **63** 66 67 **70** 75 77 82 85 94 97 ☆☆☆☆ **1995 Quinta de Roeda $$$**

Ch. La Croix [la crwah] (*Pomerol*, *Bordeaux*, France) Producer of long-lasting traditional wines.

Ch. la Croix-de-Gay [la crwah duh gay] (*Pomerol*, *Bordeaux*, France) Classy estate whose complex wines have good, blackcurranty-plummy fruit. 81 **82 83** 85 86 **88** 89 90 91 **92** 93 94 95 96

Ch. Croizet-Bages [krwah-zay bahzh] (*Pauillac 5ème Cru Classé*, *Bordeaux*, France) Underperformer showing some signs of improvement. **82** 83 85 86 87 88 **90** 92 93 94 95 96

Croser [kroh-sur] (*Adelaide Hills*, Australia) Made by *Brian Croser* of *Petaluma* in the Piccadilly Valley, this is one of the New World's most *Champagne*-like sparkling wines. ☆☆☆☆ **1996 Brut $$$**

Crouchen [kroo-shen] (France) Obscure white grape known as Clare Riesling in Australia and Paarl Riesling in South Africa.

Crozes-Hermitage [krohz ehr-mee-tahzh] (*Rhône*, France) Up-and-coming *appellation* in the hills behind supposedly greater *Hermitage*. Smoky, blackberryish reds are pure *Syrah*. Whites (made from *Marsanne* and *Roussanne*) are creamy but less impressive. And they rarely keep. Red: **83 85 88 89 90** 91 95 96 97 98 White: **89 90** 91 94 **95** 96 97 98 **Dom Belle; Chapoutier; Colombier; Combier; *Delas; Alain Graillot; Paul Jaboulet Aîné;* Dom. du Pavilion-Mercure; Pochon; Sorrel; Tain l'Hermitage Cooperative.**

Cru Bourgeois [kroo boor-zhwah] (*Bordeaux*, France) Wines beneath the *Crus Classés*, supposedly satisfying certain requirements, which can be good value for money and, in certain cases, better than more prestigious *classed growths*. Since around half the wine in the Médoc comes from Crus Bourgeois (and a quarter from *Crus Classés*), don't expect the words to mean too much. ***d'Angludet; Beaumont; Chasse-Spleen; Citran; Haut-Marbuzet; Gloria; la Gurgue; Labégorce; Labégorce-Zédé; Marbuzet; Meyney; Monbrison; de Pez; Phélan-Ségur; Pibran; Potensac; Poujeaux; Siran; Sociando-Mallet; la Tour Haut-Caussin.***

Cru Classé [kroo klas-say] (*Bordeaux*, France) The best wines of the *Médoc* are crus classés, split into five categories from first (top) to fifth growth (or *Cru*) for the Great Exhibition in 1855. The *Graves, St. Emilion* and *Sauternes* have their own classifications.

🍷 **Weingut Hans Crusius** [hans skroos-yuhs] (*Nahe*, Germany) Family-run estate prized for the quality of its highly traditional wines. Some of the best, ripest *Trocken* wines around.

Crusted Port (*Douro*, Portugal) An affordable alternative to *vintage port* – a blend of different years, bottled young and allowed to throw a deposit. ***Churchill's; Graham's; Dow's.***

🍷 **Yves Cuilleron** [Kwee-yehr-ron] (*Rhône*, France) Rising star producing great *St. Joseph* and (sweet and dry) *Condrieu*. ☆☆☆☆☆ **1996 Condrieu Les Eguets Recoltes Tardives $$$$**

🍷 **Cullen** (*Margaret River*, Australia) Brilliant pioneering estate showing off the sensitive winemaking skills of Vanya Cullen. Source of stunning *Sauvignon-Semillon* blends, *claret*-like reds, a highly individual *Pinot Noir* and a Burgundian-style *Chardonnay*. ☆☆☆☆☆ **1996 Reserve Sauvignon Blanc Semillon $$**

Cultivar [kul-tee-vahr] (South Africa) South African for grape variety.

🍷 **Ch. Curé-Bon-la-Madelaine** [koo-ray bon lah mad-layn] (*St. Emilion Grand Cru Classé, Bordeaux*, France) Very small *St. Emilion* estate next to *Ausone*. 78 81 **82** 83 **85 86** 88 **89 90 94** 95 96 97 98

Curico [koo-ree-koh] (Chile) Region in which *Torres, San Pedro* and *Caliterra* have vineyards. Now being eclipsed by *Casablanca* as a source for cool-climate whites, but still one of Chile's best wine areas for red and white. ***Caliterra*; Echeverria; la Fortuna; *Montes; Torres; Valdivieso.***

🍷 **Cuvaison Winery** [koo-vay-san] (*Napa Valley*, California) Swiss-owned winery with high-quality *Carneros Chardonnay*, increasingly approachable *Merlot*, and now good *Pinot Noir*. Calistoga Vineyards is a *second label*. ☆☆☆☆☆ **1995 Pinot Noir Napa Valley Carneros $$**

Cuve close [koov klohs] The third-best way of making sparkling wine, in which the wine undergoes secondary fermentation in a tank and is then bottled. Also called the *Charmat* or *Tank method*.

Cuvée (de Prestige) [koo-vay] Most frequently a blend put together in a process called *assemblage*. *Prestige Cuvées* are (particularly in *Champagne*) supposed to be the best of a producer's production.

🍷 **Cuvée Napa** (*Napa*, California) The Californian venture by *Mumm Champagne*, and still offering better quality and value for money than the mothership back in France.

🍷 **CVNE** [koo-nay] (*Rioja*, Spain) Compania Vinicola del Norte de Espana, a large high-quality operation, run by the owners of *Contino*, producing the excellent Viña Real in *Crianza, Reserva, Imperial* or *Gran Reserva* in the best years, and a light CVNE *Tinto*. Some recent releases have been slightly less dazzling. ☆☆☆☆ **1995 Rioja Reserva $$**

Cyprus Shifting its focus away from making ersatz *"sherry."* Even so, the best wine is still the fortified *Commandaria*.

D

🍷 **Didier Dagueneau** [dee-dee-yay dag-guhn-noh] (*Loire*, France) The iconoclastic producer of some of the best steely and oak-aged *Pouilly-Fumé*, and even the occasional *late harvest* effort that upsets the authorities. Look out for the "Pur Sang" and "Silex" bottlings. ☆☆☆☆ **1995 Silex $$$**

🍷 **Ch. Dalem** [dah-lem] (*Fronsac, Bordeaux*, France) Maker of rich full-bodied *Fronsac*. 82 83 **85** 86 88 **89 90** 91 92 93 94 95 96 97 98

🍷 **Dalwhinnie** [dal-win-nee] (*Pyrenees, Victoria*, Australia) Quietly classy producer close to *Taltarni*. Reds made to last. ☆☆☆☆ **1996 Shiraz $$$**

🍷 **Dão** [downg] (Portugal) Once Portugal's best-known regions – despite the traditional dullness of its wines. Thanks to pioneering producers like *Sogrape* and *Aliança* both reds and whites are improving. Red: **80 85 88 90 91 93** 94 95 96 97 98 **Boas Quintas; Duque de Viseu; Porta dos Cavaleiros; Quinta dos Roques; Casa de Santsr.**

🍷 **Ch. Dassault** [das-soh] (*St. Emilion Grand Cru Classé, Bordeaux*, France) Good, juicy *St. Emilion*. 82 83 **85** 86 88 89 **90** 92 93 94 95 96 97 98

🍷 **Kurt Darting** [koort dahr-ting] (*Pfalz*, Germany) New-wave producer who cares more about ripe flavor than making the tooth-scouringly dry wine favored by some of his neighbors. Great *late harvest* wines. ☆☆☆☆ **1996 Ungsteiner Bettelhaus Riesling Auslese $$$$**

🍷 **Ch. de la Dauphine** [duh lah doh-feen] (*Fronsac, Bordeaux*, France) Proof that *Fronsac* deserved its reputation in the days when it was better-regarded than *St. Emilion*. **85** 86 87 88 **89 90** 92 93 94 95 96 97 98

🍷 **Domaine d'Auvenay** [Dohv-nay] (*Burgundy*, France) Estate belonging to Lalou Bize Leroy, former co-owner of the *Dom. de la Romanée-Conti*, and now at *Dom. Leroy*. Great, if pricy, long-lived, examples of *Auxey-Duresses, Meursault, Puligny-Montrachet* and *Grands Crus* of the *Côtes de Nuits*.

🍷 **Réné and Vincent Dauvissat** [doh-vee-sah] (*Burgundy*, France) One of the best estates in *Chablis*. Watch for other Dauvissats; the name is also used by the *La Chablisienne* cooperative. ☆☆☆☆ **1997 Chablis les Preuses $$**

🍷 **Ch. Dauzac** [doh-zak] (*Margaux 5ème Cru Classé, Bordeaux*, France) Rejuvenated, following its purchase in 1993 by André Lurton of *Ch. la Louvière*. **82 83 85** 86 **88 89 90** 93 94 95 96 97 98.

🍷 **Dealul Mare** [day-al-ool mah-ray] (Romania) Carpathian region once known for whites, now producing surprizingly good *Pinot Noir.*

🍷 **Etienne & Daniel Defaix** [duh-fay] (*Burgundy*, France) Classy traditional *Chablis* producer, making long-lived wines with a steely bite. ☆☆☆☆ **1996 Chablis "Vieilles Vignes" $$**

Dégorgée (dégorgement) [day-gor-jay] The removal of the deposit of inert yeasts from *Champagne* after maturation.

🍷 **Dehlinger** (*Sonoma*, California) *Russian River Pinot Noir* and *Chardonnay* specialist that is proving highly successful with *Syrah*. ☆☆☆☆ **1994 Pinot Noir Russian River Valley Reserve $$**

Deidesheim [di-dess-hime] (*Pfalz*, Germany) Distinguished wine town noted for flavorsome *Rieslings*. QbA/Kab/Spät: **85 86 88 89 90** 91 92 93 94 95 96 97 98 Aus/Beeren/Tba: **83 85** 88 89 90 91 92 93 94 95 96 97 98 **Bassermann-Jordan; Josef Biffar; Reichsrat von Buhl; JL Wolf.**

🍷 **Deinhard** [dine-hard] (*Mosel*, Germany) See *Wegeler Deinhard*.

🍷 **Marcel Deiss** [dise] (*Alsace*, France) Tiny property producing some of the best wine in the region, including some unusually good *Pinot Noir*. ☆☆☆☆☆ **1995 Gewurztraminer Altenberg Selection de Grains Nobles $$$$**

🍷 **Delaforce** [del-lah-forss] (*Douro*, Portugal) Small *port* house with lightish but good *vintage* and *tawny*. 58 60 **63 66** 70 74 75 77 85 94 97 ☆☆☆ **1995 Quinta da Corte Vintage Port $$$**

🍷 **Delas Frères** [del-las] (*Rhône*, France) *Négoçiant* with great *Hermitage* vineyards and now promising much since its purchase by *Louis Roederer.* ☆☆☆ **1994 Hermitage Les Bessards $$$**

🍷 **Delatite** [del-la-tite] (*Victoria*, Australia) Producer of lean-structured, long-lived wines. ☆☆☆☆ **1998 Dead Man's Hill Gewürztraminer $$**

🍷 **Delegats** [del-leg-gats] (*Auckland*, New Zealand) Family firm which has hit its stride recently with impressively (for New Zealand) ripe reds, especially plummy *Merlots*. The *second label* is "*Oyster Bay*." ☆☆☆☆ **1997 Hawke's Bay Reserve Cabernet Sauvignon $$$**

🍷 **Philippe Delesvaux** [Dels-voh] (*Loire*, France) Quality-conscious *Coteaux de Layon* estate with some good red too.

🍷 **Delheim Wines** [del-hihm] (*Stellenbosch*, South Africa) A commercial estate with lean, quite traditional reds and white. ☆☆☆☆ **1998 Shiraz $$**

Demi-sec [duh-mee sek] (France) Medium-dry.

🍷 **Demoiselle** [duh-mwah-zel] (*Champagne*, France). A new *Champagne* name to watch with attractive, light, creamy wines.

🍷 **Denbies Wine Estate** [den-bees] (Surrey, England) Part tourist attraction, part winery, the largest wine estate England has so far produced. Sweet wines are the best of the batch so far. ☆☆☆☆ **Special Late Harvest $$$**

Deutsches Weinsiegel [doyt-shur vihn-see-gel] (Germany) Seals of various colors – usually neck labels – awarded for merit to German wines. Treat with circumspection.

Deutscher Tafelwein [doyt-shur tah-fuhl-vihn] (Germany) Table wine, guaranteed German as opposed to Germanic-style EC *Tafelwein*. Can be good value – and often no worse than *Qualitätswein*, the supposedly "quality" wine designation that includes every bottle of *Liebfraumilch*.

🍷 **Deutz** [duhtz] (*Champagne*, France, and also Spain, New Zealand, California) Reliable small but dynamic producer at home and abroad, now owned by *Roederer*. The *Montana Marlborough* Cuvée from New Zealand was created with the assistance of Deutz, as was the *Yalumba* 'D' in Australia. Maison Deutz is a 150-acre cool-climate vineyard joint venture in California with Nestlé and *Deutz* where unusually, a bit of *Pinot Blanc* goes into the – generally – excellent blend. The Cuvée William Deutz is the star wine.

🍷 **Devaux** [duh-voh] (*Champagne*, France) Small producer with a knack of producing fairly-priced wine and unusually good rosé and *Blanc de Noirs*. ☆☆☆☆ **1990 Distinction Brut $$$**

Dézaley [days-lay] (Vaud, Switzerland) One of the few places in the world where the Chasselas (here called the *Dorin*) makes decent wine.

Diabetiker Wein [dee-ah-beh-ti-ker vihn] (Germany) Very dry wine with most of the sugar fermented out (as in a Diat lager); suitable for diabetics.

🍷 **Diamond Creek** (*Napa Valley*, California) Big Name producer with a set of very good vineyards (Gravelly Meadow, Red Rock Terrace and Volcanic Hill) that produce toughly intense red wines which demand, but don't always repay, patience. ☆☆☆☆ **1995 Cabernet Sauvignon Napa Valley Red Rock Terrace $$$$**

🍷 **Dieu Donné Vineyards** [dyur don-nay] (*Franschhoek*, South Africa) Variable producer of quality varietals in the *Franschhoek* valley. The 1992 *Chardonnay* was legendary. ☆☆☆☆ **1997 Cabernet Sauvignon-Merlot $$$**

🍷 **Dom. Disznókó** [diss-noh-koh] (*Tokaji*, Hungary) Newly-constituted estate belonging to AXA and run by Jean-Michel Cazes of *Ch. Lynch-Bages*. Top-class modern sweet *Tokaji* and dry lemony *Furmint*. ☆☆☆☆ **1995 Tokaji Dry Furmint $$$;** ☆☆☆☆☆ **1993 Tokaji Aszu 6 Puttonyos $$$**

DLG (Deutsche Landwirtschaft Gesellschaft) (Germany) Body awarding medals for excellence to German wines – far too generously.

DO Denominac/ion/ão de Origen (Spain, Portugal) Demarcated quality area, guaranteeing origin, grape varieties, and production standards (everything, in other words except the quality of the stuff in the bottle).

DOC Denominación de Origem Controlada (Portugal) Replacing the old RD (Região Demarcada) as Portugal's equivalent of Italy"s DOCG.

DOC Denominacion de Origen Califacada (Spain) Ludicrously, and confusingly, Spain's recently launched higher quality equivalent to Italy's *DOCG* shares the same initials as Italy's lower quality *DOC* wines. So far, restricted to *Rioja* – good, bad, and indifferent. In other words, this official designation should be treated – like Italy's *DOCs* and *DOCGs* and France's *Appellation Contrôlée* – with something less than total respect.

DOC(G) Denominazione di Origine Controllata (e Garantita) (Italy) Quality control designation based on grape variety and/or origin. "Garantita" is supposed to imply a higher quality level, but all too often it does no such thing and has more to do with regional politics than with tasty wines. It is worth noting, that, while the generally dull wines of *Albana di Romagna* received the first white DOCG (ahead of all sorts of more worthy candidates), the new efforts to bring *Vini da Tavola* into the system left such internationally applauded wines as *Tignanello* out in the cold among the most basic *DOCs*.

Ch. Doisy-Daëne [dwah-zee di-yen] (*Barsac 2ème Cru Classé*, *Bordeaux*, France) Fine *Barsac* property whose wines are typically more restrained than many a *Sauternes*. The top wine is L'Extravagance. **76** 78 79 81 82 83 85 86 **88 89 90** 91 94 95 96 97 98

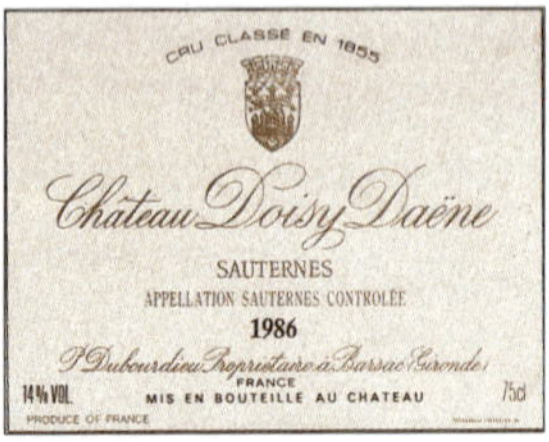

Ch. Doisy-Dubroca [dwah-zee doo-brohkah] (*Barsac 2ème Cru Classé*, *Bordeaux*, France) Underrated estate producing ultra-rich wines at often attractively low prices. **75** 76 78 79 **81 83** 85 86 87 88 89 90 95 96 97 98

Ch. Doisy-Védrines [dwah-zee vay-dreen] (*Barsac 2ème Cru Classé*, *Bordeaux*, France) Reliable *Barsac* property which made a stunningly concentrated 1989 (and a less impressive 1990). 70 **75 76** 78 79 81 **82 83** 85 86 **88** 89 90 92 93 95 96 97 98

Dolcetto (d'Alba, di Ovada) [dohl-cheh-toh] (*Piedmont*, Italy) Grape producing anything from soft everyday red to very robust and long-lasting examples. Generally worth catching quite young though. *Bests* use it to good effect in Australia ***Bava; Aldo Conterno;*** **Cortese;** ***Vajra.***

Dôle [Dohl] (Switzerland) *Appellation* of *Valais* producing attractive reds from *Pinot Noir* and/or *Gamay* grapes. Best for those with plenty of Swiss currency who like wines to knock back after a day on the ski slopes. **Germanier.**

Dom Pérignon [dom peh-reen-yon] (*Champagne*, France) *Moët et Chandon's Prestige Cuvée*, named after the cellarmaster who is erroneously said to have invented the *Champagne* method. Impeccable white and (rare) rosé. (Moët will disgorge older vintages to order.) ☆☆☆☆☆ **1990 $$$$**

Domaine (Dom.) [doh-mayn] (France) Wine estate.

Domecq [doh-mek] (*Jerez/Rioja*, Spain) Producer of (disappointing) La Ina *Fino* and the rare, wonderful 511A *Amontillado* and *Sibarita Palo Cortado*.

Ch. la Dominique [lah doh-mee-neek] (*St. Emilion Grand Cru Classé*, *Bordeaux*, France) High-flying property; one of the finest in *St. Emilion*. 70 **71** 78 79 81 **82** 83 **86** 88 89 90 93 94 95 96 97 98

Dominus [dahm-ih-nuhs] (*Napa Valley*, California) *Christian Moueix* of *Ch. Petrus*'s modestly named competitor to *Opus One* has now developed an accessibility that was lacking in early years. Even so, it is concentrated stuff that is built to last. ☆☆☆☆☆ **1994 $$$$**

Hermann Dönnhoff (*Nahe*, Germany) Brilliant winemaker who crafts great *late harvest* wine and *Eiswein* from his Hermannshöhle vineyard.

Doonkuna [doon-koo-nah] (*New South Wales*, Australia) Small winery making decent red wine close to the capital. ☆☆☆☆ **1992 Shiraz $$**

Dopff "Au Moulin" [dop-foh-moo-lan] (*Alsace*, France) Underrated *négoçiant* with concentrated *Grand Cru* wines.

Dopff & Irion [dop-fay-ee-ree-yon] (*Alsace*, France) Greatly improved; not to be confused with Dopff "Au Moulin," its namesake. ☆☆☆☆ **1994 Riesling Schoenenbourg $$$**

Vin de Pays de la Dordogne [dor-doyn] (*South West*, France) To the East of Bordeaux, this improving region offers light Bordeaux-style wines.

Dorin [doh-ran] (*Vaud*, Switzerland) The Swiss name for *Chasselas* in the *Vaud* region.

Dornfelder [dorn-fel-duh] (Germany) Sadly underrated early-ripening, juicy, berryish grape which is beginning to attract some interest among pioneering winemakers in the southern part of Germany.

Dosage [doh-sazh] The addition of sweetening syrup to naturally dry *Champagne* after *dégorgement* to replace the wine lost with the yeast, and to set the sugar to the desired level (even *Brut Champagne* requires up to 4 grams per liter of sugar to make it palatable).

Douro [doo-roh] (Portugal) The *port* region and river, producing increasingly good table wines thanks partly to the efforts of the long-established *Barca Velha, Quinta do Cotto (Grande Escolha), Sogrape*, and Australians *David Baverstock* (at *Quinta de la Rosa* and *Crasto)* and *Peter Bright*. Port house *Ramos Pinto's* Duas Quintas wines are good too.

Doux [doo] (France) Sweet.

Dow [dow] (*Douro*, Portugal) One of the big two (with *Taylor's)* and under the same family ownership as *Warre, Smith Woodhouse* and *Graham*. Great *vintage port* and similarly impressive *tawny*. The *single-quinta* Quinta do Bomfim wines offer a chance to taste the Dow's style affordably. **63 66 70** 72 75 77 85 91 94 97 ☆☆☆☆ **1995 Quinta do Bomfim Vintage Port $$$**

Drappier [drap-pee-yay] (*Champagne*, France) Small, recommendable producer. ☆☆☆☆☆ **1990 Champagne Carte d'Or Brut $$$**

Jean-Paul Droin [drwan] (*Burgundy*, France) Good, small *Chablis* producer with approachable 'modern' wines. ☆☆☆☆ **1996 Chablis Valmur $$$**

Dromana Estate [droh-mah-nah] (*Mornington Peninsula*, Australia) Viticulturalist Gary Crittenden makes good, if light, *Chardonnay* and raspberryish *Pinot Noir*. ☆☆☆☆ **1998 Chardonnay $$$**

Dom. Drouhin [droo-an] (*Oregon*, US) Top *Burgundy* producer's highly expensive investment in the US that's increasingly producing world-beating reds – thanks to Veronique Drouhin's skill and commitment and some of *Oregon's* best vineyards. ☆☆☆☆ **1995 Pinot Noir $$$$**

Joseph Drouhin [droo-an] (*Burgundy*, France) Probably *Burgundy's* best *négoçiant,* with first-class red and white wines that are unusually representative of their particular *appellations*. Also look out for the rare white *Beaune* from its own Clos des Mouches, top-class *Clos de Vougeot* and unusually (for a *négoçiant*) high-quality *Chablis*. The Marquis de Laguiche *Montrachet* is sublime. ☆☆☆☆☆ **1996 Chablis Les Clos $$$**

Pierre-Jacques Druet [droo-ay] (*Loire*, France) Wonderfully reliable *Bourgueil* producer making characterful individual *cuvées*. ☆☆☆☆ **1996 Grand Mont $$$**

Dry Creek (*Sonoma*, California) A rare example of a Californian *AVA* region whose wines have an identifiable quality and style. Look out for *Sauvignon Blanc* and *Zinfandel*. Red: 84 **85** 86 87 **90 91** 92 **93** 95 96 97 98 White: **85 90 91** 92 **95** 96 97 98. ***Beaulieu Vineyard*; *Dry Creek; Duxoup; Gallo Sonoma; Quivira; Nalle; Rafanell; Turley.***

Dry Creek Vineyard (*Sonoma*, California) Eponymous vineyard within the *Dry Creek AVA* making well-known *Fumé Blanc*, great *Chenin Blanc*, and impressive reds. ☆☆☆☆ **1995 Zinfandel $$$**

Dry River (*Martinborough*, New Zealand) Small estate with particularly impressive *Pinot Noir* and *Pinot Gris* and a delicious line in *late harvest* wines. ☆☆☆☆☆ **1995 Botrytis Riesling $$$**

Duboeuf [doo-burf] (*Burgundy*, France) The "King of *Beaujolais*," who introduced the world to the penny candy flavor of young *Gamay*. A range of good examples from individual growers, vineyards, and villages. Reliable *nouveau*, good straightforward *Mâconnais* white, single domaine *Rhônes*, and now the world's biggest plantation of *Viognier*. ☆☆☆☆ **1997 Morgon $$**

Dubreuil-Fontaine [doo-broy fon-tayn] (*Burgundy*, France) Quite traditional estate, producing full-flavored red and white individual *cuvées* from the *Corton* hillsides. ☆☆☆☆☆ **1995 Pernand Vergelesses, Ile des Vergelesses $$$**

Duckhorn (*Napa Valley*, California) Vaunted producer now making much more approachable – and to my mind far preferable – *Merlot* than in the past. ☆☆☆☆ **1995 Napa Valley Merlot $$$**

Ch. Ducru-Beaucaillou [doo-kroo boh-ki-yoo] (*St.Julien 2ème Cru Classé, Bordeaux*, France) *'Super Second'* with a decidedly less obvious style than peers such as *Léoville-Las-Cases* and *Pichon-Lalande*. Especially back on form in 1996, 1997, and (brilliantly in) 1998 after a disappointing patch in the late 1980s and early 1990s. Second wine is Croix-Beaucaillou. **70 75** 76 **78** 79 80 **81** 82 **83 85** 86 87 88 89 90 91 92 **93 94** 95 96 97 98

Dom. Bernard Dugat-Py [doo-gah pee] (*Burgundy*, France) Superstar *Gevrey-Chambertin* estate with great vineyards, from which M. Dugat makes delicious and unusually fairly priced wines *Grand Cru* ☆☆☆☆☆ **1996 Gevrey-Chambertin les Evoulles $$$**

Ch. Duhart-Milon-Rothschild [doo-ahr mee-lon rot-sheeld] (*Pauillac 4ème Cru Classé, Bordeaux*, France) Under the same management as *Lafite* and benefiting from heavy investment. 78 79 80 81 **82** 83 **85** 86 87 88 89 90 91 92 93 95 96 97 98

Dom. Dujac [doo-zhak] (*Burgundy*, France) Cult *Burgundy* producer Jacques Seysses makes fine, long-lived, and quite modern wines from *Morey-St.-Denis*, (including a particularly good *Clos de la Roche*) that are packed with intense *Pinot Noir* flavor. Now helped by Gary Farr of the excellent *Bannockburn* in Australia and busily investing time and effort into vineyards in southern France. ☆☆☆☆ **1995 Clos de la Roche $$$$**

Dumb As in dumb nose, meaning without smell.

Dunn Vineyards (*Napa Valley*, California) Randy Dunn makes tough, forbidding *Cabernets* from *Howell Mountain* for patient collectors. Give them time, though; eventually, they yield extraordinary spicy, berryish flavors. ☆☆☆☆ **1994 Cabernet Sauvignon Howell Mountain $$$$**

Durbach [door-bahk] (*Baden*, Germany) Top vineyard area of this *anbaugebiet*. **Wolf-Metternich.**

Durif [dyoor-if] See *Petite Sirah*.

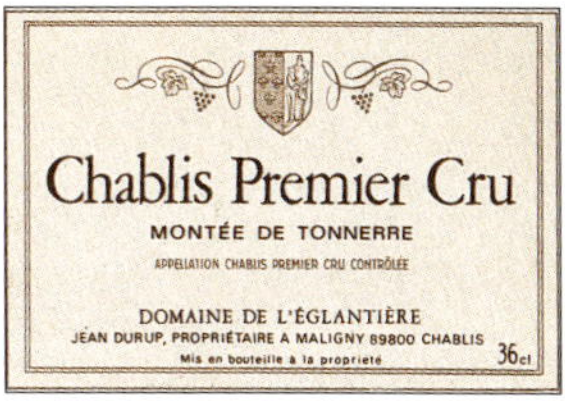

🍷 **Jean Durup** [doo-roop] (*Burgundy*, France) Modern estate whose owner controversially believes in extending vineyards of *Chablis* into what some claim to be less distinguished soil, and not using new oak. The best wines are sold as Ch. de Maligny. ☆☆☆☆ **1996 Château de Maligny Vieilles Vignes $$**

🍷 **Duxoup Wine Works** [duk-soop] (*Sonoma Valley*, California) Inspired winery-in-a-shed, producing very good characterful *Charbono* and fine *Syrah* from bought-in grapes. ☆☆☆ **1993 Charbono $$$**

E

🍷 **E&E** (*Barossa*, South Australia) One of the jewels of the *BRL Hardy* crown, producing rich, full-flavored reds and whites. ☆☆☆☆ **1994 Black Pepper Shiraz $$$**

🍷 **Maurice Ecard** [Ay-car] (*Burgundy*, France) Very recommendable *Savigny-lès-Beaune* estate with good *Premier Cru* vineyards. ☆☆☆☆ **1995 Savigny-les-Beaune les Serpentières $$$**

🍷 **Echézeaux** [ay-shuh-zoh] (*Burgundy*, France) *Grand Cru* between *Clos de Vougeot* and *Vosne-Romanée* and more or less an extension of the latter commune. *Flagey-Echézeaux*, a village on the relatively vineless side of the Route Nationale, takes its name from the "flagellation" used by the peasants to gather grain in the 6th century. Grands-Echézeaux should be finer. ***Dom. de la Romanée-Conti; Henri Jayer; Dom. Dujac;* Dom. Thierry Vigst.**

🍷 **L' Ecole No. 41** [ay-kohl] (*Washington State*, US) Stylish producer of classy *Chardonnay* and *Merlot*. Also supplies rich *Semillon*. ☆☆☆☆ **1991 Cabernet Sauvignon $$$$**

Edelfäule [ay-del-fow-luh] (Germany) *Botrytis cinerea*, or "*noble rot*."

Edelzwicker [ay-del-zwik-kur] (*Alsace*, France) Generic name for a blend of grapes. The idea of blends is coming back – but not the name (see *Hugel*).

🍷 **Edmunds St. John** (*Alameda*, California) Producer with his heart in the *Rhône* – and a taste for rich, spicy *Syrah*, and *Zinfandel* reds. ☆☆☆☆☆ **1995 Durell Vineyard Syrah $$$$**

🍷 **Edna Valley Vineyard** (California) Long-standing maker of rich, buttery *Chardonnay* in the *AVA* of the same name. In the same stable as *Chalone*, *Carmenet* and *Acacia* and now in an ambitious joint Californian venture with *Penfolds*. ☆☆☆ **1995 Brock Chardonnay $$**

Eger [eg-gur] (Hungary) Region of Hungary where *Bull's Blood* is made.

🍷 **Dom. de l'Eglise** [duh lay glees] (*Pomerol*, *Bordeaux*, France) Fairly priced, middle-of-the-range, wines. **79 82** 83 85 86 88 89 90 92 95 96 97 98

🍷 **Ch. l'Eglise-Clinet** [Lay gleez klee-nay] (*Pomerol*, *Bordeaux*, France) Terrific tiny estate that has gained – and earned – recent superstar status. 70 71 75 76 78 **79** 81 82 83 85 86 **88** 89 **90** 91 92 93 **94** 95 96 97 98 ☆☆☆☆☆ **1993 $$$$**

Egri Bikaver [eh-grih bih-kah vehr] (*Eger*, Hungary) See *Bull's Blood.*

Eiswein / Eiswein [ihs-vihn] (Germany/Austria/Canada) Ultraconcentrated *late harvest* wine, made from grapes naturally frozen on the vine. Hard to make (and consequently very pricey) in Germany but more affordable in Austria and Canada.

Eitelsbach [ih-tel-sbahk] (*Mosel*, Germany) One of the top two *Ruwer* wine towns, and the site of the famed Karthäuserhofberg vineyard.

Elaborado y Anejado Por [ay-lah-boh-rah-doh ee anay-hahdo pohr] (Spain) "Made and aged for."

Elderton (*Barossa Valley*, Australia) Highly commercial maker of big, rich, competition-winning wines, especially *Shiraz and Cabernet*.

Eléver/éléveur [ay-leh-vay/vay-leh-vuhr] To mature or "nurture" wine, especially in the cellars of the *Burgundy négoçiants,* who act as éléveurs after traditionally buying in wine made by small estates.

Elgin [el-gin] (South Africa) Coolish – *Burgundy*-like – apple-growing country which is rapidly attracting the interest of big wine producers. Watch out for the Paul Cluver reds and whites from *Neil Ellis.* May eventually overshadow all but the best parts of *Stellenbosch* and *Paarl.*

Neil Ellis (*Stellenbosch*, South Africa) New-wave *Cape* winemaker – and a pioneer of the new region of *Elgin.* ☆☆☆ **1997 Sauvignon Blanc $$**

Eltville [elt-vil] (*Rheingau*, Germany) Town housing the *Rheingau* state cellars and the German Wine Academy, producing good *Riesling* with backbone. QbA/Kab/Spät: **85** 86 **88 89 90** 91 **92 93 94** 95 96 97 98 Aus/Beeren/Tba: **83 85 88 89 90** 91 92 93 94 95 96 97 98

Elyse Wine Cellars (*Napa*, California) *Zinfandel* specialist with vineyards on *Howell Mountain*. Look out too for the Nero Misto spicy *Zinfandel, Petite Sirah* blend. ☆☆☆☆☆ **1995 Morisoli Zinfandel $$$**

Emilia-Romagna [eh-mee-lee-yah roh-ma-nya] (Italy) Region around Bologna best known for *Lambrusco;* also the source of *Albana, Sangiovese* di Romagna, and *Pagadebit.*

En primeur [on pree-muh] New wine, usually *Bordeaux*. Producers and specialist merchants buy and offer wine *en primeur* before it has been released. In the US and Australia, where producers like *Mondavi* and *Petaluma* are selling their wine in this way, the process is known as buying "futures."

Ch. l'Enclos [lon kloh] (*Pomerol*, *Bordeaux*, France) Gorgeously rich, fairly priced wines. 79 **82** 83 85 86 88 **89** 90 91 92 93 94 95 96 97 98

René Engel [On-jel] (*Burgundy*, France) Producer of rich, long-lived wines in *Vosne-Romanée* and *Clos Vougeot*. ☆☆☆☆☆ **1995 Grands Echézeaux $$$$**

English wine Quality has improved in recent years, as winemakers have moved from making semi-sweet, mock-Germanic to dry mock-*Loire* and, increasingly, sparkling, aromatic-but-dry and *late harvest*. ***Breaky Bottom; Thames Valley Vineyards;*** **Nyetimber, *Bruisyard; Three Choirs; Carr Taylor; Chiltern Valley.***

Enoteca [ee-noh-teh-kah] (Italy) Literally wine library or, now, wine shop.

Entre-Deux-Mers [on-truh duh mehr] (*Bordeaux*, France) Once a region of appalling sweet wine from vineyards between the cities of *Bordeaux* and Libourne. Now a source of basic *Bordeaux* Blanc and principally dry *Sauvignon*. Reds are sold as *Bordeaux* Rouge. Both reds and whites suffer from the difficulty grapes can have in ripening in cool years. *Ch. Bonnet* is the star.

Erath Vineyards [ee-rath] (*Oregon*, US) One of Oregon's pioneering Pinot Noir producers, now making better wine than ever. ☆☆☆☆☆ **1996 Pinot Noir $$$**

Erbach [ayr-bahkh] (*Rheingau*, Germany) Town noted for fine full *Riesling*, particularly from the Marcobrunn vineyard. QbA/Kab/Spät: **85** 86 **88 89 90** 91 92 93 94 95 96 97 98 Aus/Beeren/Tba: **83 85** 88 89 90 91 92 93 94 95 96 97 98 ***Schloss Reinhartshausen*; Schloss Schönborn.**

Erbaluce [ehr-bah-loo-chay] (*Piedmont*, Italy) White grape responsible for the light dry wines of the *Caluso*, and the sweet sun-dried *Caluso Passito*.

Erbaluce di Caluso [ehr-bah-loo-chay dee kah-loo-soh] (*Piedmont*, Italy) Dry, quite herby white wine made from the *Erbaluce* grape (*Bava* makes a good one, blending in a little *Chardonnay*). ☆☆☆ **1996 Ferrando $**

Erden [ehr-durn] (*Mosel-Saar-Ruwer*, Germany) In the *Bernkastel bereich*, this northerly village produces full, crisp, dry *Riesling* and includes the famous Treppchen vineyard. QbA/Kab/Spät: **85** 86 **88 89 90** 92 93 94 95 96 97 98 Aus/Beeren/Tba: **83 85** 88 89 90 91 92 93 94 95 97 98 ☆☆☆☆

Errazuriz [ehr-raz-zoo-riz] (*Aconcagua Valley*, Chile) One of Chile's big name producers and owner of *Caliterra*. Wines have been improved by input from *Mondavi*. Look out for the "Wild Ferment" *Chardonnay* and recently launched *Syrah*. ☆☆☆☆ **1997 Don Maximiano $$$**

Erzeugerabfüllung [ayr-tsoy-guhr-ab-foo-loong] (Germany) Bottled by the grower/estate.

Esk Valley (*Hawke's Bay*, New Zealand) Under the same ownership as *Vidal* and *Villa Maria*. Successful with *Bordeaux*-style reds and juicy rosé. ☆☆☆☆☆ **1998 Estate Chardonnay $$**

Frederic Esmonin [Ehs-moh-na'] (*Burgundy*, France) Estate with good vineyards in *Nuits-St.-Georges*, *Gevrey-Chambertin* and *Chambolle-Musigny*. ☆☆☆☆☆ **1991 Mazis-Chambertin $$$$**

Esporão [esp-per-row] (*Alentejo*, Portugal) Revolutionary wines made by Australian-born *David Baverstock*. ☆☆☆☆☆ **1997 Trincadeira Preta $$**

Espum/oso/ante [es-poom-mo-soh/san-tay] (Spain/Portugal) Sparkling.

Est! Est!! Est!!! [ehst-ehst-ehst] (*Lazio*, Italy) Red named after the repeated exclamation of a bishop's servant when he found a good wine. Apart from the ones made by Falesco, today's examples rarely offer much to exclaim about.

Esters Chemical components in wine responsible for all those extraordinary odors of fruits, vegetables, hamster cages, and sneakers.

Estremadura [ehst-reh-mah-doo-rah] (Portugal) Huge area producing mostly dull wine. Quintas da Pancas and Boavista are showing what can be done.

Estufa [esh-too-fah] (*Madeira*, Portugal) The vats in which *Madeira* is heated, speeding maturity and imparting its familiar 'cooked' flavor.

Eszencia [es-sen-tsee-yah] (*Tokaji*, Hungary) Incredibly concentrated syrup made by piling around 100kg of *late harvested*, *botrytized* grapes into *puttonyos* and letting as little as three liters of incredibly sticky stuff dribble out of the bottom. This will only ferment up to about 4 percent alcohol, over several weeks, before stopping completely. It is then stored and used to sweeten normal *Aszú* wines. The Czars of Russia discovered the joys of Eszencia, and it has been prized for its effects on the male libido. It is incredibly hard to find, even by those who can see the point in doing anything with the expensive syrup other than pouring it on ice-cream. The easier-to-find *Aszú Essencia* (one step sweeter than *Aszú* 6 *puttonyos)* is far better value.

Arnaldo Etchart [et-shaht] (*Cafayate*, Argentina) Dynamic producer, benefiting from advice by *Michel Rolland* of *Pomerol* fame, and also investment by its new owners Pernod Ricard. The key wine here, though, is the grapey white *Torrontes*. ☆☆☆ **1998 Cafayate Barrel Fermented Chardonnay $**

l'Etoile (*Jura*, France) Theoretically the best appellation in the *Jura*. *Chardonnay* and *Savagnin* whites and sparkling wines can be good, and the sherry-like *Vin Jaune* is of interest. **Ch de l'Etoile.**

Etude [ay-tewd] (*Napa*, California) Thoughtful superstar consultant Tony Soter experiments by marrying specific sites and clones of *Pinot Noir*. Apart from these wines, there are good rich *Napa* reds and *Carneros Chardonnay*. ☆☆☆☆☆ **1996 Pinot Noir Napa Valley $$$**

Ch. l' Evangile [lay-van-zheel] (*Pomerol*, *Bordeaux*, France) A classy and increasingly sought-after property that can, in great vintages like 1988, 1989 and 1990, sometimes rival its neighbor *Pétrus*, but in a more *tannic* style. 75 78 79 **82 83 85 86** 87 88 89 90 92 93 95 96 97 98 ☆☆☆☆ **1990 $$$$**

Evans Family/Evans Wine Co (*Hunter Valley*, Australia) Len Evans' (founder, ex-chairman of *Rothbury Vineyards*) own estate and company. Rich *Chardonnay* and *Semillon* as characterful and generous as their maker.

Evans & Tate (*Margaret River*, Australia) Much improved producer with good Chardonnay and Shiraz. ☆☆☆☆ **1996 Chardonnay $$$**

Eventail de Vignerons Producteurs [ay-van-tih] (*Burgundy*, France) Reliable source of *Beaujolais*. ☆☆☆☆☆ **1998 Brouilly F. Tatoux $$**

Eyrie Vineyards [ih-ree] (*Oregon*, US) Pioneering *Pinot Noir* producer in the *Willamette Valley*, whose success in a blind tasting of *Burgundies* helped to attract *Joseph Drouhin* to invest his francs in a vineyard here. ☆☆☆☆ **1996 Pinot Gris $$$**

F

Fairview Estate (*Paarl*, South Africa) Go-ahead estate where Charles Back – both under his own name and under that of Fairview – makes good-value wines more open-mindedly than some of his neighbors. One of the few South Africans responsible for genuine innovation. ☆☆☆☆ **1997 Cyril Back Zinfandel$$**

Joseph Faiveley [fay-vlay] (*Burgundy*, France) Impressive modern *négoçiant* with particular strength in vineyards in the *Côte de Nuits* and *Nuits-St.-Georges*. ☆☆☆☆ **1995 Corton Clos des Cortons $$$$**

Far Niente [fah nee-yen-tay] (*Napa Valley*, California) Well regarded producer of sometimes over-showy *Chardonnay* and *Cabernet*.

Ch. de Fargues [duh-fahrg] (*Sauternes*, *Bordeaux*, France) Elegant wines made by the winemaker at *Ch. d'Yquem* – and a good alternative. **70 71 75 76** 78 79 80 83 **85** 86 88 89 90 95 96 97 98 ☆☆☆☆ **1997 $$$$**

Gary Farrell (*Sonoma*, California) A *Russian River Pinot Noir* maker to watch. ☆☆☆☆ **1994 Pinot Noir $$$$**

Fat Has a silky texture which fills the mouth. More fleshy than meaty.

Fattoria [fah-tor-ree-ah] (Italy) Estate, particularly in *Tuscany*.

Faugères [foh-zhehr] (*Midi*, France) With neighboring *St. Chinian*, this gently hilly region is a major cut above the surrounding *Coteaux du Languedoc*, and potentially the source of really exciting red. For the moment, however, most still taste pretty rustic. **G. Alquier; Ch. des Estanilles.**

Bernard Faurie [fow-ree] (*Rhône*, France) Tournon-based producer who makes intense perfumed wines with great longevity.

Bodegas Faustino Martinez [fows-tee-noh mahr-tee-nehth] (*Rioja*, Spain) Dependable *Rioja* producer with excellent *(Gran) Reservas*, fair whites and a decent *cava*. ☆☆☆☆ **1992 Tinto Gran Reserva $$$**

Favorita [fahvoh-ree-tah] (*Piedmont*, Italy) Traditional variety from *Piedmont* transformed by modern winemaking into delicate floral whites. *Conterno;* Villa Lanata*; Bava.*

Weingut Feiler-Artinger [fih-luh arh-ting-guh] (*Rust*, Austria) Superlative innovative producer of dry and, especially, *late harvest* wines. ☆☆☆ **1997 Klaus Neuburger Essenz $$$**

Fattoria di Felsina Berardenga [fah-toh-ree-ah dee fehl-see-nah beh-rah-den-gah] (*Tuscany*, Italy) Very high-quality *Chianti* estate. ☆☆☆☆☆ **1994 Chianti Riserva $$$**

Felton Road (*Central Otago*, New Zealand) Instant superstar with what may be New Zealand's top *Pinot Noir* as well as some very smart *Riesling*.

Fendant [fon-don] (Switzerland) See *Chasselas*.

Fer [fehr] (*South-West*, France) Grape used to make *Marcillac*.

Fermentazione naturale [fehr-men-tat-zee-oh-nay] (Italy) "Naturally sparkling" but, in fact, indicates the *cuve close* method.

Fernão Pires [fehr-now pee-rehsh] (Portugal) Muscatty grape, used to great effect by *Peter Bright* of the *João Pires* winery.

Ch. Ferrand Lartique [feh-ron lah-teek] (*St. Emilion Grand Cru*, *Bordeaux*, France) Small 5-acre estate producing full-bodied rich wines.

Luigi Ferrando (*Piedmont* Italy) Producer in the Carema *DOC* of good *Nebbiolo*-based wines that are surprizingly and attractively light and elegant in style.

Ferrari [feh-rah-ree] (*Trentino*, Italy) A sexy name for some really rather sexy Champagne-method sparkling wines. The Riserva del Fondatore is the star of the show.

Ferrari-Carano (*Sonoma*, California) Improving winery best known for its oaky, crowd-pleasing Chardonnay and rich Merlot. The Italianate Sangiovese blend is more interesting.

AA Ferreira [feh-ray-rah] (*Douro*, Portugal) Traditional Portuguese *port* producer, equally famous for its excellent *tawnies* as for its *Barca Velha*, Portugal's best traditional unfortified red. ☆☆☆☆ **Duque de Braganca 20 Year Old Tawny $$**; ☆☆☆☆ **1998 Vallado Douro Tinto $$$**

Gloria Ferrer (*Sonoma*, California) New World offshoot of *Freixenet* (the people behind *Cordon Negro*) making generally unmemorable sparkling wine and rather more interesting *Pinot Noir*.

Ch. Ferrière [feh-ree-yehr] (*Margaux 3ème Cru Classé*, *Bordeaux*, France) Once small, now rather bigger, thanks to the convenience of belonging to the same owners as the *Margaux Cru Bourgeois, Ch. la Gurgue*. 89 90 91 92 93 94 95 96 97 98 ☆☆☆☆ **1995 $$$**

Ch. de Fesles [dur fel] (*Loire*, France) Classic *Bonnezeaux*. ☆☆☆☆☆ **1996 Bonnezeaux $$$$**

Sylvain Fessy [seel-van fes-see] (*Burgundy*, France) Reliable small *Beaujolais* producer with wide range of *crus*.

Henry Fessy [on-ree fes-see] (*Burgundy*, France) Consistent *négoçiant*, vineyard owner and producer of *Beaujolais*.

Fetzer [fet-zuh] (*Mendocino*, California) Underrated in the US, this is the best of the bigger Californian wineries. One of the few which really tries to make good wine at (relatively) lower prices and a pioneering producer of "Bonterra" organic wines. Recently taken over, but still run by the family. ☆☆☆☆☆ **1997 Barrel Select Viognier $$; ☆☆☆☆☆ 1997 Barrel Select Chardonnay $$**

Nicolas Feuillatte [fuh-yet] (*Champagne*, France) Quietly rising star with good-value wine. ☆☆☆☆ **1992 Palmes d'Or $$$**

William Fèvre [weel-yum feh-vr] (*Burgundy*, France) Quality *Chablis* producer who has been a revolutionary in his use of new oak. His efforts in Chile have been improving with each vintage. ☆☆☆☆ **1995 Chablis Grand Cru Bougros $$$$**

Ch. Feytit-Clinet [fay-tee klee-nay] (*Pomerol, Bordeaux*, France) A *Moueix* property with good, delicate wines. 79 81 **82** 83 **85** 86 87 88 89 90 94 95 96 97 98

Fiano [fee-yah-noh] (Italy) Herby white grape variety used to make Fiano di Avellino in the south.

Les Fiefs-de-Lagrange [fee-ef duh lag-ronzh] (*St. Julien, Bordeaux*, France) Recommendable *second label* of *Ch. Lagrange*.

Ch. de Fieuzal [duh fyuh-zahl] (*Pessac-Léognan Grand Cru Classé, Bordeaux*, France) Recently sold *Pessac-Léognan* property which has made great whites and lovely raspberryish reds. Abeille de Fieuzal is the (excellent) *second label*. Red: 75 79 81 **82** 83 **85** 86 88 89 90 91 92 93 94 **95** 96 97 98 White: **85 88 89** 90 91 **92 93 96** 97 98

Ch. Figeac [fee-zhak] (*St. Emilion Premier Grand Cru, Bordeaux*, France) Forever in the shadow of its neighbor, *Cheval Blanc*, but still one of the most characterful *St. Emilions*. **64 70** 78 **82** 83 84 **85 86** 88 89 90 92 93 **94** 95 96 97 98 ☆☆☆☆ **1994 $$$$**

Filliatreau (*Loire*, France) Exemplary producer of Saumur Champigny which shows how tasty the Cabernet Franc can be – and how it can age.

Finger Lakes (*New York State*, US) Cold region whose producers struggle (sometimes effectively) to produce good *vinifera*, including *late harvest Riesling*. *Hybrids* such as *Seyval Blanc* are more reliable. ***Fox Run.***

Fining The clarifying of young wine before bottling to remove impurities, using a number of agents including *isinglass* and *bentonite*.

Finish What you can still taste after swallowing.

Fino [fee-noh] (*Jerez*, Spain) Dry, delicate *sherry* which gains its distinctive flavor from the *flor* or yeast which grows on the surface of the wine during maturation. Drink chilled, with tapas, preferably within two weeks of opening. ***Lustau; Barbadillo; Hidalgo; Gonzalez Byass.***

Firestone (*Santa Ynez*, California) Good producer – particularly of good value *Chardonnay*, *Merlot* and *Sauvignon* and *late harvest Riesling* – in southern California. ☆☆☆☆ **1997 Chardonnay $$**

Fisher (*Sonoma*, California) Top-class producer of limited-production, single-vineyard *Cabernets* and *Chardonnays* from hillside vineyards. ☆☆☆☆☆ **1994 Wedding Vineyard Cabernet Sauvignon $$$$**

Fitou [fee-too] (*Midi*, France) Long considered to be an up-market *Corbières* but actually rather a basic southern *AC*, making reds largely from the *Carignan* grape. The wines here may have become more refined, with a woody warmth, but they never quite shake off their rustic air. **Ch. de Nouvelles; *Mont Tauch.***

Fixin [fee-san] (*Burgundy*, France) Northerly village of the *Côte de Nuits*, producing lean, tough, uncommercial reds which can mature well. **78** 79 **80** 82 83 **85** 86 87 **88 89 90** 92 95 96 97 98 ☆☆☆☆ **1996 Jadot $$$**

Flabby Lacking balancing *acidity*.

Flagey-Echézeaux [flah-jay ay-shuh-zoh] (*Burgundy*, France) Village on the wrong (non-vine) side of the Route National 74 that lends its name to the *appellations* of *Echézeaux* and *Grands Echézeaux*.

Ch. La Fleur [flur] (*St. Emilion*, *Bordeaux*, France) Small *St. Emilion* property producing softly fruity wines. **82** 83 85 86 88 **89** 90 92 94 95 96 97 98

Ch. la Fleur de Gay [flur duh gay] (*Pomerol*, *Bordeaux*, France) *Ch. Croix de Gay*'s best wine and thus heavily sought after. Showed improvement in 1998. **82 86** 88 89 90 94 95 96 97 98

Ch. la Fleur-Pétrus [flur pay-trooss] (*Pomerol*, *Bordeaux*, France) For those who find *Pétrus* a touch unaffordable, this next-door neighbor offers gorgeously accessible *Pomerol* flavor for (in *Pétrus* terms) a bargain price. 70 **75** 78 79 **81 82 83 85 86** 87 88 89 90 92 **93** 95 96 97 98

Fleurie [fluh-ree] (*Burgundy*, France) One of the 10 *Beaujolais Crus*, ideally fresh and fragrant, as its name suggests. Best vineyards include La Madonne and Pointe du Jour. Dom. Bachelard and Guy Depardon are names to watch. 90 95 96 **97 98** **Berrod; Chignard; Després; Duboeuf; Ch. Labourons; Métrat; Andre Vaisse.**

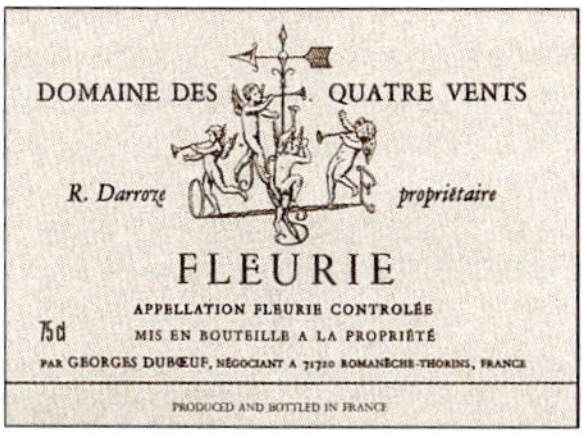

Flor [flawr] Yeast which grows naturally on the surface of some maturing sherries, making them potential *finos*.

Flora [flor-rah] A cross between *Semillon* and *Gewürztraminer*, best known in *Brown Brothers Orange Muscat* and Flora.

Flora Springs (*Napa Valley*, California) Good, unusual *Sauvignon Blanc* (Soliloquy) and classy *Merlot, Cabernet Sauvignon & Cabernet Franc* blend (Trilogy). ☆☆☆☆ **1994 Rutherford Cabernet $$$**

Emile Florentin [floh-ron-tan] (*Rhône*, France) Maker of ultra-traditional, ultra-*tannic,* chewy *St. Joseph*.

Flying winemakers Young (usually) Antipodeans who have, since the 1980s, been despatched like vinous mercenaries to wineries worldwide to make better and more reliable wine than the home teams can manage. Often, as they have proved, all it has taken to improve the standards of a European cooperative has been a more scrupulous attitude towards picking ripe grapes (rather than impatiently harvesting unripe ones) and keeping tanks and pipes clean.

Ch. Fombrauge [fom-brohzh] (*St. Emilion*, *Bordeaux*, France) Middling *St. Emilion*. **82 83 85 86 88 89 90** 92 93 **94 95** 96 97 98 ☆☆☆ **1994 $$$**

Ch. Fonplégade [fon-pleh-gahd] (*St. Emilion Grand Cru Classé*, *Bordeaux*, France) If you like your *St. Emilion* tough, this is for you. 78 **82** 83 85 86 87 88 89 90 94 95 96 97 98 ☆☆☆ **1989 $$$$**

Ch. Fonroque [fon-rok] (*St. Emilion Grand Cru Classé*, *Bordeaux*, France) Property with concentrated wines, but not always one of *Moueix's* very finest. 70 **75** 78 **79 82 83 85** 86 88 89 90 92 93 94 95 96 97 98

Fonseca Guimaraens [fon-say-ka gih-mah-rans] (*Douro*, Portugal) Now a subsidiary of *Taylor's* but still independently making great *port*. In blind tastings the 1976 and 1978 and 1984 regularly beat supposedly classier houses' supposedly finer vintages. See also *Guimaraens*. Fonseca: 60 **63 66 70** 75 77 80 83 **84** 85 95 Fonseca Guimaraens: **76 78** 82 84 88 92 94 ☆☆☆☆☆ **1984 Fonseca Guimaraens Vintage Port $$$**

JM da Fonseca Internacional [fon-say-ka in-tuhr-nah-soh-nahl] (*Setúbal* Peninsula, Portugal) Highly commercial firm whose wines include Lancers, the *Mateus*-taste-alike sold in mock-crocks.

JM da Fonseca Successores [fon-say-ka suk-ses-saw-rays] (*Estremadura*, Portugal) Unrelated to the *port* house of the same name and no longer connected to *JM da Fonseca Internacional*. Family-run firm, which with *Aliança* and *Sogrape* is one of Portugal's big three dynamic wine companies. Top reds include Pasmados, *Periquita* (from the grape of the same name), *Quinta da Camarate*, Terras Altas Dão and the *Cabernet*-influenced "TE" *Garrafeiras*. Dry whites are less impressive, but the sweet old *Moscatel de Setúbals* are luscious classics. ☆☆☆☆ **1992 Quinta da Camarate, Terras do Sado $$$$**

Dom. Font de Michelle [fon-duh-mee-shel] (*Rhône*, France) Reliable producer of medium-bodied red *Châteauneuf-du-Pape* and small quantities of brilliant, almost unobtainable, white. ☆☆☆☆☆ **1997 Châteauneuf-du-Pape $$$**

Fontana Candida [fon-tah-nah kan-dee-dah] (*Lazio*, Italy) Good producer, especially for *Frascati*. The top wine is Colle Gaio which is good enough to prove the disappointing nature of most other wines from this area. ☆☆☆☆ **1998 Frascati Superiore Terre dei Grifi $$**

Fontanafredda [fon-tah-nah-freh-dah] (*Piedmont*, Italy) Big producer with impressive *Asti Spumante* and very approachable (especially single-vineyard) *Barolo*. ☆☆☆☆ **1993 Barolo Vigna la Rosa $$$$**

Domaine de Font Sane [fon-sen] (*Rhône*, France) Producer of fine *Gigondas* in a very underrated *AC*. Very traditional and full-bodied.

Castello di Fonterutoli (*Tuscany*, Italy) Chianti Classico producer of real class, which also produces great non-DOC blends: Concerto and Siepi. ☆☆☆☆☆ **1996 Chianti Classico Riserva $$$**

Fontodi [Fon-Toh-Dee] (*Tuscany*, Italy) Classy *Tuscan* producer with Flaccianello, a good *Vino da Tavola*. ☆☆☆☆☆ **1996 Chianti Classico $$$$**

Forman (*Napa Valley*, California) Rick Forman makes good *Cabernet* and *Merlot* and refreshingly non-buttery *Chardonnay*. ☆☆☆☆ **1995 Cabernet Sauvignon $$$$**

Forst [Fawrst] (*Pfalz*, Germany) Wine town producing great concentrated *Riesling*. Famous for the *Jesuitengarten* vineyard. QbA/Kab/Spät: **85** 86 **88** 91 92 93 94 95 96 97 98 Aus/Beeren/Tba: **83 85** 88 89 90 91 92 93 94 95 96 97 98 ☆☆☆☆ **1996 Forster Jesuitengarten, Dr V Basserman-Jordan $$$**

Fortant de France [faw-tan duh frons] (*Languedoc-Roussillon*, France) Good-quality revolutionary brand owned by *Skalli* and specializing in varietal *Vin de Pays d'Oc*. ☆☆☆☆ **1998 Reserve Cabernet Sauvignon $$**

Les Forts de Latour [lay faw duh lah-toor] (*Pauillac*, *Bordeaux*, France) *Second label* of *Ch. Latour*. Not, as is often suggested, made exclusively from the fruit of young vines and wine which might otherwise have ended up in *Ch. Latour* – there are several vineyards whose grapes are grown specially for Les Forts – but, like the *second labels* of other top châteaux, this is still often better than lesser *classed growth châteaux*' top wines. **82 83 85 86** 88 **90** 91 92 **93 94** 95 96 97 98

Ch. Fourcas-Dupré [faw-kass doo-pray] (*Listrac Cru Bourgeois, Bordeaux*, France) Tough, very traditional *Listrac*. **70** 75 **78** 81 **82 83** 85 **86** 87 88 89 90 91 92 95 96 97 98

Ch. Fourcas-Hosten [faw-kass hos-ten] (*Listrac Cru Bourgeois, Bordeaux*, France) Firm, old-fashioned wine with plenty of "grip" for *tannin* fans. 75 78 81 **82 83 85 86** 87 88 89 90 91 92 95 96 97 98

Fox Run Vineyards (*New York*, US) One of the most successful producers in the Finger Lakes, offering good sparkling wine, *Riesling* and *Chardonnay*.

Foxen (*Santa Ynez*, California) *Pinot* producer now moving successfully into *Syrah*. ☆☆☆☆ **1995 Syrah $$$**

Ch. Franc-Mayne [fron-mayn] (*St. Emilion Grand Cru Classé, Bordeaux*, France) Dry, austere, traditional wines for those who like them that way. 85 86 87 88 **89 90** 94 95 96 ☆☆☆ **1990 $$$**

Franciacorta [fran-chee yah-kor-tah] (*Lombardy*, Italy) *DOC* for good, light, French-influenced reds but better noted for varied sparklers made to sell at the same price as *Champagne*, if not more than. See *Ca Del Bosco*.

Franciscan Vineyards [fran-sis-kan] (*Napa Valley*, California) Recently sold (to the huge Canandaigua), reliable *Napa* winery whose Chilean boss Augustin Huneeus, has pioneered natural yeast wines with his *Burgundy*-like "Cuvée Sauvage" *Chardonnay* and has punctured the pretentious balloons of some of his neighbors. Now also making wine in Chile – at *Veramonte*. ☆☆☆☆ **1994 Chardonnay Sauvage $$$**

Ch. de Francs [day fron] (*Côtes de Francs, Bordeaux*, France) Well-run estate which makes great-value crunchy, blackcurranty wine and, with *Ch. Puygeraud*, helps to prove the worth of this little-known region.

Franken [fran-ken] (Germany) *Anbaugebiet* making characterful, sometimes earthy, dry whites, traditionally presented in the squat flagon-shaped "*bocksbeutel*" on which the *Mateus* bottle was modeled. One of the key varieties is the *Sylvaner* which explains the earthiness of many of the wines. The weather here does make it easier to make dry wine than in many other regions.

Franschhoek [fran-shook] (South Africa) Valley leading into the mountains away from *Paarl* (and thus cooler). The soil is a little suspect, however, and the best producers are mostly clustered at the top of the valley, around the picturesque eponymous town. Red: **84** 86 **87** 89 **91 92** 93 94 95 96 White: **87 91** 92 93 94 95 96 97

Frascati [fras-kah-tee] (*Latium*, Italy) Clichéd dry or semi-dry white from *Latium*. At its best it is soft and clean with a fascinating "sour cream" flavor. Drink within 12 months of *vintage*. ***Fontana Candida*; Colli di Catone.**

Ca' dei Frati [kah day-yee frah-tee] (*Lombardy*, Italy) Fine producers, both of *Lugana* and *Chardonnay*-based sparkling wine.

Freemark Abbey (*Napa Valley*, California) Well-regarded producer of good, rather than great *Cabernet*. ☆☆☆ **1992 Cabernet Sauvignon $$$$**

Freisa [fray-ee-sah] (Italy) Characterful perfumed red wine grape with lovely cherryish, raspberryish flavors, popular with Hemingway and grown in Piedmont by producers like Gilli and *Vajra*. Drink young.

Frei Weingartener Wachau [fri-vine-gahrt-nur vah-kow] (*Wachau*, Austria) Unusually fine cooperative with great vineyards, dry and sweet versions of the indigenous *Grüner Veltliner* and gloriously concentrated *Rieslings* that outclass the efforts of many a big-name estate in Germany. ☆☆☆☆ **1993 Riesling Burgerspitalstiftung Spitz Smaragd $$$**

🍷 **Freixenet** [fresh-net] (*Catalonia*, Spain) Giant in the *cava* field and proponent of traditional *Catalonian* grapes in sparkling wine. Its dull, off-dry big-selling *Cordon Negro* made from traditional grapes is a perfect justification for adding *Chardonnay* to the blend.

🍷 **Marchesi de' Frescobaldi** [mah-kay-see day fres-koh-bal-dee] (*Tuscany*, Italy) Family estate with classy wines including *Castelgiocondo*, Mormoreto, a *Cabernet Sauvignon* based wine, the rich white *Pomino* Il Benefizio *Chardonnay*, *Pomino* Rosso using *Merlot* and *Cabernet Sauvignon*, and Nippozano in *Chianti*. Now in joint venture to make *Luce* with *Mondavi*. ☆☆☆☆ **1996 Montesodi Chianti Rufina $$$** ☆☆☆☆ **1996 Mormoreto $$$**

🍷 **Freycinet** [fres-sih-net] (*Tasmania*, Australia) Small East Coast winery with some of Australia's best *Pinot Noir* and great *Chardonnay*. Sadly, the giant Spanish sparkling wine firm *Freixenet* has striven to prevent this label appearing outside Australia, despite the facts that *Freycinet* is an historic name in *Tasmania* and that this winery makes no sparkling wine. ☆☆☆☆ **1996 Pinot Noir $$$.**

🍷 **Friuli-Venezia Giulia** [free-yoo-lee veh-neht-zee-yah zhee-yoo-lee-yah] (Italy) Northerly region containing a number of *DOC*s such as *Colli Orientali*, *Collio*, Friuli Grave and Aquileia and *Isonzo* which focus on single-variety wines like *Merlot*, *Cabernet Franc*, *Pinot Bianco*, *Pinot Grigio*, and *Tocai*. Quality varies enormously, ranging from dilute, over-cropped efforts to the complex masterpieces of producers like ***Jermann;*** **Bidoli;** ***Puiatti; Zonin.***

Frizzante [freet-zan-tay] (Italy) Semisparkling especially *Lambrusco*.

🍷 **Frog's Leap** (*Napa Valley*, California) Winery whose owners combine organic winemaking skill with a fine sense of humor (their slogan is "Time's fun when you're having flies"). Tasty *Zinfandel*, 'wild yeast' *Chardonnay* and unusually good *Sauvignon Blanc*. ☆☆☆ **1995 Chardonnay $$$**

🍷 **Fronsac/Canon Fronsac** [fron-sak] (*Bordeaux*, France) *Pomerol* neighbors, who regularly produce rich, intense, affordable wines. They are rarely subtle; however, with some good winemaking from men like *Christian Moueix* of *Ch. Pétrus* (he is a great believer in these regions), they can often represent some of the best buys in *Bordeaux*. Canon Fronsac is thought by some to be the better of the pair. **83** 85 86 **88 89** 90 94 95 96 97 98 ***Ch. Canon;*** **Cassagne;** ***Dalem;*** **Fontenil; Moulin Haut Laroque; Moulin Pey-Labrie; Vieille Cure.**

🍷 **Ch. de Fuissé** [duh fwee-say] (*Burgundy*, France) Jean-Jacques Vincent is probably the best producer in this *commune*, making wines comparable to some of the best of the *Côte d'Or*. The *Vieilles Vignes* can last as long as a good *Chassagne-Montrachet;* the other *cuvées* run it a close race. ☆☆☆☆ **1996 Pouilly Fuissé $$$**

Fumé Blanc [fyoo-may blahnk] Name originally adapted from *Pouilly Blanc Fumé* by *Robert Mondavi* to describe his California oaked *Sauvignon*. Now widely used – though not exclusively – in the New World for this style.

🍇 **Furmint** [foor-mint] (*Tokaji*, Hungary) Lemony white grape, used in Hungary for *Tokaji* and, given modern winemaking, good dry wines. See *Royal Tokaji Wine Co* and *Disznókö*. ☆☆☆☆ **1996 Disznókö Fürmint $$**

🍷 **Rudolf Fürst** [foorst] (*Fraken*, Germany) One of Germany's best producers of ripe red *Pinot Noir* Spätburgunder, and some lovely floral *Riesling*.

🍷 **Fürstlich Castell'sches Domanenamt** [foorst-likh kas-tel-shes doh-man-nehn-nahmt] (*Franken*, Germany) Prestigious producer of typically full-bodied dry whites from the German *anbaugebiet* of *Franken*.

Fûts de Chêne (élévé en) [foo duh shayne] (France) Oak barrels (aged in).

Futures See *En Primeur*

G

🍷 **Ch. la Gaffelière** [gaf-fuh-lyehr] (*St. Emilion Premier Grand Cru, Bordeaux*, France) Lightish-bodied but well-made wines. Not to be confused with *Ch. Canon la Gaffelière*. **82 83** 85 **86** 88 89 90 92 93 94 95 96 97 98

🍷 **Dom. Jean-Noël Gagnard** [jon noh-wel gan-yahr] (*Burgundy*, France) A reliable *domaine* with vineyards which spread across *Chassagne-Montrachet*. There is also some *Santenay*. ☆☆☆☆ **1995 Chassagne-Montrachet Clos de la Maltroye $$$$**

🍷 **Jacques Gagnard-Delagrange** [gan-yahr duh lag-ronzh] (*Burgundy*, France) A top-class producer to follow for those traditionalists who like their white *Burgundies* delicately oaked. ☆☆☆☆ **1992 Chassagne-Montrachet $$$$**

Gaillac [gih-yak] (*South-West* France) Light, fresh, good-value reds and (sweet, dry and slightly sparkling) whites, produced using *Gamay* and *Sauvignon* grapes, as well as the indigenous *Mauzac*. The reds can rival *Beaujolais*. **Ch. Clement Ternes; Labastide de Levis; Robert Plageoles.**

🍷 **Pierre Gaillard** [gi-yahr] (*Rhône*, France) A good producer of *Côte Rôtie, St. Joseph* and *Condrieu*. ☆☆☆☆ **1995 Côte Rôtie $$$$**

🍷 **Gainey Vineyard** [gay-nee] (*Santa Barbara*, California) Classy reds and whites, especially *Pinot* and *Chardonnay*. ☆☆☆☆ **1995 Chardonnay $$$**

🍷 **Gaja** [gi-yah] (*Piedmont*, Italy) The man who proved that wines from the previously modest region of *Barbaresco* could sell for higher prices than top-class *clarets*, let alone the supposedly classier neighbors *Barolo* (an example of which he now makes too). Individual vineyard reds are of great quality and the *Chardonnay* is the best in Italy. Asking whether they're worth these prices is like questioning the cost of a Ferrari.

Galestro [gah-less-troh] (*Tuscany*, Italy) There is no such thing as *Chianti* Bianco – the light, grapey stuff that is made in the *Chianti* region is sold as Galestro. ***Antinori; Frescobaldi.***

🍷 **E & J Gallo** [gal-loh] (*Central Valley*, California) The world's biggest wine producer; with around 60 percent of the total Californian harvest and more than the whole of Australia or *Champagne*. At the top end, there is some good *Cabernet* and (particularly impressive) *Chardonnay* from individual "ranch" vineyards and Gallo's own huge "Northern *Sonoma* Estate," a piece of land which was physically re-contoured by their bulldozers. The new Turning Leaf wines are good too, at their level. The rest of the basic range, though much improved and very widely stocked, is still pretty ordinary. ☆☆☆☆☆ **1996 Stefani Ranch Chardonnay $$$;** ☆☆☆☆ **1996 Northern Sonoma Estate Bottled Chardonnay $$$$**

🍇 **Gamay** [ga-may] (*Beaujolais*, France) Light-skinned grape traditional to *Beaujolais* where it is used to make fresh and fruity reds for early drinking, usually by the *carbonic maceration* method, and more serious *cru* wines that resemble light *Burgundy*. Also successful in California (*J Lohr*), Australia (*Sorrenberg*) and South Africa (*Fairview*).

🍇 **Gamay** [ga-may] (California) Confusingly unrelated to the *Gamay*.

Gamey Smell or taste distinctly, if oddly, reminiscent of hung game. Particularly associated with old *Pinot Noirs* and *Syrahs*. Sometimes at least partly attributable to the combination of those grapes' natural characteristics with careless use of *sulfur dioxide* by winemakers. Modern examples of both styles seem to be distinctly less gamey than in the past. Another explanation can be the presence of a vineyard infection called Brettanomyces which is feared in California but often goes unnoticed in France where gamey wines are (sometimes approvingly) said to "renarder" – to smell of fox.

🍷 **Gancia** [gan-chee-yah] (*Piedmont*, Italy) Reliable producer of *Asti Spumante* and good dry Pinot di Pinot, as well as *Pinot Blanc* sparkling wine.

Vin de Pays du Gard [doo gahr'] (*Languedoc-Roussillon*, France) Fresh, undemanding red and rosé wines from the southern part of the Rhône. Drink young, and quite possibly chilled.

Garganega [gahr-gah-nay-gah] (Italy) White grape at its best – and worst – in *Soave* in the *Veneto*. In the right site and when not overcroped, it produces interesting almondy flavors. Otherwise the wines it makes are simply light and dull.

Garnacha [gahr-na-cha blan-ka] (Spain and France) See *Grenache*.

Garrafeira [gah-rah fay rah] (Portugal) Indicates a producer's "*reserve*" wine, which has been selected and given extra time in cask (minimum 2 years) and bottle (minimum 1 year).

Vincent Gasse [gass] (*Rhône*, France) Next to La Landonne. Small production of superb, concentrated, inky black wines. ☆☆☆☆ **1991 Côte Rôtie Brune. $$$$**

Gattinara [Gat-tee-nah-rah] (*Piedmont*, Italy) Red *DOC* from the *Nebbiolo* – varying in quality but generally full-flavored and dry. 78 79 82 **85 88** 89 **90 93 94** 95 96 97 98 **Travaglini.**

Domaine Gauby [Goh-Bee] (*Côtes de Roussillon*, France) Serious *Roussillon* reds and (*Muscat*) whites. The Muntada *Syrah* is the top *cuvée*. ☆☆☆☆☆ **1997 Côtes de Roussillon Muntada $$$**

Gavi [gah-vee] (*Piedmont*, Italy) Often unexceptional white wine from the *Cortese* grape. Compared by Italians to white *Burgundy*, with which it and the creamily pleasant Gavi di Gavi share a propensity for high prices. ☆☆☆☆ **1998 Raccolto Tardivo, Villa Lanata $$$$**

Ch. le Gay [luh gay] (*Pomerol*, *Bordeaux*, France) Good *Moueix* property with intense complex wine. 70 **75 76** 78 79 **82 83 85** 86 88 89 90 94 95 96 97 98 ☆☆☆☆ **1990 $$$**

Ch. Gazin [Ga-zan] (*Pomerol*, *Bordeaux*, France) Has become far more polished since the mid 1980s. 85 86 **87** 88 89 90 92 93 94 95 96 97 98 ☆☆☆☆ **1995 $$$$**

Geelong [zhee-long] (*Victoria*, Australia) Cool region pioneered by Idyll Vineyards (makers of old-fashioned reds) and rapidly attracting notice with Clyde Park and with *Bannockburn*'s and Scotchman Hill's *Pinot Noirs*.

Geisenheim [gi-zen-hime] (*Rheingau*, Germany) Home of the German Wine Institute wine school, once one of the best in the world, but now overtaken by more go-ahead seats of learning in France, California, and Australia. Qba/Kab/Spät: **85** 86 **88 89 90** 91 92 93 94 95 96 97 Aus/Beeren/Tba: **83 85** 88 89 90 91 92 93 94 95 96 97

Ch. de la Genaiserie [Jeh-Nay-Seh-Ree] (*Loire*, France) Classy, lusciously honeyed, single-vineyard wines from *Coteaux du Layon*. ☆☆☆☆☆ **1995 Coteaux du Layon Chaume $$$$**

Generoso [zheh-neh-roh-soh] (Spain) Fortified or dessert wine.

Gentilini [zhen-tee-lee-nee] (*Cephalonia*, Greece) Nick Cosmetatos's impressive modern white wines, made using both classic Greek grapes and French varieties, should be an example to all his countrymen who are still happily making and drinking stuff which tastes as fresh as an old election manifesto. ☆☆☆ **1997 Gentilini Fumé $$$$**

JM Gerin [ger-an] (*Rhône*, France) A producer of good modern *Côte Rôtie* and *Condrieu*; uses new oak to make powerful, long-lived wines. ☆☆☆☆☆ **1996 Côte Rôtie Les Grandes Places $$$$**

Gevrey-Chambertin [zheh-vray shom-behr-tan] (*Burgundy*, France) Best-known big red *Côte de Nuits commune;* very variable, but still capable of superb, plummy, cherryish wine. The top *Grand Cru* is *Le Chambertin* but, in the right hands, *Premiers Crus* like Les Cazetiers can beat this and the other *Grands Crus.* 78 83 **85 88 89 90** 92 95 96 97 98 ***Denis Bachelet; Alain Burguet; P. Damoy; Dujac; Denis Mortet; Henri Rebourseau; Roty; Rossignol-Trapet; Armand Rousseau; Vallet Frères.***

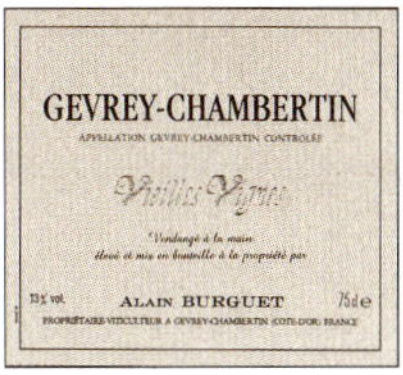

Gewürztraminer [geh-voort-strah-mee-nehr] White (well, slightly pink) grape, making dry-to-sweet, full, oily-textured, spicy wine. Best in *Alsace* (where it is spelled Gewurztraminer, without the umlaut accent) but also grown in Australasia, Italy, the US, and Eastern Europe. Instantly recognizable by its parma-violets-and-lychees character. ***Alsace; Casablanca.***

Geyser Peak [Gih-Suhr] (*Alexander Valley*, California) Australian winemaker Darryl Groom revolutionized Californian thinking in this once Australian-owned winery with his *Semillon-Chardonnay* blend ("You mean *Chardonnay*'s not the only white grape?"), and with reds which show an Australian attitude towards ripe *tannin*. A name to watch. Canyon Creek is the good-value *second label.* ☆☆☆☆ **1995 Alexander Valley Reserve Cabernet Sauvignon $$**

Ghemme [gem-may] (*Piedmont*, Italy) Spicy Nebbiolo usually unfavorably compared to its neighbor Gatinara. Cantalupo is the star producer.

Ghiaie della Furba see *Capezzana.*

Giaconda [zhee-ya-kon-dah] (*Victoria*, Australia) Small winery hidden away high in the hills. Sells out of its impressive *Pinot Noir* and *Chardonnay en primeur.* ☆☆☆☆☆ **1997 Pinot Noir $$$**

Bruno Giacosa [zhee-yah-koh-sah] (*Piedmont*, Italy) Stunning winemaker with a large range, including *Barolos* (Vigna Rionda in best years) and *Barbarescos* (Santo Stefano, again, in best years). Recent success with whites, including a *Spumante.* ☆☆☆☆ **1993 Barolo $$$**

Gie les Rameaux [lay ram-moh] (*Corsica*, France) One of this island's top producers.

Giesen [gee-sen] (*Canterbury*, New Zealand) Small estate, with particularly appley *Riesling* from *Canterbury,* and *Sauvignon* from *Marlborough.* ☆☆☆☆ **1997 Sauvignon Blanc $$**

Gigondas [zhee gon-dass] (*Rhône*, France) *Côtes du Rhône commune,* with good-value, spicy/peppery, blackcurranty reds which show the *Grenache* at its best. A good competitor for nearby *Châteauneuf.* 78 79 **83 85 88** 89 90 93 94 95 96 **Brusset; Font-Sane; *Guigal;* Saurel.**

Ch. Gilette [gil-lette] (*Sauternes*, *Bordeaux*, France) Eccentric, unclassified but of classed-growth quality *Sauternes* kept in tank (rather than cask) for 20 or 30 years. Rare, expensive, worth it. 49 53 59 **61 62 67 70 75 76 78**

Gippsland [gip-sland] (*Victoria*, Australia) Up-and-coming coastal region where *Bass Philip* and *Nicholson River* are producing fascinating and quite European-style wines. Watch out for some of Australia's finest *Pinot Noirs.*

🍷 **Vincent Girardin** [van-son zhee-rahr-dan] (*Burgundy*, France) Reliable *Santenay* producer with vines in several other *communes*. ☆☆☆☆ **1996 Santenay Malardière $$$**

Giropalette [zhee-roh-pal-let] Large machine which, in *méthode champenoise*, automatically and highly efficiently replaces the human beings who used to perform the task of *remuage*. Used by almost all the bigger *Champagne* houses which, needless to say, prefer to conceal them from visiting tourists.

🍷 **Camille Giroud** [kah-mee zhee-roo] (*Burgundy*, France) Laudably old-fashioned family-owned *négoçiant* with no love of new oak and small stocks of great mature wine that go a long way to prove that good *Burgundy* really doesn't need it to taste good. ☆☆☆☆ **1995 Volnay $$$$**

Gisborne [giz-bawn] (New Zealand) North Island vine-growing area since the 1920s. Cool, wettish climate, mainly used for New Zealand's best *Chardonnay*. An ideal partner for *Marlborough* in blends. White: **89 91** 94 **95 96 97** 98 ***Coopers Creek; Corbans;*** **Matawhero;** ***Matua Valley; Millton; Montana.***

🍷 **Ch. Giscours** [zhees-koor] (*Margaux 3ème Cru Classé, Bordeaux*, France) *Margaux* property which, despite the lovely blackcurranty wines it produced in the late 1970s and early 1980s, today remains on the threshold of competition with the best. **71 75** 76 **78 79 81** 82 85 86 88 89 90 91 92 96 97 98 ☆☆☆ **1982 $$$$**

🍷 **Givry** [zheev-ree] (*Burgundy*, France) *Côte Chalonnaise* commune, making typical and affordable, if rather jammily rustic, reds and creamy whites. French wine snobs recall that this was one of King Henri IV's favorite wines, forgetting the fact that a) he had many such favorites dotted all over France and b) his mistress – of whom he also probably had several – happened to live here. Red: **78 85**88 89 90 92 93 9495 96 97 98 **Steinmaier; *Joblot; Ragot;* Thénard; Mouton.**

🍷 **Glen Carlou** [kah-loo] (*Paarl*, South Africa) Small-scale winery with rich, oily, *oaky Chardonnay* and less convincing reds. ☆☆☆ **1996 Chardonnay $$**

🍷 **Glen Ellen** (*Sonoma Valley*, California) Dynamic firm producing large amounts of commercial tropical fruit juice-like *Chardonnay* under its "Proprietor's Reserve" label. Reds are good value. The *Benziger* range is better. ☆☆☆ **1997 Glen Ellen Pinot Noir $$**

Glenrowan [glen-roh-wan] (*Victoria*, Australia) Area near *Rutherglen* with a similar range of excellent *liqueur Muscats* and *Tokays*.

🍷 **Ch. Gloria** [glaw-ree-yah] (*St. Julien Cru Bourgeois, Bordeaux*, France) One of the first of the super *Crus Bourgeois*. Now back on form after a disappointing patch. **70 75 82** 83 85 86 88 89 90 92 9394 95 96 97 98

🍷 **Golan Heights Winery** [goh-lan] (Israel) Until recently almost the only non-sacramental wines in Israel were made by *Carmel*, who produced one of the least palatable *Sauvignons* I have ever encountered. Today, *Carmel* wines are greatly improved, thanks to competition from this enterprise at which Californian expertise is used to produce good *Kosher Cabernet* and *Muscat*. ☆☆☆☆ **1996 Gamla Cabernet Sauvignon $$**

🍷 **Goldwater Estate** (*Auckland*, New Zealand) *Bordeaux*-like red wine specialist on *Waiheke Island* whose wines are expensive but every bit as good as many similarly-priced Californian offerings. ☆☆☆☆ **1997 Roseland Chardonnay $$$**

🍷 **Gonzalez Byass** [gon-zah-lez bih-yas] (*Jerez*, Spain) If *sherry* is beginning to enjoy a long awaited comeback, this is the company that should take much of the credit. Producer of the world's best-selling *fino, Tio Pepe* – and a supporting cast of the finest, most complex, traditional *sherries* available to mankind. ☆☆☆☆☆ **Matusálem Oloroso Dulce Muy Viejo $$$$**

🍷 **Gosset** [gos-say] (*Champagne*, France) The oldest house in *Champagne* producing some marvelous and very long-lived *cuvées,* particularly the Celebris. ☆☆☆☆ **1990 Celebris $$$$**

🍷 **Henri Gouges** [Gooj] (*Burgundy*, France) Long-established estate, producing some truly classic long-lived wines. ☆☆☆☆☆ **1995 Nuits-St.-Georges les St.-Georges $$$$**

Goulburn Valley [gohl-boorn] (*Victoria*, Australia) Small, long-established region reigned over by the respectively ancient and modern *Ch. Tahbilk* and *Mitchelton,* both of whom make great *Marsanne,* though in very different styles. ☆☆☆☆ **1995 Mitchelton Goulburn Valley Shiraz $$$**

🍷 **Gould Campbell** [goold] (*Douro*, Portugal) Underrated member of the same stable as *Dow's, Graham's and Warre's*. 60 63 66 70 75 77 80 83 85 91 94 97 ☆☆☆ **1994 Late Bottled Vintage Port $$$**

🍷 **Goundrey** [gown-dree] (*Western Australia*) Winery in the up-and-coming region of *Mount Barker,* bought by an American millionaire who has continued the founder's policy of making impressively fruity but not overstated *Chardonnay* and *Cabernet*. ☆☆☆☆ **1996 Reserve Shiraz $$**

Graach [grahkh] (*Mosel-Saar-Ruwer*, Germany) *Mittelmosel* village producing fine wines. Best known for its *Himmelreich* vineyard. QbA/Kab/Spät: **85** 86 **88 89 90 92 93 94** 95 96 97 98 Aus/Beeren/Tba: **83 85 88 89 90** 92 93 94 95 96 97 98 ***Deinhard; JJ Prum; Max Ferd Richter; Von Kesselstadt.***

🍷 **Graham** [gray-yam] (*Douro*, Portugal) Sweetly delicate wines, sometimes outclassing the same stable's supposedly finer but heftier *Dow's*. Malvedos is the Single *Quinta*. **55** 60 **63 66 70** 75 77 85 91 94 97 ☆☆☆☆ **1994 Late Bottled Vintage Port $$$** ☆☆☆☆ **1988 Malvedos $$$**

🍷 **Alain Graillot** [al-lan grih-yoh] (*Rhône*, France) Producer who should be applauded for shaking up the sleepy, largely undistinguished *appellation* of *Crozes-Hermitage,* using grapes from rented vineyards. All the reds are excellent, and La Guiraude is the wine from the top vineyard. ☆☆☆☆ **1996 Crozes Hermitage la Guiraude $$$**

Grampians (*Victoria*, Australia) New name for *Great Western.*

Gran Reserva [gran rays-sehr-vah] (Spain) Quality wine aged for a designated number of years in wood and, in theory, only produced in the best vintages. Can be dried out and less worthwhile than *Crianza* or *Reserva.*

Grand Cru [gron kroo] (France) Prepare to be confused. Term referring to the finest vineyards and the – supposedly – equally fine wine made in them. It is an official designation in *Bordeaux*, *Burgundy, Champagne,* and *Alsace*, but its use varies. In *Alsace* where there are 50 or so Grand Cru Vineyards, some are more convincingly grand than others. In *Burgundy* Grand Cru vineyards with their own *ACs,* e.g. *Montrachet*, do not need to carry the name of the village (e.g., *Chassagne-Montrachet*) on their label. Where these regions apply the designation to pieces of soil, in *Bordeaux* it applies to *châteaux* whose vineyards can be bought and sold. More confusingly, still *St. Emilion* can be described as either *Grand Cru, Grand Cru Classé* – or both – or *Premier Grand Cru Classé.*

🍷 **Ch. Grand Mayne** [Gron-Mayn] (*St. Emilion Grand Cru, Bordeaux*, France) Producer of rich, deeply flavorsome, modern *St. Emilion*. Not for traditionalists perhaps, but still due for promotion to *Premier Grand Cru* status. 82 83 85 86 87 88 89 90 92 93 94 95 96 97 98

🍷 **Ch. du Grand Moulas** [gron moo-lahs] (*Rhône*, France) Very classy *Côtes du Rhône* property with unusually complex wines. ☆☆☆☆ **1995 $$**

Grand Vin [gron van] (*Bordeaux*, France) The first (quality) wine of an estate – as opposed to its *second label.*

🍷 **Ch. Grand-Pontet** [gron pon-tay] (*St. Emilion Grand Cru Classé, Bordeaux*, France) Rising star with showy wines. **86** 88 89 90 92 93 94 95 96 97 98.

🍷 **Ch. Grand-Puy-Ducasse** [gron pwee doo-kass] (*Pauillac 5ème Cru Classé, Bordeaux*, France) Excellent wines from fifth growth *Pauillac* property. 79 81 **82** 83 **85 86** 88 89 90 91 92 93 94 **95** 96 **97** 98

🍷 **Ch. Grand-Puy-Lacoste** [gron pwee lah-kost] (*Pauillac 5ème Cru Classé, Bordeaux*, France) Top-class fifth growth owned by the Borie family of *Ducru-Beaucaillou* and now right up there among the *Super Seconds*. 79 81 **82 83 85** 86 88 89 90 91 92 **93** 94 95 96 97 98 ☆☆☆☆☆ **1996 $$$**

🍷 **Grande Rue** [grond-roo] (*Burgundy*, France) Recently promoted *Grand Cru* in *Vosne-Romanée,* across the way from *Romanée-Conti* (hence the promotion). Sadly, the Dom. Lamarche to which this *monopole* belongs is an improving but long-term under-performer.

Grandes Marques [grond mahrk] (*Champagne*, France) Once-official designation for"big name" *Champagne* houses, irrespective of the quality of their wines. Now, although the "Syndicat" of which they were members has been disbanded, the expression is still quite widely used.

🍷 **Grands-Echézeaux** [grons AY-sheh-zoh] (*Burgundy*, France) One of the best *Grand Crus* in *Burgundy;* see *Echézeaux*.

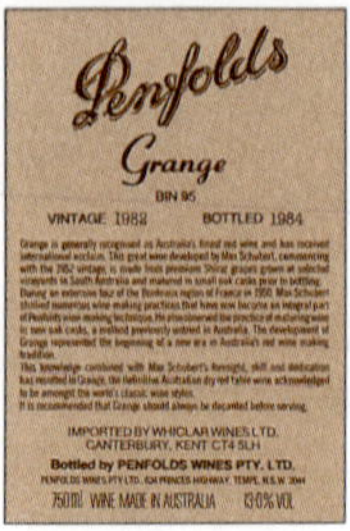

🍷 **Grange** [graynzh] (South Australia) *Penfolds'* and Australia's greatest wine – "The Southern Hemisphere's only first growth" – pioneered by Max Schubert in the early 1950s following a visit to Europe. From the outset, although Schubert was aiming to match top Bordeaux, he used *Shiraz* and American (rather than French) oak barrels and a blend of grapes from 70-year-old vines sited in several South Australian regions. Recently discovered in the US and thus a collector's item that sells out as soon as each vintage hits the streets. **55 63 66 71 76 78 81 83 86 88** 90 91 93 ☆☆☆☆☆ **1993 $$$$**

🍷 **Grangehurst** [graynzh-huhrst] (*Stellenbosch*, South Africa) Exceptionally concentrated modern reds from a small winery converted from the family squash court! Expanding. Good *Cabernet* and *Pinotage*. ☆☆☆☆ **1996 Pinotage $$**

🍷 **Weingut Grans-Fassian** [grans-fass-yan] (*Mosel*, Germany) Improving estate with some really fine, classic wine – especially at a supposedly basic level. ☆☆☆☆ **1997 Riesling $$**

🍷 **Yves Grassa** [gras-sah] (*South-West,* France). Pioneering producer of *Vin de Pays des Côtes de Gasçogne* – now moving from *Colombard* and *Ugni Blanc* into *Sauvignon Blanc*. ☆☆☆ **1997 Dom. de Tariquet $**

🍷 **Alfred Gratien** [gras-see-yen] (*Champagne*, France) Good *Champagne* house, using traditional methods. Also owner of *Loire* sparkling winemaker Gratien et Meyer, based in *Saumur.* ☆☆☆ **1989 Vintage Champagne $$$**

🍇 **Grauerburgunder** [grow-urh-buhr-goon-duhr] (Germany) Another name for *Pinot Gris*. ***Müller-Cattoir.***

🍷 **Dom. la Grave** [lah grahv] (*Graves*, *Bordeaux*, France) Small property in the *Graves* with a growing reputation for 100 percent *Sémillon* whites.

Grave del Friuli [grah-veh del free-yoo-lee] (*Friuli-Venezia Giulia*, Italy) *DOC* for young-drinking reds and whites. *Cabernet*, *Merlot* and *Chardonnay* are increasingly successful.

Graves [grahv] (*Bordeaux*, France) Large region producing vast quantities of red and white, ranging from good to indifferent. The best whites come from *Pessac-Léognan* in the northern part of the region and are sold under that appellation. Reds can have a lovely raspberryish character. Red: **70** 78 79 81 82 83 85 86 88 89 90 94 95 97 98 96 White: 78 79 82 **83 85 86** 88 **89 90 93** 94 95 96 97 98 **Ch. d'Archambeau; de Chantegrive; *Clos Floridène;* Rahoul; du Seuil; Villa Bel Air.**

Gravner [grahv-nehr] (*Friuli-Venezia-Giulia*, Italy) Innovative producer with brilliant oaked Chardonnay and Sauvignon Blanc produced in Collio but not under the rules of that denomination. The blended white Breg is good too.

Great Western (*Victoria*, Australia) Old name for region noted for *Seppelt's* sparkling wines including the astonishing "Sparkling *Burgundy*" *Shirazes*, for *Best's* and for the wines of *Mount Langi Ghiran*. Now renamed Grampians, though I suspect it will take time for enthusiasts to get used to the new name.

Grechetto [grek-keh-toh] (Italy) Subtly spicy white grape used to fine effect in Umbria by Adanti and Goretti.

Greco di Tufo [greh-koh dee too-foh] (*Campania*, Italy) From *Campania*, best-known white from the ancient Greco grape; dry, characterfully herby southern wine. **Botomagno; Librandi; Mastroberardino; Vignadora.**

Greece Finally, if belatedly, beginning to modernize its wine industry – and to exploit the potential of a set of grapes grown nowhere else. Unfortunately, as Greece begins to rid itself of its taste for the stewed, oxidized styles of the past, the modern wines are so popular in the smart restaurants in Athens that they tend to be both expensive and hard to find overseas. Oddbins and the Greek Wine Center in the UK have a good range. **Amethystos; Antonopoulos; *Boutari; Ch. Carras;* Gaia; *Gentilini;* Gerovassilou; *Hatzimichalis;* Ktima; Lazarides; Papantonis; Skouras; Strofilia.**

Green Point (*Yarra Valley*, Australia) See *Dom. Chandon*.

Green & Red (*Napa Valley*, California) Fast-rising star with impressive *Zinfandel*. ☆☆☆☆ **1996 Chiles Mill Vineyard Unfiltered Zinfandel $$$**

Grenache [greh-nash] Red grape of the *Rhône* (aka Garnacha in Spain) making spicy, peppery, full-bodied wine, provided yields are kept low. Also used to make rosés across Southern France, Australia and California.

Marchesi de Gresy [mah-kay-see day greh-see] (*Piedmont*, Italy) Good producer of single-vineyard *Barbaresco*. ☆☆☆☆ **1990 Martinenga Camp Gros $$$$**

Grgich Hills [guhr-gich] (*Napa Valley*, California) Pioneering producer of *Cabernet Sauvignon, Chardonnay* and *Fumé Blanc*. The name is a concatenation of the two founders – Mike Grgich and Austin Hills, rather than a topographical feature. ☆☆☆☆ **1997 Napa Valley Chardonnay $$$**

Grignolino [green-yoh-lee-noh] (*Piedmont*, Italy) Red grape and modest but refreshing cherryish wine, e.g. the *DOC* Grignolino d'Asti. Drink young.

Ch. Grillet [gree-yay] (*Rhône*, France) *Appellation* consisting of a single estate and producer of improving *Viognier* white. Neighboring *Condrieu* is still better value. ☆☆☆ **1996 Ch. Grillet $$$$**

🍷 **Marqués de Griñon** [green-yon] (*La Mancha, Rioja, Ribera del Duero*, Spain/Argentina) Dynamic exception to the dull *La Mancha* rule, making wines, with the help of *Michel Rolland*, which can outclass *Rioja*. The juicy *Cabernet Merlot* and fresh white *Rueda* have been joined by Durius, a blend from *Ribera del Duero*, an exceptional new *Syrah* and an extraordinary *Petit Verdot*. Look out too for new wines from Argentina. ☆☆☆☆☆ 1996 Domino de Valdespusa Petit Verdot 1996 $$ ☆☆☆☆ 1994 Rioja Reserva $$

🍷 **Bernard Gripa** [gree-pah] (*Rhône*, France) Maker of top-notch *St. Joseph* – ripe, thick, *tarry* wine that could age forever. ☆☆☆☆ 1997 St. Joseph $$$

🍷 **Jean-Louis Grippat** [gree-pah] (*Rhône*, France) An unusually great white *Rhône* producer in *Hermitage* and *St. Joseph*. His reds in both *appellations* are less stunning, but still worth buying in their subtler-than-most way. Look out too for his ultra-rare Cuvée des Hospices, *St. Joseph* Rouge ☆☆☆☆ 1996 Hermitage $$$$

🍷 **Dom. Jean Grivot** [gree-voh] (*Burgundy*, France) Top-class *Vosne-Romanée* estate whose winemaker Etienne has recently escaped from the spell of Lebanese guru enologist Guy Accad, whose advice made for some curious wines in the 1980s. ☆☆☆☆ 1996 Vosne-Romanée $$$$

🍷 **Robert Groffier** [grof-fee-yay] (*Burgundy*, France) Up-and-coming estate, with top-class wines from *Chambolle-Musigny*. ☆☆☆☆☆ 1996 Bonnes Mares $$$$

🍷 **Groot Constantia** [khroot-kon-stan-tee-yah] (*Constantia*, South Africa) Government-run, 300-year-old wine estate and national monument that is finally making worthwhile wines. ☆☆☆ 1995 Cabernet Sauvignon $$$

🍷 **Dom. Anne Gros** [groh] (*Burgundy*, France) Unfortunately for one's wallet, the best wines from this *Vosne-Romanée domaine* are as expensive as they are delicious – but they are worth every cent. ☆☆☆☆ 1996 Vosne Romanée $$$$

🍷 **Jean Gros** [groh] (*Burgundy*, France) Slightly less impressive *Vosne-Romanée* producer, but the *Clos Vougeots* are good. ☆☆☆☆ 1995 Clos du Vougeot $$$$

🍇 **Gros Lot/Grolleau** [groh-loh] (*Loire*, France) The workhorse black grape of the *Loire*, particularly in *Anjou*, used to make white, rosé, and sparkling *Saumur*.

🍇 **Gros Plant (du Pays Nantais)** [groh-plon doo pay-yee non-tay] (*Loire*, France) Light, sharp white *VDQS* wine from the western *Loire*. In all but the best hands, serves to make even a poor *Muscadet* look good.

🍷 **Grosset** [gros-set] (*Clare Valley, South Australia*) Terrific white (*Chardonnay, Semillon* and especially *Riesling*) specialist now making great reds too (the Gaia red *Bordeaux*-blend and lovely *Pinot Noir*). Give all wines time to develop. ☆☆☆☆ 1998 Polish Hill Riesling $$$

Grosslage [gross-lah-guh] (Germany) Wine district, the third subdivision after *anbaugebiet* (e.g. *Rheingau*) and *bereich* (e.g. *Nierstein*). For example, *Michelsberg* is a *grosslage* of the *bereich Piesport*.

🍷 **Groth** [grahth] (*Napa Valley*, California) Serious producer of quality *Cabernet* and *Chardonnay*. ☆☆☆☆ 1994 Napa Valley Cabernet Sauvignon Reserve $$$

🍷 **Grove Mill** (New Zealand) Young Marlborough winery with good *Sauvignon Blanc, Chardonnay* and *Riesling*. ☆☆☆☆ 1998 Sauvignon Blanc $$

🍷 **Ch. Gruaud-Larose** [groo-oh lah-rohz] (*St. Julien 2ème Cru Classé, Bordeaux*, France) One of the stars of the *Cordier* stable. Rich but potentially slightly unsubtle. The second wine is "Le Sarget."

🍇 **Grüner Veltliner** [groo-nuhr felt-lee-nuhr] Spicy white grape of Austria and Eastern Europe, producing light, fresh, aromatic wine – and for *Willi Opitz* an extraordinary *late harvest* version. Knoll; *Kracher;* Lang; Metternich-Sándor; *Opitz;* Pichler; Prager; Schuster; Steininger.

🍷 **Bodegas Guelbenzu** [guhl-bent-zoo] (*Navarra*, Spain) Starry new-wave producer of rich red wines using local grapes and *Cabernet*. ☆☆☆☆ 1998 Garnacha $$; ☆☆☆☆ 1996 Guelbenzu Evo $$

🍷 **Guerrieri-Rizzardi** [gwer-reh-ree rit-zar-dee] (*Veneto*, Italy) Solid organic producer, with good rather than great *Amarone* and single-vineyard *Soave Classico*. ☆☆☆☆ **1996 Soave Classico Costeggiola $$$**

🍷 **Guffens-Heynen** [goof-fens ay-na(n)] (*Burgundy*, France) Rising star in *Pouilly-Fuissé*. ☆☆☆☆ **1996 Mâcon Pierreclos $$$**

🍷 **E Guigal** [gee-gahl] (*Rhône*, France) Still the yardstick for *Rhône* reds, despite increased competition from *Chapoutier*. His extraordinarily pricy single-vineyard La Mouline, La Landonne, and La Turque wines from *Côte Rôtie* are still ahead of the young turks and the "Brune et Blonde" blend of grapes from two hillsides remains a benchmark for this *appellation*. The basic red and white *Côtes du Rhône* are also well worth looking out for. ☆☆☆☆☆ **1991 Condrieu la Landonne $$$$;** ☆☆☆☆ **1996 Côte Rôtie Brune et Blonde $$**

🍷 **Guimaraens** [gee-mah-rens] (*Douro*, Portugal) Associated with *Fonseca*; underrated *port*-house making good wines. ☆☆☆☆☆ **1984 Fonseca Guimaraens Vintage Port $$$$**

🍷 **Ch. Guiraud** [gee-roh] (*Sauternes Premier Cru Classé, Bordeaux*, France) *Sauternes classed growth*, recently restored to original quality. Good wines but rarely among the most complex sweet *Bordeaux*. 67 79 81 82 **83** 85 **86** 87 88 89 90 92 93 94 95 96 97 98 ☆☆☆☆ **1997 $$$$**

🍷 **Weingut Gunderloch** [goon-duhr-lokh] (*Rheinhessen*, Germany) One of the few estates to make *Rheinhessen* wines of truly reliable quality. ☆☆☆☆ **1997 Nackenheimer Rothenbergl Riesling Gold Cap Auslese $$$**

🍷 **Gundlach-Bundschu** [guhnd-lakh buhnd-shoo] (*Sonoma Valley*, California) Good, well-made, juicy *Merlot* and spicy *Zinfandel*. ☆☆☆☆ **1991 Rhinefarm Vineyard Zinfandel $$$**

🍷 **Louis Guntrum** [goon-troom] (*Rheinhessen*, Germany) Family-run estate with a penchant for *Sylvaner*. ☆☆☆☆ **1997 Oppenheimer Herrenberg Silvaner Eiswein $$$$**

🍷 **Ch. la Gurgue** [lah guhrg] (*Margaux Cru Bourgeois, Bordeaux*, France) *Cru Bourgeois* across the track from *Ch. Margaux*. Less impressive since the same owner's *Ch. Ferrière* has both improved and increased its production. Coincidence presumably. **83 85** 86 88 89 90 94 95 96

🍇 **Gutedel** [goot-edel] (Germany) German name for the *Chasselas* grape.

🍷 **Friedrich-Wilhelm Gymnasium** [free-drikh vil-helm-gim-nahz-yuhm] (*Mosel*, Germany) Big-name estate that ought to be making better wine. ☆☆☆☆ **1996 Graacher Himmelreich Riesling Spätlese $$$**

H

🍷 **Weingut Fritz Haag** [hahg] (*Mosel-Saar-Ruwer*, Germany) Superlative small estate with classic *Rieslings*. ☆☆☆☆☆ **1997 Brauneberger Juffer Sonnenuhr Riesling Auslese Gold Cap $$$$**

🍷 **Weingut Reinhold Haart** [rihn-hohld hahrt] (*Mosel*, Germany) Fast rising *Piesport* star. ☆☆☆☆ **1997 Piesporter Goldtröpfchen Riesling Auslese $$$**

Halbtrocken [hahlb-trok-en] (Germany) Off-dry. Usually a safer buy than *Trocken* in regions like the *Mosel, Rheingau,* and *Rheinhessen,* but still often aggressively acidic. Look for *QbA* or *Auslese* versions.

Hallgarten [hal-gahr-ten] (*Rheingau*, Germany) Important town near *Hattenheim* producing robust wines including the (in Germany) well-regarded produce from *Schloss Vollrads*. QbA/Kab/Spät: **85** 86 **88 89 90** 91 92 93 95 96 97 98 Aus/Beeren/Tba: **83 85 88 89 90** 92 93 94 95 96 97 98

Hamilton Russell Vineyards (*Walker Bay*, South Africa) Pioneer of impressive *Pinot Noir* and *Chardonnay* at a winery in Hermanus at the southernmost tip of the *Cape*. Now expanded to include a *second label* – Southern Right – to produce a varietal *Pinotage*, and a *Chenin*-based white. ☆☆☆☆ **1998 Chardonnay $$$**

Handley Cellars (*Mendocino*, California) Fine sparkling wine producer with a particularly good pure *Chardonnay Blanc de Blancs*. The still *Chardonnay* is pretty impressive too.

Hanging Rock (*Victoria*, Australia) As in the movie, "Picnic at....," this winery makes Australia's biggest, butteriest sparkling wine and some pretty good reds and whites. ☆☆☆☆ **1997 Heathcote Shiraz $$$**

BRL Hardy (*South Australia*) The second biggest wine producer in Australia, encompassing *Houghton* and *Moondah Brook* in *Western Australia, Leasingham* in the *Clare Valley, Redman* in *Coonawarra, E& E* in Barossa, Hardy's itself, and *Ch. Reynella*. Hardy's reliable range includes the commercial Nottage Hill, new Bankside and Banrock Station, and multi-regional blends, but the wines to look for are the top-of-the-range Eileen and Thomas Hardy. The *Ch. Reynella* wines from *McLaren Vale* fruit (and, in the case of the reds, using basket presses) are good, quite lean examples of the region. Hardy's ventures in Italy (d'Istinto) and France (la Baume) are less impressive. ☆☆☆☆☆ **1998 Banrock Station Chardonnay $$$;** ☆☆☆☆☆ **1996 Eileen Hardy Shiraz $$$**

Harlan Estate (*Napa Valley*, California) Fiercely pricy, small quantities of *Bordeaux*-style reds, made with input from *Michel Rolland*, and using grapes from hillside vineyards. ☆☆☆☆ **1995 Proprietory Red $$$$**

Hárslevelü [harsh-leh-veh-loo] (Hungary) White grape used in *Tokaji* and for light table wines.

Harveys (*Jerez*, Spain) Maker of the ubiquitous *Bristol Cream*. Other styles are unimpressive apart from the 1796 range and Club Classic.

Hattenheim [hat-ten-hime] (*Rheingau*, Germany) One of the finest villages in the Rheingau, with wines from producers such as *Balthasar Ress*, Von Simmern, *Schloss Rheinhartshausen,* and *Schloss Schönborn.*

Hatzimichalis [hat-zee-mikh-ahlis] (Atalanti, Greece) The face of future Greek winemaking? Hopefully. This self-taught producer's small estate makes top-notch *Cabernet Sauvignon, Merlot, Chardonnay,* and fresh dry Atalanti white. ☆☆☆☆ **1997 Merlot $$;** ☆☆☆☆ **1997 Cabernet Sauvignon $$**

Ch. Haut-Bages-Averous [oh-bahj-aveh-roo] (*Pauillac Cru Bourgeois*, *Bordeaux*, France) *Second label* of *Ch. Lynch-Bages*. Good-value blackcurranty *Pauillac*. **82** 83 **85** 86 88 89 90 93 94 95 96 97 98

Ch. Haut-Bages-Libéral [oh-bahj-lib-ay-ral] (*Pauillac 5ème Cru Classé*, *Bordeaux*, France) Classy small property in the same stable as *Chasse-Spleen*. **75** 78 **82** 83 85 **86** 87 88 89 90 91 93 94 95 96 97 98

Ch. Haut-Bailly [oh bih-yee] (*Pessac-Léognan Cru Classé*, *Bordeaux*, France) Recently sold: brilliant *Pessac-Léognan* property consistently making reliable, excellent-quality, long-lived red wines. A stunning 1998. **61** 64 **70** 78 **79** 81 83 **85** 86 87 88 89 90 92 **93** 94 95 96 97 98

Ch. Haut-Batailley [oh-ba-tih-yee] (*Pauillac 5ème Cru Classé, Bordeaux*, France) Subtly-styled wine from the same stable as *Ducru-Beaucaillou* and *Grand-Puy-Lacoste* **85 86** 88 89 90 91 92 93 **95 96** 97 98

Ch. Haut-Brion [oh bree-yon] (*Pessac-Léognan Premier Cru Classé*, *Bordeaux*, France) Samuel Pepys' favorite and still the only non-*Médoc* first growth. Situated in the *Graves* on the outskirts of *Bordeaux* in the shadow of the gasworks. Wines can be tough and hard to judge when young, but at their best they develop a rich, fruity, perfumed character setting them apart from their peers. 1996 and 1998 were both especially good, as – comparatively – were 1993, 1994 and 1995.The white is rare and often sublime. Red: **61 70 71 75 78 79 82** 85 86 88 89 90 91 92 93 94 95 96 97 98 White: 85 87 88 89 90 91 92 93 94 95 96 97 98

Ch. Haut-Marbuzet [oh-mahr-boo-zay] (*St. Estèphe Cru Bourgeois*, *Bordeaux*, France) *Cru bourgeois* which thinks it's a *cru classé*. Immediately imposing wine with bags of oak. Decidedly new-wave *St. Estèphe*.

Haut-Médoc [oh-may-dok] (*Bordeaux*, France) Large *appellation* which includes nearly all of the well-known *crus classés*. Basic Haut-Médoc should be better than plain *Médoc*. **82** 83 **85 86** 88 89 90 94 95 96 97 98

Haut-Poitou [oh-pwa-too] (*Loire*, France) A source of basic inexpensive *Sauvignon*. A team of Australians from *BRL Hardy* has recently shown that a dose of skillful winemaking pays dividends here.

Hautes Côtes de Beaune [oht-coht-duh-bohn] (*Burgundy*, France) Rustic wines from villages in the hills above the big-name *communes*. Worth buying in good vintages; in poorer ones the grapes have problems ripening. Much of the wine seen outside the region is made by one of *Burgundy*'s improving cooperatives.

Hautes Côtes de Nuits [oht-coht-duh-nwee] (*Burgundy*, France) Mostly red wines that are slightly tougher than *Hautes Côtes de Beaune*.

Hawke's Bay (New Zealand) Major North Island vineyard area which is finally beginning to live up to the promise of producing top-class reds. Whites can be fine too, though rarely achieving the bite of *Marlborough*. ***Babich;* Church Road; *Delegats; Esk Valley; Te Mata; Matua Valley, Mills Reef; Mission; Montana; Morton Estate; Ngatarawa; CJ Pask; Sacred Hill; Vidal; Villa Maria.***

Hedges (*Washington State*, US) Producer of good, rich, berryish reds. ☆☆☆☆ **1997 Red Mountain Reserve $$$**

Heemskerk [heems-kuhrk] (*Tasmania*, Australia) Generally underperforming winery recently bought by its neighbor *Pipers Brook*. The *Janz* sparkling wine label now belongs to *Yalumba*, while Heemskerk's own sparkling wine is now named Pirie, after the owner of *Pipers Brook*.

Dr Heger [hay-gehr] (*Baden*, Germany) A brilliant exponent of the *Grauerburgunder* which ripens well in this warm region of Germany. ☆☆☆☆ **1997 Ihringer Winkleberg Grauer Burgunder Spätlese Trocken $$$**

Heggies [heg-gees] (South Australia) Impressive *Adelaide Hills* label in the same camp as *Yalumba*. Lovely *Riesling*, *Viognier*, *Merlot*, *Pinot Noir*, and stickies. ☆☆☆☆ **1997 Botrytis-Affected Riesling $$**

Heida [hi-da] (Switzerland) Spicy Swiss grape variety, thought to be related to the *Gewürztraminer*. When carefully handled, produces wonderfully refreshing wines .

Charles Heidsieck [hihd-seek] (*Champagne*, France) Go-ahead producer whose winemaker Daniel Thibaut (*Bonnet, Piper Heidsieck*) has recently introduced the clever notion of labeling non-*vintage* wine with a "mis en cave" bottling date. Wines are all recommendable. ☆☆☆☆☆ **Brut Réserve Mis en Cave 1995 $$$**

Heidsieck Dry Monopole [hihd-seek] (*Champagne*, France) A subsidiary of *Mumm* and thus until 1999 controlled by Seagrams. Wines with the same quality aspirations as that brand. Even so, recent vintages have shown some improvement. ☆☆☆ **Diamont Bleu $$$$**

Heitz Cellars [hihtz] (*Napa Valley*, California) One of the great names of California and the source of stunning reds in the 1970s. More recent (pre 1992) releases of the flagship Martha's Vineyard *Cabernet* have tasted unacceptably musty, however, as have the traditionally almost-as-good Bella Oaks. At the winery and among some critics, such criticisms are apparently treated as lèse-majesté. Recent (post 1996) vintages of Martha's Vineyard wines are made from newly replanted (post-Californian *phylloxera*) vines.

Joseph Henriot [on-ree-yoh] (*Champagne*, France) Modern *Champagne* house producing soft, rich wines. Now also shaking things up and improving wines at its recently purchased *Bouchard Père et Fils négoçiant* in *Burgundy*. ☆☆☆☆ **Champagne Blanc de Blancs $$$$**

Henriques & Henriques [hen-reeks] (*Madeira*, Portugal) One of the few independent producers still active in *Madeira*. Top quality. ☆☆☆☆☆ **10 Year Old Sercial $$$**

Henschke [hench-kee] (*Adelaide Hills*, Australia) One of the world's best. From the long-established Hill of Grace with its 130-year-old vines and (slightly less intense) Mount Edelstone *Shirazes* to the new Abbott's Prayer *Merlot-Cabernet* from *Lenswood*, the *Riesling* and Tilly's Vineyard white blend, there's not a poor wine here; the reds last forever. ☆☆☆☆☆ **1995 Abbott's Prayer Merlot Cabernet $$$,** ☆☆☆☆☆ **1995 Cyril Henschke Cabernet Sauvignon $$$**

Vin de Pays de l'Hérault [Eh-roh] (*Languedoc-Roussillon*, France) Large region made famous by the success of Aimé Guibert's *Mas de Daumas Gassac*. Other producers such as Domaine Limbardie are following in his footsteps.

Hermitage [ayr-mee-tazh] (*Rhône*, France) Supreme Northern *Rhône appellation* for long-lived pure *Syrah*. Whites are less reliable. Red: **76 78 82 83 85 88** 89 **90** 91 95 96 97 98 White: **82 85** 87 **88 89 90** 91 94 95 96 97 98 ***Belle Père & Fils;* Michel Bernard; *Chapoutier; Chave; Dom. Colombier; Grippat; Guigal; Delas;* Bernard Faurie; *Jaboulet Aîné;* Sorrel; Cave de Tain l'Hermitage; *Tardieu-Laurent.***

James Herrick [heh-rick] (*Languedoc-Roussillon*, France) Dynamic Briton who brought an Australian philosophy to southern France, planting extensive Chardonnay vineyards and producing good-value varietal wine. As we go to press, he is negotiating a sale of the company to Southcorp (Penfolds etc).

The Hess Collection (*Napa Valley*, California) High-class *Cabernet* producer high in the *Mount Veeder* hills.named after the owner's art collection (see *Vinopolis*). The lower-priced Hess Select *Monterey* wines are worth buying too. ☆☆☆☆☆ **1997 Napa Valley Cabernet Sauvignon $$$**

Hessische Bergstrasse [hess-ishuh behrg-strah-suh] (Germany) Smallest *anbaugebiet* capable of fine *Eisweins* and dry *Sylvaners* which can surpass those of nearby *Franken*. QbA/Kab/Spät: **85 88 89 90** 91 92 93 94 95 96 97 98 Aus/Beeren/Tba: **83 85** 88 89 90 91 92 93 94 95 96 97 98

Heuriger [hoy-rig-gur] (Austria) Austria's equivalent of Beaujolais Nouveau – except that this new-born wine is white and sold by the jug in cafés. Of interest if only as a taste of the way most wine used to be drunk.

Heyl zu Herrnsheim [highl zoo hehrn-sime] (*Rheinhessen*, Germany) Organic estate in *Nierstein* with good *Riesling* from the Plettenthal vineyard.

Vinicola Hidalgo y Cia [hid-algoh ee-thia] (*Jerez*, Spain) Specialist producer of impeccable dry "La Gitana" *sherry* and a great many own-label offerings. ☆☆☆☆ **Manzanilla Pasada Pastrada Single Vineyard Sherry $$**

Hill-Smith (South Australia) Very classy firm, under the same family ownership as *Pewsey Vale, Yalumba,* and *Heggies* Vineyard, and now active in Tasmania (Janz sparkling wine), New Zealand (Nautilus) and California (where its *Voss* wines are made). ☆☆☆ **1997 Estate Chardonnay.**

Hillstowe [hil-stoh] (*South Australia*) Up-and-coming producer in the *McLaren Vale*, using grapes from various parts of the region to produce unusually stylish *Chardonnay, Sauvignon Blanc* and *Cabernet-Merlot*. ☆☆☆☆ **1997 Udy's Mill Lenswood Pinot Noir $$$**

Himmelreich [him-mel-rihkh] (*Mosel*, Germany) One of the finest vineyards in *Graach*. See *JJ Prum*. QbA/Kab/Spät: **85 86 88 89** 90 **91 92 93** 94 95 96 97 98 Aus/Beeren/Tba: **83** 85 **88 89 90 91** 92 93 94 95 96 97 98

Paul Hobbs (*Sonoma*, California) Former winemaker at *Simi*, and now a consultant at *Catena* and *Valdivieso*, Paul Hobbs makes fine *Pinot Noir*, *Cabernet* and rich *Chardonnay* from the memorably-named "Dinner Vineyard."

Hochfeinste [hokh-fihn-stuh] (Germany) "Very finest."

Hochgewächs QbA [hokh-geh-fex] (Germany) Recent official designation for *Rieslings* which are as ripe as a *QmP* but can still only call themselves *QbA*. This from a nation supposedly dedicated to simplifying what are acknowledged to be the most complicated labels in the world.

Hochheim [hokh-hihm] (*Rheingau*, Germany) Village whose fine *Rieslings* gave the English the word *"Hock."* QbA/Kab/Spät: **85** 86 **88 89 90** 91 92 93 94 95 96 97 98 Aus/Beeren/Tba: **83 85** 88 89 90 91 92 93 94 95 96 97 98 **Geh'rat Aschrott; Konigen Victoria Berg.**

Hogue Cellars [hohg] (*Washington State*, US) Highly dynamic, family-owned *Yakima Valley* producer of good *Chardonnay*, *Riesling*, *Merlot* and *Cabernet*. ☆☆☆☆ **1996 Barrel Select Merlot $$$**

Hollick (*Coonawarra*, Australia) A good, traditional producer; the *Ravenswood* is particularly worth seeking out. ☆☆☆☆ **1994 Coonawarra Cabernet-Merlot $$$**

Dom. de l'Hortus [Or-Toos] (*Languedoc-Roussillon*, France) Exciting spicy reds from *Pic St. Loup* in the *Coteaux de Languedoc* that easily outclass many an effort from big-name producers in the *Rhône*. ☆☆☆☆ **1997 $$$**

Hospices de Beaune [os-peess duh bohn] (*Burgundy*, France) Hospital whose wines (often *cuvées* or blends of different vineyards) are sold at an annual charity auction, the prices of which are erroneously thought to set the tone for the *Côte d'Or* year. In the early 1990s, wines were generally sub-standard, improving instantly in 1994 with the welcome return of winemaker André Porcheret who has since proved controversial by (in 1997) making wines that struck some critics (not this one) as too big and rich. In any case, be aware that although price lists often merely indicate "Hospices de Beaune" as a producer, all of the wines bought at the auction are matured and bottled by local merchants, some of whom are more scrupulous than others.

🍷 **Houghton** [haw-ton] (*Swan Valley*, Australia) Long-established subsidiary of *Hardy*'s. Best known for its *Chenin*-based rich white blend traditionally sold in Australia as "White *Burgundy*" and in Europe as "HWB." The Wildflower Ridge commercial wines are good, as are the ones from *Moondah Brook*. Look out too for the new *Cabernet-Shiraz-Malbec* "Jack Mann," named after one of *Western Australia's* pioneering winemakers. ☆☆☆☆ **1995 Jack Mann $$$.**

🍷 **Weingut von Hovel** [fon huh-vel] (*Mosel-Saar-Ruwer*, Germany) A 200-year-old estate with fine *Rieslings* from great vineyards. These repay the patience that they demand. ☆☆☆☆ **1997 Oberemmeler Hutte Riesling Auslese Gold Cap $$$**

🍷 **Howard Park** (*Western Australia*) John Wade is one of the best winemakers in *Western Australia* and one of the finest Riesling producers in Australia. Madfish Bay is the second label. ☆☆☆☆ **1998 Riesling $$$**

Howell Mountain [how-wel] (*Napa Valley*, California) Increasingly well-respected hillside region in the north of the *Napa Valley,* capable of fine whites and reds that justify its *AVA*. Red: **85** 86 87 **90 91** 92 93 95 96 97 98. White: **85 90 91** 92 95 96 97 98 ***Beringer; Duckhorn; Dunn; la Jota; Turley.***

🍷 **Huadong Winery** (Shandong Province, China) Dynamic joint venture producing the basic commercial Tsing Tao brand of wines. Recent vintages have shown a marked improvement.

🍷 **Alain Hudelot-Noëllat** [ood-uh-loh noh-el-lah] (*Burgundy*, France) A great winemaker whose generosity with oak is matched, especially in his *Grand Cru Richebourg* and *Romanée St.Vivant,* by intense fruit flavors. ☆☆☆☆☆ **1995 Vosne-Romanée les Suchots $$$$**

Huelva [wel-vah] (*Extremadura*, Spain) *DO* of the *Extremadura* region, producing rather heavy whites and fortified wines.

🍷 **Gaston Huët** [oo-wet] (*Loire*, France) Winemaker Noël Pinguet produces top-quality individual vineyard examples of *Sec, Demi-Sec* and *Moëlleux* wines. The non-vintage sparkling wine, though only made occasionally, is top class too. ☆☆☆☆ **1997 le Haut-Lieu Sec $$$$**

🍷 **Hugel et Fils** [oo-gel] (*Alsace*, France) Reliable *négoçiant*. Best are the *late harvest* and Jubilee wines. The wine "Gentil" revives the tradition of blending different grape varieties. ☆☆☆☆ **1996 Riesling 'Jubilee' $$$**

Hungary Country too long known for its infamous *Bull's Blood* and *Olasz Rizling*, rather than *Tokaji*. ***Disznókö;*** **Egervin; Megyer;** ***Kym Milne;*** **Nagyrede; Neszmély; Pajsos;** ***Royal Tokay; Hugh Ryman.***

Hunter Valley (*New South Wales*, Australia) The best-known wine region in Australia is ironically one of the least suitable places to make wine. When the vines are not dying of heat and thirst they are drowning beneath the torrential rains which like to fall at harvest time. Even so, the *Shirazes* and *Semillons* – traditionally sold as *"Hermitage," "Claret,"*, *'Burgundy," "Chablis,"* and *"Hunter Valley Riesling"* – develop remarkably. **Allandale; Allanmere;** ***Brokenwood; Evans Family; Lake's Folly; Lindemans; McWilliams;*** **Petersons; Reynolds;** ***Rosemount; Rothbury Estate; Tyrrells;*** **Wilderness Estate**

🍷 **Hunter's** (*Marlborough*, New Zealand) One of *Marlborough*'s most consistent producers of ripe fruity *Sauvignon Blancs* and now a quality sparkling wine. ☆☆☆☆☆ **1996 Miru Miru Brut $$$;** ☆☆☆☆☆ **1998 Sauvignon Blanc $$$**

🍇 **Huxelrebe** [huk-sel-ray-buh] Minor white grape, often grown in England but proving what it can do when harvested late in Germany. **Anselmann (Germany); Barkham Manor; Nutbourne Manor (England).**

Hybrid [hih-brid] Cross-bred grape Vitis *vinifera* (European) x Vitis *labrusca* (North American) – an example is *Seyval Blanc*.

Hydrogen sulfide Naturally occurring rotten egg-like gas produced by yeasts as a by-product of fermentation, or by *reductive* conditions. Before bottling, may be cured by *racking*. If left untreated, hydrogen sulfide will react with other components in the wine to form *mercaptans*. Stinky bottled wines may be "cleaned up" by the addition of a copper coin. Unfortunately, too many (especially in *Ribera del Duero* for some reason) go unnoticed.

I

Iambol [yam-bohl] (*Southern Region*, Hungary) Large, former cooperative which now makes commercial *Merlot* and *Cabernet Sauvignon* reds, particularly for sale overseas under the Domaines Boyar label.

Icewine Increasingly popular Anglicization of the German term *Eiswein*, used particularly by Canadian producers making luscious, spicily exotic wines from the frozen grapes of varieties like *Vidal*.

IGT - Indicazione Geografiche Tipici (Italy) New designation designed to create a home for quality non-*DOC/DOCG* wines that were previously sold as *Vino da Tavola*.

Vin de Pays de l'Île de Beauté [eel-duh-bow-tayl] (*Corsica*, France) Designation that includes varietal wines (including *Pinot Noir, Cabernet, Syrah*, and *Merlot* as well as local grapes). Often better than the island's ACs.

Imbottigliato nel'origine [im-bot-til-yah-toh neh-loh-ree-zhee-nay] (Italy) Estate-bottled.

Imperial(e) [am-pay-ray-ahl] (*Bordeaux*, France) Bottle containing almost six and a half liters of wine (eight and a half bottles). Cherished by collectors partly through rarity, partly through the longevity that large bottles give their contents.

India Source of generally execrable table wine and surprisingly reliable sparkling wine, labeled as Marquis de Pompadour or *Omar Khayam*.

Inferno [een-fehr-noh] (*Lombardy*, Italy) *Lombardy DOC*. *Nebbiolo* red that needs aging for at least five years. ☆☆☆ **1994 Nino Negri $$**

Inglenook Vineyards [ing-gel-nook] (*Napa Valley*, California) Once-great winery which, like *Beaulieu*, fell into the hands of the giant Grand Metropolitan. The Gothic building and vineyards now belong appropriately to Francis Ford-Coppola. The now far from dazzling brand has been sold to the giant Canandaigua which has also recently bought Franciscan and Simi.

Inniskillin (*Ontario*, Canada) Long-established, pioneering winery with good *Icewines* (from the *Vidal* grape), highly successful *Chardonnay*, improving *Pinot Noir*, and a rare example of a good *Maréchal Foch*. ☆☆☆☆ **1997 Icewine $$$$**

Institut National des Appellations d'Origine (INAO) (France) French official body which designates and (half-heartedly) polices quality, and outlaws sensible techniques like irrigation and the blending of *vintages*, which are permitted elsewhere. Maybe this is why *Appellation Contrôlée* wines are often inferior to – and sell at lower prices than – the newer *Vins de Pays* over which this body has no authority.

International Wine Challenge (England) Wine competition, held in London, Tokyo, China, and Singapore. (The author is founder chairman.)

International Wine & Spirit Competition (England) Wine competition, held in London.

Iphofen (*Franken*, Germany) One of the finest places to sample wines made from the Sylvaner. Modern wine drinkers may, however, prefer the Rieslings, which are fruitier and less earthy in style.

IPR - Indicação de Proveniência Regulamentada (Portugal) Designation for wines that fall beneath the top – *DOC* – grade and above the basic Vinho Regional.

Irancy [ee-ron-see] (*Burgundy*, France) Little-known light reds and rosés made near *Chablis* from a blend of grapes including the *Pinot Noir* and the little-known *César*. Curiously, Irancy has *AC* status whereas nearby *Sauvignon de St. Bris* is merely a *VDQS* region. **Brocard; Simonnet-Febvre.**

Iron Horse Vineyards (*Sonoma Valley*, California) One of the best sparkling wine producers in the New World, thanks to cool-climate vineyards. Reds and still whites are increasingly impressive too. ☆☆☆ **1993 Chardonnay Estate Cuvée Joy $$$**

Irouléguy [ee-roo-lay-gee] (*South-West*, France) Earthy, spicy reds and rosés, and improving whites from Basque country where names seem to include an abundance of the letter "x". **Dom. Brana; Etxegaraya; Irouléguy Cooperative.**

Isinglass [Ih-sing-glahs] *Fining* agent derived from sturgeon bladders.

Isole e Olena [ee-soh-lay ay oh-lay-nah] (*Tuscany*, Italy) Brilliant pioneering small *Chianti* estate with a pure *Sangiovese Super-Tuscan*, *Cepparello* and Italy's first (technically illegal) *Syrah*. ☆☆☆☆ **1995 Cepparello $$$**

Isonzo [Ih-son-zoh] (*Friuli-Venezia Giulia*, Italy) One of the best DOCs in this region, offering a wide range of varietal wines from some very go-ahead producers. **Lis Neris-Pecorari; Ronco del Gelso; Vie di Romans; Villanova.**

Israel Once the source of appalling stuff, but the new-style varietal wines are increasingly impressive. **Golan Heights; Carmel.**

Ch. d'Issan [dee-son] (*Margaux 3ème Cru Classé*, *Bordeaux*, France) Recently revived *Margaux* third growth with lovely, recognizable blackcurranty *Cabernet Sauvignon* intensity. 70 **75** 78 79 81 **82 83** 85 86 88 89 90 93 94 95 96 98

Italian Riesling/Riesling Italico [ee-tah-lee-koh] Not the great *Rhine Riesling*, but another name for an unrelated variety, which also goes by the names *Welschriesling*, *Lutomer* and *Laski Rizling*, and is widely grown in Northern and Eastern Europe. At its best in Austria.

Italy Tantalizing, seductive, infuriating. In many ways the most exciting wine nation in the world, though, as ever, in a state of change as it reorganizes its wine laws. See individual regions.

J

JP Vinhos (Portugal) See *Peter Bright*.

Paul Jaboulet Aîné [zha-boo-lay ay-nay] (*Rhône*, France) The wine world was saddened to learn of the death this year from a heart attack of Gérard Jaboulet, the highly popular international face of this family *négoçiant* which owns the illustrious *Hermitage* La Chapelle vineyard. Despite being overshadowed nowadays by *Guigal*, this remains a reliable producer of a wide range of wines apart from the La Chapelle, including white *Hermitage*, chunky *St. Joseph*, good *Côtes du Rhône* and *Châteauneuf-du-Pape*. ☆☆☆☆☆ **1996 Hermitage la Chapelle $$$**

Jackson Estate (*Marlborough*, New Zealand) Neighbor of *Cloudy Bay* and producer of *Sauvignon*, which gives that superstar estate a run for its money. The sparkling wine is good too. ☆☆☆ **1998 Riesling $$**

Jacob's Creek (*South Australia*) Brilliantly commercial South Australian wines made by *Orlando*. Try the recently launched sparkling wine.

Jacquart [zha-kahr] (*Champagne*, France) Large cooperative with some top-class wines. ☆☆☆☆ **1988 Cuvée Nominée $$$$**

Jacquère [zha-kehr] The slightly citrusy grape of *Savoie*.

Jacquesson et Fils [jak-son] (*Champagne*, France) A small *Champagne* house that ought to be better known, particularly for its delicately stylish *Blanc de Blancs*. ☆☆☆☆ **1990 Blanc de Blancs $$$$**

Louis Jadot [zha-doh] (*Burgundy*, France) Good, sometimes great, *Beaune négoçiant* with a growing number of its own top-class vineyards in *Beaune, Chassagne-* and *Puligny-Montrachet*. Jadot has also been a pioneering producer of *Rully* in the *Côte Châlonnais*. Whites are most impressive. ☆☆☆☆ **1996 Meursault Premier Cru Les Bouchères $$$**

Jaffelin [zhaf-lan] (*Burgundy*, France) Small *négoçiant*, particularly good at supposedly 'lesser' *appellations* – *Rully Blanc* and *Monthélie* are particularly good – but winemaker Bernard Repolt (who is now also responsible for the improving wines at *Bouchard Aîné*) is now showing his skills across the board. ☆☆☆☆ **1997 Borgogne du Chapitre Chardonnay $$$**

Joseph Jamet [zha-may] (*Rhône*, France) Top-class *Côte Rôtie* estate, making unusually stylish wines for this often high-profile *appellation*. ☆☆☆☆ **1994 Côte Rôtie $$$$**

Jamieson's Run (*Coonawarra*, Australia) *Mildara's* pair of prize-winning, good-value red and white wines. ☆☆☆☆ **1996 Jamieson's Run Cabernet Shiraz Merlot $$**

Dom. de la Janasse [ja-nass] (*Rhône*, France) High-quality *Châteauneuf-du-Pape* estate, producing three individual wines under this *appellation*, plus a good *Côtes du Rhône* les Garrigues. ☆☆☆☆ **1997 Côtes du Rhône les Garrigues $$$**

Janz [yantz] (*Tasmania*, Australia) See *Yalumba* and *Heemskerk*.

Vin de Pays du Jardin de la France [jar-da'n duh lah fronss] (*Loire*, France) Large Loire region that can produce alternatives to the region's appellations, but tends to offer light, unripe whites. ☆☆☆☆☆ **1997 Domaine de Cray Chardonnay 1997 $$$**

Robert Jasmin [zhas-man] (*Rhône*, France) Traditionalist *Côte Rotie* estate, eschewing new oak. ☆☆☆☆☆ **1994 Côte Rôtie $$$$**

Jasnières [zhan-yehr] (*Loire*, France) On rare occasions bone-dry and – even rarer – *Moelleux*, sweet *Chenin Blanc* wines from *Touraine*. Buy carefully. Poorly made, over-sulfured efforts offer a pricy chance to taste the *Chenin* at its worst. White: **86 88 89 90** 94 95 **96 97** 98 Sweet White: **76** 83 **85** 86 **88 89 90 94** 95 96 97 98

Jasper Hill (*Bendigo*, Australia) Winery in Heathcote with a cult following for both reds and whites – especially those from the Georgia's Paddock vineyard. ☆☆☆☆ **1995 Georgia's Paddock Riesling, Heathcote $$**

Jaume Serra [how-may seh-rah] (*Penedès*, Spain) Privately owned company which recently relocated from *Alella* to *Penedès*, and is doing good things with *Xarel-lo*.

Patrick Javillier [zha-vil-yay] (*Burgundy*, France) Reliable, small merchant making meticulous village *Meursault* and good reds. ☆☆☆☆ **1996 Meursault Clos Cromin $$$$**

Henri Jayer [zha-yay] (*Burgundy*, France) Now retired cult winemaker who is still represented on labels referring to Georges et Henri. Also an influence on the wines of *Meo Camuzet*.

Robert Jayer-Gilles [zhah-yay-zheel] (*Burgundy*, France) *Henri Jayer's* cousin, whose top wines – including an *Echézeaux* – bear comparison with those of his more famous relative. (His whites – particularly the *Aligoté* – are good too.) ☆☆☆☆☆ **1996 Echézeaux du Dessus $$$$**

Jerez (de la Frontera) [hay-reth] (Spain) Center of the *sherry* trade, giving its name to entire *DO* area. ***Gonzalez Byass; Lustau; Hidalgo; Barbadillo.***

Jermann [zhehr-man] (*Friuli-Venezia Giulia*, Italy) Brilliant winemaker who gets outrageous flavors – and prices – out of every white grape variety he touches. Look out for the Vintage Tunina blend of *Tocai, Picoli*, and *Malvasia*, and the "Dreams" white blend plus the single-vineyard Capo Martino. Also good at *Chardonnay, Pinot Gris* and *Pinot Blanc*. ☆☆☆☆ **1996 Dreams $$$**

Jeroboam [zhe-roh-bohm] Large bottle; in *Champagne* holding three liters (four bottles); in *Bordeaux*, four and a half (six bottles). Best to make sure before writing your check.

Jesuitengarten [zhes-yoo-wi-ten-gahr-ten] (*Rheingau*, Germany) One of Germany's top vineyards – well handled by *Bassermann-Jordan*. QbA/Kab/Spät: **85** 86 **88 89 90** 91 92 93 94 95 96 97 Aus/Beeren/Tba: **83 85** 88 89 90 91 92 93 94 95 96 97

Jeunes Vignes [zhuhn veen] Denotes vines too young for their crop to be sold as an *Appellation Contrôlée* wine.

Dom. François Jobard [fron-swah joh-bahr] (*Burgundy*, France) Great white wine estate in *Meursault*. ☆☆☆☆ **1995 Meursault Genevrières $$$**

Dom. Joblot [zhob-loh] (*Burgundy*, France) One of the top *domaines* in *Givry*. ☆☆☆ **1996 Cellier Aux Moines $$$**

Charles Joguet [zho-gay] (*Loire*, France) One of the finest producers of red *Loire*, making *Chinon* wines that last. He is also notable in having some of the only quality vines in France that have not been grafted onto *phylloxera*-resistant American rootstock. ☆☆☆☆ **1996 Chinon, Clos de la Cure $$**

Johannisberg [zho-han-is-buhrg.] (*Rheingau*, Germany) Village making superb *Riesling*, which has lent its name to a *bereich* covering all the *Rheingau*. QbA/Kab/Spät: **85** 86 **88 89 90** 91 **92** 93 94 95 96 97 98 Aus/Beeren/Tba: **83 85 88 89** 90 91 92 93 94 95 96 97 98

Johannisberg Riesling [rees-ling] Californian name for *Rhine Riesling*.

Weingut Karl-Heinz Johner [karl-hihntz yoh-nuh] (*Baden*, Germany) Former winemaker at *Lamberhurst*, now making exceptional *oaky Pinot Noir* in southern Germany.

Pascal Jolivet [zhol-lee-vay] (*Loire*, France) Superstar producer of modern *Sancerre* and *Pouilly-Fumé*. ☆☆☆☆ **1997 Sancerre Chêne Marchand $$$**

Nicolas Joly [Zhoh-lee] (*Loire*, France) The biodynamic owner-winemaker behind the *Coulée de Serrant* in *Savennières*.

Jordan (*Stellenbosch*, South Africa) Young winery whose Californian-trained winemakers are hitting the mark with their *Sauvignon* and *Chardonnay*. ☆☆☆☆ **1997 Jordan Estate Chardonnay $$$**

Jordan (*Sonoma Valley*, California) *Sonoma* winery surrounded by the kind of hype more usually associated with *Napa*. Table wines – from the *Alexander Valley* – are mostly good rather than great, though the sparkling wine is of *Champagne* quality. ☆☆☆☆☆ **1991 'J', Sonoma County $$$$**

Joseph (*South Australia*) *Primo Estate's* label for its top wines and olive oils.

Josmeyer [jos-mi-yur] (*Alsace*, France) Estate producing wines that are more delicate and restrained than those of some of its neighbors. ☆☆☆☆ **1997 'H' Vieilles Vignes Pinot Auxerrois $$$**

Weingut Toni Jost [toh-nee yohst] (*Mittelrhein*, Germany) A new-wave producer with (well-sited) vines in Bacharach, good reds and a penchant for experimenting (often successfully) with new oak barrels. ☆☆☆☆☆ **1997 Riesling Auslese Mittelrhein Bacharacher Hahn $$$**

La Jota [lah hoh-tah] (*Napa Valley*, California) Small *Howell Mountain* producer with stylish reds, including an unusually good *Cabernet Franc*. ☆☆☆☆ **1996 Howell Mountain Cabernet Franc $$$**

Judd's Hill (*Napa Valley*, California) Young winery with dazzling *Cabernets*. ☆☆☆☆ **1995 Cabernet Sauvignon Napa Valley $$$.**

Juffer [yoof-fuh] (*Mosel*, Germany) Famous vineyard in the village of *Brauneberg*. QbA/Kab/Spät: **85** 86 **88 89 90** 91 **92** 93 94 95 96 97 98 Aus/Beeren/Tba: **83 85 88 89 90** 91 92 93 94 95 96 97 98

Jug wine (California) American term for quaffable *Vin Ordinaire*.

Marcel Juge [zhoozh] (*Rhône*, France) Producer of one of the subtlest, classiest examples of *Cornas*. ☆☆☆☆ **1993 Cornas $$$**

Juliénas [joo-lee-yay-nas] (*Burgundy*, France) One of the ten *Beaujolais Crus*, producing classic, vigorous wine which often benefits from a few years in bottle. **85 87 88 89** 90 **91** 93 94 95 96 97 98 ***Georges Duboeuf; Eventail des Producteurs;* Ch. de Juliénas; Dom. Michel Tête**

Weingut Juliusspital [yoo-lee-yoos-shpit-ahl] (*Franken*, Germany) Top-class estate whose profits benefit the poor and sick. A good source of *Riesling* and *Sylvaner*.

Jumilla [hoo-mee-yah] (Spain) *DO* region, traditionally known for heavy high-alcohol wines but increasingly making lighter *Beaujolais*-style ones.

Jurançon [zhoo-ron-son] (*South-West*, France) Rich, dry apricoty white and excellent sweet wines made from the *Gros* and *Petit Manseng* **83** 85 86 **89 90** 92 93 95 96 **Dom. J-P Bousquet; Castera; Cauhapé; Clos Uroulat.**

Justin (*San Luis Obispo*, California) A winery to watch, with stunning reds, including a great *Cabernet Franc* and Isosceles, a *Bordeaux* blend. ☆☆☆☆ **1994 Isosceles San Luis Obispo County Reserve.**

Juvé y Camps [hoo-vay ee kamps] (*Catalonia*, Spain) The exception which proves the rule – by making and maturing decent *cava* from traditional grapes and excellent vintage *Brut*.

K

Kabinett (Germany) First step in German quality ladder, for wines which achieve a certain natural sweetness.

🍷 **Ch. Kefraya** [keh-frah-ya] (Lebanon) *Ch. Musar* is not the only Lebanese winery; this is the other one worth taking seriously. ☆☆☆ **1996 Ch. Kefraya $$**

Kaiserstuhl-Tuniberg [kih-sehr shtool too-nee-burg] (*Baden*, Germany) Supposedly finest *Baden bereich* (actually it covers a third of *Baden's* vineyards) with top villages producing rich, spicy *Riesling* and *Sylvaner* from volcanic slopes. QbA/Kab/Spät: **85 88 89 90** 91 **92** 93 94 95 96 97 98
Aus/Beeren/Tba: **83 85 88 89** 90 91 92 93 94 95 96 97 98

Kallstadt [kahl-shtaht] (*Pfalz*, Germany) Village containing the best-known and finest vineyard of Annaberg, making luscious full *Riesling*.
QbA/Kab/Spät: **85** 86 **88 89 90** 91 92 93 94 95 96 97 98
Aus/Beeren/Tba: **83 85** 88 89 90 91 92 93 94 95 96 97 98

🍷 **Kamptal** [kamp-tal] (*Niederösterreich*, Austria) Up-and-coming region for rich dry white Grüner Veltliners and Rieslings, thanks largely to the efforts of star producer Brundlmayer.

🍷 **Kanonkop Estate** [ka-NON-kop] (*Stellenbosch*, South Africa) Estate with largely traditional equipment, but a modern approach to its unusually classy *Pinotage*. The light red blend, "Kadette," is good too, and *Bordeaux*-style "Paul Sauer" is one of the *Cape's* best. ☆☆☆☆ **1995 Pinotage $$**

🍷 **Karthäuserhof** [kart-hows-sur-hof] (*Ruwer*, Germany) Impressive new-wave estate with impeccably made Rieslings. ☆☆☆☆☆ **1997 Riesling Kabinett Eitelsbacher Karthäuserhofberg Karthäuserhof $$$**

🍷 **Katnook Estate** (*Coonawarra*, Australia) Small estate making the highly commercial Deakin Estate wines as well as plenty of such innovative stuff as a *late harvest Coonawarra Chardonnay* and top-class *Coonawarra Merlot* and *Cabernet*. ☆☆☆☆ **1997 Merlot $$$**

Kellerei/kellerabfüllung [kel-luh-rih/kel-luh-rab-foo-loong] (Germany) Cellar/producer/estate-bottled.

🍷 **Kendall-Jackson** (*Clear Lake*, California) Ultra-dynamic, fast-growing producer with popular but decidedly off-dry *Chardonnay* and *Sauvignon*. Reds are better. ☆☆☆☆ **1995 Pinot Noir Vintners Reserve $$**

🍷 **Kenwood Vineyards** (*Sonoma Valley*, California) Classy *Sonoma* winery with good single-vineyard *Chardonnays* and impressive, if sometimes rather tough, *Cabernets* (including one made from the author Jack London's vineyard). The other star is the brilliant *Zinfandel*. ☆☆☆☆☆ **1994 Artist Series 20th Anniversary Cabernet Sauvignon Sonoma Valley $$$$**

Kerner [kuh-nuh] A white grape variety. A *Riesling*-cross that is grown in Germany and also widely in England. **Anselmann.**

Weingut Reichsgraf von Kesselstatt [rihkh-sgraf fon kes-sel-shtat] (*Mosel-Saar-Ruwer*, Germany) Large, impressive collection of four *Riesling* estates spread between the *Mosel*, *Saar*, and *Ruwer*. ☆☆☆☆ **Ockfener Bockstein Riesling $$**

Kiedrich [kee-drikh] (*Rheingau*, Germany) Top village high in the hills whose vineyards can produce great intense *Rieslings*. QbA/Kab/Spät: **85** 86 **88 89 90** 91 **92 93** 94 95 96 97 98 Aus/Beeren/Tba: **83 85 88 89** 90 91 92 93 94 95 **96** 97 98

Kientzheim [keents-him] (*Alsace*, France) Village noted for its *Riesling*. **71** 75 **76 83 85 86** 88 89 **90** 92 93 95 96 97 98

André Kientzler [keent-zluh] (*Alsace*, France) Classy producer with better-than-average *Pinot Blanc*. ☆☆☆☆ **1996 Pinot Blanc d'Alsace $$**

JF Kimich [kih-mikh] (*Pfalz*, Germany) Fast-rising star making rich spicy wines typical of the *Pfalz*. *Gewurztraminers* are as good as *Rieslings*. ☆☆☆☆ **1992 Forster Elster Riesling Kabinett $$$$**

King Estate (*Oregon*, US) Glitzy new investment in part of the state that has yet to produce top-class wine. ☆☆☆☆ **1995 King Estate Pinot Noir $$$**

Kingston Estate (*Murray Valley*, South Australia) Dynamic producer in the Riverland and, increasingly, cooler regions. ☆☆☆☆ **1998 Merlot $$$**

Kiona [kih-yoh-nah] (*Washington State*, US) Small producer in the middle of nowhere with a penchant for berryish reds and intensely flavored *late harvest* wines. ☆☆☆☆ **1995 Cabernet Sauvignon $$$$**

Kir (*Burgundy*, France) A mixture of sweet fortified *Crème de Cassis* (regional specialty of *Burgundy*) with simple and often rather *acidic* local white wine (*Aligoté*, or basic *Bourgogne* Blanc) to produce a delicious summertime drink. Try it with *Crème de Mûre* or *Crème de Framboise* instead.

Ch. Kirwan [keer-wahn] (*Margaux 3ème Cru Classé*, *Bordeaux*, France) Rejuvenated property belatedly coming out of prolonged doldrums. Still doesn't warrant its third growth status. 70 78 81 **82 83** 85 86 87 88 89 90 92 **93 94** 95 96 97 98

Kistler [kist-luh] (*Sonoma Valley*, California) Probably California's top *Chardonnay* producer, with a really dazzling range of uncompromizing complex single-vineyard wines and fast-improving *Pinot Noirs*. *Burgundy* quality at *Burgundy* prices. ☆☆☆☆☆ **1996 Chardonnay Carneros Hyde Vineyard $$$$**

Klein Constantia [klihn kon-stan-tee-yah] (*Constantia*, South Africa) Small go-ahead estate on the site of the great 17th-century *Constantia* vineyard. After a slightly disappointing patch, wines seem to be right back on form and proving a credit to the *Constantia* region. The star wine is the sweet "Vin de Constance" which is sadly hard to find outside South Africa. ☆☆☆☆☆ **1998 Sauvignon Blanc $$;** ☆☆☆☆☆ **1997 Shiraz $$$**

Klusserath [kloo-seh-raht] (*Mosel-Saar-Ruwer*, Germany) Small village best known in UK for *Sonnenuhr* and Konigsberg vineyards. QbA/Kab/Spät: **85** 86 **88 89 90** 91 **92 93** 94 95 96 97 98 Aus/Beeren/Tba: **83 85 88 89 90** 91 92 93 94 95 96 97 98

Knappstein [nap-steen] (*Clare Valley*, South Australia). Now part of the *Mildara-Blass* stable and no longer associated with founder Tim (see *Knappstein Lenswood*) but still producing good *Clare Valley* wines.

Knappstein Lenswood [nap-steen] (*Lenswood*, South Australia) Tim Knappstein's brilliant *Sauvignon, Semillon, Chardonnay, Pinot Noir* and *Cabernets* from *Lenswood* label. ☆☆☆☆ **1998 Semillon $$$**

🍷 **Emerich Knoll** [knowl] (*Wachau,* Austria). Maker of stunning new wave *Riesling* and *Grüner Veltliner* wines.

🍷 **Konocti Cellars** [ko-nok-tih] (*Lake County*, California) Dynamic producer with good straightforward wines.

Kosher (Israel) Wine made under complex rules. Every seventh vintage is left unharvested and non-Jews are barred from the winemaking process.

🍷 **Korbel** [Kor-BEL] (*Sonoma*, California) Big producer of basic California sparkling wine. Better wines like Le Premier Reserve show what can be done.

🍷 **Kourtakis** [koor-tah-kis] (Greece) One of Greece's growing number of dynamic wine companies with unusually recommendable whites and good examples of the characterful native *Mavrodaphne*. ☆☆☆☆ **1996 Kouros Nemea $$$**

🍷 **Weinlaubenhof Weingut Alois Kracher** [Ah-loys krah-kuh] (*Neusiedlersee*, Austria) Source of world-class, (very) *late harvest* wines including a very unusual effort which blends the *Chardonnay* with the *Welschriesling*. ☆☆☆☆☆ **1996 Chardonnay Welschriesling Nouvelle Vague Trokenbeerenauslese No.4 $$$$**

Krems [krems] (*Wachau*, Austria) Town and *Wachau* vineyard area producing Austria's most stylish *Rieslings* from terraced vineyards.

Kreuznach [kroyt-znahkh] (*Nahe*, Germany) Northern *bereich*, boasting fine vineyards situated around the town of *Bad Kreuznach*. QbA/Kab/Spät: **85** 86 **88 89 90** 91 92 93 94 95 96 97 98 Aus/Beeren/Tba: **83 85 88 89** 90 91 92 93 94 95 96 97 98

🍷 **Dom. Kreydenweiss** [krih-den-vihs] (*Alsace*, France) Top-class organic producer with particularly good *Muscat, Pinot Gris,* and *Riesling*.

🍷 **Krondorf** [kron-dorf] (*Barossa Valley*, Australia) Innovative viticulturists and winery specializing in traditional, big *Barossa* style wines. ☆☆☆☆ **1996 Semillon $$$**

🍷 **Krug** [kroog] (*Champagne*, France) The *Ch. Latour* of *Champagne*. Great vintage wine, extraordinary rosé, and pure *Chardonnay* from the *Clos de Mesnil* vineyard. Theoretically the best non-vintage, thanks to the greater proportions of aged Reserve wine. ☆☆☆☆☆ **1989 Vintage $$$$**

🍷 **Kruger-Rumpf** [kroo-gur roompf] (*Nahe,* Germany) Nahe estate, demonstrating the potential of varieties like the *Scheurebe*. ☆☆☆☆☆ **1997 Riesling Eiswein Nahe Munsterer Pittersberg Kruger-Rumpf $$$$**

🍷 **Kuentz-Bas** [koontz bah] (*Alsace*, France) Reliable producer for *Pinot Gris* and *Gewurztraminer*. ☆☆☆☆ **1998 Gewurztraminer Cuvée Tradition $$$**

🍷 **Kuhling-Gillot** [koo-ling gil-lot] (*Rheinhessen,* Germany) Hitherto little-known producer, now fast developing a reputation for rich concentrated wines. ☆☆☆☆ **1996 Oppenheimer Sackträger Riesling Spätlese $$$$**

🍷 **Kumeu River** [koo-myoo] (*Auckland*, New Zealand) Michael Brajkovich is successful with a wide range of wines, including a very unusual dry *botrytis Sauvignon* which easily outclasses many a dry wine from *Sauternes*. ☆☆☆☆☆ **1997 Mate's Vineyard Chardonnay $$$**

- **Kunde** [koon-day] (*Sonoma*, California) Producer of good *Chardonnay* and *Zinfandel*. ☆☆☆☆ **1995 Zinfandel Sonoma Valley Robusto $$$**
- **Weingut Franz Künstler** [koont-sluh] (*Rheingau*, Germany) A new superstar producer with superlative *Riesling*. ☆☆☆☆ **1996 Rheingau Hochheimer Kirchenstuck Riesling Spätlese $$**
- **KWV** (*Cape*, South Africa) Huge cooperative formed by the South African government at a time when surplus wine seemed set to flood the industry and, for a long time, maintained by the National Party when it needed to keep the members of the big wine cooperatives, well, cooperative. Winemaking has improved recently – especially the wines sold under the Cathedral Cellars label. ☆☆☆☆☆ **1996 Cathedral Cellars Shiraz $$$;** ☆☆☆☆☆ **1996 Cathedral Cellars Pinotage $$$**

L

- **Ch. Labégorce** [la-bay-gors] (*Bordeaux*, France) Good traditional *Margaux*. 75 79 81 **82 83 85** 86 88 **89** 90 94 95 96 97 98
- **Ch. Labégorce-Zédé** [la-bay-gors zay-day] (*Margaux Cru Bourgeois, Bordeaux*, France). An estate that belongs to the same Thienpont family as *Vieux Château Certan* and *le Pin*. A name to remember for wine beyond its Bourgeois class. 81 82 **83 85 86** 88 89 90 92 94 95 96 97 98
- **Labouré-Roi** [la-boo-ray rwah] (*Burgundy*, France) A highly successful and very commercial *négoçiant*, responsible for some quite impressive wines. See *Cottin Frères*. ☆☆☆☆ **1995 Meursault Clos de la Baronne $$$**
- ***Labrusca*** [la-broo-skah] *Vitis labrusca*, the North American species of vine, making wine which is often referred to as "foxy". All *vinifera* vine stocks are grafted on to *phylloxera*-resistant *labrusca* roots, though the vine itself is banned in Europe and its wines, thankfully, are almost unfindable.
- **Ch. Lacoste-Borie** [la-cost-bo-ree] (*Pauillac*, *Bordeaux*, France) The reliable *second label* of *Grand-Puy-Lacoste*. ☆☆☆ **1995 Ch. Lacoste-Borie $$$**

Lacryma Christi [la-kree-mah kris-tee] (*Campania*, Italy) Literally, "tears of Christ," the melancholy name for some amiable, light, rather rustic reds and whites. Those from Vesuvio are *DOC*. **Caputo; Mastroberardino.**

Ladoix-Serrigny [la-dwah-seh-reen-yee] (*Burgundy*, France) Village including parts of *Corton* and *Corton-Charlemagne*. The village wines are not well known and some bargains are still to be found. White: 79 **85 86 88** 89 **90 92** 95 96 97 98 Red: 78 83 **85** 87 **88 89 90** 92 **94** 95 96 97 98 **Capitain-Gagnerot; Dubreuil-Fontaine; Gay; Launay; Maréchale.**

- **Patrick de Ladoucette** [duh la-doo-set] (*Loire*, France) Fine intense *Pouilly-Fumé*, sold as "Baron de L." Other wines are greatly improved in recent years. ☆☆☆☆ **1997 Comte Lafond Blanc $$$**
- **Michel Lafarge** [la-farzh] (*Burgundy*, France) One of the very best producers in *Volnay* – and indeed *Burgundy*. Fine, long-lived, modern wine. ☆☆☆☆ **1995 Volnay Clos des Chênes $$$**
- **Ch. Lafaurie-Peyraguey** [la-foh-ree pay-rah-gee] (*Sauternes Premier Cru Classé, Bordeaux*, France) Much-improved *Sauternes* estate that has produced creamy, long-lived wines in the 1980s and in the 1990s. 78 80 **81** 82 **83** 85 **86 88 89 90 96** 95 97 98 ☆☆☆☆ **1990 $$$$**
- **Ch. Lafite-Rothschild** [la-feet roh-chihld] (*Pauillac Premier Cru Classé, Bordeaux*, France) Often almost impossible to taste young, this *Pauillac* first growth is still one of the monuments of the wine world – especially since the early 1980s. A brilliant 1998. **61 75 76** 78 79 **81 82** 83 84 85 **86** 87 88 89 90 91 92 **93 94** 95 96 97 98 ☆☆☆☆ **1994 $$$$**

Ch. Lafleur [la-flur] (*Pomerol*, *Bordeaux*, France) *Christian Moueix*'s pet *Pomerol*, often on a par with the wine *Moueix* makes at *Pétrus*. **61 62 66 70 75 78 79 82 83 85 86** 88 89 90 **92 93** 94 95 96 97 98

Ch. Lafleur-Gazin [la-flur-ga-zan] (*Pomerol*, *Bordeaux*, France) Another good *Moueix* wine. **82** 83 **85** 86 88 89 90 92 93 94 95 96 97 98

Dom. des Comtes Lafon [day comt la-fon] (*Burgundy*, France) The best domaine in *Meursault*, with great vineyards in *Volnay* and a small slice of *Montrachet*. Wines last forever. ☆☆☆☆ **1995 Meursault Clos de la Barre $$$**

Ch. Lafon-Rochet [la-fon-ro-shay] (*St. Estèphe 4ème Cru Classé*, *Bordeaux*, France) Very classy modern *St. Estèphe*. Impressive in 1998. 70 79 81 82 83 85 86 88 89 90 91 92 93 94 95 96 97 98

Alois Lageder [la-GAY-duh] (*Trentino-Alto-Adige*, Italy) New-wave producer of the kind of wine the *Alto-Adige* ought to make.

Lago di Caldaro [LA-goh dah KAHL-deh-roh] (*Trentino-Alto-Adige*, Italy) Also known as the *Kalterersee*, using the local *Schiava* grape to make cool light reds with slightly unripe, though pleasant, fruit.

Ch. Lagrange [la-gronzh] (*St. Julien 3ème Cru Classé*, *Bordeaux*, France) A once underperforming third growth rejuvenated by Japanese cash and local know-how (for a while from Michel Delon of *Léoville-Las-Cases*). Look out for *Les Fiefs de Lagrange*, the impressive *second label*. 70 82 83 84 **85 86** 88 89 90 91 92 93 94 95 96 97 98

Ch. Lagrange [la-gronzh] (*Pomerol*, *Bordeaux*, France) Yet another *Moueix* property – and yet another good wine. **70 75** 78 81 **82** 83 **85** 86 87 88 89 90 92 93 94 95 96 97 98 ☆☆☆ **1993 $$$**

Lagrein [la-grayn] (Italy) Cherryish red grape of north-east Italy.

Ch. la Lagune [la-goon] (*Haut-Médoc 3ème Cru Classé*, *Bordeaux*, France) Lovely accessible wines which last well and are worth buying even in poorer years. **70 75 78** 79 **82** 85 86 88 89 90 92 93 94 95 96 97 98

Lake County (California) Vineyard district salvaged by improved irrigation techniques and now capable of some fine wines as well as *Kendall Jackson*'s highly commercial efforts. Red: 84 **85** 86 87 **90 91** 92 93 95 96 97 98 White: **85 90 91** 92 95 96 97 98

Lake's Folly (*Hunter Valley*, Australia) Meet Max Lake, surgeon-turned-winemaker/writer/researcher who has great theories about the sexual effects of sniffing various kinds of wine. He is also a leading Australian pioneer of *Chardonnay*, with an unusually successful *Hunter Valley Cabernet Sauvignon*. Wines now made by Max's son, Stephen. ☆☆☆☆ **1994 Hunter Valley Cabernet Sauvignon $$$**

Lalande de Pomerol [la-LOND duh po-meh-rol] (*Bordeaux*, France) Bordering on *Pomerol* with similar, but less fine wines. Still generally better than similarly priced *St. Emilions*. Some good-value *Petits-Châteaux*. **70 82 83 85** 86 **88 89** 90 92 93 94 95 96 97 98

Ch. Lalande-Borie [la-LOND bo-ree] (*St. Julien*, *Bordeaux*, France) In the same stable as *Ch. Ducru-Beaucaillou*. Reliable wines. 82 85 86 88 89 90 91 92 93 94 95 **96** 97 98 ☆☆☆☆ **1989 $$$**

🍷 **Ch. Lamarque** [la-mahrk] (*Haut-Médoc Cru Bourgeois*, *Bordeaux*, France) Spectacular *château* with good traditional wines. 82 **83** 85 **86** 88 89 90 91 92 93 94 95 96 97 98 ☆☆☆ **1992 $$$; ☆☆☆ 1993 $$**

🍷 **Lamberhurst** (Kent, England) One of the first English vineyards and still one of the more reliable, though rarely the most innovative. (Other non-English wines sold by Lamberhurst are not recommendable.)

🍷 **Lamborn Family** (*Napa Valley*, California) Small *Howell Mountain* producer, focusing on rich, concentrated, long-lived *Zinfandel*.

🍷 **Dom. des Lambrays** [lom-bray] (*Burgundy*, California) Under new ownership and promising further improvements in quality. Already very worthwhile, though. ☆☆☆☆ **1995 Clos des Lambrays $$$**

🍷 **Lambrusco** [lam-broos-koh] (*Emilia-Romagna*, Italy) Famous/infamous low-strength (7.5 percent) sweet, sparkling UK and North American version of the sparkling, dry, red wine favored in Italy. The real thing – fascinating with its dry, unripe, cherry flavor – comes with a cork rather than a screw-cap. ☆☆☆ **1997 Don Bosco Escuela Vitivinicola $**

🍷 **Lamouroux Landing** [lam-moh-roh] (*New York State*, USA) Impressive young *Chardonnay* specialist in the Finger Lakes.

🍷 **Landmark** (*Sonoma*, California) Small *Chardonnay* specialist with rich, fruity, buttery wines from individual "Damaris" and "Overlook" vineyards. Not the subtlest fare, but very seductive. ☆☆☆☆ **1995 Pinot Noir Sonoma County Grand Detour $$$**

Landwein [land-vihn] (Germany) The equivalent of a French *Vin De Pays* from one of 11 named regions (*anbaugebiet*). Often dry.

🍷 **Ch. Lanessan** [la-neh-son] (*Haut-Médoc Cru Bourgeois*, *Bordeaux*, France) Old-fashioned *Cru Bourgeois* largely untouched by new oak. A long-lived argument for the way things used to be done.

Langhe [lang-gay] (*Piedmont*, Italy) A range of hills; when preceded by "*Nebbiolo* delle," indicates declassified *Barolo* and *Barbaresco*.

🍷 **Ch. Langoa-Barton** [lon-goh-wah-bahr-ton] (*St. Julien 3ème Cru Classé*, *Bordeaux*, France) *Léoville-Barton*'s (slightly) less complex kid brother. Often one of the best bargain *classed growths* in *Bordeaux*. Well made in poor years. **70 75** 76 **78** 79 **82** 83 85 **86** 88 89 90 91 92 93 **94** 95 96 97 98 ☆☆☆☆ **1993 $$$$**

Languedoc-Roussillon [long-dok roo-see-yon] (*Midi*, France) One of the world's largest wine regions and, until recently, a major source of the wine lake. But a combination of government-sponsored uprooting and keen activity by *flying winemakers* and (a few) dynamic producers is beginning to turn this into a worrying competitor for the New World. The region includes *appellations* like *Fitou, Corbières* and *Minervois, Faugères, St. Chinian, Coteaux de Languedoc, Côtes de Roussillon,* and a torrent of *Vin de Pays d'Oc*. Sadly, many of the best, more ambitious, wines are hard to find outside France.

🍷 **Lanson** [lon-son] (*Champagne*, France) Much-improved *Champagne* house with decent non-vintage "Black Label," good *Demi-Sec,* and sublime *vintage* champagne. ☆☆☆☆ **1988 Noble Cuvée Vintage $$$$**

🍷 **Casa Lapostolle** [la-pos-tol] (*Colchagua Valley*, Chile) Instant superstar. Belongs to the owners of Grand Marnier and benefits from the expertize of *Michel Rolland*. Cuvée Alexandre *Merlot* reds have been a classy instant success, though the whites need more work. The 1997 Clos Apalta Merlot-Carmenère blend is one of the (relatively) cheapest of Chile's new-wave flagship reds. It easily justifies its ($20 / $35) price tag. ☆☆☆☆☆ **1997 Clos Apalta $$$$**

🍷 **Ch. Larcis-Ducasse** [lahr-see doo-kass] (*St. Emilion Grand Cru Classé*, *Bordeaux*, France) Property whose lightish wines rarely live up to the potential of its hillside site. 66 78 79 81 **82** 83 85 86 88 89 90 94 95 96 97 98 ☆☆☆☆ **1990 $$$**

🍷 **Ch. Larmande** [lahr-mond] (*St. Emilion Grand Cru Classé*, *Bordeaux*, France) A property to watch for well-made ripe-tasting wines. 85 86 **88** **89** 90 **92 93** 94 95 96 97 98

🍷 **Dom. Laroche** [la-rosh] (*Burgundy*, France) Highly reliable *Chablis négoçiant* with some enviable vineyards of its own, including some top-class *Premiers* and *Grands Crus*. At more affordable prices, there are also reliable southern French *Chardonnay Vin de Pays d'Oc* and innovative wines from *Corsica*. ☆☆☆☆ **1997 Chablis Premier Cru Les Fourchaumes Vieilles Vignes $$$**

🍷 **Ch. Lascombes** [las-komb] (*Margaux 2ème Cru Classé*, *Bordeaux*, France) Subtle second growth *Margaux* which often exemplifies the perfumed character of this *appellation*, but could still do better. **70 75** 82 83 85 **86 88** 89 90 91 92 93 94 95 96 97 98 ☆☆☆☆ **1995 $$$$**

🍇 **Laski Riesling/Rizling** [lash-kee riz-ling] (Former Yugoslavia) Yugoslav name for white grape, unrelated to the *Rhine Riesling*, aka *Welsch*, *Olasz* and *Italico*.

🍷 **Ch. de Lastours** [duh las-toor] (*Languedoc-Roussillon*, France) Combined winery and home for people with mental disabilities which frequently provides ample proof that *Corbières* can rival *Bordeaux*. Look out for the *cuvée* Simone Descamps. ☆☆☆☆ **1995 Cuvée Fûts de Chêne $$**

Late harvest Made from (riper) grapes picked after the main vintage. Should have at least some *botrytis*.

Late-Bottled Vintage (Port) (LBV) (*Douro*, Portugal) Officially, bottled four or six years after a specific (usually non-declared) *vintage*. Until the late 1970s, this made for a *vintage port*-style wine that matured earlier, was a little lighter and easier to drink, but still needed to be decanted. Until recently, the only houses to persevere with this style were *Warres* and *Smith Woodhouse*, who labeled their efforts "*Traditional*" LBV. Almost every other LBV around, however, was of the filtered, "modern" style pioneered by *Taylors*. These taste pretty much like up-market *ruby* and *vintage character ports*, need no decanting, and bear very little resemblance to real *vintage* or even *crusted port*. Belatedly, a growing number of producers are now confusingly offering "Traditional" as well as modern LBV. Under their self-imposed laws, the port shippers infuriatingly allow themselves to use the same name for these two very different styles of wine. Which is not very surprizing really: as one very prominent retired *port* maker admitted, he and his competitors have always done well out of confusing their clients.

Latium/Lazio [lah-tee-yoom] (Italy) The vineyard area surrounding Rome, including *Frascati* and *Marino*. **Fontana Candida; Colli di Catone.**

🍷 **Louis Latour** [loo-wee lah-toor] (*Burgundy*, France) Underperforming *négoçiant* who still pasteurizes his – to my mind, consequently muddy-tasting – reds, treating them in a way no quality-conscious New World producer would contemplate. Some whites, however, including *Corton-Charlemagne*, can be sublime, and Latour deserves credit for pioneering regions such as *Mâcon Lugny* and the *Ardèche*. ☆☆☆☆ **1993 Montrachet $$$$**; ☆☆☆☆ **1995 Batard-Montrachet $$$$**

🍷 **Ch. Latour** [lah-toor] (*Pauillac Premier Cru Classé*, *Bordeaux*, France) Recently bought – from its British owners, Allied Domecq – by the same self-made French millionaire who this year bought Christie's. First growth *Pauillac* which can be very tricky to judge when young, but which develops majestically. *Les Forts de Latour* is the – often worthwhile – *second label*. The 1992 is a good example of a generally disappointing vintage. **61** 62 64 **66** 67 **70** 73 **75** 76 **78** 79 80 81 **82** 83 **85 86** 88 89 90 **91 92 93** 94 95 96 97 98

🍷 **Ch. Latour-à-Pomerol** [lah-toor ah po-meh-rol] (*Pomerol*, *Bordeaux*, France) A great-value, small (3,500-case) *Pomerol estate* under the same ownership as *Ch. Pétrus* and the same *Moueix* winemaking team. It is a little less concentrated than its big brother, but then it is around a quarter of the price, too. **82** 83 **85** 86 88 89 90 92 93 94 95 96 98 ☆☆☆☆ **1990 $$$$**

🍷 **Ch. Latour-Martillac** [la-toor mah-tee-yak] (*Graves Cru Classé*, *Bordeaux*, France) Good, sometimes overlooked reds and whites. Red: **85** 86 88 89 90 91 92 93 94 95 96 White: **89** 90 93 94 96 97 98

Laudun [loh-duhn] (*Rhône*, France) Named village of *Côtes du Rhône*, with peppery reds and attractive rosés.

🍷 **Laurel Glen** (*Sonoma* Mountain, California) Small hillside estate with *claret*-style reds that are respected by true Californian wine lovers. Terra Rosa is the accessible *second label*. ☆☆☆☆ **1994 Sonoma Mountain Cabernet $$**

🍷 **Dominique Laurent** [Loh-ron] (*Burgundy*, France) A young *négociant* founded a few years ago by a former pastry chef who has rapidly shown his skills at buying and maturing top-class wines from several *appellations*.

🍷 **Laurent-Perrier** [law-ron pay-ree-yay] (*Champagne*, France) Historically one of the more reliable larger houses, though some recent bottlings have seemed variable. Grand Siècle is the most interesting wine.

🍷 **Ch. Laville Haut-Brion** [la-veel oh-bree-yon] (*Graves Cru Classé*, *Bordeaux*, France) Exquisite white *Graves* that lasts for 20 years or more. 62 **66 75** 82 **83 85** 86 88 89 90 92 93 94 95 96 97 98

Lazio [lat-zee-yoh] (Italy) See *Latium*.

LBV (*Douro*, Portugal) See *Late-Bottled Vintage*.

Lean Lacking body.

🍷 **Leasingham** (South Australia) *BRL Hardy* subsidiary in the *Clare Valley* that makes top-flight reds and whites, including great *Shiraz*, *Cabernet* and *Chardonnay*. ☆☆☆☆ **1996 Classic Clare Cabernet Sauvignon $$$**

Lebanon Best known for the remarkable *Ch. Musar* from the *Bekaa Valley*.

🍷 **Leconfield** [leh-kon-feeld] (South Australia) Reliable producer of highly impressive intense *Coonawarra* reds. Ralph Fowler, the winemaker responsible for the award-winning recent vintages has now moved to *Chapoutier*, Australia.

Lees or lie(s) The sediment of dead yeasts that fall in the barrel or vat as a wine develops. *Muscadet* – like some other white wines – is aged *Sur Lie*. Producers of modern *Chardonnay* also leave their wine n its lees, stirring it occasionally to maximize richness the rich flavour provided by the yeasts.

🍷 **Leeuwin Estate** [loo-win] (*Margaret River*, Western Australia) Showcase winery (and concert venue) whose vineyards were originally picked out by *Robert Mondavi*. The genuinely world-class ("art label") *Chardonnay* is one of Australia's priciest and longest-lived. Other wines are less dazzling. ☆☆☆☆☆ **1994 Art Series Chardonnay $$$**

🍷 **Dom. Leflaive** [luh-flayv] (*Burgundy*, France) A new generation of Leflaives is using organic methods – and making better wines than ever. ☆☆☆☆☆ **1996 Puligny-Montrachet Les Combettes $$$$**

🍷 **Olivier Leflaive** [luh-flayv] (*Burgundy*, France) The *négoçiant* business launched by Vincent Leflaive's nephew. High-class white wines. ☆☆☆☆ **Rully Premier Cru les Clous $$$**

🍷 **Peter Lehmann** [lee-man] (*Barossa Valley*, Australia) The grand old man of the *Barossa*, Peter Lehmann and his son Doug make intense *Shiraz*, *Cabernet*, *Semillon*, and *Chardonnay* which make up in character (and value) what they lack in subtlety. Stonewell is the best red. ☆☆☆☆☆ **1993 Stonewell Shiraz $$$**

Length How long the taste lingers in the mouth.

Lenswood (South Australia) New high-altitude region near *Adelaide*, proving its potential with *Sauvignon*, *Chardonnay*, *Pinot Noir*, and even (in the case of *Henschke*'s Abbott's Prayer), *Merlot* and *Cabernet Sauvignon*. Pioneers include *Stafford Ridge*, *Shaw & Smith*, *Knappstein Lenswood* and *Nepenthe*. White: **86 87** 88 **90 91 94 95** Red: **80 82 84 85 86 87** 88 **90 91 94** 95 96 97 98

🍷 **Lenz Vineyards** [lentz] (*New York State*, US) One of the most reliable wineries on Long Island, with particularly recommenadable *Merlot* and *Chardonnay*.

León [lay-on] (Spain) Northwestern region producing acceptable dry, fruity reds and whites.

🍷 **Jean León** [zhon lay-ON] (*Catalonia*, Spain) American pioneer of *Chardonnay* and *Cabernet*, improved since its purchase by *Torres*. ☆☆☆☆ **1993 Cabernet Sauvignon $$$**

🍷 **Leonetti Cellars** [lee-oh-net-tee] (*Washington State*, US) One of the best red wine producers in the US. Now showing its skills with *Sangiovese*. ☆☆☆☆ **1994 Cabernet Sauvignon Columbia Valley $$**

🍷 **Ch. Léoville-Barton** [lay-oh-veel bahr-ton] (*St. Julien 2ème Cru Classé*, *Bordeaux*, France) The charming Anthony Barton produces one of the classiest wines in *Bordeaux*. A fairly priced, reliably stylish *St. Julien* second growth, whose wines are among the best in the *Médoc*. *Langoa Barton* is the sister property. **61 70 75** 76 **78** 81 **82** 83 85 86 87 88 89 90 91 92 93 94 95 96 97 98 ☆☆☆☆☆ **1993 $$$$**

🍷 **Ch. Léoville-Las-Cases** [lay-oh-veel kas-kahz] (*St. Julien 2ème Cru Classé*, *Bordeaux*, France) Impeccably made *St. Julien Super Second* which now often matches its neighbor *Ch. Latour*, partly through the severity of the selection process that decides how much of each year's wine will go into the Grand Vin and how much into the *Clos du Marquis "second label."* Michel Delon, the owner, knows just how good his wine is, however, and now does everything possible to raise its price to the level of his first growth neighbors. 76 **78** 81 **82 83 85** 86 88 89 90 91 92 93 94 95 96 97 98

🍷 **Ch. Léoville-Poyferré** [lay-pwah-feh-ray] (*St. Julien 2ème Cru Classé*, *Bordeaux*, France) 1995, 1996 and 1997 showed the touch of *Michel Rolland* here. A rising star. The *second label* is Moulin Riche. **82 83** 84 85 86 87 88 89 90 91 93 94 95 96 97 98 ☆☆☆☆ **1995 $$$$**

🍷 **Dom. Leroy** [luh-rwah] (*Burgundy*, France) Organic *domaine* in *Vosne-Romanée* founded by the former co-owner of the *Dom. de la Romanée-Conti* and making wines as good as those of that estate. Prices are stratospheric, but the humblest wines are better than other producers' *Grands Crus*. ☆☆☆☆☆ **1995 Musigny $$$$**

🍷 **Maison Leroy** [luh-rwah] (Burgundy) If you want to buy a really great old bottle of Burgundy, no matter the cost, this is the place to come.

🍇 **Lexia** [lex-ee-yah] See *Muscat d'Alexandrie*.

Lie(s) See *Lees/Sur Lie.*

Liebfraumilch [leeb-frow-mihlkh] (Germany) Seditious exploitation of the *QbA* system. Good examples are pleasant; most are alcoholic sugar-water bought on price alone.

🍷 **Lievland** [leev-land] (*Stellenbosch*, South Africa) Estate which has a reputation in South Africa as a high-quality specialty producer of *Shiraz* and *late harvest* wines. ☆☆☆ **1996 Shiraz $$**

🍷 **Hubert Lignier** [Lee-nee-yay] (*Burgundy*, France) Producer of classic long-lived *Morey-St.-Denis.* ☆☆☆☆☆ **1995 Morey-St.-Denis $$$**

🍷 **Limestone Ridge** (South Australia) *Lindemans'* often excellent *Coonawarra* red blend. ☆☆☆☆ **1994 Shiraz Cabernet $$$**

Limousin [lee-moo-zan] (France) Oak forest that provides barrels that are high in wood *tannin.* Better, therefore, for red wine than for white.

Limoux [lee-moo] (*Midi*, France) (Relatively) cool-climate, chalky soil *appellation* that was recently created for increasingly *Chardonnay* which was previously sold as *Vin de Pays d'Oc.* Stories of tankers of wine being driven north by night to Burgundy are hotly denied (in the latter region). See *Blanquette.*

🍷 **Lindauer** [lin-dowr] (*Marlborough*, New Zealand) Good-value *Montana* sparkling wine. ☆☆☆☆ **Special Reserve $$**

🍷 **Lindemans** (South Australia) Once *Penfolds'* greatest rival, now (like so many other once-independent Australian producers) its subsidiary. Noted for long-lived *Hunter Valley Semillon* and *Shiraz*, *Coonawarra* reds, and good-value multi-region blends, such as the internationally successful Bin 65 *Chardonnay*, Bin 45 *Cabernet* and Cawarra wines.

🍷 **Weingut Karl Lingenfelder** [lin-gen-fel-duh] (*Pfalz*, Germany) Great new-wave *Rheinpfalz* producer of a special *Riesling, Dornfelder, Scheurebe* and an unusually successful *Pinot Noir.* ☆☆☆☆ **1997 Freisenheimer Riesling Spätlese $$**

🍷 **Jean Lionnet** [lee-oh-nay] (*Rhône*, France) Classy *Cornas* producer whose Rochepertius is a worthwhile buy. The *St. Péray* is an unusually good example of its *appellation* too. ☆☆☆☆ **1997 Cornas $$$**

🍷 **Ch. Liot** [lee-yoh] (*Barsac*, *Bordeaux*, France) Good light and elegant *Barsac.* 75 76 82 83 86 88 89 90 92 94 96 97 98 ☆☆☆☆ **1996 $$$**

Liqueur Muscat (*Rutherglen*, Australia) A wine style unique to Australia. Other countries make fortified *Muscats*, but none achieve the caramelized marmalade and Christmas pudding flavors that *Rutherglen* can achieve. **Mick Morris; Campbell's.**

Liqueur d'Expedition [lee-kuhr dex-pay-dees-see-yon] (*Champagne*, France) Sweetening syrup for *dosage.*

Liqueur de Tirage [lee-kuhr duh tee-rahzh] (*Champagne*, France) The yeast and sugar added to base wine to induce secondary fermentation (and hence the bubbles) in bottle.

Liquoreux [lee-koh-ruh] (France) Rich and sweet.

Liquoroso [lee-koh-roh-soh] (Italy) Rich and sweet.

🍷 **Lirac** [lee-rak] (*Rhône*, France) Peppery, *Tavel*-like rosés, and increasingly impressive, deep berry-fruit reds. Red: 90 95 96 97 98 **Ch. D'Aqueria; Bouchassy; Delorme; Ch. Mayne Lalande; André Méjan; Perrin.**

🍷 **Listel** [lees-tel] (*Languedoc-Roussillon*, France) Recently taken over, improving pioneer with vineyards on beaches close to Sète. Best wines: rosé ("Grain de Gris") and sparkling *Muscat* (Pétillant de Raisin).

Listrac-Médoc [lees-trak] (*Bordeaux*, France) Small *Haut-Médoc commune* near *Moulis*, though quite different in style. Clay makes this *Merlot* country, though this isn't always reflected in the vineyards. Wines tend to be toughly unripe and fun-free even in warm vintages. 82 83 85 86 88 89 90 94 95 96 97 98 **Ch. Clarke; Fonréaud; Fourcas-Dupré; Fourcas-Hosten.**

Livermore (Valley) [liv-uhr-mohr] (California) Warm-climate vineyard area with fertile soil producing full rounded whites, including increasingly fine *Chardonnay.* Red: 84 **85** 86 87 **90 91** 92 93 95 96 97 98 White: **92** 95 **96** 97 98 **Bonny Doon; Concannon; Livermore Cellars; Wente.**

Ɏ **Los Llanos** [los yah-nos] (*Valdepeñas*, Spain) Commendable modern exception to the tradition of dull *Valdepeñas*, with quality mature reds.

Ɏ **De Loach** [duh lohch] (*Sonoma*, California) Look for the letters OFS – Our Finest Selection – on the *Chardonnay* and *Cabernet*. But even these rarely surpass the stunning individual vineyard *Zinfandels*.

Ɏ **J Lohr** [lohr] (Santa Clara, California) Winery noted for its well-made affordable wines, particularly the Wildflower and now more classic noble styles. ☆☆☆☆ **1995 Hilltop Paso Robles Cabernet Sauvignon $$**

Loire [lwahr] (France) An extraordinary variety of wines come from this area – dry whites such as *Muscadet* and the classier *Savennières, Sancerre* and *Pouilly-Fumé*; grassy summery reds; – *Chinon* and *Bourgueil;* buckets of rosé – some good, most dreadful; glorious sweet whites – *Vouvray* etc, – and very acceptable sparkling wines (also *Vouvray* plus *Crémant de Loire*). Stick to growers and *domaines*. White: **86 88 89 90 94** 95 97 98 Sweet White: **76** 83 **85** 86 **88 89** 90 94 95 **96 97.** Red: **78** 83 **85** 86 **88 89 90** 95 **96 97** 98

Lombardy [lom-bahr-dee] (Italy) Region (and vineyards) around Milan, known mostly for sparkling wine but also for increasingly interesting reds, such as Valcalepio and *Oltrepò Pavese* and the whites of *Lugana*. Red: **78 79 82 85 88 90** 94 95 **96** 97 98 ☆☆☆☆ **1998 Lugana Ca' Dei Frati $$$$**

Long Island (*New York State*, US) A unique microclimate where fields once full of potatoes are now yielding classy *Merlot* and *Chardonnay.* **Bridgehampton; Hargrave; Lenz; Palmer Vineyards.**

Ɏ **Longridge** (*Stellenbosch*, South Africa) Designer winery tailoring three ranges (Longridge, Bay View, and Capelands) to export markets.

Lontue [lon-too-way] (Chile) Region where some of Chile's best *Merlots* are being made. **Lurton; San Pedro; Santa Carolina; Valdevieso.**

Ɏ **Weingut Dr. Loosen** [loh-sen] (*Mosel-Saar-Ruwer*, Germany) New-wave *Riesling* producer. Probably the best and most reliable in the *Mosel* (I only wish he'd use a little less *sulfur dioxide*). ☆☆☆☆ **1998 Erdener Prälat Riesling Auslese $$$$**

Ɏ **Lopez de Heredia** [loh-peth day hay-ray-dee-yah] (*Rioja*, Spain) Ultra-traditional winery producing old-fashioned Viña Tondonia white and *Gran Reserva* reds. ☆☆☆ **1993 Vina Tondonia Tinto Crianza $$$**

Ɏ **Louisvale** [loo-wis-vayl] (*Stellenbosch*, South Africa) Once avowed *Chardonnay* specialists, Louisvale's range has expanded to include some *Cabernet*-based reds. ☆☆☆ **1995 Cabernet Merlot $$**

Ɏ **Loupiac** [loo-peeyak] (*Bordeaux*, France) *Sauternes* neighbor with similar but less fine wines. **83 85 86 88** 89 90 95 96 97 98 **Ch. Loupiac-Gaudiet.**

Ɏ **Ch. Loupiac-Gaudiet** [loo-pee-yak goh-dee-yay] (*Loupiac*, *Bordeaux*, France) A good producer of *Loupiac*. **83** 85 **86 88** 89 90 95 **96 97**

Ɏ **Ch. la Louvière** [lah loo-vee-yehr] (*Graves*, *Bordeaux*, France) André Lurton's best known *Graves* property. Reliable, rich, modern whites and reds. The second wine is called 'L' de Louvière. Red: 81 **82** 83 **85 86** 88 89 90 91 92 93 94 95 96 97 98 White: 86 88 **89 90** 91 92 93 94 95 96 97 98 ☆☆☆☆ **1996 Red $$$**

🍷 **Van Loveren** [van loh-veh-ren] (*Robertson*, South Africa) Large family-owned estate producing good value for money wine. Concentrating primarily on classic fresh whites and also soft reds. ☆☆☆ **1998 Binnode Noir Muscadelle $$**

Côtes du Lubéron [koht doo LOO-bay-ron] (*Rhône*, France) Reds like light *Côtes du Rhône*, pink and sparkling wines and *Chardonnay*-influenced whites. A new *appellation* and still good value.

🍷 **Luce** [loo-chay] (*Tuscany*, Italy) Coproduction between *Mondavi* and *Frescobaldi* who have combined forces to produce a pleasant but overpriced red.

🍷 **Lugana** [loo-gah-nah] (*Lombardy*, Italy) Potentially appley, almondy whites made from the *Trebbiano*, grown on the shores of Lake Garda. ☆☆☆☆ **1998 Villa Flora, Zenato $$**

Lugny [loo-nee] (*Burgundy*, France) See *Mâcon*.

🍷 **Pierre Luneau** [loo-noh] (*Loire*, France) A rare beast: a top-class *Muscadet* producer. M. Luneau likes to try out wacky ideas with his wines, like keeping juice under nitrogen for a few years to see what happens.

🍷 **Cantine Lungarotti** [kan-tee-nah loon-gah-roh-tee] (*Umbria*, Italy) One of the most innovative producers in Italy, and the man who more or less single-handedly created the *Torgiano* denomination. ☆☆☆☆ **1986 Il Vessillo Rosso Dell'Umbria $$$$**

🍷 **Jacques & François Lurton** [loor-ton] Having made a success at his father's *Ch. la Louvière* and *Ch. Bonnet* in *Entre-Deux-Mers* (especially with the whites), Jacques now makes wine all over the world. Look out for Hermanos Lurton labels from Spain and Bodega Lurton wines from Argentina. ☆☆☆☆ **1997 Gran Araucano Cabernet Sauvignon Reserva $$**

🍷 **Ch. de Lussac** [loo-sak] (*Lussac St. Emilion*, *Bordeaux*, France) A name to watch out for in *Lussac St. Emilion*. 86 **89** 90 **94** 95 96 97 98

🍷 **Lussac St. Emilion** [loo-sak sant-ay-mee-yon] (*Bordeaux*, France) Potentially worthwhile satellite of *St. Emilion*. **82** 83 **85** 86 **88** 89 90 94 95 96

🍷 **Emilio Lustau** [loos-tow] (*Jerez*, Spain) Top-class *sherry* producer with great *almacanista* wines. ☆☆☆☆ **Palo Cortado Almacenista Vides $$**

Lutomer [loo-toh-muh] (Slovenia) Area still known mostly for its (very basic) Lutomer *Laski Riesling*. Now doing better things with *Chardonnay*.

Luxembourg [luk-sehm-burg] Source of some pleasant, fresh, white wines from *Alsace*-like grape varieties, and generally dire sparkling wine.

Ch. Lynch-Bages [lansh bazh] (*Pauillac 5ème Cru Classé, Bordeaux*, France) Reliably over-performing fifth growth *Pauillac* belonging to Jean-Michel Cazes of *Ch. Pichon-Longueville*. The (very rare) white is worth seeking out too. 70 75 78 **82 83 85 86** 88 89 90 91 92 93 94 95 96 97 98

Ch. Lynch-Moussas [lansh moo-sahs] (*Pauillac 5ème Cru Classé, Bordeaux*, France) Slowly improving. **85** 86 88 89 **90** 91 **94 95 96**

M

Macération carbonique [ma-say-ra-see-yon kahr-bon-eek] Technique of fermenting uncrushed grapes under pressure of a blanket of carbon dioxide gas to produce fresh fruity wine. Used in *Beaujolais*, southern France and, increasingly, the New World.

Machard de Gramont [ma-shahr duh gra-mon] (*Burgundy*, France) Producer of superb *Nuits-St.-Georges, Vosne-Romanée* and *Savigny-lès Beaune*. ☆☆☆☆ **1996 Vosne-Romanée Clos des Réas $$$**

Mâcon/Mâconnais [ma-kon/nay] (*Burgundy*, France) Avoid unidentified "rouge" or "blanc" on wine lists. Mâcons with the suffix *Villages, Superieur,* or Prissé, *Viré, Lugny* or Clessé should be better. The region contains the *appellations St.-Véran* and *Pouilly-Fuissé*. For straight Mâcon try *Jadot* or *Duboeuf*, but the *Dom. Thevenet Dom. de la Bongran* from Clessé is of *Côte d'Or* quality. Red: **95 96 97 98** White: **90 92 95 96 97** 98. **Roger Lasserat; Caves de Lugny; Cave de Prissé.**

Maculan [mah-koo-lahn] (*Veneto*, Italy) A superstar producer of blackcurranty *Cabernet* Breganze, an oaked *Pinot Bianco-Pinot Grigio-Chardonnay* blend called Prato di Canzio and the lusciously sweet *Torcolato*. ☆☆☆☆ **1995 Breganze Torcolato Maculan $$**

Madeira [ma-dee-ruh] (Portugal) Atlantic island producing fortified wines, usually identified by style: *Bual, Sercial, Verdelho,* or *Malmsey*. Most is ordinary stuff for use by mainland European cooks and, more rarely, finer fare for those who appreciate the unique marmalady character of good Madeira. **Blandy; Cossart-Gordon; Barros e Souza; Henriques & Henriques.**

Maderization [mad-uhr-ih-zay-shon] Deliberate procedure in *Madeira*, produced by the warming of wine in *estufas*. Otherwise undesired effect, commonly produced by high temperatures during storage, resulting in a dull flat flavor, tinged with a *sherry* taste and color.

Madiran [ma-dee-ron] (*South-West*, France) Robust country reds made from the *Tannat* grape; *tannic* when young, but worth aging. **Bouscassé; Dom. du Crampilh; Ch. Montus; Producteurs de Plaimont.**

🍷 **Ch. Magdelaine** [Mag-duh-layn] (*St. Emilion Premier Grand Cru, Bordeaux*, France) *St. Emilion* estate owned by JP *Moueix* and neighbor to *Ch. Ausone*, producing impeccable, perfumed wines. **61 70 71** 75 78 79 81 **82 83** 85 86 88 **89** 90 92 93 94 95 96 97 98 ☆☆☆☆ **1989 $$$**

🍷 **Maglieri** [mag-lee-yeh-ree] (*McLaren Vale*, South Australia) Dynamic *Shiraz* specialist recently taken over by *Mildara-Blass*.

Magnum Large bottle containing the equivalent of two bottles of wine (one and a half liters in capacity).

Maipo [mih-poh] (Chile) Historic region in which are found many good producers. Reds are most successful, especially *Cabernet* and *Merlot*, and softer *Chardonnays* are also made.Watch out for new varieties and enterprizing organic vineyards. **Aquitania (Paul Bruno); Canepa; Carmen; Concha y Toro; Cousino Macul; Peteroa; Santa Carolina; Santa Inés; Santa Rita; Undurraga; Viña Carmen.**

Maître de Chai [may-tr duh chay] (France) Cellar master.

Malaga [ma-la-gah] (Spain) A semimoribund Andalusian *DO* producing raisiny dessert wines of varying degrees of sweetness, immensely popular in the 19th century. **Lopez Hermanos.**

🍷 **Ch. Malartic-Lagravière** [mah-lahr-teek lah-gra-vee-yehr] (*Pessac-Léognan Cru Classé, Bordeaux*, France) Previously slumbering estate, bought in 1994 by *Laurent Perrier*, improving new-wave whites; reds need time. Red: 81 **82** 83 85 **86** 88 89 90 91 92 93 94 95 96 97 98 White: 85 **87** 88 89 90 91 92 94 95 96 97 98

🍇 **Malbec** [mal-bek] Red grape, now rare in *Bordeaux* but widely planted in Argentina, the *Loire* (where it is known as the *Côt*), *Cahors* and also in Australia. Producing rich, plummy, silky wines.

🍷 **Ch. Malescasse** [ma-les-kas] (*Haut-Médoc Cru Bourgeois, Bordeaux*, France) Watch this space; since 1993, wines have been made by the former cellarmaster of *Pichon-Lalande*. 82 83 85 86 88 89 90 93 94 95 96

🍷 **Ch. Malescot-St-Exupéry** [ma-les-koh san tek-soo-peh-ree] (*Margaux 3ème Cru Classé, Bordeaux*, France) Understated but sometimes quite classy wines. 70 **82** 83 86 87 88 89 90 91 92 94 95 96 97 98 ☆☆☆ **1996 $$$**

🍷 **Ch. de Malle** [duh mal] (*Sauternes 2ème Cru Classé, Bordeaux*, France) Good *Sauternes* property near Preignac, famous for its beautiful *château*. 76 78 **81** 82 **83** 85 **86** 88 89 90 91 94 95 96 97 98 ☆☆☆☆ **1990 $$$$**

Malolactic fermentation [ma-loh-lak-tik] Secondary "fermentation" in which appley *malic acid* is converted into the "softer," creamier *lactic* acid by naturally present or added strains of bacteria. Almost all red wines undergo a malolactic fermentation. For whites, it is common practice in *Burgundy*. It is varyingly used in the New World, where natural acid levels are often low. An excess is recognizable in wine as a buttermilky flavor.

🍷 **Ch. de la Maltroye** [mal-trwah] (*Burgundy*, France) Classy modern *Chassagne*-based estate with fingers in fourteen *AC* pies around *Burgundy*, all of whose wines are made by *Dom. Parent*. ☆☆☆☆ **1996 Chassagne-Montrachet les Grandes Ruchottes $$$$**

🍇 **Malvasia** [mal-vah-see-ah] *Muscatty* white grape vinified dry in Italy (as a component in *Frascati* for example), but far more successfully as good, sweet, traditional *Madeira*, where it is known as *Malmsey*. It is not the same grape as Malvoisie.

La Mancha [lah man-cha] (Spain) Huge region known for mostly dull and old-fashioned wines, but in recent times producing increasingly clean, modern examples. Also the place where the *Marquès de Griñon* is succeeding in his experiments with new vine-growing techniques and grapes, especially *Syrah*.

🍷 **Albert Mann** (*Alsace*, France) Top grower who always manages to express true varietal character without overblown alcohol flavors. ☆☆☆☆ **1996 Riesling Alsace Grand Cru Schlossberg $$$**

🍇**Manseng (Gros M. & Petit M.)** [man-seng] (*South-West*, France) Two varieties of white grape grown in southwestern France. The Gros M. is a flavorsome workhorse for much of the dry white of the Armagnac region, whereas Petit M. is capable of extraordinary apricot-and-cream concentration in the great *vendange tardive* wines of *Jurançon*. The Manseng is one of the few noble varieties not to have found wide favor across the globe, possibly because it is low-yielding and hard to grow. ***Dom. Cauhapé; Grassa; Producteurs de Plaimont.***

Manzanilla [man-zah-nee-yah] (*Jerez*, Spain) Dry tangy *sherry* – a *fino* style widely (though possibly mistakenly) thought to take on a salty tang from the coastal *bodegas* of Sanlucar de Barrameda. ***Don Zoilo; Barbadillo; Hidalgo.***

🍷 **Maranges** [mah-ronzh] (*Burgundy*, France) A new hillside *appellation* promising potentially affordable, if a little rustic, *Côte d'Or* wines. White: **92** 95 96 97 98 Red: **90** 92 95 96 97 98 **Bachelet; Chevrot; *Drouhin.***

Marc [mahr] (France) The residue of seeds, stalks, and skins left after the grapes are pressed – and often distilled into a fiery brandy of the same name, e.g. Marc de Bourgogne.

🍷 **Marcassin** (*Sonoma*, California) Helen Turley produces expressive – and, for some, a touch overblown – *Côte d'Or Grand Cru*-quality *Chardonnays* in tiny quantities from a trio of vineyards. Almost unobtainable.

Marches [MAHR-kay] (Italy) Central wine region on the Adriatic coast, below Venice. Best known for *Rosso Conero* and good, dry, fruity *Verdicchio* whites. **Fazi Battaglia; Garofoli; *Umani Ronchi.***

🍷 **Marcillac** [mah-see-yak] (*South-West*, France) Full-flavored country reds, made principally from the *Fer*, possibly plus some *Cabernet* and *Gamay*.

🍇**Maréchal Foch** [mah-ray-shahl fohsh] A *hybrid* vine producing red grapes in Canada and Eastern North America. ***Inniskillin.***

Margaret River (*Western Australia*) Cool(ish) vineyard area on the coast of *Western Australia*, gaining notice for *Cabernet Sauvignon* and *Chardonnay*. Also one of Australia's only two *Zinfandels*. White: **85 86 87** 88 90 91 93 94 95 96 97 98 Red: **80 82 83 85 86 87** 88 **90** 91 92 93 94 95 96 97 98 **Brookland Valley; *Cape Mentelle; Cullen; Devil's Lair; Evans & Tate; Moss Wood; Leeuwin; Pierro; Vasse Felix;* Voyager Estate; *Ch. Xanadu.***

🍷 **Margaux** [mahr-goh] (*Bordeaux*, France) Large *commune* with a concentration of *crus classés* including *Ch. Margaux, Palmer, Lascombes*. Sadly, other wines which should be deliciously blackberryish are variable, partly thanks to the diverse nature of the soil, and partly through the producers' readiness to sacrifice quality for the sake of yields. Curiously, though, if you want a good 1983, this vintage succeeded better here than elsewhere in the *Médoc*; 1995s are good too. Also worth hunting out are generic Margaux from reputable *négoçiants*. 70 75 **78** 81 **82 83 85 86** 88 89 90 **94** 95 96 97 98

🍷 **Ch. Margaux** [mahr-goh] (*Margaux Premier Cru Classé, Bordeaux*, France) Peerless *first growth*, back on form since the dull 1970s, and producing intense wines with cedary perfume and velvet softness when mature. The second wine, *Pavillon Rouge* (red and matching white), is worth buying too. **61 78** 79 **81** 82 83 84 85 86 87 88 89 90 91 **92** 93 **94** 95 96 97 98 ☆☆☆☆☆ **1996 $$$$**

Markham (*Napa Valley*, California) A producer to watch for fairly priced reds and whites. ☆☆☆☆ **1995 Napa Valley Reserve Chardonnay $$$; ☆☆☆☆ 1995 Petite Sirah $$$**

Marlborough [morl-buh-ruh] (New Zealand) An important wine area with cool climate in the South Island producing excellent *Sauvignon*, *Chardonnay*, and improving *Merlot* and *Pinot Noir*, as well as a number of impressive sparkling wines. White: **89 91** 92 96 97 98 ***Babich Cellier le Brun; Cloudy Bay; Corbans Giesen; Grove Mill; Hunter's; Jackson Estate; Montana; Stoneleigh; Vavasour.***

Marne et Champagne [mahr-nay-shom-pan-y] (*Champagne*, France) Huge cooperative which owns the Besserat de Bellefon, *Lanson* and Alfred Rothschild labels, and can provide really good own-label wines for merchant and superstore buyers who are prepared to pay the price.

Ch. Marquis-de-Terme [mahr-kee duh tehrm] (*Margaux 4ème Cru Classé*, *Bordeaux*, France) Traditional property with quite tough wines. **81** 82 **83** 85 **86** 87 88 89 90 93 95 96 98 ☆☆☆ **1996 $$$**

Marsala [mahr-sah-lah] (*Sicily*, Italy) Dark, rich, fortified wine from *Sicily* essential for use in recipes such as Zabaglione. ***De Bartoli*; Cantine Florio; Pellegrino; Rallo.**

Marsannay [mahr-sah-nay] (*Burgundy*, France) Northernmost village of the *Côte de Nuits* with a range of largely undistinguished but, for *Burgundy*, affordable *Chardonnay* and *Pinot Noir* (red and rosé). White: **79** 84 **85 86** 87 **88** 89 **90 92** 95 96 97 98 Red: 76 **78** 79 **80** 83 **85** 86 87 **88 89 90** 92 95 96 97 98 ***Bruno Clair*, Fougeray de Beauclair; *Louis Jadot*.**

Marsanne [mahr-san] (*Rhône*, France) The grape usually responsible (in blends with *Roussanne*) for most of the northern *Rhône* white wines. Also successful in the *Goulburn Valley* in *Victoria* for *Ch. Tahbilk* and *Mitchelton* and in California for *Bonny Doon*. It has a delicate perfumed intensity when young and fattens out with age. Look out for un-oaked versions from Australia. ***Tahbilk; Mitchelton; Bonny Doon; Guigal*.**

Martinborough (New Zealand) Up-and-coming North Island region for *Pinot Noir* and *Chardonnay*. White: 87 88 **89 91** 92 **94** 96 97 98 Red: **83 85 87 89** 90 **91 92** 93 94 95 96 97 98 ***Ata Rangi*; Alana Estate; *Dry River; Martinborough Vineyard; Palliser Estate*.**

Martinborough Vineyard (*Martinborough*, New Zealand) Producer of the best Kiwi *Pinot Noir* and one of the best *Chardonnays*. Wines can be so *Burgundian* in style that the 1991 *Pinot Noir* was refused an export licence for being untypically "farmyardy" until a delegation of wine-loving politicians intervened. ☆☆☆☆ **1996 Martinborough Vineyard Reserve Pinot Noir $$$**

Martinelli (*Sonoma*, California) Century-old *Zinfandel* specialists, making rich intense reds from this variety and juicy *Pinot Noirs*.

Bodegas Martinez Bujanda [mahr-tee-neth boo-han-dah] (*Rioja*, Spain) New-Wave producer of fruit-driven wines sold as *Conde de Valdemar*. Probably the most consistently recommendable producer in *Rioja*. ☆☆☆☆ **1994 Finca Valpiedra Reserva $$$**

Martini (*Piedmont*, Italy) Good *Asti Spumante* from the producer of the vermouth house which invented "lifestyle" advertising – still, we're all guilty of something. ☆☆☆ **Asti Fratelli Martini $$**

Louis Martini (*Napa Valley*, California) Grand old name right on form at the moment. Superlative long-lived *Cabernet* from the Monte Rosso vineyard. ☆☆☆☆ **1997 Sangiovese Heritage Collection 1997 $$$; ☆☆☆☆☆ 1995 Russian River Valley Reserve Merlot $$$**

Marzemino [mahrt-zeh-mee-noh] (Italy) Grape making spicy-plummy wines.

Mas Amiel [mahs ah-mee-yel] (*Provence*, France) The producer of wonderful rich almost *port*-like wine in the small *appellation* of Maury in the west of *Provence*. ☆☆☆☆ **Maury 15 Ans d'Age $$$**

Mas de Daumas Gassac [mas duh doh-mas gas-sac] (*Midi*, France) Ground-breaking *Herault Vin de Pays* red, compared by some to top *claret*. Its flavors come from an eclectic blend of up to half a dozen varieties, including *Pinot Noir, Syrah, Mourvèdre* and *Cabernet* – and a unique "*terroir*". Approachable when young, but lasts for ages. A white blend including *Viognier* is similarly impressive. ☆☆☆☆ **1998 White $$$**

Mas Jullien [mas joo-lye'n] (*Languedoc-Roussillon*, France) The most stylish wines in the Coteaux du Languedoc (or elsewhere in southern France)? Classic individual reds and whites from classic traditional grapes.

Bartolo Mascarello [mas-kah-reh-loh] (*Piedmont*, Italy) Great ultra-traditional *Barolo* specialist whose rose-petaly wine proves that the old ways can compete with the new. But they do call for patience.

Giuseppe Mascarello [mas-kah-reh-loh] (*Piedmont*, Italy) Top-class *Barolo* estate (unconnected with that of *Bartolo Mascarello*), producing characterful wine from individual vineyards. Succeeds in tricky vintages. Great *Dolcetto*. ☆☆☆☆ **1995 Monprivato $$$$**

Masi [mah-see] (*Veneto*, Italy) Producer with reliable, affordable reds and whites and single-vineyard wines which serve as a justification for *Valpolicella's* denomination. ☆☆☆☆☆ **1995 Osar $$$**

Massandra [mahsan-drah] (*Crimea*, CIS) Famous as the source of great, historic, dessert wines which were sold at a memorable Sotheby's auction in 1991, this is now the place to find good but not great *Cabernet*.

Master of Wine (MW) One of a small number of people (around 250) internationally who have passed a grueling set of wine exams.

Mastroberadino [maas tro be rah dino] (*Campania*, Italy) Top producer of rich Taurasi in Italy's south. ☆☆☆☆ **1993 Taurasi Radici $$$**

Matanzas Creek [muh-tan-zuhs] (*Sonoma Valley*, California) Top-class complex *Chardonnay*, good *Sauvignon*, and high-quality accessible *Merlot*. ☆☆☆☆ **1995 Chardonnay $$$$**

Mataro [muh-tah-roh] See *Mourvèdre*.

Mateus [ma-tay-oos] (Portugal) Highly commercial pink and white off-dry *frizzante* wine made by *Sogrape*, Portugal's biggest producer, sold in bottles traditional in *Franken*, Germany, and with a label depicting a palace with which the wine has no connection. A 50-year-old marketing masterpiece. The name is now being used for *Sogrape's* more serious reds.

Thierry Matrot [tee-yer-ree ma-troh] (*Burgundy*, France) Top-class white producer with great white and recommendable red *Blagny*. ☆☆☆☆ **1992 Meursault Les Charmes $$$$**

Matua Valley [ma-tyoo-wah] (*Auckland*, New Zealand) Reliable maker of great (*Marlborough*) *Sauvignon*, (Judd Estate) *Chardonnay* and *Merlot*. Also producer of the even better *Ararimu* red and white. Shingle Peak is the *second label*. ☆☆☆☆ **1997 Dartmoor Smith Cabernet Sauvignon $$$**

Yvon Mau [ee-von moh] (*Bordeaux* & *South-West*, France) Highly commercial producer of *Bordeaux* and other, mostly white, wines from South-West France. Occasionally good. ☆☆☆☆ **1996 Premius $$**

Ch. Maucaillou [mow-kih-yoo] (*Moulis Cru Bourgeois*, *Bordeaux*, France) *Cru Bourgeois* in the *commune* of *Moulis* producing approachable wines to beat some *crus classés*. **75 82** 83 **85 86** 88 **89 90 92 93** 94 95 96 97 98

Maule [mow-lay] (Chile) Up-and-coming *Central Valley* region especially for white wines but warm enough for red. ***Santa Carolina*; Carta Vieja.**

Bernard Maume [Mohm] (*Burgundy*, France) Small *Gevrey-Chambertin* estate run by a biology professor and his son and making long-lived wines. ☆☆☆☆ **1996 Gevrey-Chambertin Premier Cru $$$**

Bodegas Mauro [mow-roh] (Spain) Just outside the *Ribera del Duero DO*, but making very similar rich red wines.

Maury [moh-ree] (*Languedoc-Roussillon*, France) Potentially rich sweet wine to compete with Banyuls and port. Sadly, too many examples are light and feeble. ☆☆☆☆ **1995 Mas Amiel Vintage Reserve $$$**

Mauzac [moh-zak] (France) White grape used in southern France for *Vin de Pays* and *Gaillac*. Can be characterful and floral or dull and earthy.

Mavrodaphne [mav-roh-daf-nee] (Greece) Characterful indigenous Greek red grape, and the wine made from it. Dark and strong, it needs ageing to be truly worth drinking. ☆☆☆☆ **Kourtakis Mavrodaphne of Patras $$**

Mavrud [mah-vrood] (Bulgaria) Traditional red grape and the characterful, if rustic, wine made from it.

Maximin Grünhaus [mak-siee min groon-hows] (*Mosel-Saar-Ruwer*, Germany) Dr. Carl von Schubert's 1,000-year-old estate producing intense *Rieslings*. ☆☆☆☆☆ **1996 Abtsberg Riesling Spätlese $$$$**

Maxwell (*McLaren Vale*, Australia) Reliable producer of *Shiraz, Merlot* and *Semillon,* and good mead ☆☆☆☆ **1992 Ellen Street Shiraz $$$**

Mayacamas [mih-yah-kah-mas] (*Napa Valley*, California) Long-established winery on *Mount Veeder* with *tannic* but good old-fashioned *Cabernet* and long-lived rich *Chardonnay*. ☆☆☆☆ **1994 Cabernet Sauvignon $$$$**

McGuigan Brothers (*Hunter Valley*, Australia) Commercial and occasionally quite impressive stuff from the former owners of *Wyndham Estate*. ☆☆☆☆ **1997 McGuigan Shareholders Shiraz $$**

McLaren Vale (South Australia) Region close to Adelaide renowned for European-style wines, but possibly too varied in topography, soil and climate to create its own identity. White: **86 87** 88 **90 91 94** 95 97 98 Red: **80 82 84 85 86 87** 88 90 **91** 94 95 96 97 98 ***D'Arenberg; Hardy's; Kays Amery, Maglieri; Geoff Merrill; Ch. Reynella; Wirra Wirra.***

McWilliams (*Hunter Valley*, Australia) *Hunter Valley*-based, evidently non-republican firm with great traditional ("Elizabeth") *Semillon* and ("Philip") *Shiraz* which are now sold younger than previously and so may need time. Fortified wines can be good, too, as are the pioneering *Barwang* and improved *Brand's* wines. Surprizingly good at "Bag-in-box" wines! ☆☆☆☆ **1994 Elizabeth Semillon $$$**

Médoc [may-dok] (*Bordeaux*, France) Area encompassing the region of *Bordeaux* south of the *Gironde* and north of the town of *Bordeaux* in which the *Cru Classés* as well as far more ordinary fare are made. Should be better than basic *Bordeaux* and less good than *Haut-Médoc,* which tend to have more flavor: experience, however, suggests that this is not always the case. **82** 83 **85 86** 88 89 90 92 93 94 95 96 **97 98**

Meerlust Estate [meer-loost] (*Stellenbosch*, South Africa) One of the *Cape's* best estates. Classy *Merlots* and a highly rated *Bordeaux*-blend called "Rubicon," both of which will hopefully one day, benefit from being bottled on the estate rather than by the *Bergkelder*. ☆☆☆☆ **1994 Rubicon $$$**

Gabriel Meffre [mef-fr] (*Rhône*, France) Sound commercial *Rhône* and, now, southern France producer under the Galet Vineyards and Wild Pig labels. However, a tradition of producing reliable, more classy wines is maintained. ☆☆☆ **1997 Seguret Les Village des Papes $$**

Ch. Megyer [meg-yer] (*Tokaji*, Hungary) French-owned pioneer of *Tokaji* and *Furmint*.

Melon de Bourgogne [muh-lon duh boor-goyn] (France) Grape originally imported from *Burgundy* (where it is no longer grown) to the *Loire* by Dutch brandy distillers who liked its resistence to frost. Amazingly, good producers now contrive to make decent *Muscadet* from it.

Charles Melton (*Barossa Valley*, Australia) Small-scale producer of lovely still and sparkling *Shiraz* and world-class rosé called "Rose of Virginia," as well as Nine Popes, a wine based on, and mistakenly named after, *Châteauneuf-du-Pape*. ☆☆☆☆ **1995 Shiraz Barossa Valley $$$**

Mendocino [men-doh-see-noh] (California) Northern, coastal wine county known for unofficial marijuana farming and for its laid back winemakers who successfully exploit cool microclimates to make "European-style" wines. Red: 84 **85** 86 87 **90 91** 92 93 95 96 9798 White: **85 90 91** 92 95 96 97 **98** ***Fetzer; Handley Cellars;*** **Hidden Cellars; Lazy Creek; Parducci; Roederer;** ***Scharffenberger.***

Mendoza [men-doh-zah] (Argentina) Capital of a now up-and-coming principal wine region. Source of good rich reds from firms producing traditional-style reds but with more uplifting fruit. **La Agricola; Bianchi;** ***Catena; Etchart;*** **Finca Flichman;** ***Norton;*** **Lurton;** ***Morande;*** **la Rural; San Telmo;** ***Trapiche; Weinert.***

Menetou-Salon [men-too sah-lon] (*Loire*, France) Bordering on *Sancerre*, making similar if earthier, less pricy *Sauvignon*, as well as some decent *Pinot Noir. Henri Pellé* makes the best. White: 94 95 96 **97** 98 Red: **90** 91 92 93 94 **95** 96 97 98 ☆☆☆☆ **1998 Menetou Salon Blanc $$**

Dom. Méo-Camuzet [may-oh-ka-moo-zay] (*Burgundy*, France) Brilliant *Côte de Nuits* estate with top-class vineyards and intense, oaky wines, made, until his retirement, by the great *Henri Jayer.* ☆☆☆☆ **1995 Vosne-Romanée aux Brûlées $$$$**

Mercaptans [mehr-kap-ton] See *hydrogen sulfide*.

Mercier [mehr-see-yay] (*Champagne*, France) Subsidiary, or is it sister company, of *Moët & Chandon* and producer of improving but pretty commercial sparkling wine which, according to the advertisements, is the biggest seller in France. ☆☆☆☆ **Champagne Mercier Demi-Sec $$$**

Mercurey [mehr-koo-ray] (*Burgundy*, France) Village in the *Côte Chalonnaise*, where *Faiveley* makes high-quality wine. Red: **78** 80 **85** 86 87 **88 89** 90 92 95 96 97 98 White: 84 **85 86** 87 **88** 89 **90 92** 95 96 97 98 **Dom Brintet; Marguerite Carillon; Ch. de Chamirey;** ***Dom. Faiveley;*** **Genot-Boulanger; Michel Juillot; Olivier Leflaive; Meix-Foulot;** ***Pillot.***

Meridian (*San Luis Obispo*, California) Unusually good-value *Pinot Noir* from *Santa Barbara*. The *Merlot* and *Chardonnay* are pretty impressive too.

Merlot [mehr-loh] "Flavor of the Month," if the ludicrous orgy of planting in California's *Central Valley* is anything to go by. Soon to be everyone's unloved child, when grapegrowers and winemakers discover that this red variety only produces appealing soft, honeyed, even toffeeish wine with plummy fruit when it is planted in the right (ideally clay) soil, and kept to very moderate yields. In other words, quite the opposite of what it will get in the *Central Valley*. It is traditionally used to balance the more tannic *Cabernet Sauvignon* throughout the *Médoc*, where it is actually the most widely planted grape; as it is in *Pomerol* and *St. Emilion*, where clay also prevails. Also increasingly – though not spectacularly – successful in the *Languedoc* in southern France. California's best efforts include *Newton, Matanzas Creek,* and (recently) *Duckhorn*. Australia, South Africa, and New Zealand have had few real successes, but there are impressive efforts from *Washington State* and Chile.

Merricks Estate (*Mornington Peninsula*, Australia) Small estate specializing in *Shiraz*. ☆☆☆☆ **1994 Shiraz**

Geoff Merrill (*McLaren Vale*, Australia) The ebullient moustachioed winemaker who has nicknamed himself "The Wizard of Oz." Impressive if restrained *Semillon, Chardonnay,* and *Cabernet* in *McLaren Vale* under his own label, plus easier-going Mount Hurtle wines (especially the rosé). ☆☆☆☆ **1995 Reserve Cabernet Sauvignon $$$**

Merryvale (*Napa Valley*, California) Starry winery with especially good Reserve and Silhouette *Chardonnay* and Profile *Cabernet*. ☆☆☆☆ **1995 Napa Valley Reserve Chardonnay $$$**

Louis Métaireau [meht-teh-roh] (*Loire*, France) The Cadillac of Muscadet, which comes here in the form of several individual *cuvées*. Cuvée One is the star.

Méthode Champenoise [may-tohd shom-puh-nwahz] Term now outlawed by the EU from wine labels but still used to describe the way *Champagne* and all other quality sparkling wines are produced. Labor intensive, because bubbles are made by secondary fermentation in bottle, rather than in a vat or by the introduction of gas. Bottles are individually given the "*dégorgémont* process,", topped up and recorked!

Methuselah Same size bottle as an *Imperiale* (six liters). Used in *Champagne*.

Meursault [muhr-soh] (*Burgundy*, France) Superb white *Burgundy*; the *Chardonnay* ideally showing off its nutty, buttery richness in full-bodied dry wine. Like *Nuits-St.-Georges* and *Beaune*, it has no *Grands Crus* but great *Premiers Crus* such as Charmes, Perrières, and Genevrières. There is a little red here too, some of which is sold as *Volnay-Santenots*. White: 89 **90 92** 95 96 97 98 ***Ampeau; d'Auvenay; Coche-Dury; Drouhin;* Henri Germain; Ropiteau; *Jobard; Comtes Lafon; Michelot; Pierre Morey; Jacques Prieur; Ch. de Puligny-Montrachet; Roulot; Roux Père et Fils; Verget.***

Ch. de Meursault [muhr-soh] (*Burgundy*, France) One of Burgundy's few *châteaux* and well worth a visit. The wines – far better than most produced by its owner, *Patriarche* – are good too. ☆☆☆☆☆ **1994 Meursault $$$**

Mexico See *Baja California*.

Ch. Meyney [may-nay] (*St. Estèphe Cru Bourgeois, Bordeaux*, France) Improving *St. Estèphe* property, with wines that are richer in flavor than some of its neighbors. 81 **82** 83 85 **86** 88 89 90 91 92 93 94 95 96 **97 98**

Peter Michael (*Sonoma*, California) UK-born Sir Peter Michael produces stunning *Sonoma*, *Burgundy*-like *Chardonnays*, *Sauvignons*, and *Cabernets*. ☆☆☆☆ **1994 Cabernet Sauvignon "Les Pavots," Knights Valley $$$**

Louis Michel et Fils [mee-shel] (*Burgundy*, France) Top-class *Chablis* producer. ☆☆☆☆ **1996 Chablis Montée de Tonnerre $$$$**

Robert Michel (*Rhône*, France) Produces softer *Cornas* than most from this sometimes tough *appellation:* beautiful, strong yet silky wines. ☆☆☆☆ **1995 Cornas la Geynale $$$**

Alain Michelot [mee-shloh] (*Burgundy*, France) Producer of perfumed, elegant *Nuits-St.-Georges* that can be enjoyed young – but is well worth keeping too. ☆☆☆☆☆ **1994 Nuits-St.-Georges Vaucrains $$$$**

Dom. Michelot-Buisson [mee-shloh bwee-son] (*Burgundy*, France) One of the great old *Meursault* properties. A pioneer of estate bottling – and of the use of new oak. Wines are rarely subtle, but then they never lack typical *Meursault* flavor either. ☆☆☆☆ **1995 Meursault Les Genevrières $$$$**

Mildara Blass [mil-dah-rah] (*South Australia*) Dynamic,unashamedly "market-driven" Fosters-owned company whose varied portfolio of styles and (sometimes derivative labels) includes *Rothbury, Yarra Ridge, Yellowglen, Wolf Blass, Balgownia,* Mount Helen, *Stonyfell, Saltram,* and *Maglieri. Coonawarra* wines, including the very commercial *Jamieson's Run*, are best..
☆☆☆☆ **1995 Mildara Coonawarra Cabernet Sauvignon $$$**

Millton Estate (*Auckland*, New Zealand) James Millton is an obsessive, not to say a masochist. He loves the hard-to-make *Chenin Blanc* and uses it to make first-class organic wine in *Gisborne*. Sadly, it seems, most people would rather buy his *Chardonnay*.
☆☆☆☆ **1997 Barrel-Fermented Chenin Blanc $$**

Milmanda [mil-man-dah] (*Conca de Barbera*, Spain) *Torres'* top-label *Chardonnay*. Classy by any standards. ☆☆☆☆☆ **1997 $$$**

Kym Milne Antipodean *flying winemaker* who has been quietly expanding his empire with great success, particularly with Vinfruco in *South Africa*, at Le Trulle in southern *Italy*, and at *Nagyrede* in *Hungary*.

Minervois [mee-nehr-vwah] (*South-West*, France) Fast leaving its neighbor *Corbières* behind with its improving reds, Minervois still confuses with styles and qualities which vary, depending on the part of the region, the grape and the maker. Wines made from old-vine Carignan can be richly intense; *maceration-carbonique* wines from younger *Carignan* can compete with *Beaujolais; Mourvèdre* can be perfumed, and *Syrah*, spicy. Some of the best wines come from a newly-recognized subregion called la Livinière, where the leading producer Jean--Christophe Piccinini is based. Elsewhere, an enterprising Australian called Nerida Abbott is labeling a pure *Syrah* as "*Shiraz*"' (a term that is apparently not recognized in France as a synonym for this variety). Whites and rosés are considerably less interesting. **Abbott's Cumulus; Clos Centeilles; Gourgazaud; Ch d'Oupia; Piccinini; Ste. Eulalie; la Tour Boisée; Villerambert-Julien.**

Mis en Bouteille au Ch./Dom. [mee zon boo-tay] (France) Estate-bottled.

Mission (*Hawke's Bay*, New Zealand) Still run by monks, nearly 150 years after its foundation, this estate is now one of the best in Ne w Zealand.
☆☆☆☆ **1997 Jewelstone Mission Cabernet Merlot $$$**

Mission Hill (*British Columbia*, Canada) Dynamic producer of various styles, ranging from *Riesling icewine* to *Merlot*.

Ch. la Mission-Haut-Brion [lah mee-see-yon oh-bree-yon] (*Pessac-Léognan Cru Classé, Bordeaux*, France) Tough but rich reds which rival and – possibly in 1998 – even overtake its supposedly classier neighbor *Haut-Brion*. **78 79 81 82 83** 84 **85 86 87** 88 89 90 91 92 **93 94** 95 96 97 98

Mitchell (*Clare Valley*, Australia) Good producer of *Riesling* and of the Peppertree *Shiraz*, one of the *Clare Valley's* best reds. Also good for powerful *Grenache, Riesling, Semillon*, and sparkling *Shiraz*. ☆☆☆☆ **1997 Growers Grenache $$**

Mitchelton (*Goulburn Valley*, Australia) A modern producer of *Marsanne* and *Semillon* which now belongs to *Petaluma. Late harvest Rieslings* are also good, as is a *Beaujolais*-style red, known as Cab Mac. The Preece range – named after the former winemaker – is also well worth seeking out owing to its French style. ☆☆☆☆ **1998 Thomas Mitchell Marsanne $$$**

Mittelhaardt [mit-tel-hahrt] (*Pfalz*, Germany) Central and best *bereich* of the *Rheinpfalz*. QbA/Kab/Spät: **85** 86 **88 89 90** 91 92 93 94 95 96 97 98 Aus/Beeren/Tba: **83 85** 88 89 90 91 92 93 94 95 96 97 98

Mittelmosel [mit-tel-moh-zuh] (*Mosel-Saar-Ruwer*, Germany) Middle and best section of the *Mosel*, including the *Bernkastel bereich*. QbA/Kab/Spät: **85** 86 **88 89 90** 91 92 93 94 95 96 97 98 Aus/Beeren/Tba: **83 85** 88 89 90 91 92 93 94 95 96 97 98

Mittelrhein [mit-tel-rihne] (Germany) Small, northern section of the *Rhine*. Good *Rieslings* that sadly are rarely seen outside Germany. QbA/Kab/Spät: **85** 86 **88 89 90** 91 92 93 94 95 96 97 98 Aus/Beeren/Tba: **83 85** 88 89 90 91 92 93 94 95 96 97 98 ***Toni Jost***

Mittnacht-Klack [mit-nakt-clack] (*Alsace*, France) Seriously high-quality wines with particular accent on "*vendage tardive*" and *late havest* wines. ☆☆☆☆ **1996 Gewurztraminer Rosacker $$$$**

Moelleux [mwah-luh] (France) Sweet.

Moët & Chandon [moh-wet ay shon-don] (*Champagne*, France) The biggest producer in *Champagne. Dom Pérignon*, the top wine, and *vintage* Moët are reliably good and new *cuvées* of "Brut Imperial Non-Vintage" though not always brilliant, show a welcome reaction to recent criticism. Watch out too for a good *Brut* rosé. ☆☆☆☆ **1993 Vintage $$$**

Clos Mogador [kloh MOH-gah-dor] (*Priorato*, Spain) Juicy, modern, and more importantly, stylish red wine from the once ultra-traditional and rustic region of *Priorato*. The shape of things to come. ☆☆☆☆ **1995 Clos Mogador $$$**

Moillard [mwah-yar] (*Burgundy*, France) Middle-of-the-road *négoçiant* whose best wines are sold under the "Dom. Thomas Moillard" label.

Moldova Young republic next to Romania whose as yet uncertain potential is being tested by *Hugh Ryman* at the Hincesti winery.

Monbazillac [mon-ba-zee-yak] (*South-West*, France) *Bergerac AC* using the grapes of sweet *Bordeaux* to make improving alternatives to *Sauternes*.

Ch. Monbousquet [mon-boo-skay] (*St. Emilion Grand Cru Classé*, *Bordeaux*, France) Newly taken over and now producing rich, concentrated wines. The 1994 was specially successful. **78** 79 82 **85** 86 88 89 90 92 93 94 95 96 97 98 ☆☆☆ **1995 Ch. Monbousquet, St. Emilion $$$**

Ch. Monbrison [mon-bree-son] (*Margaux*, *Bordeaux*, France) Reliable, constant overperformer in this often disappointing *appellation*. A great 1998. **78** 79 82 **85** 86 88 89 90 92 94 95 96 97 98 ☆☆☆☆ **1990 $$$$**

Mönchof [moon-chof] (*Mosel*, Germany) Top *Mosel* producer with vineyards in *Urzig*.

Ch. de Moncontour [mon-con-toor] (*Loire*, France) One of the more recommendable – and affordable – sources of still and sparkling *Vouvray*. ☆☆☆ **1995 Vouvray Demi-Sec $$**

🍷 **Robert Mondavi** [mawn-dah-vee] (*Napa Valley*, California) Pioneering producer of great Reserve *Cabernet* and *Pinot Noir,* and *Chardonnay*, and inventor of *oaky Fumé Blanc Sauvignon*. The Coastal wines are good but the Woodbridge wines, though pleasant, are less interesting. Co-owner of *Opus One* and now in a joint venture with *Caliterra* in Chile and *Frescobaldi* in *Tuscany.* ☆☆☆☆ **1997 Robert Mondavi Napa Valley Zinfandel $$$**

🍷 **Mongeard-Mugneret** [mon-zhahr moon-yeh-ray] (*Burgundy*, France) A source of invariably excellent and sometimes stunningly exotic red *Burgundy*. ☆☆☆☆ **1995 Vosne-Romanée $$$**

🍇 **Monica (di Cagliari/Sardegna)** [moh-nee-kah] (*Sardinia*, Italy) Red grape and wine of *Sardinia* producing drily tasty and fortified spicy wine.

🍷 **Marqués de Monistrol** [moh-nee-strol] (*Catalonia*, Spain) Single-estate *cava*. Also producing noble varietals. ☆☆☆☆ **1994 Merlot $$**

Monopole [mo-noh-pohl] (France) Literally, exclusive – in *Burgundy* denotes single ownership of an entire vineyard.

🍷 **Mont Gras** [mon gra] (*Colchagua*, Chile) Fast-improving winery. ☆☆☆☆☆ **1997 Cabernet Sauvignon Reserva $$$**

🍷 **Clos du Mont Olivet** [Mo(n)-toh-lee-vay] (*Rhône*, France) Good *Châteauneuf-du-Pape* producer. Cuvée du Pape is the top wine. ☆☆☆☆ **1995 Châteauneuf-du-Pape $$$**

🍷 **Les Producteurs du Mont Tauch** [mon-tohsh] (*Midi*, France) Southern cooperative with surprisingly good, top-of-the-range wines. ☆☆☆☆☆ **1998 Fitou l'Exception $$**

🍷 **Montagne St. Emilion** [mon-tan-yuh san tay-mee-yon] (*Bordeaux*, France) A "satellite" of *St. Emilion*. Often good-value reds which can outclass supposedly finer fare from *St. Emilion* itself. Drink young. **82 83 85 86 88 89** 90 **94** 95 96 **97** 98

🍷 **Montagny** [mon-tan-yee] (*Burgundy*, France) Small hillside *Côte Chalonnaise commune* producing good lean *Chardonnay* that can be a match for many *Pouilly-Fuissés*. *Premier Crus* are not from better vineyards; they're just made from riper grapes. White: **90 92 93** 95 96 **97** 98 **J-M Boillot; Caves de Buxy; *Louis Latour; Olivier Leflaive; Michel; Antonin Rodet; Vachet.***

🍷 **Montalcino** [mon-tal-chee-noh] (*Tuscany*, Italy) Village near Sienna known for *Brunello di Montalcino, Chianti's* big brother, whose reputation was largely created by *Biondi Santi*, whose wines no longer deserve the prices they command. *Rosso di Montalcino* is lighter. **78 79 82 85 88 90 94** 95 96 97 98 ***Altesino; Banfi; Costanti; Frescobaldi; Poggio Antico.***

🍷 **Montana** (*Marlborough*, New Zealand) Impressively consistent, huge firm with tremendous *Sauvignons*, improving *Chardonnays*, and good-value *Lindauer* and *Deutz Marlborough Cuvée* sparkling wine. Reds still tend to be on the green side. Look out for the Church Road wines and the smartly packaged single-estate wines such as the Brancott *Sauvignon*. ☆☆☆☆ **1996 Patutahi Estate Gewürztraminer $$$**

🍷 **Monte Real** [mon-tay ray-al] (*Rioja*, Spain) Made by Bodegas Riojanos; generally decent, richly flavored and tannic *Rioja*.

🍷 **Montecarlo** [mon-tay car-loh] (*Tuscany*, Italy) The place to find interesting Italian-Rhône blends such as Sangiovese-Syrah. **Carmignani; Wandanna.**

🍷 **Bodegas Montecillo** [mon-tay-thee-yoh] (*Rioja*, Spain) Classy wines including the oddly named Viña Monty. The Cumbrero Blanco white is good, too. ☆☆☆ **1989 Viña Monty Gran Reserva $$**

Montée de Tonnerre [mon-tay duh ton-nehr] (*Burgundy*, France) Excellent *Chablis Premier Cru*.

Montefalco Sagrantino [mon-teh-fal-koh sag-ran-tee-noh] (*Umbria*, Italy) Intense cherryish red made from the local Sagrantino grape.

Ch. Montelena [mon-teh-lay-nah] (*Napa Valley*, California) Its two long-lived *Chardonnays* (from *Napa* and the rather better *Alexander Valley*) make this one of the more impressive producers in the state. The vanilla-and-blackcurranty *Cabernet* is too impenetrable, however. I prefer the Zinfandel.

Montepulciano [mon-tay-pool-chee-yah-noh] (Italy) Confusingly, both a red grape used to make red wines in central and southeastern Italy (Montepulciano *d'Abruzzi*, etc) and the name of a town in *Tuscany* (see *Vino Nobile di Montepulciano*). **Poliziano.**

Monterey [mon-teh-ray] (California) Underrated region south of San Francisco, producing potentially good if sometimes rather grassy wines. ***Jekel; Sterling Redwood Trail; Estancia.***

The Monterey Vineyard (*Monterey*, California) Reliable inexpensive varietal wines now under the Redwood Trail label overseas. Go for the "Classic" range. Read the labels carefully though; the small print has on occasion revealed the contents to have been produced in the *Languedoc* region in France rather than California.

Viña Montes [mon-tehs] (*Curico*, Chile) Leading Chilean enologist, Aurelio Montes' go-ahead winery with improving reds (including the flagship Alpha M) and improved *Sauvignon*. ☆☆☆☆ **1997 Alpha Merlot $$$**

Fattoria di Montevertine [mon-teh-ver-TEE-neh] (*Tuscany*, Italy) Less famous outside Italy than *Antinori* and *Frescobaldi* perhaps, but just as instrumental in the evolution of modern Tuscan wine, and of the rediscovery of the *Sangiovese* grape. Le Pergole Torte is the long-lived top wine. Il Sodaccio is fine too, however.

Montevina [mon-tay-veen-yah] (*Amador County*, California) *Sutter Home* subsidiary, making exceptionally good *Zinfandel* from *Amador County* and reliable *Cabernet, Chardonnay* and *Fumé Blanc*. ☆☆☆ **1995 Chardonnay $$**

Monthélie [mon-tay-lee] (*Burgundy*, France) Often overlooked *Côte de Beaune* village producing potentially stylish reds and whites. The appropriately named Dom. Monthélie-Douhairet is the most reliable estate. White: **85 86 88** 89 **90 92 95** 96 97 98 Red: **78** 80 83 **85** 86 87 **88 89 90** 92 95 96 97 98 ***Coche-Dury; Jaffelin; Comtes Lafon; Olivier Leflaive; Leroy; Monthélie-Douhairet; Ch. de Puligny-Montrachet; Roulot.***

Montilla-Moriles [mon-tee-yah maw-ree-lehs] (Spain) *DO* region producing *sherry*-type wines in *solera* systems, often so high in alcohol that fortification is unnecessary. Good examples easily match *sherry*, offering far better value for money. Occasional successes, though, achieve far more. **Pérez Barquero; Toro Albalá.**

Dom. de Montille [duh mon-tee] (*Burgundy*, France) A lawyer-cum-winemaker whose *Volnays* and *Pommards*, if rather tough and astringent when young, are unusually fine and long-lived. Classy stuff. ☆☆☆☆ **1995 Volnay Taillepieds $$$**

Montlouis [mon-lwee] (*Loire*, France) Neighbor of *Vouvray* making similar, lighter-bodied, dry, sweet, and sparkling wines. **Berger; Delétang; Levasseur; Moyer; la Taille aux Loups.**

Le Montrachet [luh mon-ra-shay] (*Burgundy*, France) Shared between the villages of *Chassagne-* and *Puligny-Montrachet*, with its equally good neighbours *Bâtard-M.*, Chevalier-M., *Bienvenue-Bâtard-M*,.and Criots-Bâtard-M. Potentially the greatest, biscuitiest white *Burgundy* – and thus dry white wine – in the world. ***Marc Colin; Drouhin*** **(Marquis de Laguiche)*****; Comtes Lafon; Leflaive; Ramonet; Domaine de la Romanée-Conti; Sauzet.***

Montravel [mon'-ravel] (South West France) Region with three separate appellations: Montravel, for dry *Sémillon/Sauvignon*; Côtes de Montravel and Haut-Montravel for semi-sweet, medium-sweet and *late harvest* whites. **Ch du Bloy, Pique-Serre, la Roche-Marot, Viticulteurs de Port Ste Foy.**

Ch. Montrose [mon-rohz] (*St. Estèphe 2ème Cru Classé, Bordeaux*, France) Back-on-form *St. Estèphe* renowned for its longevity. More typical of the *appellation* than *Cos d'Estournel* but often less approachable in its youth. However, still maintains a rich, tarry, inky style. Especially good in 1994, though less so in 1995 and 1996. **61 64** 66 **70 75** 76 78 79 81 **82** 83 85 86 88 89 90 91 92 93 94 95 96 97 98

Ch. Montus [mon-toos] (*South-West*, France) Ambitious producer in *Madiran* with carefully oaked examples of *Tannat* and *Pacherenc de Vic Bilh*. *Bouscassé* is a cheaper, more approachable label.

Moondah Brook (*Swan Valley*, Australia) An atypically (for the baking *Swan Valley*) cool vineyard belonging to *Houghtons* (and thus *Hardys*). The stars are the wonderful tangy *Verdelho* and richly oaky *Chenin Blanc*. The *Chardonnay* and reds are less impressive.

Moorilla Estate [moo-rillah] (*Tasmania*, Australia) Long-established, recently reconstituted estate with particularly good *Riesling*.

Morande [moh-ran-day] (Argentina/Chile) Impressive winemaker, producing wine often from pioneering varieties on both sides of the Andes. ☆☆☆☆ **1998 Vitisterra Merlot $$**

Morellino di Scansano [moh-ray-lee-noh dee skan-sah-noh] (*Tuscany*, Italy) Amazing cherry and raspberry, young-drinking red made from a clone of *Sangiovese*. **Cantina Cooperativa; Motta; le Pupile.**

Dom. Marc Morey [maw-ray] (*Burgundy*, France) Estate producing stylish white *Burgundy*. ☆☆☆☆ **1996 Chassagne-Montrachet Morgeot $$$**

Dom. Pierre Morey [maw-ray] (*Burgundy*, France) Top-class *Meursault* producer known for concentrated wines in good vintages. ☆☆☆☆ **1996 Meursault les Tessons $$$**

Bernard Morey et Fils [maw-ray] (*Burgundy*, France) Top-class producer in *Chassagne-Montrachet* with good vineyards here and in *St. Aubin*. ☆☆☆☆ **1996 Puligny-Montrachet La Truffière $$$$**

Morey-St.-Denis [maw-ray san duh-nee] (*Burgundy*, France) *Côtes de Nuits* village which produces deeply fruity, richly smooth reds, especially the *Grand Cru* "Clos de la Roche." Best producer is *Domaine Dujac*, which virtually makes this *appellation* its own. 76 **78** 79 **80** 82 83 **85** 86 87 **88 89 90** 92 95 96 ***Bruno Clair; Dujac; Faiveley;* Georges Lignier; Hubert Lignier; *Ponsot.***

Morgon [mohr-gon] (*Burgundy*, France) One of the ten *Beaujolais Crus*. Worth maturing, as it can take on a delightful chocolate/cherry character. **89** 90 **91** 93 94 95 **96** 97 98 Dom. Calon; ***Georges Duboeuf (aka Marc Dudet);* Jean Descombes; *Sylvain Fessy;* Jean Foillard; Lapierre; Piron; Savoye.**

Morio Muskat [maw-ree-yoh moos-kat] White grape grown in Germany and Eastern Europe and making simple grapey wine.

Mornington Peninsula (*Victoria*, Australia) Some of Australia's newest and most southerly vineyards on a perpetual upward crescent. Close to Melbourne and under threat from housing developers. Good *Pinot Noir*, minty *Cabernet* and juicy *Chardonnay*, though the innovative T'Gallant is leading the way with other varieties. ***Dromana;* Paringa; *Stonier;* T'Gallant.**

Morris of Rutherglen (*Rutherglen*, Australia) Despite the takeover by *Orlando* and the retirement of local hero and champion winemaker Mick Morris, this is still an extraordinarily successful producer of delicious *Liqueur Muscat* and *Tokay* (seek out the Show Reserve). Also worth buying is a weird and wonderful *Shiraz-Durif* sparkling red. ☆☆☆☆ **Liqueur Muscat $$$**

Denis Mortet [mor-tay] (*Burgundy*, France) Fast up-and-coming producer with straight *Gevrey-Chambertin* that is every bit as good as some of his neighbors' *Grands Crus*. ☆☆☆☆ **1995 Gevrey-Chambertin $$$**

Morton Estate (*Waikato*, New Zealand) Producer of fine *Sauvignon, Chardonnay*, *Loire* and *Bordeaux* styles. ☆☆☆☆ **1997 Colefield Sauvignon $$**

Moscatel de Setúbal [mos-kah-tel day say-too-bahl] (Portugal) See *Setúbal*.

Moscato [mos-kah-toh] (Italy) The Italian name for *Muscat*, widely used across Italy in all styles of white wine from *Moscato d'Asti*, through the more serious *Asti Spumante*, to dessert wines like Moscato di Pantelleria.

Moscato d'Asti [mos-kah-toh das-tee] (Italy) Delightfully grapey, sweet, and fizzy low alcohol wine from the *Muscat*, or *Moscato* grape. Far more flavorsome (and cheaper) than designer alcoholic lemonade. Drink young.

Moscato Passito di Pantelleria [pah-see-toh dee pan-teh-leh-ree-yah] (*Sicily*, Italy) Gloriously traditional sweet wine made on an island off Sicily from grapes that are dried out of doors until they have shriveled into raisins.

Mosel/Moselle [moh-zuhl] (Germany) River and term loosely used for wines made around the Mosel and nearby Saar and Ruwer rivers. Equivalent to the "*Hock*" of the Rhine. (Moselblumchen is the equivalent of Liebfraumilch.) Not to be confused with the uninspiring *Vins de Moselle* made on the French side of the river. The wines tend to have flavors of green fruits when young but develop a wonderful ripeness as they fill out with age. Arguably, the best wine region in Germany today. QbA/Kab/Spät: **89 90** 91 92 93 94 95 96 97 98 Aus/Beeren/Tba: **83 85** 88 89 90 91 92 93 94 95 96 97 98 ***Dr Loosen;* JJ Chriastobel; Jakoby-Mathy; Freiher von Heddesdorff; Willi Haag; Heribert Kerpen; Weingut Karlsmuhle; Karp-Schreiber; *Immich Batterieberg.***

Lenz Moser [lents moh-zur] (Austria) Big producer with a range including crisp dry whites and luscious dessert wines. Best efforts come from the Klosterkeller Siegenfdorf.

Moss Wood (*Margaret River*, Australia) Pioneer producer of *Pinot Noir*, *Cabernet*, and *Semillon*. The wines have long cellaring potential and have a very French feel to them. The *Semillon* is reliably good in both its oaked and unoaked form; the *Chardonnay* is big and forward and the *Pinot Noir* never quite living up to the promise of the early 1980s. ☆☆☆☆ **1995 Cabernet Sauvignon Reserve $$$**

La Motte Estate [la mot] (*Franschhoek*, South Africa) Best known for top *Shiraz*. ☆☆☆☆ **1994 La Motte Millennium $$$**

J.P. Moueix [mwex] (*Bordeaux*, France) Top-class *négoçiant*/producer, Christian *Moueix* specialises in stylishly traditional *Pomerol* and *St. Emilion* and is responsible for *Pétrus*, *La Fleur-Pétrus*, *Bel Air*, Richotey and *Dominus* in California. (Do not confuse with any other Moueix's).

Moulin Touchais [moo-lan too-shay] (*Loire*, France) Producer of intensely honeyed, long-lasting, sweet white from *Coteaux du Layon*.

Moulin-à-Vent [moo-lan-na-von] (*Burgundy*, France) One of the ten *Beaujolais Crus* – big and rich at its best and, like *Morgon*, can benefit from a few years' ageing. **85 88 89** 90 **91** 93 94 95 96 97 98. ***Charvet; Degrange; Duboeuf; Paul Janin; Janodet; Lapierre; Ch. du Moulin-à-Vent; la Tour du Bief.***

Ch. Moulin-à-Vent [moo-lan-na-von] (*Moulis Cru Bourgeois*, *Bordeaux*, France) Leading *Moulis* property. **82** 83 **85** 86 89 90 94 96

Ch. du Moulin-à-Vent [moo-lan-na-von] (*Burgundy*, France) Reliable producer of *Moulin-à-Vent*. **85 88 89** 90 **91** 93 94 95 96 97 **98**

Moulis [moo-lees] (*Bordeaux*, France) Red wine village of the *Haut-Médoc*; often paired with *Listrac*, but making far more approachable good-value *Crus Bourgeois*. 76 **78** 79 81 **82** 83 **85 86** 88 89 90 94 95 96 97 98 **Ch. Anthonic; *Chasse-Spleen; Maucaillou;* Moulis; *Poujeaux.***

Mount Barker (Western Australia) Cooler-climate, southern region with great *Riesling*, *Verdelho*, impressive *Chardonnay*, and restrained *Shiraz*. White: 90 91 93 **94 95** 96 97 98 Red: **80 82 83 85 86 87** 88 **90** 91 92 93 94 95 96 97 98 **Frankland Estate; *Goundrey; Howard Park; Plantagenet; Wignalls.***

Mount Horrocks (*Clare Valley*, Australia) Inventive *Shiraz* and *Riesling* producer that has made a speciality out of reviving an old method of winemaking called "Cordon Cut," which concentrates the flavor of the Riesling juice by cutting the canes some time before picking the grapes. ☆☆☆☆ **1998 Watervale Cordon Cut Riesling $$$**

Mount Hurtle (*McLaren Vale*, South Australia) See *Geoff Merrill*.

Mount Langi Ghiran [lan-gee gee-ran] (*Victoria*, Australia) A maker of excellent cool-climate *Riesling*, peppery *Shiraz* and very good *Cabernet*. ☆☆☆☆☆ **1996 Shiraz, Grampians $$$**

Mount Mary (*Yarra Valley*, Australia) Dr Middleton makes *Pinot Noir* and *Chardonnay* that are astonishingly and unpredictably *Burgundy*-like in the best and worst sense of the term. The *clarety-like* Quintet blend is more reliable. ☆☆☆☆☆ **1996 Quintet $$$**

Mount Veeder (*Napa Valley*, California) Convincing hillside *appellation* producing impressive reds, especially from *Cabernet Sauvignon* and *Zinfandel*. Red: 84 **85** 86 87 **90 91** 92 **93** 95 96 97 98 White: **85 90 91** 92 95 96 97 98 ***Hess Collection; Mayacamas; Mount Veeder Winery;* Ch. Potelle.**

🍷 **Mountadam** (*High Eden Ridge*, Australia) Son of *David Wynn*, Adam makes classy Burgundian *Chardonnay* and *Pinot Noir* (both still and sparkling) and an impressive blend called "The Red." Also worth seeking out are the *Eden Ridge* organic wines, the fruity *David Wynn* range and the "Samuel's Bay" second label. ☆☆☆☆ **1997 Chardonnay $$$**

🍇 **Mourvèdre** [mor-veh-dr] (*Rhône*, France) Floral-spicy *Rhône* grape usually found in blends. Increasingly popular in France and California where, as in Australia, it is called *Mataro*. ***Jade Mountain; Penfolds; Ridge.***

Mousse [mooss] The bubbles in *Champagne* and sparkling wines.

Mousseux [moo-sur] (France) Sparkling wine – generally cheap and unremarkable.

🍷 **Mouton-Cadet** [moo-ton ka-day] (*Bordeaux*, France) A brilliant commercial invention by Philippe de Rothschild who used it to profit handsomely from the name of *Mouton-Rothschild*, with which it has no discernible connection. The recently introduced "Reserve" is better than the basic and recently launched white Graves Reserve creditable in its own right.

🍷 **Ch. Mouton-Baronne-Philippe** [moo-ton ba-ron-fee-leep] (*Pauillac, 5ème Cru Classé, Bordeaux*, France) See *Ch.d'Armailhac*.

🍷 **Ch. Mouton-Rothschild** [moo-ton roth-child] (*Pauillac Premier Cru Classé, Bordeaux*, France) The only *château* to be elevated to a first growth from a second, Mouton can have gloriously rich, complex flavors of roast coffee and blackcurrant. Current vintages have been eclipsed by *Margaux*, *Lafite* and *Latour* but the 1998 shows a return to form. **61 62 66 70 75** 76 78 81 82 83 **85** 86 88 89 90 91 92 93 **94** 95 96 97 98 ☆☆☆☆☆ **1990 $$$$**

Mudgee [mud-zhee] (*New South Wales*, Australia) Australia's first *appellation* region, a coolish-climate area now being championed by *Rosemount* as well as by *Rothbury*. **Botobolar; Huntington Estate.**

🍷 **Bodegas Muga** [moo-gah] (*Rioja*, Spain) Producer of good old-fashioned *Riojas*, of which Prado Enea is the best. ☆☆☆ **1991 Rioja Torre Reserva $$**

🍷 **Jacques-Frederic Mugnier** [moo-nee-yay] (*Burgundy*, France) *Chambolle-Musigny* estate that makes long-lived wines from great vineyards, including Bonnes-Mares and *Musigny*. ☆☆☆☆ **1995 Chambolle-Musigny $$$**

🍷 **Mulderbosch** [mool-duh-bosh] (*Stellenbosch*, South Africa) South Africa's answer to *Cloudy Bay*: exciting *Sauvignon* and *Meursault*-like *Chardonnay*, not to mention a red blend called Faithful Hound. ☆☆☆☆ **1997 Chardonnay $$**

🍷 **Weingut Müller-Catoir** [moo-luh kah-twah] (*Pfalz*, Germany) Great new-wave producer using new-wave grapes as well as *Riesling*. Wines of all styles are impeccable and packed with flavor. Search out powerful Grauburgunder, Rieslaner, and *Scheurebe* wines. ☆☆☆☆☆ **1993 Haardter Herrenletten Riesling Spätlese $$**

🍷 **Egon Müller-Scharzhof** [moo-luh shahtz-hof] (*Mosel-Saar-Ruwer*, Germany) Truly brilliant *Saar* producer. ☆☆☆☆ **1997 Scharzhofberger Riesling Spätlese $$$**

🍇 **Müller-Thurgau** [moo-lur-toor-gow] (Germany) Workhorse white grape, a *Riesling* x *Sylvaner* cross – also known as *Rivaner* – making much unremarkable wine in Germany, but yielding some gems for producers like *Müller-Catoir*. Very successful in England.

🍷 **Mumm/Mumm Napa** [murm] (*Champagne*, France/California) Maker of slightly improved Cordon Rouge *Champagne* and far better *Cuvée Napa* from California. Newly (1999) sold by its owners, Seagram. Hopefully new owners will have greater ambitions. ☆☆☆☆ **1990 Grand Cordon $$$**

🍷 **Réné Muré** [moo-ray] (*Alsace*, France) Producer of full-bodied wines, especially from the Clos St. Landelin vineyard. ☆☆☆☆ **1996 Riesling Vorbourg, Clos St. Landelin $$$**

Murfatlar [moor-fat-lah] (Romania) Major vineyard and research area that is having increasing success with *Chardonnay*.

Murphy-Goode (*Alexander Valley*, California) Classy producer of quite Burgundian style whites which sell at – for California – affordable prices.

Murray Valley (South Australia) Irrigated area producing much of the Antipodes' cheapest wine – and some increasingly impressive rather pricier fare. ***Angoves;*** **Banrock Station;** ***Kingston Estate.***

Bodegas Marqués de Murrieta [mar-kays day moo-ree-eh-tah] (*Rioja*, Spain) Until recently the best old-style *oaky* white (sold as Castillo Ygay), though recent efforts have been slightly disappointing. The red, at its best, is one of the most long-lived, elegant *Riojas* – look out for the old Castillo Ygays from the 1960s with their distinctive old-style labels. ☆☆☆☆ **1994 Ygay Reserva Especial Tinto $$$**

Murrietta's Well (*Livermore*, California) Blends of *Zinfandel* and *Cabernet, Merlot* are rare, but the berryish red sold by *Wente* under this name proves that it is an experiment more producers should try.

Ch. Musar [moo-sahr] (*Ghazir*, Lebanon) *Serge Hochar* makes a different red every year, varying the blend of *Cabernet, Cinsault*, and *Syrah*. The style veers wildly between *Bordeaux*, the *Rhône*, and Italy, but there's never a risk of becoming bored. Good vintages easily keep for a decade. The *Chardonnay*-based whites are less than dazzling, though. **86** 88 89 91 93 95

Muscadelle [mus-kah-del] Spicy ingredient in white *Bordeaux*. See *Tokay*.

Muscadet des Coteaux de la Loire / Côtes de Grand Lieu / de Sèvre et Maine [moos-kah-day day koh-toh dur lah lwar / koht dur gron lyur / dur say-vr' eh mayn] (*Loire*, France) Emphatically non-aromatic wines made from the *Melon de Bourgogne*. Worthwhile examples are briefly matured and bottled on their dead yeasts or *lees* ("*sur lie*"). The recently created Côtes de Grand Lieu is worth looking for, as can be the rare Coteaux de la Loire. Sèvre et Maine is less reliable. 97 98 ***Dom. de Chasseloir;*** **Bossard;** ***Chéreau-Carré;*** **Couillaud; Guindon; Marquis de Goulaine;** ***Pierre Luneau; Metaireau;*** **Marcel Sautejeau; Sauvion.**

Muscat [mus-kat] Generic name for a species of white grape (aka *Moscato* in Italy) of which there are a number of different sub-species.

Muscat à Petits Grains [moos-kah ah puh-tee gran] Aka *Frontignan*, the best variety of Muscat and the grape responsible for *Muscat de Beaumes de Venise, Muscat de Rivesaltes, Asti Spumante, Muscat of Samos, Rutherglen* Muscats, and dry *Alsace* Muscats.

Muscat de Cap Corse / Frontignan / Mireval / Rivesaltes / St. Jean de Minervois (*Languedoc-Roussillon*, France) Potentially luscious fortified Muscats of which Rivesaltes and Minervois are possibly the best.

Muscat of Alexandria [moos-kah] Grape responsible for *Moscatel de Setúbal, Moscatel de Valencia*, and sweet South Australians. Also known as *Lexia*, and in South Africa it satisfies the sweet tooth of much of the Afrikaner population as *Hanepoot*.

Muscat Ottonel [moos-kah ot-oh-nel] Muscat variety grown in Middle and Eastern Europe.

Musigny [moo-zee-nyee] (*Burgundy*, France) Potentially wonderful *Grand Cru* from which *Chambolle-Musigny* takes its name. 76 79 82 83 **88 89 90** 91 92 93 **94** 95 96 97 98 ***De Vogüé; Groffier; Leroy; Mugnier; Prieur.***

Must Unfermented grape juice.

MW See *Master of Wine*.

N

Nackenheim [nahk-ehn-hime] (*Rheinhessen*, Germany) Village in the *Nierstein bereich*, sadly best known for its debased *grosslage*, Gütes Domtal. QbA/Kab/Spät: **0** 91 92 93 94 95 96 97 98 Aus/Beeren/Tba: 90 91 92 93 94 95 96 **97** 98 ***Gunderloch; Kürfurstenhof;*** **Heinrich Seip.**

Nahe [nah-huh] (Germany) *Anbaugebiet* producing wines which can combine delicate flavor with full body. QbA/Kab/Spät: **88 89 90** 91 **92 93** 94 95 96 97 98 Aus/Beeren/Tba: **83 85** 88 89 90 91 92 **93 94** 95 96 97 98. **Crusius;** ***Schlossgut Diel;*** **Hermann Donnhoff; Hehner Kiltz;** ***Kruger-Rumpf.***

Ch. Nairac [nay-rak] (*Barsac 2ème Cru Classé, Bordeaux*, France) Delicious, lush, long-lasting wine sometimes lacking a little complexity.

Nalle (*Sonoma*, California) Great *Dry Creek* producer of some of California's (and thus the world's) greatest *Zinfandel*.

Naoussa [nah-oosa] (Greece) Region producing dry red wines, often from the Xynomavro grape. ***Boutari.***

Napa [na-pa] (California) Named after the Native American word for "plenty," this is a region with plentiful wines ranging from ordinary to sublime. Too many are hyped; none is cheap and the region as a whole is far too varied in altitude and conditions to make sense as a single *appellation*. The 20 or so smaller *appellations* within Napa, such as *Carneros, Stag's Leap, Howell Mountain,* and *Mt. Veeder* deserve greater prominence – as do nearby regions like *Sonoma*. Red: 86 87 **90 91** 92 **93 94** 95 96 97 98 White: 85 **90 91** 92 **95** 96 97 98 ***Atlas Peak; Beaulieu; Beringer; Cain; Cakebread; Caymus; Chimney Rock; Clos du Val; Crichton Hall; Cuvaison; Diamond Creek; Dom. Chandon; Duckhorn; Dunn; Flora Springs; Franciscan; Frog's Leap; Heitz; Hess Collection; Ch. Montelena; Monteviña; Mumm; Newton; Niebaum-Coppola; Opus One; Ch. Potelle; Phelps; Schramsberg; Screaming Eagle; Shafer; Stag's Leap; Sterling; Turley.***

Napa Ridge (California) Highly successful brand, most of whose pleasant, commercial wines are made with juice from grapes grown outside *Napa*. (Exports are less confusingly labeled as "Coastal Ridge").

Nautilus Estate [naw-tih-luhs] (*Marlborough*, New Zealand) *Yalumba's* New Zealand offshoot. Sparkling wine and *Sauvignon*. ☆☆☆ **Nautilus Cuvée $$**

Navajas [na-VA-khas] (*Rioja*, Spain) Small producer making impressive reds and *oaky* whites worth keeping. ☆☆☆☆ **1993 Blanco Crianza $$**

Navarra [na-VAH-rah] (Spain) Northern *DO*, traditionally renowned for rosés and heavy reds but now producing wines to rival those from neighboring *Rioja*, where prices are often higher. Look for innovative *Cabernet Sauvignon* and *Tempranillo* blends. **81** 82 **83 85 87** 89 90 91 92 94 95 96 97 98 ***Chivite; Guelbenzu; Castillo de Monjardin; Vinicola Murchantina; Nekeas; Ochoa; Palacio de la Vega;*** **Senorio de Sarria.**

Nebbiolo [neh-bee-oh-loh] (*Piedmont*, Italy) Grape of *Piedmont*, producing wines with tarry, cherryish, spicy flavors that are slow to mature but become richly complex – epitomized by *Barolo* and *Barbaresco*. Quality and style vary enormously depending on soil. Aka *Spanna*.

Nederburg [neh-dur-burg] (*Paarl*, South Africa) Huge commercial producer. The Edelkeur *late harvest* wines are the gems of the cellar. Sadly, the best wines are only sold at the annual Nederburg Auction.

Négociant [nay-goh-see-yon] (France) Merchant who buys, matures, and bottles wine. See also *Eléveur*.

Négociant-manipulant (NM) [ma-nih-pyoo-lon] (*Champagne*, France) Buyer and blender of wines for *Champagne*, identifiable by the NM number which is mandatory on the label.

Negroamaro [nay-groh-ah-mah-roh] (*Puglia*, Italy) A Puglian grape whose name means "bitter-black" and produces fascinating, spicy-gamey reds. Found in *Salice Salentino* and *Copertino*.

Nelson (New Zealand) Small region, a glorious bus ride to the north-west of *Marlborough*. *Neudorf* and *Seifried/ Redwood Valley* are the stars. White: **89 91** 94 **96** 97 98 Red: **87 89** 90 **91 92 94** 95 96 97 98

Nemea [nur-may-yah] (Peloponnese, Greece) Improving cool(ish) climate region for reds made from Agiorgitiko. ***Boutari; Semeli; Tsantalis.***

Nepenthe [neh-pen-thi] (*Adelaide Hills*, South Australia) Instant star with dazzling *Chardonnay, Semillon, Sauvignon, Pinot Noir, Cabernet-Merlot* and *Zinfandel*. ☆☆☆☆ **1997 Pinot Noir $$$**

Ch. La Nerthe [nurf] (*Rhône*, France) One of the most exciting estates in *Châteauneuf-du-Pape*, producing rich wines with seductive dark fruit.

Ch. Nenin [nay-nan] (*Pomerol, Bordeaux*, France) A *château* to watch since its recent purchase by Michel Delon of *Ch. Léoville-Las-Cases*.

Neuchâtel [nur-sha-tel] (Switzerland) Lakeside region. Together with Les Trois Lacs, a source of good red and rosé, *Pinot Noir*, and *Chasselas* and *Chardonnay* whites. **Ch. d'Auvernier; Porret.**

Neudorf [noy-dorf] (*Nelson*, New Zealand) Pioneering small-scale producer of beautifully made *Chardonnay*, *Semillon, Sauvignon, Riesling* and *Pinot Noir*. ☆☆☆☆☆ **1997 Moutere Sauvignon $$$**

Neusiedlersee [noy-zeed-lur-zay] (Austria) *Burgenland* region on the Hungarian border. Great *late harvest* and improving whites and reds. ***Fieler-Artinger; Kracher; Lang; Willi Opitz;*** **Tschida.**

Nevers [nur-vehr] (France) Subtlest oak – from a forest in *Burgundy*.

New South Wales (Australia) Major wine-producing state, which is home to the famous *Hunter Valley*, along with the *Cowra, Mudgee, Orange*, and *Murrumbidgee* regions. White: **85 86 87 88** 90 **91** 94 **95 96** 97 98 Red: 82 83 **85 86 87 88** 90 91 93 94 95 96 97 98

New Zealand Instant superstar with proven *Sauvignon Blanc* and *Chardonnay* and – despite most expectations – increasingly successful *Merlots* and *Pinot Noirs*. Vintages vary, however (1998 was not a great year for Marlborough). See *Marlborough, Martinborough, Hawke's Bay, Gisborne, Auckland*.

Newton Vineyards (*Napa Valley*, California) High-altitude vineyards with top-class *Chardonnay, Merlot*, and *Cabernet*, now being made with help from *Michel Rolland*.

Ngatarawa [na-TA-ra-wah] (*Hawke's Bay*, New Zealand) Small winery that can make impressive reds and even better *Chardonnays* and *late harvest* whites.

Niagara (*Ontario*, Canada) Area close to the Falls and to Lakes Ontario and Erie where the *Vidal* is used to make good *Icewine*. The *Chardonnnay, Riesling* and – though less successfully – red varieties such as *Pinot Noir* and *Merlot* are now being used too. ***Ch. des Charmes;* Henry of Pelham; *Inniskillin;* Magnotta; *Reif; Southbrook.***

Nicholson River (*Gippsland*, Australia) The temperamental *Gippsland* climate makes for a small production of stunning *Chardonnays*. ☆☆☆☆ **1993 Chardonnay $$$**

Niebaum-Coppola [nee-bowm coh-po-la] (*Napa Valley*, California) You've seen the movie. Now taste the wine. The "Dracula" and "Godfather" director's estate now includes the appropriately Gothic *Inglenook* winery, has some of the oldest vines about and makes intensely concentrated *Cabernets* to suit the patient. ☆☆☆☆ **1995 Rubicon Napa Valley $$$**

Niederhausen Schlossböckelheim [nee-dur-how sen shlos-bok-ehl-hime] (*Nahe*, Germany) State-owned estate producing highly concentrated *Riesling* from great vineyards.

Dom. Michel Niellon [nee-el-lon] (*Burgundy*, France) Estate ranking consistently in the top five white *Burgundy* producers and making highly concentrated wines. ☆☆☆☆ **1995 Chassagne-Montrachet Champs Gain $$$**

Niepoort [nee-poort] (*Douro*, Portugal) Small, independent *port* house making subtle *vintage* and particularly impressive *colheita tawnies*. A name to watch. ☆☆☆☆ **1985 Colheita Port $$$**

Nierstein [neer-stine] (*Rheinhessen*, Germany) Village and (with *Piesport*) *bereich* best known in the UK. Some fine wines, obscured by the notoriety of the reliably dull Niersteiner Gütes Domtal. QbA/Kab/Spät: **85** 86 **88 89 90** 91 92 93 94 95 96 97 98 Aus/Beeren/Tba: **83 85 88 89 90** 91 92 93 94 95 96 97 98 ***Balbach; Gunderloch; Heyl zu Herrnsheim.***

Weingut Nikolaihof [nih-koh-li-hof] (*Niederösterreich*, Austria) One of the producers of some of the best *Grüner Veltliners* and *Rieslings* in Austria. ☆☆☆☆ **1997 Riesling Smaragd Wachau Vom Stein $$$**

Nipozzano [nip-ots-zano] (*Tuscany*, Italy) *See Frescobaldi*.

Nobilo [nob-ih-loh] (Huapai, New Zealand) Family-owned firm making good *Chardonnay* from *Gisborne, "Icon"* wines from *Marlborough* including a pleasant, commercial off-dry *White Cloud* blend.

Noble rot Popular term for *botrytis cinerea*.

Normans (*McLaren Vale*, Australia) Fast-improving *Cabernet* and *Shiraz* specialist. ☆☆☆☆☆ **1996 Signature Cabernet Sauvignon Cabernet Franc $$$**

Bodega Norton [naw-ton] (Argentina) One of Argentina's most recommendable producers, producing a wide range of *varietal* wines. The "Privada" wines are the cream of the crop. ☆☆☆☆ **1997 Malbec Reserva $$**

Nouveau [noo-voh] New wine, most popularly used of *Beaujolais*.

Quinta do Noval (*Douro*, Portugal) Fine and potentially finer estate. The ultra-rare Nacional *vintage ports* are the jewel in the crown, made from ungrafted vines. Also of note are great *colheita tawny ports*. ☆☆☆☆ **1964 Colheita Port $$$**

Albet i Noya [al-bet-ee-noy-ya] (Spain) Innovative producer with red and white traditional and imported varieties. A superstar in the making. ☆☆☆☆☆ **1995 Reserva Marti $$$**

Nuits-St.-Georges [noo-wee san zhawzh] (*Burgundy*, France) *Commune* producing the most *claret*-like of red *Burgundies*, properly tough and lean when young but glorious with age. Whites are good but ultra-rare. Red **78** 79 **80** 82 83 **85** 86 87 **88 89 90** 91 92 93 **94** 95 96 97 98 ***Dom. de l'Arlot; Robert Chevillon; Jean-Jacques Confuron; Faiveley; Henri Gouges; Jean Grivot; Leroy; Alain Michelot; Patrice Rion; Henri & Gilles Remoriquet.***

Nuragus di Cagliari [noo-rah-goos dee ka-lee-yah-ree] (*Sardinia*, Italy) Good-value, tangy, floral wine from the Nuragus grape.

NV Non-vintage, meaning a blend of wines from different years.

O

Oakville Ranch (*Napa Valley*, California) Potentially one of the Napa's most exciting red wine producers, but wines have so far been a little too tough.

Oaky Flavor imparted by oak casks which will vary depending on the source of the oak (American is more obviously sweet than French). Woody is usually less complimentary.

Vin de Pays d'Oc [pay-doc] (*Languedoc-Roussillon*, France) The world's biggest wine region, encompassing appellations such as *Corbières* and *Minervois* and several smaller *Vins de Pays* regions.

Bodegas Ochoa [och-oh-wah] (*Navarra*, Spain) New-wave producer of creamy, fruitily fresh *Cabernet*, *Tempranillo* and *Viura*. ☆☆☆☆ **1990 Navarra Tinto Reserva $$**

Ockfen [ok-fehn] (*Mosel-Saar-Ruwer*, Germany) Village producing some of the best, steeliest wines of the *Saar-Ruwer bereich*, especially *Rieslings* from the *Bockstein* vineyard. QbA/Kab/Spät: **85** 86 **88 89 90** 91 **92 93 94 95** 96 97 98 Aus/Beeren/Tba: **83 85 88 89 90** 91 **92 93 94 95** 96 97 98 ☆☆☆ **1996 Ockfener Bockstein Riesling Reichsgraf von Kesselstadt $$**

Oechsle [urk-slur] (Germany) Scale indicating the sugar level in grapes or wine.

Oenology/ist The science of wine/one who advises winemakers.

Oeste [wes-teh] (Portugal) Western region in which a growing number of fresh, light, commercial wines are being made, of which the most successful has undoubtedly been Arruda. Red:93 94 95 96 97 98

Oestrich [ur-strihckh] (*Rheingau*, Germany) Source of good *Riesling*. QbA/Kab/Spät: **85** 86 **88 89 90** 91 **92 93** 94 95 96 97 98 Aus/Beeren/Tba: **89 90** 92 93 94 95 96 97 98 ***Wegeler Deinhard; Balthazar Ress.***

Michel Ogier [ogee-yay] (*Rhône*, France) *Côte Rôtie* producer, making less muscular wines than most of his neighbors. ☆☆☆☆ **1996 Côte Rôtie $$$**

Oïdium [oh-id-ee-yum] Fungal grape infection, shriveling them, and turning them gray.

Ojai Vineyard [oh-high] (*Santa Barbara*, California) The specialties here are a *Sauvignon-Semillon* blend and – more interestingly – a *Rhône*-like *Syrah*. ☆☆☆☆ **1995 Syrah Bien Nacido Vineyard $$$**

Okanagan (*British Columbia*, Canada) Principal wine region in the west of Canada. Despite frosts, *Pinot Noir* can produce good wine here. **Mission Hill.**

Olasz Rizling [oh-lash-riz-ling] (Hungary) Term for the *Welschriesling*.

Ch. Olivier [oh-liv-ee-yay] (*Pessac-Léognan Cru Classé, Bordeaux*, France) An underperformer which has yet to join the *Graves* revolution. Red: 82 83 85 86 88 89 90 91 92 93 94 95 96 98 White: 90 92 93 94 96 98

Oloroso [ol-oh-roh-soh] (*Jerez*, Spain) Style of full-bodied *sherry*, that is either dry or semi-sweet.

Oltrepò Pavese [ohl-tray-poh pa-vay-say] (*Lombardy*, Italy) Still and sparkling *DOC* made from local grapes including the characterfully spicy red Gutturnio and white Ortrugo. **Ca' Di Frara; Tenuta Il Bosco; Cabanon; Fugazza; Mazzolina; Bruno Verdi.**

Omar Khayyam (Champagne India) [oh-mah-ki-yam] (Maharashtra, India) *Champagne*-method wine which, when drunk young, has more than novelty value. The producer's cheeky name, "*Champagne* India," is a source of considerable annoyance to the Champenois, but they, in the shape of *Piper Heidsieck*, were happy enough to sell the Indians their expertise.

Willi Opitz [oh-pitz] (*Neusiedlersee*, Austria) Oddball pet food-manufacturer-turned-producer of a magical mystery tour of *late harvest* and straw-dried wines, including an extraordinary *botrytis* red briefly labeled – to the discomfort of some Californians – "Opitz One." ☆☆☆☆☆ **1995 Pinot Gris Trockenbeerenauslese $$$**

Oppenheim [op-en-hime] (*Rheinhessen*, Germany) Village in *Nierstein bereich* best known – unfairly – for unexciting wines from the Krottenbrunnen. Elsewhere produces soft wines with concentrated flavor. QbA/Kab/Spät: **85** 86 **88 89 90** 91 **92 93** 94 95 96 97 98 Aus/Beeren/Tba: **83 85** 88 89 90 91 92 93 94 95 **96 97** 98

Opus One (*Napa Valley*, California) 20-year old co-production between *Mouton-Rothschild* and *Robert Mondavi*. Classy *claret*-like blackcurranty wine that sells at an appropriately classy *claret*-like price. ☆☆☆☆☆ **1995 $$$$**

Orange (*New South Wales*, Australia) Coolish region which, with *Cowra*, is likely to eclipse the nearby *Hunter Valley*. Try the Orange *Chardonnay* made by Philip Shaw of *Rosemount* from vineyards of which he is proud co-owner.

Orange Muscat Another highly eccentric member of the *Muscat* family, best known for dessert wines in California by *Quady* and in Australia for the delicious *Brown Brothers Late Harvest* Orange Muscat and *Flora*.

Oregon (US) Fashionable cool-climate state, some of whose winemakers grow marijuana as keenly as their specialty, *Pinot Noir*. The *Chardonnay*, *Riesling*, *Pinot Gris*, and sparkling wines show promise too. ***Adelsheim; Amity; Argyle; Beaux Freres; Cameron;*** **Chehalem;** ***Dom Drouhin; Duck Pond; Erath; Eyrie;*** **Henry Estate;** ***King Estate; Ponzi; Rex Hill;*** **Sokol Blosser.**

🍷 **Oriachovitza** [oh-ree-ak-hoh-vit-sah] (Bulgaria) Major source of reliable *Cabernet Sauvignon* and *Merlot*.

🍷 **Orlando** (*South Australia*) Huge, French-owned (Pernod-Ricard) producer of the world-beating and surprisingly reliable *Jacob's Creek* wines. The RF range is good but the harder-to-find Gramps and Flaxmans wines are more exciting, as are Jacaranda Ridge, Centenary, and the "Saints" series. ☆☆☆☆ **1994 St Hugo Cabernet Sauvignon $$$**

Orléanais [aw-lay-yo-nay] (*Loire*, France) A vineyard area around Orléans in the Central Vineyards region of the *Loire*, specializing in unusual white blends of *Chardonnay* and *Pinot Gris*, and reds of *Pinot Noir* and *Cabernet Franc*. White: **95 96 97** 98 Red: **90 95** 96 97 98

🍷 **Ch. Les Ormes-de-Pez** [awm dur-pay] (*St. Estèphe Cru Bourgeois*, *Bordeaux*, France) Often underrated stable-mate of *Lynch-Bages* and made with similar skill. **82 83** 85 **86** 88 89 90 92 93 94 95 96 97 98

🍷 **Tenuta dell'Ornellaia** [teh-noo-tah del-aw-nel-li-ya] (*Tuscany*, Italy) *Bordeaux*-blend *Bolgheri Super-Tuscan* from the brother of *Piero Antinori*. This is serious wine that is worth maturing. ☆☆☆☆ **1995 Ornellaia $$$$**

Ortega [aw-tay-gah] Recently developed variety, and grown in Germany and England, though rarely to tasty advantage. *Biddenden* makes a good one, however, as does *Denbies*, which uses it to produce *late harvest* wine.

🍷 **Orvieto** [ohr-vee-yet-toh] (*Umbria*, Italy) White Umbrian *DOC* responsible for a quantity of dull wine. Orvieto *Classico* is better. Look out for *Secco* if you like your white wine dry; *Amabile* if you have a sweet tooth. ***Antinori;* Bigi; La Carraia; Covio Cardetto; Palazzone.**

🍷 **Osbourne** [os-sbaw-nay] (*Jerez*, Spain) Producer of a good range of *sherries* including a brilliant *Pedro Ximenez*.

🍷 **Dom. Ostertag** [os-tur-tahg] (*Alsace*, France) Poet and philosopher André Ostertag's superb *Alsace domaine*. ☆☆☆☆ **1996 Riesling Moenchberg $$$**

Oxidation The effect (usually detrimental, occasionally – as in *sherry* – intentional) of oxygen on wine.

Oxidative The opposite to *reductive*. Certain wines – most reds, and whites like *Chardonnay* – benefit from limited exposure to oxygen during their fermentation and maturation, such as barrel aging.

🍷 **Oyster Bay** (*Marlborough*, New Zealand) See entry for *Delegats*. ☆☆☆ **1997 Sauvignon Blanc $$**

P

Paarl [pahl] (South Africa) Warm region in which *Backsberg* and *Boschendal* make a wide range of appealing wines. Hotter and drier than neighboring *Stellenbosch*. Red: **82 84** 86 **87** 89 **91 92** 93 94 95 96 97 98 White: **95** 97 98 ***Charles Back/Fairview; KWV; Backsberg; Glen Carlou; Villiera; Plaisir de Merle.***

🍷 **Pacherenc du Vic-Bilh** [pa-shur-renk doo vik beel] (*South-West*, France) Rare, dry or fairly sweet white wine made from the *Petit* and *Gros Manseng*. A specialty of *Madiran*. ☆☆☆☆☆ **1997 Alain Brumont les Jardins du Bouscasse Pacherenc du Vic-Bihl $$**

Padthaway [pad-thah-way] (South Australia) Vineyard area just north of *Coonawarra* specializing in *Chardonnay* and *Sauvignon*, though reds work well here too. White: **94** 95 96 97 98 Red: **86 87** 88 **90 91** 94 95 96 97 98 Angove's ***Hardys; Lindemans; Orlando; Penfolds.***

Pagadebit di Romagna [pah-gah-deh-bit dee roh-man-ya] (*Emilia-Romagna*, Italy) Dry, sweet, and sparkling whites from the Pagadebit grape.

Pahlmeyer (*Napa Valley*, California) One of California's most interesting winemakers, producing Burgundian *Chardonnay* and a complex *Bordeaux*-blend red. ☆☆☆☆ **1996 Napa Valley Chardonnay $$$**

Ch. Pajzos [pah-zhohs] (*Tokaji*, Hungary) Serious French-owned producer of new-wave *Tokay*. ☆☆☆☆ **1993 Tokay Aszú 5 Puttonyos $$$**

Bodegas Palacio [pa-las-see-yoh] (*Rioja*, Spain) Underrated *bodega* with stylish, fruit-driven reds and distinctively oaky whites. Also helped by wine guru *Michel Rolland*. ☆☆☆☆ **1997 Cosme Palacio Rioja Red $$**

Alvaro Palacios (*Catalonia*, Spain) Young Priorato superstar estate producing individual wines with rich, concentrated flavors. L'Ermita is the top wine.

Palate Nebulous, not to say ambiguous, term describing the apparatus used for tasting (ie, the tongue) as well as the skill of the taster ("he has a good palate").

Palette [pa-let] (*Provence*, France) *AC* rosé and creamy white, well liked by vacationers in St. Tropez who are so used to extortionate prices for cups of coffee that they don't notice paying more for a pink wine than for a serious red. The white, which can be very perfumed, is better value.

Palliser Estate [pa-lih-sur] (*Martinborough*, New Zealand) Source of classy *Sauvignon Blanc*, *Chardonnay* and – increasingly – *Pinot Noir* from *Martinborough*. ☆☆☆☆ **1997 Pinot Noir $$**

Ch. Palmer [pahl-mur] (*Margaux 3ème Cru Classé*, *Bordeaux*, France) The success story of the late Peter Sichel who died in 1998, this third growth *Margaux* stands alongside the best of the *Médoc* and often outclasses its more highly ranked neighbors. Wonderfully perfumed. **61 66 70 71 75** 76 **78 79** 80 82 **83** 84 85 **86** 87 **88 89** 90 91 92 93 **94** 95 96 97 98

Palo Cortado [pah-loh kaw-tah doh] (*Jerez*, Spain) Rare *sherry* pitched between *amontillado* and *oloroso*. **Gonzalez Byass; Hidalgo; Lustau; Osborne; Pedro Romero; Valdespino.**

Palomino [pa-loh-mee-noh] (*Jerez*, Spain) White grape responsible for virtually all fine *sherries* – and almost invariably dull white wine, when unfortified. Also widely grown in South Africa.

Ch. Pape-Clément [pap klay-mon] (*Pessac-Léognan Cru Classé*, *Bordeaux*, France) Great source of rich reds since the mid 1980s and, more recently, small quantities of delicious peach-oaky white. Red: 70 **75** 82 83 85 **86** 88 89 90 92 **93** 94 95 96 97 98

Parducci [pah-doo-chee] (*Mendocino*, California) Steady producer whose *Petite Sirah* is a terrific bargain. ☆☆☆☆ **1996 Petite Sirah $$$**

Dom. Alain Paret [pa-ray] (*Rhône*, France) Producer of a great *St. Joseph* and *Condrieu*, in partnership with one of the world's best-known winemakers. (Though, to be fair, Gérard Dépardieu does owe his fame to the cinema rather than his efforts among the vines.) ☆☆☆☆ **1997 Condrieu les Ceps du Nebadon $$$$**

Parker Estate (*Coonawarra*, Australia) Small producer sharing its name with the US guru, and calling its (very pricy) red "First Growth." Marks for chutzpah. ☆☆☆☆ **1996 Terra Rossa First Growth $$$$**

Pasado/Pasada [pa-sah-doh/dah] (Spain) Term applied to old or fine *fino* and *amontillado sherries*. Worth seeking out.

🍷 **C.J. Pask** [pask] (*Hawke's Bay*, New Zealand) *Cabernet* pioneer with excellent *Chardonnay* and *Sauvignon*. One of New Zealand's very best. ☆☆☆☆ **1997 Reserve Cabernet Merlot $$$**

Paso Robles [pa-soh roh-blays] (*San Luis Obispo*, California) Warmish, long-established region, good for *Zinfandel* (especially *Ridge*), *Rhône*, and Italian varieties. Plus increasingly successful *Chardonnays* and *Pinots*. Red: 85 86 87 90 91 92 93 95 White: 85 90 91 92 94 95 96 97 98

🍷 **Pasqua** [pas-kwah] (*Veneto*, Italy) Producer of fairly priced, reliable wines. ☆☆☆ **1998 Soave Superiore Sagramoso $**

Passetoutgrains [pas-stoo-gran] (*Burgundy*, France) Wine supposedly made from two-thirds *Gamay*, one third *Pinot Noir* - though few producers respect these proportions. Once the Burgundians' daily red – until they decided to sell it and drink cheaper wine from other regions.

🍷 **Passing Clouds** (*Bendigo*, Australia) "We get clouds, but it never rains ..." Despite a fairly hideous label, this is one of Australia's most serious red blends.

Passito [pa-see-toh] (Italy) Raisiny wine, usually made from sun-dried *Erbaluce* grapes in Italy. This technique is now used in Australia by *Primo Estate*.

🍷 **Ch. Patache d'Aux** [pa-tash-doh] (*Médoc Cru Bourgeois*, *Bordeaux*, France) Traditional, toughish stuff. 83 85 88 89 90 93 95 96 97 98 ☆☆☆ **1996 $$$**

🍷 **Frederico Paternina** [pa-tur-nee-na] (*Rioja*, Spain) Ernest Hemingway's favorite *bodega*.

🍷 **Luis Pato** [lweesh-pah-toh] (*Bairrada*, Portugal) One of Portugal's rare superstar winemakers, proving, amongst other things, that the *Baga* grape can make first-class spicy, berryish red wines. ☆☆☆☆ **1997 Quinta do Ribeirinho Primeira Escolha $$**

🍷 **Patriarche** [pa-tree-arsh] (*Burgundy*, France) Huge merchant whose name is not a watchword for great *Burgundy*. The *Ch. de Meursault domaine*, however, is worthwhile.

🍷 **Patz & Hall** (*Napa Valley*, California) The maker of delicious, unashamedly full-flavored *Chardonnays*.

🍷 **Pauillac** [poh-yak] (*Bordeaux*, France) One of the four famous "*communes*" of the *Médoc*, Pauillac is the home of Châteaux *Latour*, *Lafite*, and *Mouton-Rothschild*, as well as the two *Pichons* and *Lynch-Bages*. The epitome of full-flavored blackcurranty *Bordeaux*; very classy (and pricy) wine. 70 75 76 78 79 82 83 85 86 88 89 90 94 95 96 97 98

🍷 **Clos de Pauililles** [poh-leey] (*Languedoc-Roussillon*, France) Top-class producer of *Banyuls* and of the little-known *appellation* of *Collioure*.

🍷 **Neil Paulett** [paw-let] (South Australia) Small, top-flight *Clare Valley Riesling* producer. ☆☆☆☆ **1995 Polish Hill River Riesling $$**

🍷 **Dr Pauly-Bergweiler** [bur-gwi-lur] (*Mosel-Saar-Ruwer*, Germany) Ultra-modern winery with good modern *Riesling*. ☆☆☆☆ **1997 Wehlener Sonnenuhr Riesling Käbinett $$**

🍷 **Ch. Pavie** [pa-vee] (*St. Emilion Premier Grand Cru Classé*, *Bordeaux*, France) Recently purchased, impeccably made, plummily rich *St. Emilion* wines. 79 81 82 83 85 86 87 88 89 90 91 93 94 95 96 98

🍷 **Ch. Pavie-Decesse** [pa-vee dur-ses] (*St. Emilion Grand Cru Classé*, *Bordeaux*, France) Neighbor to *Ch. Pavie*, but a shade less impressive. 82 83 85 86 88 89 90 92 94 95 96

🍷 **Ch. Pavie-Macquin** [pa-vee ma-kah'] (*St. Emilion Grand Cru Classé*, Bordeaux) Returned to form since the late 1980s – and the producer of a startlingly good 1993.

🍷 **Le Pavillon Blanc de Ch. Margaux** [pa-vee-yon blon] (*Bordeaux*, France) The (rare) *Sauvignon*-dominated white wine of *Ch. Margaux* which still acts as the yardstick for the growing number of *Médoc* white wines. 85 86 89 **90 91** 92 95 96 97 ☆☆☆☆ **1994 Pavillon Blanc $$$$**

🍷 **Ca' del Pazzo** [kah-del-pat-soh] (*Tuscany*, Italy) Ultra-classy, oaky *Super-Tuscan* with loads of ripe fruit and oak.

Pécharmant [pay-shar-mon] (*South-West*, France) In the *Bergerac* area, producing light, *Bordeaux*-like reds. Worth trying.

🍇 **Pedro Ximénez (PX)** [peh-droh khee-MEH-nes] (*Jerez*, Spain) White grape, dried in the sun to create a sweet, curranty wine, which is used in the blending of the sweeter *sherry* styles, and in its own right by *Osbourne*, and by *Gonzalez Byass* for its brilliant Noe. Also produces a very unusual wine at *De Bortoli* in Australia. ☆☆☆☆ **Cream Of Creams, Manuel de Argueso $$$**

🍷 **Viña Pedrosa** [veen-ya pay-droh-sah] (*Ribera del Duero*, Spain) Modern blend of *Tempranillo* and classic *Bordelais* varieties. The Spanish equivalent of a *Super-Tuscan*.

🍷 **Clos Pegase** [kloh-pay-gas] (*Napa Valley*, California) Showcase winery with improving but historically generally overpraised wines. ☆☆☆ **1996 Merlot Napa Valley $$$**

🍷 **Dom. Henry Pellé** [on-ree pel-lay] (*Loire*, France) Reliable producer of fruitier-than-usual *Menetou-Salon*. ☆☆☆☆ **1998 Menetou-Salon $$$**

🍷 **Pelorus** [pe-law-rus] (*Marlborough*, New Zealand) Showy, big, buttery, yeasty, almost Champagnois-style New Zealand sparkling wine from *Cloudy Bay*.

Pemberton (Western Australia) Up-and-coming cooler climate region for more restrained styles of *Chardonnay* and *Pinot Noir; Picardy, Plantagenet* and *Smithbrook* are the names to look out for.

🍷 **Peñaflor** [pen-yah-flaw] (Argentina) Huge, dynamic firm producing increasingly good-value wines. ☆☆☆☆☆ **1998 Malbec Barricas $$$**

Penedés [peh-neh-dehs] (*Catalonia*, Spain) Largest *DOC* of *Catalonia* with varying altitudes, climates and styles ranging from *cava* to still wines pioneered by *Torres* and others, though some not as successfully. The use of *varietals* such as *Cabernet Sauvignon*, *Merlot*, and *Chardonnay* allows more French style winemaking without losing intrinsic Spanish character. Belatedly living up to some of its early promise. White: **95 96 97 98** Red: **85 87** 88 89 90 **91** 93 **94** 95 96 97 98 ***Albet i Noya;*** **Can Feixes;** ***Can Ráfols dels Caus; Freixenet; Cavas Hill; Juve y Camps; Jean Leon; Monistrol; Puig i Roca; Torres.***

🍷 **Penfolds** (*South Australia*) The world's biggest premium wine company with a high-quality range, from Bin 2 to *Grange*. Previously a red wine specialist but now rapidly becoming a skillful producer of still white wines such as the improving Yattarna (good but not yet living up to its supposed role as the "White *Grange*"). Under the same ownership as *Wynns, Seaview, Rouge Homme, Lindemans, Tullochs, Leo Buring, Seppelt*, and now James Halliday's *Coldstream Hills* and *Devil's Lair* in the *Margaret River*. ☆☆☆☆ **1996 Bin 389 Cabernet Shiraz $$;** ☆☆☆☆☆ **1996 128 Coonawarra Shiraz $$$**

🍷 **Penley Estate** (*Coonawarra*, Australia) High-quality *Coonawarra* estate with rich *Chardonnay* and very blackcurranty *Cabernet*. ☆☆☆☆ **1996 Coonawarra Cabernet Sauvignon $$$**

Comte Peraldi [peh-ral-dee] (*Corsica*, France) High-class *Corsican* wine producer, now also making good wine in Romania. ☆☆☆☆ **1995 Dom. Comte Peraldi Ajaccio $$**

Le Pergole Torte [pur-goh-leh taw-teh] (*Tuscany*, Italy) Long-established pure *Sangiovese, oaky Super-Tuscan*. ☆☆☆☆☆ **1995 Montevertine $$**

Periquita [peh-ree-kee-tah] (Portugal) Spicy, tobaccoey grape – and the wine *J.M. da Fonseca* makes from it.

Perlé/Perlant [pehr-lay/lon] (France) Lightly sparkling.

Perlwein [pehrl-vine] (Germany) Sparkling wine.

Pernand-Vergelesses [pehr-non vehr-zhur-less] (*Burgundy*, France) *Commune* producing rather jammy reds but fine whites, including some *Côte d'Or* best buys. White: **85 86** 87 **88** 89 **90 92** 95 96 97 98 Red: **78** 83 **85** 87 **88 89 90** 92 95 96 97 98 **Arnoux; Champy; *Chandon de Briailles; Dubreuil-Fontaine; Germain (Château de Chorey); Jadot; Laleure-Piot; Pavelot; Rapet; Dom. Rollin.***

André Perret (*Rhône*, France) Producer of notable *Condrieu* and some unusually good examples of *St. Joseph*. ☆☆☆☆ **1996 Condrieu Coteau de Chery $$$**

Joseph Perrier [payh-ree-yay] (*Champagne*, France) Family-run producer whose long-lasting elegant *Champagnes* have a heavy *Pinot Noir* influence. ☆☆☆☆ **1990 Cuvée Royale Brut $$$$**

Perrier-Jouët [payh-ree-yay zhoo-way] (*Champagne*, France) Sadly underperforming *Champagne* house which, like *Mumm*, has just been sold by Canadian distillers, Seagram. Sidestep the non-vintage for the genuinely worthwhile – and brilliantly packaged – Belle Epoque prestige cuvée white and rosé sparkling wine. ☆☆☆☆ **1990 Belle Epoque $$$$**

Pesquera [peh-SKEH-ra] (*Ribera del Duero*, Spain) Robert Parker dubbed this the *Ch. Pétrus* of Spain. Well, maybe. I'd say it's a top-class *Tempranillo* often equal to *Vega Sicilia* and the best of *Rioja*. ☆☆☆☆ **1996 Tinto $$**

Pessac-Léognan [peh-sak lay-on-yon] (*Bordeaux*, France) *Graves commune* containing most of the finest châteaux. ***Ch. Fieuzal; Domaine de Chevalier; La Louvière; Haut Brion; Smith-Haut-Laffite.***

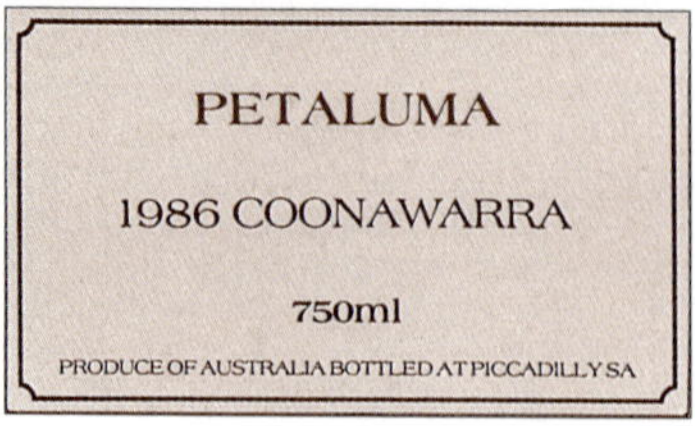

Petaluma [peh-ta-loo-ma] (*Adelaide Hills*, Australia) High-tech creation of *Brian Croser* and role model for other producers in the New World who are interested in combining innovative winemaking with the fruit of individually characterful vineyards. Classy *Chardonnays* from Piccadilly in the *Adelaide Hills, Clare Rieslings* (particularly good *late harvest*) and *Coonawarra* reds. Now owns *Smithbrook* and *Mitchelton*, ☆☆☆☆ **1997 Chardonnay $$$**

Pétillant [pur-tee-yon] Lightly sparkling.

Petit Chablis [pur-tee shab-lee] (*Burgundy*, France) (Theoretically) less fine than plain *Chablis* – though plenty of vineyards that were previously designated as Petit Chablis can now produce wines sold as *Chablis*. Often poor value. 95 96 97 98 ***La Chablisienne.***

Petit Verdot [pur-tee vehr-doh] (*Bordeaux*, France) Spicy, *tannic* variety used in small proportions in red *Bordeaux*, California (rarely) and now as a pure varietal in Australia (*Kingston Estate, Leconfield, Pirramimma*), Italy and Spain (*Marqués de Griñon*). ☆☆☆☆ **1996 Marqués de Griñon Domaine de Valdepusa $$$**

Ch. Petit Village [pur-tee vee-lahzh] (*Pomerol*, *Bordeaux*, France) Classy, intense, blackcurranty-plummy *Pomerol* now under the same ownership as *Ch. Pichon-Longueville*. Worth keeping. **75** 78 79 81 **82** 83 **85** 86 88 89 90 92 **93** 94 95 96 97 98 ☆☆☆☆ **1990 $$$$**

Petite Sirah [peh-teet sih-rah] Spicy red cousin of the Syrah grown in California and Mexico and as *Durif* in the *Midi* and Australia. ***LA Cetto; Carmen; Fetzer; Morris; Parducci; Ridge; Turley.***

Petrolly A not unpleasant overtone often found in mature *Riesling*. Arrives faster in Australia than in Germany.

Ch. Pétrus [pay-trooss] (*Pomerol*, *Bordeaux*, France) Until recently the priciest of all *clarets* (until *le Pin* came along). Voluptuous *Pomerol* hits the target especially well in the US, and is finding a growing market in the Far East. **61** 62 **64** 66 **70 71 75** 76 78 **79** 81 82 83 85 86 88 89 90 92 93 94 95 96 97 98 ☆☆☆☆☆ **1989 $$$$**

Pewsey Vale [pyoo-zee vayl] (*Adelaide Hills*, Australia) Classy, cool-climate wines from winery under the same ownership as *Yalumba*, *Hill-Smith* and *Heggies*. ☆☆☆☆ **1998 Riesling $$**; ☆☆☆☆ **1998 Cabernet Sauvignon $$$**

Ch. de Pez [dur pez] (*St. Estèphe Cru Bourgeois*, *Bordeaux*, France) Fast-improving *St. Estèphe*, especially since its recent purchase by *Louis Roederer*. In good vintages, well worth aging. 78 79 **82** 83 85 **86** 88 89 **90 93** 94 95 96 97 98

Pfalz [*Pfaltz*] (Germany) Formerly known as the *Rheinpfalz*, and before that as the *Palatinate*. Warm, southerly *anbaugebiet* noted for riper, spicier *Riesling*. Currently competing with the *Mosel* for the prize of best of Germany's wine regions. QbA/Kab/Spät: **85** 86 **88 89 90** 91 92 93 94 95 96 97 98 Aus/Beeren/Tba: **83 85** 88 89 90 91 92 93 94 95 97 98 ***Kurt Darting; Lingenfelder; Müller-Cattoir.***

Ch. Phélan-Ségur [fay-lon say-goor] (*St. Estèphe Cru Bourgeois, Bordeaux*, France) A good-value property since the mid-1980s, with ripe, well-made wines. Could do better. 75 **82** 85 88 89 90 92 93 **94** 95 96 97 98

Joseph Phelps (*Napa Valley*, California) Pioneer *Napa* user of *Rhône* varieties (*Syrah* and *Viognier*), and a rare source of *late harvest Riesling*. *Cabernet* is a strength. ☆☆☆☆ **1994 Insignia Napa Valley $$$$**

Philipponnat [fee-lee-poh-nah] (*Champagne*, France) Small producer famous for Clos des Goisses, but also notable for *vintage* and rosé.

Phylloxera Vastatrix [fih-lok-seh-rah] Root-eating louse that wiped out Europe's vines in the 19th century. Foiled by grafting *vinifera* vines onto resistant American *labrusca* rootstock. Pockets of pre-phylloxera and/or ungrafted vines still exist in France (in a *Bollinger* vineyard and on the south coast – the louse hates sand), Portugal (in *Quinta do Noval*'s "Nacional" vineyard), Australia and Chile. Elsewhere, phylloxera recently devastated *Napa Valley* vines planted (despite warnings from French experts) on insufficiently resistant rootstock.

Piave [pee-yah-vay] (*Veneto*, Italy) *DOC* in *Veneto* region, including reds made from a *Bordeaux*-like mix of grapes.

Ch. Pibarnon [pee-bah-non] (*Bandol*, France) Top-class producer of modern *Bandol*. 88 **89 90** 92 93 95 **96** 97 98 ☆☆☆☆☆ 1996 **$$$**

Ch. Pibran [pee-bron] (*Pauillac Cru Bourgeois*, *Bordeaux*, France) Small but high-quality and classically *Pauillac* property. 88 **89** 90 92 94 95 96 97 98

Picardy (*Pemberton*, Western Australia) Impressive new *Pinot Noir* and *Shiraz* specialist by the former winemaker of *Moss Wood*.

Pic St. Loup [peek-sa'-loo] (*Languedoc-Roussillon*, France) Up-and-coming region within the *Coteaux du Languedoc* for *Syrah*-based, *Rhône*-style reds and whites. **Dom. l'Hortus; Mas Bruguière.**

Ch. Pichon-Lalande [pee-shon la-lond] (*Pauillac 2ème Cru Classé, Bordeaux*, France) The new name for Pichon-Longueville-Lalande. Famed *super second* and tremendous success story, thanks to top-class winemaking and the immediate appeal of its unusually high *Merlot* content. A great 1996, but surprizingly a slightly less exciting 1998. **61 66 70 75 78 79 82 83 85 86** 88 89 **90** 91 92 **93 94** 95 96 97 98 ☆☆☆☆ **1989 $$$$**

Ch. Pichon-Longueville [pee-shon long-veel] (*Pauillac 2ème Cru Classé, Bordeaux*, France) New name for Pichon-Longueville-Baron. An underperforming second growth *Pauillac* until its purchase by *AXA* in 1988. Now level with, and sometimes ahead of, *Ch. Pichon-Lalande*, once the other half of the estate. Wines are intense and complex. Les Tourelles, the *second label*, is a good-value alternative. **86** 88 89 90 91 **92 93 94** 95 96 97 98

Picolit [pee-koh-leet] (*Friuli*, Italy) Grape used to make both sweet and dry white wine. *Jermann* makes a good one.

Piedmont/Piemonte [pee-yed-mont/pee-yeh-mon-tay] (Italy) Ancient and modern northwestern region producing old-fashioned, tough *Barolo* and *Barbaresco* and brilliant modern fruit-packed wines. Also makes *Oltrepò Pavese, Asti Spumante* and *Dolcetto d'Alba*. See *Nebbiolo*.

Pieropan [pee-yehr-oh-pan] (*Veneto*, Italy) *Soave*'s top producer, which more or less invented single-vineyard wines here and is still a great exception to the dull *Soave* rule. Lovely almondy wine. ☆☆☆☆ **1998 Vigneto $$**

Pieroth [pee-roth] Huge company whose salesmen visit clients' homes offering wines that are rarely recommended by this or any other critic.

Pierro [pee-yehr-roh] (*Margaret River*, Australia) Small estate producing rich, buttery, *Meursault*-like *Chardonnay*. ☆☆☆☆ **1996 Chardonnay $$$**

Piesport [pees-sport] (*Mosel-Saar-Ruwer*, Germany) Produced in the *grosslage Michelsberg*, a region infamous for dull German wine and bought by people who think themselves above *Liebfraumilch*. Try a single-vineyard – Gunterslay or Goldtröpchen – for something more memorable. QbA/Kab/Spät: **85** 86 **88 89 90** 91 **92 93 94 95** 96 97 98 Aus/Beeren/ Tba: **83 85** 88 89 90 91 **92** 93 **94** 95 96 97 98 ***Reichsgraf von Kesselstadt.***

Pikes (*Clare Valley*, South Australia) Top-class estate with great *Riesling, Shiraz, Sangiovese* and *Sauvignon*. ☆☆☆☆ **1998 Sauvignon Blanc $$**

Jean Pillot [pee-yoh] (*Burgundy*, France) There are three estates called Pillot in *Chassagne-Montrachet*. This one is the best – and makes the best red.

Ch. le Pin [lur pan] (*Pomerol, Bordeaux*, France) Ultra-hyped, small, recently formed estate whose – admittedly delicious – wines sell at increasingly silly prices in the US and the Far East. The forerunner of a string of other similar honey-traps (see *Ch. Valandraud* and *la Mondotte*), and one of the wines that is helping to create a burgeoning trade in forged bottles. **81 82 83 85 86** 87 88 89 90 92 93 94 95 96 97 98 ☆☆☆☆☆ **1990 $$$$**

Pine Ridge (*Napa Valley*, California) Greatly improved *Stag's Leap* producer that is now also making good quality reds on *Howell Mountain*.

Pineau de Charentes [pee-noh dur sha-ront] (*South-West*, France) Fortified wine produced in the Cognac region.

Pingus [pin-goos] (*Ribeiro del Duero*, Spain) Probably the finest wine now being made in this region. Sadly, a large proportion of the great 1995 vintage was lost at sea. ☆☆☆☆☆ **1996 $$$$**

Pinot Blanc / Bianco [pee-noh blon] Rather like *Chardonnay* without all that fruit, and rarely as classy or complex. Fresh, creamy and adaptable. At its best in *Alsace* (Pinot d'Alsace), the *Alto-Adige* in Italy (as *Pinot Bianco*), and in Germany and Austria (as *Weissburgunder*). In California, confusingly, a synonym for *Melon de Bourgogne*.

Pinot Chardonnay (Australia) Misleading name for *Chardonnay*, still used by *Tyrrells*. Don't confuse with *Pinot Noir/Chardonnay* sparkling wine blends such as the excellent *Seaview* and *Yalumba*.

Pinot Gris / Grigio [pee-noh gree] (*Alsace*, France) White grape of uncertain origins, making full, rather heady, spicy wine. Best in *Alsace* (also known as *Tokay d'Alsace*), Italy (as *Pinot Grigio*) and Germany (as *Rülander* or *Grauburgunder*). **Ernst Brun; Bott-Geyl; *Dopff & Irion; Kreydenweiss; Ostertag;* Schleret; Sorg; *Cave de Turckheim; Weinbach (Faller); Zind–Humbrecht*.**

Pinot Meunier [pee-noh-mur-nee-yay] (*Champagne*, France) Dark pink-skinned grape. Plays an unsung but major role in *Champagne*. Can also be used to produce a still varietal wine. **Best's; *Bonny Doon; William Wheeler*.**

Pinot Noir [pee-noh nwahr] Black grape responsible for all red *Burgundy* and in part for white *Champagne*. Also grown in the New World with increasing success in sites whose climate is neither too warm nor too cold. Winemakers need the dedication which might otherwise have destined them for a career in nursing. Buying is like Russian Roulette - once you've got a taste for that complex raspberryish flavor, you'll go on pulling the expensive trigger. See *Oregon, Carneros, Yarra, Santa Barbara, Tasmania, Burgundy*.

Pinotage [pee-noh-tazh] (South Africa) *Pinot Noir* x *Cinsault* cross with a spicy, plummy character, used in South Africa and (now very rarely) New Zealand. Good old examples are brilliant but rare; most taste muddy and rubbery. New winemaking and international demand are making for more exciting wines. **Beyerskloof; Clos Malverne; Fairview; *Grangehurst; Kanonkop; Saxenberg; Simonsig; Warwick*.**

Piper Heidsieck [pi-pur hide-sehk] (*Champagne*, France) Greatly improved *Champagne* made by Daniel Thibaut of *Charles Heidsieck*. The "Rare" is worth looking out for.

Pipers Brook Vineyards (*Tasmania*, Australia) Dr. Andrew Pirie, who has just bought *Heemskerk*, is a pioneering producer of fine *Burgundian Chardonnay, Pinot Noir*, and *Pinot Gris*. Ninth Island, the *second label*, includes an excellent unoaked *Chablis*-like *Chardonnay*. The Pirie sparkling wine is good too. ☆☆☆☆ **1998 Pinot Gris $$$**

Pira [pee-rah] (*Piedmont*, Italy) Chiara Boschis's impressive small *Barolo* estate makes long-lived wines from top-class vineyards.

Producteurs Plaimont [play-mon] (*South-West*, France) Reliable cooperative in *Côtes de St. Mont* producing *Bordeaux*-lookalike reds and whites with some use of local grapes. See also *Pacherenc du Vic-Bilh* and *Madiran*. ☆☆☆ **1997 Vivian Ducorneau VdP Côtes de Gascogne $$**

Plaisir de Merle [play-zeer dur mehrl] (*Paarl*, South Africa) Paul Pontallier of *Ch. Margaux* is helping to make ripe, soft reds and New World-style whites for *Stellenbosch Farmers' Winery* in this new showcase operation. ☆☆☆☆ **1997 Chardonnay $$**

Plantagenet (*Mount Barker*, Western Australia) Good producer of *Chardonnay, Riesling, Cabernet,* and lean *Shiraz* in this increasingly successful region in the south-west corner of Australia. ☆☆☆☆ **1996 Mount Barker Cabernet Sauvignon $$$**

Il Podere dell'Olivos [eel poh-deh-reh del-oh-lee-vohs] (California) Pioneering producer of Italian varietals.

Poggio Antico [pod-zhee-yoh an-tee-koh] (*Tuscany*, Italy) Ultrareliable *Brunello* producer. ☆☆☆☆ **1993 Brunello di Montalcino $$$$**

Pol Roger [pol rod-zhay] (*Champagne*, France) Consistently fine producer, with an unusually subtle non-vintage that improves with keeping. The Cuvée Winston Churchill (named in honor of a faithful fan) is spectacular, and the *Demi-Sec* is a rare treat. ☆☆☆☆☆ **1990 Winston Churchill $$$$**

Poliziano [poh-leet-zee-yah-noh] (*Tuscany*, Italy) Apart from a pack-leading *Vino Nobile di Montepulciano*, this is the place to find the delicious Elegia and Le Stanze *Vini da Tavola*. ☆☆☆☆☆ **1995 Vino Nobile di Montepulciano Vigna Asinone $$$**

Pomerol [pom-meh-rohl] (*Bordeaux*, France) With *St. Emilion*, the *Bordeaux* for lovers of the *Merlot*, which predominates in its rich, soft, plummy wines. *Ch. Pétrus* and *le Pin* are the big names but wines like *Petit Village* and *Clos René* abound. None are cheap because production is often limited to a few thousand cases (in the *Médoc*, 20–40,000 is more common). Quality is far more consistent than in *St. Emilion*. See *Pétrus, Moueix* and individual *châteaux*. 79 81 **82 83 85** 86 **88 89** 90 **93** 94 95 96 97 98

Pomino [poh-mee-noh] (*Tuscany*, Italy) Small *DOC* within *Chianti Rufina;* virtually a monopoly for *Frescobaldi* who make a delicious buttery unwooded white *Pinot Bianco/Chardonnay*, the oaky-rich Il Benefizio and a tasty *Sangiovese/Cabernet*. ☆☆☆ **1996 Pomino Rosso $$**

Pommard [pom-mahr] (*Burgundy*, France) Very variable quality *commune*, theoretically with a higher proportion of old vines, making slow-to-mature, then solid and complex reds. 78 **85** 86 87 **88 89 90** 92 93 94 95 96 97 98 ***Comte Armand; Jean-Marc Boillot; Girardin; Dominique Laurent; Leroy; Château de Meursault; de Montille; Mussy; Dom. de Pousse d'Or.***

Pommery [pom-meh-ree] (*Champagne*, France) Returned-to-form big-name with rich full-flavored style. The top-label Louise Pommery white and rosé are tremendous. ☆☆☆☆☆ **1988 Cuvée Louise $$$$**

Pongràcz [pon-gratz] (South Africa) Brand name for the *Bergkelder*'s (excellent) *Cap Classique* sparkling wine. ☆☆☆☆ **Cap Classique $$**

Dom. Ponsot [pon-soh] (*Burgundy*, France) Top-class estate noted for *Clos de la Roche, Chambertin* and (rare) white *Morey-St.-Denis*. More affordable is the excellent *Gevrey*. ☆☆☆☆ **1995 Clos de la Roche $$$**

Ch. Pontet-Canet [pon-tay ka-nay] (*Pauillac 5ème Cru Classé*, *Bordeaux*, France) Rich, concentrated, up-and-coming *Pauillac* benefitting since the early 1980s from the dedicated ambition of its owners who also have *Lafon-Rochet*. **82** 83 85 **86** 88 89 90 91 92 **93 94** 95 96 97 98

Ponzi [pon-zee] (*Oregon*, US) The ideal combination: a maker of good *Pinot Noir, Chardonnay* and even better beer. ☆☆☆☆ **1994 Pinot Noir Reserve $$$**

Port (*Douro*, Portugal) Fortified wine made in the upper *Douro* valley. Comes in several styles; see *Tawny, Ruby, LBV, Vintage, Crusted* and *White port*.

Viña Porta [veen-yah por-ta] (*Rapel*, Chile) Dynamic winery that specializes in juicy *Cabernet* and *Merlot*. The *Chardonnay* is good too.

Ch. Potelle (*Napa Valley*, California) *Mount Veeder* winery that won fame when its stylish wines were served at the White House. Great Zinfandel.

Ch. Potensac [po-ton-sak] (*Médoc Cru Bourgeois, Bordeaux*, France) Under the same ownership as the great *Léoville-Las-Cases*, and offering a more affordable taste of the winemaking that goes into that wine.

Pouilly-Fuissé [poo-yee fwee-say] (*Burgundy*, France) Variable white often sold at vastly inflated prices. Pouilly-Vinzelles, Pouilly-Loché, and other *Mâconnais* wines are often better value, though top-class Pouilly-Fuissé from producers like *Ch. Fuissé*, Dom. Noblet, or Dom. Ferret can compete with the best of the *Côte d'Or*. **88** 89 **90 92 95** 96 97 98 ***Barraud; Corsin***; **Ferret;** ***Ch. Fuissé;*** **Lapierre; Noblet; Philibert;** ***Verget.***

🍷 **Pouilly-Fumé** [poo-yee foo-may] (*Loire*, France) Potentially ultra-elegant *Sauvignon Blanc* with classic gooseberry fruit and "smoky" overtones derived from flint ("*silex*") subsoil. Like *Sancerre*, rarely repays cellaring. See *Ladoucette* and *Didier Dagueneau*. **94** 95 96 97

🍷 **Ch. Poujeaux** [poo-joh] (*Moulis Cru Bourgeois*, *Bordeaux*, France) Up-and-coming plummy-blackcurranty wine. **79 82 83 85 86** 88 89 90 91 92 93 94 **95 96** 97 98 ☆☆☆ **1993 $$$**

Pourriture noble [poo-ree-toor nohbl] (France) See *botrytis cinerea* or *noble rot*.

🍷 **Dom. de la Pousse d'Or** [poos-daw] (*Burgundy*, France) One of the top estates in *Volnay*. (The *Pommard* and *Santenay* wines are good too.) ☆☆☆☆ **1995 Volnay Clos de la Bousse d'Or $$$$**

Prädikat [pray-dee-ket] (Germany) As in Qualitätswein mit Prädikat (*QmP*), the (supposedly) higher quality level for German and Austrian wines, indicating a greater degree of natural ripeness.

🍷 **Franz Prager** [prah-gur] (*Wachau*, Austria) Top class producer of a wide range of impressive *Grüner-Veltliners*, and, now, *Rieslings*.

Precipitation The creation of a harmless deposit, usually of *tartrate* crystals, in white wine, which the Germans romantically call "diamonds."

Premier Cru [prur-mee-yay kroo] In *Burgundy*, indicates wines that fall between village and *Grand Cru* quality. Some major communes such as *Beaune* and *Nuits-St.-Georges* have no *Grand Cru*. Wine simply labeled Meursault Premier Cru, for example is probably a blend from two or more vineyards.

🍷 **Premières Côtes de Blaye** See *Côtes de Blaye*

🍷 **Premières Côtes de Bordeaux** [prur-mee-yay koht dur bohr-doh] (*Bordeaux*, France) Up-and-coming riverside *appellation* for reds and (often less interestingly) sweet whites. Whites: 76 **83** 85 **86 88 89 90 95** 96 **97** 98 ***Carsin;*** **Grand-Mouëys;** ***Reynon.***

Prestige Cuvée [koo-vay] (*Champagne*, France) The top wine of a *Champagne* house. Expensive and elaborately packaged. Some, like *Dom Pérignon*, are brilliant; others less so. Other best-known examples include *Veuve Clicquot's* Grand Dame and *Roederer's* Cristal.

🍷 **Preston Vineyards** (*Sonoma*, California) Winery making the most of *Dry Creek Zinfandel* and *Syrah*. A white Meritage blend is pretty good too but the *Viognier* needs more work.

🍷 **Dom. Jacques Prieur** [pree-yur] (*Burgundy*, France) Estate with fine vineyards. Increasingly impressive since takeover by *Antonin Rodet*.

🍷 **Ch. Prieuré-Lichine** [pree-yur-ray lih-sheen] (*Margaux 4ème Cru Classé*, *Bordeaux*, France) Recently (1999) sold *château* making reliable if rarely subtle blackcurranty wine which benefits from input by *Michel Rolland*. One of the only *châteaux* with a gift shop and a helicopter landing pad on its roof. 70 **82 83** 85 **86** 88 89 90 **93 94** 95 96 97 98

Primeur [pree-mur] (France) New wine, e.g. *Beaujolais* Primeur (the same as *Beaujolais Nouveau*) or, as in *en primeur*, wine which is sold while still in barrel. Here in the US, known as "Futures."

🍷 **Primitivo** [pree-mih-tee-voh dee man-doo-ra] (*Puglia*, Italy) Another name for the *Zinfandel*.

Primo Estate [pree-moh] (South Australia) Extraordinarily imaginative venture among the fruit farms of the Adelaide Plains. Passion-fruity *Colombard*, sparkling *Shiraz*, and *Bordeaux* blends made *Amarone*-style, using grapes partially dried in the sun. The olive oil is good too. ☆☆☆☆ **1997 Joseph Cabernet Merlot $$$**

Prinz zu Salm-Dalberg [zoo sahlm dal-burg] (*Nahe*, Germany) Historic but innovative producer with successful red *Spätburgunder* and (especially) *Scheurebe*.

Priorato [pree-yaw-rah-toh] (*Catalonia*, Spain) Traditionally, hefty alcoholic reds and (rare) whites from *Cariñena* and *Garnacha* grapes grown in a very warm region. New-Wave producers are bringing real class now with lighter modern reds. ***Clos Mogador*; Mas Martinet; *Alvaro Palacios;* Clos i Terrasses; Scala Dei; Vilella de la Cartoixa.**

Propriétaire (Récoltant) [pro-pree-yeh-tehr ray-kohl-ton] (France) Vineyard owner-manager.

Prosecco di Conegliano-Valdobbiàdene [proh-sek-koh dee coh-nay-lee-anoh val-doh-bee-yah-day-nay] (*Veneto*, Italy) Soft, slightly earthy, dry and sweet sparkling wine made from the *Prosecco* grape. Less boisterous and fruity than *Asti Spumante*. Drink young. **Bisol; Bortolin; Canevel; Produttori de Valdobbiadene; Ruggeri; Zardetto.**

Provence [proh-vons] (France) Southern region producing fast-improving wine with a number of minor ACs. Rosé de Provence should be dry and fruity with a hint of peppery spice. See *Bandol, Coteaux d'Aix en-Provence, Palette*.

J.J. Prüm [proom] (*Mosel-Saar-Ruwer*, Germany) Top *Riesling* producer with fine *Wehlen*er vineyards. ☆☆☆☆ **1997 Wehlener Sonnenuhr Riesling Auslese $$$**

Dom. Michel Prunier [proo-nee-yay] (*Burgundy*, France) Best estate in *Auxey-Duresses*. ☆☆☆☆ **1995 Premier Cru Clos du Val $$$**

Alfredo Prunotto [proo-not-toh] (*Piedmont*, Italy) Good *Barolo* producer recently bought by *Antinori*. ☆☆☆☆ **1993 Barolo Cannubi $$$**

Puglia [poo-lee-yah] (Italy) Hot region, now making pretty cool wines, thanks partly to *flying winemakers* like *Kym Milne*. Also see *Salice Salentino* and *Copertino*.

Puiatti [pwee-yah-tee] (*Friuli-Venezia Giulia*, Italy) Producer of some of Italy's most stylish *Chardonnay, Pinot Bianco, Pinot Grigio*, and *Tocai Friulano*. The Archetipi wines are the cream of the crop.

Puisseguin St. Emilion [pwees-gan san tay-mee-lee-yon] (*Bordeaux*, France) Satellite of *St. Emilion* making similar, *Merlot*-dominant wines which are often far better value. **82 83 85** 86 **88 89** 90 94 95 97 98

Puligny-Montrachet [poo-lee-nee mon-ra-shay] (*Burgundy*, France) Aristocratic white *Côte d'Or commune* that shares the *Montrachet* vineyard with *Chassagne*. Should be complex buttery *Chardonnay* with a touch more elegance than *Meursault*. *Carillon, Sauzet, Ramonet, Drouhin,* and *Dom. Leflaive* are all worth their money. **85 86 88** 89 **90 92** 95 96 97 98 ***D'Auvenay; Carillon; Chavy; Drouhin; Leflaive (Olivier & Domaine);*** **Marquis de Laguiche; Ch de Puligny-Montrachet;** ***Ramonet; Sauzet.***

Putto [poot-toh] (Italy) See *Chianti*.

Puttonyos [poot-TOH-nyos] (*Tokaji*, Hungary) The measure of sweetness (from 1 to 6) of *Tokaji*. The number indicates the number of puttonyos (baskets) of sweet *aszú* paste that are added to the base wine.

Ch. Puygeraud [Pwee-gay-roh] (*Bordeaux*, France) Perhaps the best property on the *Côtes de Francs*. 85 86 88 **89** 90 **94 95** 96 97 98

Pyrenees (*Victoria*, Australia) One of the classiest regions in *Victoria*, thanks to the efforts of *Taltarni* and *Dalwhinnie*. White: **92 94 95 96** 97 98 Red: **85 86 87 88 90 91 92 94 95** 96 97 98

Pyrus [pi-rus] (Australia) See *Lindemans*. ☆☆☆☆ **1994 Pyrus $$$**

Q

QbA (Germany) Qualitätswein bestimmter Anbaugebiet: [kvah-lih-tayts-vine behr-shtihmt-tuhr ahn-bow-geh-beet] Basic-quality German wine from one of the 11 ***anbaugebiet***, e.g. *Rheinhessen*.

QmP (Germany) Qualitätswein mit Prädikat: [pray-dee-kaht] *QbA* wine (supposedly) with "special qualities." The QmP blanket designation is broken into five sweetness rungs, from *Kabinett* to *Trockenbeerenauslese* plus *Eiswein*.

Quady [kway-dee] (*Central Valley*, California) Quirky producer of the wittily named "Starboard" (hint: serve it in a decanter), *Orange Muscat* Essencia (great with chocolate), *Black Muscat* Elysium, low-alcohol Electra, and now, the brilliant Vya Sweet Vermouth. ☆☆☆☆ **Quady's Starboard Batch 90 $$$**

Quarles Harris [kwahrls] (*Douro*, Portugal) Underrated *port* producer with a fine 1980 and 1983. ☆☆☆☆ **1983 Vintage Port $$$**

Quarts de Chaume [kahr dur shohm] (*Loire*, France) Luscious but light sweet wines, uncloying, aging beautifully, from the *Coteaux du Layon*. The *Dom. des Baumard* is exceptional. Sweet white: **76** 83 **85** 86 **88 89** 90 **94** 95 96 97 98 **Dom des Baumard;** ***Pierre Soulez.***

Quilceda Creek [kwil-see-dah] (*Washington State*, US) Producer of one of the best, most blackcurranty *Cabernets* in the Northwest.

Quincy [kan-see] (*Loire*, France) Dry *Sauvignon*, lesser-known and sometimes good alternative to *Sancerre* or *Pouilly-Fumé*. **Joseph Mellot.**

Quinta [keen-ta] (Portugal) Vineyard or estate, particularly in the *Douro*, where "single Quinta" ***vintage ports*** are increasingly being taken as seriously as the big-name blends. See *Crasto, Vesuvio* and *de la Rosa*.

Guiseppe Quintarelli [keen-ta-reh-lee] (*Veneto*, Italy) Old-fashioned *Recioto*-maker producing some of the quirkiest, most sublime *Valpolicella*. Try the more affordable Molinara. ☆☆☆☆☆ **1995 Molinara $$**

Quivira (*Sonoma*, California) Great *Dry Creek* producer of intense *Zinfandel* and *Syrah* and a deliciously clever *Rhône*-meets-California blend that includes both varieties.

Qupé [kyoo-pay] (*Central Coast*, California) Run by one of the founders of *Au Bon Climat*, this *Santa Barbara* winery produces brilliant *Syrah* and *Rhône*-style whites. ☆☆☆☆ **1996 Hillside Select Syrah $$$**

R

Ch. Rabaud Promis [rrah-boh prraw-mee] (*Sauternes Premier Cru Classé, Bordeaux*, France) Under-performing until 1986; now making top-class wines. **83 85 86 87 88 89 90 95** 96 97 98 ☆☆☆☆☆ **1990 $$$**

Racking The drawing off of wine from its *lees* into a clean cask or vat.

A Rafanelli [ra-fur-nel-lee] (*Sonoma*, California) Great Dry River winery with great Cabernet Sauvignon. The *Zinfandel* is the jewel in the crown though. ☆☆☆☆ **1995 Zinfandel $$$**

Olga Raffault [ra-foh] (*Loire*, France) There are several Raffaults in *Chinon*; this is the best – and the best source of some of the longest-lived examples of this *appellation*.

Raïmat [ri-mat] (*Catalonia*, Spain) Innovative *Codorníu*-owned winery in the *Costers del Segre* region. *Merlot*, a *Cabernet/Merlot* blend called Abadia and *Tempranillo* are interesting and *Chardonnay* – both still and sparkling – are good. ☆☆☆☆ **1994 Cabernet Sauvignon Mas Castell $$**

Rainwater (*Madeira*, Portugal) Light dry style of *Madeira* popular in the US. ☆☆☆ **Berry Bros & Rudd's Selected Rainwater $$**

Ch. Ramage-la-Batisse [ra-mazh la ba-teess] (*Haut-Médoc Cru Bourgeois, Bordeaux*, France) Good-value wine from St. Laurent, close to *Pauillac*.

Ramitello [ra-mee-tel-loh] (*Molise*, Italy) Spicy-fruity reds and creamy citric whites produced by di Majo Norante in Biferno on the Adriatic coast.

Adriano Ramos Pinto [rah-mosh pin-toh] (*Douro*, Portugal) Family-run winery that belongs to *Roederer. Colheita tawnies* are a delicious specialty, but the *vintage* wines and *single quintas* are good too.

Dom. Ramonet [ra-moh-nay] (*Burgundy*, France) Supreme *Chassagne-Montrachet* estate with top-flight *Montrachet, Bâtard* and *Bienvenues-Bâtard-Montrachet* and fine complex *Premiers Crus*. Pure class; worth waiting for too. ☆☆☆☆☆ **1995 Bâtard-Montrachet $$$$.**

Castello dei Rampolla [kas-teh-lohday-ee ram-poh-la] (*Tuscany*, Italy) Good *Chianti*-producer whose wines need time to soften. The berryish Sammarco *Vino da Tavola* is also impressive.

Rancio [ran-see-yoh] Term for the peculiar yet prized *oxidized* flavor of certain fortified wines, particularly in France (e.g. *Banyuls*) and Spain.

Randersacker [ran-dehr-sak-kur] (*Franken*, Germany) One of the most successful homes of the *Sylvaner*, especially when made by Weingut Juliuspital.

Rapel [ra-pel] (*Central Valley*, Chile) Important subregion of the *Central Valley*, especially for reds. Includes *Colchagua* and *Cachapoal*.

Rapitalà [ra-pih-tah-la] (*Sicily*, Italy) Estate producing a fresh, peary white wine from a blend of local grapes.

Kent Rasmussen (*Carneros*, California) One of California's too-small band of truly inventive winemakers, producing great *Burgundy*-like *Pinot Noir* and *Chardonnay* and Italianate *Sangiovese* and *Dolcetto*. ☆☆☆☆ **1997 Chardonnay $$$**

Rasteau [ras-stoh] (*Rhône*, France) Southern village producing peppery reds with rich, berry fruit. The fortified *Muscat* can be good too. Red: **88** 89 **90 95 96** 97 98 **Bressy-Masson; Rabasse-Charavin; La Soumade.**

Renato Ratti [rah-tee] (*Piedmont*, Italy) One of the finest, oldest producers of *Barolo*. ☆☆☆☆ **1993 Barolo $$$**

Rauenthal [row-en-tahl-tee] (*Rheingau*, Germany) *Georg Breur* is the most interesting producer in this beautiful village. Other names to look for include *Schloss Schonborn* and *Schloss Rheinhartshausen*.

Ch. Rauzan-Ségla [roh-zon say-glah] (*Margaux 2ème Cru Classé*, *Bordeaux*, France) For a long time an under-performing *Margaux*. Now, since its purchase by Chanel in 1994, one of the best buys in *Bordeaux*. 70 82 **83** 85 **86** 88 89 90 91 92 **93 94** 95 96 97 98

Ch. Rauzan-Gassies [roh-zon ga-sees] (*Margaux 2ème Cru Classé*, *Bordeaux*, France) Compared to *Rauzan-Ségla* its neighbor, this property is still underperforming magnificently.

Jean-Marie Raveneau [rav-noh] (*Burgundy*, France) The long-established king of Chablis, with impeccably made *Grand* and *Premier Cru* wines that last brilliantly. ☆☆☆☆☆ **1995 Chablis Montée de Tonnerre $$$**

Ravenswood (*Sonoma Valley*, California) Brilliant *Zinfandel*-maker whose individual-vineyard wines are wonderful examples of this variety. The *Merlots* and *Cabernet* are fine too. ☆☆☆☆ **1995 Zinfandel $$$**

Ravenswood (South Australia) Label confusingly adopted by *Hollick* for its top *Coonawarra* reds (no relation to the above entry).

Raventos i Blanc [ra-vayn-tos ee blank] (*Catalonia*, Spain) Josep Raventos' ambition is to produce the best sparkling wine in Spain, adding *Chardonnay* to local varieties. ☆☆☆☆ **Cava l'Hereu $$$**

Ch. Rayas [rih-yas] (*Rhône*, France) The only chance to taste *Châteauneuf-du-Pape* made solely from the *Grenache*. Pricy but good.

Raymond (*Napa Valley*, California) Tasty, intense *Cabernets* and *Chardonnays*.

Ch. Raymond-Lafon [ray-mon la-fon] (*Sauternes*, *Bordeaux*, France) Very good small producer whose wines deserve keeping. **75 80** 82 **83** 85 **86 89** 90 92 94 95 96 97 98

Ch. de Rayne-Vigneau [rayn VEEN-yoh] (*Sauternes Premier Cru Classé*, *Bordeaux*, France) *Sauternes* estate, located at *Bommes*, producing a rich complex wine. 85 86 88 89 90 92 94 95 96 97 98 ☆☆☆☆ **1990 $$$$**

RD (*Champagne*, France) Récemment Dégorgée – a term invented by *Bollinger* for their delicious *vintage Champagne*, which has been allowed a longer-than-usual period (as much as fifteen years) on its *lees*.

Ignacio Recabarren [ig-na-see-yoh reh-ka-ba-ren] (Chile) Superstar wine-maker and *Casablanca* pioneer.

Recioto [ray-chee-yo-toh] (*Veneto*, Italy) Sweet or dry alcoholic wine made from semi-dried, ripe grapes. Usually associated with *Valpolicella* and *Soave*.

Récoltant-manipulant (RM) [ray-kohl-ton ma-nih-poo-lon] (*Champagne*, France) Individual winegrower and blender, identified by mandatory RM number on label.

Récolte [ray-kohlt] (France) Vintage, literally 'harvest'.

Dom de la Rectorie [rehc-toh-ree] (*Languedoc-Roussillon*, France) One of the two top names (with *Mas Blanc*) in *Banyuls*, and also a brilliant producer of *Collioure*.

🍷 **Redman** (*South Australia*) Improved *Coonawarra* estate with intense reds. ☆☆☆☆ **1996 Cabernet Sauvignon $$**

🍷 **Redwood Valley Estate** See *Seifried.*

Refosco [re-fos-koh] [(*Friuli-Venezia Giulia*, Italy) Red grape and its dry and full-bodied *DOC* wine. Benefits from aging.

🍷 **Regaleali** [ray-ga-lay-ah-lee] (*Sicily*, Italy) Ambitious aristocratic estate, using local varieties to produce *Sicily's* most serious wines. ☆☆☆☆ **1995 Rosso del Conte Tasca d'Almerita $$$**

Régisseur [rey-jee-sur] (*Bordeaux*, France) In *Bordeaux*, the cellar-master.

🍷 **Régnié** [ray-nyay] (*Burgundy*, France) Once sold as *Beaujolais Villages,* Régnié now has to compete with *Chiroubles, Chénas* and the other *crus*. It is mostly like an amateur competing against pros. Fortunately for *Régnié,* those pros often aren't on great form. *Duboeuf* makes a typical example. 90 **91** 93 94 95 96 97 98 ***Duboeuf;* Dubost; Piron; Sapin; Trichard.**

🍷 **Reguengos** (*Alentejo*, Portugal) Richly flavorsome reds pioneered by Esporão and the Reguengos de Monsaraz cooperative.

Reichensteiner [rike-en-sti-ner] Recently developed white grape, popular in England (and Wales).

🍷 **Reif Estate Winery** [reef] (*Ontario*, Canada) Impressive *icewine* specialist. ☆☆☆☆ **1997 Vidal Icewine $$$$**

🍷 **Remelluri** [ray-may-yoo-ree] (*Rioja*, Spain) For most modernists, this is the nearest *Rioja* has got to a top-class, small-scale organic estate. Wines are more serious (and *tannic*) than most, but they're fuller in flavor too and they're built to last. ☆☆☆☆ **1996 Rioja $$**

Remuage [reh-moo-wazh] (*Champagne*, France) Part of the *méthode champenoise,* the gradual turning and tilting of bottles so that the yeast deposit collects in the neck ready for *dégorgement.*

Reserva [ray-sehr-vah] (Spain) Wine aged for a period specified by the relevant *DO:* usually one year for reds and six months for whites and pinks.

Réserve [reh-surv] (France) Legally meaningless, as in "Réserve Personelle," but implying a wine selected and given more age.

Residual sugar Term for wines which have retained grape sugar not converted to *alcohol* by yeasts during fermentation. In France 4 grams per liter is the threshold. In the US, the figure is 5 and many so-called "dry" white wines contain as much as 10 and some supposedly dry red Zinfandels definitely have more than a trace of sweetness. New Zealand *Sauvignons* are rarely bone dry, but their *acidity* balances and conceals any residual sugar.

🍷 **Weingut Balthasar Ress** [bul-ta-zah rress] (*Rheingau*, Germany) Good producer in *Hattenheim*, blending delicacy with concentration. ☆☆☆☆ **1996 Hattenheimer Riesling Qualitätswein Halbtrocken $$$**

Retsina [ret-see-nah] (Greece) Wine made the way the ancient Greeks used to make it – resinating it with pine to keep it from spoiling. Today, it's an acquired taste for non-vacationing, non-Greeks. Pick the freshest examples you can find (though this isn't easy when labels mention no vintage).

Reuilly [rur-yee] (*Loire*, France) (Mostly) white *AC* for dry *Sauvignons*, good-value, if sometimes rather earthy alternatives to nearby *Sancerre* and *Pouilly-Fumé* and spicy *Pinot* rosé. ***Henri Beurdin.***

Rex Hill Vineyards (*Oregon*, US) Greatly improved *Pinot* specialist.

Chateau Reynella [ray-nel-la] (*McLaren Vale*, Australia) *BRL Hardy* subsidiary, mastering both reds and whites. ☆☆☆☆ **1996 Basket-Pressed Cabernet Sauvignon-Merlot $$**

Ch. Reynon [ray-non] (*Premier Côtes de Bordeaux*, France) Fine red and especially recommendable white wines from *Denis Dubourdieu*.

Rheingau [rine-gow] (Germany) Traditional home of the finest *Rieslings* of the 11 *Anbaugebiete*, but now often overshadowed by the *Pfalz* and *Mosel*. There are still great things to be found, however. QbA/Kab/Spät: **85** 86 **88 89 90** 92 93 94 95 96 97 98 Aus/Beeren/Tba: **83 85** 88 89 90 92 93 94 95 96 97 98 ***Künstler; Balthasar Ress; Domdechant Werner'sches;*** **HH Eser.**

Rheinhessen [rine-hehs-sen] (Germany) Largest of the 11 *anbaugebiete*, now well known for *Liebfraumilch* and *Niersteiner*. Fewer than one vine in 20 is now *Riesling*; throughout the region, easier-to-grow varieties, and lazy cooperative wineries prevail. Pick and choose to get the good stuff. Keller is a star. QbA/Kab/Spät: **85** 86 **88 89 90** 91 **92 93** 94 95 96 97 98 Aus/Beeren/Tba: **83 85 88 89 90** 91 92 93 94 95 96 97 98 ***Balbach;*** **Keller;** ***Gunderloch.***

Rhône [rohn] (France) Fast-improving, exciting, packed with the newly sexy *Grenache, Syrah* and *Viognier varietal* wines. See *St. Joseph, Crozes-Hermitage, Hermitage, Condrieu, Côtes du Rhône, Châteauneuf-du-Pape, Tavel, Lirac, Gigondas, Ch. Grillet, Beaumes de Venise*. White: **88 89 90** 91 **94** 95 96 97 98 Northern Rhône Red: **76 78 82 83 85 88** 89 90 91 95 96 Southern Rhône Red: **78 82 83 85 88** 89 **90 95** 96 97 98

Rias Baixas [ree-yahs bi-shahs] (*Galicia*, Spain) The place to find spicy *Albariño*. **Lagar de Cervera; Pazo de Barrantes; Santiago Ruiz; Valdamor.**

Ribatejo [ree-bah-tay-joh] (Portugal) *DO* area north of Lisbon where *Peter Bright* and the cooperatives are beginning to make highly commercial white and red wine, but traditional *Garrafeiras* are worth watching out for too.

Ribera del Duero [ree-bay-rah del doo-way-roh] (Spain) Potentially the region to watch in Spain for good reds. Unfortunately, despite the established success of *Vega Sicilia* and of producers like *Pesquera, Arroyo*, and *Alion*, there is still far too much poor winemaking. 82 **83 85 87** 89 90 91 92 94 95 96 97 98 **Arroyo; Pago de Carraovejas; Balbas;** ***Pesquera; Pedrosa; Pingus;*** **Hermanos Sastre; Valtravieso;** ***Vega Sicilia.***

Dom. Richeaume [ree-shohm] (*Provence*, France) Dynamic producer of good, earthy, long-lived, organic *Cabernet* and *Syrah*. Sadly, as with many other smaller organic wineries, quality can vary from bottle to bottle. Recommendable, nonetheless. ☆☆☆☆ **1996 Cuvée Columelle Rouge $$$**

Richebourg [reesh-boor] (*Burgundy*, France) Top-class *Grand Cru* vineyard just outside *Vosne-Romanée* with a recognizable floral-plummy style. 76 **78** 79 **80** 82 83 **85** 86 87 **88 89 90** 92 93 94 95 96 97 98 ***Grivot; Anne Gros; Leroy;*** **Méo-Camuzet; D&D Mugneret;** ***Noëllat; Romanée-Conti.***

Richou [ree-shoo] (*Loire*, France) Fine *Anjou* producer with reliable reds and whites and fine, affordable, sweet whites from Coteaux de l'Aubance.

Weingut Max Ferd Richter [rikh-tur] (*Mosel-Saar-Ruwer*, Germany) Excellent producer of long-lived concentrated-yet-elegant *Mosel Riesling*s from high-quality vineyards. The *cuvée* Constantin is the unusually successful dry wine, while at the other end of the scale, the *eisweins* are sublime. ☆☆☆☆☆ **1996 Brauneberger Juffer Riesling Kabinet $$$**

John Riddoch (South Australia) Classic *Wynn's Coonawarra* red. One of Australia's best and longest-lasting wines. (Not to be confused with the wines that *Katnook Estate* sells under its own "Riddoch" label.)

Ridge Vineyards (*Santa Cruz*, California) Paul Draper, and Ridge's hilltop *Santa Cruz* and *Sonoma* vineyards, consistently produce some of California's very finest *Zinfandel, Cabernet, Mataro,* and *Chardonnay*. ☆☆☆☆☆ **1996 Lytton Springs $$$$**

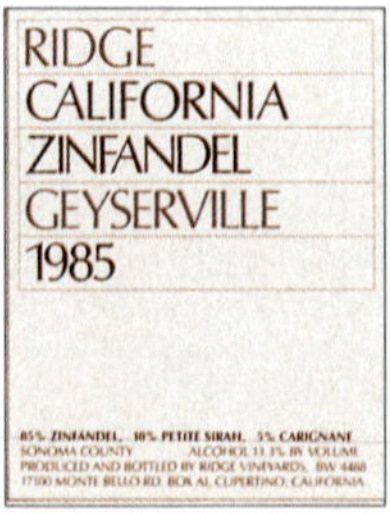

Riecine [ree-eh-chee-nay] (*Tuscany*, Italy) Modern estate with fine *Chiantis* and an even more impressive la Gioia *Vino da Tavola*. ☆☆☆☆ **1995 Chianti Classico Riserva $$$**

Riesling [reez-ling] The noble grape responsible for Germany's finest offerings, ranging from light, floral, everyday wines, to the delights of *botrytis*-affected sweet wines which retain their freshness for decades. Reaching its zenith in the superbly balanced racy wines of the *Mosel*, and the richer offerings from the *Rheingau*, it also performs well in *Alsace*, California, South Africa, and Australia. Watch out for the emergence of the *Wachau* region as a leader of the Austrian *Riesling* pack.

Riesling Italico See *Italian Riesling*, etc.

Ch. Rieussec [ree-yur-sek] (*Sauternes Premier Cru Classé, Bordeaux*, France) Fantastically rich and concentrated *Sauternes*, often deep in color and generally at the head of the pack chasing *d'Yquem*. Now owned by the Rothschilds of *Lafite*. R de Rieussec is the unexceptional dry white wine. **75** 79 82 **83 85 86** 88 89 90 92 93 94 95 **96** 97 98

Rioja [ree-ok-hah] (Spain) Spain's best-known wine region is split into three parts. The Alta produces the best wines, followed by the Alavesa, while the Baja is by far the largest. Most Riojas are blends made by large *bodegas* using grapes grown in two or three of the regions. Small *Bordeaux*- and *Burgundy*-style estates are rare, thanks to restrictive Spanish rules which require wineries to store unnecessarily large quantities of wine. Things are happening in the vineyards, however, including plantings of "experimenta"' *Cabernet* alongside the traditional *Tempranillo* and lesser-quality *Garnacha*. Such behavior breaks all sorts of local rules – as does the irrigation which is also now in evidence – but is already paying off for producers like *Martinez Bujanda*. With luck, this kind of innovative thinking will help the region as a whole to live up to its reputation. Reds: **79 80 81** 82 **83 85 87** 89 90 91 92 94 95 ***Amezola de la Mora; Ardanza; Artadi; Baron de Ley; Berberana;*** **Breton;** ***Campillo; Campo Viejo; Contino; El Coto; Lopez de Heredia; Marqués de Griñon; Marqués de Murrieta; Marqués de Riscal;*** **Marqués de Vargas;** ***Martinez Bujanda; Montecillo;*** **Ondarre;** ***Palacio; Remelluri; La Rioja Alta;*** **Riojanos.**

La Rioja Alta [ree-ok-hah ahl-ta] (*Rioja*, Spain) Of all the big companies in *Rioja*, this is the name to remember. Its Viña Ardanza, Reserva 904, and (rarely produced) Reserva 890 are all among the most reliable and recommendable wines in the region. ☆☆☆ **1990 Viña Ardanza Reserva $$$**

Dom. Daniel Rion [ree-yon] (*Burgundy*, France) Patrice Rion produces impeccably made modern *Nuits-St.-Georges* and *Vosne-Romanées*. ☆☆☆☆ **1992 Nuits-St-Georges Premier Cru Les Vignes Rondes $$$**

Ripasso [ree-pas-soh] (*Veneto*, Italy) Method whereby newly made *Valpolicella* is partially refermented in vessels recently vacated by *Recioto* and *Amarone*. *Ripasso* wines made in this way are richer, alcoholic, and raisiny. Increases the *alcohol* and *body* of the wine. ***Tedeschi; Quintarelli; Masi.***

Marqués de Riscal [ris-KAHL] (*Rioja*, Spain) Historic *Rioja* name now back on form thanks to more modern winemaking for both reds and whites. The Baron de Chirel is the recently launched top wine.

Riserva [ree-ZEHR-vah] (Italy) *DOC* wines aged for a specified number of years – often an unwelcome term on labels of wines like *Bardolino*, which are usually far better drunk young.

Rivaner [rih-VAH-nur] (Germany) The name used for *Müller-Thurgau* (a cross between *Riesling* and *Sylvaner*) in parts of Germany and *Luxembourg*.

Rivera [ree-vay-ra] (*Puglia*, Italy) One of the new wave of producers who are turning the southern region of *Puglia* into a source of interesting wines. The red Riserva il Falcone is the star wine here.

Riverina [rih-vur-ee-na] (*New South Wales*, Australia) Irrigated *New South Wales* region which produces basic-to-good wine, much of which ends up in "*South-East Australian*" blends. *Late harvest Semillons* can, however, be surprisingly spectacular. ***Cranswick Estate.***

Rivesaltes [reev-zalt] (*Languedoc-Roussillon*, France) Fortified dessert wine of both colors. The white made from the *Muscat* is lighter and more lemony than *Beaumes de Venise*, while the *Grenache* red is like liquid Christmas pudding and ages wonderfully. ***Cazes;* Ch. de Corneilla; Força Réal; Ch. de Jau; Sarda-Malet.**

Riviera Ligure di Ponente [reev-ee-yeh-ra lee-goo-ray dee poh-nen-tay] (*Liguria*, Italy) Little-known northwestern region, close to Genoa, where local grapes like the *Vermentino* produce light aromatic reds and whites.

Robertson (South Africa) Warm area where new-wave *Chardonnays* and *Sauvignons* are grabbing the spotlight from the *Muscats* that used to be the region's pride. ***Graham Beck;* Springfield; *Robertson Winery; Van Loveren;* Weltevrede.**

Rocca delle Macie [ro-ka del leh mah-chee-yay] (*Tuscany*, Italy) Reliable if unspectacular *Chianti* producer.

La Roche aux Moines [rosh oh mwahn] See *Nicolas Joly*.

Joe Rochioli [roh-kee-yoh-lee] (*Sonoma*, California) Brilliant *Russian River Pinot Noir* and *Chardonnay* producer whose name also appears on single-vineyard wines from *Williams Selyem*.

Rockford (*Barossa Valley*, Australia) Robert "Rocky" O'Callaghan makes a great intense *Barossa Shiraz* using 100-year-old vines and 50-year-old equipment. There's a mouthfilling *Semillon*, a wonderful Black *Shiraz* sparkling wine, and a magical *Alicante Bouschet* rosé, which is sadly only to be found at the winery. ☆☆☆☆ **1996 Basket Press Shiraz, Barossa Valley $$$**

Antonin Rodet [on-toh-nan roh-day] (*Burgundy*, France) Very impressive *Mercurey*-based *négoçiant*, which has also improved the wines of the *Jacques Prieur* domaine in *Meursault*. **Ch. de Chamery; de Rully.**

Louis Roederer [roh-dur-rehr] (*Champagne*, France) Family-owned, and still one of the most reliable *Champagne* houses, whose delicious non-vintage wine benefits from being cellared for a few years. Roederer's prestige Cristal remains a most deliciously "wine-like" Champagne. ☆☆☆☆☆ **1990 Cristal $$$$**

Roederer Estate [roh-dur-rehr] (*Mendocino*, California) No longer involved with the *Janz* sparkling wine in *Tasmania* but making top-class wine in California which is sold in the US as Roederer Estate and in the UK as Quartet. ☆☆☆☆ **Quartet Anderson Valley $$$**

Roero [roh-weh-roh] (*Piedmont*, Italy) *Nebbiolo* red and *Arneis* white (sold as Roero Arneis) which are now among Italy's most interesting wines. ***Ceretto;* Bruno Giacosa; *Prunotto;* Serafino; *Vietti.***

Michel Rolland [ROH-lon] Based in *Pomerol*, *St. Emilion*, and now increasingly international guru-enologist, whose taste for ripe fruit flavors is influencing wines from Ch. *Ausone* to Argentina and beyond.

Rolly-Gassmann [rroh-lee gas-sman] (*Alsace*, France) Fine producer of subtle, long-lasting wines which are sometimes slightly marred by an excess of *sulfur dioxide*.

Dom. de la Romanée-Conti [rroh-ma-nay kon-tee] (*Burgundy*, France) Aka "DRC." Small *Grand Cru* estate. The jewel in the crown is the Romanée-Conti vineyard itself, though *La Tâche* runs it a close second. Both can be extraordinary, ultraconcentrated spicy wine, as can the *Romanée-St.-Vivant*. The *Richebourg*, *Echézeaux*, and *Grands Echézeaux* and *Montrachet* are comparable to those produced by other estates – and sold by them for less kingly ransoms. ☆☆☆☆☆ **1994 La Tâche $$$$**

Romania Traditional source of sweet reds and whites, now developing drier styles from classic European varieties. *Flying winemakers* are helping, as is the owner of the *Comte Peraldi* estate in *Corsica*. Note that Romania's well-praised *Pinot Noirs* may be made from a different variety mistaken for the Pinot.

Romarantin [roh-ma-ron-tan] (*Loire*, France) Interesting, limey grape found in obscure white blends in the *Loire*. See *Cheverny*.

Romerlay [rroh-mehr-lay] (*Mosel*, Germany) One of the *grosslagen* in the *Ruwer* river valley. QbA/Kab/Spät: **85 86 88 89 90** 91 **92 93 94** 95 96 97 98 Aus/Beeren/Tba: **83 85** 88 89 90 91 **92 93 94** 95 96 97 98

Rongopai [ron-goh-pi] (Te Kauwhata, New Zealand) Estate in a region of the North Island pioneered by *Cooks*, but which has fallen out of favor with that company and with other producers. The specialty here is *botrytis* wines, but the dry *Sauvignons* are good too.

La Rosa (Chile) One of the fastest-growing wineries in Chile, with new vineyards and great winemaking from *Ignacio Recabarren*. Las Palmeras is a *second label*.

Quinta de la Rosa (*Douro*, Portugal) Recently established estate producing excellent *port* and exemplary dry red wine, under guidance from David Baverstock, Australian-born former winemaker at *Dow's* and now filling a similar role at the nearby *Quinta do Crasto*. ☆☆☆☆ **1995 Vintage Port $$$**

Rosato (Italy) Rosé.

Rosé d'Anjou [roh-zay don-joo] (*Loire*, France) Widely exported, usually dull, semi-sweet pink from the *Malbec*, *Groslo,t* and (less usually) *Cabernet Franc*.

Rosé de Loire [roh-zay duh-lwahr] (*Loire*, France) The wine *Rosé d'Anjou* ought to be. Dry, fruity stuff. ***Richou; Cave des Vignerons de Saumur.***

Rosé de Riceys [roh-zay dur ree-say] (*Champagne*, France) Rare and occasionally delicious still rosé from the *Pinot Noir*. Pricy. **Alexandre Bonnet.**

Rosemount Estate (*Hunter Valley*, Australia) Ultradynamic company which introduced the world to *oaky Hunter Chardonnay* with its Show Reserve and Roxburgh. Reliably good-value blends from other areas have followed, including impressive *Syrahs* and *Chardonnays* from the newly developed region of *Orange* and *Mountain Blue* from *Mudgee*. ☆☆☆☆☆ **1996 Roxburgh Chardonnay $$$;** ☆☆☆☆☆ **1996 GSM $$$**

Rosenblum (*Alameda*, California) Terrific characterful *Zinfandels* from a wide variety of individual vineyards in *Napa, Sonoma, Contra Costa,* and *Paso Robles*. There are also some great multi-regional Californian blends.

Rossese di Dolceaqua [ros-seh-seh di dohl-chay-ah-kwah] (*Liguria*, Italy) Attractive, generally early-drinking wines made from the Rossese. Single-vineyard examples like Terre Bianche's Bricco Arcagna are more serious.

Dom. Rossignol-Trapet [ros-seen-yol tra-pay] (*Burgundy*, France) Once old-fashioned, now more recommendable estate in *Gevrey-Chambertin*.

Rosso Conero [ros-doh kon-neh-roh] (*Marches*, Italy) Big, *Montepulciano* and *Sangiovese* red, with a rich, herby flavor. Good-value characterful stuff. ☆☆☆☆ **1995 Umani Ronchi Cumaro $$$**

Rosso di Montalcino [ros-soh dee mon-tal-chee-noh] (*Tuscany*, Italy) *DO* for lighter, earlier-drinking versions of the more famous *Brunello di Montalcino*. Often better – and better value – than that wine. **82** 85 88 90 91 93 **94** 95 96 97 93 ***Altesino; Caparzo*; Fattoria dei Barbi; Talenti.**

Rosso Piceno [ros-soh pee-chay-noh] (*Marche*, Italy) Traditionally rustic red made from a blend of the *Montepulciano* and *Sangiovese*.

René Rostaing [ros-tang] (*Rhône*, France) Producer of serious northern *Rhône* reds, including a (somewhat) more affordable alternative to *Guigal's* la Landonne. ☆☆☆☆ **1995 Côte Rôtie la Landonne $$$**

Rothbury Estate (*Hunter Valley*, Australia) Founded by *Len Evans,* Svengali of the Australian wine industry and now – via *Mildara* – a subsidiary of Fosters, this is a great source of *Shiraz, Semillon,* and *Chardonnay* from the *Hunter Valley*. There are also wines from nearby *Cowra* and first-class *Sauvignon* from the bit of the estate that surfaces in *Marlborough*, New Zealand. ☆☆☆☆ **1996 Brokenback Chardonnay $$**

Joseph Roty [roh-tee] (*Burgundy*, France) Superstar producer of a range of intensely concentrated but unsubtle wines in *Gevrey-Chambertin*. ☆☆☆☆ **1995 Gevrey Chambertin $$$$**

Rouge Homme (*Coonawarra*, Australia) Founded by the linguistically talented *Mr. Redman*, but now under the same ownership as *Penfolds* and *Lindemans*. This is increasingly one of the most reliable producers in *Coonawarra*. ☆☆☆☆ **1996 Rouge Homme Coonawarra Cabernet $$$**

Dom. Guy Roulot [roo-loh] (*Burgundy*, France) One of the greatest domaines in *Meursault*. ☆☆☆ **1996 Meursault Charmes $$$**

Georges Roumier [roo-me-yay] (*Burgundy*, France) Blue-chip winery with great quality at every level, from village *Chambolle-Musigny* to the *Grand Cru,* Bonnes Mares, and (more rarely seen) white *Corton-Charlemagne*. ☆☆☆☆ **1995 Chambolle-Musigny les Amoureuses $$$$**

Round Hill (*Napa*, California) A rare source of Californian bargains. Large-production, inexpensive *Merlots* and *Chardonnays* that outclass many a pricier offering from smart boutique wineries.

Roussanne [roos-sahn] (*Rhône*, France) With the *Marsanne*, one of the key white grapes of the northern *Rhône*.

Armand Rousseau [roos-soh] (*Burgundy*, France) *Gevrey-Chambertin* estate on top form with a range of *Premiers* and *Grands Crus*. Well-made, long-lasting wines. ☆☆☆☆ **1996 Chambertin $$$$**

Roussillon [roos-see-yon] (*Languedoc-Roussillon*, France) Vibrant up-and-coming region, redefining traditional varieties, especially *Muscat*.

Ch. Routas [roo-tahs] (*Provence*, France) Impressive producer of intense reds and whites in the Coteaux Varois. **1995 Rouvier $$$**

Royal Oporto Wine Co. (*Douro*, Portugal) Occasionally (very occasionally) successful, large producer.

The Royal Tokaji Wine Co. (*Tokaji*, Hungary) Recently-founded company that has – with other foreign investors – helped to drag *Tokaji* into the late 20th century with great single-vineyard wines. ☆☆☆☆ **Aszú 5 Puttonyos Szt Tamas $$$**

Rubesco di Torgiano [roo-bes-koh dee taw-jee-yah-noh] (*Umbria*, Italy) Modern red *DOCG*; more or less the exclusive creation of *Lungarotti*. ☆☆☆☆ **1987 Vigna Monticchio Riserva $$$**

Ruby (*Douro*, Portugal) Cheapest, basic *port*; young, blended, sweetly fruity.

Ruby Cabernet [roo-bee k-behr-nay] (California) A *Cabernet Sauvignon* and *Carignan* cross producing unsubtly fruity wines in California, Australia, and South Africa.

Ruche [roo-kay] (*Piedmont*, Italy) Raspberryish red grape from northern Italy producing early-drinking wines. Best from *Bava*.

Rüdesheim [rroo-des-hime] (*Rheingau*, Germany) Tourist town producing powerful *Rieslings*. QbA/Kab/Spät: **85** 86 **88 89 90** 91 **92 93** 94 95 96 97 98 Aus/Beeren/Tba: **83 85 88 89** 90 91 92 93 94 95 96 97 98 ***Georg Breuer.***

Rueda [roo-way-dah] (Spain) *DO* in northwest Spain for clean, dry whites from the local *Verdejo*. Progress is being led most particularly by the *Lurtons*, *Marqués de Riscal* and *Marqués de Griñon*.

Ruffino [roof-fee-noh] (*Tuscany*, Italy) Big *Chianti* producer with impressive top-of-the-range wines, including the reliable Cabreo *Vino da Tavola*. **93 94** 95 96 97 98 ☆☆☆☆ **1993 Riserva Ducale Gold $$$**

Rufina [roo-fee-na] (*Tuscany*, Italy) A subregion within *Chianti*, producing supposedly classier wine. **78 79** 81 **82 85 88 90** 94 95 96 97 98

Ruinart [roo-wee-nahr] (*Champagne*, France) High-quality sister to *Moët & Chandon*, with superlative *Blanc de Blancs*. ☆☆☆☆☆ **1990 R. de Ruinart $$$**

Rülander [roo-len-dur] (Germany) German name for *Pinot Gris*.

Rully [roo-yee] (*Burgundy*, France) *Côte Chalonnaise commune* producing rich white and a red that's been called the "poor man's" *Volnay*. See *Antonin Rodet*, *Jadot* and *Olivier Leflaive*. Red: 86 87 **88 89 90** 92 95 96 97 98 White: **85** **88** 89 90 92 95 96 97 98 ***Faiveley;* Jacqueson; *Jadot; Olivier Leflaive; Antonin Rodet.***

Ruppertsberg [roo-purt-sbehrg] (*Pfalz*, Germany) Top-ranking village with a number of excellent vineyards making vigorous fruity *Riesling*. QbA/Kab/Spät: **88 89 90** 91 **92 93** 94 95 96 97 98 Aus/Beeren/ Tba: **83 85 88 89 90** 91 **92** 93 94 95 96 97 98 **Bürklin-Wolf; Kimich; Werlé.**

Russe [rooss] (Bulgaria) Danube town best known in Britain for its reliable red blends but vaunted in *Bulgaria* as a source of modern whites.

Russian River Valley (California) Cult, cool-climate area to the north of *Sonoma* and west of *Napa*. Ideal for apples and good fizz, as is proven by the excellent *Iron Horse*, which also makes impressive table wines. Great *Pinot Noir* country. Red: **90 91 92** 93 95 96 97 98 White: 92 **95** 96 97 98 ***Dehlinger; de Loach; Iron Horse; Kistler; Martinelli; Rochioli; Sonoma-Cutrer; Joseph Swann; Marimar Torres; Williams Selyem.***

Rust [roost] (*Burgenland*, Austria) Wine center of *Burgenland*, famous for Ruster *Ausbruch* sweet white wine.

Rust-en-Vrede (*Stellenbosch*, South Africa) Well-regarded producer but could improve. ☆☆☆ **1994 Tinta Barocca $$**

Rustenberg (*Stellenbosch*, South Africa) On a roll since 1996, this is now a leading light in the Cape. The lower-priced Brampton efforts are good too. ☆☆☆☆☆ **1996 Stellenbosch Cabernet Merlot $$$**

Rutherford (California) *Napa* region in which some producers believe sufficiently to propose it – and its geological "bench" – as an *appellation*. Red: **85** 86 87 **90 91** 92 **93 95** 96 97 98 White: **90 91** 92 **94 95** 96 97 98

Rutherglen (*Victoria*, Australia) Hot area on the *Murray River* pioneered by gold miners. Today noted for rich *Muscat* and *Tokay* dessert and *port*-style wines.The reds are often tough and the *Chardonnays* are used by cool-region winemakers to demonstrate why *port* and light dry whites are hard to make in the same climate. **All Saints; Campbells; Chambers; Morris; Seppelt..**

Ruwer [roo-vur] (*Mosel-Saar-Ruwer*, Germany) *Mosel* tributary alongside which is to be found the *Romerlay grosslage*, and includes Kasel, *Eitelsbach* and the great *Maximin Grunhaus* estate. QbA/Kab/Spät: **85** 86 **88 89 90 92 93 94** 95 96 97 98 Aus/Beeren/Tba: 83 **85 88 89 90 92** 93 94 95 **96 97** 98

Hugh Ryman [ri-man] *Flying winemaker* whose team turns grapes into wine under contract in *Bordeaux*, *Burgundy*, southern France, Spain, Germany, Moldova, Chile, California, South Africa, and Hungary. Wines tend to bear the initials HDR at the foot of the label – or one of Ryman's own brands: Santara, Kirkwood, Richemont, Rafael Estate.

Rymill [ri-mil] (South Australia) One of several *Coonawarra* wineries to mention *Riddoch* on its label (in its Riddoch Run) and a rising star. Rymill at least has the legitimacy of a family link to *John Riddoch*, the region's founder. The *Shiraz* and *Cabernet* are first class, as are the whites and the sparkling wine. ☆☆☆☆ **1996 Old Penola Merlot-Cabernets $$$**

S

Saale-Unstrut [zah-luhr oon-strurt] (Germany) Remember East Germany? Well, this is where poor wines used to be made there in the bad old days. Today good ones are being produced, by producers like Lützkendorf.

Saar [zahr] (*Mosel-Saar-Ruwer*, Germany) The other *Mosel* tributary associated with lean, slatey *Riesling*. Villages include *Ayl, Ockfen,* Saarburg, Serrig and *Wiltingen*. QbA/Kab/Spät: **85 88 89 90** 91 **92 93** 94 95 96 97 98 Aus/Beeren/Tba: **83 85 88 89 90** 91 **92** 93 94 95 96 97 98

Sablet [sa-blay] (*Rhône*, France) Good *Côtes du Rhône* village. Red: **78** 81 **82 83 85 88** 89 **90 95** 96 97 98

Sachsen [zak-sen] (Germany) Revived former East German region where Klaus Seifert is producing good Riesling.

St. Amour [san ta-moor] (*Burgundy*, France) One of the ten *Beaujolais Crus* – usually light and fruity. 94 95 **96 97** 98 **Billards; la Cave Lamartine; *Duboeuf*; Patissier; Revillon.**

St. Aubin [san toh-ban] (*Burgundy*, France) Underrated *Côte d'Or* village for (jammily rustic) reds and rich, nutty, rather classier white; affordable alternatives to *Meursault*. White: **86 88** 89 **90 92 95 96** 97 98 Red: **85** 86 87 **88 89 90** 92 95 96 97 98 ***Marc Colin; Olivier Leflaive;* Roux Père et Fils; *Gérard Thomas.***

St. Chinian [san shee-nee-yon] (*South-West*, France) Neighbor of *Faugères* in the *Coteaux du Languedoc*, producing mid-weight wines from *Carignan* and other *Rhône* grapes. **Ch. Babeau; Mas Champart; Mas de la Tour; Maurel Fonsalade; Ch. Quartironi de Sars.**

St. Clement (*Napa Valley*, California) Japanese-owned winery whose best wine is the Oroppas red blend. In case you were wondering, the name isn't a Native American word, but that of the owner spelled backward.

St. Emilion [san tay-mee-lee-yon] (*Bordeaux*, France) Large *commune* with varied soils and wines. At best, sublime *Merlot*-dominated *claret*; at worst dull, earthy and fruitless. 170 or so "*Grand Cru*" St. Emilions are made in better-sited vineyards and have to undergo a tasting every vintage to be able to use these words on their labels and too few fail. *Grand Cru Classé* refers to 68 *châteaux*, of which two – *Ausone* and *Cheval-Blanc* – are rated as "Premier *Grands Crus Classés*'" and 11 are "Premiers *Grands Crus Classés* 'B'." These ratings are reviewed every decade. Supposedly "lesser" satellite neighbors – *Lussac, Puisseguin, St. Georges* etc. – often make better value wine than basic St. Emilion. **70 75** 78 79 81 **82 83 85** 86 **88 89** 90 94 95 **96** 97 98 ***Angelus; Ausone; Beau-Séjour-Bécot; Beauséjour; Belair; Canon; Canon la Gaffelière; Cheval Blanc; Clos des Jacobins; Clos Fourtet; Figeac; Franc Mayne; Grand Mayne; Larcis Ducasse; Magdelaine; la Mondotte; Pavie; Tertre Roteboeuf; Troplong Mondot; Trottevieille; Valandraud.***

St. Estèphe [san teh-stef] (*Bordeaux*, France) Northernmost *Médoc commune* with clay soil and wines which can be a shade more rustic than those of neighboring *Pauillac* and *St. Julien*, but which are often longer-lived and more structured than some of the juicy, easy-to-drink *St. Emilions* and *Pomerols* that tend to win approval from critics. **78 82** 83 **85 86** 88 89 90 92 93 94 95 96 97 98 ***Calon-Ségur; Cos d'Estournel; Haut-Marbuzet; Lafon-Rochet; Marbuzet; Montrose; de Pez; Ormes de Pez; Phélan-Ségur.***

St. Francis (*Sonoma*, California) Innovative winery with great *Zinfandels*, and Reserve *Chardonnays* and *Cabernets*. The first Californian to introduce artificial corks to protect wine drinkers from faulty bottles. ☆☆☆☆☆ **1996 Cabernet Sauvignon $$$;** ☆☆☆☆☆ **1996 Old Vines Zinfandel $$$**

St. Georges-St.Emilion [san jorrzh san tay-mee-lee-yon] (*Bordeaux*, France) Satellite of *St. Emilion* with good *Merlot*-dominant reds, often better value than *St. Emilion* itself. **Ch. Maquin St. Georges; St. Georges.**

St. Hallett (*Barossa Valley*, Australia) Superstar *Barossa* winery specializing in wines from old ('old block') *Shiraz* vines. Whites (especially *Semillon* and *Riesling*) are good too. ☆☆☆☆ **1997 Faith Shiraz $$$**

St. Hubert's (*Victoria*, Australia) Pioneering *Yarra* winery with ultra-fruity *Cabernet* and mouth-filling *Roussanne* whites. ☆☆☆☆ **1996 Roussanne $$**

Chateau St. Jean [jeen] (*Sonoma*, California) Named after the founder's wife; now Japanese-owned and a source of good single-vineyard *Chardonnays, late harvest Rieslings* and *Bordeaux*-style reds. ☆☆☆☆ **1993 Sonoma County Reserve Cabernet Sauvignon $$$**

St. Joseph [san joh-sef] (*Rhône*, France) Potentially vigorous, fruity *Syrah* from the northern *Rhône*. Whites range from flabby to fragrant *Marsannes*. Red: **82 83 85 88** 89 **90** 91 **95** 96 97 98 ***Chapoutier; Chave; Courbis;*** **Coursodon;** ***Cuilleron; Delas;*** **de Fauturie; Gacho-Pascal;** ***Gaillard; Graillot; Gripa; Grippat; Perret; Pichon; St.-Désirat;*** **Trollo;** ***Vernay.***

St. Julien [san-joo-lee-yen] (*Bordeaux*, France) Aristocratic *Médoc commune* producing classic rich wines, full of cedar and deep, ripe fruit. 70 75 76 **78** 79 81 **82** 83 **85 86** 88 89 90 94 95 96 97 98 ***Beychevelle; Branaire; Ducru-Beaucaillou; Gruaud-Larose; Lagrange; Langoa-Barton; Léoville-Barton; Léoville-Las-Cases; Léoville-Poyferré; Talbot.***

St. Laurent [sant loh-rent] (Austria) *Pinot Noir*-like berryish red grape, mastered, in particular, by *Umathum*.

St. Nicolas de Bourgueil [san nee-koh-lah duh boor-goy] (*Loire*, France) Lightly fruity *Cabernet Franc*; needs a warm year to ripen its raspberry fruit, but then can last for up to a decade. Lighter than *Bourgueil*. ***Caslot; Jamet;*** **Mabileau; Vallée.**

St. Péray [san pay-reh] (*Rhône*, France) *AC* near Lyon for full-bodied, still white and *méthode champenoise* sparkling wine, at risk from encroaching housing. ***Auguste Clape; Jean Lionnet; Alain Voge.***

Ch. St. Pierre [san pee-yehr] (*St. Julien 4ème Cru Classé, Bordeaux*, France) Reliable *St. Julien* under the same ownership as *Ch. Gloria*.

St. Romain [san roh-man] (*Burgundy*, France) *Hautes Côtes de Beaune* village producing undervalued fine whites and rustic reds. **Alain Gras;** ***Jaffelin;*** **Thevenin-Monthelie.**

St. Véran [san vay-ron] (*Burgundy*, France) Once sold as *Beaujolais* Blanc; affordable alternative to *Pouilly-Fuissé;* better than most *Mâconnais* whites. Ch. Fuissé is worth keeping an eye out for. White: **92 93** 94 **95 96** 97 98 ***Corsin;* Dom des Deux Roches; *Duboeuf;* Luquet; Pacquet.**

Ste. Croix-du-Mont [sant crwah doo mon] (*Bordeaux*, France) Never as luscious, rich and complex as the better efforts of its neighbor *Sauternes* – but often a far more worthwhile buy than wines unashamedly sold under that name. Sweet white: **88 90 92 93 94 95** 96 97 98

Saintsbury (*Carneros*, California) Superstar *Carneros* producer of unfiltered *Chardonnay* and – more specially – *Pinot Noir.* The slogan: "*Beaune* in the USA" refers to the winery's Burgundian aspirations! The Reserve *Pinot* is a world-beater, while the easy-going Garnet is the good *second label.* ☆☆☆☆ **1995 Carneros Pinot Noir $$$**

Sakar [sa-kah] (Bulgaria) Long-time source of much of the best *Cabernet Sauvignon* to come from *Bulgaria.*

Castello della Sala [kas-tel-loh del-la sah-lah] (*Umbria*, Italy) *Antinori's* over-priced but sound *Chardonnay, Sauvignon.* Also good *Sauvignon*/Procanico blend. ☆☆☆☆ **1996 Sauvignon della Sala $$**

Ch de Sales [duh sahl] (*Pomerol*, Bordeaux) Good but generally unexciting wine for relatively early drinking.

Salice Salentino [sa-lee-chay sah-len-tee-noh] (*Puglia*, Italy) Spicy, intense red made from the characterful *Negroamaro.* Great value, especially when mature. **Candido; Leone de Castris; Taurino; Vallone.**

Salon le Mesnil [sah-lon lur may-neel] (*Champagne*, France) Small, traditional subsidiary of *Laurent Perrier* with cult following for pure long-lived *Chardonnay* sparkling wine. Only sold in the form of a single-vintage cuvée.

Saltram [sawl-tram] (South Australia) Fast-improving part of the *Mildara-Blass* empire. Rich, fairly priced *Barossa* reds and whites (also under the Mamre Brook label) and top-flight "*ports.*" ☆☆☆☆ **1996 Saltram No 1 Shiraz $$$**

Samos [sah-mos] (Greece) Aegean island producing sweet, fragrant, golden *Muscat* once called "the wine of the Gods."

Cellier des Samsons [sel-yay day som-son] (*Burgundy*, France) Source of better-than-average *Beaujolais.*

San Luis Obispo [san loo-wis oh-bis-poh] (California) Californian region gaining a reputation for *Chardonnay* and *Pinot Noir.* Try *Edna Valley.* Red: 84 **85** 86 87 **90 91** 92 **93 95** 96 97 98 White: 92 **95 96** 97 98

Viña San Pedro [veen-ya san-pay-droh] (*Curico*, Chile) Huge *Curico* firm whose wines are quietly improving thanks to the efforts of consultant *Jacques Lurton.* ☆☆☆☆ **1999 35 Sur Sauvignon Blanc $$**

Sancerre [son-sehr] (*Loire*, France) At its best, the epitome of elegant, steely dry *Sauvignon;* at its worst, oversulfured and fruitless. Reds and rosés, though well regarded and highly priced by French restaurants, are often little better than quaffable *Pinot Noir.* **90** 94 **95 96 97** 98 **Bailly-Reverdy; Bourgeois; *Cotat;* Crochet; Pierre Dézat; Fouassier; Gitton; Jolivet; de Ladoucette; Mellot; Natter; Vincent Pinard; Jean-Max Roger; Vacheron; Vatan.**

Sandeman (Spain/Portugal) North American-owned, generally underperforming but occasionally dazzling *port* and *sherry* producer. Port: **55** 57 58 **60 62 63** 65 66 67 68 **70** 72 75 80 94 97 ☆☆☆☆☆ **Royal Ambrosante Sherry $$$**

Sanford Winery (*Santa Barbara*, California) *Santa Barbara* superstar producer of *Chardonnay* and especially distinctive, slightly horseradishy *Pinot Noir*. ☆☆☆☆ **1997 Pinot Noir $$$**

Sangiovese [san-jee-yoh vay-seh] (Italy) The tobaccoey, herby-flavored red grape of *Chianti* and *Montepulciano*, now being used increasingly in *Vino da Tavola* and – though rarely impressively – in California. ***Antinori; Atlas Peak; Bonny Doon; Isole e Olena.***

Santa Barbara (California) Successful southern, cool-climate region for *Pinot Noir* and *Chardonnay*. ***Au Bon Climat; Byron; Ojai; Qupé; Sanford.***

Viña Santa Carolina [ka-roh-lee-na] (Chile) Greatly improved producer, thanks to *Ignacio Recabarren* and vineyards in *Casablanca*. Good reds. ☆☆☆☆☆ **1996 Cabernet Gran Reserva $$$**

Santa Cruz Mountains [krooz] (California) Exciting region to the south of San Francisco. See *Ridge* and *Bonny Doon*. Red: 84 **85** 86 87 **90 91** 92 **93** 95 **96** 97 98 White: **91** 92 95 96 97 98

Santa Emiliana (*Aconcagua*, Chile) Large producer with good Andes Peak offerings from *Casablanca*, and wines from the new southern region of Mulchen. ☆☆☆☆ **1997 Andes Peak Casablanca Chardonnay $$**

Santa Maddalena [san-tah mah-dah-LAY-nah] (*Alto Adige*, Italy) Light spicy-fruity red made from the Schiava. Rarely found outside the region, but well worth seeeking out. **Cantina Produttori Sta. Maddalena; Gojer.**

Santa Rita [ree-ta] (*Maipo*, Chile) Back on track after a slightly bumpy patch. The Casa Real is not only one of Chile's best and most fairly priced reds; it is also truly world class. ☆☆☆☆☆ **1995 Casa Real $$$**

Santenay [sont-nay] (*Burgundy*, France) Southern *Côte d'Or* village, producing pretty whites and good, though occasionally rather rustic, reds. Look for *Girardin* and *Pousse d'Or*. White: **88** 89 **90 92 95** 96 97 98 Red: 78 79 **80** 83 **85** 86 87 **88 89 90** 92 95 96 97 98 **Roger Belland; *Fernand Chevrot; Marc Colin; Colin-Deléger; Girardin; Olivier Leflaive; Bernard Morey; Lucien Muzet; Claude Nouveau; Pousse d'Or; Prieur Brunet.***

Caves São João [sow-jwow] (*Bairrada*, Portugal) Small company which produces high-quality *Bairrada*.

Sardinia (Italy) Traditionally the source of powerful reds (try *Santadi*) and whites, increasingly interesting *DOC* fortified wines, and new-wave modern reds to match the best *Super Tuscans*. **Sella e Mosca.**

Sarget de Gruaud-Larose [sahr-jay dur groowoh lah-rohs] (*St. Julien, Bordeaux*, France) *Second label* of *Ch. Gruaud-Larose*.

Sassicaia [sas-see-ki-ya] (*Tuscany*, Italy) World-class *Cabernet*-based *Super Tuscan* with more of an Italian than a *claret* taste. No longer a mere *Vino da Tavola* since the *DOC* Bolgheri was introduced in 1994.

Saumur [soh-moor] (*Loire*, France) Heartland of variable *Chenin*-based fizz and still wine, and potentially more interesting *Saumur-Champigny*. Red: **85 88 89 90 95** 96 97 98 White: **90** 94 95 96 **97** 98 Sweet White: **76** 83 85 86 **88 89 90 94 95** 96 97 98 **Ch. du Hureau; Langlois-Château; Roches Neuves; Vatan; Cave des Vignerons de Saumur; Villeneuve.**

Saumur-Champigny [soh-moor shom-pee-nyee] (*Loire*, France) Crisp *Cabernet Franc* red; best served slightly chilled. Good examples are worth cellaring.**88 89 90 95** 96 97 98 ***Bouvet-Ladubay; Couly-Dutheil;*** **Filliatreau; Foucault; Ch. du Hureau; Langlois-Château; Targé; Vatan; de Villeneuve.**

Sauternes [soh-turn] (*Bordeaux*, France) Rich, honeyed dessert wines from *Sauvignon* and *Sémillon* (and possibly *Muscadelle*) blends. Should be affected by *botrytis* but the climate does not always allow this. That's one explanation for disappointing Sauternes; the other is careless winemaking, and, in particular, a tendency to be heavy-handed with *sulfur dioxide*. 78 79 80 81 82 **83 85 86 88 89 90 91** 92 95 97 98 ***Bastor-Lamontagne; Doisy-Daëne; Fargues; Filhot; Guiraud; Rieussec; Suduiraut; Yquem.***

Sauvignon Blanc [SOH-vin-yon-BLON] "Grassy," "catty," "asparagussy," "gooseberryish" grape grown the world over, but rarely really loved, so often blended, oaked or made sweet. In France at home in the *Loire* and *Bordeaux*. New Zealand gets it right – especially in *Marlborough*. In Australia, *Knappstein, Cullens, Stafford Ridge*, and *Shaw & Smith* are right on target. *Mondavi's* oaked *Fumé Blanc* and *Kendall Jackson's* sweet versions are successful but *Monteviña, Quivira, Dry Creek, Simi*, and – in blends with the *Semillon* – *Carmenet* are the stars. Chile is making better versions every year, despite starting out with a lesser variety. See *Caliterra, Casablanca, Canepa, Sta. Carolina*, and *Villard*. In South Africa, see *Thelema, Klein Constantia* and *Neil Ellis*.

Sauvignon de St. Bris [SOH-vin-yon-dur san BREE] (*Burgundy*, France) *Burgundy's* only *VDQS*. An affordable and often worthwhile alternative to *Sancerre*, produced in vineyards near *Chablis*. **95** 96 97 98 ***Jean-Marc Brocard;*** **Moreau.**

Etienne Sauzet [SOH-zay] (*Burgundy*, France) First-rank estate whose white wines are almost unfindable outside collectors' cellars and Michelin-starred restaurants. ☆☆☆☆ **1995 Montrachet $$$$**

Savagnin [sa-van-yan] (*Jura*, France) No relation of the *Sauvignon*; a white *Jura* variety used for *Vin Jaune* and blended with *Chardonnay* for *Arbois*. Also, confusingly, the Swiss name for the *Gewürztraminer*.

Savennières [sa-ven-yehr] (*Loire*, France) Fine, if sometimes aggressively dry *Chenin Blanc* whites. Very long-lived. **86 88 89 90 94 95** 96 97 98 **des Baumard; Bise; du Closel; *Coulée de Serrant;* d'Epiré; *La Roche aux Moines;* de Plaisance; *Soulez.***

Savigny-lès-Beaune [sa-veen-yee lay bohn] (*Burgundy*, France) Distinctive whites (sometimes made from *Pinot Blanc*) and raspberry reds. At their best can compare with *Beaune*. White: 89 **90 92** 95 96 97 98 Red: **78** 80 83 **85** 86 87 **88 89 90** 92 95 96 97 98 ***Simon Bize; Chandon de Briailles; Ecard; Girard-Voillot; Girardin;*** **Pavelot; *Tollot-Beaut.***

Savoie [sav-wah] (Eastern France) Mountainous region near Geneva producing crisp floral whites such as Abymes, *Apremont, Seyssel* and *Crépy.*

🍷 **Saxenburg** (*Stellenbosch*, South Africa) Wines for those who prefer ripely flavorsome wines to some of the mean fare on offer in South Africa. Particularly good *Pinotage* and *Sauvignon Blanc*.

🍷 **Scavino** [ska-vee-noh] (*Piedmont*, Italy) Terrific New-Wave, juicy reds, including single-vineyard *Barolos, Barberas* and *Dolcettos*. ☆☆☆☆ **1993 Barolo Canubi $$$**

🍷 **Scharffenberger** [shah-fen-bur-gur] (*Mendocino*, California) *Pommery*-owned, independently-run producer of top-class, top-value sparkling wine. ☆☆☆☆ **Scharffenberger Brut $$$**

Scharzhofberg [shahts-hof-behrg] (*Mosel-Saar-Ruwer*, Germany) Top-class *Saar* vineyard, producing great *Riesling*. QbA/Kab/Spät: **85** 86 **88 89 90** 91 **92 93 94 95** 96 97 98 Aus/Beeren/Tba: **83 85 88 89 90** 91 **92 93** 94 95 96 97 98 ***Reichsgraf von Kesselstadt.***

Schaumwein [showm-vine] (Germany) Low-priced sparkling wine.

🍇 **Scheurebe** [shoy-ray-bur] (Germany) *Riesling* x *Sylvaner* cross, grown in Germany and in England. Tastes deliciously like pink grapefruit. In Austria, where it makes brilliant sweet wines, they sometimes call it Samling 88. ***Kurt Darting;* Hafner; Kadlec; *Alois Kracher; Lingenfelder.***

🍇 **Schiava** [skee yah-vah] (*Alto-Adige*, Italy) Grape used in *Lago di Caldaro* and *Santa Maddalena* to make light reds.

Schilfwein [shilf-vine] (Austria) Luscious "reed win'" – Austrian *vin de paille* pioneered by *Willi Opitz*.

🍷 **Schiopetto** [skee yoh-peh-toh] (*Friuli-Venezia-Giulia*, Italy) Gloriously intense, perfumed *Collio* white varietals to rival those of *Jermann*. ☆☆☆☆☆ **1996 Malvasia $$$;** ☆☆☆☆☆ **1996 Tocai Friulano $$$**

Schloss [shloss] (Germany) Literally "castle," vineyard or estate.

Schloss Böckelheim [shloss boh-kell-hime] (*Nahe*, Germany) Varied southern part of the *Nahe*. Wines from the Kupfergrübe vineyard and the State Wine Domaine are worth buying. QbA/Kab/Spät: **85** 86 **88 89 90** 91 92 93 94 95 96 97 98 Aus/Beeren/Tba: **83 85 88 89** 90 91 92 93 94 95 96 97 98

🍷 **Schloss Reinhartshausen** [shloss rine-harts-how-zehn] (*Rheingau*, Germany) Innovative estate, successful with *Pinot Blanc* and *Chardonnay* (the latter introduced following a suggestion by *Robert Mondavi*). The *Rieslings* are good too. QbA/Kab/Spät: **85 88 89 90** 91 **92 93** 94 95 96 97 98 Aus/Beeren/Tba: **83 85 88 89 90** 91 **92** 93 94 95 96 97 98

🍷 **Schloss Saarstein** [shloss sahr-stine] (*Mosel-Saar-Ruwer*, Germany) High-quality *Riesling* specialist in *Serrig*. QbA/Kab/Spät: **85** 86 **88 89 90** 91 92 93 94 95 96 97 98 Aus/Beeren/Tba: **83 85 88 89 90** 91 **92 93 94** 95 96 97 98

🍷 **Schloss Schönborn** [shloss sahr-stine] (*Mosel-Saar-Ruwer*, Germany) Unreliable but sometimes brilliant estate.

🍷 **Schloss Vollrads** [shloss fol-rahts] (*Rheingau*, Germany) Long-time under-performing *Charta* pioneer. Following the death of the man behind it – Graf Matuschka-Greiffenclau – things may change.

Schlossbockelheim [shloss bok-el-hime] (*Nahe*, Germany) Village which gives its name to a large *Nahe bereich*, producing elegant *Riesling*. QbA/Kab/Spät: **88 89 90** 91 92 93 94 95 96 97 98 Aus/Beeren/Tba: **83 85 88** 89 90 91 92 93 94 95 96 97 98 **Staatsweingut Niederhausen.**

🍷 **Schlossgut Diel** [deel] (*Nahe*, Germany) Armin Diel is both wine writer and winemaker. Co-author of the excellent German Wine Guide, his Dorsheimer Goldloch wines are worth seeking out.

Dom. Schlumberger [shloom-behr-jay] (*Alsace*, France) Great, sizeable estate whose subtle top-level wines can often rival those of the somewhat more showy *Zind-Humbrecht*. ☆☆☆☆ **1997 Riesling Kesler $$$;** ☆☆☆☆ **1996 Pinot Gris Les Prince Abbés $$$**

Schramsberg [shram-sberg] (*Napa Valley*, California) The winery that single-handedly put Californian sparkling wine on the quality trail. Wines used to be too big for their boots, possibly because too many of the grapes were from warm vineyards in *Napa*. The J Schram is aimed at *Dom Pérignon* and gets pretty close to the target. ☆☆☆☆ **1992 J Schram $$$$**

Scotchman's Hill (*Victoria*, Australia) *Pinot Noir* specialist in *Geelong*. *Sauvignons* and *Chardonnays* have been less exciting.

Screaming Eagle (*Napa Valley*, California) Miniscule winery the size of many people's living room, and producing around 200 of intense *Cabernet* per year since 1992 – and selling them at $100 a bottle. The owners are avowedly trying to make California's greatest wine. Sadly most people will only ever read about it.

Seaview (South Australia) *Penfolds* brand for brilliantly reliable sparkling wine and (less frequently) *McLaren Vale* red table wines. Look out for the Edwards & Chaffey label too. ☆☆☆☆ **1995 Pinot Noir/Chardonnay $$$**

Sebastiani/ Cecchetti Sebastiani [seh-bas-tee-yan-nee] (*Sonoma Valley*, California) Sebastiani makes unexceptional wine from *Central Valley* grapes. The associated but separate Cecchetti Sebastiani however, like the top end of *Gallo*, makes really good stuff in *Sonoma*. The Pepperwood Grove wines are good too. ☆☆☆☆ **1994 Cecchetti Sebastiani Cabernet Sauvignon $$$**

Sec/secco/seco [se-koh] (France/Italy/Spain) Dry.

Second label (*Bordeaux*, France) Wine from a producer's (generally a *Bordeaux Château*) lesser vineyards, younger vines, and/or lesser *cuvées* of wine. Especially worth buying in good vintages. See *Les Forts de Latour*.

Segura Viudas [say-goo-rah vee-yoo-dass] (*Catalonia*, Spain) The quality end of the *Freixenet Cava* giant. ☆☆☆ **Brut Reserva $$$**

Seifried Estate [see-freed] (*Nelson*, New Zealand) Also known as *Redwood Valley Estate*. Superb *Riesling*, especially *late harvest* style, and very creditable *Sauvignon* and *Chardonnay*.

Sekt [zekt] (Germany) Very basic sparkling wine – best won in carnival games. Watch out for anything that does not state that it is made from *Riesling* – other grape varieties almost invariably make highly unpleasant wines. Only the prefix "Deutscher" guarantees German origin.

Selaks [see-lax] (*Auckland*, New Zealand) Large company in Kumeu best known for the piercingly fruity *Sauvignon* originally made by a young man called Kevin Judd, who went on to produce *Cloudy Bay!*

Weingut Selbach-Oster [zel-bahkh os-tehr] (*Mosel-Saar-Ruwer*, Germany) Archetypical *Mosel Riesling*.

Sélection de Grains Nobles (SGN) [say-lek-see-yon day gran nohbl] (*Alsace*, France) Equivalent to German *Beerenauslese*; rich, sweet *botrytized* wine from specially selected grapes.

Sella e Mosca [seh-la eh mos-kah] (*Sardinia*, Italy) Dynamic firm with a good *Cabernet* called Villamarina, the rich *Anghelu Ruju* and traditional *Cannonau*. ☆☆☆☆ **1994 Tanca Farra' Alghero $$$**

Fattoria Selvapiana [fah-taw-ree-ya sel-va-pee-yah-nah] (*Tuscany*, Italy) Benchmark *Chianti Rufina, vin santo*, and olive oil. ☆☆☆☆ **1994 Riserva $$$**

Sémillon [in France: say-mee-yon; in Australia: seh-mil-lon and even seh-mih-lee-yon] Peachy grape generally blended with *Sauvignon* to make sweet and dry *Bordeaux*, and vinified separately in Australia, where it is also sometimes blended with *Chardonnay*. Rarely as successful in other New World countries where many versions taste more like *Sauvignon*. ***Carmenet; Geyser Peak; McWilliams; Rothbury; Tyrrell; Xanadu.***

Seña [sen-ya] (Chile) A *Mondavi* and *Caliterra* coproduction. A Mercedes of a wine: impeccably put together but, so far, somehow unexciting.

Seppelt (South Australia) *Penfolds* subsidiary and pioneer of the *Great Western* region where it makes rich still and sparkling *Shiraz*. Other Seppelt sparkling wines are recommendable too, though the once-fine Salinger seems to have lost its way. ☆☆☆☆ **1998 Moyston Cabernet-Shiraz $$$**; ☆☆☆☆ **1987 Show Reserve Sparkling Shiraz $$$**

Serasin [seh-ra-sin] (*Marlborough*, New Zealand) New venture launched by a British movie cameraman. Impeccable vineyards and really impressive *Chardonnay, Sauvignon*, and a promising *Pinot Noir*.

Servir frais (France) Serve chilled.

Setúbal [shtoo-bal] (Portugal) *DOC* on the *Setúbal Peninsula*.

Setúbal Peninsula (Portugal) Home of the *Setúbal DOC*, but now notable for the rise of two new wine regions, Arrabida and Palmela, where *JM Fonseca Succs* and *JP Vinhos* are making excellent wines from local and international grape varieties.The lusciously rich *Moscatel de Setúbal*, however, is still the star of the show.

Seyssel [say-sehl] (*Savoie*, France) *AC* region near Geneva producing light white wines that are usually enjoyed in après-ski mood when no-one is overly concerned about value for money. ***Varichon et Clerc.***

Seyval Blanc [aay-vahl blon] *Hybrid* grape – a cross between French and US vines – unpopular with EU authorities but successful in eastern US, Canada, and England, especially at *Breaky Bottom*.

Shafer [shay-fur] (*Napa Valley*, California) Top *Cabernet* producer in the *Stag's Leap* district, and maker of classy *Chardonnay* and *Merlot* from *Carneros*. ☆☆☆☆ **1997 Hillside Select Cabernet Sauvignon Stag's Leap District $$$**

Shaw & Smith (*Adelaide Hills*, Australia) Recently founded winery producing one of Australia's best *Sauvignons* and a pair of increasingly Burgundian *Chardonnays* that demonstrate how good wines from this variety can taste with and without oak. ☆☆☆☆☆ **1998 Sauvignon Blanc $$$**

Sherry (*Jerez*, Spain) The fortified wine made in the area surrounding *Jerez*. Wines made elsewhere – Australia, England, South Africa, etc. – may no longer use the name. See also *Almacenista; Fino; Amontillado; Manzanilla; Cream Sherry*. ***Barbadillo; Gonzalez Byass; Hidalgo; Lustau.***

Shiraz [shee-raz] (Australia, South Africa) The *Syrah* grape in Australia and South Africa, named after its supposed birthplace in Iran. South African versions are lighter (and generally greener) than the Australians, while the Australians are usually riper and *oakier* than efforts from the *Rhône*. The move to cooler sites is broadening the range of Australian Shiraz, however. ***Hardy's; Henschke; Maglieri; Lindemans; Rockford; Rothbury; Penfolds; Picardy; Plantagenet; St. Hallett; Saxenburg; Wolf Blass.***

Sicily (Italy) Historically best known for *Marsala* and sturdy "southern" table wine. Now, however, there is an array of other unusual fortified wines and a fast-growing range of new-wave reds and whites, many of which are made from grapes grown nowhere else on earth. ***de Bartoli; Corvo;* Planeta; *Regaleali;* Terre di Ginestra.**

Sieur d'Arques [see-uhr dark] (*Languedoc-Roussillon*, France) High-tech cooperative in *Limoux* that ought to serve as a role model to its neighbors. Good *Blanquette de Limoux* sparkling wine and truly impressive *Chardonnays* sold under the Toques et Clochers label.

Siglo [seeg-loh] (*Rioja*, Spain) Good brand of modern red (traditionally sold in a burlap "sack") and old-fashioned whites.

Signorello (*Napa Valley*, California) Small winery making Burgundian *Chardonnay* with lots of yeasty richness, *Bordeaux*-style *Semillon* and *Sauvignon* as well as *Cabernets* that are both blackcurrranty and stylish.

Silex [see-lex] (France) Term describing flinty soil, used by *Didier Dagueneau* for his oak-fermented *Pouilly-Fumé*.

Silver Oak Cellars (*Napa Valley*, California) Superb specialist *Cabernet* producers favoring fruitily accessible, but still classy, wines which benefit from long aging in (American oak) barrels and bottle before release. Look out for older vintages of the single-vineyard Bonny's Vineyard wines, the last of which was made in 1991.

Silverado [sil-veh-rah-doh] (*Napa Valley*, California) Reliable *Cabernet*, *Chardonnay* and now *Sangiovese* winery that belongs to Walt Disney's widow. ☆☆☆☆ **1996 Art Cuvée Chardonnay $$$**

Simi Winery [see-mee] (*Sonoma Valley*, California) Recently sold (to the giant Canandaigua) and made famous by the thoughtful Zelma Long and her complex, long-lived Burgundian *Chardonnay*, archetypical *Sauvignon*, and lovely, blackcurranty *Alexander Valley Cabernet*. The current (excellent) Kiwi-born winemaker is staying on apparently.

Bert Simon (*Mosel-Saar-Ruwer*, Germany) Newish estate in the *Saar* river valley with super-soft *Rieslings* and unusually elegant *Weissburgunder*.

Simonsig Estate [see-mon-sikh] (*Stellenbosch*, South Africa) A big estate with a very impressive commercial range, and the occasional gem – try the *Shiraz*, *Cabernet*, *Pinotage*, *Chardonnay* the Kaapse Vonkel sparkler. ☆☆☆ **1997 Chardonnay $$**

Sin Crianza [sin cree-an-tha] (Spain) Not aged in wood.

Sion [see-yo'n] (*Valais*, Switzerland) One of the proud homes of the grape the Swiss call the Fendant and outsiders know as *Chasselas*. Dull elsewhere, it can produce creditable (and even occasionally ageworthy) wines.

Ch. Siran [see-ron] (*Margaux Cru Bourgeois*, *Bordeaux*, France) Beautiful *château* outperforming its classification and producing increasingly impressive and generally fairly priced wines. 70 **75** **78** 81 **82** 83 85 86 88 89 90 93 94 95 96 97 98

Skillogalee [skil-log-gah-lee] (*Clare Valley*, Australia) Well-respected *Clare* producer, specializing in *Riesling*, but also showing his skill with reds. ☆☆☆☆ **1997 The Cabernets $$**

Skin contact The longer the skins of black grapes are left in with the juice after the grapes have been crushed, the greater the *tannin* and the deeper the color. Some non-aromatic white varieties (*Chardonnay* and *Semillon* in particular) can also benefit from extended skin contact (usually between six and twenty-four hours) to increase flavor.

Sliven [slee-ven] Bulgarian region offering good-value, simple reds and better-than-average whites.

Slovakia Up-and-coming source of wines from grapes little seen elsewhere, such as the Muscatty Irsay Oliver.

Slovenia Former Yugoslavian region in which *Laski Rizling* is king. Other grapes show greater promise.

🍷 **Smith & Hook** (*Mendocino*, California) Winery with a cult following for its zippy blackcurranty Cabernet Sauvignon. These lack the ripe richness sought by most US critics, however.

🍷 **Smith-Madrone** (*Napa*, California) Long-established winery which bucks the trend by using the *Riesling* (which is being uprooted elsewhere) to make good wine. *Chardonnay* is good too.

🍷 **Smith Woodhouse** (*Douro*, Portugal) Part of the same empire as *Dow's, Graham's*, and *Warre's* but often overlooked. *Vintage ports* can be good, as is the house specialty *Traditional Late Bottled Vintage Port*. 60 **63 66 70** 75 **77** **85** 94 97 ☆☆☆☆ **1984 Traditional Late Bottled Vintage Port $$$**

🍷 **Ch. Smith-Haut-Lafitte** [oh-lah-feet] (*Pessac-Léognan Cru Classé, Bordeaux*, France) Estate flying high since its purchase by a former French sportsman and his wife. Increasingly classy reds and (specially) pure *Sauvignon* whites. Grape seeds from the estate are also used to make an anti-aging skin cream called Caudalie. Red: **82** 85 86 **89 90** 93 94 95 96 97 98 White: 92 **93** 94 **95** 96 97 98 ☆☆☆☆ **1996 White $$$$**

🍷 **Smithbrook** (Western Australia) *Pinot Noir* specialist in the new southerly region of *Pemberton*. Now owned by *Petaluma*. ☆☆☆☆ **1998 Sauvignon Blanc $$$**

🍷 **Soave** [swah-veh] (*Veneto*, Italy) Mostly dull stuff, but Soave *Classico* is better; single-vineyard versions are best. Sweet *Recioto* di Soave is delicious. *Pieropan* is almost uniformly excellent. ***Anselmi; Masi; Pieropan; Pra; Tedeschi; Zenato.***

🍷 **Ch. Sociando-Mallet** [soh-see-yon-doh ma-lay] (*Haut-Médoc Cru Bourgeois, Bordeaux*, France) A *Cru Bourgeois* whose oaked, fruity red wines are way above its status. **82** 83 **85 86 88 89 90** 91 92 93 94 95 96 97 98

🍷 **Sogrape** [soh-grap] (Portugal) Having invented *Mateus* Rosé half a century ago, this large firm is now leading the way in modernizing the wines of *Dão, Douro* and *Bairrada*, and *Alentejo* (with the new Vinha do Monte) bringing out flavors these once-dull wines never seemed to possess. *Sogrape* also owns the *port* house of *Ferreira* and is thus also responsible for *Barca Velha*, Portugal's top red table wine. The *Penfolds* of Portugal. ☆☆☆☆☆ **1996 Duque de Viseu $$**

🍷 **Sokol Blosser** (*Oregon*, US) Highly successful makers of rich Chardonnay. The *Pinot* is good too. ☆☆☆☆☆ **1994 Redland Chardonnay $$$**

🍷 **Solaia** [soh-li-yah] (*Tuscany*, Italy) Yet another *Antinori Super Tuscan*. A phenomenal blend of *Cabernets Sauvignon* and *Franc*, with a little *Sangiovese*. Italy's top red? ☆☆☆☆☆ **1994 Solaia Antinori $$$$**

Solera [soh-leh-rah] (*Jerez*, Spain) Aging system involving older wine being continually "refreshed" by slightly younger wine of the same style.

🍷 **Bodegas Felix Solís** [fay-leex soh-lees] (*Valdepeñas*, Spain) By far the biggest, most go-ahead winery in *Valdepeñas*.

Somontano [soh-mon-tah-noh] (Spain) *DO* region in the foothills of the Pyrénées in Aragon, now experimenting with international grape varieties. **COVISA; Enate; Pirineos; Viñas Del Vero.**

Sonnenuhr [soh-neh-noor] (*Mosel*, Germany) Vineyard site in the famous village of *Wehlen*. See *Dr Loosen*. QbA/Kab/Spät: **85** 86 **88 89 90** 91 **92 93 94 95** 96 97 98 Aus/Beeren/Tba: **83 85 88 89 90** 91 **92** 93 94 95 96 97 98

Sonoma Valley [so-NOH-ma] (California) Despite the *Napa* hype, this lesser-known region not only contains some of the state's top wineries, it is also home to *E&J Gallo's* super-premium vineyard and *Dry Creek*, home of some of California's best *Zinfandels*. The region is sub-divided into the *Sonoma*, *Alexander* and *Russian River Valleys* and *Dry Creek*. Red: **85 0 91** 92 93 95 96 97 98 White: **90 91** 92 **95** 96 97 98 Adler Fels; *Arrowood; Carmenet; Ch. St Jean Clos du Bois; Dry Creek; Duxoup; E&J Gallo; Geyser Peak; Gundlach Bundschu; Cecchetti Sebastiani; Iron Horse; Jordan; Kenwood; Kistler; Laurel Glen; Matanzas Creek; Peter Michael; Quivira; Ravenswood; Ridge; St. Francis; Sonoma-Cutrer; Simi; Marimar Torres; Joseph Swan.*

🍷 **Sonoma-Cutrer** [soh-noh-ma koo-trehr] (*Sonoma Valley*, California) Recently sold producer of world-class single-vineyard *Chardonnay* from that can rival *Puligny-Montrachet*. The "Les Pierres" is the pick of the litter.

🍷 **Marc Sorrel** [sor-rel] (*Rhône*, France) *Hermitage* producer who is – unusually – as successful in white as red. The "le Gréal" single-vineyard red is the wine to buy, though the "les Roccoules" white ages well.

🍷 **Pierre Soulez** [soo-layz] (*Loire*, France) Producer of *Savennières* from several vineyards. The Clos du Papillon and Roche-aux-Moines *late harvest* wines are the ones to buy.

South Africa The wine revolution is as dramatic as the ones affecting the rest of South African society. Quality is patchy but improving and better producers are leading the way toward producing riper, more characterful wine that apes neither France nor Australia. Elsewhere, look for inexpensive, simple dry and off-dry *Chenins*, lovely *late harvest* and fortified wines, and surprisingly good *Pinotages*; otherwise very patchy. Red: 86 **87** 89 **91 92** 93 94 **95** 96 97 98 White: 92 93 94 **95** 96 97 98 *Fairview; Grangehurst; Klein Constantia; Jordan; Kanonkop; Mulderbosch; Plaisir de Merle; Saxenburg; Simonsig; Thelema; Vergelegen.*

South Australia Home of almost all the biggest wine companies, and still producing over 50 percent of Australia's wine. The *Barossa Valley* is one of the country's oldest wine producing regions, but like its neighbors *Clare* and *McLaren Vale*, faces competition from cooler areas like the *Adelaide Hills, Padthaway* and *Coonawarra*. Red: **82 84 85 86 87** 88 **90 91 94** 95 96 97 98 White: **87** 88 **90 91 94** 95 96 97 98

South-East Australia A cleverly meaningless regional description which sidesteps Europe's pettier *appellation*-focused rules. Technically, it covers around 85 percent of Australia's vineyards.

South-West France An unofficial umbrella term covering the areas between *Bordeaux* and the *Pyrénées, Bergerac, Madiran, Cahors, Jurançon* and the *Vins de Pays de Côtes de Gascogne*.

Spanna [spah-nah] (*Piedmont*, Italy) The *Piedmontese* name for the *Nebbiolo* grape and the more humble wines made from it.

Pierre Sparr (*Alsace*, France) Big producer offering a rare chance to taste traditional *Chasselas*. ☆☆☆☆ **1996 Tokay Pinot Gris Reserve $$**

Spätburgunder [shpayt-bur-goon-dur](Germany) German name for Pinot Noir.

Spätlese [shpayt-lay-zeh] (Germany) Second step in the *QmP* scale, *late harvested* grapes making wine a notch drier than *Auslese*.

Spottswoode (*Napa Valley*, California) Excellent small producer of complex *Cabernet* and unusually good *Sauvignon Blanc*. Deserves greater recognition. ☆☆☆☆☆ **1994 Cabernet Sauvignon Napa Valley $$$**

Spring Mountain (*Napa Valley*, California) Revived old winery with great vineyards and classy berryish *Cabernet*.

Spritz/ig [shprit-zig] Slight sparkle or sparkling wine. Also *pétillance*.

Spumante [spoo-man-tay] (Italy) Sparkling.

Squinzano [skeen-tzah-noh] (*Puglia*, Italy) Traditional, often rustic reds from the warm south. The Santa Barbara cooperative makes the best wines.

Staatsweingut [staht-svine-goot] (Germany) A state-owned wine estate such as Staatsweinguter *Eltville (Rheingau)*, a major cellar in *Eltville*.

Stafford Ridge (*Adelaide Hills*, Australia) Fine *Chardonnay* and especially *Sauvignon* from *Lenswood* by Geoff Weaver, former winemaker of *Hardys*.

Stag's Leap District (*Napa Valley*, California) A long-established hillside region, specializing in blackcurranty *Cabernet Sauvignon*. Red: 84 **85** 86 87 **90 91** 92 93 95 96 ***Shafer; Clos du Val; Stag's Leap.***

Stag's Leap Wine Cellars (*Napa Valley*, California) Pioneering supporter of the *Stag's Leap appellation*, and one of the finest wineries in California. The best wines are the Faye Vineyard, SLV and Cask 23 *Cabernets*. ☆☆☆☆☆ **1997 SLV-FAYE Cabernet Sauvignon $$$**

Stalky or stemmy Flavor of the stem rather than of the juice.

Stanton & Killeen (*Rutherglen*, Australia) Reliable producer of *Liqueur Muscat*. ☆☆☆☆ **Rutherglen Liqueur Muscat $$**

Steele (*Lake County*, California) The former winemaker of *Kendall Jackson* and a master when it comes to producing fruitily crowd-pleasing *Chardonnays* from various regions and more complex *Zinfandel*.

Steely Refers to young wine with evident *acidity*. A compliment when paid to *Chablis* and dry *Sauvignons*.

Steen [steen] (South Africa) Local name for (and possibly odd *clone* of) *Chenin Blanc*. Widely planted (over 30 percent of the vineyard area). The best come from *Boschendal* and *Fairview*.

Steiermark / Styria (Austria) Sunny southern region where the Chardonnay is now being used (under the name of "Morillon") to produce rich, buttery but often quite Burgundian wines.

Stellenbosch [stel-len-bosh] (South Africa) Center of the *Cape* wine industry, and climatically and topographically diverse region that, like the *Napa Valley*, is taken far too seriously as a regional *appellation*. Hillside sub-regions like Helderberg make more sense. Red: 82 84 86 **87** 89 **91 92** 93 94 **95** 96 97 98 White: **95 96** 97 98 ***Bergkelder; Delheim; Neil Ellis; Grangehurst;*** **Hartenburg;** ***Jordan; Kanonkop; Meerlust; Mulderbosch; Rustenberg; Saxenburg; Stellenzicht; Thelema; Warwick.***

Stellenbosch Farmers' Winery (*Stellenbosch*, South Africa) South Africa's biggest producer; wines include Sable View, Libertas, *Nederburg*, and, now, *Plaisir de Merle*.

Stellenzicht Vineyards [stel-len-zikht] (*Stellenbosch*, South Africa) Sister estate of *Neethlingshof*, with a good *Sauvignon* and a *Shiraz* good enough to beat *Penfolds Grange* in a blind tasting. ☆☆☆☆ **1997 Shiraz $$$**

Sterling Vineyards (*Napa Valley*, California) Founded by Peter Newton (now at *Newton* vineyards) and once the plaything of Coca-Cola, this showcase estate now belongs to Canadian liquor giant Seagram. Among the current successes are the Reserve *Cabernet*, *Pinot Noir*, and fairly priced Redwood Trail wines. ☆☆☆☆ **1994 Cabernet Sauvignon $$**

Weingut Georg Stiegelmar [stee-gel-mahr] (*Burgenland*, Austria) Producer of pricy, highly acclaimed, dry whites from *Chardonnay* and *Pinot Blanc*, *late harvest* wines, and some particularly good reds from *Pinot Noir* and *St. Laurent*. ☆☆☆☆☆ **1995 Juris Trockenbeerenauslese $$$**

Stoneleigh (*Marlborough*, New Zealand) Reliable *Marlborough* label used by *Cooks/Corbans*. ☆☆☆☆ **1997 Sauvignon Blanc $$**

Stonestreet (*Sonoma*, California) Highly commercial wines from the *Kendall-Jackson* stable.

Stony Hill (*Napa Valley*, California) Unfashionable old winery with the guts to produce long-lived, complex *Chardonnay* that tastes like unoaked *Grand Cru Chablis*, rather than follow the herd in apeing buttery-rich *Meursault*. Individual wine for individualist winedrinkers.

Stonyridge (*Hawke's Bay*, New Zealand) Rapidly rising star on the fashionable Waiheke Island, making impressive, if pricy, Bordeaux-style reds.

Stonier's [stoh-nee-yurs] (*Mornington Peninsula*, Australia) Small *Mornington* winery, successful with impressive *Pinot Noir*, *Chardonnay* and *Merlot*. (Previously known as Stoniers-Merrick.) ☆☆☆☆ **1997 Reserve Pinot Noir $$**

Storybook Mountain (*Napa Valley*, California) Great individual-vineyard *Zinfandels* that taste good young but are built for the long haul. The *Howell Mountain* vines are – after the 1997 vintage – being replanted with *Cabernet Sauvignon*. ☆☆☆☆ **1996Estate Zinfandel $$$**

Structure The "structural" components of a wine include *tannin*, *acidity*, and *alcohol*. They provide the skeleton or backbone that supports the "flesh" of the fruit. A young wine with good structure should age well.

Ch. de Suduiraut [soo-dee-rroh] (*Sauternes Premier Cru Classé*, *Bordeaux*, France) Producing greater things since its purchase by French insurance giant, *AXA*. Top wines: "*Cuvée* Madame," "Crème de Tête." 75 **76** 78 **79** 81 **82** **83** 85 86 **88** **89** 90 94 96 97 98 ☆☆☆☆ **1998 $$$$**

Suhindol [soo-win-dol] (Bulgaria) One of *Bulgaria's* best-known regions, the source of widely available, fairly-priced *Cabernet Sauvignon*.

Sulfites US labeling requirement alerting those suffering from an (extremely rare) allergy to the presence of *sulfur dioxide*. Curiously, no such requirement is made of cans of baked beans and dried apricots, which contain twice as much of the chemical.

Sulfur dioxide/SO2 Antiseptic routinely used by food packagers and winemakers to protect their produce from bacteria and *oxidation*.

Super Second (*Bordeaux*, France) *Médoc* second growths: *Pichon-Lalande*, *Pichon-Longueville*, *Léoville-Las-Cases*, *Ducru-Beaucaillou*, *Cos d'Estournel*; whose wines are thought to rival – and cost nearly as much as – the first growths. Other over-performers include: *Rauzan-Ségla* and *Léoville-Barton*, *Lynch-Bages*, *Palmer*, *La Lagune*, *Montrose*.

Super Tuscan (Italy) New-Wave *Vino da Tavola* (usually red) wines, pioneered by producers like *Antinori*, which stand outside traditional *DOC* rules. Generally *Bordeaux*-style blends or *Sangiovese* or a mixture of both.

Supérieur/Superiore [soo-pay-ree-ur/soo-pay-ree-ohr-ray] (France/Italy) Often relatively meaningless in terms of discernible quality. Denotes wine (well or badly) made from riper grapes.

Sur lie [soor-lee] (France) The aging "on its *lees*" – or dead yeasts – most commonly associated with *Muscadet,* but now being used to make other fresher, richer and sometimes slightly sparkling wines in southern France.

Süssreserve [soos-sreh-zurv] (Germany) Unfermented grape juice used to bolster sweetness and fruit in German and English wines.

🍷 **Sutter Home Winery** (*Napa Valley*, California) Home of robust red *Zinfandel* in the 1970s, and responsible for the invention of successful sweet "white" (or, as the non-color-blind might say, pink) *Zinfandel. Amador County Zinfandels* are still good, but rarely exceptional. The M Trinchero Founders Estate Cabernet and Chardonnay are worth looking out for.

🍷 **Joseph Swan** (*Sonoma*, California) Small Burgundian-scale winery whose enthusiastic winemaker, Rod Berglund, produces great single-vineyard, often attractively quirky, *Pinot Noir* and *Zinfandel*.

Swan Valley (*Western Australia*) Hot old vineyard area; good for fortified wines and a source of fruit for *Houghton's* successful *HWB*. *Houghton* also produces cooler-climate wines in the microclimate of *Moondah Brook*.

🍷 **Swanson** [swon-son] (*Napa Valley*, California) Top-flight, innovative producer of *Cabernet, Chardonnay*, *Sangiovese, Syrah* and *late harvest Semillon*. ☆☆☆☆☆ **1996 Syrah $$$**

Switzerland Produces mostly enjoyable but expensive light, floral wines mostly for early drinking. See *Dôle, Fendant, Chablais.* Also the only country to use screw caps for much of its wine, thus facilitating recycling and avoiding the problems of faulty corks. Clever people, the Swiss.

🍇 **Sylvaner/Silvaner** [sihl-vah-nur] Relatively non-aromatic white grape, originally from *Austria* but adopted by other European areas, particularly *Alsace* and *Franken*. Elsewhere, wines are often dry and earthy, though there are some promising efforts with it in South Africa.

🍇 **Syrah** [see-rah] (*Rhône*, France) The red *Rhône* grape, an exotic mix of ripe fruit and spicy, smoky, gamey, leathery flavors. Skillfully adopted by Australia, where it is called *Shiraz* and in southern France for *Vin de Pays d'Oc*. Increasingly popular in California, thanks to "*Rhône* Rangers" like *Bonny Doon* and *Phelps*. See *Qupé, Marqués de Griñon* in Spain and *Isole e Olena* in Italy, plus *Côte Rôtie, Hermitage, Shiraz*.

T

🍷 **La Tâche** [la tash] (*Burgundy*, France) Wine from the La Tâche vineyard, exclusively owned by the *Dom. de la Romanée Conti*. Frequently as good as the rarer and more expensive "La Romanée Conti." ☆☆☆☆☆ **1994 $$$$**

Tafelwein [tah-fel-vine] (Germany) Table wine. Only the prefix "Deutscher" guarantees German origin.

🍷 **Ch. Tahbilk** [tah-bilk] (*Victoria*, Australia) Old-fashioned winemaking in the *Goulbourn Valley*. Great long-lived *Shiraz* from 130-year-old vines, surprizingly good *Chardonnay*, and lemony *Marsanne* which needs a decade. The second wine is Dalfarras. ☆☆☆☆ **1995 Marsanne $$**

🍷 **Cave de Tain L'Hermitage** (*Rhône*, France) Reliable cooperative for *Crozes-Hermitage*, and *Hermitage*. ☆☆☆ **1993 Crozes-Hermitage $$**

🍷 **Taittinger** [tat-tan-jehr] (*Champagne*, France) Producer of reliable non-vintage, and fine Comtes de *Champagne Blanc de Blancs* and Rosé. ☆☆☆☆ **1993 Comtes de Champagne Blanc de Blancs $$$$**

🍷 **Ch. Talbot** [tal-boh] (*St. Julien 4ème Cru Classé*, *Bordeaux*, France) Reliable, if sometimes slightly jammy, wine. Connétable Talbot is the *second label*. 75 **78** 79 81 **82 83** 84 **85** 86 88 89 90 92 93 94 95 96 97 98.

Talley (*San Luis Obispo*, California) Serious small producer of elegant *Chardonnay* and *Pinot Noir* that lasts.

Taltarni [tal-tahr-nee] (*Victoria*, Australia) Until his recent departure, Dominique Portet made great European-style *Shiraz Cabernets* in this beautiful *Pyrénées* vineyard. ☆☆☆☆ **1997 Merlot Cabernet $$$**

Tannat [ta-na] (France) Rustic French grape variety, traditionally widely used in the blend of *Cahors* and in South America, principally *Uruguay*.

Tannic See *Tannin*.

Tannin *Astringent* component of red wine which comes from the skins, seeds, and stalks and helps the wine to age.

Tardy & Ange [tahr-dee ay onzh] (*Rhône*, France) Partnership producing classy *Crozes-Hermitage* at the Dom. de Entrefaux.

Tarragona [ta-ra-GO-nah] (*Catalonia*, Spain) *DO* region south of *Penedés* and home to many cooperatives. Contains the better-quality *Terra Alta*.

Tarrawarra [ta-ra-wa-ra] (*Yarra Valley*, Australia) Increasingly successful *Pinot* pioneer in the cool-climate region of the *Yarra Valley*. *Second label* is Tunnel Hill. ☆☆☆☆☆ **1997 Chardonnay $$$**

Tarry Red wines from hot countries often have an aroma and flavor reminiscent of tar. The *Syrah* and *Nebbiolo* exhibit this characteristic.

Tartaric Type of acid found in grapes. Also the form in which acid is added to wine in hot countries whose legislation allows this.

Tartrates [tar-trayts] Harmless white crystals often deposited by white wines in the bottle. In Germany, these are called "diamonds."

Tasmania (Australia) Cool-climate island, showing potential for sparkling wine, *Chardonnay, Riesling* and *Pinot Noir*. White: **92 94 95** 96 97 98 Red: **91 92 94 95** 96 97 98 ***Freycinet; Heemskerk; Moorilla; Piper's Brook.***

Tastevin [tat-van] The silver *Burgundy* tasting-cup used as an insignia by vinous brotherhoods (*confréries*), as a badge of office by sommeliers and as ashtrays by the author. The *Chevaliers de Tastevin* organize annual tastings, awarding a mock-medieval Tastevinage label to the best wines. *Chevaliers de Tastevin* attend banquets, often wearing similarly mock-medieval clothes.

Taurasi [tow-rah-see] (*Campania*, Italy) Big old-fashioned *Aglianico*. Needs years to soften and develop a burned, cherry taste. ***Mastroberardino.***

Tavel [ta-vehl] (*Rhône*, France) Dry rosé. Often very disappointing. Seek out young versions and avoid the bronze color revered by traditionalists. **Ch. d'Aquéria; Dom. de la Mordorée; du Prieuré.**

Tawny (*Douro*, Portugal) In theory, pale browny-red *port* that acquires its mature appearance and nutty flavor from long aging in oak casks. *Port* houses, however, legally produce "'tawny" by mixing basic *ruby* with *white port* and skipping the tiresome business of barrel-aging altogether. The real stuff comes with an indication of age, such as 10 or 20-year-old, but these figures are approximate. A 10-year-old *port* only has to "'taste as though it is that old." *Port* shippers incidentally get terribly aerated if anyone ever describes an Australian, genuinely wood-aged, tawny) as "*port*-style" or even "*port*-like." I love real tawny *port* (and good *port*-style tawnies, from elsewhere!) – and heartily recommend them to anyone who gets a hangover from *vintage port*. *Colheita ports* are tawnies of a specific vintage (also derided by most traditionalist *port* shippers). ***Noval; Taylor's; Graham's; Cockburn's; Dow's; Niepoort; Ramos Pinto; Calem.***

Taylor (Fladgate & Yeatman) (*Douro*, Portugal) With *Dow's*, one of the "first growths" of the *Douro*. Outstanding *vintage port*, "modern" *Late Bottled Vintage*. Also owns *Fonseca* and *Guimaraens*, and produces the excellent *Quinta de Vargellas* Single-*Quinta port*. **55 60 63 66 70 75 77** 83 85 92 94 97 **1986 Quinta de Vargellas $$$**

🍷 **Te Mata** [tay mah-tah] (*Hawke's Bay*, New Zealand) Pioneer John Buck proves what *New Zealand* can do with *Chardonnay* (in the Elston Vineyard) and pioneered reds with his Coleraine and (lighter) Awatea.

🍷 **Fratelli Tedeschi** [tay-dehs-kee] (*Veneto*, Italy) Reliable producer of rich and concentrated *Valpolicellas* and good *Soaves*. The *Amarones* are particularly impressive. ☆☆☆☆ **1995 Capitel Recioto Classico Monte Fontana $$$**

🍷 **Tement** [teh-ment] (*Steiermark*, Austria) Producer of a truly world-class barrel-fermented *Sauvignon Blanc* which competes directly with top *Pessac-Léognan* whites. Chardonnays are impressive too.

🍷 **Dom. Tempier** [tom-pee-yay] (*Provence*, France) *Provence* superstar estate, producing single-vineyard red and rosé *Bandols* that support the claim that the *Mourvèdre* (from which they are largely made) ages well. Curiously, in recent years the rosé seems to be more reliable than the red.

🍇 **Tempranillo** [tem-prah-nee-yoh] (Spain) The red grape of *Rioja* – and just about everywhere else in Spain, thanks to the way in which its strawberry fruit suits the vanilla/oak flavors of barrel-aging. In *Navarra*, it is called *Cencibel*; in *Ribera del Duero,* Tinto Fino; in the *Penedès*, *Ull de Llebre;* in *Toro*, Tinto de Toro; and in Portugal – where it is used for *port* – it's known as *Tinto Roriz*. So far, though, it is rarely grown outside Spain.

Tenuta [teh-noo-tah] (Italy) Estate or vineyard.

🍷 **Terlano/Terlaner** [tehr-LAH-noh/tehr-LAH-nehr] (*Trentino-Alto-Adige*, Italy) Northern Italian village and its wine: usually fresh, crisp and carrying the name of the grape from which it was made.

🍇 **Teroldego Rotaliano** [teh-ROL-deh-goh roh-tah-lee-AH-noh] (*Trentino-Alto-Adige*, Italy) Dry reds, quite full-bodied, with lean, slightly bitter berry flavors which make them better accompaniments to food. **Foradori.**

Terra Alta [tay ruh al-ta] (*Catalonia*, Spain) Small *DO* within the much larger *Tarragona DO,* producing wines of higher quality due to the difficult climate and resulting low yields. **Pedro Rovira.**

🍇 **Terret** [tehr-ret] (France) Suddenly fashionable, herby, grassy white grape. Possibly best in blends, but a welcome new arrival on the scene. *Jacques Lurton* is a particularly keen – and successful – user.

🍷 **Ch. du Tertre** [doo tehr-tr] (*Margaux 5ème Cru Classé*, *Bordeaux*, France) Recently restored to former glory by the owners of *Calon-Ségur.*

🍷 **Ch. Tertre-Rôteboeuf** [Tehr-tr roht-burf] (*St. Emilion Grand Cru Classé*, *Bordeaux*, France) Good, rich, concentrated if sometimes atypical, crowd-pleasing wines. 85 86 88 89 90 91 **93 94** 95 96 97 98

Tête de Cuvée [teht dur coo-vay] (France) An old expression still used by traditionalists to describe their finest wine.

🍷 **Thackrey** (*Marin County*, California) Rich, impressively concentrated wines that seek to emulate the *Rhône,* but actually come closer to Australia in style.

🍷 **Thames Valley Vineyard** (Reading, England) England's most reliable and dynamic winery – and consultancy – thanks to Australian expertise.

🍷 **Dr H Thanisch** [tah-nish] (*Mosel-Saar-Ruwer*, Germany) Two estates with confusingly similar labels. The best of the pair which has a *VDP* logo offers decent though not always great examples of *Bernkasteler* Doctor, one of the finest vineyards in Germany.

🍷 **Thelema Mountain Vineyards** [thur-lee-ma] (*Stellenbosch*, South Africa) One of the very best wineries in South Africa, thanks to Gyles Webb's skill and to stunning hillside vineyards. *Chardonnay* and *Sauvignon* are the stars, though Webb is coming to terms with his reds too.

🍷 **Thermenregion** [thehr -men-ray-gee-yon] (Austria) Big region close to Vienna, producing good reds and sweet and dry whites.

Ch. Thieuley [tee-yur-lay] (*Entre-Deux-Mers, Bordeaux*, France) Classy property forging the way for concentrated *Sauvignon*-based, well-oaked whites, and silky reds. With *Château Bonnet*, this is one of the leading lights of this region. White: **95** 96 97 98
☆☆☆☆ **1998 Cuvée Francis Courselle Blanc $$**

Paul Thomas (*Washington State*, US) Dynamic brand now under the same ownership as Columbia Winery, and producing a broad range of wines, including good *Chardonnay* and *Semillon* whites and *Cabernet-Merlot* reds.

Three Choirs Vineyard (Gloucestershire, England) Named for the three cathedrals of Gloucester, Hereford, and Worcester, this is one of England's most reliable estates. Try the oaky "Barrique-matured" 1997 whites that are being served on British Airways, and the annual "New Release" *Nouveau*.

Ticino [tee-chee-noh] (Switzerland) One of the best parts of Switzerland to go looking for easy-drinking and (relatively) affordable reds, the best of which are made from Merlot.

Tiefenbrunner [TEE-fen-broon-nehr] (*Trentino-Alto-Adige*, Italy) Consistent producer of fair-to-good *varietal* whites, most particularly *Chardonnay* and *Gewurztraminer.*

Tignanello [teen-yah-neh-loh] (*Tuscany*, Italy) *Antinori's Sangiovese – Cabernet Super Tuscan* is one of Italy's original superstars. Should last for a decade. 82 83 **85** 88 **90** 93 **94** 95 96 97 ☆☆☆☆ **1994 $$$$**

Tinta Roriz [teen-tah roh-reesh] (Portugal) *See Tempranillo*

Tio Pepe [tee-yoh peh-peh] (*Jerez*, Spain) Ultra-reliable *fino sherry* from *Gonzalez Byass*. ☆☆☆☆ **$$**

Tocai [toh-kay] (Italy) Lightly herby Venetian white grape, confusingly unrelated to others of similar name. Drink young.

Tokaji [toh-ka-yee] (Hungary) Not to be confused with Australian *liqueur Tokay*, Tocai Friulano or *Tokay d'Alsace*, *Tokaji Aszú* is a dessert wine made in a specific region of Eastern *Hungary* (and a small corner of *Slovakia*) by adding measured amounts (*puttonyos*) of *eszencia* (a paste made from individually-picked, overripe, and/or *botrytis*-affected grapes) to dry wine made from the local *Furmint* and *Hárslevelu* grapes. Sweetness levels, which depend on the amount of *eszencia* added, range from one to six *puttonyos*, anything beyond which is labeled *Aszú Eszencia*. This last is often confused with the pure syrup which is sold – at vast prices – as *Eszencia*. Wines have become fresher and finer (less *oxidized*) since the arrival of outside investment, which has also revived interest in making individual-vineyard wines from the best sites. ***Disznókö; Royal Tokaji Wine Co; Ch. Megyer; Pajzos.***

Tokay [*in France:* to-kay; *in Australia:* toh-ki] Various different regions have used Tokay as a local name for other grape varieties. In Australia it is the name of a fortified wine from *Rutherglen* made from the *Muscadelle;* in *Alsace*, it is *Pinot Gris;* while the Italian *Tocai* is quite unrelated. Hungary's Tokay – now helpfully renamed *Tokaji* – is largely made from the *Furmint*.

Tokay d'Alsace [toh-ki dal-sas] (*Alsace*, France) See *Pinot Gris*.

Tollana [to-lah-nah] (South Australia) Another part of the Southcorp (*Penfolds, Lindeman etc*) empire – and a source of great value. ☆☆☆☆ **1996 TR222 Cabernet Sauvignon $$;** ☆☆☆☆ **1998 Eden Valley Riesling $$**

Dom. Tollot-Beaut [to-loh-boh] (*Burgundy*, France) Wonderful *Burgundy* domaine in *Chorey-lès-Beaune*, with top-class *Corton* vineyards and a mastery over modern techniques and new oak. Wines have lots of rich fruit flavor. ☆☆☆☆ **1995 Chorey-lès-Beaune $$$**

Torcolato [taw-ko-lah-toh] (*Veneto*, Italy) See *Maculan*.

Torgiano [taw-jee-yah-noh] (*Umbria*, Italy) Zone in *Umbria* and modern red wine made famous by *Lungarotti*. See *Rubesco*.

Toro [TO-roh] (Spain) Up-and-coming region on the *Douro*, close to Portugal, producing intense reds such as Fariña's *Collegiata* from the *Tempranillo*, confusingly known here as the Tinta de Toro. Fariña, **Vega Saúco.**

Torre de Gall [to-ray day-gahl] (*Catalonia*, Spain) *Moët & Chandon's* Spanish sparkling wine. As good it gets using traditional *cava* varieties. ☆☆☆☆ **$$**

Torres [TO-rehs] (*Catalonia*, Spain) *Miguel Torres* revolutionized Spain's wine industry with reliable wines like Viña Sol, Gran Sangre de Toro, Esmeralda, and Gran Coronas, before doing the same for Chile. Today, while these wines face heavier competition, efforts at the top end of the scale, like the *Milmanda Chardonnay*, Fransola *Sauvignon Blanc* and Mas Borras ("Black Label") *Cabernet Sauvignon*, still look good. ☆☆☆☆☆ **1995 Milmanda $$$**

Marimar Torres [TO-rehs] (*Sonoma*, California) *Miguel Torres'* sister is producing some of the most impressive *Pinot Noir* and *Chardonnay* from a spectacular little vineyard in *Russian River*. ☆☆☆☆ **1995 Chardonnay $$$**

Miguel Torres [TO-rehs] (*Curico*, Chile) Improving offshoot of the Spanish giant. The Santa Digna *Cabernet* and the new Manso de Velasco are the star wines. ☆☆☆☆☆ **1996 Manso de Velasco $$$**

Torrontes [to-ron-TEHS] (Argentina) Aromatic grape variety related to the *Muscat*, and highly successful in *Argentina*. *Etchart* is a star producer. Smells sweet even when the wine is bone dry.

Toscana [tos-KAH-nah] (Italy) See *Tuscany*.

Ch. la Tour Blanche [lah toor blonsh] (*Sauternes Premier Cru Classé*, *Bordeaux*, France) Since the late 1980s, one of the finest, longest-lasting *Sauternes*. Also a well-run wine school. 86 **88** 89 90 92 94 95 96 97 98

Ch. la Tour-Carnet [lah toor kahr-nay] (*Haut-Médoc 4ème Cru Classé*, *Bordeaux*, France) Picturesque but *Cru Bourgeois*-level fourth growth.

Ch. la Tour-de-By [lah toor dur bee] (*Médoc Cru Bourgeois*, *Bordeaux*, France) Reliable, especially in ripe years. **85** 86 88 89 90 91 94 95 96 98.

Ch. Tour-du-Haut-Caussin [toor doo oh koh-sa'n] (*Haut-Médoc Cru Bourgeois*, *Bordeaux*, France) Highly reliable modern estate.

Ch. Tour-du-Haut-Moulin [toor doo oh moo-lan] (*Haut-Médoc Cru Bourgeois*, *Bordeaux*, France) An under-appreciated producer of what often can be *cru classé* quality wine. **82** 83 **85** 86 88 **89** **90** 92 94 95 96 97 98

Ch. la Tour-Martillac [lah toor mah-tee-yak] (*Graves Cru Classé*, *Bordeaux*, France) Recently revolutionized organic *Pessac-Léognan* estate with juicy reds and fine whites. **82** 83 85 86 88 89 90 91 **92** 93 94 95 96 97 98.

Touraine [too-rayn] (*Loire*, France) Area encompassing the ACs *Chinon*, *Vouvray* and *Bourgueil*. Also an increasing source of quaffable *varietal* wines – *Sauvignon*, *Gamay* de Touraine, etc. White: 96 97 98 Red: **88** **89** **90** 95 96 97 98 **Briare; Charmoise; Octavie; Oisly & Thésée.**

🍷 **Les Tourelles de Longueville** [lay too-rel dur long-ur-veel] (*Pauillac*, *Bordeaux*, France) The *second label* of *Pichon-Longueville*.

🍇 **Touriga (Nacional/Francesa)** [too-ree-ga nah-see-yoh-nahl/fran-say-sa] (Portugal) Red *port* grape, also (though rarely) seen in the New World.

Traditional Generally meaningless term, except in sparkling wines where the "méthode traditionelle" is the new way to say "*méthode champenoise*" and in Portugal where "Traditional *Late Bottled Vintage*" refers to *port* that unlike non-traditional LBV, hasn't been filtered.

🍇 **Traminer** [tra-mee-nur; *in Australia*: trah-MEE-nah] A less aromatic variant of the *Gewürztraminer* grape widely grown in Eastern Europe and Italy, although the term is confusingly also used as a pronouncable, alternative name for the latter grape – particularly in Australia.

Transfer Method A way of making sparkling wine, involving a second fermentation in the bottle, but unlike the *méthode champenoise* in that the wine is separated from the *lees* by pumping it out of the bottle into a pressurized tank for clarification before returning it to another bottle.

🍷 **Bodegas Trapiche** [tra-pee-chay] (Argentina) Big go-ahead producer with noteworthy barrel-fermented *Chardonnay* and *Cabernet/Malbec*.

Tras-os-Montes [tras-ohsh-montsh] (*Douro*, Portugal) Wine region of the *Upper Douro*, right up at Spanish border and source of *Barca Velha*.

🍇 **Trebbiano** [treh-bee-YAH-noh] (Italy) Ubiquitous white grape in Italy. Less vaunted in France, where it is called *Ugni Blanc*.

🍷 **Trebbiano d'Abruzzo** [treh-bee-YAH-noh dab-ROOT-zoh] (*Abruzzo*, Italy) A *DOC* region where they grow a clone of *Trebbiano*, confusingly called Trebbiano di Toscana, and use it to make unexceptional dry whites.

🍷 **Trefethen** [treh-feh-then] (*Napa Valley*, California) Pioneering estate whose *Chardonnay* and *Cabernet* now taste oddly old-fashioned. The Eshcol wines, though cheaper, are curiously often a better buy.

Trentino [trehn-TEE-noh] (Italy) Northern *DOC* in Italy. *Trentino* specialties include crunchy red *Marzemino*, nutty white Nosiola, and excellent *Vin Santo*. Winemaking here often suffers from overproduction, but less greedy winemakers can offer lovely, soft, easy-drinking wines. **Càvit; *Ferrari;* Foradori; Pojer & Sandri; San Leonardo; Vallarom; Roberto Zeni.**

Trentino-Alto-Adige [trehn-tee-noh al-toh ah-dee-jay] (Italy) Northern region confusingly combining the two *DOC* areas *Trentino* and *Alto-Adige*.

🍷 **Dom. de Trévallon** [treh-vah-lon] (*Provence*, France) Superstar long-lived blend of *Cabernet Sauvignon* and *Syrah* that was sold under the *Les Baux de Provence appellation* but has now (because of crazily restrictive rules) been demoted to *Vin de Pays des Bouches du Rhône*. ☆☆☆☆ **1995 $$$**

🍷 **Dom. Frédéric-Emile Trimbach** [tram-bahkh] (*Alsace*, France) Distinguished grower and merchant with subtle complex wines. Top *cuvées* are the Frédéric Emile, Clos St. Hune, and Seigneurs de Ribeaupierre. ☆☆☆☆☆ **1994 Riesling Alsace Cuvée Frédéric Emile $$$**

Trittenheim [trit-ten-hime] (*Mosel-Saar-Ruwer*, Germany) Village whose vineyards are said to have been the first in Germany planted with *Riesling*, making honeyed wine. QbA/Kab/Spät: **85 88 89 90** 91 **92 93 94 95** 96 97 98 Aus/Beeren/Tba: **83 85 88 89 90** 91 92 93 **94** 95 96 97 98

Trocken [trok-ken] (Germany) Dry, often aggressively so. Avoid Trocken *Kabinett* from such northern areas as the *Mosel*, *Rheingau* and *Rheinhessen*. *QbA* (*chaptalized*) and *Spätlese* Trocken wines (made,by definition, from riper grapes) are better. See also *Halbtrocken*.

Trockenbeerenauslese [trok-ken-beh-ren-ows-lay-zeh] (Austria/ Germany) Fifth rung of the *QmP* ladder, wine from selected dried grapes which are usually *botrytis*-affected and full of natural sugar. Only made in the best years, rare and expensive, though less so in Austria than Germany.

Trollinger [trroh-ling-gur] (Germany) The German name for the Black Hamburg grape, used in *Württemburg* to make light red wines.

Tronçais [tron-say] (France) Forest producing some of the best oak for barrels.

Ch. Tronquoy-Lalande [trron-kwah-lah-lond] (*St. Estèphe Cru Bourgeois, Bordeaux*, France) Traditional wines to buy in ripe years. 79 **82** 83 85 86 88 **89 90** 93 94 95 96 97 98 ☆☆☆☆ **1990 $$$**

Ch. Troplong-Mondot [trroh-lon mondoh] (*St. Emilion Grand Cru Classé, Bordeaux*, France) Brilliantly-sited, top-class property whose wines now sell for top-class prices. **82** 83 **85** 86 88 89 90 91 92 93 94 95 96 98

Ch. Trotanoy [trrot-teh-nwah] (*Pomerol, Bordeaux*, France) Never less than fine and back on especially roaring form since the beginning of the 1990s to compete with *Pétrus*. Some may, however, prefer the lighter style of some of the 1980s. **61 64 67 70 71 75** 76 78 79 81 **82** 83 **85** 86 **88 89** 90 **93 94** 95 96 97 98 ☆☆☆☆ **1994 $$$$**

Ch. Trottevieille [trrott-vee-yay] (*St. Emilion Premier Grand Cru, Bordeaux*, France) Improving but still middle-grade property. **79** 81 **82** 83 **85** 86 88 89 90 91 92 93 94 95 96 97 98 ☆☆☆☆ **1989 $$$$**

Trousseau [troh-soh] (Eastern France) Grape variety found in *Arbois*.

Tsantalis [tsan-tah-lis] (*Nemea*, Greece) Increasingly impressive producer, redefining traditional varieties.

Tulloch [tul-lurk] (*Hunter Valley*, Australia) Under-performing backwater of the *Penfolds* empire.

Tunisia [too-nee-shuh] Best known for dessert *Muscat* wines.

Cave Vinicole de Turckheim [turk-hime] (*Alsace*, France) Cooperative whose top wines can often rival those of some the region's best estates. ☆☆☆☆ **1996 Riesling Brand $$$**

Turkey Flat (South Australia) Small *Barossa Shiraz* and *Grenache* maker. ☆☆☆☆☆ **1994 Grenache Noir, Barossa Valley $$$**

Turley Cellars (*Napa Valley*, California) US guru *Robert Parker* favorite, Helen Turley, who is winemaker here and consultant elsewhere, makes intense but not overblown *Petite Sirahs* and *Zinfandels*, including small quantities from very old vines.

Tuscany (Italy) Major region, the famous home of *Chianti* and reds such as *Brunello di Montalcino* and the new wave of *Super Tuscan Vini da Tavola*. Red: **78 79** 81 **82 85 88 90 94** 95 **96** 97 98

Tyrrell's (*Hunter Valley*, Australia) *Chardonnay* (confusingly sold as *Pinot Chardonnay*) pioneer, and producer of old-fashioned *Shiraz* and (probably most impressively) *Semillon* and even older-fashioned *Pinot Noir* which tastes curiously like old-fashioned *Burgundy*. ☆☆☆☆ **1993 Vat 1 Semillon $$$;** ☆☆☆☆ **1996 Vat 8 Shiraz Cabernet $$$**

U

Ugni Blanc [oo-nee blo*n*] (France) Undistinguished white grape whose neutrality makes it ideal for distillation. It needs modern winemaking to produce a wine with flavor. In Italy, where it is known as the *Trebbiano*, it takes on a mantle of (spurious) nobility. Try *Vin de Pays des Côtes de Gascogne*.

Ull de Llebre [ool dur yay-bray] (Spain) Literally "hare's eye." See *Tempranillo*.

Ullage Space between surface of wine and top of cask or, in a bottle, the cork. The wider the gap, the greater the danger of *oxidation*. Older wines almost always have some degree of ullage; the less the better.

Umani Ronchi [oo-MAH-nee RON-kee] (*Marches*, Italy) Innovative producer whose wines, like the extraordinary new Pelago, prove that *Tuscany* is not the only exciting region in Italy. ☆☆☆☆☆ **1996 Pelago $$$**

Umathum [oo-ma-toom] (*Neusiedlersee*, Austria) Producer of unusually good red wines including a brilliant *St. Laurent*.

Umbria [uhm-bree-ah] (Italy) Central wine region, best known for white *Orvieto* and *Torgiano*, but also producing the excellent red *Rubesco*.

Viña Undurraga [oon-dur-rah-ga] (*Central Valley*, Chile) Family-owned estate with a range of single *varietal* wines, including good *Carmenère*.

Unfiltered Filtering a wine can remove flavor – as can *fining* it with egg white or *bentonite*. Most winemakers traditionally argue that both practices are necessary if the finished wine is going to be crystal-clear and free from bacteria that could turn it to vinegar. Many quality-conscious New-Wave winemakers, however, are now cutting back on *fining* and filtering.

Uruguay Outside consultants are turning this into a new source of *Cabernet Sauvignon* and *Tannat*. **Castel Pujol; Castillo Viejo; Juanico.**

Urzig [oort-zig] (*Mosel-Saar-Ruwer*, Germany) Village on the *Mosel* with steeply sloping vineyards and some of the very best producers, including Christoffel, *Mönchhof*, and *Dr. Loosen*. QbA/Kab/Spät: **88 89 90** 92 93 **94** 95 96 97 98 Aus/Beeren/Tba: **83 85 88 89 90** 91 92 93 **94** 95 96 97 98

Utiel-Requena [oo-tee-yel reh-kay-nah] (*Valencia*, Spain) *DO* of *Valencia*, producing heavy red and good fresh rosé from the Bobal grape.

V

Dom. Vacheron [va-shur-ro*n*] (*Loire*, France) Reliable, if unspectacular, producer of *Sancerre* – including a better-than-average red.

Vacqueyras [va-kay-ras] (*Rhône*, France) *Côtes du Rhône* village with full-bodied, peppery reds which compete with (pricier) *Gigondas*. Red: 90 95 **96** 97 98. **Cazaux; Combe; Couroulu; Fourmone; *Jaboulet Aîné;* Dom. de Mont Vac; Montmirail; de la Soleïade; Tardieu-Laurent; Ch. des Tours; Cave de Vacqueyras; *Vidal-Fleury*.**

Aldo Vajra [vi-rah] (*Piedmont*, Italy) Producer of rich, complex *Barolo* and the deliciously different gamey Freisa delle Langhe.

Val/Valle d'Aosta [val-day-yos-tah] (Italy) Small, spectacularly beautiful area between *Piedmont* and the French/Swiss border. Better for tourism than wine.

Vignerons du Val d'Orbieu [val-dor-byur] (*Languedoc-Roussillon*, France) Would-be innovative association of over 200 cooperatives and growers. Apart from the excellent Cuvée Mythique, however, too many wines leave room for improvement. Reds are far better than whites.
☆☆☆☆ **1997 Cuvée Mythique $$**

Valais [va-lay] (Switzerland) Vineyard area on the upper *Rhône*, making good *Fendant* (*Chasselas*) which surmounts the usual innate dullness of that grape. There are also some reasonable – in all but price – light reds made from the *Pinot Noir*.

Ch. Valandraud [va-lon-droh] (*St. Emilion*, *Bordeaux*, France) An instant superstar launched in 1991 as competition for *le Pin*. Production is small (of *Pomerol* proportions) and the price really astronomical. Values have quintupled following demand from the US and Far East, where buyers seem uninterested in the fact that these wines are actually no finer than Médoc classics costing far less.

Valdeorras [bahl-day-ohr-ras] (*Galicia*, Spain) A barren and mountainous *DO* in *Galicia* beginning to exploit the *Cabernet Franc*-like local grape Mencia and the indigenous white Godello.

Valdepeñas [bahl-deh-pay-nyass] (*La Mancha*, Spain) *La Mancha DO* striving to refine its rather hefty strong reds and whites. Progress is being made, particularly with reds. ***Los Llanos; Felix Solis.***

Valdespino [bahl-deh-spee-noh] (*Jerez*, Spain) Old-fashioned *sherry* company that uses wooden casks to ferment most of its wines. Makes a classic *fino* Innocente and an excellent *Pedro Ximénez*.

Valdevieso [val-deh-vee-yay-soh] (*Curico*, Chile) Dynamic winery with good commercial wines, high-quality *Chardonnay* and *Pinot Noir* and an award-winning blend of grapes, regions, and years called Caballo Loco whose heretical philosophical approach gives Gallic traditionalists apoplexy.

Valençay [va-lon-say] (*Loire*, France) *AC* within *Touraine*, near *Cheverny*, making comparable whites: light and clean, if rather sharp.
85 86 88 89 90 94 95 96 97

Valencia [bah-LEN-thee-yah] (Spain) Produces quite alcoholic red wines from the Monastrell and also deliciously sweet grapey *Moscatel de Valencia*.

Vallet Frères [va-lay frehr] (*Burgundy*, France) Good, small, traditional – not to say old-fashioned – merchant based in *Gevrey-Chambertin*. Also known as Pierre Bourrée. ☆☆☆☆ **1987 Charmes-Chambertin $$$**

Valpolicella [val-poh-lee-cheh-lah] (*Veneto*, Italy) Over-commercialized, light, red wine which should – with rare exceptions – be drunk young to catch its interestingly bitter-cherryish flavor. Bottles labeled *Classico* are better; best are *Ripasso* versions, made by refermenting the wine on the *lees* of an earlier vat. For a different experience, buy *Amarone* or *Recioto*. **86 88 90 91 93 94** 95 96 97 98 ***Allegrini;*** **Bertani;** ***Bolla; Boscaini;*** **dal Forno;** ***Guerrieri-Rizzardi, Masi;*** **Mazzi;** ***Quintarelli;*** **Le Ragose;** ***Serego Alighieri; Tedeschi;*** **Villa Spinosa; Fratelli Zeni.**

Valréas [val-ray-yas] (*Rhône*, France) Peppery, inexpensive red wine from a *Côtes du Rhône* village. 78 **83 85 88** 89 **90** 95 96 97 **Earl Gaia**

Valtellina [vat-teh-lee-na] (*Lombardy*, Italy) Red *DOC* mostly from the *Nebbiolo* grape, of variable quality. Improves with age. The raisiny Sfursat, made from dried grapes, is more interesting.

Varichon et Clerc [va-ree-shon ay klayr] (*Savoie*, France) OK sparkling wine.

Varietal A wine made from and named after one or more grape variety, e.g., California *Chardonnay*. The French authorities are trying to outlaw such references from the labels of most of their *appellation contrôlée* wines. "*Shiraz*" has so far escaped this edict because it is considered a foreign word.

Viña Los Vascos [los vas-kos] (*Colchagua Valley*, Chile) Estate belonging to Eric de *Rothschild* of *Ch. Lafite*, and shamelessly sold with a *Lafite*-like label. The *Cabernet* Grande Reserve has improved but the standard *Cabernet* is uninspiring and the white disappointing, not to say downright poor.

Vasse Felix [vas-fee-liks] (*Margaret River*, Australia) Very classy *Margaret River* winery belonging to the widow of millionaire Rupert Holmes à Court, specializing in juicy, high-quality *Cabernet, Shiraz, Semillon*, and *Riesling*. ☆☆☆☆☆ **1997 Heytesbury $$$**

Vaucluse [voh-klooz] (*Rhône*, France) *Côtes du Rhône* region with good *Vin de Pays* and peppery reds and rosés.

Vaud [voh] (Switzerland) Swiss wine area on the shores of Lake Geneva, famous for unusually tangy *Chasselas* (Dorin) and light reds.

Vaudésir [voh-day-zeer] (*Burgundy*, France) Possibly the best of the seven *Chablis Grands Crus*.

Vavasour [va-va-soor] (*Marlborough*, New Zealand) Pioneers of the Awatere Valley sub-region of *Marlborough*, hitting high standards with *Bordeaux*-style reds, powerful *Sauvignons*, and impressive *Chardonnays*. Dashwood is the *second label*. ☆☆☆☆ **1998 Chardonnay $$$**

VDP (Germany) Association of high-quality producers. Look for the eagle.

VDQS (France) *Vin Délimité de Qualité Supérieur*. Official, neither-fish-nor-fowl, designation for wines better than *Vin de Pays* but not fine enough for an *AC*. Enjoying a strange half-life (amid constant rumors of its imminent abolition), this includes such oddities as *Sauvignon de St. Bris*.

Vecchio [veh-kee-yoh] (Italy) Old.

Vecchio Samperi [veh-kee-yoh sam-peh-ree] (*Sicily*, Italy) Best *Marsala* estate, belonging to *De Bartoli*. Although not *DOC*, a dry aperitif similar to an *amontillado sherry*.

Vega Sicilia [bay-gah sih-sih-lyah] (*Ribera del Duero*, Spain) Spain's top wine is a long (10 years) barrel-matured, eccentric *Tempranillo-Bordeaux* blend called Unico sold for extravagant prices. For a cheaper, slightly fresher taste of the Vega Sicilia-style, try the supposedly lesser Valbuena. 62 64 66 67 69 **70** 72 74 75 76 79 80 82 83 ☆☆☆☆☆ **1992 Valbuena $$$**

Vegetal Often used of *Sauvignon Blanc*, like "grassy." Can be complimentary – though not in California or Australia, where it is held to mean "unripe."

Caves Velhas [kah-vash-vay-yash] (Portugal) Large merchants who blend wine from all over the country, almost single-handedly saved the *Bucelas DO* from extinction. Wines are good, but rarely outstanding.

Velho/velhas [vay-yoh/vay-yas] (Portugal) Old, as of red wine.

Velletri [veh-leh-tree] (Italy) Town in the Alban hills (*Colli Albani*), producing mainly *Trebbiano* and *Malvasia*-based whites, similar to *Frascati*.

Veltliner See *Grüner Veltliner.*

Vendange [Von-donzh] (France) Harvest or vintage.

Vendange tardive [von-donzh tahr-deev] (France) Particularly in *Alsace*, wine from *late harvested* grapes, usually lusciously sweet.

Vendemmia/Vendimia [ven-DEH-mee-yah/ven-DEE-mee-yah] (Italy, Spain) Harvest or vintage.

Venegazzú [veh-neh-GAHT-zoo] (*Veneto*, Italy) Fine, understated *claret*-like *Cabernet Sauvignon Vino da Tavola* "Super-Veneto" to compete with those *Super Tuscans*. Needs five years. The black label is better.

Veneto [veh-neh-toh] (Italy) Northeastern wine region, the home of *Soave, Valpolicella* and *Bardolino*.

Veramonte [vay-rah-mon-tay] (*Casablanca*, Chile) New venture by Augustin Huneeus of *Franciscan Vineyards* in *California*, already producing impressive reds, especially the *Merlot* (which, like many others, is actually *Carmenère*).

Verdejo [vehr-de-khoh] (Spain) Interestingly herby white grape; confusingly not the *Verdelho* of *Madeira* and Australia, but the variety used for new-wave *Rueda*.

Verdelho [*in Madeira:* vehr-deh-yoh; *in Australia:* vur-DEL-loh] (Madeira/Australia) White grape used for fortified *Madeira* and *white port* and for limey, dry, table wine in Australia. **Capel Vale; Chapel Hill; Moondah Brook; Sandalford.**

Verdicchio [vehr-dee-kee-yoh] (*Marches*, Italy) Spicy white grape seen in a number of *DOCs* in its own right, the best of which is *Verdicchio dei Castelli di Jesi*. In *Umbria* this grape is a major component of *Orvieto*.

Verdicchio dei Castelli di Jesi [vehr-dee-kee-yoh day-ee kas-tay-lee dee yay-zee] (*Marches*, Italy) Light, clean, and crisp wines to drink with seafood. **Bucci; Garofoli; Monacesca; *Umani Ronchi.***

Verduzzo [vehr-doot-soh] (*Friuli-Venezia Giulia*, Italy) White grape making a dry and a fine *amabile*-style wine in the *Colli Orientale*.

Vergelegen [vehr-kur-lek-hen] (*Somerset West*, South Africa) Hi-tech winery producing some of the Cape's more reliable wines.

Verget [vehr-jay] (*Burgundy*, France) Young negoçiant based in the Mâconnais and producing impeccable white wines ranging from *Mâcon Villages* to *Meursault* and *Chablis*.

Vermentino [vayr-men-tee-noh] (*Liguria*, Italy) The spicy, dry white grape of the Adriatic and, increasingly, in southern French *Vin de Table*.

Vernaccia [vayr-naht-chah] (*Tuscany*, Italy) White grape making the Tuscan *DOCG* Vernaccia di San Gimignano (where it's helped by a dash of *Chardonnay*) and *Sardinian* Vernaccia di Oristano. At best with a distinct nut 'n' spice flavor. **Casale-Falchini; Teruzzi & Puthod.**

🍷 **Georges Vernay** [vayr-nay] (*Rhône*, France) The great master of *Condrieu* who can do things with *Viognier* that few seem able to match. ☆☆☆☆☆ **1996 Condrieu Coteau de Vernon $$$**

🍷 **Noël Verset** [vehr-say] (*Cornas*, Rhône) Top-class Cornas producer.

🍷 **Quinta do Vesuvio** [veh-soo-vee-yoh] (*Douro*, Portugal) Single *quinta port* from the family that owns *Dow's*, *Graham's*, *Warre's*, etc.

🍷 **Veuve Clicquot-Ponsardin** [vurv klee-koh pon-sahr-dan] (*Champagne*, France) The distinctive orange label is the mark of reliable non-vintage *Brut*. The *prestige cuvée* is called Grand Dame after the famous Widow Clicquot, the *Demi-Sec* is a lovely honeyed wine and the vintage rosé is now one of the best pink wines in the region. ☆☆☆☆☆ **1990 Rosé $$$$**

Victoria (Australia) Huge variety of wines from the *Liqueur Muscats* of *Rutherglen* to the peppery *Shirazes* of *Bendigo* and the elegant *Chardonnays* and *Pinot Noirs* of the *Yarra Valley*.

🍷 **Vidal** [vee-dahl] (*Hawke's Bay*, New Zealand) One of New Zealand's top four red wine producers. Associated with *Villa Maria* and *Esk Valley*. *Chardonnays* are the strongest suit. ☆☆☆☆ **1996 Reserve Cabernet Merlot $$$**

🍇 **Vidal** [VI-dal] (Canada) A *hybrid* and highly frost-resistant variety looked down on by European authorities but widely and successfully grown in *Canada* for spicily exotic *icewine*. ***Iniskillin; Rief Estate.***

🍷 **J. Vidal-Fleury** [vee-dahl flur-ree] (*Rhône*, France) High-quality grower and shipper that belongs to *Guigal*.

VIDE [vee-day] (Italy) Syndicate supposedly denoting finer estate wines.

Vieilles Vignes [vee-yay veeñ] (France) Wine (supposedly) made from a producer's oldest vines. (In reality, while real vine maturity begins at 25, Vieilles Vignes can mean anything between 15 and 90 years of age.)

🍷 **Vieux Château Certan** [vee-yur-cha-toh-sehr-tan] (*Pomerol*, *Bordeaux*, France) Ultra-classy, small *Pomerol* property, known as "VCC" to its fans, producing reliable, concentrated, complex wine. ☆☆☆☆☆ **1995 $$$$**

🍷 **Dom. du Vieux-Télégraphe** [vee-yor tay-lay-grahf] (*Rhône*, France) Modern *Châteauneuf-du-Pape* domaine now back on form after a dull patch. Great whites too. ☆☆☆☆ **1995 Châteauneuf-du-Pape $$$**

🍷 **Ch. Vignelaure** [veen-yah-lawrr] (*Provence*, France) Pioneering estate, now owned by David O'Brien, son of Vincent the Irish racehorse trainer.

Vignoble [veen-yohbl] (France) Vineyard; vineyard area.

🍷 **Villa Maria** (*Auckland*, New Zealand) One of New Zealand's biggest producers, and one which is unusual in coming close to hitting the target with its reds as well as its whites. *Riesling* is a particular success.

🍷 **Villa Sachsen** [za-shehn] (*Rheinhessen*, Germany) Estate with good-rather-than-great, low-yielding vineyards in *Bingen*.

Villages (France) The suffix "villages" e.g., *Côtes du Rhône* or *Mâcon* generally – like *Classico* in Italy – indicates a slightly superior wine from a smaller delimited area encompassing certain village vineyards.

Villany [vee-lah-nyee] (Hungary) Warm area of Hungary with a promising future for soft young drinking reds.

Villard [vee-yarr] (Chile) Improving wines from French-born Thierry Villard, especially *Chardonnays* from *Casablanca*.

Ch. Villemaurine [veel-maw-reen] (*St. Emilion Grand Cru Classé, Bordeaux*, France) Often hard wines which are not helped by heavy-handedness with oak. **82** 83 **85** 86 88 **89** 90 92 94 96 98

Villiera Estate [vil-lee-yeh-rah] (*Paarl*, South Africa) Reliable range of affordable sparkling and still wines from the go-ahead Grier family. The *Sauvignons* and Cru Monro red and now a very impressive Merlot are the wines to buy. ☆☆☆☆☆ **1997 Merlot $$$**

Vin de Corse [van dur kaws] (*Corsica*, France) *Appellation* within *Corsica*. Good sweet *Muscats* too. **Gentile; Peraldi; *Skalli; Toraccia.***

Vin de garde [van dur gahrd] (France) Wine to keep.

Vin de l'Orléanais [van dur low-lay-yon-nay] (*Loire*, France) Small *VDQS* in the Central Vineyards of the *Loire*. See *Orléanais*.

Vin de Paille [van dur piy] (*Jura*, France) Traditional, now quite rare regional specialty; sweet golden wine from grapes dried on straw mats.

Vin de Pays [van dur pay-yee] (France) Lowest/broadest geographical designation. In theory, these are simple country wines with certain regional characteristics. In fact, the producers of some of France's most exciting wines – such as *Dom. de Trévallon* and *Mas de Daumas Gassac* – prefer this designation and the freedom it offers from the restrictions imposed on *appellation contrôlée* wines. See *Côtes de Gascogne* and *Vin de Pays d'Oc*.

Vin de Savoie [van dur sav-wah] (Eastern France) Umbrella mountainous appellation encompassing sub-appellations such as *Aprémont* and Chignon.

Vin de table [van dur tahbl] (France) Table wine from no particular area.

Vin de Thouarsais [twar-say] (*Loire*, France) *VDQS* for a soft light red from the *Cabernet Franc*; whites from the *Chenin Blanc*.

Vin doux naturel [doo nah-too-rrel] (France) Fortified – so not really "naturel" at all – dessert wines, particularly the sweet, liquorous *Muscats* of the south, such as *Muscat de Beaumes de Venise, Mireval* and *Rivesaltes*.

Vin Gris [van gree] (France) Chiefly from *Alsace* and the *Jura*, pale rosé from red grapes pressed after crushing or following a few hours of *skin contact*.

Vin Jaune [van john] (*Jura*, France) Golden-colored *Arbois* specialty; slightly *oxidized* – like *fino sherry*. See *Ch. Chalon*.

Vin ordinaire (France) A simple local wine, usually served in carafes.

Vin Santo [vin sahn-toh] (Italy) Powerful, highly traditional white dessert wine made from bunches of grapes hung to dry in airy barns for up to six years, especially in *Tuscany* and *Trentino*. Often very ordinary, but at its best competes head-on with top-quality medium *sherry*. Best drunk with sweet almond ("Cantuccine") biscuits. ***Altesino; Avignonesi; Badia a Coltibuono; Berardenga; Felsina Isole e Olena; Poliziano; Selvapiana.***

Vin vert [van vehrr] (*Languedoc-Roussillon*, France) Light, refreshing, acidic white wine.

Viña de Mesa [vee-nah day may-sah] (Spain) Spanish for table wine.

Vinho Verde [vee-noh vehrr-day] (Portugal) Literally "green" wine, confusingly red or pale white often tinged with green. At worst, dull and sweet. At best delicious, refreshing and slightly sparkling. Drink young.

Vinícola Navarra [vee-NEE-koh-lah na-VAH-rah] (*Navarra*, Spain) Ultramodern winemaking and newly-planted vineyards beginning to come on stream. Owned by *Bodegas y Bebida*.

Vinifera [vih-nih-feh-ra] Properly *Vitis vinifera*: Species of all European vines.

Vino da Tavola [VEE-noh dah TAH-voh-lah] (Italy) Table wine, but the *DOC* quality designation net is so riddled with holes that producers of many superb – and pricey – wines have contented themselves with this "modest" ***appellation***. Now being replaced by *IGT*.

Vino de la Tierra [bee-noh day la tyay rah] (Spain) Spanish wine designation which can offer interesting, affordable, regional wines.

Vino Nobile di Montepulciano [vee-noh NOH-bee-lay dee mon-tay-POOL-chee-AH-noh] (*Tuscany*, Italy) *Chianti* in long pants; potentially truly noble (though not often), and made from the same grapes. Can age well. Rosso di Montepulciano is the lighter, more accessible version. The *Montepulciano* of the title is the *Tuscan* town, not the grape variety.

Vino novello [vee-noh noh-vay-loh] (Italy) New wine; equivalent to French ***nouveau***.

Vinopolis Recently (1999) launched London wine museum / theme park.

Vintage Year of production.

Vintage Champagne (*Champagne*, France) Wine from a single "declared" year.

Vintage Character (port) (*Douro*, Portugal) Smartly packaged up-market ***ruby*** made by blending various years' wines.

Vintage (port) (*Douro*, Portugal) Produced only in "declared" years, aged in wood then in the bottle for many years. In "off" years, ***port*** houses release wines from their top estates as single ***quinta ports***. This style of ***port*** must be decanted, as it throws a sediment.

Viognier [vee-YON-nee-yay] (*Rhône*, France) Infuriating white variety which, at its best, produces floral peachy wines that startle with their intensity and originality. Once limited to the *Rhône* – *Condrieu* and *Ch. Grillet* – but now increasingly planted in southern France, California and Australia. Benefits from a little – but not too much – contact with new oak. ***Calera; Duboeuf; Guigal; Heggies; Andre Perret; Georges Vernay.***

Viré [vee-ray] (*Burgundy*, France) *Mâconnais* village, famous for whites.

Virgin Hills [*Victoria*, Australia] A single red blend that is unusually lean in style for Australia and repays keeping. Making valiant efforts to make sulfur-free wine. ☆☆☆☆ **1996 $$$**

Viticulteur (-Propriétaire) (France) Vine grower/vineyard owner.

Viura [vee-yoo-ra] (Spain) Dull white grape of the *Rioja* region and elsewhere, now being used to greater effect.

Dom. Michel Voarick [vwah-rik] (*Burgundy*, France) Old-fashioned wines that avoid the use of new oak. Fine *Corton-Charlemagne*.

Dom. Vocoret [vok-ko-ray] (*Burgundy*, France) Classy *Chablis* producer whose wines age well. ☆☆☆☆☆ **1995 Chablis Blanchot $$$**

Roberto Voerzio [vwayrt-zee-yoh] (*Piedmont*, Italy) One of the new-wave producers of juicy, spicy reds, including a first-rate *Barolo*. ☆☆☆☆ **1996 Vignaserra $$$**

Alain Voge [vohzh] (*Rhône*, France) Traditional *Cornas* producer who also makes good *St. Péray*.

De Vogüé [dur voh-gway] (*Burgundy*, France) *Chambolle-Musigny* estate whose ultra-concentrated red wines deserve to be kept – for ages. Not cheap, but nor are many of life's true luxuries.

Volatile acidity (VA) Vinegary character evident in wines which have been spoiled by bacteria.

Volnay [vohl-nay] (*Burgundy*, France) Red wine village in the *Côte de Beaune* (the Caillerets vineyard, now a *Premier Cru*, was once ranked equal to *le Chambertin*). This is the home of fascinating, plummy, violety reds. **78** 80 83 **85 88 89 90 92** 93 94 95 96 97 98 ***Ampeau; d'Angerville; J-M Boillot;*** **Francois Buffet;** ***Lafarge; Lafon; Leroy; Dom de Montille; Pousse d'Or.***

Castello di Volpaia [vol-pi-yah] (*Tuscany*, Italy) Top-quality *Chianti* estate with *Super Tuscans* Coltassala and Balifico. ☆☆☆☆ **1994 Coltassala $$$**

Vosne-Romanée [vohn roh-ma-nay] (*Burgundy*, France) *Côte de Nuits* red wine village with *Romanée-Conti* among its many grand names, and many other potentially gorgeous, plummy, rich wines, from a variety of different producers. 78 79 80 82 83 **85** 86 87 **88 89 90** 92 95 96 97 98 ***Confuron-Cotetidot; Engel; Anne Gros; Grivot; Hudelot-Noëllat; Jayer; Laurent; Leroy; Méo-Camuzet; Mongeard-Mugneret; Rion; Romanée-Conti; Rion.***

Voss (*Sonoma*, California) Californian venture by *Yalumba*, producing lovely intense *Zinfandel*.

Vougeot [voo-joh] (*Burgundy*, France) *Côte de Nuits commune* comprizing the famous *Grand Cru Clos de Vougeot* and numerous growers of varying skill. Red: 78 79 83 **85 88 89 90** 92 93 95 96 97 98. ***Bertagna;* Chopin-Groffier; *Engel; Drouhin; Anne Gros; Leroy; Méo-Camuzet; Rion;* de la Tour.**

la Voulte Gasparets [voot-gas-pah-ray] (*Languedoc-Roussillon*, France) Unusually ambitious estate with single-vineyard bottlings (Romain Pauc is the best) that show just how good *Corbières* can be from the best sites.

Vouvray [voov-ray] (*Loire*, France) White wines from the *Chenin Blanc*, ranging from clean dry whites and refreshing sparklers to *Demi-Secs* and honeyed, long-lived, sweet *Moelleux* wines. Often spoiled by massive doses of *sulfur dioxide*. Sweet white: **76** 83 **85** 86 **88 89 90** 94 95 96 97 98 White: 83 **85 86 88 89 90 94** 95 96 97 98 ***Des Aubuisières; Champalou; Huët;* Foreau; Fouquet; Gaudrelle; Jarry; Mabille; Clos de Nouys; Pichot; Vaugondy.**

VQA (Canada) Acronym for Vintners Quality Alliance, a group of Canadian producers with a self-styled quality designation.

Vriesenhof [free-zen-hof] (*Stellenbosch*, South Africa) Tough, occasionally classic reds and so-so *Chardonnay*. ☆☆☆ **1995 Kallista Red $$**

W

Wachau [vak-kow] (Austria) Major wine region producing some superlative *Riesling* from steep, terraced vineyards. **Alzinger; Pichler; Hirtzberger; Jamek; Nikolaihof; Prager; *Freie Weingärtner Wachau.***

Wachenheim [vahkh-en-hime] (*Pfalz*, Germany) Superior *Mittelhaardt* village which should produce full, rich, unctuous *Riesling*. QbA/Kab/Spät: **85 88 89 90** 91 **92 93** 94 95 96 97 98 Aus/Beeren/Tba: **83 85 88 89 90** 91 92 93 94 95 96 97 98 ***Biffar; Bürklin-Wolf.***

Waiheke Island (*Auckland*, New Zealand) Tiny island off Auckland where holiday cottages compete for space with vineyards. Land – and the resulting wines – is pricy, but this microclimate does produce some of New Zealand's best reds. ***Goldwater Estate;*** **Stonyridge; Te Motu.**

🍷 **Waipara Springs** [wi-pah-rah] (*Canterbury*, New Zealand) Tiny producer offering the opportunity to taste wines from this southern region at their best.

🍷 **Wairau River** [wi-row] (*Marlborough*, New Zealand) Classic Kiwi *Chardonnays* and *Sauvignons* with piercing fruit character. ☆☆☆☆ **1996 Sauvignon Blanc $$**

Walker Bay (South Africa) Promising southerly region for *Pinot Noir* and *Chardonnay*. Established vineyards include *Hamilton Russell* and *Bouchard-Finlayson*.

🍷 **Warre's** [waw] (*Douro*, Portugal) Oldest of the big seven *port* houses and a stablemate to *Dow's*, *Graham's*, and *Smith Woodhouse*. Traditional *port* which is both rather sweeter and more *tannic* than most. The old-fashioned *Late-Bottled Vintage* is particularly worth seeking out too. **55** 58 60 **63 66** 70 75 77 83 85 91 94 97 ☆☆☆☆☆ **1990 Bottle Matured LBV $$$**

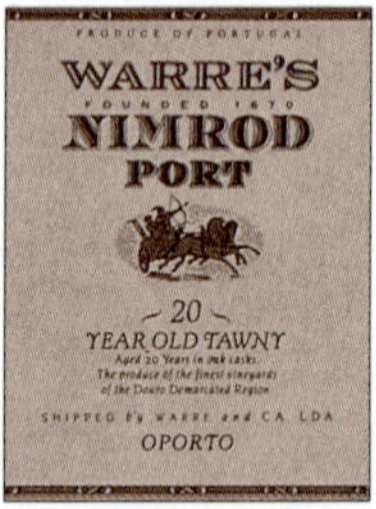

🍷 **Warwick Estate** [wo-rik] (*Stellenbosch*, South Africa) Source of some of South Africa's best reds, including a good *Bordeaux*-blend called Trilogy. The *Cabernet Franc* grows extremely well here.

Washington State (US) Underrated (especially in the US) state whose dusty irrigated vineyards produce classy *Riesling*, *Sauvignon*, and *Merlot*. Red: 85 88 **89** 91 92 94 **95** 96 97 98 White: **95 96** 97 98 ***Columbia; Columbia Crest; 'Ecole 41; Hedges; Hogue; Kiona; Paul Thomas; Leonetti Cellars; Quilceda Creek; Staton Hills; Ch. Ste. Michelle; Andrew Will; Woodward Canyon.***

Jimmy Watson Trophy (*Victoria*, Australia) Coveted trophy given annually to the best young (still-in-barrel) red at the Melbourne Wine Show. Apparently "worth" $(Aus) 1,.000,000 in increased sales to the winner, it is often criticized for hyping stuff that is not necessarily representative of what you'll actually be drinking when the wine gets in the bottle.

🍷 **Geheimrat J. Wegeler Deinhard** [vayg-lur-dine-hard] (*Rheingau*, Germany) Once family-owned producer recently bought by the huge sparkling wine producer Henkell Söhnlein. Wines that made Deinhard famous include recommendable top *Mosels* such as *Bernkasteler Doctor* and *Wehlener Sonnenuhr*. It remains to be seen whether the new owners continue to produce wines of the same standard.

Wehlen [VAY-lehn] (*Mosel-Saar-Ruwer*, Germany) *Mittelmosel* village making fresh, sweet, honeyed wines; look for the *Sonnenuhr* vineyard. QbA/Kab/Spät: **85** 86 **88 89 90** 91 92 93 94 95 Aus/Beeren/Tba: **83 85** 88 89 90 91 92 93 94 95 96 ***Dr Loosen; JJ Prum; SA Prum; Richter; Wegeler Deinhard; Selbach-Oster.***

🍷 **Weingut Dr Robert Weil** [vile] (*Rheingau*, Germany) Suntory-owned, family-run winery with stunning dry and *late harvest* wines. ☆☆☆☆☆ **1996 Rheingau Riesling Halbtrocken $$$**

🍷 **Dom. Weinbach** [vine-bahkh] (*Alsace*, France) Laurence Faller regularly turns out wonderful, concentrated, but gloriously subtle wines. The Cuvée Laurence is a personal favorite. ☆☆☆☆☆ **1994 Gewurztraminer Furstentum Selection de Grains Nobles $$$$**

🍷 **Bodegas y Cavas de Weinert** [vine-nurt] (Argentina) Excellent *Cabernet Sauvignon* specialist, whose soft, ripe wines last extraordinarily well. ☆☆☆☆ **1995 Cabernet Sauvignon $$**

Weingut [vine-goot] (Germany) Wine estate.

Weinkellerei [vine-keh-lur-ri] (Germany) Cellar or winery.

🍇 **Weissburgunder** [vi-sbur-goon-dur] (Germany/Austria) The *Pinot Blanc* in Germany and Austria. Relatively rare, so often made with care.

🍷 **Weissherbst** [vi-sairb-st] (*Baden*, Germany) Spicy, berryish dry rosé made from various different grape varieties.

🍇 **Welschriesling** [velsh-rreez-ling] Aka *Riesling Italico*, *Lutomer*, *Olasz*, *Laski Rizling*. Dull grape, unrelated to the Rhine Riesling, but with many synonyms. Comes into its own when affected by *botrytis*.

🍷 **Wendouree** (*Clare*, Australia) Small winery with a cult following for its often *Malbec*-influenced reds. Wines are very hard to find outside Australia but are well worth seeking out. ☆☆☆☆ **1992 Cabernet Malbec $$$**

🍷 **Wente Brothers** (*Livermore*, California) Improving family company which, despite – or perhaps because of – such distracting enterprises as producing cigars and joint ventures in Mexico, Israel, and Eastern Europe, is still trailing in quality and value behind firms like *Fetzer*. *Murrieta's Well* is the strongest card in the Wente pack. ☆☆☆☆ **1997 Riva Ranch Reserve Chardonnay $$**

🍷 **Domdechant Werner'sches Weingut** [dom-dekh-ahnt vayr-nehr-ches vine-goot] (*Rheingau*, Germany) Excellent vineyard sites at *Hochheim* and *Riesling* grapes combine to produce a number of traditional wines that age beautifully.

🍷 **De Wetshof Estate** [vets-hof] (*Robertson*, South Africa) *Chardonnay* pioneer, Danie de Wet makes up to seven different styles of wine for different markets.

🍷 **William Wheeler Winery** (*Sonoma*, California) Inventive producer whose Quintet brings together such diverse grapes as the *Pinot Meunier*, the *Pinot Noir*, *Grenache*, and *Cabernet Sauvignon*. ☆☆☆☆☆ **1995 Napa Valley Reserve Cabernet Sauvignon $$**

🍷 **White Cloud** (New Zealand) Commercial white made by *Nobilo*.

White port (*Douro*, Portugal) Semi-dry aperitif, drunk by its makers with tonic water and ice, which shows what they think of it. *Churchill's* make a worthwhile version. ☆☆☆☆ **Churchill's White Port $$**

🍷 **Whitehall Lane** (*Napa Valley*, California) Impressive *Merlots* and *Cabernets*. ☆☆☆☆☆ **1994 Cabernet Sauvignon Napa Valley Morisoli Vineyard.**

🍷 **Wien** [veen] (Austria) Region close to the city of Vienna, producing ripe-tasting whites and reds. **Mayer; Wieninger.**

🍷 **Wild Horse** (*San Luis Obispo*, California) *Chardonnays, Pinot Blancs* and *Pinot Noirs* are all good, but the perfumed *Malvasia Bianca* is the star.

Willamette Valley [wil-AM-et] (*Oregon*, US) The heart of *Oregon's* *Pinot Noir* vineyards.

🍷 **Williams Selyem** [sel-yem] (*Sonoma*, California) Recently dissolved partnership producing world-class Burgundian-style *Chardonnay* and *Pinot Noir*.

Wiltingen [vihl-ting-gehn] (*Mosel-Saar-Ruwer*, Germany) Distinguished *Saar* village, making elegant, slatey wines. Well known for the *Scharzhofberg* vineyard. QbA/Kab/Spät: **85** 86 **88 89 90** 91 **92 93 94** 95 96 97 98 Aus/Beeren/Tba: **83 85 88 89** 90 91 92 93 94 95 96 97 98

🍷 **Wing Canyon** (*Mount Veeder*, California) Small *Cabernet Sauvignon* specialist with vineyards high in the hills of *Mount Veeder*. Great, intense, blackcurranty wines. ☆☆☆☆ **1993 Mount Veeder Cabernet Sauvignon $$$$**

Winkel [vin-kel] (*Rheingau*, Germany) Village with a reputation for complex delicious wine, housing *Schloss Vollrads* estate. QbA/Kab/Spät: **85** 86 **88 89 90** 91 **92 93** 94 95 96 97 98 Aus/Beeren/Tba: **83 85 88 89** 90 91 **92 93** 94 95 96 97 98

Winzerverein/Winzergenossenschaft [vint-zur-veh-RINE/vint-zur-geh-NOSH-en-shaft] (Germany) Cooperative.

🍷 **Wirra Wirra Vineyards** (*McLaren Vale*, Australia) Reliable producer making first-class *Riesling* and *Cabernet* which, in best vintages, is sold as The Angelus. Recently joined by Dr. Tony Jordan ex-Domaine Chandon .

🍷 **WO (Wine of Origin)** (South Africa) Official European-style certification system that is taken seriously in South Africa.

🍷 **J.L. Wolf** [volf] (*Pfalz*, Germany) A recently reconstituted estate producing good wine in *Wachenheim*.

🍷 **Wolff-Metternich** [volf met-tur-nikh] (*Baden*, Germany) Good, rich *Riesling* from the granite slopes of *Baden*.

🍷 **Woodward Canyon** (*Washington State*, US) Small producer of characterful but subtle *Chardonnay* and *Bordeaux*-style reds that compete with the best of California. *Semillons* are pretty impressive too. ☆☆☆☆ **1995 Cabernet Sauvignon Washington Canoe Ridge Vineyard Artist Series $$$**

Württemburg [foor-thm-burg] (Germany) *Anbaugebiet* surrounding the Neckar area, producing more red than any other German region.

🍷 **Würzburg** [foor-ts-burg] (*Franken*, Germany) Great Sylvaner country, though there are some fine Rieslings too. **Bürgerspital; Juliusspital.**

🍷 **Wyndham Estate** (*Hunter Valley*, Australia) Ultra-commercial *Hunter/Mudgee* producer which, like *Orlando*, now belongs to Pernod-Ricard. Quite what that firm's French customers would think of these often rather jammy blockbusters is anybody's guess. ☆☆☆☆ **1997 Bin 555 Shiraz $$**

🍷 **Wynns** (*Coonawarra*, Australia) Subsidiary of *Penfolds*, based in *Coonawarra* and producer of the *John Riddoch Cabernet* and Michael *Shiraz*, both of which are only produced in good vintages and sell fast at high prices. There is also a big buttery *Chardonnay* and a commercial *Riesling*. ☆☆☆☆☆ **1996 Coonawarra Estate Cabernet Shiraz Merlot $$$**

X

🍷 **Ch. Xanadu** [za-na-doo] (*Margaret River*, Australia) The reputation here was built on *Semillon*, but the *Cabernet* is good too. ☆☆☆☆ **1996 Cabernet Reserve $$$**

🍇 **Xarel-lo** [sha-REHL-loh] (*Catalonia*, Spain) Fairly basic grape exclusive to *Catalonia*. Used for *Cava*; best in the hands of *Jaume Serra*.

Y

🍷 **"Y" d'Yquem** [ee-grek dee-kem] (*Bordeaux*, France) Hideously expensive dry wine of *Ch. d'Yquem* which, like other such efforts by *Sauternes châteaux*, is of greater academic than hedonistic interest.

Yakima Valley [YAK-ih-mah] (*Washington State*, US) Principal region of *Washington State*. Good for *Merlot*, *Riesling* and *Sauvignon*. Red: 85 88 **89** 91 92 94 95 96 97 98 White: **90 91 92 94 95** 96 97 98 ***Columbia Crest; Columbia Winery; Kiona; Ch. Ste. Michelle.***

🍷 **Yalumba** [ya-LUM-ba] (*Barossa Valley*, Australia) Associated with *Hill-Smith, Heggies, Pewsey-Vale,* and *Janz* in Australia, *Nautilus* in New Zealand and *Voss* in California. Producers of good-value reds and whites under the Oxford Landing label; more serious vineyard-designated reds and dry and sweet whites, fortified wines (including *Rutherglen Muscat)* and some of Australia's most appealing sparkling wine, including *Angas Brut* and the brilliant Cuvée One *Pinot Noir-Chardonnay*. ☆☆☆☆ **1996 The Signature Cabernet Sauvignon Shiraz $$$;** ☆☆☆☆ **1998 Growers Limited Release Viognier $$$**

🍷 **Yarra Ridge** [ya-ra] (Australia) *Mildara-Blass* label with wines from beyond the *Yarra Valley*.

Yarra Valley [ya-ra] (*Victoria*, Australia) Historic wine district whose "boutiques" make top-class *Burgundy*-like *Pinot Noir* and *Chardonnay* (*Coldstream Hills* and *Tarrawarra)*, some stylish *Bordeaux*-style reds and, at *Yarra Yering*, a brilliant *Shiraz*. **de Bortoli; Coldstream Hills; Dom. Chandon (Green Point); Mount Mary; St Huberts; Seville Estate; Tarrawarra; Yarra Yering.**

🍷 **Yarra Yering** [ya-ra yeh-ring] (*Yarra Valley*, Australia) Bailey Carrodus proves that the *Yarra Valley* is not just *Pinot Noir* country by producing a complex *Cabernet* blend, including a little *Petit Verdot* (Dry Red No.1) and a *Shiraz* (Dry Red No.2), in which he puts a bit of *Viognier*. Underhill is the *second label*. ☆☆☆☆ **1994 Underhill Shiraz $$$**

🍷 **Yellowglen** (*South Australia)* Producer of uninspiring basic sparkling wine, and some really fine top-end fare, including the "Y" which looks oddly reminiscent of a sparkling wine called "J" from *Jordan* in California.

🍷 **Yonder Hill** (*Stellenbosch*, South Africa) New winery making waves with well-oaked reds. ☆☆☆☆ **1997 Merlot $$**

Yonne [yon] (*Burgundy*, France) Northern *Burgundy* département in which *Chablis* is to be found.

🍷 **Ch. d'Yquem** [dee-kem] (*Sauternes Premier Cru Supérieur*, *Bordeaux*, France) Sublime *Sauternes*. The grape pickers are sent out several times to select the best grapes. Not produced every year. Recently bought by the giant Louis-Vuitton Moët Hennessy group which wants to sell the wine through its duty-free shops in the Far East. Such is the wine world in 1999. **67 71** 73 **75 76** 77 78 79 **80 81 82** 83 84 85 86 87 88 89 90 91 93 94 95 96 97 98 ☆☆☆☆☆ **1989 $$$$**

Z

🍷 **Zaca Mesa** [za-ka may-sa] (*Santa Barbara*, California) Fast-improving winery with a focus on spicy *Rhône* varietals.

Zell [tzell] (*Mosel-Saar-Ruwer*, Germany) *Bereich* of lower *Mosel* and village, making pleasant, flowery *Riesling*. Famous for the *Schwarze Katz* (black cat) *grosslage*. QbA/Kab/Spät: **85 88 89 90** 91 **92** 93 94 95 96 97 98 Aus/Beeren/Tba: **83 85 88 89** 90 91 **92** 93 94 95 96 97 98

🍷 **Zenato** [zay-NAH-toh] (*Veneto*, Italy) Successful producer of modern *Valpolicella* (particularly *Amarone*), *Soave*, and *Lugana*. ☆☆☆☆☆ **1996 Ripassa Valpolicella Classico Superiore $$$**

Zentralkellerei [tzen-trahl-keh-lur-ri] (Germany) Massive central cellars for groups of cooperatives in six of the *anbaugebiet* – the *Mosel-Saar-Ruwer* Zentralkellerei is Europe's largest cooperative.

Zibibbo [zee-BEE-boh] (*Sicily*, Italy) Good, light *Muscat* for easy summer drinking.

🍷 **Zilliken** [tsi-li-ken-] (*Saar*, Germany) Great *late harvest Riesling* producer. ☆☆☆☆☆ **1997 Riesling Beerenauslese Gold Cap Saarburger Rausch $$$**

Zimbabwe An industry started by growing grapes in ex-tobacco fields is slowly attaining a level of international adequacy.

🍷 **Dom. Zind-Humbrecht** [zind-hoom-brekht] (*Alsace*, France) Extraordinarily consistent producer of ultra-concentrated, single-vineyard wines and good *varietals* that have won numerous awards from the *International Wine Challenge* and drawn *Alsace* to the attention of a new generation of wine drinkers. ☆☆☆☆ **1997 Wintzenheim Gewurztraminer $$$**

🍇 **Zinfandel** [zin-fan-del] (California, Australia, South Africa) Versatile red grape, producing everything from dark, jammy, leathery reds in California, to (with a little help from sweet Muscat) pale pink "blush" wines, and even a little fortified wine that bears comparison with *port*. Also grown by *Cape Mentelle* and *Nepenthe* in Australia, and *Blauwklippen* in South Africa. **Chateau Potelle; Cline; *De Loach;* Gary Farrell; *Lamborn Family Vineyards; Quivira, Rafanelli; Ravenswood; Ridge;* Rocking Horse; *Rosenblum; St. Francis; Steele; Storybook Mountain, Turley; Wellington.***

🍷 **Don Zoilo** [don zoy-loh] (*Jerez*, Spain) Classy *sherry* producer. ☆☆☆☆ **Don Zoilo Oloroso $$**

🍷 **Zonin** [zoh-neen] (*Veneto*, Italy) Dynamic company producing good wines in the *Veneto*, *Piedmont* and *Tuscany*.

🍇 **Zweigelt** [zvi-gelt] (Austria) Distinctive berryish red wine grape, more or less restricted to Austria and Hungary. **Kracher.**

U.S. RETAILERS

Where to Buy

The following section has been conceived in order to help you to find almost everything – short of a congenial companion – you are likely to need to enjoy wine. If you are looking for a good local retailer, a wine from a specific region/country, or perhaps a wine course/school, vacation, tour, cellar, rack, or chiller, this is the place to look.

Wine Retailers

Arizona

Anna's Cafe

5618 East Thomas Road, Phoenix. AZ 85018. ☎ 480 945 4503. FAX 480 423 5771. Pre-arrivals, delivery, tastings, credit cards.
Friendly and cozy atmosphere and quality, well-priced wines. Specialists in Burgundy.

Colonial Bottle Shop

11601 West Markham, Little Rock AZ 72211. ☎ 501 223 3120. FAX 501 224 3120. E-mail: ctrim@arkansas.net.. Wine futures, books, credit cards, accessories.
Services include party and wedding planning and food/wine pairing.

Drinkwater's Liquor & Fine Wine

10802 North Scottsdale Road, Scottsdale, AZ 85254. ☎ 602 948 0520. FAX 602 998 5247. Delivery, tastings, credit cards, accessories.
Specializing in upscale spirits, boutique wines and beers. Tastings are held in the store's wine bar.

House Wine & Cheese

7001 North Scottsdale Road, Scottsdale, AZ 85253. ☎ 480 922 3470. FAX 480 922 3269.
E-mail: pour@housewines.com
Website: www.housewines.com
Wine futures, books, delivery, tastings, newsletters, credit cards, accessories.
Stacks of domestic boutique wines, specially imported cheeses and unique hand-made chocolates.

California

Bel-Air Wine Merchant

10421 Santa Monica Boulevard West, Los Angeles, CA 90025. ☎ 310 474 9518. FAX 310 475 2836.
E-mail: sales@belair2020.com
Wine futures, books, delivery, newsletters, cellarage, credit cards, wine club.
Wide range focusing on the finer end of the market, particularly Bordeaux. Also boasts a good wine club.

David Berkley Fine Wines & Specialty Foods

515 Pavilions Lane, Sacramento, CA 95825. ☎ 916 929 4422. FAX 916 929 0066. E-mail: dberkley@dberkley.com Website: dberkley.com
Wine futures, books, glass rental, delivery, tastings, newsletters, credit cards, Riedel glassware, accessories, wine gifts, shipping.
Strong range in both breadth and depth, plus regular wine dinners, tastings, presentations, and seminars.

Beltramo's Wines & Spirits

1540 El Camino Real, Menlo Park, CA 94025. ☎ 650 325 2806. FAX 650 323 8450.
Website: www.beltramos.com
Wine futures, books, delivery, tastings, newsletters, credit cards, accessories.
Trading since 1882, with a very good selection of imports.

Briggs Wine & Spirits

13038 San Vincents Boulevard, Los Angeles, CA 90049. ☎ 310 395 9997. FAX 310 393 7279. Wine futures, delivery, newsletters, credit cards, gift wrapping, baskets, accessories.
Good merchant focusing on delivery.

Bristol Farms

880 Apollo, El Segundo, CA 90245. ☎ 310 726 1300. Website: www.bristolfarms. com. E-mail: GNicoll@bristolfarms.com. Books, delivery, tastings, credit cards, accessories.
Grocery chain offering over 3000 wines and spirits. Domestic wines include California Merlots and a lot of obscure, harder-to-find lines.

Calistoga Wine Stop

1458 Lincoln Avenue, Suite Two, Calistoga, CA 94515. ☎ 707 942 5556. FAX 707 942 4528. California wine futures, books, delivery, cellarage, credit cards, accessories.
The oldest continually-owned wine store in the Napa Valley. Only wine is sold here – mostly from the Napa or Sonoma valleys.

Coit Liquor
585 Columbus Avenue, San Francisco, CA 94133. ☎ 415 986 4036. FAX 415 296 7825. Website: www.coitliquor.com Wine futures, books, delivery, credit cards, accessories.
A great range with a selection of fine wines and a well-run wine club.

Cost Plus World Market
101 Clay Street, Oakland, CA 94607. ☎ 510 834 4440. FAX 510 763 9993. Delivery, credit cards, accessories.
Chain spreading across the USA, with a fine, ever-changing range.

D & M Wine & Liquor Co.
2200 Fillmore Street, San Francisco, CA 94115. ☎ 415 346 1325. FAX 415 346 1812. E-mail: wine@dnai.com Books, delivery, newsletters, credit cards, accessories, wine clubs.
Six different clubs are run here, devoted to Champagne, Single Malt, Armagnac, Cognac, and Calvados.

Draeger's Supermarkets Inc.
1010 University Drive, Menlo Park, CA 94025. ☎ 650 688 0682. FAX 650 326 3718. E-mail:draegers@aol.com Website: www.draegers.com Stores also in San Mateo & Los Altos. Wine futures, books, delivery, wine tasting bar, dinners, glass loan, newsletters, credit cards, accessories, gift packs and baskets, cellar appraisal.
Check out the wines and the one-day and ten-week wine courses. 1998 Leader in Wine and Spirits Retailing (Market Watch Magazine.)

Duke of Bourbon
20908 Roscoe Boulevard, Canoga Park, CA 91304. ☎ 818 341 1234. FAX 818 341 9232. E-mail: duke@dukeofbourbon.com Website: dukeofbourbon. com Wine futures, books, delivery, mail order, tastings, newsletters, credit cards, accessories.
Services include a recommendable wine tasting/ dinner group.

Enoteca Wine Shop
1345 Lincoln Avenue, Suite C, Calistoga, CA 94515. ☎ 707 942 1117. FAX 707 942 1118. Website: www.neteze.com/enoteca. Newsletters, mail order, shipping, credit cards, accessories.
Classy wines with customer-friendly tasting and vinification notes.

Epicurus
625 Montana Avenue, Suite B, Santa Monica, CA 90403. ☎ 310 395 1352. FAX 310 260 9733. E-mail: epiwine@gateway.net Wine futures, books, delivery, tastings, newsletters, credit cards, accessories.
Wines from California and around the world – including some old and rare.

Fireside Cellars
1421 Montana Avenue, Santa Monica, CA 90403. ☎ 310 393 2888 FAX 310 458 4360. E-mail: fred@firesidecellars.com Website www.firesidecellars.com Wine futures, delivery, credit cards, accessories.
Store dealing mainly in domestic and French wines, and an extensive range of spirits.

Gourmet Au Bay
PO Box 1175, 913 Coast Highway One, Bodega Bay, CA 94923. ☎ 707 875 9875. FAX 707 875 9800. E-mail: gourmet@monitor.net Website: www.GourmetAuBay.com Credit cards, accessories.
Gold Medal and 90+ rated California wines. Guests can taste on the seaside deck at the very water's edge.

Hi-Time Wine Cellars
250 Ogle Street, Costa Mesa, CA 92627. ☎ 949 650 8463 / 800 331 3005 FAX 949 631 6863. Website www.hitime.com Wine futures, books, delivery, tastings, newsletters, cellarage, accessories, wine club, gift baskets, shipping.
Wine store offering a wide and upscale range.

Jonathan's of La Jolla
7611 Fay Avenue, La Jolla, CA 92037. ☎ 619 459 2677. FAX 619 459 2854. Glassware, delivery, newsletters, credit cards, accessories. tastings.
20 year-old wine and gourmet food store, with a good California selection

Kermit Lynch, Wine Merchant of Berkeley
1605 San Pablo Avenue, Berkeley, CA 94702 ☎ 510 524 1524. FAX 510 528 7026. E-mail: klwmgb@aol.com Wine futures, books, newsletters, credit cards,
Long-established merchant with a cult following for wines by top-class French producers. Provence is a specialty – for wine and gourmet foods.

Mediterranean Market Inc.

Ocean Avenue, Mission Street, Carmel, CA 93921. ☎ 831 624 2022. FAX 831 624 7354. Wine futures, books, glass-rental, delivery, tastings. credit cards, accessories.
40 year-old family store, specializing in top of the range California wines.

Michaels Wine & Spirits

2198 Union Street, San Francisco, CA 94123. ☎ 415 921 5700. FAX 415 554 0289. Delivery, credit cards, accessories.
Wines, single malts, Cognacs, Tequila, and cigars.

Mill Valley Market

12 Corte Madera Avenue, Mill Valley, CA 94941. ☎ 415 388 8466. FAX 415 388 8824. Wine futures, glass rental/loan, delivery, tastings, newsletters, credit cards, accessories.
Good value wines, Argentinian, Chardonnay, and Portuguese reds.

North Berkeley Wine

1505 Shattuck Avenue, Berkeley, CA 94709. ☎ 510 848 8910. FAX 510 848 0841. E-mail: nbw@slip.net.Wine futures, books, delivery, newsletters, credit cards, accessories.
Fine French and Italian barrel selections.

Oakville Grocery Co.

7856 St Helena Highway, Oakville, CA 94562. ☎ 707 944 8802. FAX 707 944 1844. E-mail:ogccorp@aol.com Website:www.oakvillegrocery.com Stores in five locations, books, delivery, tastings, newsletters, credit cards, accessories.
Ultra-premium California wines with tastings given by producers.

Old Bridge Cellars

1212 Market Street, Suite 100, San Francisco, CA 94102. ☎ 415 863 9463. FAX 415 863 9487. Website: www.oldbridgecellars.com E-mail: info@oldbridgecellars.com Credit cards.
Unashamed Australia obsessives, importing many exclusive lines.

Old Doc's

8070 North Cedar, Fresno, CA 93720. ☎ 559 224 3627. FAX 559 224 3636. Wine futures, mail order, wine club delivery, tastings, cellarage, credit cards.
Wide-ranging specialist with good value wines and a wine publication library

Pebble Beach Co.

Cyprus at 17 Mile Drive, Pebble Beach, CA 93953. ☎ 831 625 8528. FAX 831 622 8793. Books, national and local delivery, newsletters, credit cards, accessories.
Upscale California reds, which account for three fourths of sales.

Piedmont Grocery Co.

4038 Piedmont Avenue, Oakland, CA 94611. ☎ 510 653 8187. FAX 510 653 0308. Wine futures, delivery, newsletters, credit cards, accessories.
A 100-year-old company specializing in upscale and hard-to-find items, and wine and food gift baskets.

Premier Cru

5890 Christie Avenue, Emeryville, CA 94608. ☎ 510 655 6691. FAX 510 547 5405. Website: www.premier-cru.com Wine futures, mail order, delivery, newsletters, credit cards.
Broad range, with top range Burgundies and California rarities.

Prima

1522 North Main Street, Walnut Creek, CA 94596. ☎ 925 945 1800. FAX 925 935 0519. Wine futures, books, delivery, tastings, glass loan, newsletters, cellarage, credit cards.
Wine store and restaurant with particularly hard-to-get Californian and Australian wines.

Stafford Fine Wine

17801 Main Street, Suite F, Irvine, CA 92614. ☎ 949 474 4416. FAX 949 474 5303. Wine futures, books, delivery, tastings, newsletters, cellarage, credit cards, accessories.
Wines and beers only.

Vintage Wine & Spirits

67 Thruckmorton Avenue, Mill Valley, CA 94941. ☎ 415 388 1626. FAX 415 388 4249. Wine futures, delivery, tastings, newsletters, credit cards.
Specializing in a wide range of the pick of California.

John Walker & Co.

175 Suiter Street, San Francisco, CA 94104. ☎ 415 986 2707. FAX 415 421 5820. Wine futures, delivery, newsletters, cellarage, credit cards, accessories.
Imported and domestic wines feature heavily in the broad selection offered here.

Wally's
2107 Westwood Boulevard, Los Angeles, CA 90025. ☎ 310 475 0606. FAX 310 474 1450. E-mail: wallywine@aol.com Website: www.wallywine. com Wine futures, books, delivery, glass loan, tastings, newsletters, cellarage, credit cards, accessories.
Wine store and deli, with rare French, Australian, and California wines.

The Wine Exchange
2368 North Orange Mall, Orange, CA 92865. ☎ 714 974 1454 / 800 769 4639. FAX 714 974 1792. E-mail:wines@winex.com Website: www.winex.com Wine futures, books, local delivery, tastings, newsletters, credit cards, accessories, mail order.
A very competitively priced discount store with a large and varied range.

The Wine Exchange of Sonoma
452 First Street East Sonoma, CA 95476. ☎ 707 938 1794. FAX 707 938 0969. Wine futures, books, delivery, tastings, newsletters, credit cards, accessories.
California, Oregon, and Washington specialists par excellence (plus hard to find sherries and ports).

COLORADO

Argonaut Wine & Liquor
718 East Colefax, Denver, CO 80203. ☎ 303 831 7788. FAX 303 839 8305. E-mail: argonautwl@aol.com Website: www.argonautliquor.com Wine futures, books, delivery, tastings, newsletters, credit cards, accessories.
Specializes in small Italian producers, and domestic boutique wines.

Bonnie Brae Wine & Liquor Mart
785 University Boulevard, Denver, CO 80209. ☎ 303 733 7261. FAX 303 733 7264. Delivery, tastings, credit cards.
Very broad range of wines from all over the world.

Chamber's Wine & Liquor
15260 East Iliff Avenue, Aurora, CO 80014. ☎ 303 751 6935. FAX 303 751 5089. E-mail: chamberswl@aol.com.Books, delivery, tastings, credit cards, accessories.
Good all-around store, with all the mainstream lines rubbing shoulders with hard to get specialty wines.

Heritage Wines & Liquors
74/75 East Arapahoe Road, Englewood, CO 80112. ☎ 303 770 8212. FAX 303 770 3494. Delivery, tastings, newsletters, accessories.
Large range, covering a broad range of countries and styles.

Mayfair Liquors Inc.
1385 Krameria Street, Denver, CO 80220. ☎ 303 322 0810. FAX 303 321 3393. E-mail: lmouton61@aol.com
Books, delivery, newsletters, accessories.
Eighty percent of the wines sold here are Californian, especially older vintages, including the 70s and 80s.

Pringle's Fine Wines & Spirits
2100 West Drake, Fort Collins, CO 80526. ☎ 970 221 1717. FAX 970 221 2890. 3000 wine choices, accessories, wine and food pairing classes, wine club, glassware, tastings, limited delivery, credit cards.
Trained staff imparting knowledge on a wide range to suit all pockets. Also 60 Agave Tequilas, 100 Single Malts, and a good range of fine cigars.

Wild Oats Community Market
3375 Mitchell Lane, Boulder, CO 80301. ☎ 303 440 5220. FAX 303 440 5280.
Tastings, newsletters, accessories.
A chain of wine and food stores offering a good mix of wines in selected stores..

CONNECTICUT

Amity Wines, Beers & Spirits
95 Amity Road, New Haven, CT 6515. ☎ 203 387 6725. FAX 203 397 1414.
Website: www.amitywine.com
E-mail: Amtywine@amitywine.com
Books, delivery, tastings, newsletters, credit cards, accessories.
A broad range, but with an emphasis on hard-to-get wines. Wine dinners organized.

The Bottle Shop
520 South Main Street, Middletown, CT 06457. ☎ 860 346 8246.
Books, delivery, tastings, credit cards, accessories.
A broad selection of wines and spirits, offering good value and choice across the board.

Castle Wine & Spirits
1439 Post Road East, Westport, CT 06880. ☎ 203 259 5948. FAX 203 259 7351. E-mail: cws1439@aol.com
Tastings, newsletters, credit cards, accessories.
Over 100 tastings a year held in restaurants and homes.

Fairground's Wine & Spirits
19A Sugar Hollow Road, Danbury, CT 06810. ☎ 203 792 2152. FAX 203 744 1756. Newsletters, credit cards, accessories.
From boxed wines to the finest bottles. Huge Spanish and Riesling selections, plus many import exclusives.

DELAWARE

The Wine & Spirit Co. of Greenville
4025 Kennett Pike, Greenville, DE 19807. ☎ 302 658 5939. FAX 302 658 0808. E-mail: wnsco.@aol.
Wine futures, newsletters, credit cards, accessories.
Specialists in Californian and French wine. Services include in-store tastings and dinners at local restaurants.

DISTRICT OF COLUMBIA

Bell Wine & Liquor
1821 M Street Northwest, Washington, DC 20036. ☎ 202 223 4727. FAX 202 466 8070. E-mail: 74001.3503@compuserve.com
Wine futures, delivery, tastings, credit cards, accessories, mail order.
2000 wines and around 850 spirits. Specialists in California, Oregon, Portugal, Bordeaux and Argentina.

Calvert Woodley
4339 Connecticut Avenue Northwest, Washington, DC 20008. ☎ 202 966 0445. FAX 202 537 5086.
Wine futures, books, tastings, newsletters, credit cards, accessories, cheese and deli.
Specializing in rare mature Bordeaux and quality international wines.

Chevvy Chase Wines & Spirits
5544 Connecticut Avenue Northwest, Washington, DC 20015. ☎ 202 363 4000. FAX 202 537 6067.
Wine futures, delivery, tastings, newsletters, credit cards., free parking in rear.
Knowledgeable yet non-stuffy store with wines from all over, plus a large range of beers and spirits.

D & G Inc. DBA Central Liquor
917 F Street Northwest, Washington, DC 20004. ☎ 202 737 2800. FAX 202 347 9463. E-mail: centrallic@aol.com For auctions of wines www.auctionvine.com Wine futures, mail order, delivery, tastings, credit cards, accessories.
Strength in depth here, with a large single malt Scotch section.

Schneider's of Capitol Hill
300 Massachussetts Avenue Northeast, Washington, DC 20002. ☎ 202 543 9300. FAX 202 546 6289. 1-800 377 1461.
E-mail: schneid2@ix.netcom.com
Website: www.cellar.com Wine futures, delivery, tastings, newsletters, credit cards, accessories.
Specialists in old and rare Bordeaux, Burgundy and Cabernets.

FLORIDA

67 Wine & Spirits
5360 North Federal Highway, Lighthouse Point, FL 33064. ☎ 954 428 6255. FAX 954 725 0837.
Wine futures, books, delivery, tastings, cellarage, credit cards, accessories.
Family merchants with top French and dessert wines, and whiskies.

Bern's Fine Wines & Spirits
1002 South Howard Avenue, Tampa, FL 33606. ☎+FAX 813 250 9463.
Books, delivery, tastings, newsletters, cellarage, credit cards, accessories.
Great selection of domestic wines, including California Cabernets, old vine Zinfandel, and West Coast Pinots.

The Dorn Companies
4140 Northwest 16th Boulevard, Gainesville, FL 32606. ☎ 352 378 0229. FAX 352 375 3010. E-mail: tommydorn@aol.com Books, delivery, tastings, credit cards, accessories.
Chain whose flagship store specializes in microbrewed beers and whiskies.

Island Tobacco & Trade Inc.
3 South Third Street, Ferdandina Beach, FL 32034. ☎ 904 261 7222. FAX 904 261 6911. E-mail: islandtobacco@net.magic.net Glassware, wine tastings, credit cards, full line of tobacco products.
Cozy, friendly operation with large array of services.

Laurenzo's International Food & Wine Centre
16385 West Dixie Highway, North Miami Beach, FL 33160. ☎+FAX 305 945 6381. Wine futures, books, delivery, tastings, newsletters, credit cards, accessories.
The largest independent wine retailer in Florida. Special annual tutored Champagne tasting.

Park Avenue Wine & Cheese Cellar
323 South Park Avenue, Winter Park, FL 32789. ☎ 407 628 3963. FAX 407 628 3876. Website: www.parkavwine.com Wine futures, books delivery, tastings, newsletters, credit cards, accessories.
Oldest wine retailer in central Florida.Very good across the board.

Sunset Corners Fine Wines & Spirits
8701 Sunset Drive, Miami, FL 33156. ☎ 305 271 8492. FAX 305 271 5390. E-mail: mbwine@aol.com Wine futures, books, delivery, tastings, newsletters, credit cards, accessories.
44-year-old operation specializing in classy imports.

Wine Castle
11728 North Fifty-Sixth Street, Tampa, FL 33617. ☎ 813 985 0455. Delivery, tastings, newsletters, credit cards, accessories.
Concentrating on an across-the-board, mainstream selection.

Wine Watch
901 Progresso Drive, Fort Lauderdale, FL 33304. ☎ 954 523 9463. FAX 954 523 9213. E-mail: winewatch@msn.com Website:www.winewatch.com Wine futures, books, tastings, newsletters, cellarage, credit cards, accessories.
Good wines, and personalized gift boxes.

GEORGIA

Mink Wines & Spirits
2565 Delk Road, Marietta, GA 30067. ☎ 770 952 2337. FAX 770 952 6150. E-mail: minks@mindspring.com Books, tastings, newsletters, credit cards, accessories.
Selection includes a range of beers and single malts. A walk-in humidor, a temperature controlled wine cellar, and an upstairs smoking room!

Sherlock's Fine Wine
2156 Roswell Road, Marietta, Atlanta, GA 30062. ☎ 770 971 6333. FAX 770 977 9235. E-mail: sherlock@mindspring.com Website: www.sherlocks.com Books, glass rental/loan, tastings, newsletters, cellarage, credit cards, accessories.
Two large stores offering a wide variety of wines, spirits, and beers and advice on cellar-building.

Tower Package Store
2161 Piedmont Road, Atlanta, GA 30324. ☎ 404 881 0902. FAX 404 881 0301. Credit cards, accessories.
Full beverage selection/service, (liquor, beer, wine). Fine wine emphasis. Event-planning.

HAWAII

Kihei Wine & Spirits
300 Ohukai Road, Kihei, HI 96753. ☎+FAX: 808 879 0555. Delivery, newsletters, credit cards, accessories.
Gourmet food and quality wines.

ILLINOIS

Binny's Wines
5100 West Dempster, Skokie, IL 60077 ☎ 847 674 4200. FAX 847 459 4207.
Wine futures, books, tastings, newsletters, cellerage (selected stores), credit cards, accessories.
Part of a chain offering a wide range of services.

International House of Wine & Cheese
11302 Route 12, Richmond, IL 60071. ☎ 815 678 2500. FAX 815 678 3100. Books, delivery, tastings, newsletters, cellarage, credit cards, accessories, wine club.
Wine store, deli, and restaurant with a wine club and mail order service.

Knightsbridge Wine Shoppe & Epicurean Centre Ltd.
824 Sunset Bridge Road, Northbrook, IL 60062. ☎ 847 498 9300. FAX 847 498 4263 Website: Knightsbridgewine.com Wine futures, books, delivery, tastings, newsletters, cellarage, accessories, gift service and gourmet centre.
Only sell fine wines above $10, and specialize in large and half bottles. 100 wines are available to taste daily.

Mainstreet
5425 South Lagrange Road, Countryside, IL 60525. ☎ 708 354 0355/1-888 354 0355. FAX 708 354 3933. Website: www.mainstreetwine.com
Wine futures, glass rental, delivery, tastings, newsletters, cellarage, credit cards, accessories.
The second biggest drinks store in Illinois, specializing in France, California, Italy, and Spain.

Sam's Wine & Spirits
1720 North Marcey Street, Chicago, IL 60614. ☎ 312 664 4394. FAX 312 664 7037. E-mail: sams@sams-wine.com Website: www.sams-wine.com
Wine futures, books, delivery, tastings, newsletters, credit cards, accessories, shipping, corporate delivery.
Largest independent wine store in the US. Walk-in cigar humidor, deli and great wines, spirits, port, and beers.

Savway Liquors, Fine Wines & Spirits
3821 South York Road, Oakbrook, Illinois, IL 60523. ☎ 630 325 6550. FAX 630 989 0059. Wine futures, books, glass rental/loan, delivery, tastings, newsletters, credit cards, accessories.
Broad range of wines from throughout the world, whiskies, and cigars.

Wine Discount Center
1826 North Elston Avenue, Chicago, IL 60622. ☎ 773 489 3454. FAX 773 489 3589. Wine futures, newsletters, credit cards, accessories.
Well-priced and ever evolving selection. Free tastings every Saturday.

Indiana

John's Fine Wine & Spirits
25 N.Pennsylvania St., Indianapolis, IN 46204. ☎ 317 637 5759. FAX 317 786 1877. Newsletters, tastings, credit cards, accessories, delivery.
This store offers a good broad range of wines to suit all pockets.

Kentucky

Cork 'N Bottle
501 Crescent Ave, Covington, Kentucky, KY 41011. ☎ 606 261 8333. FAX 606 261 0062. Delivery, tastings, newsletters, mail order, credit cards.
Specialists in Champagne as well as Italian, French, and California wine.

The Party Source
95 Riviera Drive, Bellevue, KY 41073. ☎ 606 291 4007. FAX 606 291 4147. E-mail: bellevue@thepartysource.com. Website: www.thepartysource.com
Credit cards, Riedel glassware, gift baskets.
Largest wine store in the state with over 5,000 wines, and gourmet foods.

Louisiana

Dorignac's Food Centre
710 Veteran Highway, Metairie, LA 70005. ☎ 504 837 6548. FAX 504 837 6532. E-mail: Butch@dorignac.com Website: www.Dorignac.com. Wine futures, books, delivery, tastings, credit cards, accessories.
Wine and food store selling a wide range of domestic and imported wines.

Maine

Clayton's Gourmet Market
189 Main St, Yarmouth, ME 04096. ☎ 207 846 1117. FAX 207 846 6950.
Books, monthly tastings, newsletters, credit cards, accessories.
Specializing in wines from Australia, France, Italy, and Spain. Also offering specialities, cheeses, and in-store café.

Maryland

Calvert Discount Liquor
10128 York Road, Hunt Valley, MD 21030. ☎ 410 628 2320. FAX 410 628 1830.
Books, glass rental/loan, delivery, tastings, cellarage, credit cards,accessories.
Featuring a hand-picked selection of wines from throughout the globe.

Jason's Wines & Spirits
9339 Baltimore National Pike, Ellicott City, MD 21042. ☎ 410 465 2424. FAX 410 750 1565.
Books, tastings, credit cards, accessories.
A broad range of mainstream brands at very fair prices.

Mills Wine & Spirits Mart
87 Main Street, Annapolis, MD 21401. ☎ 410 263 2888. FAX 410 268 2616. E-mail: millswine@toad.net. Website: www.millswine.com
Wine futures, books, delivery, monthly wine dinners, newsletters, credit cards, accessories.
Bordeaux is the specialty of this 52-year-old store. French regional wines, California, Australian, and Spanish.

Rotunda Wines & Spirits

711 West 40th Street, Baltimore, MD 21211. ☎ 410 467 7777 / 800 349 6786. FAX 410 889 8187. Website: www.the-wine-source.com. Wine futures, books, local delivery, tastings, newsletters, credit cards, accessories.

Specialists in fine wine from all over the world with particular emphasis on Italy, France, United States, Australia, South Africa, and Spain.

Silesia Liquors

10909 Livingstone Road, Fort Washington, MD 20744. ☎ 301 292 1542. FAX 301 203 9417. Website: www.silesiawine.com. Wine futures, books, delivery, tastings, newsletters, credit cards, accessories.

Check out the choice older vintages. Dinners and wine and food pairings are on offer here.

Wells Discount Liquors

6310 York Road, Baltimore, MD 21212. ☎ 410 435 2700. FAX 410 323 0912. E-mail: wellswine@aol.com Website: www.wellswine.com Wine futures, delivery, tastings, newsletters, credit cards, accessories.

Discount store offering pretty much everything.

MASSACHUSSETTS

All Star Wine

1220 Chestnut Street, Upperfalls Newton, MA 2464. ☎ 617 332 9400. FAX 617 332 8225. Wine futures, delivery, tastings, newsletters, credit cards, accessories.

Strong on fine Italian wines and single malts.

Andover Liquors Inc.

209 North Main Street, Andover, MA 01810. ☎ 978 470 0500. FAX 978 470 1944. Wine futures, delivery, tastings,newsletters, credit cards, accessories.

Every wine here is pre-selected by a tasting panel.

Bauer Wine & Spirits

330 Newberry Street, Boston, MA 02115. ☎ 617 262 0083. FAX 617 266 0871 Website:www.bauerwines.com. Delivery, tastings, newsletters, credit cards, accessories.

General wine store with particular emphasis on New World, Spain, and Italy.

Table and Vine

122 North King Street, Northampton, MA 1060. ☎ 800 474 2449. FAX 413 584 7732. E-mail: staff@tableandvine.com Website: www.tableandvine.com Wine futures, books, delivery, tastings, newsletters, cellarage, credit cards, glass sale.

Gourmet wines and foods.

Blanchards of Allstone Liquors

103 Harvard Avenue, Allstone, MA 02134. ☎ 617 782 5588. FAX 617 782 9504. E-mail: blanchrds@aol.com Wine futures, books, delivery, tastings, newsletters, credit cards.

Broad-based discount store with a range that is constantly changing.

Charles Street Liquor

143 Charles Street, Boston, MA 02114. ☎ 617 523 5051. FAX 617 523 6066. E-mail: csliquors@aol.com Books, delivery, tastings, newsletters, credit cards, accessories.

Upscale store with delivery and corporate sales services. Tastings are held every Friday and Saturday.

Colonial Spirits

69 Great Road, Acton, MA 1720. ☎ 978 263 7775. FAX 978 263 0403. Website: www.colonialspirits.com Delivery, tastings, newsletters, credit cards.

Friendly store, with staff imparting knowledge on everything from domestic boutique wines to imported beers.

Dub's Discount Liquors

30 Chauncy Street, Mansfield, MA 02048. ☎ 508 339 3454. FAX 508 339 3941. E-mail:dubs@freshcatchinc.com Website: www.freshcatchinc.com Local delivery, tastings, newsletters, credit cards, accessories, gift baskets, cigars.

Specialities include single barrel Bordeaux bottlings, single malt whiskies, microbrew beers, and cigars.

Kappy's Liquors

296 Main Street, Everett, MA 2149. ☎ 617 389 7600. FAX 617 387 1905. E-mail: lsb@kappys.com Website: www.kappys.com Wine futures, books, newsletters, credit cards, wine club.

Discount store with huge range on all price levels. Some stock imported specially. The wine club is also worth checking out.

Liquor World

365 West Central Street, Franklin, MA 2038. ☎ 508 528 0138. FAX 508 528 6989. E-mail: wine38d@aol.com Wine futures, books, delivery, tastings, newsletters, credit cards, accessories.

A good range, with tasting samples available anytime!

Marty's Liquors

675 Washington Street, Newton, MA 2160. ☎ 617 332 1230. FAX 617 332 5437. Wine futures, books, glass rental, tastings, delivery, newsletters, credit cards, accessories.

Importer, distributor, and retailer. Tastings led by both staff and well-known wine professionals.

Merchant's Wine & Spirits

6 Water Street, Boston, MA 2109. ☎ 617 523 7425. FAX 617 523 0196. E-mail: Villawines.com\villawines@aol.com. Website: www.Vinomon.com Wine futures, delivery, tastings, newsletters, cellarage, credit cards, accessories.

Friendly enterprise dedicated to searching out the wines of the moment.

Michigan

G.B. Russo & Son

2770 Twenty-Ninth Street Southeast, Grand Rapids, MI 49512. ☎ 616 942 2980. FAX 616 942 2295. Website: www.gbrusso.com E-mail:drusso@gbrusso.com Wine futures, delivery, tasting, credit cards, accessories.

Also offer gourmet food.

Minnesota

Byerly's Beveridges

13081 Ridgedale Drive, Minnetonka, MN 55305. ☎ 612 541 1412. FAX 612 541 0089. Books, delivery, tastings, newsletters, credit cards, accessories.

Wide ranging selection throughout five stores, focusing on domestic wines.

France 44 Wines & Spirits

4351 France Avenue South, Minneapolis, MN 55410. ☎ 612 925 3252. FAX 612 925 5870. Website: www.france44.com Local delivery, newsletters, accessories.

Large store majoring in premium California reds and whites; Italian, Rhone and Australian , plus specialty single malt Scotch and Cognac.

Haskell's Inc.

81 South Ninth Street, Minneapolis, MN 55402. ☎ 800 486 2434\612 333 2434. FAX 612 342 2440. E-mail:tfarrell@haskells.com.Website: www.haskells.com Wine futures, books, glass rental/loan, delivery, tastings, newsletters, cellarage, credit cards, accessories.

Small chain of stores whose wine society happily organizes tastings.

Hennepin Lake Liquors

1200 West Lake Street, Minneapolis, MN 55408. ☎ 612 825 4411. Tastings, accessories.

Genuine emphasis on the top range wine, examples of which can be sampled at daily in-store tastings.

Missouri

Berbiglia Wines & Spirits

1101 East Bannister, Kansas City MO 64131. ☎ 816 942 0070. FAX 816 942 1777. E-mail: Berbwine@aol.com Wine futures, delivery, tastings, gourmet dinners newsletters, credit cards, accessories.

The finest wine selection in Kansas City.

The Cheese Place

9755 Manchester Road, St Louis, MO 63119. ☎ 314 962 6464. FAX 314 962 850. E-mail: cheesepl@swbell.net Wine futures, delivery, tastings, newsletters, credit cards, accessories, 2 more stores in Clayton and Baldwin.

Over 1500 wines. Occasional informative wine classes are held.

Gomer's Fine Wines & Spirits

9902 Holmes Road, Kansas City, MO 64131. ☎ 816 942 6200. FAX 816 942 7753. E-mail: moody47@aol.com Wine and spirits, books, glass rental, delivery, tastings, credit cards, accessories.

Largest single outlet in Missouri, with a wide-range of wines and cigars.

The Wine Chateaux

12 Clarkson Wilson Centre, Chesterfield, MO 63017. ☎ 314 532 6069. FAX 314 532 6069. E-mail: wineshat@win1.net Wine futures, books, glass rental/loan, delivery, tastings, newsletters, credit cards, accessories.

A recommendable, intimate venture offering two tastings a week, a walk-in cigar humidor, and a cellar installation service.

MONTANA

The Liquor Store

404 E 9th Libby, MT 59923.
☎ 406 293 4856. FAX 406 293 4856.
Books, delivery, credit cards, accessories, mixers.
Retailer offering the largest selection of fine wines in NW Montana.

NEBRASKA

The Winery

741 North 98th Street, Omaha, NE 68114. ☎ 800 884 WINE.
FAX 402 391 2713. Wine futures, books, glass rental/loan, tastings, newsletters, credit cards, accessories.
Super-premium California wines, and highly trained and intelligent staff.

NEW JERSEY

Canals Bottlestop

10 West Route 70, Marlton, NJ 08053. ☎ 609 983 4991. FAX 609 596 2640. E-mail: canalsmarlton@msn.com Website: canalsforwine.com
Bordeaux wine futures, delivery, tastings, newsletters, cellarage, accessories, gift baskets
Good on French, German, California, and New Zealand wines.

Carduner's Wines & Spirits

8 Princeton-Hightstown Road, East Windsor, NJ 8520. ☎ 609 448 0574.
FAX 609 448 1420. Website: www.carduners.com Wine futures, books, glass rental/loan, local delivery, newsletters, credit cards, accessories.
Store concentrating on those hard-to-get California boutique wines.

Clinton Wine & Gourmet

57 Wallmart Plaza, Clinton, NJ 08809.
☎ 908 735 9655. FAX 908 735 0627.
Website: www.wineaccess.com/clinton
Wine futures, books, delivery, tastings, newsletters, credit cards, accessories.
Store co-owned by a Master of Wine, stocking a wide range of wines, beers, cheeses, and patés.

Liquor Fair Inc.

Route 38, Lumberton Shopping Plaza, Mount Holly, NJ 8060.
☎ 609 267 4012. FAX 609 267 4482.
Futures, books, delivery, newsletters, credit cards.
Good range of wines and vodkas. Also advice on setting up a cellar.

Phillips Fine Wines & Liquors

Bridge Street, Stockton, NJ 08559.
☎ 609 397 0587. FAX 609 397 2899.
Wine futures, books, delivery, newsletters, credit cards, accessories.
Very good broad range of over 5,000 different wines.

Rickards Liquors

121 Waters Street, New Jersey, NJ 7860. ☎ 973 383 4484.
FAX 973 383 5864. Books, newsletters, cellarage, credit cards, accessories.
A broad range of well-chosen wines.

Shoppers Wine Library

8 Milburn Avenue, Springfield, NJ 7081. ☎ 973 376 0005.
FAX 973 376 8577. E-mail: swl@winelibrary.comWebsite: www.winelibrary.com Wine futures, books, delivery, tastings, newsletters, credit cards, accessories.
They claim they'll do anything they legally can to sell you the wine you want. 800 Cabernets, 125 Zinfandels...

True Value Wine & Spirits

12 Lyons Shopping Mall, Basking Ridge, NJ 7920. ☎ 908 766 0830.
FAX 908 766 5606. E-mail:rawine@aol.com Books, newsletters, credit cards, accessories.
Two stores specializing in California Chardonnay, Cabernet, and Zinfandel. Many hard-to-get boutique wines.

NEW HAMPSHIRE

The Wine Cellar

650 Amherst St, Nashua, NH 03063.
☎ 603 883 4114. FAX 603 883 5981.
E-mail: Winecell@aol.com.
Bi-monthly tastings, delivery, newsletters, credit cards, accessories.
A wide range of fine wines selected by "Les Chevaliers du Grand Vin" wine society. Gourmet foods and cigars.

NEW YORK

Acker Merrall & Condit

160 West 72nd Street, New York, NY 10023. ☎ 212 787 1700.
FAX 212 799 1984. E-mail: vinogod@aol.com Wine futures, books, glass rental/loan, tastings, newsletters, credit cards, accessories.
Wide-ranging specialists in tastings, and cellarage for customers. Also run online auctions, live auctions, a wine club, and a mail order service.

Armonk Wines & Spirits

383 Main Street, Armonk, NY 10504. ☎ 914 273 3044. FAX 914 273 5420. Wine futures, delivery,tastings, credit cards, accessories.

Taste before you buy at the in-store tastings every Saturday.

Astor Wines & Spirits

12 Astor Place, New York, NY 10003. ☎ 212 674 7500. FAX 212 673 1218. Website: www.astoruncorked.com Books, delivery, newsletters, credit cards, accessories.

A great range, with tutored tastings in-store, wine and cheese on the last Saturday of the month. One of the best sake selections in New York..

Beacon Wines & Spirits

2120 Broadway, New York NY 10023. ☎ 212 877 0028. FAX 212 501 7172. Website: www. Beaconwines.com Delivery, credit cards.

Wide ranging stock roughly split down the middle between Old and New Worlds.

Beekman Liquor

500 Lexington Avenue, New York, NY 10017. ☎ 212 759 5857. FAX 212 753 4534. Website: www .beekmanliquors.com Wine futures, delivery, newsletters, credit cards, accessories.

A fine selection of wines, spirits, and champagnes, with access to rare Bordeaux and Bordeaux futures.

Best Cellars

1291 Lexington Ave. New York, NY 10128. ☎ 212 426 4200. FAX 212 426 9597. Website: www. bestcellars.net Delivery, tastings, credit cards, accessories.

Great value everyday wines, with nothing over $10. Saturday food and wine pairings with guest chef in store.

Bristol Farms

454 South Riverside Avenue, Croton-on-Hudson, NY 90245. ☎ 914 271 3200. FAX 914 271 7890. Glass rental, delivery, tastings, newsletters, credit cards, accessories.

Chain with an extensive range of wines. Domestic offerings include plentiful Zinfandels, over 80 California Merlots and a lot of obscure, harder-to-find lines.

Burgundy Wine Company Ltd.

323 West 11th Street, New York, NY 10014. ☎ 212 691 9092. FAX 212 691 9244. Website: www.Burgundywine company.com Delivery, newsletters, credit cards.

Intimate upscale store specializing in Burgundy and Cotes du Rhone, also Oregon and California wines from Burgundy and Rhone varieties. Vignerons-led seminars are held in store and in local restaurants.

The Chelsea Wine Vault Ltd.

75 Ninth Avenue, New York, NY 10011. ☎ 212 462 4244. FAX 212 463 9589. E-mail: chelseawinevault@erols.com Website: www.chelseawinevault.com Wine futures, newsletters, cellarage, credit cards, accessories.

Broad-based store owned by one of the only Masters of Wine in the US. Check out the tastings and seminars.

Crossroads Wines

55 West 14th Street, New York, NY 10011. ☎ 212 924 3060. FAX 212 633 2863. Wine futures, delivery, credit cards

The best and broadest range in Manhattan? Dedicated to uncovering esoteric wines others tend to ignore.

Diplomat Wines & Spirits

939 Second Avenue, New York, NY 10022. ☎ 212 832 5080 FAX 212 832 5084. Books, delivery, tastings, newsletters, credit cards, accessories.

3,500 wines with a strong international flavor, as you would expect from a store close to the UN Building.

Dodd's Liquor City

Intersection of Routes 100 + 133, Millwood, NY 10546. ☎ 914 762 5511. FAX 914 762 4957. Wine futures, delivery, credit cards.

All the top California boutique wines are carried, as well as many imports at discounted prices.

Embassy Wines and Spirits.

796 Lexington Avenue, New York City, NY 10021. ☎ 212 838 6551. FAX 212 832 4896. Delivery, tastings, cellarage, credit cards.

Regular importer and distributor, sponsored tastings are a feature here, as are their wine courses and regular parties.

Garnet Wines & Liquors
929 Lexington Avenue, New York, NY 10021. 212 772 3211. FAX 212 517 4029.
E-mail: Garnetwin@aol.com.
Website: www.Garnetwine.com
Wine futures, nationwide delivery, tastings, newsletters, credit cards, mail order.
Low prices on quality lines. Vast selection from around the world.

Heights Chateau Wines & Spirits
131 Atlantic Avenue, Brooklyn, NY 11201. 718 330 0963. FAX 718 522 0236. E-mail: htschateau@aol.com Tastings, newsletters, credit cards, accessories.
Good all-round selection with an emphasis on "undiscovered" good value wines. Also good single malts, single-barrel Bourbons, and Tequilas.

Liquor Square Inc.
P.O.Box 6333 Syracuse, NY 13224. 315 445 0445. FAX 315 445 2829.
Books, tastings, delivery, credit cards, accessories, holiday gift baskets.
Largest wine and spirit retailer in Central New York, with more than 5,000 wines and 2,000 spirits. Emphasis is on California, Australia, and South America.

Liquorama Wine Cellars
Hyde Park Mall, Hyde Park, NY 12538. 914 229 8177. FAX 914 229 8194. E-mail: gephard@idsi.net
Wine futures, books, delivery, credit cards, accessories.
The main areas of specialty here include Zinfandels and single malts.

Manley's Wines & Spirits Inc.
35 Eighth Avenue, New York, NY 10014. 212 242 3712
E-mail: Manleyswine@att.net.
Books, delivery, credit cards.
Family owned business established in 1934. Wide range, with good older vintages a specialty. Services include temperature-controlled cellars and fully working model trains!

Marketview Liquor
1100 Jefferson Road, Rochester, NY 14623. + FAX 716 427 2480
Tastings, credit cards, accessories.
Wide-ranging discount store focusing firmly on California wines.

Montauk Liquors & Wines
The Plaza, Montauk, NY 11954. 516 668 5454. FAX 516 668 4610.
Books, delivery, credit cards, accessories.
Big on wine from around the world, and over 100 single malts. Knowledgable and enthusiastic staff are always happy to help.

P. J. Liquor Warehouse
4898 Broadway, New York, NY 10034. 212 567 5500. FAX 212 567 2743. Wine futures, delivery, newsletters, credit cards, wine club.
Fine wine specialist with particular emphasis on California, Bordeaux, Spain, and Grand Cru Burgundy.

Park Avenue Liquor Shop
292 Madison Avenue, New York, NY 10017. 212 685 2442. FAX 212 689 6247. E-mail: info@parkaveliquor.com.superlink.net
Website: www.parkaveliquor.com
Wine futures, books, delivery, tastings, newsletters, credit cards.
Hold three or four auctions per year. Range includes 360 single malts, 150 ports, 80 Armagnacs, and 60 bourbons. Also specialize in over and undersized bottles.

Pines Liquor Shop
Harbour Walk, Fire Island, NY 10074. 516 597 6442. FAX 212 268 9441. Tastings, credit cards.
Popular local, intimate store offering top end wines, and regular in-store tastings.

Raeders Wine Merchants
1029 Willis Avenue, Albertson, NY 11507. 516 747 0004. FAX 516 747 0942.
Website: www.Raederswine.com
Wine futures, books, delivery, tastings, newsletters, credit cards, accessories, wine club.
Fine wines at discount prices, with 7,000 wines in stock. Wine classes and dinners.

Rochambeau Wines & Liquors
389 Broadway, Dobbs Ferry, NY 10522. 914 693 0034. FAX 914 693 0039. Wine futures, delivery, books, tastings, newsletters, credit cards, accessories.
Regular wine dinners and tastings organized. Specialists in California wines as well as Bordeaux and Burgundy.

Sherry-Lehmann Inc.
679 Madison Avenue, New York, NY 10021. 212 838 7500
800 811 WINE. Wine futures, books, delivery, tastings,
catalog, cellarage, credit cards, accessories.
Seven million dollars worth of smart wines in the store, its temperature-controlled cellars, and at the firm's auctions. Bordeaux is the best seller.

Silver Spirits
248 Lake Avenue, St. James, NY 11780. 516 584 7696.
516 584 6407. Website: www.silver spirits.com Wine futures, books, credit cards.delivery, tastings, newsletters, cellarage.
Full set of services include auctions (buying and selling of cellars of all sizes), and mail order.

D. Sokolin
25 North Sea Road, Southampton, NY 11968. 516 283 0505.
516 287 3739. E-mail:dsokolin@sokolin.com Wine futures, delivery, tastings, newsletters, cellarage, cellar appraisal, credit cards, America's only wine investment specialist.
Older vintage specialists who buy and sell anything from rarer Bordeaux to domestic boutique wines.

Town Centre Liquors
1620 Route 22, Brewster, NY 10509.
914 278 7741. 914 278 7742.
Website: www.wineo.com
Wine futures, books, newsletters, credit cards.
Discount store offering all the better well-known brands.

Union Square Wines & Spirits
33 Union Square West, New York, NY 10003. 212 675 8100.
212 675 8663. Website: www.unionsquarewines.com. Books, delivery, tastings, credit cards, accessories.
Fine store with over 4,000 wines, an extensive selection of premium spirits and a mail order service.

Villa Wines & Liquors
2461 Jericho Tpke, Garden City Park, NY 11040. 516 294 9110.
516 2944221.
Website: www.villawines.com Wine futures, books, delivery, tutored tastings, newsletters, cellarage, credit cards.
Many lines are specially imported. Services include monthly tastings and a recommendable wine club.

Village Wine & Spirits
486 Sixth Avenue at 12th Street, New York, NY 10011.
FAX 212 255 0539. 212 807 7305.
Wine futures, wine classes, books, delivery, credit cards, accessories, cellar consultation.
Arguably the Village's most outstanding selection of Californian wines – not to mention an unusually good range of fine spirits.

Winetasters of Larchmont
100 Chatsworth Avenue, Larchmont, NY 10538.
914 834 0800. 914 834 0903.
Books, free local delivery, tastings, newsletters, credit cards, accessories.
Among the range of services on offer here include gift baskets, party planning, and wine dinners.

Young's Fine Wines & Liquors
505 Plandome Road, Manhasset, NY 11030. 516 627 1234.
516 627 2822. French wine futures, local delivery, credit cards.
This is the place to find a really extensive range of laudably well-chosen wines from around the globe.

North Carolina

Asheville Wine Market Inc.
65 Biltmore Avenue, Asheville, NC 28801. 828 253 0060.
828 251 0609.
Website:www.ashvillewine.com
Wine futures, books, glass rental, tastings, newsletters, cellarage, credit cards, accessories.
A very personable operation with the distinction of offering a broad range of fine quality yet affordable French wines.

Fowler's Gourmet
112 South Duke Street, Durham, NC 27701. 919 683 2555.
919 956 8403.
E-mail:fowlersfood@mindspring.com
Website: www.fowlersfoodandwine.com
Wine futures, books, delivery, credit cards, accessories.
One of North Carolina's few specialists in English food, with a newly opened wine bar and tastings every Saturday.

OHIO

Gentile's, The Wine Sellers

6867 Flags Center Drive, Columbus, OH 43229. ☎ 614 891 3284. FAX 614 891 3286. E-mail: gentiles@netwalk.com Website: www.gentiles.com Delivery, tastings, newsletters, credit cards, accessories, wine club.

See website for details on their weekly tastings and wine dinners. They also boast a great little wine club.

Pat O'Briens Fine Wines & Gourmet Food

30800 Pine Tree Road, Pepper Pike, OH 44124. ☎ 216 831 8680. FAX 216 765 8887. Books, delivery, tastings, newsletters, credit cards, accessories, wine club.

Now in its 29th year of trading, "Best Wine Store" (Cleveland Magazine Silver Spoon award). Offering a good range and advice on anything from a simple purchase to cellar construction.

Vintage Wine & Coffee

11804 Springfield Pike, Cincinatti, OH 45246. ☎ 513 671 2085. Tastings, newsletters, credit cards, accessories.

Also offering a wine bar which serves hors d'oeuvres, quality wines, beer, and great coffee!

OKLAHOMA

Edmond Wine Shop

1532 Sth Boulevard, Edmond, OK 73013. ☎ 405 341 9122. FAX 405 341 2456.
E-mail: thewineshop@msn.com
Cellar consultation, books, tastings by invitation, newsletters, credit cards.

A thoughtful selection of wines often from small artisan producers and importers. Emphasis is on California, Southern France, and Italy, provided for sale in a relaxed, friendly atmosphere and with experienced service.

OREGON

Burlingame Grocery

8502 South West Terwilliger Boulevard, Portland, OR 97219. ☎ 503 246 0711. FAX 503 246 0723.
Website: www.porland.citysearch.com
Wine futures, books, delivery, tastings, newsletters, credit cards, accessories.

Dynamic but easy-going store, offering a broad-based selection of wines.

Sundance Wine Cellars / Oregon Wine Merchants

2470 Alder Street, Eugene, OR 97401. ☎ 541 687 9463 \ 1-800 679 4637. FAX 541 342 1660.
E-mail: orwines@efn.org
Website:www.orwines.com
Wine futures, tastings, newsletters, credit cards.

The right place to go looking for limited-production, hard-to-come-by Oregon Pinot Noirs and northwest wines.

RHODE ISLAND

Campus Fine Wines

127 Brook Street, Providence, RI 2906. ☎ 401 621 9650. FAX 401 454 8193.
E-mail: camwine@aol.com
Website: www.campuswines.com.
Wine futures, books, glass rental, tastings, newsletters, credit cards, accessories.

Large range of wines to suit all tastes. Also offering accessories and other services.

TENNESSEE

Arthur's Wine & Spirits

964 June Road, Memphis, TN 38119. ☎ 901 767 9463. FAX 901 682 9463.
Wine futures, credit cards.

A very solid range of wines from a worldwide selection of well-known producers.

Bluegrass Beverages

555 East Main Street, Hendersonville, TN 37075. ☎ 615 824 6600. FAX 615 822 7517.
Tastings, newsletters, credit cards, accessories.

Broad-based and competitively priced wines, and great customer service. Selection of spirits, single malts, single-barrel bourbons, fine wines, imported and craft beers, keg beer, and delicatessen specialities.

Cool Springs Wine & Spirits

2000 Mallory Lane, Suite 210, Franklin, TN 37064. ☎ 615 771 7436. FAX 615 771 7925.
Website: www.coolspringswine.com
Newsletters, credit cards.

Intimate little store that firmly believes in matching up the right wine with the right customers at the right price.

Mt. Moriah Liquors Inc.

5782 Mount Moriah, Memphis, TN 38115. ☎ 901 794 9463. FAX 901 794 0733. E-mail: eshidester@msn.com / winehawk@aol.com Website: www.mtmoriah.com Wine futures, tastings, credit cards.

Specialists in a selection of classy French and California wines, together with fine single malt scotches.

TEXAS

The Austin Wine Merchant

512 West 6th Street Austin, TX 78701. ☎ 512 499 0512. FAX 512 499 0558 Website: www.austinwinemerchant.com Fine wines, spirits and accessories, service, selection, delivery available within the Austin area, cash, check, American Express line

Great service from "The Texan Expert."

The Cellar

3520 Bee Caves Road, Austin, TX 78746. ☎ 512 328 6464. FAX 512 327 8333. E-mail: wine@alicia.ausinfo.com Website: www.thecellar.ausinfo.com Books, delivery, tastings, newsletters, credit cards, accessories, personal and corporate accounts, case discounts.

Cozy little store owned by a friendly English couple.

Liquid Town

4141 South Alameda, Corpus Christi, TX 78411. ☎ 512 854 1030. FAX 512 854 6979. E-mail: liquidtown@aol.com Wine futures, books, glass rental/loan, tastings, newsletters, credit cards.

Large store majoring in California Chardonnay and Cabernet. They also have a selection of around 200 Bordeaux.

Gabriel's Wine & Spirits

4445 Walzem Road, San Antonio, TX 78218.
☎ 210 654 1123. FAX 210 655 5763. E-mail: gabriel's@txdirect.net. Wine futures, books, delivery, newsletters, tastings, accessories.

Small chain with over 5,000 wines. Specializing in Bordeaux, Burgundy, Tuscany, Germany, California, and Australia. Full climate-control retail space in the three main stores.

H E B Central Market

4001 North Lamar, Austin, TX 78756. ☎ 512 206 1000. FAX 512 206 1010. Website: www.centralmarket.com Books, delivery, newsletters, credit cards, accessories.

3,000 lines and knowledgable staff to help match wines with food bought in-store. Selection of fine cigars.

Po Go's Wine & Spirits

5360 West Lovers, Suite 200, Dallas, TX 75209. ☎ 214 350 8989. FAX 214 350 8670. Wine futures, books, delivery, tastings, newsletters, credit cards, accessories.

World-class range from Burgundy, Bordeaux and California boutique wineries.

Richards Liquor

2565 Kirby Drive, Houston, TX 77019. ☎ 713 529 6266. FAX 713 529 3884. Website: www.richardsliquors.com Wine futures, delivery, tastings, accessories.

Chain with a friendly atmosphere, well informed staff and upscale wines. Walk-in humidor and gift baskets

Spec's Liquor Stores

2410 Smith Street, Houston, TX 77006. ☎ 713 526 8787. FAX 713 526 6129. E-mail: beardalton@specsonline.com Website: www.specsonline.com Bordeaux wine futures, delivery, tastings, newsletters, credit cards, accessories.

Around 9,000 wines, all of which are also available by mail order.

Wiggy's

1130 West 6th Street, Austin, TX 78703. ☎ 512 474 9463. FAX 512 474 5384. E-mail:wiggys@austin360.com Wine futures, books, delivery, credit cards, accessories.

Good range across the board, with selections of Cognac, Armagnac, and port. Library of older vintages in vault.

Wines of America

2055 Westheimer, Suite 155, Houston, TX 77098. ☎ 713 524 3397. FAX 713 524 1304. E-mail: woa@houstonwines.com. Website: www.houstonwines.com. Private & general tastings, delivery, newsletters, accessories, credit cards

Good selection of California boutique wines, French, Italian, South American, Australian, and Spanish.

VERMONT

Cheese Outlet Fresh Market

400 Pine Street, Burlington, Vermont 05401. ☎ 802 863 3968. FAX 802 865 1705. Website: www.cheeseoutlet.com

Credit cards.

Gourmet food emporium with wines especially from Italy, Spain, Australia, France, and New Zealand. Also cheese, prepared foods, bakery, specialty foods, and beverages.

VIRGINIA

Arrowine

4508 Lee Highway, Arlington, VA 22207. ☎ 703 525 0990. FAX 703 525 2218

E-mail: drosen@arrowine.com.

Wine futures, books, delivery, tastings, newsletters, credit cards, accessories.

Very hands-on approach to service: almost everything sold is tasted first. Wine dinners.

Cecile's Wine Cellars

1351 Chain Bridge Road, McLean VA 22101. ☎ 703 356 6500. FAX 703 356 6502. E-mail: cwc@finewine.com Website: finewine.com

Glass hire/loan, delivery, free weekly tastings, newsletters, gift baskets shipped or delivered, credit cards, accessories, wine and food pairing services, corporate accounts and seminars.

From everyday wine to collector cravings. Exceptional service and wonderful staff. "We avoid grocery store plonk and taste everything we bring into the store. Not a bad selection in the place...guaranteed."

Sutton Place Gourmet

600 Franklin Street, Alexandria, VA 22314. ☎ 703 549 6611. FAX 703 549 1138. Books, wine futures, local delivery, tastings, newsletters, credit cards, accessories, case discounts.

Chain of gourmet stores with wide-ranging wine department which specializes in California, Italy, Burgundy, and Rhone.

The Wine Seller

304 Elden Street, Herndon,VA 20170. ☎ 703 471 9649. FAX 703 733 0202.

Website: www.thewineseller.com

Books, delivery, credit cards, accessories.

Mail order service available (Virginia only). Cigar selection.

WASHINGTON

Fred Meyer

2041 148th Avenue Southeast, Bellevue, WA 98007. ☎ 425 865 8563.

FAX 425 641 6749.

Website: www.fredmeyer.com

Wine futures, books, credit cards, accessories.

Large chain of department stores with well-stocked wine departments specializing in California premiums and Washington wines.

La Cantina Wine Merchants

5436 Send Point Way, NE,Seattle,WA 98105. ☎ 206 525 4340.

FAX 206 729 7466. Wine futures, books, delivery, tastings, newsletters, credit cards, accessories.

Exclusive range of French wines boosted by annual selection trips. Also strong on Northwestern domestic wines.

McCarthy & Schiering Wine Merchants

2209 Queen Anne Avenue North, Seattle, WA 98109. ☎ 206 282 8500. FAX 206 284 2498. E-mail: msqa@sprynet.com Wine futures, books, delivery, tastings, newsletters, mail order, credit cards, accessories.

Two stores in Seattle, one of whose owners is the author of a book on the wines of Oregon and Washington. Not surprisingly, the range of both is highly recommendable. Specializing in the Northwest, Greece, France, Italy, Spain, and Australia.

Pete's Wine Shops

58 East Lynn, Seattle, WA 98102. ☎ 206 322 2660. FAX 206 322 1391.

Website: www.petesfinewines.com.

Wine futures, books, delivery, tastings, credit cards, accessories, also a second store located in Bellevue.

You will find 1,800 wines here from all corners of the globe. Mail order is available.

QFC (Quality Food Center)

University Village, 2746 NE 45th, Seattle,WA 98105. ☎ 206 523 5160.

Credit cards, accessories, also a second store in Bellevue.

QFC is a state-wide food market chain with high volume, and a good selection of premium wines.

Wine Specialists

CHAMPAGNE

FINE & RARE

FRANCE

GERMANY

ITALY

NEW ZEALAND

OREGON

SPAIN

Auctioneers

Acker Merrall & Condit ☎ 212 787 1700 FAX 212 799 1984 Website: www.vinogod.comaol E-mail: ackerbids@aol.com
The Chicago Wine Co. (Online auctions) ☎ 847 647 8789 FAX 847 647 7265 E-mail: tcwc@aol.com
Christie's New York ☎ 212 546 5830 FAX 212 317 2470 Website: www.christies.com E-mail: brobinson@christies.com
Fine & Rare Wines ☎ 415 861 7500 tel. ext 319 FAX 415 861 1450 Website: www.butterfields.com
Morrell & Co ☎ 212 307 4200 FAX 212 247 5242 E-mail: Morrellvin@aol.com
Sherry-Lehmann Inc ☎ 212 838 7500 FAX 212 838 9285
Sothebys, Los Angeles ☎ 310 274 0340 FAX 310 274 0899 E-mail: Fred.backlar@sothebys.com
Sothebys, New York ☎ 212 774 5330 FAX 212 774 5347 Website: www.sothebys.com E-mail: wine@sothebys.com
Winebid.com (online auction house) ☎ 630 876 1414 http://www.winebid.com or call: (877) Winebid
Zachys ☎ 914 723 0241 FAX 914 723 1033 Website: www.zachys.com E-mail: info@zachys.com

Wine Racks, Cellars & Fittings

Apex ☎ 1-800 462 2714 Website: www.apex-sauna-wine.com E-mail: apex@isomedia.com
Buckhead Fine Wines ☎ 404 231 8566
Kedco ☎ 516 454 7800
Koolspace ☎ 888 274 8813 www.koolspace.com
Robinson & Sons ☎ 1-800 773 8775 Website: www.winejazz.com
Vaults ☎ 561 776 1713
Vinotemp Intl. ☎ 1-800 777 8466 FAX 310 886 3310 Website: www..vinotemp.com E-mail:info@ vinotemp.com
Vintage Cellars ☎ 1-800 876 8789 Website: www.vintagecellars.com E-mail: vintage@znet.com
Wine Appreciation Guild ☎ 800 231 9463
Wine Cellar Concepts ☎ 703 356 3742 Website: www.winecellarcon-cepts.com
Wine Cellars Limited ☎ 1-800 250 8050
Wine Cellar Solutions ☎ 888 649 9463 Website: www.winehome.com
Wine Cellar Innovations ☎ 1-800 229 9813 Website: www. winecellarinnovations.com
Wine Chillers of California ☎ 1-800 331 4274 E-mail: winechillers@earthlink.net
The Wine Enthusiast ☎ 1-800 356 8466 FAX 1-800 833 8466 Website: www.wineenthusiast.com
Wine Environments ☎ 303 788 0470
Wine Racks & More ☎ 888 547 1706
Zipco ☎ 215 592 4744

TEMPERATURE / HUMIDITY MONITORS

Mannix Testing & Measurement ☎ 516 887 7979 FAX 516 887 7844 Website: www. instrumentmart.com

FRIDGE-TO-WINE-CELLAR CONVERSION KITS

BH Enterprises ☎ +FAX 510 943 7311 Website: www.winestat.com E-mail: bh@winestat.com

Wine Storage

Bel-Air 2020 Wine Merchants ☎ 310 447 2020 FAX 310 475 2836 Website: www.Belair2020wine.com
Extra Space Storage ☎ 415 333 3191 FAX 415 333 1256
John Walker & Co. ☎ 415 986 2707 FAX 415 421 5820
International Wine Storage ☎ 305 856 1208 FAX 305 858 6124
K&L Wine Merchants ☎ 650 364 8544 FAX 650 364 4687 Website: www.KLwines.com E-mail: questions@KLwines.com
Vintage Wine Warehouse ☎ 212 245 4889 FAX 212 245-4839

L.A. Fine Arts & Wine Storage ☎ 310 447 7700 FAX 310 447 7070 Website: www.LAfineart.com.
Morgan Manhattan ☎ 718 786 3304 FAX 718 786 2969 Website: www.morganmanhattan.com
My Cellar ☎ 215 625-3928 FAX 215 592 4741
Sam's Wines & Spirits ☎ 312 664 4394 FAX 312 664 7037 Website: www.sams-wine.com
Subterraneum Private Wine Storage ☎ 510 451 3939 / 888 277 7777 FAX 510 451 5753 Website: www.subterraneum.com
The Strongbox Wine Cellar ☎ 312 787 2800 Website: www.winestorage.com.
The Wine House ☎ 310 479 3731 FAX 310 478 5609 E-mail: winehse@wavenet.com
Vintage Wine Warehouse ☎ 212 245-4889 FAX 212 245-4839
Wine East Bank Storage ☎ 312 644 2000 FAX 312 644 7878 E-mail: eastbankstorage.ameritech.net
Wine Services Inc. ☎ 1-800 955 WINE Website: www.alstop.com/wine

ACCESSORIES

GENERAL ACCESSORIES

IWA ☎ 1-800 527 4072
Wine Appreciation Guild ☎ 800 231 9463
The Wine Enthusiast ☎ 1-800 356 8466 ` 1-800 833 8466 Website: www.wineenthusiast.com.

GLASSES

Absolutely Riedel ☎ 516 234 5314 FAX 516 234 5583 Website: www.wineglasses.com
ABC Fine Wine & Spirits ☎ 407 851 0000 FAX 407 857 5500
Brown Derby International Wine Center ☎ 417 883 4066 FAX 417 883 3073 E-mail:bdwine@dialnet.net
L'Esprit et le Vin ☎ 201 222 1080 FAX 201 656 7876 E-mail: selex-inc@msn.com
Wine Stuff ☎ 516 234 5314 FAX 516 234 5583 Website: www.winestuff.com

SOFTWARE

Apex ☎ 1-800 462 2714 Website: www.apex-sauna-wine.com
Cellar Savant ☎ 1-800 594 5228
Wine Guild ☎ 1-800 231 9463
Wine Professor ☎ 607 257 7610 FAX 607 257 7610 Website: www.wineprofessor.com E-mail: info@wineprofessor.com
Wine Rack Software ☎ 888 606 WINE Website: www.winerack.com.
Wine Technologies ☎ 617 323 8745 Website: www.winetech.com
Winewin ☎ 1-800 WINEWIN

WINE VACATIONS / TOURS

Arblaster Clarke ☎ 011 44 1730 893 344
Avalon Tours ☎ 714 673 7376 Website:www.travelsource.com/wine/avalon.html
France in your glass ☎ 1-800 578 0903 / 1-206 325 4324 Website: www.inyourglass.com
Gabriele's Travels to Italy ☎ 888 287 8733 Website: travelingtoitaly.com
XO Travel Consultants ☎ 1-888 262 9682 / 1-212 947 5530 FAX 1 (212) 971 0924
Wine & Dine Tours ☎ 1-800 946 3868 Website: www.wineanddinetour.com E-mail: winetour@napanet.net
Grape Adventures ☎ + FAX 978 440 9754 E-mail: agrapeline@aol.com Website: www.grapeadventures.com

LEARNING ABOUT WINE

Institute of Masters of Wine ☎ 011 44 171 236 4427
International Wine Centre ☎ 212 627 7170 FAX 212 627 7116 E-mail: iwcny@aol.com
Society of Wine Educators ☎ 301 776 8569 FAX 301 776 8578 Website: http://wine.gurus.com
Wine & Spirit Education Trust ☎ 011 44 171 236 3551
Wine School (Robert Joseph) Website: www.wine-school.com
Christie's Wine Course ☎ 011 44 171 581 3933

INDEX

An index that can be used as a supplement to the A–Z (page 97)

A

B

C

D

E

F

G

H

I

J

K

N

O

P

Q

R

S

T

U

V

W

X

Y

Z